THIRD EDITION

NEW INTRODUCTORY
Reader in Sociology

Mike O'Donnell

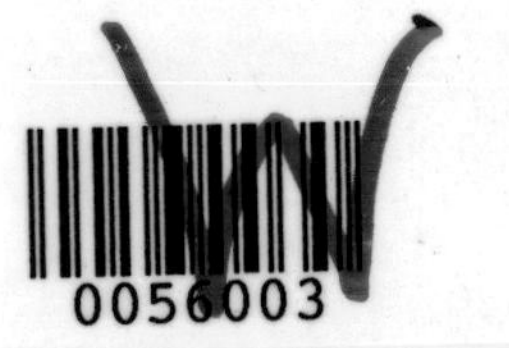

Nelson

To Eileen, my mother, with love

Thomas Nelson and Sons Ltd
Nelson House, Mayfield Road
Walton-on-Thames, Surrey
KT12 5PL UK

51 York Place
Edinburgh
EH1 3JD UK

Thomas Nelson (Hong Kong) Ltd
Toppan Building 10/F
22A Westlands Road
Quarry Bay, Hong Kong

Thomas Nelson Australia
102 Dodds Street
South Melbourne
Victoria 3205 Australia

Nelson Canada
1120 Birchmount Road
Scarborough, Ontario
M1K 5G4 Canada

First published by Thomas Nelson and Sons Ltd
1993

ISBN 0-17-448192-6

NPN 9 8 7 6 5 4 3 2 1

Printed in Hong Kong.

The author and publisher wish to thank the authors and publishers who gave their permission to reproduce copyright material in this book.

Every effort has been made to trace all the copyright holders, but if any have been inadvertently overlooked, the publishers will be pleased to make the necessary arrangements at the earliest opportunity.

PREFACE

The third edition of a *New Introductory Reader in Sociology* stands alongside rather than replaces the second edition. I hope that the second edition will remain useful for some years. More than ninety percent of the readings in this edition are new. The few that have been carried over from the second edition are mainly classics for which it is convenient to have ready access.

Why, then, have I decided to publish this edition virtually as a new book? Firstly and most obviously, people will not be keen to buy the same reading twice. This edition attempts to give maximum value for money.

Secondly, I felt it imperative to capture in this edition the main themes and trends of what increasingly seems to be a new, if not yet adequately defined, epoch. The crisis in confidence of reformist liberalism, the rise of the New Right – and its subsequent troubles – and the collapse of Soviet Communism all indicate that the world is rapidly changing. A new mood of change has been widely reflected in sociology and social commentary. In part, the new mood expresses a greater global awareness. The power of transnational corporations, concern for the global environment and for poverty and hunger worldwide, are prominent themes in this collection. On the other hand, as some strive for wider and more effective bases of cooperation, forces of fragmentation, particularly ethnic bickering and conflict, have also asserted themselves. These are also discussed here, as are developments in other sources of social identity such as class and gender.

Perhaps the sense of an epoch coming to its close is most clearly expressed in the various 'post' theories. Post-industrial society theory, post-Fordism, postmodernism and poststructuralism seems collectively to declare that one age is ending and that a new one must therefore be beginning. Put as succinctly as possible, what is ending is the 'modern' age characterised by a socio-economic system founded on heavy manufacture, a belief in material progress, and cultural self-confidence, if not certainty, based on 'Western' liberal values. What remains is capitalism globally rampant. The West is post-industrial, but certainly not postcapitalist. Capitalism's capacity for construction and destruction is greater than ever.

How the system is used and directed will determine the nature and quality of human life in the new millenium. As we approach it, new social movements are asserting themselves and less familiar voices are making themselves heard. These include Islam, anti-imperialism, the black liberation movement which has still not achieved its goals of justice and equality in most parts of the world, a regrouping feminist movement, and the poor and alienated citizenry of the West. All these matters are represented in this reader and they are the justification for a third edition.

Mike O'Donnell, January 1993

Acknowledgements

This edition differs from previous ones in that, in addition to drawing on published sources, it contains several original readings. These include contributions from my colleagues Rob Mears and Simon Cottle who also advised me about selections in their respective areas of expertise, health and the media. My thanks to them for their considerable efforts. I am also delighted to be able to include an original contribution from Sue Sharpe which is based on data which will be more fully written-up in the second edition of *Just Like a Girl* (Penguin, 1994).

I would like to thank Julia Cousins at Nelson's who managed this enterprise with both efficiency and flexibility and Mandy Green who edited the final manuscript.

References

References have only been included in the case of readings which are original to this volume. Otherwise, references can be found in the publications in which the readings first appeared.

CONTENTS

SECTION 1

SOCIOLOGICAL THEORY: THE FOUNDATIONS

SECTION 2

SOCIOLOGICAL METHODS

SECTION 3

SOCIAL CLASS AND STRATIFICATION

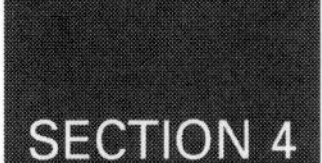

GENDER

SECTION 5

RACE AND ETHNICITY

AGE AND GENERATION

FAMILIES AND HOUSEHOLDS

EDUCATION

SECTION 9

WORK AND NON-WORK

SECTION 10

ORGANISATIONS

SECTION 11

URBANISATION AND COMMUNITY

SECTION 12

DEVELOPMENT AND UNDERDEVELOPMENT

POLITICAL SOCIOLOGY

HEALTH, WELFARE AND POVERTY

DEVIANCE

RELIGION

SECTION 17

THE SOCIOLOGY OF THE MEDIA

SECTION 18

THEORY – CURRENT DEVELOPMENTS

INDEX

SOCIOLOGICAL THEORY: THE FOUNDATIONS

Introduction: Readings 1–6

This section deals with the development of sociology in the late nineteenth and the first half of the twentieth centuries. Given the scope of time and subject matter involved, no more can be attempted than to offer some significant illustrations of what was achieved.

Marx's materialist concept of history is important because it broke with explanations of social life which depended on the will of God or the 'march of ideas' (idealism) and explained it instead in terms of the relationship of people to the material world and to each other (materialism). While many contemporary sociologists still accept the truth of religion, virtually all now explain society in broad historical and materialist terms without reference to external spiritual forces.

In Reading 2, Durkheim sketches out the distinct subject matter of sociology. He also describes two main types of society: the first characterised by mechanical solidarity (integration or 'hanging together') and the second by organic or contractual solidarity. The former tend to be traditional and the latter modern.

Like Marx and Durkheim, Freud tended to stress the power of society to form the behaviour and consciousness of individuals. Part of his contribution was to suggest how instincts and emotions as well as values, norms and ideas are moulded by social institutions. In Reading 3, he describes how an individual's conscience and sense of guilt is structured through socialisation.

Max Weber deliberately sought to reassert the importance of individually meaningful action in order to balance what he considered was the excessive stress put by Marx on the formative effect of society. George Herbert Mead similarly intended that social science should not develop an 'over-socialised' conceptualisation of human beings. In Reading 5, he stresses that the relatively autonomous 'I' can act freely despite the constraint of the socialised 'Me'

Frederick von Hayek carries the notion of individual freedom further still – too far for his critics. For him, there are virtually no legitimate social constraints on the free individual other than those imposed by the state to protect the freedom of others. For sociologists, this by-passes the whole social dimension to existence but, then, von Hayek is pre-eminently an economist.

Karl Marx: Production, Consciousness, Historical Conflict and Change

The reason for presenting this extract here is that in it Marx outlines much of the core of his analysis of social change. It is work, the main practical activity, out of which people construct society and from which their own frame of thought and reference develop. Therefore, the economy is the 'base' from which culture, the 'superstructure', emerges.

Marx perceives a fundamental conflict in all types of society (other than communist). This conflict is between those who own the means of production and those who have to work them. Out of this conflict a new system develops, but the new system only takes over from the old when the mode of production on which it is based is sufficiently developed or mature. Thus, the capitalist system replaced the feudal system, just as Marx considered that the communist system would replace the capitalist system. At that point, this process of conflict ceases and people can begin to create a society of fulfilment.

It is probably accurate to say that, for better or worse, this agenda dominated global consciousness and history throughout most of the twentieth century. In the last decade of the century, actual historical events may have dealt a mortal blow to the predictive aspect of Marx's theory. Much of his sociological analysis, however, still merits consideration.

Reading 1 From Karl Marx in T. B. Bottomore and M. Rubel *eds., Karl Marx: Selected Writings in Sociology and Social Philosophy* (Penguin, 1956), pp. 67–69

> This point is fundamental to Marx's theory of society and history. Every society must produce to survive. Some own the means of production (land, factories), others have to work the means of production.

> In this famous statement, Marx is saying that social experience, including the work we do, determines our thinking rather than vice-versa. So, culture is built upon the economy rather than the other way round. Evidently, this is a view with which one can agree or disagree.

> This is another of Marx's celebrated statements. His analysis is that a new kind of society emerges only when a new system of production is ready to take over from the previous one.

In the social production which men carry on they enter into definite relations that are indispensable and independent of their will; these relations of production correspond to a definite stage of development of their material powers of production. The totality of these relations of production constitutes the economic structure of society – the real foundation, on which legal and political superstructures arise and to which definite forms of social consciousness correspond. The mode of production of material life determines the general character of the social, political, and spiritual processes of life. It is not the consciousness of men that determines their being, but, on the contrary, their social being determines their consciousness. At a certain stage of their development, the material forces of production in society come in conflict with the existing relations of production, or – what is but a legal expression for the same thing – with the property relations within which they had been at work before. From forms of development of the forces of production these relations turn into their fetters. Then occurs a period of social revolution. With the change of the economic foundation the entire immense superstructure is more or less rapidly transformed. In considering such transformations, the distinction should always be made between the material transformation of the economic conditions of production which can be determined with the precision of natural science, and the legal, political, religious, aesthetic or philosophical – in short, ideological – forms in which men become conscious of this conflict and fight it out. Just as our opinion of an individual is not based on what he thinks of himself, so can we not judge of such a period of transformation by its own consciousness; on the contrary, this consciousness must rather be explained from the contradictions of material life, from the existing conflict between the social forces of production and the relations of production. No social order ever disappears before all the productive forces for which there is room in it have been developed; and new, higher relations of production never appear before the material conditions of their existence have matured in the womb of the old society. Therefore, mankind always sets itself only such problems as it can solve; since, on closer examination, it will always be found that the problem itself arises only when the material conditions necessary for its solution already exist or are at least in the process of formation. In broad outline we can designate the Asiatic, the ancient, the feudal, and the modern bourgeois modes of production as progressive epochs in the economic formation of society. The bourgeois relations of production are the last antagonistic form of the social process of production; not in the sense of individual antagonisms, but of conflict arising from conditions surrounding the life of individuals in society. At the same time the productive forces developing in the womb of bourgeois society create the material conditions for the solution of that antagonism. With this social formation, therefore, the prehistory of human society comes to an end.

Preface (1859)

Emile Durkheim: Sociology and Society – Mechanical and Organic Solidarity

This reading divides into two main sections: 'The Nature of Sociology'; and 'Mechanical and Organic (contractual) Solidarity'. Although they come from separate parts of Durkheim's work, they can be read as complementary.

In the first brief section, Durkheim charts what he considers to be the distinctive subject domain of sociology. Sociology focuses on the level of the group, people in interaction (be it two individuals or two societies or more). Elsewhere, he describes the formation and observance (or not) of norms and values (i.e. of social order) as of particular concern to sociology. Weber's analysis of social action (Reading 4) which stresses the prime importance of 'subjectively (individually) meaningful action' (my brackets) as the prime concern of sociology may be considered as balancing what is sometimes thought of as Durkheim's over-emphasis on social factors just as Marx emphasised the centrality of social conflict rather than order (Reading 1).

Durkheim's distinction between mechanical and organic solidarity (social integration) is at the core of his developmental or evolutionary theory of society. Mechanical solidarity occurs because members of a society believe that the rules of social conduct have been spiritually or divinely ordained. Organic solidarity occurs because members of a society agree to observe certain mutually established or negotiated rules or laws. The former type of society tends to be traditional and communal and the latter modern and individualistic.

Despite the differences between societies based on mechanical and organic solidarity, both conform to Durkheim's definition of society. Both involve a necessary collective dimension to individual action.

Reading 2 From Emile Durkheim in K. Thompson *ed., Readings from Emile Durkheim* (Tavistock Publications, 1985), pp. 21–22, 47–49

The nature of sociology

Now on first consideration, sociology might appear indistinguishable from psychology; and this thesis has in fact been maintained, by Tarde, among others. Society, they say, is nothing but the individuals of whom it is composed. They are its only reality. How, then, can the science of societies be distinguished from the science of individuals, that is to say, from psychology?

If one reasons in this way, one could equally well maintain that biology is but a chapter of physics and chemistry, for the living cell is composed exclusively of atoms of carbon, nitrogen, and so on, which the physico-chemical sciences undertake a study. But that is to forget that a whole very often has very different properties from those which its constituent parts possess. Though a cell contains nothing but mineral elements, these reveal, by being combined in a certain way, properties which they do not have when they are not thus combined and which are characteristic of life (properties of sustenance and of reproduction); they thus form, through their synthesis, a reality of an entirely new sort, which is living reality and which constitutes the subject matter of biology. In the same way, individual consciousnesses, by associating themselves in a stable way, reveal, through their interrelationships, a new life very different from that which would have developed had they remained uncombined; this is social life. Religious institutions and beliefs, political, legal, moral, and economic institutions – in a word, all of what constitutes civilization – would not exist if there were no society.

In effect, civilization presupposes cooperation not only among all the members of a single society, but also among all the societies which interact with one another . . .

Organic and mechanical (contractual) solidarity

[W]e shall recognize only two sorts of positive solidarity, distinguishable by the following characteristics:

Throughout this section, 'the first kind' refers to mechanical solidarity and 'the second kind' to organic solidarity.

1 The first kind links the individual directly to society without any intermediary. With the second kind, the individual depends on society, because he depends on the parts which make the whole.

2 Society is not viewed in the same way in the two cases. In the first case, what we call society is a more or less organised totality of beliefs and sentiments common to all the members of the group: this is the collective type. On the other hand, the society in which we are integrated in the second case is a system of different, special functions which are linked by precise relationships. These two societies are but one. They are two faces of one and the same reality, but which none the less need to be distinguished.

3 Out of this second difference there arises another which will help us to describe and name these two sorts of solidarity.

The first kind can be strong only to the extent that the ideas and inclinations common to all the members of the society are greater in number and intensity than those which belong personally to each of them; the greater the excess, the stronger the solidarity. Now, our personality is made up of everything that is peculiar to and characteristic of us, everything that distinguishes it from others. This solidarity can, therefore, only increase in inverse proportion to the personality. As we have said, there are in the consciousness of each of us two consciousnesses: one which is common to our whole group, which, consequently, is not ourselves, but is society living and acting within us; the other represents us at our most personal and distinctive, in everything that makes us an individual. The solidarity that derives from similarities is at its maximum when the collective consciousness completely envelops our total consciousness and coincides with it at every point: but, at that moment, our individuality is nil. Our individuality can come into being only if the community takes up less place within us. There are two contrary forces, one centripetal, the other centrifugal, which cannot both increase at the same time. We cannot develop at the same time in two such opposing directions. If we have a strong inclination to think and act for ourselves, we cannot also be strongly inclined to think and act like others. If the ideal is to make a distinct, personal character for oneself, then it would not be ideal to resemble everyone else. Furthermore, at the very moment when this solidarity exercises its influence, our personality collapses, one might say, by definition; for we are no longer ourselves; we are a collective being.

The social molecules which would cohere only in this way could act together only to the extent that they have no movements of their own, as do molecules in inorganic bodies. This is why we suggest calling this type of solidarity 'mechanical'. The word does not imply that it is produced by mechanical, artificial means. We only use this term by analogy to the cohesion which unites the elements of raw materials, as opposed to the cohesion which brings about the unity of living bodies. What justifies this term is that the link which binds the individual to society is wholly analogous to the link between a thing and a person. Individual consciousness, considered from this viewpoint, is simply dependent on the collective type and follows all its movements, in the same way as the possessed object follows those required by its owner. In societies where his solidarity is highly developed, the individual is not his own master, as we shall see later, quite literally, he is a thing at the disposal of the society. Also in these same social types, personal rights are not yet distinguished from real rights.

The solidarity produced by the division of labour is quite different. Whereas the preceding type implies that individuals resemble each other, this type assumes that they are different from each other. The first is possible only to the extent that the individual personality is absorbed into the collective personality; the second is possible only if each has its own sphere of action, and therefore a personality. The collective consciousness must therefore leave open a part of the individual consciousness, so that these special functions which it cannot regulate may be established; the more this area is extended, the stronger is the cohesion which results from its solidarity. In fact, on the one hand, the more labour is divided up, the greater the dependence on society, and, on the other hand, the more specialized the activity of each individual, the more personal it is. Circumscribed though that activity may be, it is never completely original; even in the exercise of our profession, we conform to usages and practices which are common to the entire professional body. But, even in this case, the burden that we accept is less heavy than when the whole of society weighs on us, and it leaves much more room for the free play of our initiative. So, the individuality of the whole increases at the same time as the individuality of its parts; the society becomes more capable of collective movement, at the same time as each of its elements has more freedom of movement of its own. This resembles the solidarity that is observed in higher animals. Each organ, in fact, has its special characteristics, its autonomy, and yet, the greater the unity of the organism, the more marked is the individuation of its parts. Using this analogy, we propose to call the solidarity due to the division of labour 'organic'.

The increasing preponderance of organic solidarity and its consequences

If there is one truth that history has settled beyond all question, it is that religion embraces an ever-diminishing part of social life. Originally it extended to everything; everything social was religious; the two words were synonymous. Then gradually political, economic and scientific functions freed themselves from the religious function, became established separately, taking on an increasingly pronounced temporal character. God, if we may express it in this way, at first present in all human relationships, gradually withdrew from them; he abandoned the world to men and their disputes. At least, if he did continue to dominate it, it was from on high and at a distance, and the influence which he exercised, becoming more general and imprecise, left more room for the free play of human forces. The individual feels himself to be, and is, in fact, less 'acted upon'; he becomes more a source of spontaneous activity. In short, not only does the sphere of religion not increase at the same time and to the same extent as the sphere of temporal life, but it progressively diminishes. This regression did not begin at a precise moment in history, but one can follow its phases going back to the origins of social evolution. It is therefore bound up with the fundamental conditions of the development of societies, and it thus demonstrates that there is an ever-decreasing number of collective beliefs and sentiments which are both sufficiently collective and strong to assume a religious character. This means that the average intensity of the common consciousness progressively weakens . . .

Sigmund Freud: Conscience and Guilt – The Social Control and Use of Aggression

Who made the greatest contribution to social science, Marx or Freud? I ask this question, not because I propose to answer it – answers will vary – but to highlight the stature of Freud's work. It stands in scale alongside that of Marx and Darwin in terms of its contribution to social science and social biology.

Why, then, has no extract from Freud appeared in the previous two editions of this Reader? The fact is that it is no simple matter to translate the implications of Freud's psychoanalytic model into sociology even though the psychological–sociological linkage was always intrinsic to Freud's thinking. (This linkage is sometimes referred to as 'metapsychology'.) Freud's best known attempt to present the relationship of the individual to society is his *Civilisation and Its Discontents* (1929). In the following passage, he describes how the instincts of eros (love/sex) and aggression are translated from being personal (potentially 'selfish'/socially disruptive 'needs') into socially constructive energy/functions. His initial reference to eros is brief but he clearly considers that sexual love can be expressed more generally as 'love' for a larger group – family, community, nation, human kind, a particular idea etc.

Freud's analysis of the relationship of conscience to love and aggression is central to his concept of 'civilisation' or society. He argues that conscience develops in two stages from being potentially selfish and socially disruptive into socially constructive channels. In the first stage, guilt is felt as a result of fear that others will withdraw love and punish us if we do what they consider 'bad'. It is fear of 'the loss of love' that motivates anxiety. In the second stage, morality has been 'internalised' in the form of the superego which 'operates' its own control over egoistic, anti-social instincts. In this stage, aggression is turned back by the superego against the ego (self or individual) and fuels feelings of guilt. Thus, instead of being expressed in a socially disruptive or destructive way, 'aggression' is transformed into socially useful guilt. It is 'useful' because it now functions to control individuals and to reinforce conformity. This rather complex process is described as early as the second paragraph of this extract but much of what follows serves to clarify Freud's position.

The diagram provided on p. 8 should assist in interpreting Freud's metapsychology. The left side of the diagram provides a model of the individual psyche or self. The central part of the diagram indicates that the instincts of sex and aggression are socialised into socially acceptable forms of behaviour. The right side of the diagram indicates that work and structured reproduction are key forms of socially acceptable behaviour. Although Freud does not discuss the concepts of the 'pleasure' and 'reality principles' in this extract, they are included in the diagram because they are fundamental to his thinking. It will be useful to describe them briefly here.

The bottom left of the diagram indicates the reality principle and the pleasure principle. The reality principle refers to the (realistic) need to survive, to work and to accept social control. The pleasure principle refers to the need for sex, enjoyment, freedom and, beyond, for fantasy and utopia. Freud himself, 'took the side of' the reality principle against the pleasure principle. He considered that the unbridled pursuit of instinctual pleasure would cause social chaos.

Not all writers influenced by Freud have reached quite the same conclusion. Indeed, the desire for a more fulfilling and enjoyable society – for the 'lost' pleasure principle – has been something of an obsession for some neo-Marxist and radical writers such as sixties philosopher, Herbert Marcuse, and, rather differently, humanist psychologist, Abraham Maslow. Marcuse, certainly, could not accept Freud's 'virtuous' bargain that 'the price of progress in civilisation is paid in forfeiting happiness through the heightening of the sense of guilt' (*Civilisation and Its Discontents*, p. 123).

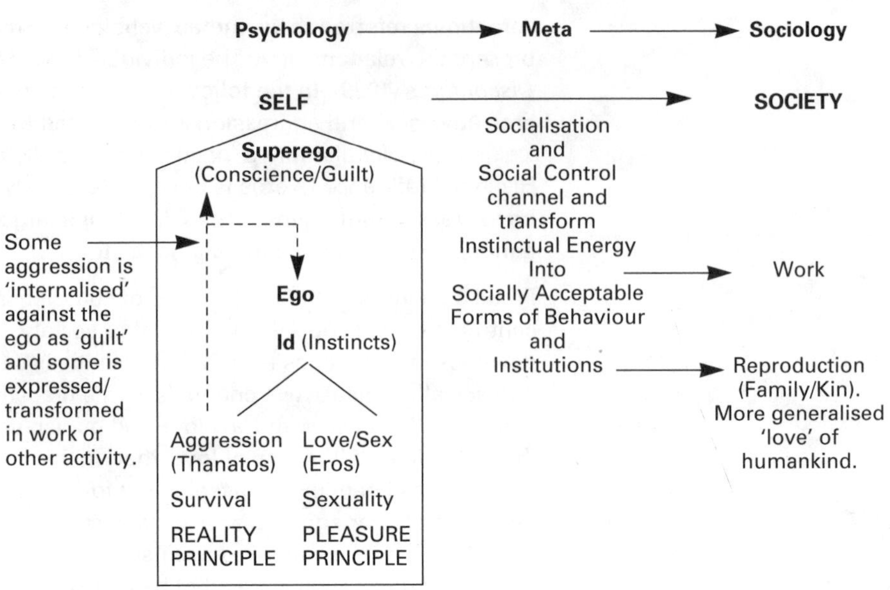

The Socialisation of the Instincts into Socially Acceptable Forms – According to Freud

Freud's work remains controversial. Even his language is patriarchal to the point of being difficult to read. Yet, he is a seminal influence in social science. In addition to his influence on the Frankfurt school, including Marcuse, he greatly influenced American Functionalism through Talcott Parsons (see my *A New Introduction to Sociology,* 3rd Edition, p. 498). If it is true that, in one sense, all psychology is social psychology, equally, sociology requires a psychological dimension. Patriarchal and over-deterministic Freud may have been, but his metapsychology remains a fruitful source for social science.

Reading 3

From Sigmund Freud, *Civilisation and Its Discontents* (Hogarth Press, 1929), pp. 102, 105, 107–8, 109, 111–12

'the process' i.e. culture

In all that follows I take up the standpoint that the tendency to aggression is an innate, independent, instinctual disposition in man, and I come back now to the statement that it constitutes the most powerful obstacle to culture. At one point in the course of this discussion the idea took possession of us that culture was a peculiar process passing over human life and we are still under the influence of this idea. We may add to this that the process proves to be in the service of Eros, which aims at binding together single human individuals, then families, then tribes, races, nations, into one great unity, that of humanity. Why this has to be done we do not know; it is simply the work of Eros. These masses of men must be bound to one another libidinally; necessity alone, the advantages of common work, would not hold them together. The natural instinct of aggressiveness in man, the hostility of each one against all and of all against each one, opposes this programme of civilization . . .

What means does civilization make use of to hold in check the aggressiveness that opposes it, to make it harmless, perhaps to get rid of it? Some of these measures we have already come to know, though not yet the one that is apparently the most important. We can study it in the evolution of the individual. What happens in him to render his craving for aggression innocuous? Something very curious, that we should never have guessed and that yet seems simple enough. The aggressiveness is introjected, 'internalized'; in fact, it is sent back where it came from, *i.e.* directed against the ego. It is there taken over by a part of the ego that distinguishes itself from the rest as a superego, and now, in the form of 'conscience', exercises the same propensity to harsh aggressiveness against the ego that the ego would have liked to enjoy against others. The tension between the strict super-ego and the subordinate ego we call the sense of guilt; it manifests itself as the need for punishment. Civilization therefore obtains the mastery over the dangerous love of aggression in individuals by enfeebling and disarming it and setting up an institution within their minds to keep watch over it, like a garrison in a conquered city . . .

> 'internalisation' is explained in the introduction to this reading.

> 'an institution in the mind' i.e. conscience

It is easy to discover this motive in man's helplessness and dependence upon others; it can best be designated the dread of losing love. If he loses the love of others on whom he is dependent, he will forfeit also their protection against many dangers, and above all he runs the risk that this stronger person will show his superiority in the form of punishing him. What is bad is, therefore, to begin with, whatever causes one to be threatened with a loss of love; because of the dread of this loss, one must desist from it. That is why it makes little difference whether one has already committed the bad deed or only intends to do so; in either case the danger begins only when the authority has found it out, and the latter would behave in the same way in both cases.

We call this state of mind a 'bad conscience'; but actually it does not deserve this name, for at this stage the sense of guilt is obviously only the dread of losing love, 'social' anxiety. In a little child it can never be anything else, but in many adults too it has only changed in so far as the larger human community takes the place of the father or of both parents. Consequently such people habitually permit themselves to do any bad deed that procures them something they want, if only they are sure that no authority will discover it or make them suffer for it; their anxiety relates only to the possibility of detection. Present-day society has to take into account the prevalence of this stage of mind.

> For those familiar with the social psychology of George Mead, there is a clear parallel between what Freud refers to as 'the larger human community' and Mead's 'Generalised other' and between 'parents' and 'significant others'.

A great change takes place as soon as the authority has been internalised by the development of a super-ego. The manifestations of conscience are then raised to a new level; to be accurate, one should not call them conscience and sense of guilt before this. At this point the dread of discovery ceases to operate and also once for all any difference between doing evil and wishing to do it, since nothing is hidden from the super-ego, not even thoughts . . .

At this second stage of development, conscience exhibits a peculiarity which was absent in the first and is not very easy to account for. That is, the more righteous a man is the stricter and more suspicious will his consicence be, so that ultimately it is precisely those people who have carried holiness farthest who reproach themselves with the deepest sinfulness . . .

Hence we know of two sources for feelings of guilt: that arising from the dread of authority and the later one from the dread of the super-ego. The first one compels us to renounce instinctual gratification; the other presses over and above this towards punishment, since the persistence of forbidden wishes cannot be concealed from the super-ego. We have also heard how the severity of the super-ego, the rigour of conscience, is to be explained. It simply carries on the severity of external authority which it has succeeded and to some extent replaced. We see now how renunciation of instinctual gratification is related to the sense of guilt. Originally, it is true, renunciation is the consequence of a dread of external authority; one gives up pleasures so as not to lose its love. Having made this renunciation, one is quits with authority, so to speak; no feeling of guilt should remain. But with the dread of the super-ego the case is different. Renunciation of gratification does not suffice here, for the wish persists and is not capable of being hidden from the super-ego. In spite of the renunciations made, feelings of guilt will be experienced, and this is a great disadvantage economically of the erection of the super-ego, or, as one may say, of the formation of conscience. Renunciation no longer has a completely absolving effect; virtuous restraint is no longer rewarded by the assurance of love; a threatened external unhappiness – loss of love and punishment meted out by external authority – has been exchanged for a lasting inner unhappiness, the tension of a sense of guilt.

Thus, 'discontent' is seen by Freud as the price of 'civilisation' – discontent (guilt) because of what the instincts 'want' but cannot have.

Max Weber: Four Types of Social Conduct (Action)

Weber argues that the purpose of sociology is to understand (*verstehen*) 'subjectively meaningful action . . . whose intent is related by the individuals involved to the conduct of others and is oriented accordingly'. In other words, sociology is about why human beings interact as they do.

Weber's 'ideal type' model of social conduct or action helps to bring some coherence to the variety of individual motive and behaviour. He suggests that the main types of social action are:

1 Rational
2 Value-related
3 Affectual (emotional)
4 Traditional

The basis of meaning in each type of conduct is different. Sometimes both affectual and traditional behaviour may be more reactive than intentionally meaningful.

In stressing the central importance in sociology of understanding social action, Weber did much to counterbalance tendencies to determinism within the developing discipline.

Reading 4 From Max Weber, *Basic Concepts in Sociology* (Greenwood Press, 1962), pp. 59–62

Characteristic forms of social conduct

Like any other form of conduct, social conduct may be determined in any one of the following four ways. *First*: It may be classified rationally and oriented toward a goal. In this instance the classification is based on the expectation that objects in the external situation or other human individuals will behave in a certain way, and by the use of such expectations as "conditions" or "means" for the successful achievement of the individual's own rationally chosen goals. Such a case will be called *goal-oriented* conduct. *Second*: Social conduct may be classified by the conscious belief in the absolute worth of the conduct, as such, independent of any ulterior motive and measured by some such standard as ethics, esthetics or religion. Such a case of rational orientation toward an absolute value will be called *value-related* conduct. *Third*: Social conduct may be classified affectually, especially emotionally, the result of a special configuration of feelings and emotions on the part of the individual. *Fourth*: Social conduct may be classified traditionally, having been accustomed to by long practice.

1 Strictly traditionalist behavior – just as the reactive type of imitation discussed above (see par. 1) lies altogether on the borderline and sometimes even crosses what can be called meaningfully oriented conduct. Frequently it is simply a dull reaction – almost automatic – to accustomed stimuli that have led behavior repeatedly along a routine course. The greater part of all routine duties performed habitually by people every day is of this type; consequently it is not just as a marginal case that it belongs in this classification but also, as will be shown later, because its attachment to what are accustomed forms can be upheld with varying degrees of self-consciousness and in a variety of senses: in that case the type may approach that of number two (value-relatedness).

2 Strictly affectual behavior also straddles the line of what may be considered "meaningfully" oriented, and frequently it, too, crosses the line; for instance, it may be an uninhibited reaction to some extraordinary stimulus. It is a case of sublimation when affectually conditioned behavior issues in the form of conscious release of emotional tensions. When this happens, it is usually, though not always, well on its way either toward value-related or goal-oriented rational conduct or both.

> i.e. emotion 'harnessed' in a rational or moral cause is meaningful.

3 Value-related conduct is distinguished from affectual conduct by its conscious formulation of the ultimate values governing such conduct and its consistent planned orientation to these values. At the same time these two types share in the fact that the meaning of the conduct does not lie in the achievement of some goal ulterior to it, but in engaging in the specific type of behavior for its own sake. Affectually determined behavior is the kind which demands the immediate satisfaction of an impulse, regardless of how sublime or sordid it may be, in order to obtain revenge, sensual gratification, complete surrender to a person or ideal, blissful contemplation, or finally to release emotional tensions.

Examples of pure value-related conduct would be the behaviour of persons who, regardless of the consequences, conduct themselves in such a way as to put into practice their convictions of what appears to them to be required by duty, honor, beauty, religiosity, piety or the importance of a "cause", no matter what its goal. Within our terminology such value-related behavior is always pursuant to commands or demands whose fulfilment are believed by the person engaging in it to constitute an obligation for him. Only insofar as human conduct is oriented exclusively toward such unconditional demands – and this is true to a very modest degree – will it be considered as "value-related", i.e., oriented toward absolute values. It will be seen that this type of conduct is important enough to justify its being singled out as a special type; though it should be noted that no attempt is made here to formulate in any way an exhaustive classification of certain types of behavior.

Religiously motivated behaviour is the main example of this type.

4 Rational conduct is of the goal-oriented kind when it is engaged in with due consideration for ends, means, and secondary effects; such conduct must also weigh alternate choices, as well as the relations of the end to other possible uses of the means and, finally, the relative importance of different possible ends. The classification of conduct either in affectual or traditional terms is thus incompatible with this type. The decision between competing and conflicting ends and results may in turn be determined by a consideration of absolute values: in that case, such conduct is goal-oriented only in respect to the choice of means. Or, the person engaged in such conduct may, rather than decide between conflicting or competing ends in terms of value-related orientation, merely take them as given subjective wants and arrange them on a scale in order of priority. He may then orient his conduct according to this scale in such a way that it conforms as far as possible to the order of priority as prescribed by the principle of "marginal utility".

Even absolute values can be rationally calculated on the basis of their relative usefulness (marginal utility) – or so Weber suggests.

This value-oriented conduct can be variously related to goal-oriented conduct. From the point of view of the latter, however, value-orientation acquires more irrationality the more absolute it becomes. For, the more unconditionally the individual devotes himself to such value for its own sake – be it because of sentiment, beauty, absolute kindness, or devotion to duty – the less is there any thought of the consequences of such devotion. Absolute goal-oriented conduct – i.e., pure expediency, without any reference to basic values – is essentially only a constructive exception.

5 Rarely is conduct, especially social conduct, oriented only in one or the other of these ways. Nor does this represent an exhaustive classification of the types of conduct now existing; it is meant merely to arrive at certain conceptually pure forms of sociologically important types, to which social conduct is more or less closely approximated, or as is much more usual, which constitute the elements joining to make it up. Only its future success can justify the usefulness of this classification for the purposes of our investigation.

Although Weber's four-part 'ideal-type' model of social action helps us understand 'reality', in reality action often does not fit into a single 'pure' category.

George Mead: The Action of the 'I'

George Mead distinguished two aspects of the 'self': the 'I' and the 'me'. The 'me' is that part of the self which has internalised society's norms and demands. The 'I', although it develops its capacity for role-play through social experience, is the source of free action within the self. I have chosen this reading to illustrate Mead's analysis of the 'I's capacity for freedom. However, it is worth noting that the 'I' is never wholly free of the 'me' (one never entirely escapes from one's socialisation and society), and that the extent to which people act freely varies between individuals.

Mead also indicates that 'free' action can sometimes be destructive as well as original and creative.

Reading 5 From George Mead, *Mind, Self, and Society* (The University of Chicago Press, 1934), pp. 209–11

The contributions of the "me" and the "I"

I have been undertaking to distinguish between the "I" and the "me" as different phases of the self, the "me" answering to the organized attitudes of the others which we definitely assume and which determine consequently our own conduct so far as it is of a self-conscious character. Now the "me" may be regarded as giving the form of the "I". The novelty comes in the action of the "I", but the structure, the form of the self is one which is conventional.

By describing the 'form of the self' as 'conventional', Mead means that the self is shaped by socialisation.

This conventional form may be reduced to a minimum. In the artist's attitude, where there is artistic creation, the emphasis upon the element of novelty is carried to the limit. This demand for the unconventional is especially noticeable in modern art. Here the artist is supposed to break away from convention; a part of his artistic expression is thought to be in the breakdown of convention. This attitude is, of course, not essential to the artistic function, and it probably never occurs in the extreme form in which it is often proclaimed. Take certain of the artists of the past. In the Greek world the artists were, in a certain sense, the supreme artisans. What they were to do was more or less set by the community, and accepted by themselves, as the expression of heroic figures, certain deities, the erection of temples. Definite rules were accepted as essential to the expression. And yet the artist introduced an originality into it which distinguishes one artist from another. In the case of the artist the emphasis upon that which is unconventional, that which is not in the structure of the "me", is carried as far, perhaps, as it can be carried.

This same emphasis also appears in certain types of conduct which are impulsive. Impulsive conduct is uncontrolled conduct. The structure of the "me" does not there determine the expression of the "I". If we use a Freudian expression, the "me" is in a certain sense of censor. It determines the sort of expression which can take place, sets the stage, and gives the cue. In the case of impulsive conduct this structure of the "me" involved in the situation does not furnish to any such degree this control. Take the situation

> Although generally critical of Freud, here Mead seems to draw on Freud's theory of 'natural aggression' to explain the more destructive type of ego ('I') assertion.

of self-assertion where the self simply asserts itself over against others, and suppose that the emotional stress is such that the forms of polite society in the performance of legitimate conduct are overthrown, so that the person expresses himself violently. There the "me" is determined by the situation. There are certain recognized fields within which an individual can assert himself, certain rights which he has within these limits. But let the stress become too great, these limits are not observed, and an individual asserts himself in perhaps a violent fashion. Then the "I" is the dominant element over against the "me". Under what we consider normal conditions the way in which an individual acts is determined by his taking the attitude of the others in the group, but if the individual is not given the opportunity to come up against people, as a child is not who is held out of intercourse with other people, then there results a situation in which the reaction is uncontrolled.

> Here Mead recognises that the expression of the ego can distinguish an individual from 'the rest of the crowd'. Incidentally, the aspect of Mead's social psychology which emphasises individuality accords very well with individualistic American cultural values.

Social control is the expression of the "me" over against the expression of the "I". It sets the limits, it gives the determination that enables the "I", so to speak, to use the "me" as the means of carrying out what is the undertaking that all are interested in. Where persons are held outside or beyond that sort of organized expression there arises a situation in which social control is absent. In the more or less fantastic psychology of the Freudian group, thinkers are dealing with the sexual life and with self-assertion in its violent form. The normal situation, however, is one which involves a reaction of the individual in a situation which is socially determined, but to which he brings his own responses as an "I". The response is, in the experience of the individual, an expression with which the self is identified. It is such a response which raises him above the institutionalized individual.

Frederick von Hayek: Individual Freedom, Coercion and the State

Hayek is better known as an economist and political philosopher than as a sociologist – and that is almost certainly how he would have wanted it. However, there is a clear, implicit sociology in his writings. As is apparent from the passage below, his view of society is that it is (or ought to be) the sum of the mutual activities of free individuals within an agreed framework of law. The main and essential purpose of the law is to protect individuals from each other, i.e. to ensure individual liberty. In turn, the main purpose of the state is to enforce the law. The state is entitled to use coercion to prevent individuals from coercing other individuals. Hayek also considers that it is the function of the state to provide certain common services, which should be kept to the minimum, otherwise the state itself becomes a costly and complex burden on individuals.

Hayek's work is included as a theoretical perspective in this section largely because of his immense, worldwide influence in recent years. In particular, he was an inspiration to Margaret Thatcher and Ronald Reagan even though neither pursued his analyses with the radicalism with which he stated them.

Hayek differs from sociologists proper in that the latter invariably consider that there is a natural social aspect or level to human life (the study of which is sociology). In contrast, Hayek sees human life exclusively in terms of individual freedom or coercion (by other individuals or the state). It may be more accurate to describe his perspective as 'anti-sociological' than as implicitly sociological. Nevertheless, we have seen that when applied by politicians and policy-makers, Hayek-inspired analysis can have an enormous effect on what sociologists refer to as 'society', but what Hayek prefers to think of as many individuals acting simply on the basis of self-interest.

Reading 6 From Frederick von Hayek, *The Constitution of Liberty* (Routledge and Kegan Paul, 1960), pp. 11–12, 139–40

We are concerned in this book with that condition of men in which coercion of some by others is reduced as much as is possible in society. This state we shall describe throughout as a state of liberty or freedom. These two words have been also used to describe many other good things of life. It would therefore not be very profitable to start by asking what they really mean. It would seem better to state, first, the condition which we shall mean when we use them . . . only in order to define more sharply that which we have adopted.

The state in which a man is not subject to coercion by the arbitrary will of another or others is often also distinguished as "individual" or "personal" freedom, and whenever we want to remind the reader that it is in this sense that we are using the word "freedom", we shall employ that expression . . .

Even our tentative indication of what we shall mean by "freedom" will have shown that it describes a state which man living among his fellows may hope to approach closely but can hardly expect to realise perfectly. The task of a policy of freedom must therefore be to minimise coercion or its harmful effects, even if it cannot eliminate it completely . . .

'data' means conditions

Since coercion is the control of the essential data of an individual's action by another, it can be prevented only by enabling the individual to secure for himself some private sphere where he is protected against such interference. The assurance that he can count on certain facts not being deliberately shaped by another can be given to him only by some authority that has the necessary power. It is here that coercion of one individual by another can be prevented only by the threat of coercion.

The existence of such an assured free sphere seems to us so much a normal condition of life that we are tempted to define "coercion" by the use of such terms as "the interference with legitimate expectations", or "infringement of rights", or "arbitrary interference". But in defining coercion we cannot take for granted the arrangements intended to prevent it. The "legitimacy" of one's expectations or the "rights" of the individual are the result of the recognition of such a private sphere. Coercion not only would exist but would be much more common if no such protected sphere existed. Only in a society that has already attempted to prevent coercion by some demarcation of a protected sphere can a concept like "arbitrary interference" have a definite meaning.

If the recognition of such individual spheres, however, is not itself to become an instrument of coercion, their range and content must not be determined by the deliberate assignment of particular things to particular men. If what was to be included in a man's private sphere were to be determined by the will of any man or group of men, this would simply transfer the power of coercion to that will. Nor would it be desirable to have the particular contents of a man's private sphere fixed once and for all. If people are to make the best use of their knowledge and capacities and foresight, it is desirable that they themselves have some voice in the determination of what will be included in their personal protected sphere.

The solution that men have found for this problem rests on the recognition of general rules governing the conditions under which objects or circumstances become part of the protected sphere of a person or persons. The acceptance of such rules enables each member of a society to shape the content of his protected sphere and all members to recognize what belongs to their sphere and what does not.

We must not think of this sphere as consisting exclusively, or even chiefly, of material things. Although to divide the material objects of our environment into what is mine and what is another's is the principal aim of the rules which delimit the spheres, they also secure for us many other "rights", such as security in certain uses of things or merely protection against interference with our actions.

Marx would have regarded Hayek's emphasis on private property as 'bourgeois'. The former's emphasis on communal property marks a fundamental difference between the two. 'Several', in this context, means 'separate'.

The recognition of private or several property is thus an essential condition for the prevention of coercion, though by no means the only one. We are rarely in a position to carry out a coherent plan of action unless we are certain of our exclusive control of some material objects; and where we do not control them, it is necessary that we know who does if we are to collaborate with others. The recognition of property is clearly the first step in the delimitation of the private sphere which protects us against coercion; and it has long been recognised that "a people averse to the institution of private property is without the first element of freedom" and that "nobody is at liberty to attack several property and to say at the same time that he values civilization".

SOCIOLOGICAL METHODS

Introduction: Readings 7–10

This section covers the main sociological methods. The first extract, by Alan Bryman, differs from the others in that it is a theoretical overview of issues related to quantitative methods, whereas the others are all drawn directly from methodological sections of pieces of empirical work. In addition to describing a range of quantitative methods, Bryman discusses the relationship between natural science, social science and positivism. He avoids the simplifications of many introductory discussions and, in particular, points out that positivism is not the only model for either quantitative social science *or* natural science. (For another discussion of natural scientific approaches, see Kuhn, Reading 81). Bryman also rejects the tendency to polarise quantitative and qualitative methods.

Although the extract from Eileen Barker has been selected to illustrate the main qualitative method, participant observation, it further demonstrates that research methods cannot be described in terms of water-tight boxes. Indeed, Barker herself used quantitative methodology as well as participant observation in her study of the religious sect, the Moonies. Her study also shows that the process of research does not always progress as expected, and that sometimes researchers have to improvise according to circumstances. The question is, how much do such improvisations affect the reliability and validity of research?

The reading from Ian Warwick and his colleagues runs mildly counter to the tendency to reconcile quantitative and qualitative methods evinced in the rest of this section. They argue that the quality of data on complex and sensitive matters such as attitudes to HIV and AIDS is heavily dependent on the methods of enquiry adopted. They argue that semi-structured interviews rather than structured questions provide a more effective tool of research in this area.

The final reading in this section is included because of the excellent practical advice Helen Simons gives on how to carry out open-ended (unstructured) interviews.

Alan Bryman:
• An Overview of Quantitative Methods
• The Positivist Position
• Combining Quantitative and Qualitative Research

The first of the three sections in this reading is a succinct summary of the main quantitative methods used by sociologists. It also raises the question – pursued in the second section – why do certain sociologists seek to copy the approach of natural scientists?

In the second section, Bryman neatly summarises the positivist position, while pointing out that few, if any, sociologists would subscribe to all of the five points he associates with positivism. These are:

1 Positivism entails a belief that the methods and procedures of the natural sciences are appropriate to the social sciences.
2 Positivism entails a belief that only those phenomena that can be directly observed can be validly considered as knowledge.
3 Positivism tends to suggest that scientific knowledge is arrived at through the accumulation of verifiable facts.
4 Positivism considers that scientific theories are required to be empirically tested.
5 Positivism aspires to value neutrality in the process of research.

It is important to be aware that Bryman considers that positivism is merely one, not the only, approach to natural science. Further, while he concedes that some social scientists have been over-imitative in adopting positivist assumptions, he stresses that many others have not. His third section illustrates how many sociologists have used both quantitative and qualitative methods without getting 'stuck' in a doctrinaire version of the positivist approach. Overall, this is a much more balanced and accurate account of the relationship between natural science, positivism and social science than that which obtains in many textbooks.

Reading 7 From Alan Bryman, *Quantity and Quality in Social Research* (Unwin Hyman, 1988), pp. 11–12, 13, 14–16, 18, 127–28

A brief overview of quantitative methods

Quantitative research is associated with a number of different approaches to data collection. In sociology in particular, the social survey is one of the main methods of data collection which embodies the features of quantitative research to be explored below. The survey's capacity for generating quantifiable data on large numbers of people who are known to be representative of a wider population in order to test theories or hypotheses has been viewed by many practitioners as a means of capturing many of the ingredients of a science . . . Most survey research is based on an underlying research design which is called 'correlational' or 'cross-sectional'. This means that data are collected on a cross-section of people at a single point in time in order to discover the ways and degrees to which variables relate to each other.

The social survey approach contrasts with experimental designs, which constitute the main approach to data collection within the tradition of quantitative research in social psychology. In an experiment, there are at least two groups to which subjects have been randomly allocated: an experimental and a control group. The logic of experimental design is that the former group is exposed to an experimental stimulus (the independent variable) but the control group is not. Any observed differences between the two groups is deemed to be due to the independent variable alone, since the two groups are identical in all other aspects. Thus an investigator may be interested in whether autonomy or close control leads to more rapid task attainment. Experimental subjects will be randomly allocated to each of the two conditions, but the two groups will differ only in that one group will be allowed autonomy in how it accomplishes the assigned task, whereas the other group will receive clear instructions and be closely supervised. In all other respects (such as the nature of the task, the experimental setting, and so on) the experiences of the two groups will be identical, so that if there are any differences in time taken to accomplish the task, it can be assumed that this is due to the experimental treatment. The term 'control group' is a little misleading in that, as in this hypothetical study, it is not without an experimental treatment. Both groups are exposed to an experimental stimulus – either autonomy or close control.

Surveys and experiments are probably the main vehicles of quantitative research but three others are worthy of a brief mention. The analysis of previously collected data, like official statistics on crime, suicide, unemployment, health, and so on, can be subsumed within the tradition of quantitative research. Indeed, Durkheim's (1952) analysis of suicide statistics is often treated as an exemplar of research within this tradition (e.g. Keat and Urry, 1975). Secondly, structured observation, whereby the researcher records observations in accordance with a pre-determined schedule and quantifies the resulting data, displays many of the characteristics of quantitative research. It is often used in the examination of patterns of interaction such as studies of teacher-pupil interaction (Flanders, 1970) or in Blau's (1955) study of patterns of consultation among officials in a government bureaucracy. Finally, as Beardsworth (1980) had indicated, content analysis – the quantitative analysis of the communication content of media such as newspapers – shares many of the chief features of quantitative research.

Quantitative research is, then, a genre which uses a special language which appears to exhibit some similarity to the ways in which scientists talk about how they investigate the natural order – variables, control, measurement, experiment. This superficial imagery reflects the tendency for quantitative research to be under-pinned by a natural science model, which means that the logic and procedures of the natural sciences are taken to provide an epistemological yardstick against which empirical research in the social sciences must be appraised before it can be treated as valid knowledge . . .

The foregoing discussion, of course, begs the question: why should students of society copy the approach of natural scientists whose subject matter appears so different? In part, the enormous success of the sciences this century in facilitating our understanding of the natural order has probably played a part. So too has the view of writers subscribing to the doctrine of positivism (about which more will be said below) that the natural sciences provide a standard against which knowledge should be gauged and that there is no logical reason why its procedures should not be equally applicable to the study of society. In addition, as social scientists have been looked to increasingly by governments and other agencies to provide policy-relevant research (or alternatively have sought to present themselves in this light), they have either been compelled to adopt a supposedly scientific approach or have sought to display an aura of scientific method in order to secure funding. The reasons are undoubtedly legion and since this is a somewhat speculative topic it is not proposed to dwell any further on it. Rather, it is more fruitful to examine the precise nature of the scientific method that forms the bedrock of quantitative research. In order to do this it is necessary to introduce the notion of *positivism*, which is invariably credited with providing the outline of the social scientist's understanding of what science entails, especially by the opponents of quantitative research (e.g. Walsh, 1972).

The positivist position

There are a number of problems with the term 'positivism', one of which can be readily discerned in the more recent writing on philosophical issues in relation to the social sciences. This problem is simply that in the context of the critique of quantitative research that built up in the 1960s, and which was carried forward into the subsequent decade, the attribution 'positivist' was used glibly and indiscriminately by many writers and in fact became a term of abuse. Nowadays writers on positivism bemoan this exploitation of the term and seek to distance themselves from the tendency to treat it as a pejorative designation (e.g. Giddens, 1974; Cohen, 1980; Bryant, 1985). Thus in the eyes of many authors the term has become devalued as a description of a particular stance in relation to the pursuit of knowledge.

A further difficulty is that even among more sophisticated treatments of positivism a wide range of meanings is likely to be discerned. Different versions of positivism can be found; Half-penny (1982) identifies twelve. Even when there is a rough overlap among authors on the basic meaning of the term, they rarely agree precisely on its essential components. Consequently, in the explication of positivism that follows can be found not a complete catalogue of the constituents which have been identified by various writers but an extraction of those which are most frequently cited. The basic point about positivism is that it is a philosophy which both proclaims the suitability of the scientific method to all forms of knowledge and gives an account of what that method entails, divergent versions notwithstanding. Thus in following the widely held convention of regarding quantitative research as founded on positivism one is presumably subscribing to the view that the former reflects the aims and tenets of the latter. What then is positivism supposed to comprise?

1 First and foremost, positivism entails a belief that the methods and procedures of the natural sciences are appropriate to the social sciences. This view involves a conviction that the fact that the objects of the social sciences – people – think, have feelings, communicate through language and otherwise, attribute meaning to their environment, and superficially appear to be uniquely different from one another in terms of their beliefs and personal characteristics – qualities not normally held to describe the objects of the natural scientist – is not an obstacle to the implementation of the scientific method. This position is often referred to as the principle of *methodological monism* or *methodological naturalism* (von Wright, 1971; Giedymin, 1975).

2 Like the first constituent, this second one is rarely omitted from expositions of positivism. Positivism entails a belief that only those phenomena which are observable, in the sense of being amenable to the senses, can validly be warranted as knowledge. This means that phenomena which cannot be observed either directly through experience and observation or indirectly with the aid of instruments have no place. Such a position rules out any possibility of incorporating metaphysical notions of 'feelings' or 'subjective experience' into the realms of social scientific knowledge unless they can be rendered observable. This aspect of positivism is often referred to as the doctrine of *phenomenalism* and sometimes as *empiricism*, although some writers would probably challenge the treatment of these two terms as synonyms.

3 Many accounts of positivism suggest that scientific knowledge is arrived at through the accumulation of verified facts. These facts feed into the theoretical edifice pertaining to a particular domain of knowledge. Thus theory expresses and reflects the accumulated findings of empirical research. Such findings are often referred to as 'laws', that is, empirically established regularities. The notion of science, and in particular scientific theories, being a compendium of empirically established facts is often referred to as the doctrine of *inductivism*.

4 Scientific theories are seen by positivists as providing a kind of backcloth to empirical research in the sense that hypotheses are derived from them – usually in the form of postulated causal connections between entities – which are then submitted to empirical test. This implies that science is *deductive*, in that it seeks to extract specific propositions from general accounts of reality. The logic involved might entail seeking to construct a scientific theory to explain the laws pertaining to a particular field; a hypothesis (or possibly more than one) is derived in order to enable the scientist to test the theory; if the hypothesis is rejected when submitted to rigorous empirical examination the theory must be revised.

5 Positivism is also often taken to entail a particular stance in relation to *values*. This notion can be discerned in explications of positivism in two senses. The first is the more obvious sense of needing to purge the scientist of values which may impair his or her objectivity and so undermine the validity of knowledge. Clearly, within the domain of the social sciences, in which moral or political predispositions may exert a greater influence than in the natural sciences, this aspect of positivism has special relevance. The second aspect of positivism's posture on values is to draw a sharp distinction between scientific issues and statements on the one hand and normative ones on the other. Positivism denies the appropriateness of the sphere of the normative to its purview because normative statements cannot be verified in relation to experience. While positivists recognize that they can investigate the implications of a particular normative position, they cannot verify or falsify the position itself. In a sense, this standpoint is a special instance of the doctrine of phenomenalism, but it has been taken to have a particular relevance in the context of the social sciences (Keat, 1981), though it figures in more general treatments too (Kolakowski, 1972).

A number of liberties have been taken in this exposition: there is no single treatment of positivism which entails all of these principles and not all positivists (living or dead) would subscribe to all of them. Some points have been treated in a fairly cavalier manner in order to cut a swath through a very dense undergrowth of debate. The first two ingredients probably come closest to what most people mean by positivism and are also the ones which recur most strikingly in the various expositions of it . . .

Combining quantitative and qualitative research

The rather partisan, either/or tenor of the debate about quantitative and qualitative research may appear somewhat bizarre to an outsider, for whom the obvious way forward is likely to be a fusion of the two approaches so that their respective strengths might be reaped. The technical version of the debate more readily allows this solution to be accommodated because it is much less wedded than the epistemological version to a view that the two traditions reflect antagonistic views about how the social sciences ought to be conducted. In this chapter, the focal concern will be the ways in which the methods associated with quantitative and qualitative research can be, and have been, combined. As noted in Chapter 3, there are examples of investigations carried out by investigators who locate their work largely within the tradition of qualitative research, but who have used survey procedures in tandem with participant observation (e.g. Woods, 1979; Ball, 1981). Such research will be employed as an example of the combination of quantitative and qualitative research, because the chief concern of the present chapter is with the *methods* with which each is associated.

The focus on methods of investigation should not lose sight of the significance of a distinction between quantitative and qualitative *data*. For example, some of the findings associated with an ethnographic study may be presented in a quantified form. In their research on the de-skilling of clerical work, Crompton and Jones (1988) collected much detailed qualitative information, in the form of verbatim reports, on the work of their respondents. In spite of considerable reservations about coding these data, they aggregated people's accounts of their work in terms of the amounts of control they were able to exercise in their work. Even among qualitative researchers who prefer to resist such temptations, the use of quasi-quantitative terms like 'many', 'frequently', 'some', and the like, is common (e.g. Gans, 1982, p. 408). Further, survey researchers provide the occasional verbatim quotation from an interview, or one or two case examples of respondents who exemplify a particular pattern. Sometimes, the reporting of qualitative data deriving from a survey can be quite considerable. In addition, researchers sometimes use a structured interview for the simultaneous collection of both quantitative and qualitative data. For example, Ford *et al.* (1982) employed such a structured interview schedule to investigate employers' recruitment practices. Quantitative data were collected on such topics as the frequency of use of particular methods of recruitment. The schedule also permitted qualitative data to be collected on employers' reasons for the use and non-use of particular recruitment channels. Such cases may be viewed as indicative of a slight limitation in discussing quantitative and qualitative research largely in terms of methods of data collection. However, there is little doubt that methods like surveys and participant observation are typically seen as sources of quantitative and qualitative data respectively, so that it is not proposed to challenge this convention but merely to alert the reader to the lack of a hard and fast distinction.

Note Several extracts in this book are based on original social surveys or draw heavily on existing social surveys. These include: Readings 14, 15 and 32.

Eileen Barker: Participant Observation

I have chosen this section from Eileen Barker's enquiry into the religious sect, the Moonies, because it raises many of the key issues of participant observation in a few pages. The thorough and disciplined way in which Barker carried out her research should dispel any notion that this method is an easy option. In fact, to obtain the full range of data she sought, Barker adopted three main methodologies: in-depth interviews, questionnaires and participant observation. Only the latter is included here. A second extract from the findings of this piece of research into the Moonies is given later in this book (Reading 76).

Reading 8 From Eileen Barker, The *Making of a Moonie: Choice or Brainwashing* (Basil Blackwell, 1984), pp. 18–21, 22, 24–26

Participant observation

Between interviews, and at odd periods throughout the next six years, I was also engaged in 'participant observation'. This entailed living in various centres with the members. I also attended a whole series of seminars or 'workshops' some of which were for potential members, but others were for academics or for parents, and there were yet others which were normally confined to the members themselves. I visited numerous Unification centres in North America. On the West Coast, early in the study, I nervously left instructions with a friend in San Francisco to rescue me if I did not return from a weekend at the notorious Camp K (see chapter 4). Later I was to go, this time without a second thought, to the equally notorious farm at Boonville (sometimes spelled Booneville). On the East Coast I visited various centres in New York City and New York State. I stayed at the Unification Seminary in Barrytown, and I was taken on a tour of a 'Home-Church' area in Harlem. I got a supplementary grant to study new religious movements in all four Scandinavian countries, and whenever I happened to be in any other country I would make a point of trying to visit the local Unification centre.

Although many of their interests and methods overlap, the social sciences are unlike the natural sciences in a number of ways. This is partly because they ask different kinds of questions. The chemist does not try to find out what molecules 'feel' when they are subjected to a particular process, but some degree of subjective understanding is necessary for the sociologist if he is to describe, let alone understand or explain, what his data are doing. The method employed in the attempt to gain some kind of empathetic understanding of what the world looks like from other people's point of view is frequently referred to as *Verstehen*.

The concept of *verstehen* is associated with Max Weber. It is the process of trying to understand the subjective meanings of others.

Although the two are frequently confused, empathy does not necessarily imply sympathy. *Verstehen* is a process of inquiry during which the researcher tries to put himself in other people's shoes or, to use another metaphor, to see the world through their glasses. He attempts to recognize the assumptions or 'filters' through which their world is seen, so that the actoins and perceptions of the people he is studying begin to make sense. Obviously, this is an exercise which is much easier in some instances than in others. As a mother of teenage children, I found little difficulty in empathizing fairly quickly with most of the parents I met. It took a bit longer with some of my other subjects. The first time a young Californian Moonie rushed up and flung his arms around me with declarations of eternal love, I recoiled with truly British horror and only just managed to prevent myself from protesting that I did not think we had been introduced.

Other sociologists who have adopted participant observation as a research method also refer to such stages of involvement. Thus Ronald Frankenburg (1966) refers to stages of more objective preparation, subjective involvement, and objective assessment in his research into a Welsh community.

I found that the role I played as a participant observer went through three distinct stages during the course of the study. First there was a passive stage during which I did very little except to watch and listen (doing the washing-up in the kitchen was always a good place for this). Next there was an interactive stage during which I felt familiar enough with the Unification perspective to join in conversations without jarring; Moonies no longer felt that they had to 'translate' everything for me, and those Moonies who did not know me would sometimes take me to be a member. Finally there was the active stage. Having learned the social language in the first stage and how to use it in the second, I began in the third stage to explore its range and scope, its potentialities and its limitations. I argued and asked all the awkward questions that I had been afraid to voice too loudly at an earlier stage lest I were not allowed to continue my study. I could no longer be told that I did not understand because, in one sense at least, I patently *did* understand quite a lot – and I was using Unification arguments in my questioning. In this I angered some Moonies and saddened others, but there were those who not only tolerated my probing but actually discussed the problems that they and the movement were facing with an amazing frankness.

A perennial problem in participant observation is the ethical issue of whether it is justified to lie or hide the truth if it seems to help the research. The problem is even more difficult to escape in the case of covert (hidden) as opposed to overt (open) research.

Of course, even in the interactive stage it was known that I was not a Moonie. I never pretended that I was, or that I was likely to become one. I admit that I was sometimes evasive, and I certainly did not always say everything that was on my mind, but I cannot remember any occasion on which I consciously lied to a Moonie. Being known to be a non-member had its disadvantages, but by talking to people who had left the movement I was able to check that I was not missing any of the internal information which was available to rank-and-file members. At the same time, being an outsider who was 'inside' had enormous advantages. I was allowed (even, on certain occasions, expected) to ask questions that no member would have presumed to ask either his leaders or his peers. Furthermore, several Moonies who felt that their problems were not understood by the leaders, and yet would not have dreamed of being disloyal to the movement by talking to their parents or other outsiders, could confide in me because of the very fact that I was both organisationally and emotionally uninvolved. It was not part of my duty to report which individuals were frustrated by the minor niggles of everyday life, or who was unhappily questioning some of the practices of the movement. I just listened. Fears and resentments could be expressed to someone who knew the context, yet would neither judge nor spill the beans. I found, furthermore, that I was the recipient of certain 'classified' information and, even without my asking for it, I was frequently presented with some of the less widely distributed Church literature.

My 'moles' fell into four broad categories. There were those who assumed that I knew everything anyway. Then there were those who wanted me to see everything so I would know that the 'secrets' were not as awful as I might imagine were I not to see them. There were others who, while generally loyal to the overall aims of the movement, wanted pressure to be put on the leaders by outsiders in connection with particular practices or policies about which they were worried. Finally, there were those who were generally disillusioned (and perhaps no longer members) and who wanted to expose what they considered to be the less attractive aspects of the movement without actually going to the media or the anti-cultists . . .

One question which researchers always have to ask themselves is how far they can trust their informants. I was continually being warned that, as Moonies practised 'heavenly deception' (telling permissible lies in order to further God's work in a satanic world), any information I obtained from a Moonie would be worthless.

I have not included details of the important process of cross-checking data here – but in the case of this research it was done very thoroughly.

I knew there was a problem, but I felt confident that, even if the Moonies did lie, to observe lying Moonies could produce more valuable data than would be got by confining oneself to the testimonies of ex-Moonies (see chapter 5). I did, however, need to discover which were the lies. This involved building up a very elaborate system of cross-checking between informants (particularly any discrepancies between information from those in the movement and those outside) and using several different approaches to a particular question – a procedure which was extremely time-consuming and which could not, by the very nature of the exercise, be hurried.

The issue of 'researcher effect' is another classic one of participant observation.

Finally, mention ought to be made of the fact that the people I was studying could be influenced by my presence *because* I was studying them. The observer of the natural world is not (unless he is doing experiments in which Heisenberg's Uncertainty Principle is of moment) nearly as likely as the observer of the social world to influence the data he is studying. It is impossible to know just how much my research 'disturbed' what was happening. There were several occasions on which I mediated between a Moonie and his parents, and I frequently tried to persuade the movement's leaders to see that the members kept in touch with their relations. These interventions, and the giving of information to parents, the media, members of the 'anti-cult movement', and religious and various other officials, I undertook with an awareness that what I was doing could affect the situation. There were also numerous occasions on which my influence was unintended. A couple of extreme examples will make the point.

The first incident occurred while I was on a twenty-one-day course at which the participants were expected to deliver a lecture. The subject I was allocated was 'The Purpose of the Coming of the Messiah'. I did not exactly enjoy this aspect of my research, but participant observation does involve participation, so I gave the talk, carefully punctuating its delivery with phrases such as 'The *Divine Principle* teaches that . . . ' or 'According to the *Principle* . . . '. When I had finished, a member of the audience declared that she had been extremely worried about that particular part of the doctrine, but she now understood it, and she fully accepted that the Reverend Moon was indeed the Messiah. I was horrified. 'But I don't believe it,' I insisted. 'I don't think it's true.' 'Perhaps not,' interrupted the Moonie in charge, 'but God has used Eileen to show Rosemary the truth'.

I had, from the start, excluded 'witnessing' (or 'spreading the truth') from the activities in which I was prepared to participate. I immediately vowed to refuse to give lectures in any further workshops I might attend. I have, however, given numerous talks at universities, colleges, schools, church halls and at various conferences on the subject of new religious movements in general and the Unification Church in particular. On such occasions my audience has usually consisted of people who knew little about the Unification Church – except that it was 'a bad thing'. Every once in a while, however, a Moonie . . . has stood up and made himself known (sometimes to my embarrassment and sometimes to the astonishment of his fellow students who had thought until that moment that he was an 'ordinary' student). The information about the second example of my influence on those whom I was studying came to me through a friend, one of whose students was an ex-Moonie who told him that she had heard me giving a lecture on the movement and had consequently realized for the first time that it was possible for her to take what she called 'a middle-way position'. She had reached a stage of not accepting everything that was taught or expected of her in the Unification Church, but at the same time she had felt that she could not deny the good things which she had experienced in the movement in the way that she assumed would be necessary (because of the attitudes of Moonies on the one hand and that of 'outsiders' on the other) if she were to leave. But when she had heard me give, from an outsider's perspective, what she considered to be a fairly accurate account of the movement, she had concluded that she did not have to make an absolute 'yes or no' choice but was able to leave, rather than feeling forced to stay because of her ambivalent feelings.

Of course, most of the effects of research were unlikely to be as dramatic as tipping someone into joining or leaving the movement, but it would be hard to believe that my presence in the centres did not make some difference, especially in the early years of my research when the rank-and-file Moonies very rarely talked to anyone who was not a member except for the specific purposes of fund-raising or finding new recruits. When I began the interviewing I was uncertain about the consequences of my asking difficult and searching questions which anyone, not just Moonies, would have found hard to answer. My interviewees told me that they had, in fact, enjoyed the experience, although it had often been pretty exhausting. They said that it had made them think about things they had not really thought about before; but when I pointed out inconsistencies in their arguments they were unlikely to crumble and express doubts about their faith – instead they tended to say that I had presented them with a challenge to look more deeply at the beliefs and so discover the answer, which they felt certain could be found were they only to study or think about it. I also found that I became a source of certain kinds of information for the Moonies, and, as I have already stated, I found that several Moonies would contact me for the odd chat. In this position I played the role of the 'stranger', which was, as I have already indicated, extremely useful for my research, but in so far as there was unlikely to be a 'substitute stranger' for many of those who confided in me, I must, once again, acknowledge that I could have made a difference to the situation I was studying – indeed, in some instances, I hope I did.

> Do you think the 'hope' expressed in this sentence can be justified in terms of sociological research?

> *Note* Reading 38 provides a further example of the use of participant observation.

Ian Warwick, Peter Aggleton and Hilary Homans: Semi-structured Interviews

The point of placing this extract here is to illustrate that qualitative methods can be more appropriate for eliciting certain types of data than quantitative methods. What Warwick and his colleagues show is that when young people are able to respond freely to questions about HIV infection and AIDS, they give a much fuller and more detailed account than when responding to structured questions. This is an important point in terms of sociological methodology, but it also has implications for the relationship between research and health education/policy (both of which points are bought out by the authors).

This extract is also rich in material illustrating how given groups of young people construct their own commonsense understandings of the world – in this case, of HIV and AIDS – and of how they themselves are constructed and sometimes stereotyped by others. An example of the latter is how the health issues of young lesbians in relation to HIV and AIDS seem to have been rendered almost 'invisible' because of the failure of health educators to 'see' them.

Reading 9 From Ian Warwick, Peter Aggleton and Hilary Homans, 'Constructing commonsense young people's beliefs about AIDS' in *Sociology of Health and Illness*, Vol. 10, No. 3, 1988, pp. 215–16, 217, 218, 223–26

Lay beliefs about HIV infection and AIDS

There are many ways in which an investigation into lay beliefs about HIV infection and AIDS can be carried out. Formal educational settings such as schools . . . and colleges . . . have been the most widely researched contexts so far in studies of young people's beliefs about HIV infection and AIDS. Other settings in which young people have been contacted include the home, where in one study at least, data has been collected by telephone (Strunin, and Hingson, 1987), in shopping precincts (West Midlands Regional Health Authority, 1988) and in youth groups (Millan and Ross, 1987).

Data has been collected in a variety of ways. By far the majority of studies to date have examined the extent to which young people are acquainted with mainstream medical knowledge. In DiClemente *et al*'s (1986, 1987, 1988) studies of young people's health knowledge, for example, respondents were required to indicate the extent to which they agree with a series of 'ready made' statements about HIV infection and AIDS derived from medical and media reports. Similar strategies to this were used in Strunin and Hingson's (1987) telephone survey in the United States of young people between the ages of 16 and 19, and in the study reported by Clift, Stears and Legg (1987) into the effects of the 1986 Department of Health's public information campaign on English college students' beliefs about AIDS.

Although some questionnaires have occasionally included open ended questions, rarely has a more exploratory stance been adopted in which efforts are made to access and study lay beliefs about HIV infection and AIDS on their own terms before they are contextualized against mainstream medical opinion. There is a pressing need for more open-ended and interpretative investigations of this kind, which set out to explore the complexities and contradictions within everyday understandings of AIDS. In this paper therefore we will report on a recent study of lay health beliefs which attempts to take some of these issues on board.

Method

In September 1986, as part of our work in connection with the project *Young People's Health Knowledge and AIDS*, we began a study of lay beliefs about HIV infection and AIDS. In connection with this research, we have recently completed a series of 50 in-depth interviews with young people aged between 16 and 25 involved in local authority youth provision, voluntary sector youth groups and youth training schemes. The youth clubs and youth facilities in which we have carried out this work have been urban, drawing their membership from young people living close by. Interviews were carried out by a member of the project team, Ian Warwick, who had prior experience working with young people in lesbian and gay youth groups as well as more generic types of youth provision. Equal numbers of young women and young men were included in the interviews, and data was from young people participating in lesbian and gay youth provision as well as in what we term undifferentiated youth provision.

Interviews took place in the youth centre or in respondents' homes.

It was originally intended that each interview would last about an hour although many went on considerably longer than this. In view of the exploratory nature of our investigations as well as our desire to explore young people's beliefs about HIV infection and AIDS in depth, we collected data by means of tape-recorded semi-structured interviews. Because we were interested in exploring the relationship between popular perceptions of HIV infection and AIDS and lay beliefs about health and illness in general, a series of open ended questions were constructed to enquire into a wide range of health issues. In addition to questions about HIV infection and AIDS, items were included to elicit lay beliefs about the common cold, cancer, spots and sexually transmitted diseases in general . . .

Only the *second* of these sections is included here. It follows below.

We were keen to explore a number of themes relating to what we earlier called the internal dynamics of lay beliefs about HIV infection and AIDS as well as the external relations of these. In this paper, we will report on three related sets of issues. First, we will identify some of the ways in which young people conceptualized and understood AIDS. Second, we will examine what were seen as its immediate causes. Third, we will explore what were perceived as the ultimate origins of the syndrome. Our analysis will also aim to identify similarities and differences between respondents participating in undifferentiated youth provision and respondents participating in lesbian and gay youth groups . . .

'Getting it' – beliefs about immediate causation

When young people were asked about the factors that might lead in an immediate sense to someone developing AIDS, a number of different kinds of explanation were offered. Some emphasised exogenous variables, whereas others emphasised more endogenous factors.

Amongst members of the undifferentiated sample two types of exogenous belief were apparent. The first stressed that either 'AIDS' or 'the virus' is highly contagious. Some respondents went so far as to suggest that touch alone might ensure transmission. This kind of explanation linked closely to a second set of lay beliefs which suggested that 'AIDS' or 'the virus' might be all around, floating in the air, lurking unseen and hidden, ready to descend on those who are as yet uninfected. As Steve put it:

> *Steve*: There's lot of it around this AIDS. It's everywhere. You get it from the environment you live in, (and from) the people you mix with and what have you . . .

Miasmatic beliefs such as these were linked both to the invisibility of the virus itself and to that of people who have HIV infection or AIDS.

In contrast, members of the lesbian and gay sample showed considerable resistance to the view that 'the virus' could be transmitted easily by casual contact. Indeed, respondents in this group talked disparagingly about people who still subscribed to such views: describing them variously as 'stupid', 'moralistic', 'ignorant', or as 'panic-mongers'. However, Izzy argued that the real problem was not simply a matter of ignorance or a lack of information. There were other more powerful reasons why such beliefs continued to be held:

> Izzy: . . . It's *convenient*. It's a convenient one to pull on people. It's a convenient thing to have against gay people isn't it? It's yet another good reason to think that being gay is terrible.

Amongst members of the undifferentiated youth sample, and concurrent with the view that 'the virus' might be spread miasmatically, were other beliefs which suggested that personal qualities of the individual might make them particularly susceptible to infection. These endogenous theories identified certain key groups of people who were either likely or unlikely to get 'the virus' or AIDS. Amongst those who were perceived as being especially prone to infection and especially likely to infect others were gay men, injecting drug users, prostitutes and those who are 'promiscuous'.

Respondents in lesbian and gay youth provision on the other hand made greater reference to specific sexual acts as well as to categories of person when talking about risk. Whilst everyone was felt to be 'risking it with oral (sex)', for example, this baseline risk might either increase or decrease depending on the perceived social characteristics of the partner involved. With respect to this second dimension of risk perception, the number of partners an individual had, their geographical origins, their sexual orientation, their occupation and their involvement (or otherwise) in injecting drug use were all seen as critical in determining whether or not a prospective partner posed a special risk. In this way 'the promiscuous', 'people from London', 'the promiscuous gays', 'homosexuals', 'bisexuals', 'prostitutes' and 'junkies' were all believed to be more likely than the respondent to either have 'the virus' or 'AIDS'.

Amongst the young lesbians and young gay men we interviewed, and during discussions of sexuality, it was felt that 'knowing ones sexual partner' could be a major preventative measure. Of particular importance, though, was where in Britain the prospective sexual partner came from:

> *Richie*: I'm much less aware of the dangers now that I'm not living in London. In London it was on my mind all the time because people in London are promiscuous with different people every week.
> *Mik*: It's very cosmopolitan isn't it?
> *Richie*: Yeah.

Taking precautions relating to safer sex, or being informed about safer sex, were also seen as helpful preventative measures by members of the lesbian and gay sample. However, some respondents felt that even if they were knowledgeable about 'safer sex' and even if they did take precautions, there might still have been a chance of getting 'the virus'. They realised that condoms could tear or split, and in some cases what were perceived as completely chance factors might be involved:

> *Simon*: Well, I mean that it could be any number of *completely chance factors*. If you're informed about it it's more likely to be accident or oversight, e.g. if a condom breaks or if . . . there's a cut or something that you hadn't known about and (it) opens unexpectedly, at the wrong time . . .

Reference to 'chance factors' highlights the role of serendipity in the explanations that young people used. This way of explaining the likelihood of infection was, however, seen most strikingly amongst some respondents in the undifferentiated youth sample. Whilst personal responsibility (or personal irresponsibility to be more precise) was most often identified as the reason why others might acquire HIV infection, in predicting the mechanisms by which they themselves might become infected, respondents switched logic to use more probabilistic modes of explanation. This was highlighted in a discussion with Jas:

> *Jas*: . . . Who gets the virus? I dunno. It's just the unlucky person innit?
> *Interviewer*: Right so it's luck?
> *Jas*: Bad luck I think! . . . Bad luck whoever gets it. I can't think who gets it, 'cos anybody can get it I suppose . . .
> *Interviewer*: Can you stop yourself from getting it?
> *Jas*: I dunno, 'cos you can get it from different ways innit? 'Cos I heard that you can get it from drinking out of that person's cup and if you don't know that person's got the virus and you drink out of the cup then you've got it haven't you?

This disjunction between the logic used to explain why certain categories of others (normally the supposedly 'guilty victims') might develop AIDS and that used to explain all other cases was also shown particularly clearly in a claim made by Tim:

> *Tim*: You can make yourself more at risk if you're a homosexual or a junkie, or both at the same time. You're at highest risk then and you could expect to get it. But if you're heterosexual and you're not a junkie, if you catch it (then) you're really unlucky . . .

This statement raises questions about the ways in which serendipitous logic is used to 'make sense' of AIDS. While factors associated with chance and luck appear in both groups, Tim's claims suggest that for some people these factors alone may explain heterosexual transmission. These beliefs may have important consequences for personal perceptions of risk, as well as for the perceived necessity to adopt safer sexual practices, since they suggest that perceptions of risk may be mediated by whether or not a person self-identifies as heterosexual or gay. Since there is now considerable evidence to suggest that many men who participate in homosexual acts do not consider themselves to be anything other than heterosexual (Reiss, 1961; Humphreys, 1970; Weinberg, 1983), these findings raise important THE questions about the relationship between sexual identity and risk perception.

By way of contrast with gay men, the lesbians we interviewed generally perceived themselves as unlikely to be at particular risk of HIV infection. Some stated that they were not worried at all, arguing that the only way they could get HIV would be either by 'going with men' or by sleeping with bisexual women. However, Jill's personal perceptions of risk had changed over time. She said:

> *Jill*: When the whole thing came out I didn't think that I was at any risk whatsoever, which sounds stupid I know, I know now that there is a chance and I know you've got to be careful . . .

However, most, if not all, of the information that has so far been made available about 'safer sex' was seen as irrelevant by the young lesbians interviewed. Moreover, finding out about 'safer sex' was generally perceived as difficult, since nearly all the information currently available is framed within an agenda which ascribes primacy to seminal restraint through condom use. Lou explained:

> *Lou*: They sort of tell men what to do, and they tell women to be careful and make sure that men do wear Durexes but they don't tell lesbians, I mean lesbians don't wear Durexes so I don't know what we're supposed to do . . . There's an awful lot of jokes going around about lesbians and what a woman does if she gets AIDS and what she does with the Durex . . . and you think 'God, what is the world coming to, what are we supposed to do about this?'

For the majority of the young lesbians we interviewed, this lack of information about safer sex was seen as intimately related to the processes by which lesbians and lesbian sexuality are rendered invisible and unacknowledged:

> *Diana*: . . . Well I mean everybody's had leaflets but for gay girls like lesbians there's just been no written information at all. There has been for men. There has been for heterosexual people. There hasn't been for us . . . We've just been totally ignored . . .

and Izzy continued:

> *Izzy*: . . . But that's like according to most of society lesbians don't exist anyway . . . (according to most of society) there isn't such a thing as a lesbian . . . (a) practising lesbian . . .

Conclusions

Throughout this paper, we have attempted to examine some of the complexities and contradictions within young people's beliefs about HIV infection and AIDS. Our concern has been to explore some of the ways in which young people have 'made sense' of the information to which they have had access. What is particularly clear from our findings is that mainstream medical explanations are at best moderately well understood. In this respect, it does not seem to be the case that young people are especially confused or ignorant about the issues, since in many ways their lay beliefs are comparable to those that have already been identified amongst sections fo the adult population (Vass, 1986; Mills, 1986; Campbell and Walters, 1987).

Like many adults including, sadly, a number of those who work professionally in the field of HIV infection and AIDS, some of our respondents shared the view that AIDS is either contagious or infectious, when in reality it is neither. Popular explanations that fail to make the distinction between a virus which is infectious under specific circumstances, and AIDS which is a medically diagnosed syndrome, have allowed many young people to construct their own understandings of the relationship between these two distinct phenomena. Amongst some respondents, there was a tendency to interchange the terms AIDS and 'the virus' as if they were one and the same, and when a contrast between them was drawn, this was usually dissimilar to that in mainstream medical explanations. While the young gay men who spoke to us tended to distinguish more clearly between HIV infection and AIDS, the view was expressed that more sexual contact in itself might be enough to determine whether a person got the virus in the first place, or indeed whether a person subsequently developed AIDS.

It is significant to note that even though there is a continuing popular belief that some people might wilfully pass 'the virus' on to others, the young people we interviewed stated that one of their major concerns if they had 'the virus' would be to ensure that they did not pass it on. It was also clear from the discussions we had, that young lesbians and gay men were able to articulate more clearly than others the specific steps they would take to minimise the risk of infecting other people. Their discussions of particular sexual acts relating to 'safer sex' were on the whole more accurate than those of the young people in undifferentiated youth provision. However, it was also clear that for young lesbians in particular most, if not all, the information so far available on 'safer sex' has been irrelevant. Respondents in this sub-group were aware of the many television programmes and leaflets that have addressed the needs of heterosexual women and all men by promoting condom use. However, because relevant information for lesbians does not exist at present, some of the young women interviewed were left particularly worried. Most importantly, though, our findings suggest that for many if not all the young people interviewed, mainstream medical explanations of HIV infection and AIDS may be quite insufficient to allay anxiety and help individuals acquire realistic perceptions of risk.

It is highly unlikely that the lay beliefs accessed in this study could have been identified by styles of social research which use pre-structured interview schedules to examine the extent to which people are acquainted with mainstream medical knowledge. We stated earlier, as we have done elsewhere . . . that exploratory and open-ended research into lay beliefs about HIV infection and AIDS is necessary if health educators, policy makers and others are to identify the ways in which people respond to public information campaigns and health education interventions. In developing future public health interventions, it is essential that we acknowledge the importance of differences in perception such as those identified in this paper. By doing this, we will be able to make better sense of the ways in which people actively construct beliefs about AIDS and HIV infection in particular, and health and illness in general.

Note Reading 14 provides a further example of the use of semi-structured interviews.

Helen Simons: Some Advice on How to Carry Out Open-ended (Unstructured) Interviews in a Case-study context

Many readers of this book will at some time carry out research for a sociological project or piece of coursework. My impression is that when selecting research methods, students tend to opt either for observation or questionnaires/interviews aimed mainly at generating quantitative data. Where open-ended questions occur, they tend to be tagged on to the end of questionnaires or interview schedules partly as information catch-alls and partly to provide the respondent with some 'freedom of expression'.

However, there are good practical and theoretical reasons for sometimes adopting the open-ended interview as the main tool of research – particularly in the context of a case study which requires accessing in-depth information (as in the example of the extract).

The particular research content which Helen Simons is addressing below is an educational one in which interviewees might typically involve pupils, teachers and a Head. However, her advice is broadly applicable to all research contexts in which the open-ended interview is used. The extract divides into a shorter section on 'principles of procedure' and a longer one on 'process'. The former mainly discusses the basic principle of confidentiality, and all those involved in any given piece of research of this kind need to be quite clear on how this principle is being adopted and applied. The second section – on process – is about how an open-ended interview might be conducted. Simon, of course, recognises that the process of the open-ended interview is more subjective and less predictable than in most types of sociological research. Nevertheless, she manages to give some useful concrete advice about how to conduct such interviews. Essentially, she recommends that the interviewee should be enabled to take centre stage and that the role of interviewer should be that of a skilled, sensitive but inconspicuous prompt. It is well worth mulling over her advice in detail.

Reading 10 From Helen Simons, 'Conversation Piece: the Practice of Interviewing in Case Study Research, in Clem Adelman *ed., Uttering, Muttering; Collecting, Using and Reporting Talk for Social and Educational Research* (Grant McIntyre, 1981), pp. 27, 27–28, 31–32, 33–37

The case for adopting a case study approach in educational inquiry has been well documented in recent years. Yet little has been written about *how* to do a case study or how to interview, observe or negotiate – three processes often cited as the main tools of such research. This paper looks at the first of these; in particular at some of the problems in the practice of interviewing.

Often the practice of interviewing, particularly of the unstructured kind advocated in case study research, is not discussed on the grounds that interviewing is an idiosyncratic, interpersonal process that is not susceptible to systematic analysis. Like teaching, it is seen to be a private, personal skill for which some people are suited and others are not. It takes time to develop, mostly through trial and error though the process may be helped by 'looking over the shoulder' of someone acknowledged to have the sensitivity, judgment and intellectual skills that unstructured interviewing demand. The apprenticeship analogy is often invoked to describe how people acquire such skills. But this model is expensive and inaccessible to many. If the growth of practitioners in this field is to parallel the growth of advocates I think we must begin to discuss the problems we experience in practice however self-evident, situation-specific or limited when restricted to the written word they may seem. This is not to say that personality differences are not important in interviewing – one only has to note how the same question asked by different interviewers can elicit diverse responses from the same person. It is simply to suggest that there are certain points about practice we can draw to the attention of others which may speed up the learning process.

Another reason why practice is rarely described is that discussions of the interview often never get beyond attempts to conceptualise and justify its theoretical underpinning as a research tool. In this paper I hope to circumvent debate at the theoretical level by treating some of the major premises of my practice as assumptions and so proceed, more or less directly, to explicate my experience.

I start from the following assumptions:

(a) that the justification for case study research as an appropriate mode of enquiry in the study of social situations has been established;
(b) that interviewing is a useful tool in case study research;
(c) that the recording of people's subjective definitions of experience is a normal part of case study research;
(d) that whereas structured questions are appropriate when you know what you want to find out, unstructured questions are preferable when you are not sure what you want to know but are prepared to depend on your capacity to recognise significant data on appearance;
(e) that, further, it is necessary to adopt an unstructured approach (variously called open-ended or flexible) to interviewing in the study of social situations whose complexity has to be uncovered by the research;
(f) that unstructured interviewing offers more scope for involving the interviewee in the research;
(g) that because interviewing is a most penetrative way of gaining information from and about people there is a need for rules to control both the acquisition and the subsequent use of interview data . . .

The danger of over-subjectivity is characteristic not only of open-ended interviewing but of qualitative research in general.

Principles of procedure

Open-ended interviewing challenges conventional expectations of the research process. Relying as it does a great deal on the personal skills and judgment of the interviewer it is also open to manipulation and distortion. Principles of procedure protect both interviewer and interviewee from misuse of the data, provided assumptions are shared. Perspectives, for instance, on the meaning of confidentiality may range from complete trust that the information will not go 'beyond the four walls of this room' to the assumption that the information may be shared with research colleagues but not other teachers in the school or to 'the secret that is passed on to only one person at a time'. Then there may be differences in status of people or information. Does confidentiality, for instance, mean the same for pupils as it does for teachers and the Head? Does confidentiality extend to data expressed in informal chat? Should the same or different rules apply to the use of the data obtained in and out of the interview situation or of data offered by one person about another? Should the same or different rules over the use of data apply to pupils as apply to teachers? What rights do, or should, pupils have?

Misunderstandings can easily arise if the rules of information use are not fully understood or respected equally by all parties. For example, if the researcher interviews pupils in confidence and does not reveal what they say, teachers may see the interviewer in a conspiratorial role with pupils. Since pupils in a hierarchical structure are often the last to be interviewed the researcher may be the only person at one point who has access to what pupils think as well as what the teachers think: staff may see the interviewer in a 'god-like role' which may strain previously established good relationships, if not governed by rules of procedure . . .

Process

Judging from the questions asked of case study workers both by new practitioners and by interviewees, many assume that the interview is a one-way process, for the researcher to gain information for a particular research inquiry; where the interviewer asks the questions and the interviewee 'gives' the information. But the process is much more complex than that – more dynamic, interpersonal, intangible.

Both the interviewer and the interviewee bring preconceptions to the interview which will affect what they say, hear and report, and which may be confirmed or changed in the course of the interview. Both are making judgments of each other's attitudes and expectations as well as considering the context or implications of the questions or issue under discussion. Perceptions differ too. How the interviewee perceives the interviewer, as sympathetic, critical or threatening, for example, will influence what kind of information is offered; how the interviewer perceives the interviewee, as interested, indifferent or hostile, will affect how he or she behaves. The interview, in other words, is a complex social process in which much more than information is being sought or communicated. (It can also be an educational process as interviewees begin to reflect on their own situation and, perhaps, continue the inquiry beyond the formal interview.) The interviewer should continually be responsive to the range of social and intellectual reactions in the process of engaging the person in talk: an interview should be a conversation piece, not an inquisition.

Given this emphasis, what does the interviewing process look like in practice? The following are points I try to keep in mind. They are not meant to sound prescriptive. I am simply going to try to uncover the process of interviewing as I have experienced it – to articulate what I think are the assumptions and principles I work with, or should work with, in interviewing.

It is important at the outset to establish confidence and trust so that people will speak freely. There must be some motivation to participate other than institutional expectation. On the whole, people will treat the interview seriously if they think you can change something or if they think you accept and understand their problems. Since researchers are rarely in a position to influence events directly they have to rely on demonstrating empathy with the interviewees' concerns. What can help to secure their confidence is to indicate indirectly that you have some understanding of the problems facing them. Offering confidentiality may help if this convention has meaning for them. So might informal chat around a topic of local or personal interest to the interviewee; although informal talk is sometimes perceived to be unrelated to the formal interview.

One way to engage interviewees' involvement in the study is to encourage them to talk about what interests them much as they might in a social conversation. This also helps to break down the formality of the interview over which the interviewer is perceived to have control. Reversing expectations, however, takes time and may need prompting. Try to dispossess them of any notions that you are the expert. Shift the role to them in early interviews by asking questions which touch on their concerns and which are open-ended enough to allow them scope to reply fully. Respond acceptingly so they will feel free to talk without feeling anxious about being judged or not giving the 'right response'. Let them shift from topic to topic. Counter any question to the interviewer with one which shifts the onus back to them to demonstrate that you really are interested in their perceptions and judgments.

Information people offer on their own initiative is more true, some argue, than what they say in answering questions. Whether or not this is so, interviewees' unsolicited responses frequently alert the interviewer to consider the subject under discussion in a new light and in the context central to the person interviewed. Piaget, in criticising the questionnaire as a means of obtaining access to a person's mental processes, put this point neatly when he wrote:

> But the real problem is to know how he [the subject] frames the question to himself or if he frames it at all. The skill of the practitioner consists not in making him answer questions but in making him talk freely and thus encouraging the flow of his spontaneous tendencies instead of diverting it

into the artificial channels of set question and answer. It consists in placing every symptom in its mental context rather than abstracting it from its context.

Listening is one of the most frequently neglected skills in interviewing.

In many cases where both parties to the interview share a view of the task there is no need to ask many questions; it is more important to listen. A comparison of a tape-recording where the interviewer does not speak for half an hour with one where the interviewer asks a question every second minute may illustrate the open-ended approach better than any description. (This is not to say that the interviewer is inactive. His presence, his responses, non-verbal though they may be, and how he takes notes, contribute in quite significant ways.) Usually the issues the interviewer thought of will be raised by the interviewee if the interviewer listens carefully and refrains from asking questions too soon. Take the following example related by an interviewee:

> 'It is difficult for me to hold a dialogue', he said, 'someone came to interview me once and I gave a monologue for two hours . . . I liked him. He was an easy person to talk to. Then I realised the time. "You must have some questions" I said to the interviewer. "No", the interviewer replied, "you've answered them all".'

Listening by itself, of course, does not always lead to depth of understanding. Probing is necessary to get behind the expected response or to test the significance of what you are being told. Taking up cues from the interviewees, asking them to elaborate or explain why they adopted a particular view or introducing a theme for comment are all means of extending the initial response. But these can still be pursued in a non-directed way if the aim of the research is to portray the interviewees' judgments, perceptions and theories of events.

It is evident from the emphasis given to the above points that I think one of the most common errors in open-ended interviewing is failure to listen, either by asking too many questions or interrupting to confirm one's own hypotheses. A second related error is to seek closure too soon by accepting the initial response too readily, summarising erroneously or by asking questions which give the interviewee a plausible response without committing him to reveal what he really thinks or feels. (This is a special danger when interviewing pupils.) Timely summarising of course is very useful to clarify issues and shift the interview a stage further.

Inexperienced interviewers sometimes adopt a rigid, rule-bound approach, whereas flexibility is invariably more effective.

In summary, the kind of skill flexible interviewing calls for is what the anthropologist, Hortense Powdermaker, has called 'psychological mobility', or the novelist, Sybille Bedford, 'emotional intelligence'. Sybille Bedford summarises the complex skills involved when she writes:

> 'It takes two to tell the truth.'
> 'One for one side, one for the other?'
> 'That's not what I mean. I mean one to tell, one to hear. A speaker and a receiver. To tell the truth about any complex situation requires a certain attitude in the receiver.'
> 'What is required in the receiver?'

'I would say first of all a level of emotional intelligence.'
'Imagination?'
'Disciplined.'
'Sympathy? Attention?'
'And patience.'
'All of these. And a taste for the truth – an immense willingness to *see*'.

If the study involves a series of interviews, who sets and shifts the topics may vary from interview to interview. What is appropriate at one point may not be at another, as understanding and perceptions change. At times the interviewer may want to feed in some interpretation, at other times to take up a cue from the interviewee. Towards the end of the study precisely the opposite tactic from responding to the interviewee's initiative may be appropriate, particularly if the interviewee has a habit of repeating his story over and over again. In such a case the interviewer may want to be quite assertive or exclusive about the issues he would like the interviewee to comment upon.

Interviewing encompasses more than listening, asking questions and being socially responsive. Often it is important to judge the significance of what is said by non-verbal cues such as gestures, the tone of the voice, how people dress, how they look, how and where they sit or to infer from what is not said or what is denied what the interviewee thinks or feels. At the same time acceptance of non-verbal cues may be misleading. Their significance has to be judged in relation to all the data obtained . . .

Questions and Issues

Theory and Methods: Sections 1–2

The most relevant readings are indicated in brackets after each question.

1 Describe the significance of the concept of labour in the theories of society developed by Marx and Durkheim (Readings 1–2).
2 What contributions did the founders of sociology make to our understanding of human consciousness and choice? (Readings 1–6)
3 In general, what theoretical and methodological approaches are most associated with the founders of sociology and why? (Readings 1–7; you may also want to look at Section 18 in answering this question.)
4 Why do sociologists often find it useful to adopt more than one methodology in carrying out a piece of research? (Readings 7–10)

SOCIAL CLASS AND STRATIFICATION

Introduction: Readings 11–17

This section covers classic and contemporary statements on social class and certain other aspects of stratification. It begins with a brief extract from Karl Marx on class conflict, followed by a slightly longer extract from Max Weber on class, status and party. Their disagreements about the relative significance of social class and its relationship to other aspects of stratification, notably that based on ethnicity, largely set the terms of debate about stratification for the twentieth century. Perhaps only the emergence of gender as a stratification issue has since achieved a substantive shift in the channels of discussion. The matter of ethnic/national differentiation introduced by Weber occurs again in the piece by Fiona Devine (Reading 14). Certainly, the ethnic issue is a theme for our times.

John Goldthorpe and Gordon Marshall argue that while Marxist class analysis is fundamentally flawed, class analysis itself remains of relevance (their own approach is broadly Weberian). They illustrate their argument in relation to social mobility, education and political partisanship. In Reading 14, Fiona Devine suggests that Marshall *et al.* (1988) over-emphasise the importance of class relative to other bases of identity in people's lives. In particular, she argues that people's sense of regional and national identity has tended to be neglected by sociologists.

John Goldthorpe and Clive Payne focus on the pattern of social mobility between 1972 and 1983. Their data suggest that the pattern during this decade remained similar to that of the previous post-war period, i.e. one of increased opportunity for upward mobility, but also of substantial inequality of opportunity between the classes. However, they note that the increase in unemployment, if prolonged, would severely reduce opportunities for upward mobility for this group.

This observation chimes with the theme of the 'underclass', the subject of the next reading. The long-term unemployed and their families are the largest group in the underclass, yet rather than examining their disadvantage in the employment market, Ralf Dahrendorf chooses to analyse the cultural values that he controversially associates with this group. The section concludes with a discussion of class from a neo-Marxist perspective by Richard Scase.

Karl Marx: Class Conflict

Marx's following statement on social class belongs more to the tradition of political pamphleteering than studied academic thesis. This gives it clarity. Societies are characterised by class conflict, and, in the capitalist or bourgeois epoch, conflict was sharpening or polarising. Readers who seek a more subtle appreciation of Marx's analysis of the formation and development of classes should go back to the first reading in this book. However, here it is enough to note that Marx defined class in terms of a person's relation to the means of production – they are either owners or non-owners.

I place Marx's celebrated statement on class conflict here in order to invite the reader's judgement upon it. The claims and influence of Marx's analysis of class are so enormous that they cannot be treated as of merely analytical interest. It is well over a hundred years since Marx's death and you may feel, as I do, that it is time to judge the accuracy and quality of his theory and predictions. Was he right about 'class antagonisms' becoming more 'simplified' in Britain? Was he right in the importance he attached to social class and in the importance he thought others should and, in certain conditions, would attach to it? To what extent was Marx responsible for the deeds done in his name? How far was his vision of the future correct? Was there some deep, perhaps tragic, flaw in his theory? Is Marxism now more or less finished or could it be that as Marxism falters as a political movement, the world is actually becoming more as Marx predicted?

Reading 11 From Karl Marx and Friedrich Engels, *The Communist Manifesto* (Penguin, 1981), p. 79

The history of all hitherto existing society is the history of class struggles.

Freeman and slave, patrician and plebeian, lord and serf, guildmaster and journeyman, in a word, oppressor and oppressed stood in constant opposition to one another, carried out an uninterrupted, now hidden, now open fight that each time ended, either in a revolutionary reconstitution of society at large, or in the common ruin of the contending classes.

In the earlier epochs of history, we find almost everywhere a complicated arrangement of society into various orders, a manifold gradation of social rank. In ancient Rome we have patricians, knights, plebeians, slaves; in the Middle Ages, feudal lords, vassals, guild-masters, journeymen, apprentices, serfs; in almost all of these classes, again, subordinate gradations.

The modern bourgeois society that has sprouted from the ruins of feudal society has not done away with class antagonisms. It has but established new classes, new conditions of oppression, new forms of struggle in place of the old ones.

Our epoch, the epoch of the bourgeoisie, possesses, however, this distinctive feature. It has simplified the class antagonisms. Society as a whole is more and more splitting up into two great hostile camps, into two great classes directly facing each other – bourgeoisie and proletariat . . .

Max Weber: Class, Status and Party

Weber's contribution to stratification theory is of fundamental importance in its own right, but it is in comparison and contrast to Marx's class theory that it becomes of even more profound significance.

Whereas Marx believed that class is ultimately the most important and, indeed, the only 'true' form of stratification, Weber did not. He argued that status and party (political difference/stratification) are distinct forms of stratification and in certain circumstances may be more important than class. He also defined class somewhat differently from Marx, including an individual's position in the labour market as well as their access to income and wealth as a key defining feature.

Most of this extract is devoted to Weber's discussion of status and, particularly to ethnic stratification and caste. I have made this emphasis because of the growth in ethnic and national consciousness and conflict in many parts of the world during recent years. A conspicuous example of this is the Serbs 'ethnic cleansing' of Muslims in Bosnia – an ugly phrase to describe a deeply ugly form of behaviour. These themes are pursued in greater detail in Section 5, but Reading 14 in this section describes aspects of national and regional consciousness in Britain.

To a contemporary reader, what is conspicuously absent from both Marx and Weber's analysis of stratification, is any mention of women.

Reading 12 From Max Weber, *ed.*, C. Wright Mills, *From Max Weber* (Oxford University Press, New York; 1970), pp. 181, 184, 185, 185–86, 187, 189

Determination of class-situation by market-situation

In other words, people who share the same market situation (class) may or may not act collectively (i.e. as a community). In contrast, Marx argued that a class whose members were fully conscious of their own shared interests would act as a community.

In our terminology, 'classes' are not communities; they merely represent possible, frequent, bases for communal action. We may speak of a 'class' when (1) a number of people have in common a specific causal component of their life chances, in so far as (2) this component is represented exclusively by economic interests in the possession of goods and opportunities for income, and (3) is represented under the conditions of the commodity or labor markets. (These points refer to 'class situation', which we may express more briefly as the typical chance for a supply of goods, external living conditions, and personal life experiences, in so far as this chance is determined by the amount and kind of power, or lack of such, to dispose of goods or skills for the sake of income in a given economic order. The term 'class' refers to any group of people that is found in the same class situation.) . . .

Status honor

In contrast to classes, *status groups* are normally communities. They are, however, often of an amorphous kind. In contrast to the purely economically determined 'class situation' we wish to designate as 'status situation' every typical component of the life fate of men that is determined by a specific, positive or negative, social estimation of *honor*. This honor may be connected with any quality shared by a plurality, and, of course, it can be knit to a class situation: class distinctions are linked in the most varied ways with status distinctions. Property as such is not always recognised as a status qualification, but in the long run it is, and with extraordinary regularity. In the subsistence economy of the organised neighborhood, very often the richest man is simply the chieftain. However, this often means only an honorific preference. For example, in the so-called pure modern 'democracy,' that is, one devoid of any expressly ordered status privileges for individuals, it may be that only the families coming under approximately

Weber's crucial point is, then, that individuals of very different wealth may belong to the same status group – and treat each other as equals within it.

the same tax class dance with one another. This example is reported of certain smaller Swiss cities. But status honor need not necessarily be linked with a 'class situation.' On the contrary, it normally stands in sharp opposition to the pretensions of sheer property . . .

Guarantees of status stratification

In content, status honor is normally expressed by the fact that above all else a specific *style of life* can be expected from all those who wish to belong to the circle. Linked with this expectation are restrictions on 'social' intercourse (that is, intercourse which is not subservient to economic or any other of business's 'functional' purposes). These restrictions may confine normal marriages to within the status circle and may lead to complete endogamous closure. As soon as there is not a mere individual and socially irrelevant imitation of another style of life, but an agreed-upon communal action of this closing character, the 'status' development is under way . . .

The reverse side of the 'community' of status group members is the exclusion of others.

'Ethnic' segregation and 'caste'

Where the consequences have been realised to their full extent, the status group evolves into a closed 'caste'. Status distinctions are then guaranteed not merely by conventions and laws, but also by *rituals*. This occurs in such a way that every physical contact with a member of any caste that is considered to be 'lower' by the members of a 'higher' caste is considered as making for a ritualistic impurity and to be a stigma which must be expiated by a religious act. Individual castes develop quite distinct cults and gods.

In general, however, the status structure reaches such extreme consequences only where there are underlying differences which are held to be 'ethnic'. The 'caste' is, indeed, the normal form in which ethnic communities usually live side by side in a 'societalised' manner. These ethnic communities believe in blood relationship and exclude exogamous marriage and social intercourse. Such a caste situation is part of the phenomenon of 'pariah' peoples and is found all over the world. These people form communities, acquire specific occupational traditions of handicrafts or of other arts, and cultivate a belief in their ethnic community. They live in a 'diaspora' strictly segregated from all personal intercourse, except that of an unavoidable sort, and their situation is legally precarious. Yet, by virtue of their economic indispensability, they are tolerated, indeed, frequently privileged, and they live in interspersed political communities. The Jews are the most impressive historical example.

A 'status' segregation grown into a 'caste' differs in its structure from a mere 'ethnic' segregation: the caste structure transforms the horizontal and unconnected coexistences of ethnically segregated groups into a vertical social system of super– and subordination. Correctly formulated: a comprehensive societalisation integrates the ethnically divided communities into specific political and communal action. In their consequences they differ precisely in this way: ethnic coexistences condition a mutual repulsion and disdain but allow each ethnic community to consider its own honor as the highest one; the caste structure brings about a social subordination and an acknowledgement of 'more honor' in favor of the privileged caste and status groups. This is due to the fact that in the caste structure ethnic distinctions as such have become 'functional' distinctions within the political societalisation (warriors, priests, artisans that are politically important for war and for building, and so on). But even pariah people who are most despised are usually apt to continue cultivating in some manner that which is equally peculiar to ethnic and to status communities: the belief in their own specific 'honor'. This is the case with the Jews . . .

Status privileges

For all practical purposes, stratification by status goes hand in hand with a monopolisation of ideal and material goods or opportunities, in a manner we have come to know as typical. Besides the specific status honor, which always rests upon distance and exclusiveness, we find all sorts of material monopolies. Such honorific preferences may consist of the privilege of wearing special costumes, of eating special dishes taboo to others, of carrying arms . . .

The decisive role of a 'style of life' in status 'honor' means that status groups are the specific bearers of all 'conventions.' In whatever way it may be manifest, all 'stylisation' of life either originates in status groups or is at least conserved by them. Even if the principles of status conventions differ greatly, they reveal certain typical traits, especially among those strata which are most privileged. Quite generally, among privileged status groups there is a status disqualification that operates against the performance of common physical labor . . .

Parties

Whereas the genuine place of 'classes' is within the economic order, the place of 'status groups' is within the social order, that is, within the sphere of the distribution of 'honor'. From within these spheres, classes and status groups influence one another and they influence the legal order and are in turn influenced by it. But 'parties' live in a house of 'power'.

Their action is oriented toward the acquisition of social 'power,' that is to say, toward influencing a communal action no matter what its content may be. In principle, parties may exist in a social 'club' as well as in a 'state'. As over against the actions of classes and status groups, for which this is not necessarily the case, the communal actions of 'parties' always mean a societalisation. For party actions are always directed toward a goal which is striven for in a planned manner. This goal may be a 'cause' (the party may aim at realising a program for ideal or material purposes), or the goal may be 'personal' (sinecures, power, and from these, honor for the leader and the followers of the party). Usually the party action aims at all these simultaneously. Parties are, therefore, only possible within communities that are societalised, that is, which have some rational order and a staff of persons available who are ready to enforce it.

'A societalisation' means rational organisation to achieve a social goal.

J. H. Goldthorpe and G. Marshall: Why Class Analysis is Still Relevant – After Marx

Despite the quite demanding nature of some of this extract, my introduction can be brief because the abstract and introduction provided by Goldthorpe and Marshall clearly outline the contents and purpose of their article. Primarily, they seek to reassert the validity of class analysis, but, in the light of considerable criticism of class analysis generally and their own work in particular, they are advocating class analysis of a specified and limited kind only. They clearly indicate the scope and methodological principles of their 'research programme.'

Their 'central concern' is 'the study of relationships between class structures, class mobility, class-based inequalities, and class-based action.' In a section not included here, they specify 'the requirements in conceptualisation, data analysis and data collection' which must be met if their research programme is to meet the standards which they stipulate. These are notably clear and vigorous. It will be obvious from the section on Marxist class analysis included here that they do not consider that the latter remotely reaches adequate standards in these areas.

In the second part of their article, Goldthorpe and Marshall argue the case for the continuing relevance of class analysis by reviewing findings in the areas of class and social mobility, education and political partisanship.

Reading 13 From J. H. Goldthorpe and G. Marshall, 'The Promising Future of Class Analysis: A Response to Recent Critiques' in *Sociology*, Vol. 26, No. 3, 1992, pp. 381–82, 383, 383–84, 384–85, 387–92, 393–94

Abstract

Class analysis has recently been criticised from a variety of standpoints. In this paper we argue that much of this criticism is misplaced and that, as a research programme, the promise of class analysis is far from exhausted. The first part of the paper clarifies the nature and purpose of class analysis, as we would understand it, and in particular distinguishes it from the class analysis of Marxist sociology. The second part then makes the case for the continuing relevance of class analysis, in our conception of it, by reviewing findings from three central areas of current research.

Keywords: class analysis, social mobility, education, politics.

Introduction

What are the prospects for class analysis? Of late, the enterprise has been widely dismissed as unconvincing and unproductive by prominent critics writing from a variety of different standpoints. Our own work has been a frequent target. In the present paper, however, our primary aim is not to reply to such charges on our own behalf, but rather to uphold the kind of class analysis that our work can be taken to represent – since it is our contention that its promise is far from exhausted.

The paper comprises two parts. In the first, we seek to clarify the nature and purpose of class analysis as we would understand it, and in particular to distinguish it from the class analysis of Marxist sociology. This is necessary because some critics – including Hindess (1987), Holton and Turner (1989), and Sørensen (1991) – have not, in our view, made this distinction adequately, while others, most notably Pahl (1989), have failed to make it at all. In addition, several instances can be noted of authors who, having lost faith in the Marxist class analysis that had once commanded their allegiance, or at least sympathy, now find evident difficulty in envisaging any other kind. Gorz (1982), Hobsbawm (1981), Bauman (1982), Lukes (1984), and Offe (1985) are obvious examples.

In the second part of the paper we then go on to make the case for the continuing relevance of class analysis, in our own conception of it, by reviewing findings from three central areas of current research. Here we seek to take issue more specifically with the assertions made by Pahl (1989:710) that, in modern societies, 'class as a concept is ceasing to do any useful work for sociology', and by Holton and Turner (1989:196) that we are now 'in a situation where the persistence of the class idiom is explicable more in terms of the metaphorical character of class rhetoric than any clear intellectual persuasiveness.'

Class analysis as a research programme

Class analysis, in our sense, has as its central concern the study of relationships among class structures, class mobility, class-based inequalities, and class-based action. More specifically, it explores the interconnections between positions defined by employment relations in labour markets and production units in different sectors of national economies; the processes through which individuals and families are distributed and redistributed among these positions over time; and the consequences thereof for their life-chances and for the social identities that they adopt and the social values and interests that they pursue. Understood in this way, class analysis does not entail a commitment to any particular theory of class but, rather, to a *research programme* – in, broadly, the sense of Lakatos (1970) – within which different, and indeed rival, theories may be formulated and then assessed in terms of their heuristic and explanatory performance.

> 'heuristic' means providing a fruitful focus (for research)

It may be asked, and critics have indeed done so (see, for example, Holton and Turner 1989:173), why such a programme should be pursued in the first place. We would think the answer obvious enough. The programme is attractive in that it represents a specific way of investigating interconnections of the kind that have always engaged the sociological imagination: that is, between historically formed macrosocial structures, on the one hand, and, on the other, the everyday experience of individuals within their particular social milieux, together with the patterns of action that follow from this experience. These are precisely the sort of interconnections that, in Wright Mills' (1959) words, allow one to relate biography to history and 'personal troubles' to 'public issues'. From an analytical standpoint, the programme also promises economy of explanation: the ability to use a few well-defined concepts such as class position, class origins, class mobility or immobility, in order to explain a good deal both of what happens, or does not happen, to individuals across different aspects of their social lives and of how they subsequently respond.

But *a priori* there is only attraction and promise. Whether the research programme of class analysis proves worthwhile . . . must be decided by the results it produces. No *assumption* of the pre-eminence of class is involved. To the contrary, it is integral to the research programme that specific consideration should also be given to theories holding that class relations are in fact of diminishing importance for life-chances and social action or that other relations and attributes – defined, for example, by income or consumption, status or lifestyle, ethnicity or gender – are, or are becoming, of greater consequence.

It ought to be readily apparent that class analysis, thus conceived, differs significantly from the class analysis of Marxist sociology . . . Before proceeding further, therefore, we think it important to spell out four elements, in particular, that class analysis as we would understand it does *not* entail – although they are found in most Marxist versions.

First, our conception of class analysis entails no theory of history according to which class conflicts serves as the engine of social change, so that at the crisis point of successive developmental stages a particular class (under capitalism the working class) takes on its 'mission' of transforming society through revolutionary action. In fact, among those sociologists who have been actively engaged in what we would regard as the research programme of class analysis, a strong opposition to all such historicism, whether of a Marxist or a liberal inspiration, can be found (see, for example, Goldthorpe 1971, 1979, 1992; Korpi 1978; Marshall *et al.* 1988:ch. 10; Esping-Andersen 1990: ch 1; Haller 1990). The emphasis is, rather, on the diversity of the developmental paths that nations have followed to modernity and on the very variable – because essentially contingent – nature of the part played in this respect by class formation and action.

Secondly, class analysis as we understand it implies no theory of class exploitation, according to which all class relations must be necessarily and exclusively antagonistic, and from which the objective basis for a 'critical' economics and sociology can be directly obtained. Although exponents of class analysis in our sense would certainly see conflict as being inherent within class relations, this does not require them to adhere to a labour theory of value, or indeed any other doctrine entailing exploitation as understood in Marxist discourse. Nor must they suppose, as is suggested by Sørensen (1991:73), that what is to the advantage of one class must *always* and *entirely* be to the disadvantage of another. In fact, much interest has of late centred on theoretical discussion of the conditions under which class relations may be better understood as a positive-sum (or negative-sum) rather than as a simple zero-sum game. And this interest has then been reflected in substantive studies in a concern with the part that may be played by 'class compromises', in, for example, labour relations or the development of national political economies and welfare states (*cf.* the papers collected in Goldthorpe (ed.) 1984).

Furthermore, arguments advanced from a liberal standpoint, whether by functionalist sociologists or neo-classical economists, to the effect that class inequalities are, through various mechanisms, conducive to the greater welfare of all would be seen as calling for empirical investigation rather than mere ideological rejection. And, in turn, the results of such investigation would be recognised as directly relevant to any moral evaluation of class inequalities that might be made . . .

This view, of course, echoes that of Weber, as expressed in the first sentence of Reading 12.

Thirdly, the version of class analysis that we would endorse takes in no theory of class-based collective action, according to which individuals holding similar positions within the class structure will thereby automatically develop a shared consciousness of their situation and will, in turn, be prompted to act together in the pursuit of their common class interests. In fact, awareness of developments in the general theory of collective action, from the time of Olson's (1965) crucial study onwards, has led those engaged in class analysis as a research programme effectively to reverse the traditional Marxist perspective. Instead of expecting class-based collective action to occur (and then having to resort to 'false consciousness' arguments when it does not), they have concentrated on establishing the quite special conditions that must apply before such action can be thought probable – because rational for the individuals concerned – *even where* shared interests are in fact recognised. Thus, when Pahl (1989:711) represents class analysts as mindlessly repeating the 'mantra' of 'structure-consciousness-agency', with the links in the chain being 'rarely seen as problematic', this is in fact essentially the opposite of what has happened over the last decade or more . . .

Finally, class analysis as we understand it does not embrace a reductionist theory of political action – collective or individual – according to which such action can be understood simply as the unmediated expression of class relations and the pursuit of structurally-given class interests. At the same time as they have come to a much changed understanding of the consciousness-agency link, so also have many class analysts sought to move to a new view of the relationship between consciousness (or at least consciousness of interests) and structure, again under the influence of more general theoretical developments (see, for example, Berger (ed.) 1981). What has been rejected is, precisely, the idea that an awareness of and concern with class interests follows directly and 'objectively' from class position. Rather, the occupancy of class positions is seen as creating only potential interests, such as may also arise from various other structural locations. Whether, then, it is class, rather than other, interests that individuals do in fact seek to realise, will depend in the first place on the social identities that they take up, since – to quote a maxim attributed to Pizzorno – 'identity precedes interest'. And although in the formation of such identities various social processes, for example those of mobility, will be important, it is emphasised that for class interests to become the basis of political mobilisation, a crucial role must be played by political movements

In a section not included here Goldthorpe and Marshall make the three points about good empirical research on class referred to in my introduction to this reading.

and parties themselves, through their ideologies, programmes and strategies (see Pizzorno 1978; Korpi 1983; Esping-Andersen 1985; Marshall *et al.* 1988: ch. 7; Heath *et al.* 1991: ch.5) . . .

Some illustrative results

In this second part of our paper we draw attention, albeit in a very summary way, to findings from three areas within the research programme of class analysis which, we would argue, any serious critique would need to address – and especially if its ultimate aim were to establish that class analysis no longer has a useful part to play in the study of modern societies. We will discuss in turn class mobility; class and education; and class and political partisanship.

Class mobility

To study social mobility within the context of a class structure, rather than, say, that of a status hierarchy, is a conceptual choice that must be made *a priori* (Goldthorpe 1985). However, where this perspective has been taken, results have been produced that are of no little sociological significance.

For present purposes, what may chiefly be stressed is that, across diverse national settings, classes have been shown to display rather distinctive 'mobility characteristics': that is, in inflow perspective, in the homogeneity of the class origins of those individuals who make up their current membership; and in outflow perspective, in their degree of retentiveness or 'holding power', both over individual lifetimes and intergenerationally (Featherman and Selbee 1988; Featherman, Selbee and Mayer 1989; Mayer *et al.* 1989; Jonsson 1991b; Erikson and Goldthorpe 1992:ch. 6). Thus, for example, the service classes, or salariats, of modern societies tend to be highly heterogenous in their composition but tend also to have great retentiveness both intra- and intergenerationally. In comparison, working classes are more homogeneous in composition, and farm classes far more so, but both these classes reveal lower holding power, especially in intergenerational terms. In other classes, such as among the petty bourgeoisie and routine nonmanual employees, the combinations of homogeneity and of worklife and intergenerational retentiveness are different again.

Such mobility characteristics can be shown to have a twofold origin. First, they reflect the fact that classes – defined in terms of employment relations within different sectors of national economies – tend to follow rather distinctive trajectories, or 'natural histories', of growth or decline in relation to the structural development of these economies (in a way that strata defined in terms of status or prestige do not). And secondly, they reflect the fact that different classes tend to be associated with specific 'propensities' for immobility or mobility independently of all structural effects. This last finding, it may be noted, is one made possible only by technical advances in the analysis of mobility tables, which have allowed the crucial conceptual distinction between 'absolute' and 'relative' rates to be drawn (*cf.* Hauser *et al.* 1975; Hauser 1978; Goldthorpe 1980/1987).

That classes can be shown to display such distinctive mobility characteristics would then in itself suggest that they are capable of being defined in a way that is more than merely arbitrary, and that the 'boundary problems' which some critics have sought to highlight are a good deal more tractable than they seek to imply. Certainly, one may question the grounds of assertions such as that made by Holton and Turner (1989:174), that it is 'very hard to aggregate the multiplicity of class positions into categories, without having recourse to evaluative cultural criteria.'

Furthermore, it is in terms of such mobility characteristics that class formation can be assessed at its basic 'demographic' level (Goldthorpe 1980/1987); that is, in terms of the extent and the nature of the association that exists between individuals or families and particular class positions over time. And this in turn may be seen as determining the potential for classes, as collectivities, also to develop distinctive subcultures and a 'capacity for socialisation', which are themselves the key prerequisites for class identities to be created (Featherman and Spenner 1990). In other words, an approach is here provided, and is being actively pursued, for investigating processes of class formation, or decomposition, through systematic empirical inquiry. It is not supposed, in the manner of dogmatic Marxism, that class formation is in some way historically scheduled. But neither, in the manner of Pahl or Holton and Turner is it assumed that in modern societies class decomposition is a quite generalised phenomenon. And, as we have indicated, the evidence thus far produced does indeed point to the existence of a situation of a clearly more complex kind.

Class and education

The countervailing force that has most often been cited in arguments claiming that the influence of class on individual life-chances is in decline is that of education. According to those theories of industrial society which could, in Holton and Turner's phrase, be seen as posing 'the challenge of liberalism' to class analysis, the very 'logic' of industrialism requires both that the provision of, and access to, education should steadily widen, and further that educational attainment should become the key determinant of success in economic life. In turn, then, it is expected that the association between class origins and educational attainment will weaken, while that between educational attainment and class destinations strengthens, and itself mediates (and legitimates) most of whatever association between class origins and destinations may continue to exist (see, for example, Kerr *et al.* 1960; Blau and Duncan 1967; Treiman 1970; Kerr 1983). In other words, there is a progressive movement away from a 'closed' class society towards a meritocratic society of a supposedly far more 'open' kind.

However, in the light of the research results that have so far accumulated, support for this liberal scenario can scarcely be thought impressive. Long-term changes in the interrelations between class and education of the kind envisaged turn out in most national societies to be scarcely, if at all, detectable (see especially Blossfeld and Shavit (eds.) 1992). Moreover, a further major problem is raised by another cross-nationally robust finding from the side of mobility research: namely, that relative rates of intergenerational class mobility typically show a high degree of temporal stability (Erikson and Goldthorpe 1992:ch. 3). In the case of Britain, for example, at least four independent analyses have revealed little change at all in such rates over the course of the present century – and certainly none in the direction of greater fluidity (Goldthorpe 1980/1987:chs. 3 and 9; Hope 1981; Macdonald and Ridge 1987; Marshall *et al.* 1988: ch. 5). Thus, even if it could be established that social selection has become more meritocratic, there is little indication of this having had any effect in producing more equal class mobility chances.

In the British case, where research on this issue has been perhaps more extensive than elsewhere, it was initially suggested by Halsey (1977) that although some evidence of a 'tightening bond' between education and worklife success was apparent over the middle decades of the century, this had been offset by widening class differentials in educational attainment, accompanied by little or no reduction in the strength of the 'direct' effects (those not mediated via education) of class origins on class destinations. In the light of subsequent research based on more extensive longitudinal data and more refined analytical techniques, the claim of actually widening class differentials in education would seem difficult to uphold; and the issue has rather become that of whether these differentials have remained essentially unaltered or have in some respects shown a degree of narrowing (Heath and Clifford 1990; Jonsson and Mills 1991). But what then also emerges is greater doubt about the supposed secular tendency for educational attainment to become more important as a determinant of destination class. Increasing occupational selection by merit, at least in so far as this is defined by educational credentials, is not easy to discern (see Heath, Mills and Roberts 1991; and Jonsson 1991a, for similar results for Sweden).

In sum, the evidence for education operating as a force of 'class abatement' remains slight. Rather, what is suggested by the research to which we have referred is that a high degree of resistance can be expected to any tendency favouring a reduction of class inequalities via 'meritocracy'. If education does become somewhat more important in determining worklife chances, then members of relatively advantaged classes will seek to use their superior resources in order to ensure that their children maintain a competitive edge in educational attainment; or, as Halsey (1977: 184) puts it, 'ascriptive forces find ways of expressing themselves as "achievement".' Alternatively, and as seems perhaps the more likely occurrence, if class differentials in educational attainment are to some extent diminished, then within more advantaged classes family resources can be applied through *other* channels, in order to help children preserve their class prospects against the threat of meritocratic selection (see Marshall and Swift 1992). We do not, we would stress, seek to argue here that class inequalities can *never* be mitigated through changes in educational systems and their functioning: only that there is no reason to suppose, as liberal theorists would wish to do, that this is likely to occur as the automatic and benign outcome of social processes that are in some way inherent in the development of industrial societies.

Class and political partisanship

For those who believe that in modern societies the impact of class on life-chances is in decline, there is a natural progression to the further claim that class is also of reduced importance in shaping the response of individuals to their social situation, in particular through political action. During the 1950s and 1960s liberal sociologists were pleased to describe the participation of citizens in the electoral politics of western nationals as representing 'the democratic translation of the class struggle' (Lipset 1960: ch. 7). However, under the influence of political as much as of social developments from the later 1970s onwards, a much stronger position was taken up. Class, it was now held, was (finally) dissolving as the basis of political partisanship, and this was most evident in the declining support from the working class for parties of the Left (see, for example, Lipset 1981; Clark and Lipset 1991). Moreover, such a diagnosis has also come to be accepted by many of the former leaders of *marxisant* social commentary, in their despairing *adieux* to the working class in particular and to class analysis in general.

In the British case, the thesis of 'class dealignment' in party politics has perhaps a longer history than elsewhere, and following the Conservative electoral triumphs of 1979 and 1983 it was enthusiastically revived by a series of authors (for example, Butler and Kavanagh 1984; Robertson 1984; Crewe 1984; Franklin 1985; Rose and McAllister 1986). Among the latter it was widely believed that the counterpart to the declining effect of class on vote was a tendency for party political conflicts to become organised more around 'issues' than socially structured 'interests' of any kind. However, in the view of certain other commentators, class was giving way to new structural cleavages as the basis of party support – in particular, cleavages which divided individuals and families, considered as either producers or consumers, according to their location in the public or the private sector of the economy (see Dunleavy 1979, 1980; Dunleavy and Husbands 1985; Saunders 1984; Duke and Edgell, 1984).

Critics of class analysis such as Pahl and Holton and Turner have, apparently, looked little beyond this range of literature. They write as if the thesis of class dealignment were securely established within electoral sociology and the 'new structuralism' now provides the paradigm to be reckoned with (Pahl 1989:713; Holton and Turner 1989:177, 186–90). What they quite fail to recognise, however, is the extent to which both the 'new structuralism' and the underlying claim of class dealignment have in fact been empirically challenged and on the basis of research and analysis that has significantly raised technical standards in the field.

Most importantly, Heath and his associates have shown the necessity of introducing into the debate on dealignment a distinction between absolute and relative rates of class voting, analogous to that between absolute and relative rates of social mobility (Heath, Jowell and Curtice 1985; Heath *et al.* 1991; Evan, Heath and Payne 1991). Applying this distinction to data on voting in British elections from 1964 to 1987, they are able to show that changes in absolute (or, that is, actually observed) class voting patterns are almost entirely attributable to two factors: on the one hand, changes in the 'shape' of the class structure, most importantly the growth of the service class or salariat and the decline in size of the industrial working class; and, on the other hand, changes in the number of political parties contesting elections and in their general effectiveness (that is, in their capacity to win support 'across the board', in equal degree from members of all classes alike). In contrast, changes in relative class voting – or, in other words, in the *net* association between class membership and vote – turn out to be rather slight. Moreover, in so far as such changes can be detected, they show no secular tendency for the class-vote association to decline, and appear more open to explanation in political than sociological terms (see especially Heath *et al.* 1991:ch 5). Although, for some, these findings have proved disturbingly counter-intuitive, it is important to note that they are confirmed in their essentials by those of a number of quite independent, if more restricted, analyses (see Hibbs 1982; Marshall *et al.* 1988:ch. 9; Weakliem 1989).

As Heath and his colleagues then go on to argue, their results bring out clearly the dangers of 'dualistic historical thinking' on the issue of class formation, of the kind in which critics of class analysis have tended to engage. So far at least as the evidence of political partisanship is concerned, there is in fact no reason to suppose that over recent decades, classes in Britain – the working class included – have shown any weakening in either their social cohesion or their ideological distinctiveness. This conclusion is also consistent with a variety of their findings on, for example, trends (or their absence) in patterns of class mobility, in levels of class identification, and in class differences in political attitudes and values (Heath *et al.* 1991:chs. 5, 6; *cf.* also Heath 1990) . . .

Conclusion

We have sought in this paper to respond to recent critiques of class analysis on two principal grounds. First, we argued that critics have not adequately distinguished between class analysis in its Marxist versions and class analysis understood and engaged in as a research programme. Various objections that may be powerful raised against the former simply do not apply to the latter. This is scarcely surprising, given the extent to which class analysis viewed as a field of empirical sociological inquiry freed from entanglements with the philosophy of history and 'critical theory' did in fact develop as a reaction against Marxism. Secondly, we have attempted to show, by reference to three central topics, that the research programme of class analysis has in fact yielded results permitting a flat rejection of the claims of Pahl and of Holton and Turner that class as a concept no longer does useful work, and retains only a rhetorical and not a scientific value.

Finally, we may note that the two main lines of argument that we have pursued, do in a sense converge. For Marxists, class analysis was the key to the understanding of long-term social change: class relations and specifically class conflict provided the engine of this change, and the study of their dynamics was crucial to obtaining the desired cognitive grasp on the movement of history. However, class analysis as a research programme is not only a quite different kind of intellectual undertaking from the class analysis of Marxism, but also generates results which give a new perspective on the substantive significance of class relations in contemporary society. A common theme in the research findings now accumulating is, as we have seen, that of the *stability* rather than the dynamism of class relations. What is revealed is a remarkable persistence of class-linked inequalities and of class-differentiated patterns of social action, even within periods of rapid change at the level of economic structure, social institutions, and political conjunctures. The disclosure of such stability – made possible largely by the advances in techniques of data analysis and in the construction of data sets to which we have referred – would in turn appear to carry two major implications. Most obviously, problems are created for liberal theorists of industrial society who would anticipate the more or less spontaneous 'withering away' of class, and of class analysis likewise. But at the same time the need is indicated for the theoretical concerns of proponents of class analysis to be radically reoriented. They must focus, not on the explanation of social change via class relations, but rather on understanding the processes that underlie the profound resistance to change that such relations offer.

Fiona Devine: Not only Class, but Regional and National Identities, too

The usefulness of this extract is in its emphasis on forms of identity in addition to that of social class. In particular, it is quite clear that interview respondents regard their local/regional origins and their sense of their own nationality as very important. Indeed, it is arguable that they have a clearer sense of these identities than they do of their class identity. Although the respondents generally see their class identity as significant, they are often inconsistent in their understanding of it. (Detailed material on class identity is not included in this extract.)

I have included both the 'abstract' or summary of Devine's article and the introduction to it in order to set the wider context of the debate to which this article is an interesting and helpful contribution. On the issue of whether or not the importance of social class has declined, Devine achieves a 'compromise' while maintaining a coherent position – class identity remains important but other identities have perhaps been underestimated. In order to produce data with which to examine this issue, Devine retreads the path of Goldthorpe *et al.*'s famous study, *Affluent Worker* (see below). However, her qualitative methodology contrasts with the latter's generally more quantitative approach.

Reading 14 From Fiona Devine 'Social identities, class identity and political perspectives' in *The Sociological Review*, 1992, pp. 229–31, 232–38, 248–49

Abstract

There has been considerable controversy over the extent to which class is a salient social identity, and the importance of other social identities. Marshall and his colleagues (1988) argue that class identity remains a salient frame of reference in people's daily lives while Saunders (1989; 1990) and Emmison and Western (1990) argue that class identity is not as strong as they claim, and the importance of other social identities cannot be denied. However, proponents and opponents in the debate are agreed that the salience of social identities depends upon the context in which they are found which cannot be fully explored in highly-structured interviews. Drawing on data from a 'qualitative re-study' of the *Affluent Worker* series, it will be argued that people have many different identities, including a strong class identity, which co-exist at the same time. That said, their class identity is the most important influence on the formation of political perspectives. This finding concurs with the Essex team *and* Saunders even though he has sought to distance himself from this conclusion.

Introduction

See Reading 13.

Publication of the main findings of the British Class Project in *Social Class in Modern Britain* by Gordon Marshall, David Rose, Howard Newby and Carolyn Vogler (1988) has generated a number of controversies in the field of class analysis. One such debate focuses on the relative salience of class and other social identities in shaping people's frames of reference in general, and their political perspectives in particular. The disagreement lies essentially between Marshal *et al.*, who argue that class remains a salient social identity, and Saunders (1989; 1990) and Emmison and Western (1990) who argue that other social identities are more significant than class.

In this paper, it will be argued that participants in the debate have agreed that the relative salience of class and other social identities depends upon contextual issues. No one identity enjoys an *a priori* salience over other social identities. Despite this consensus, however, disagreements persist on the significance of social identities, the form and nature of class awareness and the salience of class identity in the context of contemporary British politics. In other words, the debate has reached something of an impasse as the protagonists seem as far apart as ever. Drawing on data from a qualitative re-study of the *Affluent Worker* series, it will be argued, as Emmison and Western suggest, that national and regional identities are significant in shaping people's frames of reference. Moreover, class awareness is high as well although it is not as clear and coherent as Marshall and his colleagues suggest. That said, class remains a salient social identity in the domain of contemporary British politics, a conclusion from which Saunders does not seriously detract.

The debate on identities

Marshall and his colleagues argue that 'class is still the most common source of social identity and retains its salience as such' (1988: 143). Sixty per cent of their respondents thought they belonged to one particular social class, and ninety per cent of these people were willing to place themselves into a specific class category. The level of class awareness amongst their respondents was, therefore, high, suggesting 'that social identities are widely and easily constructed in class terms' (Marshall *et al.*, 1988: 145). While occupation and employment, income and status were the most commonly used criteria for assigning people to different social classes, most of their respondents used more than one characteristic to describe class, illustrating that 'class is widely perceived to be a multi-faceted or complex phenomenon' (Marshall *et al.*, 1988: 146–47). On the causes of class and class processes, three-quarters of their sample believed that people are born into particular classes, that it is difficult to move from one class to another, and that class is an inevitable feature of society. Fifty per cent agreed that there is still a dominant class with economic and political control and a subordinate class which lacks such control. In sum, the class structure, and the processes which sustain its existence, is perceived as 'ubiquitous and largely unchanging' (Marshall *et al.*, 1988: 147).

When asked what other social groups they belonged to, only nineteen per cent identified with another social grouping, the most frequently mentioned groups being business and religious groups. Even when references to 'them' and 'us' mentioned in the interview were explored further, the distinction invariably referred to different classes or the surrogates of class. From this evidence Marshall and his colleagues conclude, first, that 'social class is by far the most common, and seemingly the most salient frame of reference employed in the construction of social identities' (1988: 149), and second, sectoral cleavages, gender, ethnic and other social identities, often identified as undermining class, have failed to do just that.

These two conclusions have been fiercely contested by Saunders (1989; 1990), and Emmison and Western (1990) (members of the Australian team involved in the international study of class) who specifically criticise aspects of the methodology – the way in which the Essex team constructed its questionnaire – from which Marshall *et al*'s conclusions are drawn. Given the large number of questions relating to class which preceded the explicit discussion on class in the interview schedule, it is not surprising, Saunders argues, that the Essex team's respondents easily identified themselves with a particular class and were unable to place themselves in any other social grouping in a follow up question. The extent of class awareness was probably an artefact of the questions asked. Saunders (1989: 4) also argues that the importance of other social identities cannot be so easily disregarded either for the salience of a range of competing social identities depends on contextual issues . . .

The debate reconsidered

It appears, then, that proponents and opponents in the debate agree on a number of points. All of the participants acknowledge the methodological difficulties of using highly structured questionnaires to uncover some of the complex issues surrounding the study of class and other social identities. Given these shortcomings, the significance of other social identities cannot be denied. Finally, there is no doubt amongst the protagonists that the salience of social identities depends upon the context in which they are found.

Yet, despite the consensus on these issues, differences remain. Marshall and Rose argue that there is a high level of class awareness in Britain, and that this finding suggests that class is 'a common source' of social identity which is 'readily and easily' employed by people in their daily lives. It is not an artefact of the methodology they used. The critics, however, see this as tantamount to denying the significance of other social identities. Whether this is the case or not is, of course, a moot point. In other words, the debate has reached an impasse with the protagonists continuing to take their different stands.

This issue is also discussed in Reading 10.

One possible way out of this impasse is to draw upon qualitative interviews on a similar range of topics. The findings derived from qualitative interviews may overcome some of the methodological difficulties of using highly structured questionnaires to unravel these complex issues. Qualitative interviews, where interviewees can speak freely and develop their own ideas, concepts and arguments without links, consistencies and inconsistences being inferred by the interviewer, could throw light on the form, nature and meaning of class identity in people's lives, and, of course, our understanding of these issues. Similarly, it could enhance our understanding of the form, nature and meaning of other social identities. Finally, qualitative interviews which take account of contextual issues could highlight the relative salience of class and other social identities in people's daily lives. Now this is not to suggest that qualitative data alone can resolve the debate on identities. As Davies (1979) has noted, unstructured interviews can also suffer from the problem of researchers imposing an order on the material which may be inappropriate, if an order exists at all. That said, qualitative data still provides detail on the meaning and importance of issues in people's lives which quantitative interviews neglect. With this caveat in mind, the findings of qualitative interviews, conducted as part of a study on working-class life-styles, provide an opportunity to take the current debate about class and other social identities forward.

Privatism and the working class

The in-depth interviews to which I refer were carried out as part of a qualitative re-study of the *Affluent Worker* series (Devine, 1990; 1992 forthcoming). The aim of the research was to explore the extent to which members of the working class lead privatised life-styles as Goldthorpe and his colleagues described nearly thirty years ago, or whether they enjoy a more communal existence associated with the 'traditional' working class, and the meaning of those life-styles. A secondary aim of the research was to explore the ways in which people's daily lives may generate their social and political perspectives. Of course, the interviews, which were carried out in 1986–87, were undertaken in very different economic circumstances to the buoyant climate of the early 1960s. While Vauxhall had employed over 20,000 people in Luton in the 1960s, redundancies throughout the 1970s and 1980s reduced its workforce in the town to approximately 6,000 employees.

Interviews were conducted with thirty-two working-class couples living in Luton where the husbands worked in shop-floor jobs at the Vauxhall plant. The interviews with husbands and wives were conducted on separate occasions, and each lasted approximately two hours. With the use of an aide-memoire which acted as a checklist of topics to be discussed, the interviews covered a wide range of issues including geographical mobility, sociability with kin, neighbours and workmates (to tap family-centredness), conjugal roles and leisure (to consider home-centredness), and aspirations; class imagery and industrial and political attitudes (to examine social and political perspectives). On class imagery, for example, the interviewees were asked if they thought there were different classes and they were then allowed to develop their own ideas and concepts about class and present their own arguments. Usually, but not always, this introductory question led the interviewees to talk about the class structure, how it may or may not have changed, their own class position and how it affected their lives and so forth. If the topic generated a conversation of this kind, additional questions on class, such as the causes of class and the opportunities for mobility, were asked for comparability across the interviews. In the semi-structured interviews which took a conversational form, therefore, it was possible to explore social identities, the extent and nature of class awareness and the factors which shape political attitudes and behaviour.

Undoubtedly, over the course of the interviews, the interviewees identified with a wide range of social groups. As Saunders suspected, they identified themselves as male or female, young or old, as parents and children and so forth. As Emmison and Western found (1990: 249), one of the most salient social identities which was frequently mentioned by all of the interviewees was their identity with a place. However, it was not Luton with which they identified but their regions of origin. The salience of this regional/national identity and all of the characteristics associated with a place can only be fully understood in the context in which many of the interviewees moved to Luton and the life-styles which they subsequently adopted.

Regional and national identities

It will be recalled that Goldthorpe *et al.* (1968a; 1968b; 1969) saw geographical mobility as an important catalyst in the decline of the 'traditional' working-class community and the rise of privatised life-styles. Their sample comprised a highly mobile group of people who, they argued, had moved to Luton in search of highly-paid manual work and good standards of cheap housing which the town offered. In doing so, they invariably left the main body of kin, neighbours and friends behind them, being forced, as a consequence, to adopt a life-style which centred around the immediate family in the home. In the post-war period of prosperity, which fuelled new aspirations for material well-being and domestic comfort, this life-style was not unwanted (Goldthorpe *et al.*, 1969: 104).

While not recent migrants to Luton, my sample also consisted of a highly mobile group of people and first-generation Lutonians as Table 1 shows.

Table 1 The interviewees' region of upbringing

Region of Upbringing[a]	Interviewees
Luton area[b]	32
London and the South East	11
Northern Ireland and Eire	9
Abroad	5
Other parts of Britain	5
Total	62

a In keeping with the Luton team's definition of region of upbringing, the term refers to the locale in which the interviewee grew up.

b The Luton area is defined as the town and all land within a ten mile radius of the town's boundaries.

Not surprisingly, they had moved from regions like London and the South-East and Ireland and Northern Ireland from which many of Goldthorpe *et al*'s respondents also originated. However, the circumstances in which they moved to Luton were very different from those described by the Luton team. Rather than being propelled into mobility by an instrumental attitude to work, the search for employment *per se*, and not highly-paid manual work, dictated the move to Luton for the interviewees from Eire and Northern Ireland and abroad in particular. Similarly, the search for *affordable* housing also propelled the interviewees from London towards Luton as the nearest town where they could afford to buy their own homes.

Against this background, many of the migrants to the town followed or were followed by kin, neighbours and friends since they were an important source of information about jobs and accommodation. They moved within close proximity to family and friends, and the men often worked alongside each other in the Vauxhall plant. Of course, kin and friends were also an important source of companionship in their new locale so they socialised with them rather than adopt home and family-centred life-styles. Indeed, the companionship of siblings or long-standing friends was greatly valued if parents were absent from the locality. Sharing the same geographical origin often facilitated new companions as well. As one interviewee, who had moved from London to Luton in search of a house with her husband and two children explained, her closest friends were Londoners and 'we all talk about London, living in London and the reasons for moving to Luton'. Socialising with people of the same geographical origin was, for some, also reinforced by shared religious affiliations. Sociability with fellow Irish men and women, for example, was facilitated by the Catholic church and its social clubs.

Thus, rather than adopt a home and family-centred life-style, many of the interviewees socialised with kin, long-standing friends and new friends as well. While the high levels of sociability associated with the 'traditional' working class were not evident amongst the interviewees, there was a re-grouping of people with the same geographical origins in the town. Not surprisingly, then, the interviewees invariably identified themselves according to their geographical origins and the subcultural differences associated with them. Employing popular stereotypes of people, for example, the Irish described themselves in terms of their way of life or attitude to life, as friendly and informal people, as members of the Catholic church, as closely attached to their families or whatever in the same way that the Scots or Welsh highlighted their cultural distinctiveness. The way in which they saw themselves and interacted with other people was influenced by this significant identity which they readily used.

As a consequence, in a town whose districts were easily equated with different waves of migrants from particular places like Stacey's Banbury (1960), being a native Lutonian was an important identity, a status to which many of the interviewees referred. They identified themselves as a small and dwindling social group – 'we're pretty hard to find, you know, there's not many of us left' – with deep roots in the town, and they fondly recalled Luton before it had expanded to cater for the large influx of people. As one native Lutonian suggested:

> Luton has changed a lot. If I went down the road I was out in the country. All these new estates didn't exist but they were built for all the people coming into the town. I find that people who move to different towns tend to find their own people. They mix with lots of people but they still stay very close to their own.

In this instance, finding 'their own' people referred to a social group with a shared sense of place.

Interestingly, in their discussion about the 'demographic characteristics of Luton *as a community*', Goldthorpe and his colleagues (1968a: 151–52, emphasis in original) noted that native Lutonians were often outnumbered by migrant families whose 'subcultural differences' gave them 'a certain distinctiveness'. The interviews and debate in the *Luton News* about natives versus migrants led them to argue that 'it was apparent that in Luton consciousness of such differences was quite a definite influence on individuals' attitudes and behaviour towards each other (Goldthorpe *et al.*, 1968a: 152). Despite the intervening thirty-year period since the Luton team conducted their interviews, this 'consciousness' was apparent amongst my interviewees. Against the background of their geographical origins and histories, this social identity – a regional identity – influenced the way in which they defined themselves, how they viewed others and interacted with them.

However, in one important respect, Luton and its residents were different to the town which the Luton team, and Zweig (1961) before them, visited in the early 1960s. In the late 1960s and 1970s, a new influx of people from India (via East Africa), Pakistan and Bangladesh moved to Luton. Like the migrants from other parts of Britain and Ireland, they invariably moved to Luton in search of a livelihood – a job and a home – although the circumstances in which they moved were far less favourable than those of earlier migrants to the town. Like them as well, they relied on kin and friends to find them jobs, temporary and then permanent accommodation and, as a consequence, re-grouped in the town (centre) as well. Again, kin and friends were an important source of companionship and support. Clearly, their identity with their country, its people and their hopes and plans, fears and aspirations, their way of life and their culture was significant. And, of course, being non-white was a particularly important dimension of this identity, heightened by racial conflict in the town. As one interviewee from Kenya, but of Indian origin, who had moved to Luton with his parents in the 1970s, recalled:

> When we first came here, there were a lot of racial attacks on people. There were a lot of National Front people, a lot of problems. Basically, we never used to get out of the house after 7 pm. It was better to stay at home.

He now felt that Luton had changed for the better, one reason being that 'a mosque has been built which is good for us being Muslims. It is somewhere for us to go and pray'. Even so, he also identified himself as British, referring to India, his parents' country of origin, as an ex-colony of Britain, and still a Commonwealth country.

Discussion on the influx of people of different origins into the town, and of the Indian or Pakistani communities in particular, led almost all of the British/Irish interviewees to assert their British identity, their Christianity and, of course, their whiteness. While the distinctions between people of different geographical origins from Britain and Ireland had been drawn light-heartedly, the divisions between them and 'coloured immigrants' were discussed in distinctly pejorative terms. Racist beliefs were prevalent. They spoke of the decline of the residential areas in which they lived with the proliferation of families living together in the same house. The 'immigrants'' poor housing and the way in which they stayed so close to their family and friends indicated their failure to assimilate themselves into the town in particular, and into Britain in general, and to adopt the respectable life-styles of the British. As one native Lutonian explained:

> Too many overseas people have congregated in the area. Of all the towns with jobs, they have congregated in small patches, spreading out, taking over all the shops and ruining the area. B . . . used to be a different area with nice houses, gardens and trees but now it looks as if a bomb's been dropped. If I went to their country, we would have to abide by their rules. They have brought in their own rules, their own culture.

> This comment and, indeed, the whole of this section on nation/ethnic identity/racism illustrates the increased sensitivity of sociology to ethnic variety which, in my view, is beginning to emerge.

Thus, affiliation with a nation, and sometimes different nations simultaneously, was a significant dimension of the interviewees' identity. While identities based on geographical origins within Britain and Ireland were typically latent, a national identity was extremely pronounced. Their national identity was heightened because it was the basis of different and seemingly conflicting beliefs and attitudes – at least amongst the white Irish and British interviewees. It was also the source of conflict over the distribution of resources such as council houses and jobs.

Given that the majority of the interviewees felt very strongly about immigration (concurring with Sarlvik and Crewe's (1983: 242) finding that those who think they live in a 'high immigrant area' are more likely to feel very strongly about the issue than those who do not), it might have been expected that attitudes on the issue would shape political affiliations and party choice. After all, Luton's two MPs – John Carlisle and Graham Bright – are well known for their tough stands on immigration. However, this was not the case even though the interviewees were well aware of where the political parties stood on immigration. They knew that the Conservative Party wanted to restrict immigration while the Labour Party took a more liberal stand. It was mentioned only by the long-standing Conservative Party supporters in the sample as a justification for their political allegiances and why they did not vote Labour. Referring to conflict over the distribution of resources, an interviewee who had always voted Conservative said:

> I agree that we shouldn't allow more immigrants in. The Labour Party would let more in. We have youngsters of our own who want jobs. It gets harder for those here.

As we shall see, however, the majority of the interviewees were Labour Party supporters or disillusioned Labour Party supporters who justified their present or past party choice on a class basis. The interviewees' national identity did not translate into party choice, remaining, instead, a 'dormant' frame of reference in the political arena.

In sum, the interviewees identified with a range of social groups as Saunders suggested. Moreover, as Emmison and Western also found, an affiliation with 'a sense of place' was a particularly important social identity. It shaped the way in which the interviewees saw themselves and interacted with other people. The importance of social identities, other than class, therefore, cannot be denied. However, all of the interviewees also identified with a class. Indeed, their class identity brought them together whereas their regional/national identities differentiated them. Their regional/national identity, however, did not prohibit their class identity or vice-versa. This implies that people identify with many different and sometimes contradictory social groups. In turn, this suggests, as Marshall's and Rose's position implies, that a high level of class awareness can co-exist with other social identities. Asserting that class is a common source of reference is not tantamount to denying the significance of other social identities as the critics claim. That said, it will be seen that the interviewees' awareness of class was not as clear and coherent as the Essex team suggested.

Conclusion

The qualitative data, which were used to provide some insights into the debate about class and other social identities, suggest that people hold a variety of social identities which influence the way in which they see themselves, the ways in which they interact with other people, and their beliefs, attitudes, hopes and plans, fears and misgivings. One of the most important of these social identities is with a sense of place. These findings are in line with the criticisms (Saunders, 1989; 1990; Emmison and Western, 1990) of some of the findings reported in *Social Class in Modern*

Britain although two of the authors (Marshall and Rose, 1989) argue that they never denied the significance of other social identities. Moreover, it was found that other social identities, such as a regional or national identity, coexist with a high level of class awareness. It did not prohibit or undermine the interviewees' ability to distinguish between 'them' and 'us' in class terms. Finally, even though the interviewees did not hold a clear and coherent picture of class, as others (Mann, 1973; Parkin, 1972) concluded in the debate on class imagery, this did not inhibit them from invoking the importance of class on their political beliefs, attitudes and vote. Class was clearly a salient social identity in the political domain although it did not always translate into votes.

The section covering the political perspectives of respondents is not included in this extract.

The main finding to emerge from the qualitative data is that a high level of class awareness can coexist with other significant social identities. Class identity does not prohibit other social identities and vice-versa. If this finding is correct, and the debate is to go forward, the significance and relative salience of class and other social identities on people's ways of thinking and acting must be specified still further. Further consideration must be given to the ways in which social identities interact with each other, and the contexts in which they interact. These concerns also raise theoretical issues about the social construction of the self. If, as Mead (1934) argues, the self emerges through interaction which involves role-taking, trying to interpret the perceptions of others and reacting and adapting our actions in relation to others, our understanding of both individual and collective identities and interests can only be strengthened by a deeper analysis of the whole process of social interaction as well.

John Goldthorpe with Clive Payne: Social Mobility and Class Structure in the Decade following the Oxford Mobility Survey (1972–83)

The purpose of this piece is to update the findings of the Oxford Survey on Social Mobility which produced data up to 1972. The findings of the Oxford survey are well known, but I have extracted Goldthorpe's own simple summary of them as a convenient lead into his analysis of mobility and class structure between 1972 and 1983. The Oxford Survey was designed by Goldthorpe and his colleagues whereas the data used for the later period come from the British General Election Survey of 1983. Readers may feel that this only provides the basis for a partial updating. However, it does bring us well into the Thatcher era and also deals with the issue of 'double-digit' unemployment. Much of what Goldthorpe writes about the early 1980s is equally applicable to the early 1990s when the percentage of unemployed is again in double figures.

Conveniently, Goldthorpe finds that there is 'a very large measure of continuity' between the earlier and later periods. In analysing the trends, Goldthorpe takes the opportunity of emphasising what he sees as the inaccuracy and inadequacy of both the Marxist 'degradation of work' thesis and the opposing liberal position which maintains that the occupational structure in 'post-industrial' society has been generally 'upgraded'.

Reading 15 From John Goldthorpe *et al.*, *Social Mobility and Class Structure in Modern Britain*, 2nd ed. (Clarendon Press, 1987), pp. 253–54, 270–73 by permission of Oxford University Press

[The findings of the Oxford Mobility Survey] could be summarized as follows.

(i) From at least the inter-war years through to the time of the 1972 inquiry, men of *all* class origins had become progressively more likely to move into professional, administrative, and managerial positions – or, we would say, into the service class of modern British society, and, at the same time, they had become less likely to be found in the manual wage-earning positions of the working class.
(ii) These trends could be attributed, more or less entirely, to changes in the shape of the class structure – that is, to the growth of the service class and the contraction of the working class; they were, in other words, the result of changes in objective mobility opportunities, and did not reflect any changes in relative mobility rates or changes in the direction of greater equality of opportunity or 'openness'.
(iii) Thus, while upward mobility into the service class from other class origins steadily increased across successive birth cohorts, downward mobility from service-class origins to other class positions steadily decreased; and correspondingly, while the working class became somewhat less stable intergenerationally, the stability of the service class was enhanced.

The central concern of the present chapter is, then, to investigate whether these elements of change and constancy in the pattern of intergenerational class mobility have persisted for a further decade since 1972. That year has in fact a good claim to be regarded as the last of the post-war period – the period of the 'long boom' during which, it seemed, the sustained and relatively balanced growth of capitalist economies had become successfully institutionalized. In October 1973, war broke out in the Middle East, and the winter of 1973–4 saw the first major oil price increases. In the following summer came the most severe international economic crisis since 1929 and, from the vantage point of the present, this would appear to have signalled the start of a new phase in the economic history of the western world: one characterized by more intractable macro-economic relationships between inflation and unemployment and by generally reduced rates of growth. In this new context, moreover, Britain has fared worse than most other western nations, and especially in regard to 'de-industrialization' and job losses. Not only has the proportion of the work-force unemployed at any one time been unusually high (reaching an official figure of over 12 per cent by 1983); but further, from around 1975 onwards, a steady build-up has occurred in the numbers of the *long-term* unemployed. In 1983 a million persons had been registered as unemployed for a year or more. The structural change which was the key dynamic element in mobility patterns in the years up to 1972 has usually been understood as a feature of general economic expansion. Thus, one issue which becomes of evident interest is that of whether, in the economic conditions that have more recently prevailed, the creation of favourable mobility opportunities via structural change has been maintained, or whether such opportunities have become increasingly restricted and the risks of unfavourable mobility outcomes have grown . . .

Mobility and the changing class structure

The main outcome of our comparison of intergenerational class mobility tables for 1972 and 1983 is then that, despite the transition from one economic era to another which occurred between these dates, a very large measure of continuity can be observed. Relative mobility rates have remained essentially constant on the same pattern that they would appear to have displayed for most of the century; and since the evolution of the class structure has proceeded in much the same direction as throughout the post-war years, it must follow that the same trends in absolute mobility rates as were observed in 1972 will also have extended to 1983. However, we have also shown that the return of large-scale and long-term unemployment does have certain implications for mobility chances. New risks are created of downward mobility into a condition of serious social deprivation, although exposure to them is greatest by far among men who are found in, or who have a high probability of entering, manual wage-earning jobs.

> Here Goldthorpe signals the significance for mobility and stratification theory of new, very high rates of unemployment (see also Reading 44).

It would thus seem essential both to the description and the interpretation of our findings on mobility trends for the period 1972–83 to recognize that the changing structural context is of prime importance, and that this is one in which a heightening of both opportunities *and* risks occurs. What may then further be remarked is that such a conjunction is something quite unprovided for in – and hence must be a source of doubt about – two current and well-rehearsed theories of apparent relevance: the Marxist 'labour process' theory of class structural change which claims a necessary 'degrading' of work and a progressive proletarianization of the work-force under capitalism; and the liberal theory of post-industrial' society which claims a general 'upgrading' of the occupational structure, generated by technological advance and the development of a 'service economy'.

The thesis of the degrading of work would in fact appear to be rather flatly contradicted by trends that are consistently revealed in the census statistics of capitalist nations, whatever allowances may be made for the crudity or inaccuracy of these data. It is professional, administrative, and managerial occupations that are in expansion, while the greatest decline is found in manual wage-labour – above all in unskilled grades – and with an incipient decline being in some cases also apparent among more routine nonmanual occupations. Britain is certainly no exception to these trends and, as we have shown, they have continued to be the major source of change in mobility rates and patterns over the last decade, just as they were throughout the post-war years.

This discrepancy between the degrading thesis and the evidence of census data might, however, in some part be attributed to the fact that changes in occupational and class distributions at the societal level can come about quite independently of changes in the organization of production within particular enterprises: that is, through shifts in the division of total employment *among* different industries and sectors, which themselves possess different occupational structures. Thus, in Britain – as, it would appear, in other western societies – the growth of numbers in professional, managerial, and administrative occupations during the post-war period did to a substantial extent result from the increasing importance of the services sector of the economy, within which these occupational groupings have always been more prominent than within manufacturing. And in so far as in more recent years of economic difficulty the decline of British manufacturing has been accelerated, it would seem that the expansion of higher-level class positions via such 'shift' effects can only have been enhanced.

More sophisticated adherents of 'labour-process' theories have therefore been able to suggest that, for a time, the consequences of the systematic degrading of work for the shape of the class structure are likely to be masked by an offsetting industrial redistribution of employment. But, they then contend, as the service economy nears its full development, such shift effects must weaken and the reality of widespread proletarianization, together with its very negative implications for mobility opportunities, will at this point become apparent. However, this argument has of late been seriously undermined – as some of its former exponents have in fact come to acknowledge. Analyses of the American, and likewise of the British, experience in the course of the 1970s reveal that in this period professional, administrative, and managerial occupations were still in overall expansion, and manual ones in contraction, *even when* all inter-industry shifts were allowed for. That is to say, in quite direct opposition to what the thesis of the degrading of work would predict, the major trends apparent in census data were generated not only by industrial and sectoral changes in employment but further by the (net) effects of technological, organizational and other changes determining the occupational 'mix' within production units.

As a last line of defence for the 'degrading' thesis, it may be maintained that some sizeable part of the expansion of administrative and managerial positions in particular should be recognized as more apparent than real. This is so because many of these positions either have been themselves degraded into essentially subordinate ones, involving only routine tasks, or have been created by an upgrading of such subordinate positions of no more than nominal or cosmetic kind. And it has in turn been contended that when such processes are taken into account, the increased upward mobility that is typically displayed in survey-based inquiries must be regarded as in some part spurious. But what has to be pointed out here is, first of all, that no systematic empirical support for such arguments has so far been brought forward, while contrary evidence is growing; and further, that the case made out is one on which our findings can in fact throw serious doubt. If degrading or 'dilution' of the kind claimed *had* gone on over recent decades within the service class of our analyses, one would then expect this to show up in some deterioration of the mobility chances of men originating in this class, relative to those of men of other origins. But, as we have seen, there is no indication of this whatever. Rather, we find still further confirmation of what has elsewhere been referred to as the 'undiminished capacity of the service class to "reproduce" itself, even as its numbers have increased'.

The foregoing might then be taken to imply not only that the degrading thesis is seriously mistaken but, further, that the upgrading thesis is vindicated. However, if this thesis is not, in the same way as the degrading thesis, empirically unsustainable, it is still one which, at least in the economic conditions of present-day Britain, must appear to reflect an unduly partial view. It was a product, one must remember, of the period of the long boom in which employment levels were typically high; and the liberal account of the development of industrial economies and societies of which it forms part was not one that seriously entertained the possibility that unemployment might return and persist on a mass scale.

Thus, it is difficult to accommodate to the upgrading thesis the existence of 'double-digit' unemployment and of a growing pool of men who have been out of work for many months. And in so far as the expansion of professional, administrative and managerial occupations is being promoted by the sectoral shifts involved in the de-industrialization of the British economy, it must appear that the counterpart of this process is not simply that the proportion of the work-force in manual jobs declines, but further that the number of those who have no work at all is enlarged. Furthermore, present economic conditions bring out sharply the continuing differentiation between men in service-class positions and those engaged in manual wage-labour in the degree to which they are threatened by loss of work and, hence, in the nature of the employment relationships in which they are involved.

What then is unacceptable, in the British case at least, is the idea of upgrading as a generalized process at work throughout all levels of the occupational structure and leading towards what has been envisaged as 'the professionalization of everyone'. Even while the expansion of the service class remains a major feature of the structural context of mobility in present-day British society, as it was throughout the post-war period, unemployment is now, as we have seen, another feature of this context which cannot be neglected. For men of working- and intermediate-class origins in particular, the pattern of their possible mobility experience has been significantly reshaped over recent years as unemployment, rather than occupational immobility or decline, has come to represent the alternative pole to gaining entry to a higher-level class position.

We may then conclude that if the upgrading thesis is taken to refer simply to the growth of professional, administrative, and managerial occupations, it captures an important aspect of the changing class structure of advanced industrial societies; but that, on its own, it suggests an over-optimistic perspective on recent economic history, or at all events on the British case. However, the important counter-tendency to be recognized, so far at least as the understanding of current rates and patterns of class mobility is concerned, is not one towards the degrading of work within the capitalist organization of production, as 'labour process' theorists would insist. It is, rather, the elimination of work opportunities of any kind for large numbers of the active population, heavily concentrated among those who had previously been within the ranks of manual wage-earners.

Ralf Dahrendorf: More Questions than Answers – the Great 'Underclass' Debate

By far the most difficult selection for this Reader was to find a suitable article on the so-called 'underclass'. There is considerable literature on the underclass, but no clear agreement on how the term should be defined or even whether it should be used at all. It may help to indicate briefly some of the main issues in relation to the underclass before introducing Dahrendorf's piece.

In the 1960s and 1970s, the term underclass was used by, among others, John Rex to describe the almost caste-like exclusion of the majority of black people from social opportunity and mobility. More recently, the term has been used differently and more widely to describe those who, whatever their colour, appear 'cut-off' from the class system.

In 1989, the right-wing American policy theorist, Charles Murray, made an influential contribution to the debate, *The Emerging British Underclass* (IEA, Health and Welfare Unit, 1990). What characterises the underclass for Murray is their behaviour: a tendency to avoid work, to produce 'illegitimate' children, and for these children to be violent teenagers (particularly the males). The main cause of this behaviour specified by Murray is 'welfare dependency' which saps the need and desire to work and removes the material need for marriage and the nuclear family.

In replying critically to Murray, Frank Field accepted that 'Britain does now have a group of poor who are so distinguished from others on low income that it is appropriate to use the term "underclass" to describe their position in the social hierarchy' (*The Emerging British Underclass*, p. 37). He considers that the underclass is composed of three groups: 'the very frail, elderly pensioner, the single parent with no chance of escaping welfare under the existing rules and with prevailing attitudes, and the long-term unemployed' (*ibid.*, pp. 38–39). Field's inclusion of elderly pensioners in the underclass perhaps confuses matters (see below). As far as the other two groups are concerned he seeks solutions in more effective employment and training policies and in mechanisms to ensure that fathers provide financial support for their children.

The extract from Ralf Dahrendorf re-published here is one of several in a collection entitled *Understanding the Underclass* (1992). The articles in the collection were originally presented as conference papers. I have selected Dahrendorf's contribution mainly because he asks questions rather than prematurely attempting to tie-up answers about the vexed issue of the underclass. Nevertheless, Dahrendorf does make some statements which are controversial. Above all, he takes the view that it is the attitudes and culture of the underclass that are its defining characteristic.

In an article in the same collection, David J. Smith cites evidence that, in fact, the attitudes of the underclass to work and to children and the family are not significantly different from those of other members of society. Smith's own preferred explanation for the emergence of the underclass is structural rather than cultural: the main reason is the increase in long-term unemployment, although he recognises that even fuller employment would not touch the problems of many single parents. On the issue of who belongs to the underclass, Smith usefully adopts the concept of a life-cycle. Thus, pensioners and prospective students are not part of the underclass because they have a past or prospective relationship to paid employment.

It is worth summarising Dahrendorf's four footnotes:

1 There is a group of the 'excluded' in Britain.
2 People 'drop out of' society sometimes through choice and sometimes through circumstances.
3 The underclass is not a class.
4 Education and opportunities for participation as citizens may help 'to solve the problem' of the underclass.

The last point is perhaps particularly important. In linking the underclass with citizenship theory, Dahrendorf begins to suggest a way in which its members may remain attached to (the rest of) society (see Reading 58).

Finally, it is perhaps prudent to record Robert Moore's caveat against the use of the term underclass (ATSS Conference, 1991). He associates the use of the term with Nazism and theories of biological inferiority and eugenics and he concludes that it is therefore best avoided.

Reading 16 From Ralf Dahrendorf, 'Footnotes to the Discussion' in David J. Smith *ed., Understanding the Underclass* (P.S.I., 1992), pp. 55–58

I propose to add four footnotes to the discussion. They may, in part, turn out to be land mines but they are certainly not intended to kill.

Nature and significance of the underclass

First, in every age there are those who drop through the net which catches full members of society. I have at home Charles Booth's *Map of London Poverty*; in the 1890s people spoke in much more candid language, so that the map shows ink-coloured blots where people lived who were 'vagrants, drunks, unemployables, criminals', in other words horrible people with whom nobody wanted to live. There were quite a few areas in London at that time which are painted in that particular colour, and if you go 40 years further back and read Mayhew, you get some beautiful stories about the underclass. In other words, there is nothing new about the phenomenon of people who are not a part of life as those who represent the dominant values of a society would like to see it. I agree entirely with David Smith that it would be nice to find a minimal, or even an operational definition. One might try David Willett's proposal and talk about the long-term claimants of public support or even those who are entitled to public support; something of that kind might be useful. Certainly I believe that it makes sense to talk about people in human societies who are not able, or perhaps willing, or both, to participate fully in the economic, the political and the social life of the communities in which they are living. This means, incidentally, that if there are formal systems of social support, these are not likely to reach them in quite the way in which they are intended to reach them. Moneys are likely to be used for objectives which have little to do with the objectives for which these systems have been created.

The question of whether such groups exist seems to me spurious. I am quite sure that these groups are not classes in any technical sense, a subject to which I shall return. I have no difficulty with the word underclass because I can accommodate my language to everyday language, but there is no technical or proper sociological sense in which this particular category can ever be called a class. Even that is neither here nor there; the interesting questions, as David Smith put it so well, are the empirical questions: is the underclass large or small? I have a hunch that in the 19th century it was very much larger than it is today. Is it growing or shrinking? I was very interested in the empirical papers this morning because they seem to indicate that it may be growing in Britain today. Is it hard or soft? I think this is William Julius Wilson's term. In other words, is the underclass a soft category with permeable boundaries, so that it is easy for some to move out and others to drop back into it; or is it a solid, fixed group of people with their own culture? Does it correlate with other important features of social life or doesn't it? Is there something random about membership of this category or is it systematic? Does race matter or doesn't it matter? In this context, the discussion of the differences between American cities and British cities is quite important; even the race issues presents itself very differently. For example, one of Wilson's important theses is that in some of the black ghettos, what he calls the 'role models' have disappeared, so that while there is a group of successful blacks, those who grow up in Chicago, or in the Bronx, never see any black person who has been successful. Now, that is fortunately not true in Britain; it is still the case that if you grow up as a minority youngster you are able to see members of your minority who have done rather well, so that there is not this total dissociation from the opportunities of a society in which you are living.

However, my first footnote really says that there is a serious issue of the category of those who are excluded, but in Britain things are not quite as bad as they might be, and as they are in other parts of the world. The possibility – or impossibility – of making general statements about the category is itself an interesting fact and if one has to grope for general statements and finds it difficult to discover sensible things to say which are true for a significant number of people, one does not need to worry quite as much as in other parts of the world. I think the American underclass and especially the ghetto underclass problem is one of the most serious problems in the entire civilised world; I am not blaming Americans because they have tried very hard to cope with it, much harder than we have at anything, but it is nevertheless still there.

Why people fall into the underclass

Here Dahrendorf suggests that some members of the underclass want employment but cannot get it and that others simply do not want it.

Second footnote: why do people drop through this net which societies have? They do so because for some reason they do not want to or do not find it possible to comply with the dominant values of a society. In my own analysis, there are two sets of values which are particularly relevant in this connection: one of these has to do with work and the other has to do with families. The issue of work has been alluded to a number of times this morning, with rather important statements. One issue that needs to be looked at closely when discussing the category of those who drop out is to what extent a developed modern economy needs everybody who could conceivably be employed, to what extent it could do quite well with two, five, ten, fifteen, twenty per cent unemployment and nevertheless produce satisfactory growth rates. I think this is a very important issue, and one which has a lot to do with the ability of those who have dropped out of the labour market to come back in. Incidentally, even within Europe different countries seem to deal with this issues in rather different ways. Germany has had two million unemployed for quite a long time now, to say nothing of another million who are either conscripts or students, and are, therefore, taken off the labour market. And yet economic development in Germany is very satisfactory. So something is changing about the nature of work, and our values which emphasise work and the need for work do not seem to tally with the economic basis of our society. This is one of the reasons why many people have but a tenuous hold on the labour market.

Similar observations could be made about the family, especially the old ideal of a complete family with two children. Things have changed quite significantly. David Willets has made a dramatic point, the Pat Moynihan point about American blacks. The change in their family structures is quite extraordinary and is one which is very hard to explain, for among them the complete family is almost the total exception, it describes 10–15 per cent of all blacks, not many more. There are other changes, for instance the fact that two incomes are needed to sustain a family nowadays. This too has something to do with poverty and who drops into poverty. Thus dominant values, which still exist somewhere, do not satisfy the needs of all people in our societies and because they do not satisfy these needs some people drop through the net. Not surprisingly, we do not quite know what to do about them as we get these phenomena of persistent unemployment, perisistent poverty, poverty of single parent families, and so on.

Not a class but a challenge to dominant values

Perhaps the term underclass does succeed in conveying the point that the underclass is not a class but largely 'outside of' or 'beneath' the class structure.

Third footnote: The key point in theoretical terms about the underclass seems to me to be that it is precisely not a class. Classes are essentially necessary social forces. It is no accident that Marx tried to link classes, not just to relations but to forces of production; he saw classes as being based on certain central social needs, one class which presides over the existing values and laws and rules and mode of production and the other class which represents some new opportunity for the future, some chances of development. The whole point about the underclass or the category of those who have dropped through the net is that they are not needed in this sense. Can I say in parenthesis that the real equivalent of the underclass on an international scale is the very poor countries. Their position in a world society and the extent to which they are needed or not needed presents analogous challenges, as does the extent to which there is an actual interest on the part of the richer countries in doing something for the poor or not. There may not be such an interest; there certainly is no massive and identifiable interest on the part of the official classes of the advanced societies to do something about the underclass. They could live quite happily with an underclass of 5, 10, 12, 15 per cent for a very long time and if they are rich enough and have arrangements like the Federal Republic of Germany, they can feed the underclass and not bother about the fact that they are not a part of the labour market or indeed may not be a part of political or social life in general. At the same time, it seems to me that tolerating a group of people for whom this is true, while professing values like those of work or the family, means that one tolerates a not insignificant group which has no stake in the accepted general values. If one tolerates a group which has no stake in the accepted general values, one cannot be surprised if people at the margin, and many others, increasingly cast doubt on these values and the values themselves begin to become much more tenuous and precarious than is sustainable for any length of time.

> Is Dahrendorf correct in stating that the underclass challenges conventional family and work values (see my introduction)? Arguably, the phenomenon of the travellers gives support to his view.

I never argued that football hooligans are themselves a part of the underclass, but I did argue that football hooliganism and similar phenomena, including many of the breaches of law and order in our cities, express a disdain for prevailing values which is legitimised by a society that tolerates a group which is excluded from many of its areas of participation, and from many of its basic rights of participation. So my argument would not be that the underclass is going to march on Westminster or start a new class war; but that the underclass is the living doubt in the prevailing values which will eat into the texture of the societies in which we are living. In fact, it has already done so, which is why there is a very strong moral case for doing something about it.

Policies to meet this challenge

Finally, there are two ways of dealing with a phenomenon like the category called underclass. One is to try and make them a part of the official society, and here I am sure the key is education rather than church membership. That is to say I would send teachers rather than missionaries to the inner cities to try and persuade people to accept the usefulness of elementary skills. As we have heard this morning, qualifications are crucial in order to be a part of the labour market and, perhaps more than the labour market, of the social universe in which we are living.

Beyond that, I feel very strongly that the values of citizenship have a lot of power in them, and citizenship means that human beings have certain entitlements as members of the society in which we are living. In this connection, I believe that one of these entitlements should consist in basic income guarantees. I am, of course, aware of the Seattle and Denver studies to which David Willetts referred, and to the fact that they have demonstrated certain adverse effects of guaranteed incomes; but it still seems to me that extending the notion of citizenship to this area of social participation is very much in line with the kind of values which I foresee as being dominant once we have abandoned the emphatic insistence on either work or the traditional family as dominant values of our society. However, I say this with considerable hesitation and with the sure knowledge that even a society which is genuinely based on citizenship values will have its dropouts and in that sense its underclass.

Richard Scase: Does Social Class Still Matter? A Neo-Marxist View

In the following extract, Richard Scase puts his finger on a central dilemma for sociologists. Whereas most sociologists consider that 'class' is important, non-specialists generally do not. Should sociologists, then, downgrade the importance of social class as a descriptive and explanatory concept?

Richard Scase is quite clear that as far as sociologists themselves are concerned, they should not 'downgrade' the importance of the concept. On the contrary, he argues that class relations remain central to capitalist society – the latter cannot be understood without understanding the former. As will be apparent from reading the extract, Scase considers that Marx's definition of class is the most appropriate to capitalist society. However, in principle, his argument about the continuing relevance of class also applies to Weberian and perhaps other definitions of class. They, too, explain important aspects of the workings of capitalist society – whether non-sociologists appreciate this or not.

Crucially, however, Scase accepts that the fact that many (most?) non-sociologists do not think class is particularly significant, is itself of great relevance to sociology. He cites a number of arguments and developments which explain why many people are inclined to accept capitalism and class as 'given' facts – and therefore as not particularly controversial or significant.

Scase's distinction between the sociological usefulness of the concept of class and its perceived unimportance by many non-sociologists, provides a contemporary perspective on the established sociological distinction between *objective* and *subjective* class (or Marx's description of a class *in itself* and a class *for itself*). These terms describe, on the one hand, an individual's class position according to some pre-determined criteria (such as relationship to the means of production) and, on the other, what an individual considers his or her class position to be. Although Scase himself accepts the objectivity of Marx's class scheme, he sees it as profoundly significant for sociological analysis that most people do not – and do not appear likely to for the forseeable future.

Reading 17 From Richard Scase, *Class* (Open University Press, 1992), pp. 79–83

> Ironically, perhaps, readers may feel that Scase somewhat understates here the degree of importance people attach to class.

At the beginning of this book it was suggested that class is generally regarded by most people as being of little relevance for the understanding of the everyday lives. In describing themselves, people tend to refer to such characteristics as age, gender, ethnicity, place of residence, occupation, etc., rather than class membership. Most frequently, notions of class are used to describe inequalities in the past or related to aspects of 'status' or 'snobbery'. As stated earlier, it is only with the considerable assistance of interviewers that respondents participating in social surveys are likely to refer to themselves in class terms and to allocate themselves to one of a number of class categories presented to them. Other than for those engaged in radical political activity or academic social science debate, it is unlikely that notions of social class will have much meaning for the overwhelming majority of people. At best, class is a vague, residual feature of social life. This has ramifications for the general and perceived relevance of sociology as a discipline, if only because concepts of class are central to most sociological analyses in Britain. Since the overwhelming majority of studies, whether they are of industrial shopfloor behaviour, family relations, health, deviance or voting patterns, tend to be discussed in social class terms, barriers are immediately erected between the practitioners of the discipline and others. A consequence is that sociological discourse becomes introspective and, usually, locked into a variety of academic debates which are perceived by others as largely irrelevant to the description and understanding of everyday reality.

The essential argument of this book is that, notwithstanding the subjective reality of class, it remains a concept that is vital for understanding the structure of present-day capitalist society. To reiterate what has been discussed earlier, the capitalist mode of production cannot exist without class relations and vice versa. Without these relations no surplus value can be produced and accordingly, capitalism is unable to reproduce itself. Without capital and labour as productive assets, structured within relations of exploitation, capital is unable to accumulate. Hence, relations of exploitation are expressed as control relations and reflected as job tasks and responsibilities within the occupational structure. Class relations, and the changes that occur within control relations, are the underlying forces that determine the nature of job tasks, the delineation of work roles and the structuring of occupations. Work tasks do not consist entirely of technical or expert skills since they have built within them dimensions of domination and subordination derived from class relations. This is why it has been argued that sociological approaches which begin with analyses of occupations and then proceed to aggregate these into social classes are dealing with the effects rather than the causes. No understanding of occupations and jobs can be complete without recognition of their origins within class relations. Equally, the structuring of organizations, whether they are directly or indirectly associated with the production or realization of surplus values, can only be understood by reference to relations of control (Dahrendorf, 1959). Profit-making organizations and state-owned institutions are little more than aggregates of employment relations within which control is exercised by those in positions of authority over others who are compelled to execute a variety of productive and/or unproductive tasks.

> Here Scase is criticising non-Marxist models of social class based on occupation rather than on relation to the means of production.

It is for these reasons that the analysis of social class is important for understanding the dynamics of organizational change, related as these are to the development of the capitalist mode of production (Salaman, 1981). The inherently competitive processes of capitalism, bringing about the concentration of ownership in monopoly or quasi-monopoly forms, inevitably lead to the restructuring of employment relationships. Equally, technological innovation has repercussions for the nature of work and for the delineation of job tasks. But these processes cannot be fully understood unless it is appreciated that the underlying forces are to do with the production and realization of economic surpluses. They can only be considered within the framework of class relations and how the structuring of occupations and the delineation of work roles within organizational settings are determined by these. Thus, it is clear that the analysis of class is inherent to the study of capitalist society. Western industrial societies are capitalist and, hence, their economic development is determined by the interplay of class forces of one kind or another. The fact that the prime objective of capitalist corporations is to make profits means that they are characterized by relations of exploitation and control and, hence, consist of class relations. This is the reality of economic production, irrespective of the perceptions and assumptions of participating actors. It is for this reason that social class will continue to remain central to sociological analysis. To eliminate it would be to obstruct sociologists from the analysis of the core forces of socio-economic change as they exist in capitalist society.

This is not to imply that social class will be perceived by social actors as having much bearing on their everyday lives. In a sense, why should it? There would seem to be no reason for individuals to need a sophisticated understanding of the dynamics of class for the purpose of achieving their personal goals in terms of psychological and material well-being. Indeed, most employees do recognize they are exploited – although they may rarely use such an emotive term – but view this as a taken-for-granted fact of the employment relationship (Beynon, 1980). They accept that they are hired to perform tasks that will contribute to the profits of their employing corporations and that should their labour be seen by senior management as unprofitable or unproductive, they will be fired. Most workers see nothing immoral in this and many go so far as to query the value or efficiency of non-profit-making forms of economic organization. Hence, it is unlikely that an awareness of exploitation will lead to political activism and to a personal commitment to fundamental socio-economic change. As long as employees perceive that they receive 'fair rewards' for 'fair effort', that wage differentials are reasonably legitimate, and that they are able to earn enough money to meet their personal needs, they are unlikely to become engaged in collective action directed towards the destruction of capitalism. This does not mean that workers need be satisfied with the overall distribution of economic rewards and with the pattern of wage differentials (Marshall *et al.*, 1988). Clearly, there is discontent, which becomes expressed in forms of industrial unrest, low motivation and wage demands. But such forms of protest are generally directed towards changes *within* rather than *of* the prevailing capitalist order. Equally, it is generally recognized that some groups in society are highly disadvantaged. But the explanations for this tend to be associated with personal failure and/or the actions of governments rather than with the inherent dynamics of the capitalist mode of production. Any targets of protest, then, tend to be governments rather than capitalist corporations.

Scase argues that for most people these bases of shared experience are more subjectively meaningful than social class in everyday life.

If there is collective protest, it appears in terms of various occupational, industrial, community and, sometimes, corporate interests. Thus, social protest is inclined to emphasize divisions within the working class and can sometimes reinforce ties of solidarity that cut across class boundaries. This can occur when multinational corporations threaten to close particular operating units, with the effect that local management and workers will 'unite' in their protest. More generally, corporate restructuring, the introduction of new technology and structural rationalization will elicit forms of protest that are spasmodic and localized in particular work settings. To achieve heightened levels of class consciousness among employees has been the ambition of radical activists since the nineteenth century but, with occasional exceptions, this goal has not been achieved. This is not only because of the great diversity of personal experiences encountered by those occupying similar class positions, but also for two other reasons. First, the overwhelming majority of individuals do not perceive themselves as *agents* of class in the manner that radical activists would like. Thus, their own biographical experiences, structured as these are within the context of particular intimate relationships and personal networks, will be considered by them to be more important than broader socio-political processes, irrespective of whether or not these are class related. Second, in terms of an appraisal of personal costs and benefits, the great majority of citizens in capitalist society perceive themselves as beneficiaries. They may demand more in the form of enhanced living standards and improved working conditions but, on the whole, they see themselves as enjoying greater benefits than costs. Many see themselves as exploited and view the distribution of rewards as unfair, but they take these factors for granted on the grounds that it is a price that has to be paid for better living standards and for personal non-work freedoms.

This has been a major source of legitimacy for the capitalist order, but it has been greatly strengthened by developments in Europe in the late 1980s. In the closing decade of the twentieth century, there remains no viable alternative to capitalism. Even if it is accepted that the Soviet Union and the countries of Eastern Europe were not truly state socialist, but represented repressive forms of state capitalism or bureaucratic collectivism, socio-political developments in those countries have tarnished, if not destroyed, the notion of state socialism as a model for societal development. The repressive, totalitarian nature of these countries and their socio-economic structures produced forms of society in which the majority of citizens concluded that the costs greatly outweighed the benefits. Even if the official party orthodoxy was accepted – namely, that there were no exploitative class relations – the subjective reality for most people was one of subordination and the repression of personal freedoms, individual creativity, dignity and self-respect. In this sense, the abolition of social class provided little in the form of self-enrichment.

On the basis of his arguments in this paragraph, Scase goes on to contend that revolutionary Marxist politics are now discredited in the West and that a social democratic policy and approach are the only alternative.

GENDER

Introduction: Readings 18–22

The extract from Sylvia Walby introduces the concepts of private and public patriarchy. The former is based on household production and the latter occurs in institutions external to the household (e.g. through involvement in paid work) as well as in the household itself. Walby argues that there has been a shift from private to public patriarchy during the course of the twentieth century.

Heather Joshi examines, the position of contemporary women and, as Walby puts it, the relationship between changing private and public contexts. She argues that the demands made on many women in the domestic context undermine their situation in the context of paid work. She illustrates this in considerable empirical detail.

The reading from Catherine Hakim on the levels of satisfaction experienced by women in paid work follows on very well from the Joshi extract. It has often been observed that significant numbers of those in highly subordinate (even exploited) situations report that they are satisfied with their lot and may even adopt ideological explanations of their subordination. (This is true of class as well as gender subordination and can even occur in relation to racial subordination.) Catherine Hakim reviews explanations of why, in general, women report higher levels of work satisfaction than men despite relatively lower pay, power and status.

The extract from Emily Martin examines the controversial relationship between biology and gender. She does so by discussing how childbirth, menstruation and the menopause are socially constructed and controlled. In particular, the medicalisation of childbirth is discussed.

The relationship between biology and gender is also a strong sub-theme in Reading 22 on masculinities and masculinist ideology. Like Martin, Brittan is strongly critical of biologically determinist approaches. He argues that there is no single version of masculinity – despite the apparent dominance of the macho model in the West – and that various masculinities occur. However, masculinist ideology seeks to justify male domination wherever it occurs.

Sylvia Walby: Private and Public Patriarchy – The Movement from the Former to the Latter from the Mid-Twentieth Century

This extract is taken from Sylvia Walby's book *Theorizing Patriarchy*. As this title indicates, the scope of the books is considerably wider than an analysis of patriarchy in private and public contexts. Prior to developing her analysis of these two forms of patriarchy, Walby analyses six main structures or frameworks within which patriarchy occurs. These are:

- Paid employment
- Household production
- Culture (including Religion, Media, Education)

- Sexuality
- Male violence
- The State.

Of course, patriarchy has been 'theorised' within all of these 'structures' before. What is original about Walby's perspective, however, is the way in which she relates these six *structures* to what she designates as the two *forms* of patriarchy, the private and the public. Private patriarchy refers to male dominance in familial contexts and public patriarchy refers to male dominance in wider social contexts such as paid work and politics (see paragraphs two and three of the extract). A crucial point is that the balance of patriarchal control can shift between the private and the public spheres in different historical periods.

In the extract I have selected, only one period of shift or movement in patriarchal power is described. This is the movement from private to public patriarchy which Walby considers began at about the beginning of the twentieth century and continues as we approach its close. Two main factors have contributed to this movement: the relative success of the feminist movement in decreasing the domestic (private) subordination of women and the demand of contemporary capitalism for cheap labour, especially in the service sector.

In a section not included here, Walby argues (with most other commentators) that after the early stages of the industrial revolution, women were mainly excluded from the public sphere and that patriarchy was predominantly private in form. The early twentieth century saw women begin to change this situation.

Reading 18 From Sylvia Walby, *Theorizing Patriarchy* (Basil Blackwell, 1990), pp. 178–79, 185–87, 200–1

Private and public patriarchy

I am distinguishing between two forms of patriarchy: private and public. They differ on a variety of levels: firstly, in terms of the relations between the structures and, secondly, in the institutional form of each structure. Further, they are differentiated by the main form of patriarchal strategy: exclusionary in private patriarchy and segregationist in public patriarchy. Private patriarchy is based upon household production, with a patriarch controlling women individually and directly in the relatively private sphere of the home. Public patriarchy is based on structures other than the household, although this may still be a significant patriarchal site. Rather, institutions conventionally regarded as part of the public domain are central in the maintenance of patriarchy.

In private patriarchy it is a man in his position as husband or father who is the direct oppressor and beneficiary, individually and directly, of the subordination of women. This does not mean that household production is the sole patriarchal structure. Indeed it is importantly maintained by the active exclusion of women from public arenas by other structures. The exclusion of women from these other spheres could not be perpetuated without patriarchal activity at these levels.

Public patriarchy is a form in which women have access to both public and private arenas. They are not barred from the public arenas, but are nonetheless subordinated within them. The expropriation of women is performed more collectively than by individual patriarchs. The household may remain a site of patriarchal oppression, but it is no longer the main place where women are present.

The 'six structures' are summarised in my introduction to this reading.

In each type of patriarchy the six structures are present, but the relationship between them, and their relative significance, is different. For instance, I am not arguing that in private patriarchy the only significant site is that of the household. In the different forms there are different relations between the structures to maintain the system of patriarchy.

In the private system of patriarchy the exploitation of women in the household is maintained by their non-admission to the public sphere. In a sense the term 'private' for this form of patriarchy might be misleading, in that it is the exclusion from the public which is the central causal mechanism. Patriarchal relations outside the household are crucial in shaping patriarchal relations within it. However, the effect is to make women's experience of patriarchy privatized, and the immediate beneficiaries are also located there.

In the public form of patriarchy the exploitation of women takes place at all levels, but women are not formally excluded from any. In each institution women are disadvantaged.

The second aspect of the difference between private and public patriarchy is in the institutional form of each of the structures. This is a movement from an individual to a more collective form of appropriation of women. There has also been a shift in patriarchal strategy from exclusionary to segregationist and subordinating.

I have traced the movement from private to public patriarchy within each of the six patriarchal structures during the course of this book. Within paid work there was a shift from an exclusionary strategy to segregationist one, which was a movement from attempting to exclude women from paid work to accepting their presence but confining them to jobs which were segregated from and graded lower than those of men. In the household there was a reduction in the confinement of women to this sphere over a lifetime and a shift in the main locus of control over reproduction. The major cultural institutions ceased to exclude women, while subordinating women within them. Sexual controls over women significantly shifted from the specific control of a husband to that of a broader public arena; women were no longer excluded from sexual relations to the same extent, but subordinated within them. Women's exclusion from the state was replaced by their subordination within it . . .

The movement from private to public patriarchy

There have been very important changes in gender relations taking place during the twentieth century, as I have been arguing throughout this book.

The movement towards a more intense form of private patriarchy was dramatically reversed during the period at the turn of the century. The twentieth century has seen a shift in the form of patriarchy from private to public as well as a reduction in the degree of some specific forms of oppression of women.

This is not merely a statement that there were important changes, but, further, that the very direction of change was reversed. All six patriarchal structures are involved in these changes. There was a struggle by feminists against patriarchal social practices which met with resistance. Their campaigns took place in the context of, and were shaped by, the capitalist demand for labour. The outcome of these battles was a change from one form and a high degree of patriarchy to another form together with some lessening in the degree of patriarchy in specific areas. These had complex interconnected effects on other aspects of patriarchal relations. Capital's demand for increased supplies of labour was in conflict with the private patriarchal strategy of privatizing women in the home. First-wave feminism's victories of political citizenship gave women not only the vote, but education, and hence access to the professions, property ownership and the right to leave marriages. In combination these meant that women eventually gained effective access to paid employment and the ability to leave marriages, which led to significant changes in the notions of appropriate sexual behaviour. To start with first-wave feminism achieved a victory principally at the political level of the state; the eventual changes at the economic level provided the material possibility of the mass of women taking advantage of their legal independence. The two changes, political and economic, had their impact as a result of their specific combination. In the absence of the political victory the increase in women's wage labour would have been merely additional exploitation. It was only because of the citizenship rights that women were able to use the economic changes to broaden further their sphere of operation.

Capitalism and changes in the form of patriarchy

The main basis of the tension between capitalism and patriarchy is over the exploitation of women's labour. On the one hand, capitalists have interests in the recruitment and exploitation of female labour, which is cheaper than that of men because of patriarchal structures. On the other, there is resistance to this by that patriarchal strategy which seeks to maintain the exploitation of women in the household. The first forms of capitalist industrialization saw the successful recruitment of women (and children) into the cotton textile factories in greater numbers than men. Prolonged patriarchal resistance through political pressure on the state to pass the Factory Acts and by the craft unions to bar women entry to specific jobs was not able to do more than stabilize the situation in this industry. In other occupations which entered the capitalist factory later, such as skilled manual engineering work, the men's craft organizations were successful in excluding women. Indeed there was often a strong cross-class patriarchal alliance which supported the exclusion of women, even in the absence of strong male unions. However, this cross-class alliance had weaknesses when it cut across the interests of employers to recruit the cheaper labour of women. Conflict would break out, as it did over the question of women entering the munitions factories during the First World War.

An alternative patriarchal strategy developed of allowing women into paid employment, but segregating them from men and paying them less. Clerical work is a good example of this process, where the male workers' organizations were insufficiently strong to defeat employers' insistent attempts to recruit women. The problem was resolved by a compromise in which the employers ceased trying to substitute women directly for men and instead recruited women for new sub-occupations, which were segregated from those of the men, graded lower and paid less, while maintaining the men in the upper reaches of white-collar work (see Walby, 1986). Whether the exclusionary or the segregation strategy was followed depended upon the balance of capitalist and patriarchal forces in a particular industry in a particular locality. The former was based upon a private form of patriarchy in which women were controlled by excluding them from the public sphere, especially from paid work. The latter was based upon a public form of patriarchy in which women were controlled within all spheres. The power of capital precluded the successful maintenance of the exclusionary mode, except in certain small tight pockets of patriarchal power and resistance. (For instance, the typesetters were able to sustain this until the last decade, as Cockburn (1983) has shown.) The exclusionary form of patriarchy was also under attack by a large powerful feminist movement from the middle of the nineteenth century to the first quarter of the twentieth.

It is characteristic of Walby's position that she stresses the relative independence of patriarchy from capitalism – although, of course, the two systems interact (see the conclusion to this reading).

The development of the economical structures of capitalism was not sufficient by itself to cause the shift from private to public patriarchy. This could only occur in the context of a powerful feminist movement in Britain, and indeed most of the West. Where we find capitalism in the absence of a feminist movement, there is no such change in the form of patriarchy. For instance, in some parts of the contemporary Third World young women have been pulled into wage labour for the capitalist factories of foreigners, yet are still subject to the patriarchal control of their fathers (Jayawardena, 1986; Mies, 1986). Wage labour by itself does not provide freedom from patriarchal control. In the case of Western industrialization first-wave feminism created a different balance of forces.

The tension between capital and patriarchy over the exploitation of women's labour is particularly acute when the dominant patriarchal strategy is the private one, and much less intense when it is the public one. In the latter women's labour is more readily available to capital, because there is less pressure by patriarchal forces for women to be kept domesticated. This is the situation by the second half of the twentieth century. After the Second World War there was an unprecedented increase in women's paid employment in Britain (as discussed in chapter 2). This expansion took place initially under conditions of absolute labour shortage, which strengthened the arguments against the reimposition of pre-war restrictions on the paid work of married women. However, since the 1970s this expansion has continued despite the substantial rise in male unemployment. Women are not used merely as a labour reserve when male labour is already fully utilized. While the employers' demand for labour is a necessary factor behind the increase in women's paid work it is not a sufficient condition. We need also to understand why women's labour is preferred over that of men, and why it suddenly becomes available in the post-war period. The preference for female labour is simple to understand, since women are cheaper to employ at the same level of skill because patriarchal practices depress women's wage rates.

The new availability of women's labour is more difficult to explain, but is to be understood in terms of the shift from private to public patriarchy both within the paid workplace and outside it. The reduction of patriarchy exclusionary practices in the workplace and their replacement by a segregationist strategy is the form of the shift from private to public in the workplace. This was reinforced by changes in legislation affecting and opening up possibilities for women's employment. Outside the paid workplace the shift from private to public patriarchy loosened women's total commitment to domestic labour, releasing their time for paid work.

The utilization of women in this way had implications for capital labour relations. Employers were able to take advantage both of the size of the pool of available labour and the fact that it was internally differentiated in order to depress the conditions of work. Struggles, such as that over flexibilization, are affected by the fact that labour is divided by gender. The new jobs which have been created in the last two decades have been overwhelming, and unsurprisingly, for part-time women workers, who are both available and the cheapest to employ. Gender relations affect capital labour relations . . .

Patriarchy comes in more than one form; each form can be found to different degrees. British history over the last century or so has seen a shift to a more intense form of private patriarchy and then a dramatic reversal of this with a move towards public patriarchy. This latter shift was a result of the successes of first-wave feminism against the background of an expanding capitalist economy. It took its form in the context of the international economy, and various specific forms in different ethnic groups. The British form of public patriarchy involves the market as well as the state, while there is a different sub-type of public patriarchy in Eastern Europe in which the state plays a more central part in comparison with the market.

The major historical changes are different for gender relations from those of capitalist class relations. Gender and class have independent historical dynamics, although of course they do have effects upon each other. The rise of capitalism transformed class relations, changing the very classes which constituted society. This historical shift did not have such dramatic effects upon gender relations: men remained the dominant gender; all six patriarchal structures continued across this period; only a minor shift in the relative significance of public and private sites of patriarchy occurred. The trajectory towards an intensified private form of patriarchy, which can be identified as far back as the seventeenth century (Charles and Duffin, 1985; Clark, 1919), accelerated.

Gender relations are not static, and a developed concept of patriarchy is the best way of theorizing the changes. The idea of patriarchy does not necessarily give rise to fixed, ahistoric analysis.

Women are not passive victims of oppressive structures. They have struggled to change both their immediate circumstances and the wider social structures. First-wave feminism is a much more important historical force than is usually considered. This major feminist push changed the course of history. However, it did not lead to an elimination of all the forms of inequality between men and women which it sought to eradicate. In some ways early feminists won their goals, and their successes were considerable. However, in response, patriarchy changed in form, incorporating some of the hard-won changes into new traps for women.

The form of patriarchy in contemporary Britain is public rather than private. Women are no longer restricted to the domestic hearth, but have the whole society in which to roam and be exploited.

Heather Joshi: Women, Men and Work – The Effect of Family Responsibilities and Domestic Ties on Earnings

If, as seems likely, economic inequality is the basis of much other inequality, it is important to have a clear picture of the relative economic status of women and men. This extract provides such a picture. It is empirical and analytical rather than theoretical in tone but is, perhaps, the more convincing for that.

The extract divides into two parts. The first is a lucid overview of the pattern of women's economic dependency and requires little further comment. Although there has been an increase in the numbers of women in paid work in the post-war period this has been mainly in low-paid, low-status, part-time work. The second part of the extract focuses on the specific questions: what are 'the effects of women's family responsibilities on their employment and pay, and how far can the low pay of women compared to men be explained by women's domestic ties'? Joshi's calculations of the cost to women of child-rearing are done by means of a simulated model – but they are based on economic realities.

Reading 19 Heather Joshi: 'The Changing Form of Women's Economic Dependency' in *The Changing Population of Britain, ed.* H. Joshi for the Centre for Economic Policy Research (Basil Blackwell, 1989), pp 157–62, 163–64, 168–69, 170–72, 173

It is argued here that economic autonomy is still a long way off for most British women. Replacing the old presumption of financial dependence upon husbands with one of individual self-sufficiency would be justified if men and women had equivalent earning power. This would be going further than women have in fact come. There are financial handicaps to being female which keep most women either dependent on men or disadvantaged or both. Sex-blind treatment appeals to women's self-respect, and is fine for those who have successfully seized new opportunities in education and the labour market, but as long as equal treatment extends only to paid work, it does not give proper recognition to the contribution and needs of most women. They still subordinate their cash earning potential to the demands on their unpaid time and energy from their role in the family. Society still needs a large number of its adult citizens to give caring for others a higher priority than a conventional career. The expectation that such people will normally be female is self-fulfilling, but may be neither equitable nor efficient.

This chapter reviews the evidence about the changes and continuities in the role of women and men in the British economy, and summarizes research findings about the direct and indirect effect of gender on women's earning power. It concludes by drawing lessons for effective policy to bring about equality of opportunity for each sex, and by reviewing the evidence for effects of the changes to date on family formation in Britain.

Changes over time

Table 10.1 summarizes some of the changes in women's work, or at least its statistical visibility, over the twentieth century. At censuses before the Second World War, men outnumbered women in the paid workforce by more than two to one, by the mid-1980s the ratio approaches even numbers with women accounting for 40 per cent of the labour force at the 1981 census and, in 1987, 45 per cent of employees in employment.

Table 10.1 The trend in women's participation in the paid labour force in twentieth-century Britain

	Economically active women as % of all women aged 20–64				*Women of all ages as % of labour force (men and women)*
	Total labour force	*of which Full-time*	*Part-time*	*Unemployed*	
1901	33.9				29.1
1911	32.5				29.7
1921	30.6				29.5
1931	31.6				29.7
1941					
1951	36.3	30.3	5.2	0.8	30.8
1961	42.2	32.1	9.1	1.0	32.5
1971	52.3	32.8	18.0	1.5	36.5
1981	61.1	30.4	27.1	3.7	40.2

Source: Joshi, 1985. Census data have been adjusted along the lines advocated by Joshi and Owen, 1987.

The participation rate of women of working age doubled between the 1921 and 1981 (from 30.6 per cent to 61.1 per cent among those aged 20–64).

For married women under 60 there was a five-fold increase from 12 per cent in 1931 to 57 per cent at the 1981 census.[1]

The contrasts sound even more spectacular if the changes are expressed in terms of experience over a lifetime. In the pre-war world which informed Beveridge's design for the Social Insurance system (Beveridge, 1942), a woman's labour force career usually ended upon marriage and work outside the home was normally treated as incompatible with domestic duty. During the post-war period women ceased to quit employment on marriage. Their withdrawal became temporary and increasingly associated with the presence of young children. Motherhood replaced marriage as the occasion for leaving paid work and seldom marked the end of a woman's labour force membership. The increased participation rates from the 1950s to the 1980s have been largely accounted for by reductions in the gaps in employment records around childbearing. Mothers of younger and younger children have been taking on the dual burden of paid work and child rearing (see Hunt, 1968; Martin and Roberts, 1984; Joshi, 1985).

The limits to change

Occupational segregation

There are also some respects in which little has changed. Men's and women's jobs remain largely separate. Women's employment has always been, and remains, concentrated in a few occupational categories (see Hakim, 1979: Joseph, 1983). At the 1981 Census three quarters of all female workers were in just four of the sixteen occupational orders, where they outnumbered men: personal services (e.g. cleaners, hairdressers); clerical; professional workers in education, health and welfare (i.e. school teachers and nurses); and selling (mainly shop assistants). The majority of female workers work only with other women – 63 per cent of women working with others in the 1980 Women and Employment Survey (Martin and Roberts, 1984, p. 28). Male workplaces are even more segregated (81 per cent of the husbands interviewed in the same survey in 1980 had no colleagues of the opposite sex doing the same type of work). There are some 'integrated' exceptions among the younger membership of some professions (see Crompton and Sanderson, 1986) but women are still very rare in 'top jobs'. For example, in 1984, fewer than 3 per cent of university professors were women. At that time similar proportion of Members of Parliament were female. This nearly doubled to 6 per cent when 40 female MPs were returned in the 1987 General Election. Among those jobs classified as Social Class 1 by the Registrar General at the 1981 Census, only one in ten was held by women. There is, on the other hand, a remarkable concentration of

[1]Sample surveys (which always tend to identify more women with jobs than the census; see Joshi and Owen, 1987) suggest that the trend in married women's economic activity rates levelled off in the first half of the 1980s. The General Household Survey put the activity rate of married women under 60 at 62 per cent in 1978, 1979 and 1985.

female part-time employees in a few, mainly low-status occupations, seldom followed by men.[2]

Part-time employment

Another qualification that should be made to the picture of a rising trend in women's paid work is that, as can be seen in figure 10.1, participation in full-time employment has not risen. All of the post-war increase in employment is accounted for by part-time jobs. This means that in aggregate, man-hours of paid work still outnumbered woman-hours by about two to one.[3]

Figure 10.1 The trend in female economic activity rates among women aged 20–64, Great Britain, 1921–81

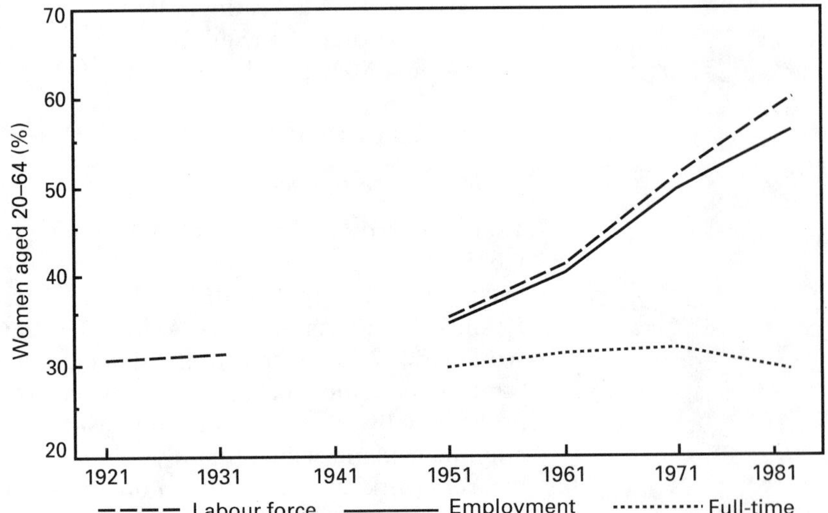

Source: Joshi (1985)

Unpaid domestic work

The picture about paid work must be set alongside that of the unpaid domestic work where the ratio of woman to man hours is reversed. Jonathan Gershuny's preliminary estimates of time spent in unpaid work (from the ESRC's time budget study in 1983/4, Gershuny *et al.*, 1986, Table 2) are that women averaged 16 hours per week more than men. The gap does seem to have been wider in the past (26 hours per week in 1961, for example) but these time budgets confirm common sense and findings from the Women and Employment survey that women do more unpaid

[2]According to the Economic Activity Tables of the 1981 census it took just seven out of a possible 549 occupational categories to account for 64 per cent of all female part-time employees. These categories were: cleaners, shop assistants, certain clerks and cashiers, domestic and school helpers, secretaries, nurses, and assistants in catering.

[3]Zabalza and Tzannatos (1985, p.116) offer an estimate of 0.52 for the ratio of woman hours to man hours employed in 1980.

work than men. Even where both spouses do full-time paid work, wives generally do more of the housework, particularly child-care.

It is also noteworthy that the policy of community care of the handi-capped relies almost exclusively on the unpaid caring work of wives, daughters and mothers (Equal Opportunities Commission, 1982; and Finch and Groves, 1983).

The relative economic status of men and women

As with men's share of unpaid household work, indicators such as the ratio of women's to men's rates of pay, plotted in figure 10.2, and women's share in household earnings, have shown some changes but still display a gulf between the sexes. Taking data on all full-time manual workers, figure 10.2 shows that the ratio of women's hourly pay to men's suddenly rose in the mid-1970s from the level it seems to have previously held over recorded history, 60 per cent, to over 70 per cent in 1977, a level more or less maintained subsequently. The pattern of change over the 1970s and 1980s is similar if one considers different definitions of pay or broader classes of worker. This once-for-all improvement in the relative wage of women coincided with the implementation of the Equal Pay Act, and this is generally thought to be more than a coincidence (see Zabalza and Tzannatos, 1985).

Figure 10.2 Women's wages relative to men's, hourly earnings, full-time manual jobs

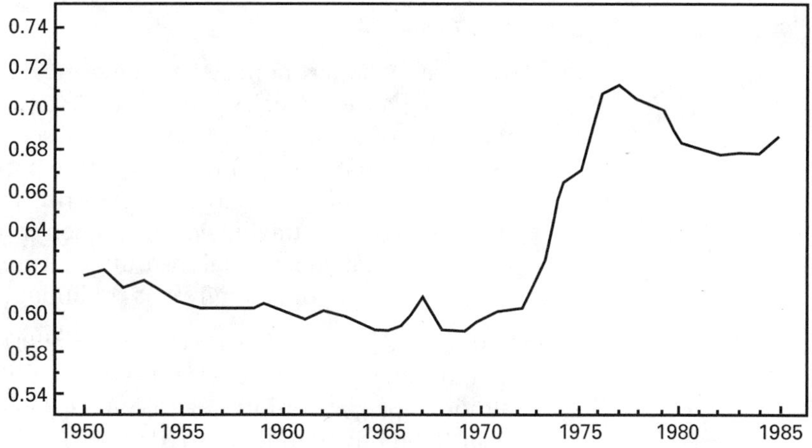

Source: Department of Employment October Enquiry, All Industries

The contribution of wife's earning to total household earnings showed some increase during the 1970s and then stabilized. Amongst non-retired married couples with an earning wife, she brought in, on average, around 30 per cent of their joint earnings – 37 per cent where there were no dependent children, or 25 per cent where there were children, according to the 1985

Family Expenditure Survey (FES). In 1980 the corresponding figures were 36 per cent and 23 per cent. There are of course a few cases where wives earn more than their husbands. This minority appears to have been on an upward trend (from 2 per cent of couples both of whom were employees in 1968 to 5 per cent in 1980 – Elias, 1983), but the conclusion of Lynne Hamill's study of the 1974 FES still stands. Breadwinner wives who are the couple's sole earners are a rarity, wives are typically joint but secondary earners . . .

Why do women earn less than men?

The lower level of wives' earnings is accounted for, in one sense, by women's lower hours of work and lower rates of pay per hour. These are in turn explained by two interacting factors, either of which is a sufficient condition for women's earnings to lag behind those of men; on one hand, the gendered division of family labour, and on the other, unequal treatment of men and women in the labour market. Both are probably deeply entrenched in our culture. Economists say that a labour market discriminates between the sexes if men and women of identical productivity are not identically remunerated. The conventional family division of labour not only reduces the number of hours a woman is available for paid work but also reduces the amount she could expect to earn per hour even in a non-discriminatory labour market. Interruptions in her employment experience, reductions in her mobility and labour market bargaining power are all ways in which family responsibilities reduce women's pay below what it might have been.

Does it matter?

There are what economists call 'efficiency' reasons, in addition to the obvious grounds of equity, to be concerned about the relative economic weakness of women. The fashionable discussion of incentives usually overlooks what may be one of the more potent of the disincentives operating on the productivity of the British labour force: the anticipation of domesticity, discouraging young women from seeking training and employers and educational institutions from providing it, even to women who do not take on a family or a traditional role within one.

Although the force of custom and prevailing values may appear sufficient to account for traditional differences in the economic roles of spouses, and although people conforming to convention need not be aware of any financial motivation to do so, customary practice is reinforced by an economic rationale.

If, for whatever reason, a husband initially commands higher rates of pay than his wife it makes economic sense for him to 'specialize' in paid work and let her shoulder the brunt of the partnership's unpaid chores (Becker, 1981, 1985; for a critique see Owen, 1987). The erosion of a woman's earning potential perpetuates the double-bind of the double burden. Why should we worry about this if the marriage remains the harmonious institution for pooling resources which is normally assumed, in economic theory as elsewhere? Should if fail so spectacularly as to break up, the 'specialist in unpaid work' is left with depleted earning power. Old fashioned alimony can be justified on these grounds, and a new fashioned proposal is on the table in Australia that divorce settlements include a lump-sum compensation for sacrificed earning potential (Macdonald, 1986). Within an unknown number of marriages as yet unbroken, marital harmony cannot always be assumed. We probably don't need Jan Pahl's pioneering research to tell us how fragile conjugal consensus is. She shows that unequal access to cash is a source of friction, and that rows about money are a common cause of the domestic violence which is now coming to light (Pahl, 1983, 1985; see also Brannen and Wilson, 1987). The 'domestic bargain' (a phrase coined by Martin and Roberts, 1984) is not always a very 'good buy'. Cain (1985) argues that it is the unreliability of marriage, no longer, as we have seen in chapter 3, a contract of total sanctity, which constitutes the economic case for policy interventions to help women in the labour force. The financial hardship of most lone mothers (see chapter 4) bears witness to the casualties of women's weak position in the labour market.

Empirical analysis of women's low incomes

My own offering to the state of knowledge about the status of British women has been to investigate two particular questions. Firstly, how great are the effects of women's family responsibilities on their employment and pay. Secondly, how far can the low pay of women compare to men be explained by women's domestic ties? On the first issue, I have taken evidence from a number of sources and some results are reviewed in Joshi, 1985, 1987a and b. This chapter therefore focuses more on the work I have done, with Marie-Louise Newell, on the question of comparing the pay of men and women . . .

Effects of family responsibility on pay

When we looked at the additional explanatory power brought to these models by information about the worker's family responsibilities we found that parenthood had little effect on men's labour force participation or pay. It was, however, a strong determinant of women's employment participation and experience. Though we found no direct effects on pay, holding other things equal, we found indirect effects of motherhood on pay. We estimated that the consequences of motherhood lowered the pay of employed mothers relative to their childless contemporaries through factors such as lost employment experience, downward occupational mobility and the low rates paid for part-time work. These three factors each accounted for similar proportions of combined effect on average pay of around 15 per cent. Note that this is only half the apparent pay advantage the average woman would reap from being paid like a man. That both sources of pay differential exist may come as no surprise, their relative size was not anticipated.

In examining the pay advantage of married men over bachelors, we tentatively concluded that for men, but not women, acquiring a spouse leads to higher pay, and perhaps productivity – an indirect contribution to the economy of wife's domestic work.

Occupational change after childbearing

A separate analysis that Marie-Louise Newell and I have done on the employment histories of women born in 1946 looked for evidence of occupational downgrading associated with childbearing (Newell and Joshi, 1986; Joshi and Newell, 1987). Close examination of these histories found similar patterns to those reported by other researchers, such as Dex (1987), Elias and Main (1982), and Stewart and Greenlagh (1984). Around three in ten of those who reported paid work within 10 years of their first birth had returned to a different type of job that was likely to have been worse paid than the one they last held before the maternity. Mothers who had left jobs in the middle of the socio-economic spectrum were most exposed to the risk of falling back on the ladder, particularly if they left a long gap in their employment record. Women with paper qualifications were more successful at re-entering their original occupation than employees of banks and public administration whose skills we surmise were more specific to the employer. It may also be that such employers were, at least in the early 1970s, less prepared to make the organizational adjustments which make it feasible for mothers to combine paid work with responsibility for young children . . .

Lifetime earnings profiles

The opportunity cost of child-rearing

A synthesis of my two strands of research is attempted for an illustrative 'typical' case in figure 10.6. This traces the simulated lifetime earnings of a person who leaves school at age 17 and faces an earnings profile of 'average' shape, rising with age and experience until a plateau somewhere round age 45 for a continuous worker. The level of this profile, for a woman, is set to pass through £6000 at age 24. Part-time employment is assumed at all times to involve a 10 per cent pay penalty reflecting the 'crummy job effect' on the pay of those with current domestic constraints. It is hypothetically assumed that if a woman marries but remains childless, she would work continuously in a full-time job until switching to part-time employment, set somewhat arbitrarily at age 54, the age when the majority of her employed contemporaries are in part-time jobs. If she has a break of, in this illustration, eight years out of employment to rear two children, and works part-time for most of the years when they are still at school, the lifetime earnings profile is given by the lower line. The difference between the bottom two lines represents, for this example, the lifetime earnings forgone as a result of having children, and amounts to £135,000.

Figure 10.6 Annual earnings over the life cycle: illustrative comparison of men and women

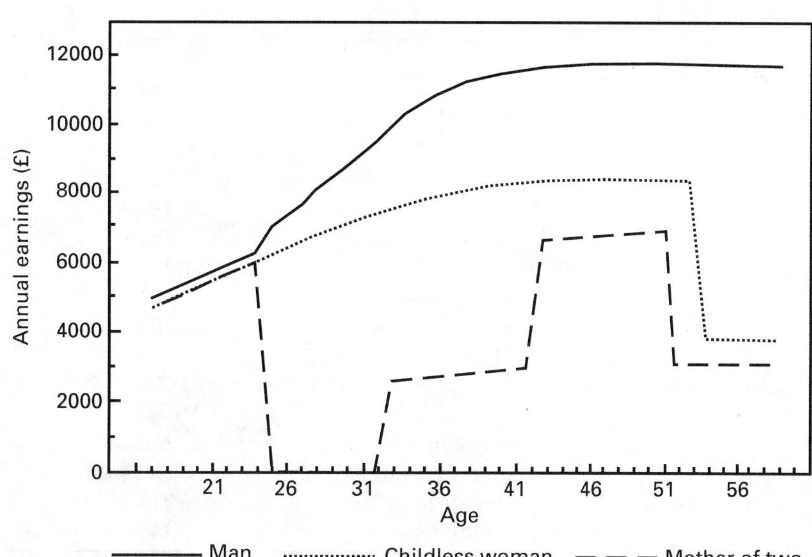

Source: Joshi 1987a

The top line on the picture is even more speculative, but informed by the analysis of 32-years-olds discussed above, it traces what the person would earn with identical characteristics other than that of being male and staying throughout in full-time employment. The area between the top two profiles is the totally hypothetical cost of being a female; it is the same order of magnitude as the hypothetical cost of a woman becoming a mother. (Each about 46 per cent of the total lifetime earnings of a woman who remains childless.) The numbers involved are also set out in table 10.3. The area between the top and bottom lines roughly corresponds with the average gaps between couples' earnings which we can observe in totally independent data like the Family Expenditure Survey discussed above.[5]

[5]This does not mean that all of the gap between men's actual income and women's is due to their gender alone. The illustrative female case is based upon a non-manual occupation, which is typical for women. Men in non-manual occupations have earnings profiles considerably above those for all men, who include a majority in lower-paid manual jobs.

Table 10.3 Simulated annual earnings at selected ages for an illustrative case

Age	*Man*	*Woman* *No child*	*Two children*
	£	£	£
19	5,891	5,035	5,035
24	7,020	6,000	6,000
29	8,622	6,897	0
34	10,403	7,649	2,628
39	11,384	8,184	2,891
44	11,750	8,447	6,770
49	11,781	8,469	6,979
54	11,781	3,828	3,159
59	11,781	3,828	3,159
Total earning from ages 17 to 59	428,000	293,000	158,000
Index numbers			
Woman with two children is 100:	271	185	100
Childless woman is 100:	146	100	54

The advantage of being male is set at 17% up to age 26, passing through 32% at age 32 and fixed at 40% from age 36 onwards. The participation, hours and wage profiles for women are derived from data on women of all ages up to 59 collected in the 1980 Women and Employment Survey.

Socio-economic variations

One of the many caveats I want to make about these still-experimental calculations is that they are not typical at all socio-economic levels. The less education a woman has, the less important are the delayed costs on later rates of pay of current absence from the labour market, but the higher is the 'cost of being female' relatively speaking. Women with more education have more to lose from becoming mothers, and perhaps less from just being women. This could well explain the fact that the trend since 1970 towards deferring first births has largely been confined to women with more education (see Joshi, 1985). The growing population of 'Dinkie' couples (dual-income no kids) was also noted in chapters 7 and 8 as providing a booming market of house purchasers. The young mothers in council housing probably face lower opportunity costs to childbearing but a stronger need to supplement family income with a low-paid part-time job.

Looking forward

Are these findings of the obstacles women face out of date? One might hope so, but the picture in figure 10.2 does not immediately support such optimism. Later generations of women have been catching up with their male contemporaries as far as the acquisition of paper qualifications is concerned. Most of them also expect to form families. Will these families be more symmetrical as far as the allocation of unpaid work is concerned? Will enlightened employer practice prevail to preserve skills of workers who are also rearing children? Or will a new generation of qualified women, some of whom are still keeping open their options, decide that the economic penalties of motherhood outweigh its attractions? Does it still 'pay' to be male as much as our estimates suggest?

New research

The evidence necessary to answer such a question would need to combine information on pay with life history. Among possible sources of such information is the proposed follow-up in their early thirties of a sample of people born in 1958 – the members of the National Child Development Study, another national cohort study similar to that of the 1946 generation described above. Another such source is the material collected in 1987 for the ESRC's studies of Economic Change and Social Life.

We know that women without male 'breadwinners' are over-represented among the statistically visible poor – the lone mothers and the lone elderly women. What we do not yet know is how women's changing opportunities for paid work have affected their relative risk of poverty. The implication of sex differences in economic activity for economic inequality are among the questions that are being pursued in my current research with John Ermisch and other colleagues. We are also looking into implications for inequality in the future of the social differentials in current demographic trends. Another important area of research is attempting to uncover female poverty that is hidden within households (Brannen and Wilson, 1987).

Policy implications

The policy implications which I have drawn from the analyses mentioned above have been set out at greater length elsewhere (Joshi, 1986). The journey to Equality of Opportunity for women has not yet been completed. Progress is still needed to reduce the sex segregation of jobs, the low pay ghettos that it permits, and the waste of potential female skills that it entails. Such progress will run into the familiar obstacles if measures are not also taken to recognize, support and share the unpaid tasks needed to maintain and reproduce the population.

Measures to improve women's access to education, training and remunerative jobs need to be complemented by measures to give families more choice about the management of their unpaid responsibilities. Examples of measures to support parents would be increases and improvements in childcare, for pre-school children and those of school age; to make parental leave available to parents of both sexes; to recognize childcare as a legitimate work expense for tax and benefit purposes.; and to encourage the participation of fathers in child-rearing. This last suggestion might be taken more seriously as the working week gets shorter and if the pay penalties for devoting time to caring were reduced. I have an even more fanciful suggestion that we challenge the age segregation of modern society which keeps young children, and their attendants, out of the adult sphere. As Charlotte Höhn remarked (in her address to the 1987 European Population Conference), modern cities are not 'kinder-freundlich'. It is time at least for the English language to take on the concept of child-friendliness.

Women, on the whole, have not achieved an equal economic footing with men in British society and they will not achieve it universally overnight. Meanwhile, it would be a mistake for legislation on divorce, tax or pensions to assume that they had. Equitable treatments must be devised that recognize economic sacrifices (whether they've been made by men or women) as well as economic achievements. For example, the Home Responsibilities Protection of pension rights under the current version of the State Earnings Related Pension Scheme (SERPS) recognizes that valuable work is being done by women who are not earning enough to pay contributions, but does not allow for the fact that the low pay of some who are contributing reflects their domestic responsibilities as well. British women are still taking better care of their families than their pension rights. It should not be beyond the wit of a woman (and man) to devise more adequate forms of compensation. The research described here should inform and stimulate the policy debate . . .

Conclusion

It is not at all clear that further progress towards improving the economic status of women would precipitate the demise of the British family or the dreaded (by some) 'twilight of parenthood'. Effective progress for women involves changes which recognize the family responsibilities of paid workers of both sexes. This should, if anything, strengthen the family and encourage childbearing. It is arguable that the Swedish policy of support for parents in the labour force, as well as similar measures in Eastern Europe, have put a brake on fertility decline and perhaps reversed it.

Catherine Hakim: Women's Satisfaction Levels in Paid Work

Catherine Hakim's article gives a fresh and fertile perspective on a long-standing social conundrum; why do women appear to be more satisfied than men with their jobs even though these are generally less well-paid and of lower status. The key to her findings and conclusion is that the work orientations of women in part-time and full-time work tend markedly to differ – with the latter tending to express levels of satisfaction at a similarly lower level as men.

In sections not included here, Hakim, discusses several other explanations, not necessarily incompatible with her own. In broad terms these are:

1 Women 'adapt to the inevitable' – they accept limited opportunities and rewards.
2 Women have different priorities from men which focus on the 'marriage career'.
3 Women 'defer' to the patriarchal attitudes of their husbands who prefer them to have less powerful jobs and to provide domestic comforts.

On the first point, Hakim comments that 'there is no obvious explanation why women should start with lower expectations for the reward of paid work or reduce their aspirations faster than men.' On the second point, Hakim's review of the evidence does show a tendency for women in Britain and the USA to have a lower commitment to paid work than men except, importantly, in higher grade (e.g. professional and managerial) work where levels of commitment between the sexes are similar. On the third point, Hakim finds that although men are somewhat more likely to have 'traditional' attitudes to women doing paid work, many women appear independently to have similar 'traditional' attitudes.

Following the above considerations, Hakim presents her own framework of explanation for the high levels of satisfaction expressed by many women in paid work. This commences under the sub-heading 'self-made women'. She relies heavily on a number of existing surveys including the National Longitudinal Surveys (NLS) carried out in the USA. Year after year, the NLS asks given age cohorts whether they plan to be working at the age of thirty-five or whether they plan to marry, keep house and raise a family at that age. The young female respondents divide into three groups:

- Career planners
- Homemaker career
- Drifters and unplanned careers

Career planners have similar, relatively lower levels of work satisfaction to the majority of men, but the homemaker group, demanding less than most men of paid work, was more satisfied with less.

As is apparent from reading the extract, Hakim strongly argues that an adequate analysis of women's orientations to work depends on understanding the varied 'choices' they make – however 'free' or otherwise these may be. The framework she develops for analysing women's choices of work could have a highly significant impact on the sociology of gender. She herself discusses its wider implications for gender research and analysis in her substantial concluding section.

Reading 20 From Catherine Hakim: 'Grateful slaves and self-made women: fact and fantasy in women's work orientations', *The European Sociological Review*, Vol.7 No. 2, September 1991, pp.101–102, 103, 111–14, 115-16 by permission of Oxford University Press

Abstract

Although job segregation concentrates women in the lowest status and lowest paid jobs in the workforce, women are disproportionately satisfied with their jobs. This paper assesses the strength of women's work commitment in Western industrial societies, and finds it to be markedly lower than men's work commitment. Work commitment is also found to be a powerful predictor of women's work decisions and job choices. The majority of women aim for a homemaker career in which paid work is of secondary or peripheral importance, with strong support from their husbands for this strategy. A minority of women are committed to work as a central life goal, achieving jobs at higher levels of status and earnings. The existence of these two discrete groups within the female workforce explains the paradox of women's high satisfaction with poor jobs, and helps explain the persistence of job segregation. We conclude that more refined and sociological indicators of workforce participation must be developed to replace the standard measures used by labour economists.

Introduction

There is a paradox in women's labour force participation. On the one hand women are concentrated in the lowest grade, least skilled and lowest paid jobs with the poorest employment benefits and prospects. On the other hand women report high levels of satisfaction with their jobs, often greater satisfaction than that reported by men with their higher status and better paid jobs. This paper seeks to reconcile these two features of women's position in the labour market. Existing research is reviewed to find an explanation for the apparently non-rational behaviour of women in being disproportionately pleased with the worst jobs. Given our starting point, explanations have to be sought among 'dispositional' factors peculiar to women rather than in 'situational' factors in the jobs they do. Explanations are sought among women's sex-role and work orientations, work commitment, and the family division of labour. It is shown that the minority of women who choose work as a central life goal achieve higher grade jobs and earnings than the majority for whom work is of secondary importance. The implications for theory, research and policy are explored.

The main focus is Britain, but the discussion extends to other Western industrial societies in Europe and North America, for which similar data is readily available and does not pose serious problems of comparability. Britain is taken as a broadly representative Western industrial society, and the results for this country are taken as applying to a greater or lesser extent to others.

The paradox of grateful slaves

That the paradox is never addressed in recent social science research literature is in itself notable. This is due in part to the separation of two streams of enquiry.

On the one hand there is an extensive literature analysing the 'objective' facts about women's position in the labour force, extending into a more polemical literature arguing the case for legislative and procedural changes to improve women's position. Using a variety of statistical and other research tools, this literature has shown labour markets to be highly segregated, with women concentrated in less skilled and lowest paid jobs. High levels of job segregation have persisted throughout the twentieth century, not just in Britain but throughout Europe, North America, and in the USSR. Equal pay and equal opportunities legislation have had an impact but most commentators express dissatisfaction with the relatively small degree of change brought about by active intervention in the labour market. New and stronger legislative measures are proposed to remedy the situation

– such as positive discrimination and equal value (comparable worth) pay assessments. The general consensus is that at the aggregate, national level the position of working women is significantly worse than that of working men; that this situation has persisted for decades despite enormous social, economic and political changes in Western societies; and that major efforts would be required to change it to any significant degree. For example, Walby concludes in a recent report that despite the increase of women in employment, job segregation has diminished little since the turn of the century, is widely deplored today as a restriction on economic efficiency, is inconsistent with social justice for women, and yet tenaciously persists (Walby, 1988: 12). The unstated assumption among sociologists is always that job segregation is *imposed* on women, unfairly and against their will, whereas economists regard job choices as reflecting personal preferences (Becker, 1985).

The other literature, on work orientations and job satisfaction, is also extensive, but is predominantly psychological and attracts little public debate. Nonetheless there is a solid body of evidence reporting a long-standing pattern of high levels of reported job and pay satisfaction among women compared with men. Given the marked discrepancies in occupational status and earnings between men and women, even *equal* levels of job satisfaction would be surprising and contrary to expectation. Yet national studies repeatedly find *higher* levels of job and pay satisfaction among British women generally than among men (Townsend, 1979: 470–75; OPCS, 1982: 85; Brown *et al.*, 1983: 28–29; Hakim, 1987a: 199–203). In other countries there is an equally persistent similarity in men and women's job satisfaction, but research only shows *higher* levels of job satisfaction among women after controls for occupational grade are introduced or when part-timers are included in the analysis (Kalleberg, 1977; Andrisani, 1978: 56; Weaver, 1979, 1980) . . .

The paradox of high job satisfaction among women in the least attractive jobs is thus a real research issue, which cannot be dismissed with reference to the poor quality of the job satisfaction data. The contradiction is observed in both national studies and at the micro-level, among homeworkers who are tenacious of their jobs. The following sections explore possible explanations in women's work orientations and life goals for this apparently non-rational behaviour. Is work a major priority for women? Or are they simply more docile and adaptable than men? Do they have the same degree of work commitment as men? What difference do husbands' views make? Are there any women who break the mould and display the same level of job satisfaction as men? . . .

These sections are briefly summarised in my introduction to this reading, but are not included here.

Self-made women

The question remains whether women ever do, in practice, determine their own destiny, and a husband to go with it, or whether they are wholly formed by the social and cultural constraints around them. The arguments presented earlier would be greatly strengthened if we can show that the

See my introduction to this reading.

obverse is true: that women with a high commitment to work, or who give priority to the work role over the domestic role, attain better jobs (on the usual job quality measures) with job satisfaction that is no different from men's in the same grade of job. To prove that women actively *choose* the jobs they do in line with their own values and work orientations, we must demonstrate that the choice of a career yields results just as effectively as the choice of the home-maker role.

To date only one study has provided the kind of longitudinal data that allows the long-term influence, or insignificance, of work orientations and work plans to be measured rigorously. The National Longitudinal Surveys (NLS) project initiated in the mid-1960s in the USA has provided a great wealth of longitudinal data on five age cohorts of young and mature women, young and older men. Of particular interest is the cohort of young women aged 14–24 in 1968 who were interviewed almost every year up to 1983 when aged 29–39 years. This cohort was asked in 1968, and again at every subsequent interview, what they would like to be doing when they were 35 years old, whether they planned to be working at age 35 or whether they planned to marry, keep house and raise a family at age 35. Compared to the length and complexity of work commitment questions included in some surveys (Bielby and Bielby, 1984), the question is crude, and conflates preferences and plans. Presumably because it asked about women's personal plans, rather than general attitudes, the question turned out to have astonishing analytical and predictive power, and was used again in the second youth cohort study initiated in 1979.

There are a number of independent analyses of the extent to which early workplans were fulfilled by age 35. They all show that women achieved their objectives for the most part, resulting in dramatic 'mark-ups' to career planners in terms of occupational grade and earnings (Mott, 1982; Rexroat and Shehan, 1984; Shaw and Shapiro, 1987). Furthermore, career planners were more likely to choose typically-male jobs, had lower job satisfaction than other women and adapted their fertility behaviour to their workplans (Waite and Stolzenberg, 1976; Stolzenberg and Waite, 1977; Spitze and Waite, 1980). Workplans were a significant independent predictor of actual work behaviour. After controlling for other factors affecting labour force participation, a woman who consistently planned to work had a probability of working that was 30 percentage points higher than did a woman who consistently planned not to work. Of the women who held consistently to their work plans, four-fifths were actually working in 1980, at age 35, compared to only half of the women who consistently intended to devote themselves exclusively to home-maker activities. Women who planned to work at age 35 were likely to do so unless they had large families or a pre-school child. Women who had planned a 'marriage career' nevertheless were obliged to work by economic factors in half the cases: the husband's low income, divorce, or the opportunity costs of not working led half to be in work despite aiming for a full-time home-maker role. On balance, career plans emerge as a *safer* bet than plans for a home-maker career.

Table 4 Long term workplans and outcomes among young women in the USA, 1970s

	Distribution of sample		*% working at age 35*
Career planners consistently anticipate working at age 35 throughout their twenties	25%		82%
Homemaker career consistently indicate no plans for work: aim is marriage, family and homemaking activities	28%		49%
Drifters and unplanned careers			
(a) switch to having future work expectations at some point in their twenties	12%	} 47%	
(b) highly variable responses over time—no clear pattern of plans for age 35	35%	} 47%	64%

Source: National Longitudinal Surveys data for cohort of young women ages 14–24 years in 1968, reported in Shaw (1987: 8–9).

Planning to work yielded a significant wage advantage. Women who had consistently planned to work had wages 30 per cent higher than those of women who never planned to work. Those women who had planned to work in the occupation they actually held at age 35 had even higher wages than women whose occupational plans were not realized. Women who make realistic plans and acquire necessary skills fare best in the labour market. Those who fare worst are women who plan an exclusive home-making career but end up working for economic reasons. A key point here is that career planners were a small minority of one-quarter of the young women cohort; the vast majority of the cohort had what might be described as 'unplanned careers' (Table 4), as did women in the older cohort aged 30–44 years at the start of the study in the late 1960s (Mott, 1978, 1982; Shaw, 1983).

Perhaps most surprisingly of all, the NLS longitudinal data has put paid to the results of cross-sectional studies showing that women's work behaviour is heavily determined by the number and ages of any children, rather than the other way round. Those who work only if their family responsibilities permit them to do so are in effect fulfilling a prior choice of emphasis on the home-maker career. Fertility expectations have only a small negative effect on young women's work-plans, whereas work-plans exert a powerful negative effect on young women's childbearing plans (Waite and Stolzenberg, 1976; Stolzenberg and Waite, 1977; Sproat *et al.*, 1985: 78).

Factors which have long been held to determine women's labour force participation, such as other family income, educational qualifications, marital status and age of youngest child are revealed as being most important in relation to women with little or no work commitment, who have so far been in the majority. Women with definite career plans manifest a rather inelastic labour supply, similar to that of men (Shaw and Shapiro, 1987).

The NLS project is monitoring changes in women's work orientations, in particular through the large new youth cohort initiated in 1979. This shows that the new cohort of young women entering the labour market in the 1980s has much stronger work expectations and work commitment than did previous cohorts. In 1979, young women were only half as likely as young women in 1968 to say they expected to be housewives not in the paid labour force at age 35, with only one quarter planning to be housewives (Sproat *et al.*, 1985: 76–78, 318, 335–6).

Overall the NLS results have repeatedly shown the importance of motivations, values and attitudes as key determinants of labour market behaviour, occupational status and even earnings, an influence that is independent of conventional human capital factors, and frequently exceeds the influence of behavioural factors (Parnes, 1975; Andrisani, 1978; Mott, 1982; Sproat *et al.*, 1985). These 'psychological' variables are too often omitted from research, so their importance has been over-looked. But the contrasting experience of the 1980 WES and the NLS project show it is crucial also to adopt meaningful questions and appropriate research designs.

Conclusions

The paradox of women's high satisfaction with comparatively poor jobs can be explained by their having different life goals from men. Most women's preference has been for the home-maker role, with paid employment regarded as a secondary activity, to be fitted in as and when home-maker activities allow it. Only a one-third minority of women dispute Becker's (1985) explanation for enduring job segregation and the continued sex differential in earnings: that 'most' married women seek less demanding jobs and invest less in paid work, due to the competing priority of their family responsibilities. The key questions are how many is 'most'?, and is that percentage changing? The evidence is that less than half of adult women give priority to their workplans, compared with a two-thirds majority of adult men. When women do choose work as a central life goal, with paid employment valued over and beyond the purely financial rewards, they achieve jobs at higher levels of status and earnings than are obtained by women for whom paid employment is a secondary or peripheral activity.

Social scientists have been using a value-laden and biased definition of job quality, one that is based on the priorities and preferences of male bread-winners. Women who have chosen a homemaker career often have some paid work as well, but their job preferences emphasize convenience factors over the high pay and security of employment conventionally valued by men. This explains women's high satisfaction with the casualized and low-paid jobs of the periphery – such as homeworking – a research finding that feminists and trade unionists have difficulty accepting (TUC, 1985; Allen and Wolkowitz 1987: 147–150; Schneider de Villegas, 1990: 428–9). More generally, this also explains women's very high satisfaction with part-time jobs *in preference to* full-time jobs throughout the European Community (Hakim, 1990: 187-197), a research finding that male workers, male-dominated trade unions and some women academics have long found difficult to accept as real and valid (Delsen, 1990; Beechey and Perkins, 1987). Research will in future need to distinguish more clearly between the job quality criteria of primary and secondary earners, full-time and part-time workers.

Readings 41 (especially) and 42 describe the primary and secondary labour markets.

More generally, future research on workforce participation, and its consequences, must recognize that working women are a heterogeneous group, comprising at least two qualitatively different groups. One group has work commitment similar to that of men, leading to long-term workplans and almost continuous full-time work, often in jobs with higher status and earnings than are typical for women. The second group has little or no commitment to paid work and a clear preference for the homemaker role; paid employment is a secondary activity, usually undertaken to earn a supplementary wage rather than as primary breadwinner, and is in low-skilled, low-paid, part-time, casual and temporary jobs more often than in skilled, permanent full-time jobs. The distinctive character of the second group is sometimes recognized in theories of a reserve army of labour, although this is often seen as applying to part-time workers only (Breugel, 1979; Beechey and Perkins, 1987). Sociologists need to recognize and refine the substantial *qualitative* differences between these two groups, rather than treating female labour supply as a single continuum measured by hours worked, as in economic theory. Even if there is no sharp boundary line between the two groups, with many women switching between groups at some point in their lives, the NLS shows that half of all young women make a firm choice between careers well before entry into the labour market. Unless sociologists are willing to recognize these qualitatively different types of working woman, employers can hardly be blamed for undifferentiating policies, and for failing to encourage those with firm workplans.

The concept of *work commitment* is central to Hakim's interpretation of women's work orientations.

The two types of worker are defined by their work commitment and workplans, with attendant consequences for occupational plans and training. Marital status is not a meaningful proxy measure, as marriage is commonplace in both groups, leading to small differences in occupational attainment between married and never-married women (Roos, 1983). Where the option of part-time and peripheral work is a real one, as in Britain (Hakim 1987b), the distinction between full-time and part-time workers may provide a proxy indicator to differentiate the two groups. In other countries, people in both groups will tend to work full-time hours and be less readily distinguishable by this criterion. For example, in the USA employers' practice of providing health insurance only for full-time workers effectively excludes part-time work as a realistic option even for women (Rotchford and Roberts, 1982: 230; Dex and Shaw, 1986: 126), and continuity of work over the year will differentiate more clearly between the two groups (Hakim, 1987b: 555).

If correct, Hakim's conclusions mean sociologists cannot routinely regard women as 'victims' of a male-dominated system – but her analysis is as controversial as it is bold.

This implies a somewhat different perspective on women as self-determining actors rather than as people whose behaviour is determined by social structural constraints and family characteristics. There are periodic pleas for better recognition of human actor and human agency in sociological theory (Homans, 1964; Wrong, 1966; Coleman, 1986) but theory and research on women's work and employment seems particularly prone to an over-socialized view of women, or with structural factors so heavily weighted that choice flies out of the window (England and McCreary, 1987; Crompton and Sanderson, 1990). In Western industrial societies at least women's lives are becoming self-made almost as much as men's lives. It is time to abandon the concept of women as so totally formed and constrained by past patterns of economic activity and sex-role stereotyping that they are unable to shape their own lives to any meaningful degree. Women may have little say in the choice of employer, but they have a large measure of freedom in the choice of occupation and of husband. Yet most still choose occupations and husbands which maintain traditional views of women's roles. Women have far more reliable methods of controlling their fertility behaviour than they have ever had in the past so that completely unintended births are now unusual (Daniel, 1980: 12). The educational system is seen to be equally accessible to women and men, in sharp contrast with the occupational system (Jowell *et al.*, 1988: 188; Sorensen, 1990: 158), and women receive about as much education as men (OECD, 1979: 45-50; England and McCreary, 1987: 152). The key missing element has been women's desire to work with some degree of long-term commitment rather than on the basis of sporadic jobs chosen within a short-term perspective. Aiming for a good job is a necessary first step towards getting one. This review has shown that women with clear employment objectives mostly achieve their plans; women who aim for specific occupations and acquire the necessary skills fare best in the labour market. Women who want to be home-makers mostly fulfil their plans too, though many end up with a job as well. It is time to bring women back into the picture as actors and agents in their own (work) lives. Women make choices as often as men do, and those choices have real effects. Those who choose domesticity, the marriage career and hence a large degree of economic dependence are self-made women just as much as those who choose, and stick with, an ongoing employment career and all that entails. The degree and pattern of job segregation in any country are historically determined, but the persistence of job segregation from now on should be regarded as a reflection of women's own preferences and choices, with an inevitable time lag for employers to modify their perception, as Becker (1985) argues rather than the outcome of patriarchal systems and male social control as Hartmann (1976) and Walby (1986) have argued for the past and as Jacobs (1989b) argues for the present. Studies of occupational segregation should in future be restricted to the workforce in *full-time* employment, excluding part-timers with no real commitment to, and investment in paid work, as in studies of the sex differential in earnings. Similarly, research should refocus on the issue of comparable worth, instead of job segregation, as the key source of the earnings gap.

Replacing the all too common view of women as downtrodden and even grateful slaves with a perspective of self-determining actors would also facilitate multi-disciplinary work on the labour force, drawing on both economic and sociological theory (England and McCreary, 1987). Economists have always noted the significance of tastes and preferences, even if they rarely find such data readily available to them, and the development of rational choice theory in the social sciences would benefit greatly from data on preferences as well as behaviour.

This does not necessarily entail wholesale conversion to methodological individualism. But at the moment surveys of the labour force typically exclude reference to choices, preferences, aims and plans. The single-minded focus on behaviour needs to be extended, for the benefit of economists as well as sociologists. Becker's thesis is of the sort that only sociologists could subject to proper empirical tests, and take further. Economists need to work more closely with sociologists in developing labour market theory.

The third, more problematic, implication of this review is that sociologists have yet to address the significance of husbands' influence on wives' work decisions, both theoretically and from the policy perspective. The most under-researched external influence on a wife's employment decision is her husband's views on the matter. We need to know how effective women are in choosing husbands to match their own workplans, just as they modify childbearing to fit in with their work life. It appears that employers (occasionally also trade unionists) are often made the scapegoats for husbands' attitudes, which restrict their wives to part-time, less responsible and typically-female jobs which do not conflict with their domestic responsibilities, pushing women into lower grade and lower-paid jobs which preserve the husband's status and power as main breadwinner. From a policy point of view it may be that it is husbands who need educating, rather than employers. But of course these two groups are actually one and the same, albeit wearing different hats and self-interests. As Pahl has pointed out, the reason core and peripheral workers are content with that pattern of labour market segmentation is that they meet as partners in bed at night (Pahl, 1988: 603).

We can now also explain why an increase in women's labour force participation does not inevitably have the wide social and economic effects commonly anticipated, such as a decline in job segregation (Walby, 1988:6), a narrowing of sex differentials in earnings (Jenson, Hagen and Reddy, 1988), heightened awareness of sex discrimination in the workforce (Sorensen, 1990) or an increase in husbands' contribution to domestic work (Huber and Spitze, 1983). By the same token, policy measures to facilitate women's return to work after childbearing, such as improved childcare services, could well result in an *increase* in job segregation and sex differentials in earnings rather than the reverse, because their main effect is to increase the labour force participation of secondary workers with little or

It is worth comparing this comment with that of Heather Joshi at the conclusion of Reading 19.

no work commitment and an insignificant investment in paid employment. It is notable that the much praised childcare services in Sweden have not dented the high level of job segregation in Sweden, which has been shown to be even higher than in Britain, France and West Germany (OECD, 1980: 41–46; Walby, 1988: 3; Jensen, Hagen and Reddy, 1988). Women's participation in paid work is not all of the same homogeneous character, so a national increase in female economic activity rates does not produce a consistent set of social and economic effects.

Work commitment is a more powerful social indicator than the economic activity rate. Sorensen recently tested the hypothesis that perceptions of gender discrimination are higher in nations with higher rates of female economic activity, concluding that the hypothesis was unsupported. It is supported, once the female economic activity rate is replaced with a national measure of work commitment. As shown earlier, work commitment stands at roughly equal levels in Britain and the USA and is substantially higher in West Germany. As expected, there are equal levels or awareness of worse occupational opportunity for women in Britain and the USA and substantially higher levels of awareness in West Germany (Sorensen, 1990: 158).

We need to develop quite different *sociological* labour market indicators rather than relying on the conventionally ones developed for labour economists by labour statisticians. Differentiating at least two separate groups among working women, as suggested above, is one option. In the absence of the necessary data, proxy measures may work better than those used by labour economists. The best readily available proxy for work commitment seems to be the percentage of women of working age who are working full-time (for countries with little part-time work, like the USA, the percentage working full-time year-round). The data are already available for both men and women, although statistics are not commonly presented in this form in national reports. But the precise relationship between this proxy variable and work commitment has yet to be mapped out.

The NLS information on work plans should be collected systematically for Europe. It may have a crucial bearing on the impact of demographic factors on the workforce, and be of policy interest (for example in relation to discussions of a guaranteed minimum income) as well as for theoretical purposes. Ideally, we need to standardize on one to two simple survey questions on work commitment and work-plans that would be used throughout Europe, to be applied to men as well as women, for example in the International Social Survey Programme (Jowell, *et al.*, 1989). The option of replicating and checking explanatory analyses across industrial societies, would enable major strides forward in understanding men and women's labour market behaviour. On the basis of research to date, we would expect to be identifying 'careerist', 'adaptive' and 'home-centred' work orientations among both men and women. Opinion polls would no longer look at attitudes towards 'working women' as an undifferentiated aggregate, and they would collect equivalent information for men and women. As well as being more sociological, labour market research needs to be more unisex in its theories and methods.

Emily Martin: Childbirth – Control and the Body

This extract has been selected as an illustration of the trend in contemporary feminist analysis to focus on how the biological reality of being female is given meaning and organised socially (i.e. socially constructed). Thus, Martin analyses three central life-experiences exclusive to females: childbirth, menstruation and the menopause (proper to females in the sense that it is the end of menstruation). Even if there were no other differences between males and females, these differences alone significantly differentiate the two sexes. Whereas, in the recent past, there was a tendency among some feminists to 'factor out' sex differences and concentrate on differential gender socialisation and roles, now the emphasis is equally on the social control and organisation of sex differences. This approach is emphatically not biologically determinist, indeed, it tends to present the control and interpretation of sex differences as an area of 'resistance' or negotiation.

Childbirth has particularly attracted the attention of feminists. Many argue that in 'modern' societies, childbirth is dominated by a scientific model which is produced and operated, overwhelmingly by males (see for instance, Paula A. Treichler, 'Feminism, Medicine, and the Meaning of Childbirth' in M. Jacobus *et al., eds., Body Politics* [Routledge, Chapman and Hall, 1990]). In the following extract, Martin adopts a class (neo-Marxist) perspective which she integrates with a critique of patriarchal scientific medicine. She draws parallels between the control and organisation of industrial production and the production of children. In this context, women are compared with workers. She also compares the *resistance* of some women to 'medicalised childbirth' with that of industrial workers to mechanisation.

It has been necessary to spell out the theoretical underpinnings of Martin's approach because the extract itself is largely made up of case studies in which the attempts of individual women to control the birth of their children are described. It is fair, though, to ask some questions in relation to Martin's findings. How representative is the 'resistance' of these women to medicalised childbirth? Do not the majority of women seek and want to give birth to their children in hospital? Despite Martin's commitment to the mother's right to choose where her child is born, do you feel she presents a representative picture of home-births? Given that Martin's data is drawn from working-class women in the United States, how applicable do you think her comments are to women in Britain?

This extract does not attempt to be quantitative. What can be said however, is that there is a wider current of opinion which reflects the concerns of the women whose words are transcribed below.

Reading 21 From Emily Martin, *The Women in the Body: A Cultural Analysis of Reproduction* (Open University Press, 1989), pp. 139–41, 142–45

How does birth look though the eyes of women? If birth is currently thought of and described by medical texts as if it were work done by the uterus, and if women's bodies are consequently subjected to the same kinds of controls as workers in the workplace, do women, as workers often have, resist their condition?

Let us look first at some forms that workers' resistance has taken. David Noble in discussing industrial production describes how workers still controlled machine tools up until after World War II: they acted as skilled operators, directing a cutting or drilling tool to produce a part of a certain size and shape. As long as this was so, they were able to control the pace of their work: "to keep time for themselves, avoid exhaustion, exercise authority over their work, avoid killing gravy piece rate jobs, stretch work to avoid layoffs, exercise creativity and last but not least, to express their solidarity and hostility to management." More dramatically, in the nineteenth and twentieth centuries, workers have waged struggles over the length of the work-day so as to limit the amount of profit that management can extract from their labor. And of course workers have used the tactic of striking (refusing to work in an establishment under unjust conditions) since the early days of industrialization. In addition, from time to time, workers' resistance has focused directly on machines. The Luddites in early-nineteenth-century England vented their anger at the machinery of industrialization by destroying the machines so that management could not use mechanization to oppress the workers further.

Like many people, Martin has mixed attitudes to new technology. It can 'allow the development of new standards', but it can also result in individuals being highly scrutinised and controlled. Here she gives a number of examples of individuals 'fighting' to keep or regain control of childbirth. This does not mean she approves of their behaviour (which might seem dangerous in some instances). It does become clear, however, that she considers that mothers should have more control and choice in relation to childbirth.

Do women's efforts to resist procedures that they experience as intrusions on their autonomy resemble the efforts of workers? Childbirth activist literature can be seen (and sometimes describes itself) as guides to "self-defense in the hospital," and the methods women have developed are strikingly similar to those that workers have tried in the workplace. First, consider the solidarity, power and organization obtainable through forming groups. Women's health groups dedicated to resisting the way birth is handled in hospitals are many and well organized, from the Childbirth Education Association (CEA) and National Association of Parents and Professionals for Safe Alternatives in Childbirth (Napsac) to C/SEC and the Cesarean Prevention Movement. Next, consider the workers' efforts to stall or slow down the rate of production. In birth, this takes the form of delaying the time at which a woman is first defined as being at each stage of labor. For example, the second stage of labor, from the time the cervix opens entirely until the baby is born, is defined by hospital as lasting only a maximum of two hours. If the woman pushes in the second stage much longer than this, doctors usually intervene, pulling the baby out with forceps or performing a cesarean section. Doctors often make laboring women very acutely aware of the clock against which the labor must progress. One woman repeated what the doctors had told her, "We'll let her labor a couple more hours and then we'll do the cesarean" (Laura Cromwell). Midwives who attend home births have a variety of ways to buy time and "avoid starting the time clock."

They do not count the second stage as starting until there is absolutely no trace of cervix visible or until the woman actually feels an urge to push (which may be delayed some time after full dilatation); or they may simply not examine the woman internally so that they do not know when she reaches full dilatation, instead letting the woman determine when she is ready for the next stage.

Martin is suggesting that by such means some women seek to keep some control over the birthing (labour) process.

Women themselves may try to reduce the amount of time they spend in the hospital by delaying admitting themselves as long as possible. Explicitly they often understand that this allows a shorter time for their labors to be defined as ineffective and the baby to be extracted operatively. Barbara Rothman has shown how the time allowed in the hospital for both first- and second-stage labor has been reduced steadily since the 1940s. In short, the uterus (as doctors see it) is being given less and less time to produce its product. One woman I interviewed was proud and satisfied at having delayed going to the hospital until she was 7 cm dilated and after that at not telling the resident she had had a previous cesarean section. (When he found out, total panic broke loose.) Another woman described herself as stalling continuously during her attempt to have a home birth, delaying by insisting an ambulance be called when the midwife decided she should go to the hospital, not divulging even to her husband the fact that the head was crowning when they reached the hospital: "a man in the elevator patted me on the head and said 'Are you having a contraction, dear?' I thought, 'No, I'm having a baby!' Then my husband asked if I could feel it in my back, and I thought, 'Of course not, the baby's coming out!' How incredibly stupid people can be" (Sarah Lasch) . . .

And then there is Luddism, workers' attack on the machines themselves. Many women report simply unstrapping external fetal monitors the minute the nurse or doctor is out of the labor room. Others go for long walks around the hospital and do not return for hours or take a shower continuously so that monitors cannot be used. And one woman described how she used physical force:

> I catch a glimpse of the flash of metal [the delivery room scissors for an episiotomy] going past me. We had done perineal massage every night [to make the perineum flexible enough to avoid tearing or the need for an episiotomy]. I grabbed the scissors; from the home birth I knew it took seventeen minutes to sterilize them. I wasn't even trying to take them out of the doctor's hand. It wasn't a logical thought at the time, I was just trying to break the sterile field. I said, "You aren't cutting me" and asked him to massage, but he didn't know how, he just went like this [gestures halfheartedly] and [after the baby emerged] said, "Well, you tore!" He wanted me to tear. (Sarah Lasch).

Finally, there is perhaps the most effective tactic of all, the equivalent of opening up your own shop or becoming your own boss: never going to the hospital at all and having your baby at home. This is as close as the birth movement gets to calling a strike on the industry of obstetrics: a more exact parallel to a strike (refusing to bear children at all) has not been necessary because, while factory owners own the means of production (machines, raw materials), leaving workers only their labor to withdraw, women have control over the means of reproduction (at least for the present, as we will see below) in the form of their own bodies. When they give birth at home, they own the whole shop and can be in charge of the entire enterprise.

The following three paragraphs echo Braverman's 'deskilling thesis' which argues that management *deliberately* uses new technology to limit and control workers.

The analogy between workers and women giving birth can be extended with a consideration of the consequences of replacing skilled workers with machines. As Noble shows, machines can seldom do everything that a human can. He describes how in machine tool industries, until very recently, management was forced to rely to some extent on the skill and knowledge of the machinist, to prevent machines under "automatic" control from destroying themselves or raw material. But whenever human labor is replaced by machines, it is likely that some of the human skills on which the machines were modeled will become lost. This is partly a result of subdividing tasks that previously were performed by one person into smaller parts, each to be performed by different people or machines.

Examples of the "depletion of irreplaceable skills" in birth are legion. Forceps themselves were introduced by male midwives in the seventeenth and eighteenth centuries and were part of what enabled these men to compete effectively against female midwives. Elizabeth Nihell, one eighteenth-century midwife, wrote that midwives who used forceps found them "at once insignificant and dangerous substitutes for their own hands, with which they were sure of conducting their operations more safely, more effectually, and with less pain to the patient." Today midwives retain a substantial store of nontechnological knowledge that, they constantly remark, doctors do not know: how to use hands instead of forceps; how to assist in the delivery of a breech baby; how to avoid an episiotomy by having the mother push only *between* contractions, not during them, for the last few contractions before delivery.

Sometimes skills can be lost and then rediscovered. Dr Brooks Ranney, who has practiced in Yankton, South Dakota, since 1949, reports on his development of "the gentle art of external cephalic version", or using one's hands to turn a baby that presents head up or sideways by pushing gently on the baby through the mother's abdomen. He notes the lack of training in the technique for young doctors, the importance of years of experience in his relearning the technique, and its success in preventing premature labors and cesarean sections associated with breech presentations.

The desperation to which women can be reduced in efforts to retain control over their own bodies is captured in the story of one woman I interviewed who attempted to do an external version herself. She had planned a vaginal birth after cesarean at home attended by a midwife, but the labor was progressing in a way the midwife found alarming. The woman herself remained confident that everything was fine, thinking that since the baby was engaged in her pelvis in posterior position, face up rather than face down, her relatively long and difficult labor was to be expected. She told me that while her husband, friends, and midwife were waiting in the living room, talking about how it was imperative to go to the hospital, "I was in the other room doing an external version myself. I got her to the side; even my doctor who is never shocked, just sat down [when I told him]. I didn't force her [the baby], I talked with her very careful in what I was doing. I really worked with her" (Sarah Lasch). An ambulance arrived, the baby turned all the way around on the ride to the hospital and was born a few minutes after arriving.

David Noble gives us the gripping story of how, through increasingly advanced technology, control of machine tools has been taken from workers, even to the point of achieving "the actual removal of the work force itself." Short of complete removal of workers, however, as workers have less and less control they lose the ability to determine the pace and process of work. In "continuous-control operations" such as oil refineries, strikes become useless because the company can continue operations at nearly full capacity even without the workers. If doctors are like managers controlling the work that women's bodies do in birthing a baby, then will they stop short of actually removing the work force, the women themselves?

The scientific model of medicine – implicitly criticised here – is further discussed in Reading 61.

This question leads us to an examination of the rapidly developing reproductive technologies. Many have suggested that these technologies contribute to birth being seen as commodity production: eggs, sperms, wombs, embryos, and even babies are increasingly being bought and sold. My analogy of birth and production shows that this analogy is a slight extension of existing tendencies: ever since labor in childbirth was defined as mechanical work done by the uterus, birth has been seen as the (re)production of goods.

What is changing is our ability to harvest components of the goods (embryo, eggs) earlier and to know in greater detail what the quality of the goods is. The new prenatal technologies of amniocentesis and sonography are creating new norms for the standard of production, which like the norms for progress in the stages of labor, are held up for women to conform to. My own second child was found by sonography to be too small for her gestational age (even though at present very little is known about the details of fetal growth). Doctors immediately raised the frightening specters of "microcephaly" or "placental insufficiency," which were only finally dissipated when she was born a normal seven pounds twelve ounces. My interviews with other women are full of anxieties, precautions, and interventions, from total bed rest to early induction of labor, that have come along with new standard expectations for fetal growth and development.

On the one hand, technology allows the development of new standards for fetal growth. On the other hand, doctors, husbands and state governments are successfully using legal sanctions to force women to involuntarily alter their diets (stop taking drugs), alter their daily activity (be confined to a hospital for the last weeks of pregnancy), or undergo cesarean section to protect the rights of the fetus. Although one could argue that at least some of these restrictions might benefit the fetus, they certainly give the woman no choice about sacrificing her rights to those of the fetus. The possibility exists that the woman, the "laborer" will increasingly drop out of sight as doctor-managers focus on "producing" perfect "products."

Arthur Brittan: Masculinities and Masculinist Ideology

For those who have not yet begun to think very seriously about the varieties of masculine identity and of the various ways males dominate and control females, the first few pages of Arthur Brittan's *Masculinity and Power* are a good place to start.

Brittan quickly dispenses with the notion that the only 'real' type of masculinity is of the type regularly portrayed by Clint Eastwood (in fact, even Eastwood's characterisations have latterly begun to evince moments of ambiguity and self-doubt). There are different ways of being masculine, and the form masculinity takes can change between historical epochs, classes and other contexts. However, whereas masculinity varies, the domination of males over females is virtually universal. Brittan refers to this system of domination as patriarchy and to the ideology which seeks to justify it as masculinism, and this, as one would expect, occurs in various forms.

A logical follow-on from Brittan's introduction to the concept of masculinist ideology, is to look for examples of it. These are not provided here but most readers will have little difficulty in finding cases from their everyday lives.

Reading 22 From Arthur Brittan: *Masculinity and Power* (Basil Blackwell, 1989), pp. 1–6.

Most discussions of masculinity tend to treat it as if it is measurable. Some men have more of it, others less. Those men who appear to lack masculinity are, by definition, sick or genetically inadequate. Gay men, for example, are often regarded as men who lack a proper hormonal balance, and who consequently are not 'real' men. This assumption – that we can know and describe men in terms of some discoverable dimension is problematic – because it suggests that masculinity is timeless and universal.

My aim in this book is to examine this assumption. My position is that we cannot talk of masculinity, only masculinities. This is not to claim that masculinity is so variable that we cannot identify it as a topic. I am not in favour of a doctrinaire relativism which would make it an almost impossible object of study. It seems to me that any account of masculinity must begin with its place in the general discussion of gender. Since gender does not exist outside history and culture, this means that both masculinity and femininity are continuously subject to a process of reinterpretation. The way men are regarded in late twentieth-century England is obviously different from the way that they were regarded in the nineteenth century. Moreover, versions of masculinity may vary over a limited time scale. In this respect, Ehrenreich (1983) has documented the changes in American men's attitudes to marriage from the fifties to the eighties.

> In the 1950s . . . there was a firm expectation . . . that required men to grow up, marry and support their wives. To do anything else was less than grown-up, and the man who willfully deviated was judged to be somehow 'less than a man'. This expectation was supported by an enormous width of expert opinion, moral sentiment and public bias, both within the popular culture and the elite centres of academic wisdom. But by the end of the 1970s and the beginning of the 1980s, adult manhood was no longer burdened with the automatic expectation of marriage and breadwinning. The man who postpones marriage even into middle age,

> who avoids women who are likely to become financial dependents, who is dedicated to his own pleasures, is likely to be found not suspiciously deviant but 'healthy'. And this judgement, like the prior one, is supported by expert opinion and by the moral sentiments and biases of a considerable sector of the American middle class. (Ehrenreich, 1983, pp.11–12)

If the 'breadwinner ethic' has indeed collapsed among large sections of middle-class American men, then is there any point in talking about masculinity in terms of a generalized category? If men are now dedicated to the cultivation of their own pleasures, does it make much sense even to attempt to theorize about masculinity? Does the concept 'masculinity' have any meaning at all when it seems to change from moment to moment? Surely this is not what is being suggested by Ehrenreich. The fact that men are rebelling against their role as breadwinners does not entail the undermining of their dominance in the political and economic spheres. Nor, for that matter, does it imply that they have surrendered authority in the family or household. What has changed is not male power as such, but its form, its presentation, its packaging. In other words, while it is apparent that styles of masculinity may alter in relatively short time spans, the substance of male power does not. Hence, men who run away from family involvements are not signalling their general abdication of power; all they are doing is redefining the arena in which that power is exercised.

The fact that masculinity may appear in different guises at different times does not entitle us to draw the conclusion that we are dealing with an ephemeral quality which is sometimes present and sometimes not. In the final analysis, how men behave will depend upon the existing social relations of gender. By this I mean the way in which men and women confront each other ideologically and politically. Gender is never simply an arrangement in which the roles of men and women are decided in a contingent and haphazard way. At any given moment, genre will reflect the material interests of those who have power and those who do not. Masculinity, therefore, does not exist in isolation from femininity – it will always be an expression of the current image that men have of themselves in relation to women. And these images are often contradictory and ambivalent.

Masculinity, from this point of view, is always local and subject to change. Obviously, some masculinities are long-lived whilst others are as ephemeral as fads in pop music. However, what does not easily change is the justification and naturalization of male power; that is, what remains relatively constant in the masculine ideology, masculinism or heterosexualism. What I am proposing here is that we must distinguish between three concepts which often tend to be confused in literature as well as in political and everyday discourse, namely masculinity, masculinism and patriarchy.

Masculinity refers to those aspects of men's behaviour that fluctuate over time. In some cases these fluctuations may last for decades – in others it may be a matter of weeks or months. For example, if we look at the fashion in male hairstyles over the past 20 years or so, we find that they range from the shoulder length vogue of the sixties, to the punk cuts of the late seventies and early eighties. During the same period men have experimented with both macho and androgynous styles of self-presentation. At the same time, we have been bombarded with stories about role reversals in marriage and the home. Men are now 'into' fatherhood. They look after their children, they sometimes change nappies and, in some cases, they stay at home and play the role of houseperson. The speed of these changes, it is sometimes suggested, has led to a crisis in masculinity. The implication here is that male identity is a fragile and tentative thing with no secure anchorage in the contemporary world. Such fragility makes it almost impossible to talk about masculinity as though it had some recognizable substantive basis. And yet, in everyday and academic discourse, we find that men are commonly described as aggresive, assertive, independent, competitive, insensitive and so on. These attributions are based on the idea that there is something about men which transcends their local situation. Men are seen as having natures which determine their behaviour in all situations.

Indeed, the habit of attributing some kind of exalted power to masculinity is so ingrained in our culture that it makes it very difficult to give credence to those explanations which stress its contextuality. This is precisely the point. Those people who speak of masculinity as an essence, as an inborn characteristic, are confusing masculinity with masculinism, masculine ideology. Masculinism is the ideology that justifies and naturalizes male domination. As such, it is the ideology of patriarchy. Masculinism takes it for granted that there is a fundamental difference between men and women, it assumes that heterosexuality is normal, it accepts without question the sexual division of labour, and it sanctions the political and dominant role of men in the public and private spheres. Moreover, the masculine ideology is not subject to the vagaries of fashion – it tends to be relatively resistant to change. In general, masculinism gives primacy to the belief that gender is not negotiable – it does not accept evidence from feminist and other sources that the relationships between men and women are political and constructed nor, for that matter, does it allow for the possibility that lesbianism and homosexuality are not forms of deviance or abnormality, but are alternative forms of gender commitment.

Masculinism as dominant ideology

However, I am not for one moment suggesting that the connection between masculinism and masculinity is tenuous. This would be absurd. If, for example, we look at the exaggerated politeness of male behaviour in some middle-class contexts, and then we observe the more direct male assertiveness in a working-class environment, this does not entitle us to draw the conclusion that middle-class and working-class masculinity are qualitatively different. Alternatively, if we examine the behaviour of men cross-culturally and discover that the number of ways of 'being a man' appears to be flexible and varied, it is then wrong to assume that this variation undermines male domination. Just as there is a large number of styles and behaviours associated with class relations so there is an almost infinite number of styles and behaviours associated with gender relations. Working-class life in the north of England is not a carbon copy of working-class behaviour in the south. This is not to say that the specificity of working-class life in different parts of Britain cannot be subsumed under the rubric of a more general view of class. Similarly, the fact that men have a multitude of ways of expressing their masculinity in different times and places does not mean that these masculinities have nothing to do with male dominance.

I realize that there are problems in talking about masculinism as a dominant ideology. To assume this is to accept without reservation that a dominant group's ideology is inevitably imposed upon everybody else. In the case of the masculine ideology, this is to claim that men have a collective ideology which they collectively force women to accept as being natural and inevitable. This implies that men constitute a class, and that they maximize their class interest. Now this is a vulgar version of ideology. It proposes that ideology is some kind of monolithic worldview which is used by a ruling group to justify and legitimate its claims to rule. By no stretch of the imagination can men be considered to be a class in this sense. One has only to look at the position of black and white men in Britain, or in the United States, to establish that their membership of a common class is problematic. Of course, it is true that black and white male workers may occupy the same class location, but this does not mean that they constitute a homogeneous class. Furthermore, it may be asked, in what ways do white working-class men have the same interests as black men workers in a country like South Africa? To assert that these men are a class sharing a common ideology poses all sorts of difficulty.

Accordingly, the proposition that masculinism is the ideology that justifies and naturalizes male domination needs to be qualified. Granted that men collectively do not form committees to ensure their continued domination, and that men themselves are exploited and dominated by other men, we can nevertheless still speak of a set of gender relations in which the power of men is taken for granted, not only in the public but in the domestic sphere as well. Masculinism is reproduced and reaffirmed in the household, in the economy and in the polity. Even when there is a great deal of gender and sexual experimentation, as was the case in the sixties and the early seventies, masculinism was never under real attack because gender relations remained relatively constant. The great amount of attention given to the increased participation of men in the household chores and the emphasis on 'democratic' family relationships did not, in any marked way, alter these gender relations. Despite the feminist analysis and demystification of patriarchy, the masculine ideology remain intact, as evidenced by the successful counter-campaign of the New Right in the United States and Britain.

> Here Brittan's analysis complements Sylvia Walby's concept of patriarchal structures (see Reading 18).

> Brittan is here referring to the anti-feminist backlash of the 1980s and early 1990s.

SECTION 5

RACE AND ETHNICITY

Introduction: Readings 23–28

The first reading in this section sets the essential context for understanding racism and ethnic conflict in contemporary Britain and Europe. In the 1950s and 1960s there was a buoyant demand for immigrant or migrant labour, but during the 1970s this demand began to contract. An increasing number of entry restrictions were placed upon people who would formerly have been welcomed.

However, the matter was never entirely an economic one. There is abundant evidence of white racism against black people in Britain, including racism in situations where black people could not be regarded as posing the slightest economic threat to whites. Mark Halstead's extract attempts to chart the varieties of racism – from sheer emotional rejection of 'the other' to well-meaning liberal failure to recognise real and legitimate difference.

Robert Miles' definition and analysis of racism contrasts sharply with Halstead's catholic approach. He argues that for an ideology to be categorised as racist it must be based on belief in the negative characteristics of a (supposed) biological group. This excludes several of the beliefs or behaviours which Halstead categorises as racist. The fourth reading, from Keith Grint, examines racism in practice – in the case of the employment market (see also Reading 53).

With my own piece, the focus shifts from 'race'/racism to ethnicity. I survey the work of several authors who argue that ethnic cultural identity is a valid form of identity, and that ethnicity differentiates black from black as well as black from white. To a significant degree, their arguments go against the grain of much established radical thinking in this area which has been critical of ethnic 'culturalism' and nationalism as anti-socialist and divisive of the working class. What the resurgence of ethnic nationalism in Eastern Europe and elsewhere seems to show is that, like it or not, ethnicity is a powerful and radical basis of identity for many people. Fiona Devine observes as much in her Luton survey (Reading 14). On the other hand, it is equally clear that an excess of ethnic nationalism can lead to the most appalling discrimination and cruelty against others, and the reading also discusses the more dangerous aspects of ethnicity.

David Marsh's article brings this section full circle. It presents an image of Western Europe almost as a fortified 'fat city' with the deprived legions at its gates. The pressures from without and within Western Europe are formidable. It is by no means certain that the forces of tolerance and liberality will prevail in the face of them.

Robin Cohen: International Labour Migration in the Post-War Period – 'Now You Need Them, Now You Don't'

Contemporary race relations in post-war Europe can only be properly understood in the context of the massive labour migration that occurred in the fifteen to twenty five years following the second world war. In view of the complexity of 'race'/ethnic relations in present day Britain and most of Europe, the story of this mass migration of labour is oddly simple. There was a demand for cheap labour in the rich and (then) economically expanding countries of northern Europe and the USA. Complementing this, was an eager supply of labour in poorer peripheral countries, mainly Eastern and Southern Europe, the Caribbean, and Mexico. Economically, it all seemed to fit conveniently.

Of course, 'units of labour' were also people who had their own individual and cultural identity. There developed social and cultural, as well as economic, tensions with some members of the indigenous communities. Robin Cohen summarises these developments very succinctly. He also describes (in a highly abbreviated extract here) how the pattern of migration changed from about the mid-1970s. Labour migration into Northern Europe has greatly declined. An issue of great human urgency has been the sharp increase in the late 1980s and early 1990s of those seeking asylum in Britain and other relatively stable European countries. This reflects a considerable increase in political and social upheaval in many parts of the world, particularly the Middle East and Eastern Europe.

People do not always learn from history but sometimes instead draw 'lessons' from it that do little more than reinforce their own prejudice. Thus, the lesson some people draw from the history of post-war migration is that 'it was a mistake to let it happen at all'. This is the way of bigotry and ethnocentrism. A larger and more generous understanding of post-war migration is to see it as but one aspect of an increasingly interdependent world. A 'one-world' view embraces a commitment to mutual responsibility and shared human rights, including the rights to life, liberty and material sufficiency.

Reading 23 From Robin Cohen, *Contested Domains: Debates in International Labour Studies* (Zed Books, 1991), pp. 151–56, 161–63, 163–65

Introduction

In a current period marked by immigration restrictions and increasingly tight definitions of nationality and citizenship, it is sometimes difficult to remember that the climate of decision-making in the immediate post-war period was far different in North America and most European countries.

In France, for example, the leading demographer at the influential *Institut National d'Études Démographiques*, Sauvy, pronounced that France needed at the minimum to import 5,290,000 permanent immigrants to renew its labour force, stabilise the skewed demographic structure arising from war-time losses and reinforce its claims to Great Power status (Freeman 1979: 69).

Across the Channel, the budding Labour Party politician, James Callaghan (later to become Prime Minister), ignored the potentially xenophobic reactions of his working-class supporters and proclaimed in the House of Commons:

> We are living in an expansionist era. Surely, this is a Socialist government committed to a policy of full employment? In a few years' time we in this

> country will be faced with a shortage of labour, and not with a shortage of jobs. Our birth rate is not increasing in sufficient proportion to enable us to replace ourselves . . . We are turning away from the shores of this country eligible and desirable young men who could be added to our strength and resources, as similar immigrants have done in the past (cited Cohen 1987: 124).

In Germany, the post-war Constitutional provision for reunification allowed millions of East Germans to cross the frontier. These expellees and refugees, together with those from the former eastern territories of the Reich and demobilised soldiers, all unprotected by the weakened labour movement, 'provided ideal conditions for capitalist expansion, and were the essential cause of the economic miracle' (Castles *et al.* 1984: 25). With expansion, West Germany's demand for labour increased dramatically. Though a more cautious attitude prevailed on the question of according citizenship to 'foreign' newcomers, a massive guestworker programme from Turkey and elsewhere was initiated.

In the US, in addition to the strong continued demand for migrant labour (flowing especially from the neighbouring areas of Central America and the Caribbean), temporary labour programmes, initiated to offset war-time shortages, were allowed to continue in the post-war period. For instance, the Bracero Program, designed to supply agricultural labourers to south-west agribusiness, commenced in 1942 with 4,203 recruits, peaked in 1957 with 450,422 labourers, and was only formally ended in 1965 (Samora & Simon 1977: 140).

Of all the major capitalist industrial powers, Japan was alone in not relying on the importation of large numbers of foreign labourers to fuel its post-war economy. This was not because of some general rule of Japanese exceptionalism, but because, unlike in the other industrial powers, there was still a large indigenous rural population which could be detached from the land, and a significant proportion of women who could be enjoined to enter employment for the first time. For instance, the number of Japanese women 'gainfully employed' increased from 3 million in 1950 to 12 million in 1970 (Mandel 1978: 171).

The end of the migrant labour boom

The authorised importation of labourers to the industrial economies mentioned above lasted roughly until the mid-1970s in Europe, when sharp restrictions were imposed. The US figures do not show similar absolute declines in legal immigration, but there were significant qualitative changes in the occupational and legal categories admitted – from immigrants to refugees and from agricultural and mass production workers to the professional, technical and independent proprietor categories (Keely & Elwell 1981: 192–3).

It is now no longer necessary to mount an elaborate argument listing the advantages conferred by the deployment of migrant labour by the host countries and employers in the post-war period, as there is now a remarkable unanimity of views between liberal (see Kindleberger 1967; Böhning 1972), Marxist (see Castles & Kosack 1973; Castells 1979) and official accounts. Perhaps one, remarkably frank, paper prepared by the West German government for a conference on 'The Future of Migration' organised by the Organisation of Economic Cooperation and Development in May 1986 is sufficient to make the point. The paper (cited in Cross 1988) accepts that the German economy had gained considerable benefits with negligible costs, and continues:

> Until far into the 1960s, the employment of foreigners helped to satisfy the rising demand for labour . . . at a time when the labour volume was getting scarcer and scarcer . . . Their considerable flexibility in the economic cycle helped to offset negative employment effects in times of recession and to avoid inflationary shortages in times of upswing. The need for infrastructural facilities, integration assistance and social benefits which followed from the employment of foreigners was almost insignificant because of the short periods of stay of the individual foreigners and the low numbers of family members who entered in the course of family reunion.

If the benefits of migrant labour were so apparent, why did the import of labour throttle off so dramatically in the mid-1970s? On this question there is no final agreement, but a number of mutually-reinforcing explanations or contingent factors may be advanced. I will briefly discuss six factors, specified below in no particular order:

The oil crisis

There is an obvious coincidence of dates in the early 1970s which may lead to a simple association between the dramatic increase in the price of oil and the end of the migrant labour boom. Certainly, the immediate wave of redundancies that followed in energy-intensive industries led to a political situation which would have made the importation of large numbers of 'alien' labourers untenable for most European governments. But, while the oil crisis can partly explain the timing of particular measures, any explanation of the end of labour migration must also be concerned with other deeper, underlying factors.

The rise of racism and xenophobia

One of the key variables, often underestimated by scholars (who frequently assumed the hegemony of 'rational' capital) and governments (who assumed their own hegemony) alike, was the rise of a virulent indigenous working-class xenophobia. This is not to argue, of course, that sentiments were only held amongst the working classes. But the opposite possibility, the belief that patterns of international class solidarity would obviate ethnic and racial allegiances, proved hopelessly idealistic.

> Events since the publication of Cohen's book further reinforce his emphatic comment. In particular, the virulence of ethnic conflict in Eastern Europe and parts of the Middle East have illustrated the vitality of nationalism.

In Britain, old protective practices, like closed shops and demarcation agreements, were used to freeze out migrant labour (Duffield 1988) while in

France, a municipal Communist Party bulldozed the hostels erected for migrant workers in response to the demands of its constituents.

In short, both capital and the state were unable to continue to employ migrant workers oblivious to the countervailing racist sentiments such a policy provoked.

The organisation of migrant workers

Much Marxist theory, particularly of the 'capital logic' tendency, depicts migrants as hopeless chaff blown about by fierce economic storms – unable to respond organisationally to the market forces arraigned against them. This picture is partly correct at the earliest stages of migration, amongst those migrants with a particularly individualist ethic and in circumstances where it was difficult to effect a bond of alliance between co-religionists or those from a similar ethnic group.

Whatever the variation in activity across the different cases, there is no doubt that community associations, religious groups and political support groups were sufficiently and increasingly active – precisely at the time when issues such as repatriation, return migration, immigration restrictions and deportations were proposed by politicians, anxious to limit what were perceived as the socially divisive consequences of the untrammelled immigration period. Migrant groups were not sufficiently influential to prevent all these measures, but they were, on the whole, powerful enough to resist the pressures to mass repatriation and to press instead for the principle of family reunification to be recognised.

The rise in the cost of reproduction

The increased assertiveness of migrants not only applied to matters of immigration policy and family reunion; immigrant associations became increasingly concerned with the full range of social and employment benefits. One should not fall into the racist trap of believing that immigrant families overclaim all benefits – the evidence indeed inclines to a contrary assertion (Rex & Tomlinson 1979: 62). However, given the demographic profile and the special language needs of many migrant communities, increased costs arose in respect of child care, language training and education. Even if we assume only a broadly converging cost of reproduction between indigenous and migrant communities, the crucial advantage accruing to the host country and employer – a minimal or wholly displaced cost of reproduction – no longer obtained as migrant communities gradually reconstituted their family life and became permanent minorities.

Economic restructuring

One way of understanding the economic restructuring of the last 15 years is to argue in terms of new technology impelling a different industrial logic – away from mass production to small-batch production, away from labouring into independent proprietorship, away from manufacturing into services (Piore & Sabel 1984). The same processes also impelled a greater comparative advantage accruing to certain newly industrialising countries (for example, Hong Kong, Korea, Taiwan and Singapore), particularly in respect of low-bulk and high-value goods where the value added by the labour component was significant.

See Reading 52.

In Chapter 8 I have explored the so-called 'new international division of labour' thesis in detail, so here, by way of summary, I simply suggest that many such theories are overly technologically determinist, and can easily confuse cause and consequence. Thus, it is at least as plausible to argue that increased levels of class composition and migrant organisation made mass production methods less attractive as to assume some exogenous new technology acted as an independent force. But whatever the exact reasons for the movement to independent proprietorship and small-batch and third world production, this development obviated the need to continue to employ factory hands imported from abroad.

The 'inefficiency' of unskilled labour

In opening the paper, I allude to a remarkable uniformity of opinion between official accounts and liberal and Marxist writers on the benefits conferred by the use of migrant labour. The orthodoxy is, in my view, largely correct, but some dissent was recorded at an early date by Misham (1970).

His argument is alarmist and based on unlikely projections of large inflows of migrant labour leading to a rise in the labour-capital ratio and a consequent fall in production. While the broad thesis makes unrealistic net migration assumptions, in some sectors, for example the textile industry, it is likely that working cheap migrant labour on a 24-hour shift pattern was used as a way of holding the line against low-cost Asian textiles, thereby avoiding the inevitable day when old machinery and tracks had to be discarded.

As Reaganomics and Thatcherism began to gain ground, and unemployment levels began to rise, arguments that importing migrants was essentially an inefficient way of reducing industrial costs became more widely heard.

Labour flows since the mid-1970s

I have given an indicative, though not an exhaustive account of the explanations for the immigration restrictions of the mid-1970s. But incomplete as this picture is, it may give the false impression that international labour migration has effectively ceased. In fact it continues largely unabated – though with significant differences in the destination areas and the kinds of migrants involved.

In Europe, the post-1970s migration is largely accounted for by family reunification, refugees and to a small degree, by illegal entrants. In the US, illegals account for a much greater proportion of post-1970s migrants. Agribusiness in the south, the sweated trades in the north-east and the service sector more generally continued to deploy imported labour, both legal and illegal. But there was also a clear movement away from employees destined for the mass occupations in the auto and steel industries, towards an acceptance of political refugees (Vietnamese, Cuban and East European) and to those who could class themselves as entrepreneurs or proprietors (for example, the Koreans and Hong Kong Chinese).

Outside the US and Europe, labour migration apparently of the more well-established kind went to the Middle East and other oil-producing countries. But even in these areas important qualitative differences appear. These differences emerge in my more detailed remarks below on migration flows to the oil-rich countries, illegal migrants, refugees and project-tied contract migrants . . .

What's in a name?

Immigrants, guestworkers, illegals, refugees, asylum-seekers, expatriates, settlers – do these labels signify anything of importance? My argument here turns on a belief that although there are considerable similarities between international migrants of all types, the modern state has sought to differentiate the various people under its sway by including some in the body politic and according them full civic and social rights, while seeking to exclude others from entering this charmed circle.

The important role of citizenship as a means of integrating dissatisfied members of the lower orders and including them in the core society was first explicitly recognised by Marshall (1950). For him, access to citizenship allowed everyone so favoured to be given some stake in the society, at least in respect of periodic elections, protection, and access to some social benefits. With the rise of welfare and distributive states in the post-war world, the social wage – unemployment benefits, social security, housing allowances, tax credits, pensions, subsidised health care – has become a much more important symbolic and economic good. By the same token, states have sought to restrict access to the social wage by deploying workers with limited entitlements. The different statuses reflected in immigrant or guestworker categories reflect the differential access of such groups to the social wage and to the protection afforded by the agencies of law and order.

If we consider the various categories mentioned, three broad categories appear – citizens whose rights are extensive, an intermediate group (the denizens) and a group which remains a subject population akin to the ancient helots who hewed wood and toiled for the Spartans without access to democratic rights, property or protection.

Some of the typical sub-groups within the different status groups mentioned are listed below (Figure 9.1).

Figure 9.1 Sub-groups of Citizens, Denizens and Helots

Citizens
Nationals by birth or naturalisation
Established Immigrants
Convention Refugees

Denizens
Holders of one or more citizenships
Recognised asylum applicants
Special entrants (e.g. ex-Hong Kong)
Expatriates

Helots
Illegal Entrants
Undocumented workers
Asylum-seekers
Overstayers
Project-tied unskilled workers

A few remarks on each of the three major categories will perhaps help to lend greater specificity to the labels.

Citizens

This group appears as an increasingly privileged one. Many states have moved from inclusive to exclusive definitions of citizenship, abandoning the principle of *jus soli* (citizenship by being born in a territory) to *jus sanguinis* (citizenship according to the parents' nationality). In the case of the European countries that once had empires (Belgium, France, Britain, Holland), binding guarantees of citizenship to colonial subjects have frequently been ignored or circumvented by subsequent legislation. While the Dutch on the whole respected the citizenship conferred on subjects of the Netherlands, the French maintained recognition only for a small number of people in the *départements* (French Guiana, Réunion, Guadeloupe and Martinique). The British, for their part, in the Nationality Act of 1982 stripped away the rights of residents of the colony of Hong Kong (and a few other places) and created a new citizenship of 'dependent territories' which conferred no right to live or work in the UK. Under the impact of the destablising events in China in 1989, however, and its consequent effects on the colony of Hong Kong, Britain has been forced to guarantee the admission of up to 50,000 Hong Kong families. The intention of this guarantee is to stabilise the last years of British rule in the colony (it reverts to Chinese rule in 1997) by buying the loyalty of key officials and entrepreneurs with the offer of settlement and full citizenship in Britain. This will require amendment of the 1982 British Nationality Act . . .

Denizens

I conceive of this group as comprising privileged aliens often holding multiple citizenship, but not having the citizenship or the right to vote in the country of their residence or domicile. Hammar (forthcoming) has produced a remarkable calculation that resident non-citizens living and working in European countries include 180,000 in Belgium, 2,800,000 in France, 2,620,000 in West Germany, 400,000 in the Netherlands, 390,000 in Sweden and 700,000 in Switzerland. Many of these alien residents may be well-paid expatriates (see above) who are not particularly concerned with exercising the franchise and have compensating employment benefits – a group, in short, that can be seen as transcending the limits of the nation-state. However, the numbers involved in Hammar's calculations suggest that many residents have been systematically excluded from citizenship and its accompanying rights without any compensating benefits deriving from their employment. These form part of the helot category.

Helots

I have used the category 'helots' in a somewhat more inclusive way in Cohen (1987). Here I refer more narrowly to people who have illegally entered the country, people who have overstayed the period granted on their entry visas, asylum-seekers who have not been recognised under the international Conventions, those who are working illegally, and those who have been granted only limited rights. A good example (cited in Castles *et al.* 1984: 77) appears in a statement given to officials as to how to operate the 1965 West German Foreigners Law:

> Foreigners enjoy all basic rights, except the basic rights of freedom of assembly, freedom of association, freedom of movement and free choice of occupation, place of work and place of education and protection from extradition abroad.

Statements such as this reveal the powerful attempt to try to exclude, detain or deport foreigners who are regarded as disposable units of labour-power to whom the advantages of citizenship, the franchise and social welfare are denied.

Conclusion

As Marshall (1950) argues, conferring citizenship is the key indicator of integration and acceptance within a nation state. This basic symbol of inclusion is signified by the right to elect periodically a new government. But the exercise of the vote has become of rather lesser significance than the other attendant benefits of citizenship – access to national insurance systems, unemployment benefits, housing support, health care and social security. In addition to these undoubted advantages, citizens of the European nations within the European Community will soon have untrammelled rights to live, work, own property and travel within a wider Europe.

Helots and denizens are, by the same token, symbolically excluded and practically denied all the advantages just listed. In the case of the denizens, this may not be particularly burdensome – a denizen may be an employee of a multinational company with access to private medical insurance. But for a helot, the denial of citizenship is usually a traumatic and life-threatening decision. Given their vulnerability, the helots have become the key means for inducing labour flexibility and provide a target for nationalist and racist outrages.

Our trichotomy leads one to speculate that a new form of stratification has emerged which in origin has little to do with income, occupation, racial or ethnic background, gender, or a particular relationship to the means of production. Of course, there are likely to be coincidences between the different patterns of stratification. A helot is likely to be a Third World migrant, a member of a stigmatised minority, with low income, holding an unskilled occupation and having limited access to housing, education and other social benefits. Similarly, a professionally-educated, urban, middle-class salary-earner, who happens to be a foreigner, is likely to be a denizen.

Migration after the 1970s to a new country will not necessarily carry the optimistic possibilities characteristic of migration at the turn of the century. Then the 'huddled masses,' that time from Europe as well as from Asia, threw off their poverty and feudal bondage to enter the American dream as equal citizens. Equally it was perfectly possible for English and Irish convicts to become landowners and gentlemen farmers in Australia. Nowadays, one's legal or national status – whether, in my terms, a citizen, helot or denizen – will increasingly operate as indelible stigmata, determining a set of life chances, access to a particular kind of employment or any employment and other indicators of privilege and good fortune.

24 *Mark Halstead: Six Types of Racism*

The question 'What is racism?' is one that can cause considerable difficulty for students. The following abbreviated version of Mark Halstead's attempt to catalogue six 'types' of racism should help. Halstead takes a very broad approach to defining racism. What the six types of racism have in common is that they all contribute to racial injustice. For him, then, racism is any belief or action that results in racial injustice. Many others, including Robert Miles (see Reading 25), would find this too broad a definition.

Halstead's typology of racism is as follows (with my own explanatory terminology in brackets):

- Pre-reflective gut racism (Emotional racism)
- Post-reflective gut racism (Ideological racism)
- Cultural racism
- Institutional racism
- Paternalistic racism
- Colour-blind racism.

While he recognises problems in including some of the above categories as types of racism, he clearly intends to generate a typology which captures all types of racial injustice.

Halstead's discussion of racism is part of his book about the controversial headteacher, Ray Honeyford, and there are one or two references to him in the extract.

Reading 24 From Mark Halstead, *Education, Justice and Cultural Diversity* (The Falmer Press, 1988), pp. 139–41, 142–43, 144, 145–46, 146–48, 151–52, 153–54, 157

In what follows, I shall distinguish and examine six different types of racism within contemporary writing on the topic. A consideration of what these six types have in common will facilitate a clarification of the concept, of its moral, social and political implications, and of the grounds on which an action or a person may be called 'racist'.

Type one: pre-reflective gut racism

Arguably, this is the commonest type of racism. It can be thought of as 'folk' or 'street' racism.

This name is being used instead of the now redundant term 'racialism', implying racial hatred. Its name suggests that it has emotional rather than rational origins and content. It can be observed in both individuals and groups. Its deep psychological roots can be traced to three main factors. First, there is a tendency to feel fear, anxiety, insecurity and suspicion in the presence of any persons and groups who are perceived as strange, foreign or unfamiliar. These emotions can provide a powerful motivation to ethnocentric action of various kinds, as Honeyford himself points out in his interview with Anthony Clare:

> Some of the offensive reactions that we get from English people towards black and coloured people might be because they themselves feel threatened (Clare, 1986, p. 13).

Secondly, there are certain motivational dispositions such as rejection, aggression, dominance and superiority which some psychologists consider fundamental to human personality. For example, Murray *et al.* (1938) include among their list of psychogenic needs the need to snub, ignore or exclude others, the need to belittle, injure or ridicule others, the need to influence, control or dominate others and the need to feel superior to others. These negative dispositions are likely to be directed primarily towards perceptibly different individuals and groups, and if it is true that children or simple-minded adults tend to notice, and put more weight on, physical differences more readily than non-physical ones (*cf* Wilson, 1986, p. 6), it is not surprising that racial minorities become particular targets. The third factor is ignorance of racial minorities, which leaves people open to the too-ready acceptance of myths, stereotypes and other fear-arousing communications. Over the centuries in Britain the black man has become an archetypal image of baseness, savagery, ignorance, ugliness and vice and has been used as a bogeyman for impressionable children rather as the reddleman was, according to Thomas Hardy, in nineteenth century Dorset.

Against this background it is easy to see how readily racial myths and stereotypes can gain acceptance. By 'racial myths' is meant statements which have no factual foundation at all or which are necessarily untrue; for example, the claim that 'they all live on social security' is incompatible with the claim that 'they're taking all our jobs'. By 'racial stereotypes' is meant the tendency to see racial groups in terms of a number of supposed distinguishing characteristics, often based on generalizations originating from limited contacts and experience, and to judge individuals in terms of group membership without allowing for individual variation. Thus West Indian children are commonly stereotyped as good at sport and music but badly behaved and unacademic, while Asian children are seen as hardworking but having unrealistic career expectations.

From these three roots racial prejudice can easily develop. Racial prejudice usually involves emotionally charged ethno-centric attitudes, including an antipathy or hostility towards other racial groups. It is extremely difficult to change by argument or the presentation of facts. It may be felt or expressed, acknowledged or hidden, directed towards an entire racial group or towards an individual because of membership of that group (*cf* Allport, 1958, p. 10). Above all, it involves a 'failure of rationality' (Schuman and Harding, 1964, p. 354).

Such prejudice is likely to be expressed in hostile behaviour and in attempts to reject or dominate racial minorities. These may be seen in positive acts of overt racism, the avoidance of social contacts and the process of scapegoating. Positive acts of overt racism include bullying, attacks on property and person, gang fights, murder, verbal abuse and name-calling, rudeness, threats and graffiti. The avoidance of social contacts manifests itself in a general spirit of unfriendliness towards members of other racial groups and often lies behind much of the discrimination in housing and employment in this country, for which there is overwhelming evidence (*cf* Hubbuck and Carter, 1980; Campbell and Jones, 1983; Eggleston *et al.*, 1986). Scapegoating involves relieving one's frustrations or sense of deprivation through displaced aggression directed towards groups of lower status who played no part in causing the initial problem. One example is the tendency to blame minority racial groups for the country's present economic situation. The process of scapegoating completes the vicious circle of gut racism by creating a new set of myths which reinforce racially prejudiced attitudes.

Although it has been assumed in the above discussion that pre-reflective gut racism originates from white people and is directed against blacks, and although white people are clearly in a better position to express certain manifestations of such racism (such as discrimination in housing and employment), there is no reason in principle why this type of racism should be limited to whites only. There may be the same degree of prejudice and hostility in a black who calls a white person 'white racist shit' as in a white who calls a black person a 'black bastard'. As the *Swann Report* (DES, 1985, pp. 27–28) points out, such racism can also exist between minority groups, and this may again take the form of violence, social avoidance or scapegoating . . .

The first two types of racism roughly equate to what most of the more exclusive definitions of racism would include (see Miles, Reading 25).

Type two: post-reflective gut racism

This type of racism is concerned to provide a *justification* for the continuation of racial privilege, and this may involve the creation of an ideology of racial superiority and domination. Whereas pre-reflective gut racism may be attacked for making arbitrary distinctions between people on the basis of irrelevant differences, post-reflective gut racism counter-attacks by claiming that the differences are not irrelevant.

Post-reflective gut racism therefore involves the *post-hoc* rationalization of practices emanating from racial prejudice, such as social avoidance, scapegoating and overt acts of racism. This rationalization may take two forms: first, the establishment and acceptance of an unfounded system of beliefs which would, if it were true, justify racial discrimination; and secondly, the misapplication of well-founded scientific theories to provide support for racist ideology. Both forms of rationalization may ultimately be the product either of conspiracy or of self-deception (*cf* Jones, 1985, pp. 227–28). Let us look at the two forms in more detail.

The first form, the establishment and acceptance of an unfounded system of beliefs, may make use of either a religious or a scientific framework. British Israelitism, for example, holds that Adam was the progenitor only of the Aryan race, the other races being already in existence when he was created. According to another old belief associated with some fundamentalist Protestant sects, negroes were the descendants of Noah's grandson Canaan and were doomed to perpetual servant status as a punishment for Ham's sin against his father (*cf Genesis* ch. 9 v. 25). In the post-Darwin eta, attempts have been made to establish through psychological, genetic and anthropological studies that there are real differences between races in terms of intelligence, personality and moral attributes, which enable the races to be ranked hierarchically and which may thus justify differential treatment and the maintenance of existing inequalities. These attempts usually entail claims that whites of North and West European ancestry are more intelligent, more responsible, more moral, less lazy, less cowardly and have a more significant culture. Thus we find John Tyndall, the former leader of the National Front, claiming

> While every race may have its particular skills and qualities, the capacity to govern and lead and sustain civilization as we understand it lies essentially with the Europeans (quoted in Walker, 1977, p. 81).

A classic example of post-reflective racism is the claim that blacks occupy a subordinate position in our society because they lack the necessary drive and moral stamina to advance themselves, and that this provides an adequate justification for the racial inequalities that currently exist. An example of an extreme form of post-reflective racism is the work in Nazi Germany relating to the distinction between Aryan and other types . . .

The second form of post-reflective racism, involving the misapplication of well-founded scientific theories to provide support for racist beliefs, may be seen in a new type of racism which has developed in recent years and which is consistent with the belief that racial differences are socially constructed.

This 'new racism' (*cf* Barker, 1981; Shallice, 1984; Gordon and Klug, 1986) involves the claim that racism, like nationalism, is simply a more sophisticated form of a natural tribal instinct to group together, to defend one's own territory, to preserve one's distinctive identity, to be loyal to one's kin and to be wary of, and if necessary antagonistic towards, outsiders. On this argument, racial conflict itself is in a sense biologically determined, as it is one aspect of the Darwinian principle of 'the survival of the fittest'. In several speeches Enoch Powell has argued that racial conflict is both natural and inevitable. In 1969, he said,

> We have an identity of our own, as we have a territory of our own, and the instinct to preserve that identity is one of the deepest and strongest implanted in mankind (quoted in Gordon and Klug, 1986, p. 19).

In 1976, he developed the point further:

> Physical and violent conflict must sooner or later supervene where an indigenous population sees no end to the progressive occupation of its heartland by aliens with whom they do not identify and who do not identify themselves with them (*ibid.*).

While such arguments do not depend on the claim that one race is inherently superior to another, they may be considered to typify post-reflective gut racism to the extent that they provide a justification for racial exclusiveness and conflict. In countering such arguments, it is not necessary to reject the underlying anthropological and socio-biological theories. For even if human nature has evolved by a process of competitiveness and aggression, it would be to commit the naturalistic fallacy to argue from this that we should live such a life today. In any case, our active participation in the world depends on much more than can be explained by biological determinism . . .

Type three: cultural racism

This term is being used with increasing frequency (Ben-Tovim, 1978; Saunders, 1982; Greenhalf, 1985b; Seidel, 1986, p. 129; Troyna and Williams, 1986, p. 89; Ashrif and Yaseen, 1987, p. 23; and Gilroy, 1987, p. 61, who applies the term directly to Honeyford) to draw attention to a shift in the focal point of much racism from physical characteristics such as skin colour to cultural characteristics such as social customs, manners and behaviour, religious and moral beliefs and practices, language, aesthetic values and leisure activities. Whereas post-reflective gut racism seeks to explain and justify racist attitudes in religious or scientific terms, cultural racism attempts the same thing in cultural terms. It involves prejudice against individuals because of their culture. The culture of minority groups is seen as flawed in some way, and thus as standing in the way of their progress (*cf* Stone, 1981). Unlike post-reflective gut racism, however, cultural racism does not involve belief in the existence of any biological incapacity to change. On the contrary, change is exactly what is sought. Minorities are encouraged to turn their back on their own culture and to become absorbed by the majority culture. Insofar as they refuse to do so, this is thought to justify inferior treatment and discrimination. Cultural racism, like gut racism, usually involves stereotyping (*cf* Fraser, 1986, p. 59) and is embodied in such statements as 'they've got really dirty habits' and 'why can't they be more like us?'.

Cultural racism demands cultural conformity where it is neither necessary nor perhaps even desirable, and penalizes people unjustly for failure to conform. It may be seen as an attempt to legitimize existing power differences. Opposition to cultural racism does not require the belief that there is no need for any shared values in society; for society would soon disintegrate if there were no respect for law, no acceptance of fundamental principles such as justice and respect for persons and no agreed procedures for resolving conflicts. Not does it involve the belief that different cultures are all equally good (*cf* Parekh, 1985, p. 23) or that one should never criticize other cultures. What it does involve is the claim that to insist on cultural conformity where such an insistence is not justified is a form of domination and oppression . . .

Halstead is observing that 'cultural racism' is based on cultural rather than biological differentiation. Can it, then, be regarded as racism? Unlike Robert Miles, Halstead considers that it is a form of racism.

In what sense can the cultural domination under discussion here be viewed as a type of *racism*? Perhaps not at all, in which case we may need to adopt a new term such as 'culturalism' (*cf* Fraser, 1986, p. 41; Seidel, 1986, p. 114), although this has not proved popular so far. On the other hand, racial differences are very frequently accompanied by cultural differences, so much so that it is often impossible to know whether prejudice and discrimination are being focussed on the former rather than the latter. A feeling of biological superiority goes hand in hand with cultural superiority in the quotation already referred to from John Tyndall who speaks of the capacity to sustain civilization lying essentially with the Europeans. In this sense, cultural differences are considered to be the natural consequence of the division of the world's population into a number of distinct racial groups, and thus hostility towards a racial group may find expression in hostility towards that group's 'alien' culture. The hostility may decline to the extent that members of a racial minority are prepared to conform to the cultural expectations of the majority; in this case, they may be accepted as honorary members of the majority group. Most teachers in multi-racial schools are familiar with situations in which white children make overtly racist comments about black people generally, yet at the same time number black children among their closest friends; indeed, the phenomenon is not limited to children. The explanation seems to be that blacks who turn their back on their own distinctive culture and who conform to the cultural values and expectations of the majority may be treated with respect, whereas those who retain their cultural differences are treated with racial hostility.

In her analysis of the early issues of *The Salisbury Review*, Seidel (1986) links cultural racism to the philosophy of the New Right, for whom, she claims (p. 111), 'the problem of race lies in the fact of cultural difference'. The presence of different cultures in a single country, in the view of the New Right, is likely to cause unacceptable social divisions; this problem can only be overcome by the assimilation of minority groups, but if they resist assimilation, the only 'radical policy that would stand a chance of success is repatriation' (Casey, 1982).

Type four: institutional racism

In one sense, this type is closely linked to type three, for the institutions of a society are a product of, and a part of, its culture. But whereas cultural racism focusses attention on the differences or supposed flaws in the culture of minority groups which are said to justify their inferior treatment, institutional racism generally refers to the way that the institutional arrangements and the distribution of resources in our society serve to reinforce the advantages of the white majority.

Since it was first coined twenty years ago (Carmichael and Hamilton, 1967; Knowles and Prewitt, 1969), the term 'institutional racism' has been used with increasing frequency by sociologists, by local authorities and especially by what Banton (1985) and others have called the 'race relations industry'. Inevitably, different writers have understood and expounded the term in different ways. For some, it involves 'manipulating the bureaucratic system to outflank the unwanted' (Humphrey and John, 1971, p. 112); for others, it includes all the material, bureaucratic, legal and ideological forms in which racism expresses itself; yet others talk of racism as 'a basic feature of the entire society, being structured into its political, social and economic institutions' (Spears, 1978). A fuller list of definitions of 'institutional racism' is provided by Troyna and williams (1986, ch. 3). For the purposes of the present analysis, however, (in order to avoid overlapping with other types of racism, especially type two), a fairly restricted use of the term will be adopted, which accords with the one provided in the *Swann Report:*

> We see institutional racism as describing the way in which a range of long-established systems, practices and procedures, both within education and the wider society, which were originally conceived and devised to meet the needs and aspirations of a relatively homogenous society, can now be seen not only to fail to take account of the multi-racial nature of Britain today but may also ignore or even actively work against the interests of ethnic minority communities. The kind of practices about which we are concerned include many which, whilst clearly originally well-intentioned and in no way racist in *intent,* can now be seen as racist in *effect,* in depriving members of ethnic minority groups of equality of access to the full range of opportunities which the majority community can take for granted or denying their right to have a say in the future of the society of which they are an integral part (DES, 1985, p. 28).

This passage draws attention to three important features of institutional racism:

(i) it refers to the adverse effects suffered by racial minorities as a result of institutional 'systems, practices and procedures';
(ii) it is usually unintentional and may be unconscious;
(iii) it is recognized by outcome.

For some criticisms of the concept of cultural racism, see Miles (Reading 25).

These three features are likely to be generally accepted as essential to the concept of institutional racism (*cf* Williams and Carter, 1985, pp. 4–5), but each is problematic and each is open to a broader or narrower interpretation . . .

Type five: paternalistic racism

This type of racism refers to the process whereby the freedom of black people is defined or restricted by generally well-intentioned regulations that are drawn up by whites. As Kirp (1979) points out,

> In all the discussions over the proper place of race in educational policy, non-white voices have seldom been heard. The government undertook to act in the best interests of a silent constituency. It acted for the racial minorities rather than with them, and in that sense was truly paternalistic (p. 64).

More recently, a minority group leader in Bradford has commented:

> The current race relations policy appears to be based on the assumption that white people have a natural right to set the agenda for black people. Such an assumption has more in common with the perpetuation of colonial relationships than the creation of racial harmony (Courtney Hay, quoted in *Yorkshire Post*, 13 June 1987).

It differs in two ways from institutional racism. First, it involves the initiation of new practices and procedures in response to the presence of racial minorities in the country, whereas institutional racism involves the failure to adapt long-standing practices and procedures to new needs. Secondly, it involves a more clear-cut wielding of power by white people, whereas it was argued above that in institutional racism it is a mistake to oversimplify the power that any individuals can wield in established institutions. Paternalistic racism implies that white people have the right to interfere in the lives of blacks for their own good and the power to define that good.

You may or may not agree that these practices actually constitute paternalistic racism.

Paternalistic racism can be seen, for example, in the provision of separate language centres for children whose first language is not English, and in the practice of 'bussing' black children (but not white) to ensure a racial mix in local authority schools. It may be seen in some forms of positive discrimination and tokenism, particularly where these are intended as a way of placating agitators and defusing protest without tackling the underlying causes of racial injustice in our society.

Type six: colour-blind racism

Evidence gathered for the *Swann Report* shows that many people believe that recognizing differences between racial groups is racially divisive and may 'constitute a major obstacle to creating a harmonious multi-racial society' (DES, 1985, p. 26). On these grounds, official policy in the UK (and in America; *cf* Glazer, 1983, p. 126f) has sometimes self-consciously played down the significance of race. In 1973, the DES discontinued the practice of gathering statistics on pupils' ethnic or racial origins (Willey, 1984, p. 95f, examines the arguments for and against this practice). For similar reasons, many teachers have deliberately sought to make no distinction between black and white pupils, but rather to treat them all equally (*cf* Little and Willey, 1983). However, the *Swann Report* concludes that such 'colour-blindness' is

> potentially just as negative as a straightforward rejection of people with a different skin colour since both types of attitude seek to deny the validity of an important aspect of a person's identity (DES, 1985, pp. 26–27).

In other words, to treat people as the same when there are significant cultural differences between them is to ignore aspects of their identity. (The argument for multi-culturalism is that it recognises such differences.)

The problem may go further, since treating racial groups equally without distinction is usually understood as treating them the same, and treating them the same usually implies treating them in accordance with assumptions based on accumulated white experience. In this sense, equal treatment can become a vehicle for white domination . . .

[Conclusion]

The central argument of this chapter is that racism *is* racial injustice. It may involve both isolated instances of injustice on the part of an individual and systematic social injustice which may permeate a whole society. It may be intentional or unintentional, conscious or unconscious. It may emanate from insecurity, from ignorance, from the belief that certain races are genetically superior to others (which, as Honeyford correctly points out, is the original meaning of racism, derived from the Italian *razzismo*), from institutional practices and procedures which were established long before Britain became a multi-racial society, from well-intentioned but misguided responses to the perceived needs and problems of racial minorities, or from the denial that such special needs and problems exist.

Robert Miles: A Marxist Analysis of Racism and Nationalism

The two examples of racism with which Miles opens this piece, lead into a discussion of some key theoretical concepts around 'racism'. In defining racism itself, Miles strongly argues that it is an *ideology* based on a belief in the negative characteristics of a (supposed) biological group. In offering this definition, he deliberately excludes negative cultural beliefs about 'others' as characteristic of racism (although some consider that such evaluations should be included).

Miles goes on to make a comparison between racism and nationalism. He describes nationalism, like racism, as an ideology based on notions of *permanent* and *inherent* difference between groups by which one group *excludes* another. However, he considers that nationalism is founded on cultural rather than biologically based ideology. Miles emphasises that both nationalism and racism vary historically in the precise form they take: nationalists and racists socially construct their respective ideologies in the context of their particular situation. The ethnic or, in Miles' terms, nationalist turmoil in Eastern Europe underlines the relevance of his analysis. Although whether, in practice, it is possible to distinguish between persecution inspired by nationalism and/or racism, is open to debate.

In quite a dense section, Miles rejects any need for the concept of institutional racism. However, from the point of view of demonstrating a more typically Marxist perspective on racism, the penultimate section in the article is more illustrative. Institutional racism aside, Marxists typically consider that in a capitalist society class is a more fundamental form of stratification than racism.

Elsewhere (Miles 1989), Miles argues that racism *within* the working class produces 'class fractions' which splinter potential working-class solidarity. This is the wider theoretical context within which Miles attempts to limit the definition of racism to a *particular* type of ideology which results in 'exclusionary practices'. Class exclusion operates differently, and needs to be clearly distinguished from racism – although the two can can occur together and reinforce each other.

It is worth mentioning here another theme in Miles' work: that of 'racialisation' (see also J. Solomos, '*Race and Racism in Contemporary Britain* [Macmillan, 1989]. Racialisation refers to how particular 'problems' – which may or may not have much to do with black minorities – are presented and explained in racial terms by certain politicians and sections of the media. Thus, unemployment, 'overpopulation' and 'urban disorder' have been presented more or less directly as the 'fault' of black poeple. It is the insidious and pervasive nature of this aspect of racism that makes it so important to highlight.

Reading 25 From Robert Miles, 'Racism, Ideology and Disadvantage' in *Social Studies Review*, Vol. 4, March 1990, pp. 148–51

During 1989, there was considerable political discussion about two events related in different ways to migration to Britain. First, the 'Rushdie Affair' has led to renewed attention being paid to the presence in Britain of people who originate from Pakistan and who adhere to the Islamic religion. A large proportion of this population has been deeply offended by Salman Rushdie's novel *The Satanic Verses.* Their protests, along with the demands from Islamic leaders in Iran for the author to be killed as punishment for what they regard as blasphemy, have received widespread publicity.

Second, the violent suppression in Beijing of a peaceful demonstration calling for greater political democracy has reactivated concern in Hong Kong about the terms negotiated for this British colony to be returned to Chinese rule in 1997. A large proportion of the population of Hong Kong hold British passports, although they have been denied the right to migrate and settle in Britain (Macdonald 1987, pp. 86–7, 94). The events in Tieneman Square were followed by a renewal in both Hong Kong and Britain of the demand that all British nationals (as signified by possession of a British passport) should have the right to live in Britain.

A British Conservative MP, Mr John Townsend (who represents the constituency of Bridlington) linked these two events in a speech in August

1989 (quoted in *The Guardian*, 29 August 1989). He argued against the admission of British passport holders from Hong Kong, claiming:

> The fact that the Hong Kong Chinese are very hard-working and hold British passports does not make them British. If millions of Chinese come to the UK they would not integrate and become yellow Englishmen. They would create another China, another Hong Kong in England, just as former immigrants have created another Pakistan in Bradford.

For Mr Townsend, this is unacceptable:

> This possibility should make us consider what has already happened to this green and pleasant land – first as a result of waves of coloured immigrants and then by the pernicious doctrine of multi-culturalism . . . Every year that goes by the English are battered into submission in their own country and more strident are the demands of ethnic nationalism. The British people were never consulted as to whether they would change from being a homogeneous society to a multi-racial society. If they had been, I am sure that a resounding majority would have voted to keep Britain an English-speaking, white country.

There is little that is new in these arguments. Mr Townsend was repeating assertions made long ago by other Conservative MPs, as well as members of neo-fascist and extreme right-wing groups and parties. Some Labour MPs have made similar claims. But Mr Townsend's speech does provide a contemporary example of a well-established discourse in Britain (Miles and Phizacklea 1984) and allows us to consider the utility and meaning of the concept of racism.

The concept of racism

The discussion of racism is the key section in Miles' article. His definition is given in the concluding paragraph of the section.

The word 'racism' is a term of political abuse as well as an analytical concept within the social sciences (Miles 1989). Although it is used today as if it were a universal concept, it was 'invented' only in the late 1930s in order to identify a central strand in fascist ideology in Germany, that which identified Jews as a distinct and inferior 'race'. Hence, since it became widely known that those who were sent to forced labour and extermination in German concentration camps were considered to be biologically inferior human beings, to label someone a racist has been to condemn them morally, to place them beyond the boundary of human acceptability.

Furthermore, since 1945, claims that the world's population is made up of a number of distinct 'races' – and that some are inherently superior to others – are rarely expressed outside the meetings and journals of neo-fascist parties. Some academics have responded to this transformation by claiming that racism is no longer expressed in contemporary societies and they conclude that the concept has no validity or use within the social sciences. In a word, racism for them is 'dead' (Banton 1970, 1987).

We should begin by acknowledging that Mr Townsend does not claim explicitly that people from Hong Kong or Pakistan are biologically inferior 'races'. But let us examine his argument more closely. He distinguishes three different populations (English/British, Chinese, Pakistanis) which are identified using a biological feature, skin colour. And there is a polarity posed between English/British people who are 'white' and immigrants (including Pakistani and Chinese people) who are 'coloured', the Chinese being identified specifically as 'yellow'. Furthermore, the presence of these latter, 'coloured' populations in Britain is considered to be undesirable. 'Our green and pleasant land' has been transformed by the presence of different 'races' and the English/British are facing defeat in some imprecise conflict, as a result of which 'our country' is no longer 'white'.

Thus, we find in this speech the view that the world's population is made up of a number of distinct populations, each biologically distinct from all others. Furthermore, each of the 'races' is attributed with a fixed character which has inevitable consequences: the populations of Chinese and Pakistani origin in Britain are necessarily recreating China and Pakistan within 'our midst', as if neither 'they' nor 'we' can do anything about it. Finally, and as a result, 'their' presence has unacceptable consequences in so far as Britain is no longer 'white' and the British population is thought to be losing a struggle for survival.

If we define racism as a set of beliefs and arguments which allege explicitly not only the existence of different 'races' but also a hierarchy of superiority and inferiority, it follows that Mr Townsend's speech is not an expression of racism. But such a definition fails to comprehend the generality that underlies these specific empirical assertions. The claims about the existence of a hierarchy of inferior and superior 'races' signify biological characteristics as a meaningful measure of human differentiation, attribute permanence and fixity to the characteristics, and predict necessary and undesirable outcomes from the social interaction of the different 'races'.

We can then define racism as any set of claims or arguments which signify some aspect of the physical features of an individual or group as a sign of permanent distinctiveness and which attribute additional, negative, characteristics and/or consequences to the individual's or group's presence. Further, it is implied or argued that the group constitutes a distinct population which is capable of reproducing itself: it is, in other words, a group that contains within itself a structure of gender relations. The central idea here is *permanence* and thereby *inherence*: the individual or group is like it is because 'nature' has made it that way.

Racism and nationalism

Racism is presented as a socially constructed ideology based on ideas of biological determinism and nationalism as a socially constructed ideology based on ideas of cultural determinism.

These ideas of permanence and inherence are also central to the ideology of nationalism which claims that the world's population is divided naturally not into 'races', but 'nations'. It is argued that each 'nation' is unique and exhibits a particular cultural profile, from which it follows that each 'people' should inhabit a territory ('its own country') within which it should ensure cultural homogeneity and govern itself (Smith 1983).

Nationalism, like racism, therefore also entails an exclusion, as is also evident in Mr Townsend's speech which refers to (in relation to the British) 'their own country' and bemoans the disintegration of cultural homogeneity. It follows that 'Chinese' people should 'stay in their own country' where they 'naturally belong'. While others have referred to claims such as the latter as instances of a 'new racism', I prefer to recognise them as instances of nationalism, but a nationalism that articulates closely with the already identified elements of racism (Miles 1987a).

What is intrinsic to both ideologies is a process of *social construction* and categorisation. What matters is not the actual characteristics of the individual or group but rather the attribution of significance to specific real characteristics or to characteristics that are alleged to exist. These may be defined as processes of nationalisation and racialisation (Nairn 1988, p. 281; Miles 1982, 1989; Green and Carter 1988). This argument is central to understanding that, with respect to racialisation, 'races' are not real biological divisions of the human species, classified by reference to skin colour or other somatic characteristics. Rather, when a person or group is defined as 'belonging to another race', this is a social artefact and depends only on acts of perception and ideological construction.

While in contemporary Britain, this process of categorisation and construction signifies skin colour as the main somatic characteristic (well illustrated by Mr Townsend's claims), it should be remembered that, historically, other characteristics have been used or invented to identify Irish and Jewish people as distinct and inferior 'races' in Britain (Curtis 1968; Holmes 1979). We can then talk about different *racisms*, evident in different historical periods and signifying differing characteristics in order to racialise different groups of people (Hall 1980).

Institutional racism

In this section Miles opposes a common definition of institutional racism and proposes an alternative.

So far, I have discussed concepts of racism that all refer to a specific form of ideology. However, some academics and political activists have redefined racism in another way, by extending its meaning to refer to all processes which, intentionally or not, result in the continued exclusion of a subordinate group or protect and advance the advantages of a dominant group. These processes are often defined as *institutional racism*. (Sivanandan 1982) to signal the argument that conscious, individual intentions may not motivate the exclusion. Rather, its origin is identified as a set of often taken-for-granted practices which result in members of a group occupying a subordinate position in society.

The origin of this inflation of the meaning of the concept lies in events in the United States in the 1950s and 1960s when sections of the Afro-American population initiated a new phase of struggle to challenge their subordinate economic and political position. In so doing, they identified themselves as 'black', and racism came to be defined as the actions of 'white' people which had the result, intentionally or otherwise, of sustaining or furthering the subordination of 'black' people (Blauner 1972). For some writers, this was transformed into a universal so that racism is by definition something that 'white' people do to 'black' people (Wellman

1977), with the corollary that 'black' people cannot be racists or practice racism.

In this inflation of its meaning, the concept of racism has come to embody a theory of stratification in which the main or sole structured division in society is presented as being between 'white' people and 'black' people. This argument was taken up in Britain during the 1970s, and has given rise to the concise definition of racism as 'prejudice + power', a definition whose succinctness assists its utilisation as a political slogan. The consequence has been that the primary emphasis has come to focus upon practices and processes, and their consequences, in order to explain 'black disadvantage'. Variants of this argument assert the significance of class and gender divisions within these two categories (Sivanandan 1983, 1985).

The 'problem' of white racism

There are a number of significant difficulties that arise from this conceptual inflation, although what is at issue here is not the evidence of disadvantage (e.g. Brown 1984) but rather its nature and the explanation for it. First, as already noted, certain populations which might be described as 'white' have been the object of beliefs and practices similar to those experienced by 'black' people. For example, the first major immigration legislation passed in the United States in 1924 was intended to prevent 'race deterioration' by stopping the arrival of people from southern and eastern Europe who were considered to have a naturally inferior intellectual ability when compared with people from northern and western Europe (Kamin 1977).

Moreover, the population that was the main (although not the exclusive) object of fascist ideology and genocide in Germany in the 1930s and 1940s were Jews. Although considered to be of a different and inferior 'race', they could often only be distinguished by the yellow stars that they were forced to wear rather than by some 'real' somatic characteristic that could be signified to differentiate them from 'Germans'. Such instances cannot be considered as racism if that concept is defined as the exclusive property of 'white' people, used to subordinate 'black' people.

Second, by defining racism in such a way that it refers to outcomes or effects rather than (or in addition to) an ideology, a simplistic explanation for patterns of disadvantage is offered. Put another way, the theory of stratification implicit in this inflated conception of racism has a number of weaknesses. For example, the 'white/black' polarity ignores or subordinates the range of economic positions occupied by both 'black' and 'white' people.

In Britain today, this may be easily understood with respect to the 'white' population, the majority of whom has little option but to seek to work for a salary or a wage in order to subsist, with a minority having control over either large or small sums of wealth which ensure either that they can employ others or that they can realise a sufficient income from their own labour and the labour of family members. But there is now considerable evidence to demonstrate that people of Caribbean and South Asian origin in Britain can also be found in all these distinct economic positions (Miles

1987b). Significant relative disadvantage remains, but it is relative rather than absolute and so serves as a negation of a theory of stratification based on a single or primary 'black/white' division.

Moreover, it proposes a misleading, monocausal explanation for the patterns of relative disadvantage that do exist. For example, it is clear that people of South Asian and Caribbean origin in Britain are more likely to be unemployed than 'white' people (Anon 1988). But to then conclude that this is to be explained exclusively in terms of racism is to obscure the complexity of determination. There is firm evidence to demonstrate that this is due in part to a willingness on the part of employers to make decisions about employment and unemployment on the basis of racist stereotypes about people of South Asian and Caribbean origin (Jenkins 1986). But there is also evidence to show that these same groups of people are more likely to be employed in sectors of the economy which have been especially vulnerable to restructuring and factory closure (Smith 1981). These latter processes are determined, in turn, by competition between capitalists, each seeking to maximise profitability, an objective that can be achieved by reducing the size of the labour force and increasing the amount of machinery and technology involved in the production process.

> Miles argues that racist ideology may be used to justify 'exclusionary' practices which have their roots in capitalist (class) exploitation.

Conclusion

Because of this, I do not consider it helpful to inflate the concept of racism to refer to processes and practices of exclusion in addition to, or to the exclusion of, ideology. Rather, the concept retains greater explanatory power if a formal distinction is made between racism as ideology, and exclusionary practices which might or might not be motivated by racism or within which racism inheres. This narrower definition allows a multiple explanation for processes of exclusion and patterns of disadvantage, one which takes account of the interplay of and interaction between class formation, gender relations, and racialisation.

Used in this way, the concept of racism is important for understanding the political discourse about political issues such as immigration, 'law and order', and the 'inner city' (all of which are central to the ideological basis upon which the nationstate is reproduced) in contemporary Britain (CCCS 1982; Gilroy 1987; Solomos 1988). It is also highly relevant to understanding the ideological basis upon which exclusionary practices are effected and/or legitimated in Britain, but is not synonymous with them.

Keith Grint: Ethnicity, Class and Occupational Recruitment

Keith Grint provides a useful summary of patterns of occupational recruitment broken down by ethnicity and gender. This exercise is something of an object lesson in the need for careful statistical analysis.

First, the data cited by Grint about black ethnic minorities must be disaggregated. The pattern of recruitment is very different for, say, Indians and Afro-Caribbeans (as well as, of course, for males and females). It has become misleading to 'lump together' black minorities even though, as a group, black people are liable to experience racism in the employment market. Second,

Grint's detailed analysis shows that the figures and percentages presented in the tables can be misleading. The *apparent* rough occupational equality of white males and Indian males disappears on closer anlaysis.

An important question, not answered by the Labour Force Survey on which Grint relies, is the extent to which the occupational position of black minorities has changed over time. In fact, earlier data from the Policy Studies Institute shows an improvement between 1974–1982 (see the second edition of this Reader, pp. 325–40). Another significant absence from this extract is a systematic discussion of the theories that seek to explain racial discrimination in the employment market. An introductory discussion of this kind is provided in my *A New Introduction to Sociology* (1992), pp. 199–203. Reading 53 relates black minority unemployment to international factors.

Reading 26 From Keith Grint, *The Sociology of Work: an Introduction* (Polity Press, 1991), pp. 259–264

Ethnic minorities make up about 4.5 per cent of the British population, and 4.8 per cent of the total labour force (with 43 per cent born in Britain) (*Employment Gazette*, March 1990). Economic activity rates are lower amongst minorities than the white population for those under 24 years old, but higher in terms of self-employment. The greatest level of ethnic differentiation emerges amongst women: the economic activity rate for West Indian or Guyanese women is 73 per cent, for whites it is 69 per cent, for Indians it is 57 per cent and for Pakistani or Bangladeshi women it is 20 per cent. Full-time employment is more prevalent amongst minority than white women (62 per cent minorities to 51 per cent whites), while the white population has a higher proportion in part-time work (26 per cent minorities to 40 per cent whites).

At the broadest level the relationships between gender and ethnic groups are represented in table 10 and figures 8 and 9.

The rather erratic summation of the groups, with several falling under the 100 per cent mark, and the absence of data on Pakistani women because the numbers involved are too small, represents the inadequacy of the existing information we have on such issues. Nevertheless, several aspects of the data are worth commenting on. First, the occupational divisons between white and Indian employees are much smaller than between Indian and other minority groups. This does not mean that Indian employees have achieved equality with the white population but it does reinforce the importance of disaggregating the minorities. Second, the West Indian/ Guyanese and Pakistani/Bangladeshi groups are very similar in occupational structure – with the obvious exclusion of Pakistani/Bangladeshi women. Within these general patterns it is noticeable that the West Indian/Guyanese men have far fewer managers and professionals and, like Pakistani/ Bangladeshi men, have a much greater proportion of 'other manual' workers. It may well be that part of the reason is the problematic categorization involved but it may also be the case that these minority groups do fulfil a disproportionate amount of the 'unskilled' and poorly rewarded jobs.

Table 10 Employment by broad occupation, ethnic origin and gender, spring 1986–8 (%)

Employment	*w/m*	*w/f*	*wi/m*	*wi/f*	*i/m*	*i/f*	*p/m*	*p/f*	*r/m*	*r/f*
Managerial & professional	35	26	15	29	42	23	27	*	40	32
Clerical & related	5	30	*	28	7	30	*	*	7	29
Other non-manual	6	10	*	*	6	9	*	*	8	*
Craft etc	25	4	29	*	19	12	17	*	15	*
General labour	1	0	*	*	*	*	*	*	*	*
Other manual	27	30	40	34	26	24	45	*	28	27

key: *w/m* – white male
w/f – white female
wi/m – West Indian/Guyanese male
wi/f – West Indian/Guyanese female
i/m – Indian male
i/f – Indian female
p/m – Pakistani/Bangladeshi male
p/f – Pakistani/Bangladeshi female
r/m – Rest male
r/f – Rest female
* – Category too small for estimate

Source: Employment Gazette, March 1990

Figure 8 Male occupation and ethnic origin 1986–8 (%)

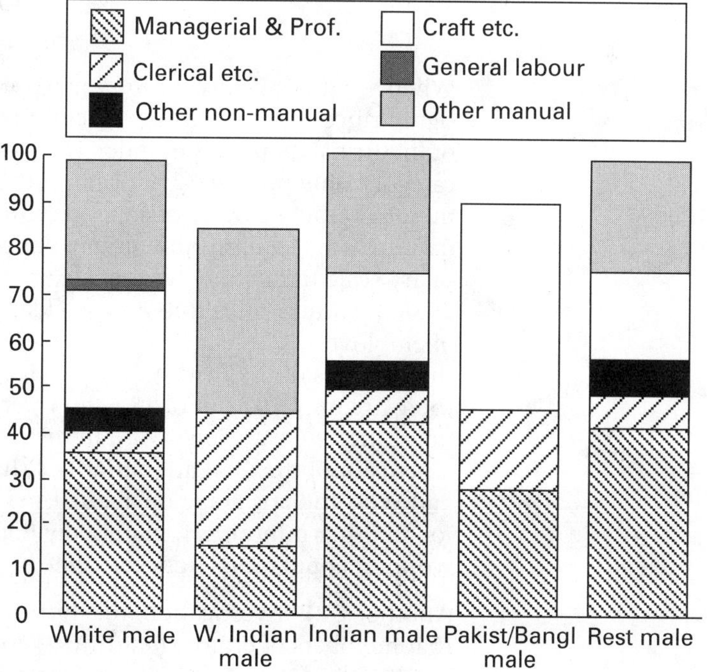

Figure 9 Female occupation and ethnic origin 1986–8 (%)

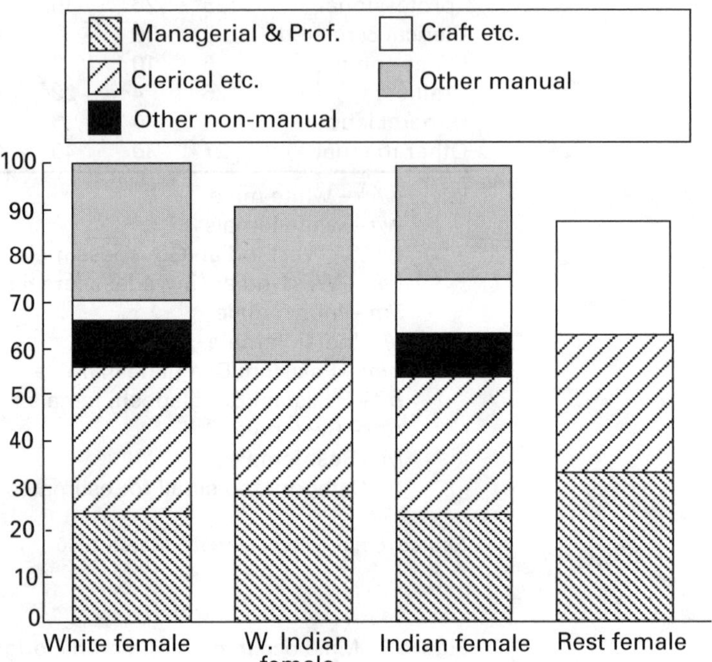

When we delve below the very general occupational categories the significance of ethnic factors is reinforced. For example, although 8 per cent of the British population under 16 is from the ethnic minorities this category only provides 2 per cent of the nation's teachers. Moreover, minority teachers were over-represented in shortage areas, or outside mainstream teaching, and more were employed at the lower end of the salary scale than white teachers (Commission for Racial Equality [CRE], 1988a). Other professions are also likely to reproduce the existing inbalance of employees. There are, for example, no ethnic minorities amongst the top three grades of the British Civil Service, and within the top seven grades there are only 207 out of 18,644 (1 per cent). This is not because ethnic minorities have avoided work in the Civil Service; on the contrary about 4 per cent of the total are minorities (Indians, Pakistanis and Bangladeshis, and West Indians make up about 1 per cent each with a further 1 per cent for all other minorities), marginally higher than the proportion for the total working population (Hencke, 1989).

Another CRE investigation, this time into chartered accountancy, found that members of ethnic minorities were three and a half times less likely to be offered a job than white applicants, and the discriminatory practices occurred at all levels of the screening process (Commission for Racial Equality, 1987). Relatedly, there are a mere 1.9 per cent of probation officers and 0.9 per cent of police officers who are minorities; only 1 per cent of solicitors derive from the minorities and most of these work in the smaller law firms, and there are only two minority circuit judges (Dyer, 1988; National Association of Probation Officers, 1988; Home Affairs Committee, 1989). The situation has caused such embarrassment that the Bar Council, and indeed the Association of Graduate Careers Advisory Services, has called for recruiters to delete requests for photographs from applicants. In sharp contrast, at the receiving end of the law, 14 per cent of prisoners are from the minorities and racism appears to be an intrinsic part of the prison service according to an unpublished study completed for the Home Office in 1986 (BBC, 1988). Even prior to conviction it appears that minorities are twice as likely as whites to be imprisoned yet twice as likely to be acquitted too (*Guardian*, 18 December 1989).

In terms of the general recruitment of non-university graduates it appears that a wide disparity exists between the 70 per cent of white graduates in employment twelve months after graduation compared to less than half the graduates from ethnic minorities (Brennan and McGeevor, 1987). Yet the informality of network recruitment also operates to perpetuate the supply of labour for ethnic businesses, and to ensure that competitors are disadvantaged, as Kim (1981) has demonstrated with regard to Korean businesses in New York, and Light and Bonacich (1988) *vis-à-vis* Korean entrepreneurial success in Los Angeles. Despite the under-representation of minorities in the professional sections of the public sector, it is still here, where recruitment is more often associated with advertising and bureaucratic procedures, that minority workers are generally more likely to receive a greater degree of equality of opportunity; though as the evidence cited above reveals, this may well be a long way short of equality of opportunity. Indeed, since it tends to be those jobs which cannot be filled by word of mouth that end up in the state employment services, and since some of these often tend to be the least attractive jobs, minority workers are provided with fewer and less attractive jobs to choose between. In addition, according to the Manpower Services Commission (MSC), almost half of the Afro-Caribbean people using Jobcentres claimed to have suffered racial discrimination in the search for employment, while almost a quarter of Asian job seekers said the same. The Youth Training Scheme (YTS) has similar overall results: less than 1 per cent of those on YTS schemes were from the minorities in 1987 or 1988, though some companies, such as Dixons, Abbey National and Marks and Spencers were radically more responsive to the needs of minority youths than were most British companies (Sousa, 1988; Hyder, 1989). Similarly, while 69 per cent of all those leaving the YTS found employment, only half of the Afro-Caribbean and Asian youths did so (Manpower Services Commission, 1987). The most recent survey reveals the Stock Exchange, Barclays, Lloyds, IBM and British Airways recruiting well, the major high street retailers, including the Co-op, doing generally badly (*Observer*, 4 March 1990).

It would seem that, under many conditions, it would be rational, that is in their own self-interests, for managers to construct a more formal and less prejudiced approach to recruitment. After all, if discrimination hinders the recruitment of the most qualified and suitable individual for the particular job then it must be against the interests of the company: not just morally but economically too. This is exactly the code of conduct spelled out in numerous Institute of Personnel Management (IPM) (1978) and Confederation of British Industry (CBI) (1970, 1981) reports. In fact, as Jewson and Mason (1986) point out, formality can actually provide the cover for more, rather than less, manipulation of the recruitment procedure. Concomitantly, reducing informal procedures may actually undermine some of the shopfloor patterns of trust between managers and workers. Since there can never be a sufficiently universal rule book to cover all contingencies there clearly is a problem regarding the manipulation or misinterpretation of rules. However, the ordinarily superior record of public employment to private employment regarding ethnic minorities suggests that formality should not be cast aside because of its inevitable problems.

Several studies have demonstrated the disadvantages associated by white employers with ethnic minorities in the recruiting world, but few more vividly than the experiments using fictitious matched pairs of identically qualified white and minority workers. The surveys of Daniel (1968), Jowell and Prescott-Clarke (1970); Smith (1977) and the 1988 BBC documentary series based in Bristol reveal the high levels of racial discrimination that masquerade behind the often liberal facades at work and in the wider community. In some areas, at least until fairly recently, discriminatory policies were much more explicit, bordering on a system not dissimilar to South African apartheid; as a representative of one engineering firm put it, the firm had: 'a policy never to employ a coloured man in a position . . . where in the course of events he would rise to a position where he would give orders to a white man' (Wright, 1968: 75–76). Another method for taking advantage of ethnic differences is that of occupational segregation. This was particularly prevalent in the USA in the early part of this century, when employers both segregated and mixed different ethnic groups with the explicit intention of increasing or decreasing levels of hostility and competition between ethnic groups. The nearest equivalent practice in the UK has been that enacted by employers in Northern Ireland to set Catholics against Protestants (Jenkins, 1988: 316–19). The undermining of any labour solidarity that appeared to be fostering union sympathies appears to have been a primary aim of this divide and rule strategy (Gordon et al., 1982: 141–43). But occupational segregation has more commonly been associated with the sucking in of immigrant labour to replace indigenous workers who refuse to undertake the most arduous and poorly paid jobs. In some circumstances this almost leads to separated labour markets, for example the pre-dominance of minority staff on the London Underground (Rex and Tomlinson, 1979). In other cases it is minority or immigrant workers who undertake specific tasks within enterprises, such as night work and shift work (Smith, 1974). But whatever the division, and however unwilling the white population appears to be to undertake certain jobs, this seldom appears to remove the resistance or discrimination of white workers (Ward, 1978).

In Britain, employers' attitudes towards ethnic minorities even seem to relate to the recognition of trade unions. Recently, union recognition in enterprises where more than 10 per cent of employees are minority shows some degree of decline. Since 1980 even fewer such employers recognize trade unions, irrespective of the general decline in trade union membership and influence. Indeed, ethnic minority workers were employed in substantial numbers in fewer enterprises, primarily because of the collapse of staple industries which employed them and because of the selective shake-out of minority labour mentioned above (Millward and Stevens, 1986: 65–99). Thus, ethnic minorities started out from a position of structured subordination in the labour market.

Mike O'Donnell: New Ethnicities – Without New Tribalism?

Little needs to be added here to the article below. The article focuses on the growing importance of the concept of ethnicity in current sociological theory which, of course, reflects the prominence of ethnic issues around the world.

However, when reading what follows, it may be useful to keep in mind an established model by which the nature of the relationship between a minority and majority population can be gauged. The terms assimilation, pluralism and separatism can be taken as points along a spectrum covering minority/majority relations. Assimilation and separatism are the two ends of the spectrum, the former indicating the total absorption of a minority into a majority and the latter their total separation. Pluralism describes a situation in which groups have distinct identities and existences but share common rights. Arguably, British Afro-Caribbeans tend more to pluralism and British Asians somewhat more to separatism – but no doubt the reader will make her or his own judgement on this matter. Although this model can be used descriptively, different individuals and groups take different views on which is the better way for ethnic groups to relate to each other.

Reading 27 From Mike O'Donnell, *Beyond Black and White: Towards a New Multi-ethnic Perspective*

A new current of opinion has been emerging since the late 1980s among many academic thinkers noted for their opposition to racism. Essentially, it gives greater emphasis to the difference and variety both between and within the ethnic groups which may be the victims of racism. This has implications for the use of the term 'black' as a routine description of both Asians and Afro-Caribbeans. This usage was adopted in the 1960s to promote solidarity against racism among black minorities. The term black is likely to be of continuing usefulness in certain general contexts particularly those concerned with racism and anti-racism but there is an increasing tendency among commentators to stress diversity among minorities and this is requiring the development of an appropriate vocabulary. Stuart Hall has used the term 'new ethnicities' to describe what he sees as this 'new phase', and the term multi-ethnic perspective is also beginning to be used. Those who adopt this approach are generally keen to distance themselves from what they see as the simplicities and naivities of multiculturalism.

Although Hall is sympathetic to the emerging emphasis on what is ethnically distinctive and unique, he stresses the need to avoid the narrowness, jingoism and exclusiveness which not infrequently characterises ethnic ideology. In particular, he is critical of the aspirations to cultural and political dominance of Thatcherism:

> We are beginning to think about how to represent a non-coercive and a more diverse concept of ethnicity, to set against the embattled, hegemonic concept of 'Englishness' which under Thatcherism, stabilises so much of the dominant political and cultural discourses and which because it is hegemonic does not represent itself as an ethnicity at all (257).

In what follows, I will first illustrate aspects of ethnic diversity and then examine the 'hegemonic' concept of 'Englishness' which typifies what used to be referred to as the 'New Right'.

Afro-Caribbean cultural variety

The great linguistic, religious and other cultural variety of Asia is perhaps at least vaguely understood by indigenous Britains, but that of the Caribbean is often scarcely appreciated at all except in so far as it impinges on popular culture. Many of the Caribbean islands reflect a variety of cultural traditions. For instance, St. Lucia changed hands between the British and the French thirteen times and Jamaica has historic connections with Spain as well as Britain. The descendants of indentured labourers from the Indian sub-Continent are prominent in parts of the Caribbean – some of them having interbred with people of African descent. Although the influence of Africa itself is profound throughout the Caribbean, it has not always been accepted uncritically. Indeed, some rivalry occurs between black Africans and Afro-Caribbeans.

The late Ken Pryce's *Endless Pressure* (1979) reflects the variety of Afro-Caribbean culture in Britain. Pryce carried out a participant observational study of the Afro-Caribbean community in Bristol, which is largely of Jamaican origin, in which he focused particularly on life-style. He designated the following terms to describe the six 'lifestyles' crystallized from his data: hustlers, teenyboppers, proletarian respectables, saints, mainliners, and in-betweeners. He further grouped these according to two major 'life-orientations': the 'expressive-disreputable' orientation and the 'stable law-abiding' orientation. These groupings can be presented in diagrammatic form as follows:

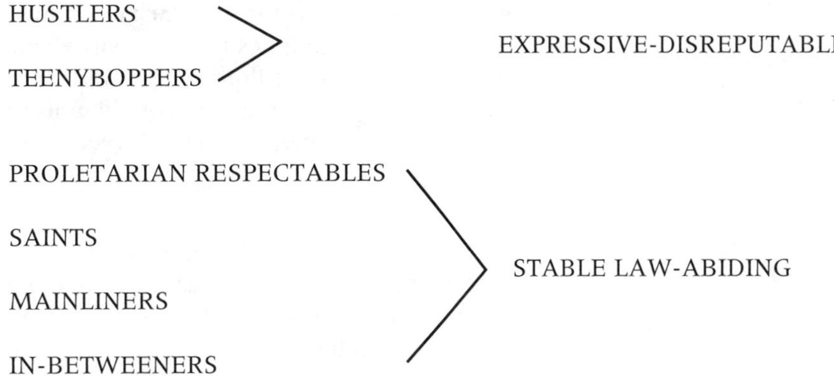

Pryce's terminology is perhaps idiosyncratic and in some respects dated, but it takes us straight into the variety and contrast of Afro-Caribbean life-style in Bristol. 'Hustlers' are male, hate 'slave labour', tend to be socially marginal, and are hedonistically inclined. 'Teenyboppers' are second generation refusers of 'slave labour' and may get involved in delinquency or black consciousness movements such as Rastafarianism. It needs to be added that because of the major recessions of the 1980s and 1990s, young black males were often not even offered low-level work and this further swelled the ranks of the black urban unemployed. In contrast to hustlers, 'proletarian respectables' tend to be in regular employment, or to be seeking it, and to be conventional in their life-style. 'Saints' are Pentecostalists who have made a peaceful orientation to British society. The term 'mainliners' refers to a small minority of white-collar black people of generally liberal or conservative–moderate inclination. 'In-betweeners' are 'young, law-abiding West Indians in the 18 to 35 age-group who would normally be mainliners but who, in keeping with their race-consciousness and Afrocentric outlook, have assimilated into their life-style certain "black culture" or Shanty Town norms which cause them to lead an existence derived from the two opposing orientations' (241).

Pryce's achievement is to describe the complexities, varieties and tensions which occur within the Afro-Carribean community. It is a picture which gives space both to the ultra-conventional 'saints' and ordinary 'respectables' as well as to the more dramatic 'hustlers' so beloved of the popular press. Pryce suggests that his description would be broadly applicable to Afro-Caribbean communities in other urban areas of Britain. Whether acknowledged or not, Pryce's work seems to foreshadow the new multi-ethnic approach.

British Asian Muslims and Salman Rushdie

Tariq Modood's article 'British Asian Muslims and the Rushdie Affair' is one of the most uncompromising among recent statements of the importance of ethnic identity and difference. Whereas Hall may be hampered by his (former?) Marxism in adopting the concept of ethnicity as the basis of his analysis of 'race'/ethnicity, Modood does not hesitate to do so. He chides indigenous Britains for their lack of knowledge about the country's Muslim community and implies that this partly explains the shocked reaction to the ritual burning in Bradford of Salman Rushdie's *Satanic Verses* in 1989. However, his main target is those liberals whose exclusive concerns in the affair he sees as the principles of freedom of expression and Rushdie's life. Modood's own concern is to explain the views and feelings of Britain's Muslim community:

> [T]he Rushdie affair is not about the life of Salman Rushdie nor freedom of expression, let alone Islamic fundamentalism or book-burning or Iranian interference in British affairs. The issue is of the rights of non-European religious and cultural minorities in the context of secular hegemony. Is the Enlightenment big enough to legitimise the existence of pre-Enlightenment religious enthusiasm or can it only exist by suffocating all who fail to be overawed by its intellectual brilliance and vision of Man? (274)

Because of his knowledge of the Asian community, Modood is able to undermine some false impressions and stereotypes of it. He reminds us that whereas the *fatwa* condemning Rushdie to death was issued in Iran, most British Muslims have their roots in Pakistan or Bangladesh. Modood argues that very few are fundamentalist, although most are traditional and conservative from a religious and social point of view. They certainly did not seek to bring about the apparent challenge to the legitimacy of the British state implied in the *fatwa*, though they do aspire to a substantial degree of cultural and religious autonomy. As he sees it, only extreme provocation drew them into the conflict centring upon the *Satanic Verses*. For him, they, rather than Rushdie, are the victims of the affair. While I disagree with Modood on the latter and several other points, his understanding of the British Muslim community provides valuable insight and perspective. Nor is his approach a narrow 'ethnic' one. Although he is critical of liberal intellectuals for their principled arrogance, he also chides many British Muslims for their naivity about racism. They tend to indulge in a 'colour-blind' wishful thinking and ignore the brute reality that racism can be triggered by colour as well as culture. Modood contends that British Asians cannot afford such isolationism and that they should make common cause with other black people in a broad anti-racist movement. It may be added that an anti-racist movement that recognises its own diversity may be more realistic and stronger in the long-run.

Data demonstrating ethnic diversity in a variety of contexts

Data about black people in relation to employment/unemployment, housing and education provides further strong evidence of highly varied and different experience. Reference to Labour Force Survey statistics (1986–88) reprinted by Keith Grint (see Reading 26), illustrates just how varied the situations of ethnic groups are in relation to employment. Variety characterises every occupational category with respect to males, with Indians and whites substantially out-numbering West Indians and Pakistanis/Bangladeshis in the managerial and professional category. The latter two groups, especially West Indian males, are more heavily concentrated in the lower status category of clerical and routine white-collar work.

The employment situation in relation to the females from the different ethnic groups surveyed is much more similar than is that of males. This has prompted Sheila Allen to argue that for females of all ethnic groups, gender rather than 'race' is the key aspect of exploitation (1987). There is substance in this analysis but I would argue the relevance of ethnic factors as well. In particular, the fact that the LFS finds too few Pakistani and Bangladeshi females to provide a base for inclusion in its published figures should not obscure the reality that tens of thousands of them are involved in 'homeworking' or 'outworking' – often in the textile industry – and usually for very low wages. Much of this work is unregistered and officially unrecorded but is done to supplement the usually low wages of their husbands. Whereas both Pakistani/Bangladeshi females and males tend to occupy low status jobs or to be unemployed, the position of West Indian women in the job market seems to be relatively better than that of West Indian males. Among the various factors which may explain this is that West Indian females tend to be somewhat better qualified than their male counterparts.

I will only refer briefly to the well-known range in the housing of ethnic groups. The main difference is that whereas a high proportion of Afro-Caribbeans are in council housing, a large majority of Asians are owner-occupiers. However, if this difference reflects a degree of choice, it is in both cases severely constrained choice. Asians occupy disproportionately older and lower quality private housing and the same is true of Afro-Caribbeans in relation to public housing. Economic and racial disadvantage partly explain these patterns. Despite this, a black bourgeoisie, with members from both these groups, is emerging, enjoying higher quality housing.

The table below indicates a wide variety of educational performance among Britain's ethnic groups. The table compares 'O' level and CSE results in 1985 of children from 11 ethnic groups (and 'Other') in the form of an average performance score for each group. The performance score is computed by giving a certain number of points for each grade from 7 for an 'O' level to 1 for a CSE 5.

It is obvious that there is no relationship between 'colour' and educational performance suggested in the table. Black groups provide the highest and lowest scores, respectively Indians and Bangladeshis. A combination of cultural and class factors probably explain most of the differences in performance between the various groups. Indian pupils are disproportionately likely to come from professional and managerial backgrounds whereas Bangladeshis are typically from rural peasant backgrounds. The former are traditionally committed to trying to achieve academic success and are generally proficient, if not fluent, in English whereas the latter often have fewer relevant cultural resources and only a limited knowledge of English.

Table Average performance of ethnic groups, 'O' level and CSE results, 1985

Ethnic group	*Average performance scores of children*	*Number*
African	16.9	426
African Asian	22.7	162
Arab	14.0	91
Bangladeshi	8.7	333
Caribbean	13.6	2,981
ESWI[1]	15.2	10,685
Greek	17.6	243
Indian	24.5	398
Pakistani	21.3	231
S.E. Asian	19.1	300
Turkish	11.9	268
Other	21.3	940
All	15.6	17,058

[1] English, Scottish, Welsh and Irish

Source: Adapted from F. Kysel, in *Education Research*, 30 (2), June 1988, pp. 83–9

The 'other side' of ethnic identity

While cultural diversity is stimulating and easy to celebrate, ethnic identification can be taken to the point where others are excluded, denigrated and even persecuted. This kind of ethnic chauvinism or nationalism is invariably intertwined with racism (some refer to the whole phenomenon as 'cultural racism'; see Barker, 1981). Nazism is the most extreme form of this phenomenon in recent history. However, the current ethnic tension throughout Europe, particularly the war in former Yugoslavia, seems to illustrate again that people are more likely to repeat history than to learn from it. Perhaps the ugliest term recently to enter the language – 'ethnic cleansing' – does, unfortunately describe what many Serbs and Croats (if not, Muslims) consider they have been doing to each other. Lord Owen has described how in residential areas in which one group strongly predominates, there are occasional gaps where the houses of families of other minority groups used to be. This is the result of so-called 'ethnic cleansing'. This phrase seems almost to legitimise what has been occurring and perhaps it should be replaced by one which is more precise such as 'ethnic slaughter'. The farce behind this tragedy is that the Serbs and Croats are both Slavic peoples who share a common language and whose only major long-standing cultural difference is religion, the former being Orthodox and the latter Catholic.

Does British nationalism run any danger of such excess? The answer to this question will depend on what is meant by 'British nationalism'. There are different degrees of nationalism. Nationalism which tends towards fascism is evidently dangerous and destructive whether this takes the form of formal political activity or of everyday racism. With vigilance, Fascism as a political movement in Britain has been uncomfortably contained but 'street' racism persists as a growing and major problem. Every year in Britain, thousands of racially motivated attacks result in injury and in some cases death to black people. Understandably, many would not wish to stretch the term nationalism to include such behaviour, but those who act in this way frequently do so in the belief that they are asserting their British identity.

Apart from such patently unacceptable and arguably perverted forms of nationalism, what are the effects of the more measured but still robust and even aggressive nationalism adopted quite widely on the British political Right? Mrs Thatcher's famous 'swamping' statement focuses the issue well:

> People are really rather afraid that this country might be rather swamped by people with a different culture . . . the British character has done so much for democracy, for law, and done so much throughout the world, that if there is any fear that it might be swamped people are going to react and be rather hostile to those coming in.
>
> (As quoted in *Daily Mail*, 31 January 1978)

It is highly arguable that such a statement is likely to provoke a sense of rejection and insecurity among black Britains and attitudes of exclusivity and intolerance among white Britains.

Norman Tebbit, a long-standing political ally of Mrs Thatcher, has been typically populist in his expressions of nationalism. He once suggested that it is possible to establish people's patriotism on the basis of what national cricket team they support: his famous 'cricket test'. Tebbit puts the nationality issue into plain language yet is subtly manipulative and divisive in his implied resolution. Apparently, people are 'English' if they support the English cricket team and not English if they support England's opponents. Such a view is radically opposed to more multi-ethnic or pluralist views of Englishness or Britishness presented above.

Tebbit's views may seem reactionary enough yet he is a senior figure in the Conservative party who has had serious aspirations to become Prime Minister. His comments on British nationality and on Britain's relationship to Europe address some of the central issues of our time. Tebbit takes himself deadly seriously and needs to be so regarded. Unlike most political progressives who tend to see Europe as an antidote to narrow nationalism, Tebbit regards Europe, particularly the Maastricht Treaty, as a threat to Britain's sovereignty and independence. At least, he is consistent in his defence of what he sees as 'English', opposing 'dilution' whether it comes from the Caribbean, Asia or Europe.

The intellectual Right and the myth of cultural superiority

Notwithstanding the populist style often adopted by leading members of the Conservative Right, they receive considerable intellectual support. Roger Scruton is one of its major interpreters and apologists. Scruton's article 'The Myth of Cultural Relativism' (1986) addresses both the question 'what is culture?' and 'what is British culture?' He describes culture as follows (with particular reference to education):

(1) Language, including dialect, speech melody, and idiom.
(2) The 'deep' customs and beliefs of religion.
(3) The 'shallow' customs of social intercourse: feasts and ceremonies, manners and courtesies.
(4) Morality, and especially sexual morality.
(5) Popular entertainment, sport and leisure.
(6) 'High' culture, in which aesthetic values are paramount.
(7) 'Political' culture, including a sense of law and justice, and expectations as to the correct way to resolve conflicts.

Scruton then goes on to argue that:

> It cannot be said that Britain is a 'multi-cultural society in all seven respects. There is a common language, a dominant religion, a settled pattern of social expectations, a shared network of entertainment and sport, a common morality and a common law. (127)

The phrase 'dominant religion' is highly indicative of Scruton's attitude to British culture. In his view there is a single dominant culture and although other cultures occur, they do not fulfil the socially unifying role of the dominant culture. For Scruton, the main function of culture is 'to bind people together in a common enterprise' or, put otherwise, to provide a means of 'belonging'. He sees it as particularly the role of education to socialise all Britains into the 'common culture'.

Scruton considers that 'high culture' should play a fundamental role in the curriculum because it embodies 'universal values'. He contends that Britain has a substantial high culture which is linked with other societies possessing a high culture. In quite a lengthy list of societies which he considers possess a high culture, Scruton pointedly fails to mention India, Pakistan, or any sub-Saharan African or Caribbean society. He does not make explicit the basis for this discrimination but presumably these societies fail to meet his criteria for 'high culture'.

However, to debate which culture is or is not 'high' on the assumption that this establishes its fitness for inclusion in a national curriculum is to play Scruton at his own exclusionist game. Judgements on matters of standards and quality are intrinsic to curriculum construction and to teaching and those who make them may aspire to reflect 'universal values'. Nevertheless, such judgements contain an irreducible element of the subjective about them – probably a very large element. Those who wish to impose a rigid and highly prescriptive curriculum are first and foremost imposing their own views. A national curriculum ought to be flexible and responsive enough to speak to the experience and meanings of all children whether their roots go back to Surrey, Barbados, or Surrey, England.

Although Scruton accuses multiculturalists of cultural relativism, he himself seems to be adopting a narrow and exclusive position, whereas they are open to cultural variety. He is saying 'what I approve of is enough' whereas they say 'let us hear what others have to say, too'. It is difficult to avoid the conclusion that under the guise of a concern with quality Scruton seeks to uphold an elitist society and elitist culture – a myth of cultural superiority.

Ironically, many liberal and socialist commentators would agree that there is a dominant culture in Britain and that to some extent it acts as a unifying force. However, such critics stress the profoundly inegaliterian nature of the dominant culture. They see it as characterised by class inequality, sexism, racism and ethnocentrism. Criticism of and opposition to these inequalities provides an alternative basis of cultural identity to the dominant culture. There is no logical reason to regard such criticism as any less 'British' than Scruton's own cultural elitism though 'Britishness' is hardly the main point about it. The working class movement, feminism, anti-racism and ethnic pluralism are all inextricably part of the British 'way of life' and as such ought to be represented in educational and other key 'national' institutions. While Scruton acknowledges that 'internal criticism' of British culture does and should occur (i.e. criticism from *within* British culture itself), he explicity excludes multicultural approaches from the National Curriculum: 'To adopt such a curriculum is to fail to transmit either the common culture of Britain or the high culture that has grown from it' (134).

To return to the question I asked earlier: what are the wider effects of some of the attitudes and ideas on 'race' and ethnicity expressed on the political Right? There are different ways of looking at this matter. On the one hand, it may be that in giving expression to a certain strain of nationalist feeling in Britain, the Conservative Right may have inadvertantly reduced the likelihood of a powerful Fascist or neo-Fascist movement developing within Britain. On the other hand, it is arguable that the Thatcher 'swamping' statement, the Tebbit 'cricket test', and Roger Scruton's cultural theorising give comfort and support to racists and are perceived as offensive, if not threatening, by many black people. It is interesting to speculate what effect a strong and uncompromising anti-racist stand by such people might have on the climate of 'race' relations in this country. It is also important to consider the effect of the nationalist ideology of the Right on Britain's relationship with Europe. The 'little England' attitudes of many of the Conservative Right could yet result in Britain's withdrawal or exclusion from the European Community. The alternative may be continued post-imperial decline and anachronistic self-obsession at a time when wider concerns urgently beckon.

Conclusion

It is clear that the development of ethnic identity can have reactionary as well as liberating effects and it is clear that any new multi-ethnic perspective has the same potential. The 'us' and 'them' tendencies of the political Right are divisive and should be avoided. Likewise there can be no return to the naivities of cruder versions of multiculturalism – 'saris, samosas and steel bands' and not much else. No one can object to anti-racism *per se*, but the anti-racist movement itself was insufficiently sensitive to and realistic about the implications of ethnic difference. The new approach to ethnicity has not yet fully developed its ideological trappings or strategy. It is likely to be anti-racist, deeply opposed to aspirations to cultural hegemony, and more sophisticated and informed in its tolerance and appreciation of cultural diversity than either the multicultural or anti-racist movements were.

References

Allen, S., 'Gender race and class in the 1980s' in C. Husband *ed., Race in Britain* (Hutchinson, 1987).

Barker, M., *The New Racism: Conservatives and the Ideology of the Tribe* (Junction, 1981).

Hall, S., 'New Ethnicities' in J. Donald, and A. Rattansi, *eds., Race, Culture and Difference* (Sage Publications, 1992).

Modood, T., 'British Asian Muslims and the Rushdie Affair' in J. Donald and A. Rattansi, *eds., Race, Culture and Difference* (Sage Publications, 1992).

O'Donnell, M., *Race and Ethnicity* (Longman, 1992).

Pryce, K., *Endless Pressure* (Penguin, 1979; also published by Bristol Classical Press, 1986).

Scruton, R., 'The Myth of Cultural Relativism' in F. Palmer *ed., Anti-Racism – an Assault on Education and Value* (Sherwood Press, 1986).

28 *David Marsh: The Spectre of Growing Racism in Western Europe*

Europe has been variously described as a 'protected zone' or 'fat city' fringed by areas of political instability, over-population, or material need. In more neutral terms, Western Europe is a stable and wealthy area of the world which acts as a magnet to some of the less fortunate.

The number of actual and would-be immigrants into Western Europe has increased in recent years for a variety of short and longer term reasons (see Reading 23). Ethnic upheaval in the former Soviet Union and what was Yugoslavia has sharply increased the numbers seeking political asylum, particularly in Germany. In the long term, the massive population increase in the North African countries compared to near nil population increase in Western Europe creates a built-in pressure. The population of the five main southern Mediterranean countries – Egypt, Algeria, Morocco, Tunisia and Turkey – used to stand at a ratio of 1 to 3 against Western Europe and is now almost 2 to 3.

Increasing demand for immigration has coincided with economic recession in Western Europe and with the disruption and readjustment caused by the re-unification of Germany (which accepts far more immigrants than any other Western European country). Taken together, these circumstances have provided fertile soil for the re-emergence of substantial racist movements in Western Europe, some of them with distinctly Fascist characteristics. David Marsh gives some examples of the 'new' racism and describes something of its wider context.

How far is fear of a 'flood' of immigrants well founded? Academic opinion is divided but much of it is cautious. Dr David Coleman suggests that 'Continued large scale immigration would lead to a fragmentation of our societies, as more and more aspirations and careers centre on sub-groups . . . while a mixed underclass of both immigrant and local origin would grow' (as quoted in the *Guardian*, 16.10.91, p. 8). On the other hand, those seeking asylum may decrease if and when Eastern Europe settles, and when Western Europe returns to economic expansion, the absorption of immigrants will be easier and the excuses for making them scape-goats less. However, these issues will not easily be resolved. Journalist Martin Woollacott perhaps strikes a more humane note than Coleman, in the conclusion to his excellent article, 'Race and Rationality within the Fat City's Gates': 'As immigration policies become politically more central (i.e. determined by the European Community), the balance between preventing undesirable levels of immigration, and maintaining some generosity and rationality, above all in dealing with emigrants from regions of risk, is likely to become increasingly difficult' (*Guardian*, 16.10.91, p. 8).

Reading 28 From David Marsh, 'Keep Out This is Western Europe' *Financial Times*, Section II, 9/10 May 1992

Along the Austrian-Hungarian border, winding through the fertile Burgenland region south of Vienna, the gaunt steel watchtowers on the eastern side are deserted, relics of the Cold War. On Austrian soil, new look-out platforms have sprung up, manned by army conscripts in sheepskin coats. They are watching not for the march of communism but for travellers from Turkey, Romania, Sri Lanka or Bangladesh seeking illegal entry. The Iron Curtain has been dismantled. But as the west attracts a growing stream of fugitives from troubled parts of the world, immigration has become the focus of Europe's fears.

In the gentle hills of the Burgenland, an immigrant's first encounter is often with a man in uniform. "They can cause disquiet among the population," says Gerhard Wild, a burly official at police headquarters in Eisenstadt, the main town in the region. Some steal local bicycles, he says. "Most are economic refugees," adds Karl Barilich, a young Austrian gendarme on patrol in his van. Captured border-crossers are taken to an impromptu reception centre in bleak rooms at a disused sugar refinery. They are questions, photographed and given medical checks. After a few hours, those without a *prima facie* case for political asylum are sent back to Hungary. "Normally, they are exhausted – they just want to sleep," says Barilich. Before going, they can take their pick from second-hand clothes donated by local residents.

Arguably, a good test of people's deeper attitudes to the Third World is their response to would-be immigrants at Europe's 'gate' rather than how they feel about media images of hunger in some safely distant land.

The fugitives are disaffected survivors of the revolutions and disruption which have swept through eastern Europe and the Third World. Instead of succour, they meet bile. Immigrants put pressure on jobs, housing and social security. The prosperous half of the continent is experiencing economic slowdown and a sharp swing to xenophobic far right-wing parties – seen in elections in France, Germany and Italy during the past few weeks. In the ugliest of ironies, the newcomers find themselves blamed for political turmoil in places they regarded as the promised land.

From all sides they come; and, on all sides, they are unwanted. Spain's *Guardia Civil* stands ready to repel immigrants from north Africa. The French *gendarmerie* are on patrol in Marseilles, while German border guards scan the wetlands of the river Oder for illicit arrivals from Poland. Most fugitives seek political asylum – even though their chances of acceptance are small. In western Europe 540,000 asylum-seekers were registered in 1991 – nearly twice the 1989 figure and more than three times 1987's. Germany alone

In Britain the numbers seeking asylum also sharply increased in 1991 to just under 50,000.

attracted a record 256,000 asylum-seekers last year. Total immigration into western Europe topped 1m (including 220,000 ethnic Germans from eastern Europe and the former Soviet Union who went to Germany and get automatic citizenship rights there). The flows have crossed to Britain too. The Home Office recorded 44,000 asylum applications in 1991. A lorryload of illegal Indian immigrants hit the headlines in March after being apprehended by police on a motorway.

Austria is the traditional gateway between east and west. But on the border, hopes of a new life can turn sour quickly. Last year, the Austrian police and army caught 12,000 illegal immigrants from Asia, Africa and eastern Europe. Many are taken to Hungary by unscrupulous international couriers and unloaded from buses and vans within walking distance of Austrian territory. Then, they are on their own.

In Austria, as across the whole of Europe, the strains are coming to the surface. Last year, 27,000 people applied for asylum – more per capita than in Germany. An additional 13,000 fugitives from the civil war in Yugoslavia – most from Croatia – were given temporary refuge in Austrian homes, hostels and church buildings. Anti-foreigner sentiment helped Austria's nationalistic Freedom Party to a sharp surge in council elections last November. Jörg Haider, the party's demagogic leader, used the slogan "Vienna for the Viennese," in his November campaign.

General elections in Switzerland and Belgium last year produced a marked far-right shift. Jean-Marie Le Pen's *Front National* (FN) in France attained 13.9 per cent of the vote in regional elections in France in March. And in Germany on April 5, the ultra-right German People's Union and Republicans parties swept into state parliaments in Schleswig-Holstein in the north and Baden-Württemberg in the south. Christian Käs, the Republicans' leader in Baden-Württemberg, accuses the country's established politicans of showering largesse on asylum-seekers while plunging east Germans into poverty.

Ballot-box support for such parties parallels an increase in racially-motivated violence. Even peaceful Sweden has seen an increase in apparently motiveless attacks on foreigners.

In Germany, where racial attacks have become almost routine since the autumn, the number of immigrants camping out in Munich has prompted fears that the city's traditional autumn beer festival could be cancelled. An Interior Ministry official in Bonn says: "The asylum problem, linked to worries about law and order, is the number one question. It's only a matter of time before this blows up."

Tension is certainly in the air at a sprawling camp for displaced foreigners in the town of Traiskirchen, near Vienna. Since 1956, the former Austrian military academy has been a transit centre. Around 300 asylum-seekers live there. They stay for a few days to complete formalities before being allotted more permanent quarters in guesthouses and hostels around the country.

Under recently-toughened laws, asylum-seekers who arrive in Austria from "safe" countries can be expelled summarily. Some immigrants throw away their identification papers to hinder the authorities. Faced with such awkward charges, the camp staff are not overly sympathetic. "The niggers are this way," said a young administrator, bustling through the building towards a group of Sudanese men cutting each other's hair in the corridor. In an attempt at heavy irony, directed at the administrator, one man grins: "The Austrians are not racists. Oh no, they are not Nazis."

The atmosphere 600 miles away, in the south of France, is only a little less chilly. Fréjus, an undistinguished, sun-specked town of 40,000 between Nice and Toulon on the Riviera, is home to 4,000 foreigners, most from North Africa. Some are new arrivals but most have lived there for years, normally in relative harmony with the locals.

In January, however, police swooped on a shanty town near the railway station housing immigrant workers. They arrested 12 people on arms or drugs charges and 18 for holding invalid identity documents. Municipal employees then pulled down some of the shacks. The *Front National* claimed the ramshackle village was not only a centre for drugs dealing but also an illegal source of cheap labour for construction companies, undercutting normal pay rates.

On the outskirts of the town is the Agachon housing estate which the local FN labels a "ghetto." It is, a fairly basic, low-rise housing complex, renovated and whitewashed in the best Mediterranean style. Many second-generation immigrants living here have parents who came to France from the Magreb during the 1960's boom. Marcel, a young mixed-race resident, tells me that one of his parents came from Africa but he has French nationality. He praises behaviour on the housing estate compared with others in the town.

Fifty miles westwards, in the port of Toulon, Jean-Marie Le Chevallier, a bespectacled European parliament deputy for the FN, who propelled the party to 29 per cent of the vote in the town in the March elections, tells a different story. Over lunch in his dusty house, he holds forth on the Front's repatriation policies. What, I inquire, would he do with Marcel? "Ask him: 'Does he love France?'" replies Le Chevallier, between mouthfuls of lamb and red wine. The implication is that, if Marcel does not, he would be deported. Le Chevallier adds: "It is less costly to spend billions to return them to Algeria and Tunisia than to have a civil war."

He claims that immigrants in France were, simultaneously, taking jobs away from the French and sponging on social security. "You earn more for doing nothing here than by working in a developing country."

As the chief destination of European immigration, Germany is at the eye of the storm. The town of Unna-Massen, an hour's drive from Düsseldorf in the prosperous state of North Rhine-Westphalia, is host to one of the country's best known refugee transit centres. Opened in 1951 for German refugees expelled from Poland, last year it was temporary home to 60,000 ethnic German from the former Soviet Union and eastern Europe.

Jügen Kraska, the camp's deputy head, thinks numbers will increase this year because of "uncertainties" in the Soviet republics. He said that more Soviet Jews – given special status in Germany – are turning up at the camp, reporting anti-Semitic attacks around Moscow and St Petersburg.

Among the roughly 2,500 inmates is Erika Ems, a wizened lady from Kazakhstan. She is glad to be here. "It is like the difference between day and night," she croaks. Peter Potempa, an engineer who says he left Poland because "nothing has changed" after the end of communism, is looking forward to getting a job in Germany. Potempa, however, speaks only Polish – and, in western Germany, jobs are growing scarcer.

To cope with growing public irritation about unkempt refugees clogging Düsseldorf, the North Rhine-Westphalian government is trying revolutionary methods to try to stem the exodus from south-east Europe. It has allocated around DM20m (£6.80m) for a programme of house-building and job creation in the Macedonian town of Skopje, and repatriated itinerant Macedonians who were camped in tents on Düsseldorf's Rhine banks. Albert Harms, the enterprising government official who negotiated the arrangement, says the deal could save money by pruning state government spending on social security for asylum-seekers.

See my qualification to this comment in the introduction to this reading.

Schemes like this offer a constructive way of easing migration pressures. In general, however, governments throughout Europe are tired of putting up funds, and are talking of putting up barriers instead. As the havens grow less secure and more unwelcoming, the tide of those seeking to come ashore shows no sign of ebbing.

AGE AND GENERATION

Introduction: Readings 29–31

The opening reading in this section is an introduction to the concept of 'life course' and an overview of it from a social constructionist perspective.

John Williams' piece on young working-class males and football hooliganism is on a very specific topic, but it also illustrates some established aspects of the analysis of youth. First, the class context of youth is now widely accepted as an essential dimension of analysis (although some recent commentators argue that this has diminished in certain aspects since about the mid-1980s). Second, the gender dimension of youth – in this case, male – is universally accepted as important. Third, cultural analysis, of the kind adopted by Williams, has become the main tool for opening the 'meanings' of youth sub-cultural rituals and styles.

The final piece in this section is about the elderly. I have selected it because it covers a wide range of key issues and concepts in relation to old age. In particular, it avoids the traps of presenting the old either as fraught with problems or as enjoying relatively untroubled the freedom and opportunities of retirement. David Field sketches a more complex but more convincing reality.

Gaynor Cohen: The Concept of Life Course – Applied to Family, Generation and Society

I have long felt that the concept of life cycle or life course, as it is now more precisely termed, is both under-defined and under-used in British sociology. What is needed is a flexible concept of age stages influenced by biology and psychology and structured by social context. Gaynor Cohen states that the concept of life course 'allows of . . . flexible biographical patterns within a continually changing social system.' Thus, a person's experience of an age stage varies both in terms of her or his individuality and in terms of the way that age stage is socially structured.

Cohen briefly demonstrates how age stages are socially constructed in contemporary society by reference to the work of a variety of authors (most of whom are contributors to the book from which this extract is taken and which she edits). Class and gender emerge as factors which substantially affect the life course (to which ethnicity can also be added). Cohen also interestingly explores the concept of generation, particularly with respect to cross-generational relationships.

Reading 29 From Gaynor Cohen *ed.*, 'Editor's Introduction' to *Social Change and the Life Course* (Tavistock Publications, 1987), pp. 1–2, 3–8

This book attempts to explore the nature of recent changes in the life course in contemporary British society. The term 'life course' is used here rather than the more familiar 'life cycle', as the latter implies fixed categories in the life of the individual and assumes a stable social system, whereas the former allows of more flexible biographical patterns within a continually changing social system. There is an extensive literature on the use of these and similar terms emanating particularly from the USA (see for example Riley, Foner, and Johnson 1972; Elder 1978). With a few outstanding exceptions, British social scientists have only recently shown interest in a life course approach to social change.

Between them, the contributors to this volume relate biographical and subjective perceptual processes to broader structural changes in the society. In particular, they explore the dynamic relations between the individual and other members of the family and the household, and the relation between the household and the changing economy within the wider society . . .

The social construction of the life course

The life course is like a bus journey punctuated by stages, with boarding and embarkation points. Authors in this book stress that these stages are not fixed, have changed in length in response to wider social change, and that new stages have emerged. The boarding and embarkation points for childhood, youth, and mid life have either lengthened or shortened over time and vary according to region or culture.

Childhood, as Busfield reminds us, is an historical novelty. Our notion of childhood has been shaped by changes in the socio-economic and political structure. Busfield traces the implication of these changes in shifting research attention from fertility, to child-rearing patterns, to the more recent emphasis on parenting. The latter again reinforces the link between the economy, career timetables, and the different parenting experiences of mothers and fathers respectively.

The extent and experience of youth, that period of metamorphosis from childhood to adulthood, has also varied both regionally and historically. In rural Wales in 1940 the youth group, collectively referred to by Alwyn Rees (1950) as *'y bechgyn'* (the boys), ranged in age from sixteen to thirty-five. Marriage brought association with the group to an end; confirmed bachelors gradually left the group as they approached middle age.

The boundaries and conceptualization of youth, as Coffield shows, have fluctuated markedly even in recent times. The imagery associated with the affluent creativity of youth in 1960 contrasts starkly with that used to describe the demoralized young unemployed of the 1980s. Coffield argues that changes in the economy are the source of these fluctuations, although not all youth will be equally affected. He notes the potential gulf between a generation of unskilled working-class young people who risk remaining unemployed and unemployable throughout their lives and younger members of their family with better training to secure new jobs generated by the economy. Unemployment in the north-east is extending the period of youth and dependency, as without a job young men and women have to remain living at home with their parents.

Adulthood is often depicted as a single stage in life's journey, undifferentiated by further boarding or embarkation points. This stage,

The psychologist, Erickson, accomodates the length of adulthood, by referring to early and middle adulthood.

which occupies the longest time span in the life course, is popularly perceived as a plateau between growing up and growing old. It does in fact incorporate numerous substages such as leaving home, getting married, setting up house, moving home, becoming a parent, parenting, maintaining a household or career. Further differentiation has been introduced by divorce, remarriage, cohabitation, and changes in the labour market structure, such as redundancy and early retirement.

From the popular literature and mass media Hepworth identifies the recent growth of yet another stage: mid life. His argument is that shifts in the timing of life phases may well be accompanied by changes in commonly held perceptions of individual capacities and abilities associated with that phase. Parents of today are likely to experience the 'empty nest' stage at a much earlier point in the life course than previous generations. They will both look and be perceived as younger than the preceding generation and because of the extension of life they will have more of their life course to live through. Assumptions of growth, development, and creativity have been associated with the early stages of the life course. Mid and late stages have been seen as heralding decline, decay and dependence. Hepworth argues that a growing emphasis on self-development and individual growth accompanying an extension of the retirement period has shifted traditional attitudes to ageing and has generated a new mid-life phase associated with creativity and growth. The extent to which the capacity for individual development can actually be realized, however, is likely to be limited by the personal and material resources which individuals have acquired over the life course.

The availability of these resources is largely related to class.

Discussions of mid life and retirement offer clear indicators of the potential quality of life in the post-retirement period. These indicators have their roots in labour market careers. Jobs offer resources (both financial and personal) and the potential for individual development which will continue to influence individual life courses beyond the career stage itself. Similarly, as Phillipson has pointed out, tensions in the immediate pre-retirement period, such as those created by recent economic upheavals like unemployment or redundancy, may well have an adverse effect on the experience of retirement itself.

Reading 31 in this volume, by David Field, takes a balanced view on this matter – the quality of life for the old can vary greatly.

Although this book does not examine old age through the eyes of the elderly themselves, recent studies are stressing the need to shift from a perception of old people that emphasizes their frailty and dependence to one which recognizes the continued capacity for individual growth and development throughout life (Wenger 1984). Certainly the old people who speak through the pages of Blythe's (1979) account of the *View in Winter* give every indication of continued activity.

Any change in one stage of the life course has implications for subsequent stages. The emerging imagery of mid life as a period of growth and development is affecting popular perceptions of post-retirement and even of old age. Personal problems and experiences too can be fully understood only with reference to the preceding life course stage. Phillipson argues that the experience of retirement needs to be analysed as part of the life course and as a sequence of interrelated stages rather than as a single stage. The quality of life in retirement will reflect continuities with working life: the level of income, or the degree of personal development. It will also reflect the quality of conjugal relationships developed earlier in life. A crisis such as redundancy or enforced early retirement experienced in the pre-retirement phase may well have a debilitating impact upon retirement itself.

The impact of extreme material inequalities influences experience throughout the life course. Burgoyne points to the contrasting life course experiences of the very rich and the very poor, while Coffield's sample is made up of young unqualified unemployed. Although it is beyond the scope of this book to trace the impact of disadvantage through the life course other studies offer evidence that extreme deprivation and discord experienced in early home life can retard later educational and social development (Rutter and Madge 1976).

It would be misleading to see each change in life experience as automatically determined by changes in preceding life course states. The process of change is dynamic and, especially within the family, may be affected by the relationship between generations. This relationship need not be one of conflict. The emphasis on conflict in much of the social science literature masks the significance of the two-way learning process. Parents may respond differently to each of their children because of the reaction and behaviour of the children themselves (Riley *et al.* 1969).

Different types of exchanges take place between generations of the same family. Because of the extension of life children are no longer likely to inherit wealth at the time when they most need it. Grandchildren are now more likely to benefit from money inherited from grandparents.

The notion of reciprocity between different generations of family members, however, goes beyond exchanges of goods or even services and is based on deep-rooted gender-related norms and values. Otherwise why should the predominantly female carers in Ungerson's survey given the increased availability of labour market jobs for women, voluntarily undertake the burden of caring for the dependent elderly? Leonard's study (1980: 9) of marriage in a South Wales town, suggested that notions of obligation and reciprocal exchanges were sown early in life. Mothers 'spoiled' their adolescent daughters because they were 'anticipating some return on parental investment by giving care or companionship in parents' old age'. Their attitudes reflect those of the Gonja people who see care of children as an investment in care by children in parents' old age: 'in infancy your mother and father fed you and cleared up your messes; when they grow old you must feed them and keep them clean' (Goody 1983: 13). It is a notion which some might perceive as more appropriate for a simple agrarian than a complex industrial economy with its demands for rationality in employment practices.

Ungerson reminds us that this view of a reciprocal exchange is more unequal than ever before. The extension of life means that services to the elderly may stretch out over a very much longer period than services to children. Moreover it is women who almost always care for older dependent relatives. The four male carers in her sample were all caring for spouses. Another significant gender difference was that, for women, caring was often an alternative to paid employment while the men carers had not interrupted their employment by caring activities. Wenger's survey (1984) of old people in north Wales found that primary care still came from the family and reflected mutual expectations although changes in the life course had meant that the children of the dependent elderly might themselves have been retired and in need of support and thus unable to provide consistent care for the over-seventy-fives.

At the same time other changes currently taking place in the life course may well extend the potential pool of carers. Recent evidence from the USA indicates that the increase in the divorce rate has encouraged greater involvement between grandparents and their grandchildren. Contact between grandparents and children whose parents are divorced is greater than with children still living with both parents. Children are often cared for by grandparents immediately following their parents' divorce. In some cases US courts have awarded custody of the children to grandparents even when neither natural parent is claimed to be unfit to care for the child. Certainly other factors such as the age of the grandparents are likely to influence the degree of contact between generations, with younger grandparents being more involved than older ones (Aldous 1985). Further research may indicate whether increasing involvement as a result of parents' divorce is likely to encourage an increase in the number of grandparents being cared for by their grandchildren at a later stage in the life course.

The dynamics of family continuities and economic change

Thus grandparents are acting as a countervailing force against the disruptive effects of divorce upon children. Indeed at every point the processes of change are resisted by basic family relations and values and their impact is thereby modified. This is why the notion of the family is so often used, particularly by politicians, to represent a support for and a haven from the destructive forces of change.

This assertion is made even in the face of such contradictory evidence as rising divorce rates and the disappearance of the stigma of illegitimate birth. There are now different family forms and the model of 'two parents – two children' can no longer be claimed to be the norm. But whatever the form, the family continues to have real as well as symbolic significance. It remains as a stubborn, complex, biological, psychological, economic, and cultural entity that exists in its own right and intervenes in the process of social change in a powerful way.

It is through the family that we gain an identity and continuity with the past: a name, physical characteristics, a 'place' in the community, and a reference point against which we are measured or can measure others. There are 'good' families offering support and comfort and 'bad' families where the weak, who are usually female and conditioned to be unaggressive (Heidensohn 1985) may be abused by the strong. Whatever its quality, the total family complex will influence the choices and experiences of its members throughout the life course.

This is a major issue which Cohen goes on to discuss in detail. It is fully dealt with in this book by Heather Joshi (Reading 19).

Individual members of the same family may have very different life course experiences. Most chapters stress the impact of gender differences upon: young people struggling for independence; parenting; personal development; and caring for elderly dependants. Women are still constrained by their commitment to their families and are therefore prevented from achieving equality with men in the labour market.

Nevertheless, as Nissel points out, the changing status of women is possibly *the* major change in our society. Evidence of the rise in women's economic activity rates (Martin and Roberts 1984) shows that the period of women's confinement to the private world of the family is now over.

John Williams: Young Working-Class Males and Football Hooliganism

This extract could have been entitled 'continuity and change in football hooliganism'. In his historical overview of mainly English football hooliganism, Williams attempts to bring out both these aspects. The continuity lies largely in the cultural values of toughness and territoriality that Williams associated with the working class. The 'lads' carry these values on to the terraces but sometimes overstate them in violent, dramatic and often clever behaviour. The change lies in the different and ingenious ways successive generations of hooligans express their sentiments and impulses. Williams takes us through from 'the Skins to the Casuals' arguing that there is a fundamental continuity despite the enormous changes in style.

In the final section of this extract, William deals with a main criticism of his thesis (which is also associated with his colleagues at the Leicester University Centre for Football Research) that football hooliganism is less and less a phenomenon of working-class youth – as, so his critics say, the involvement of the smart and expensively dressed Casuals shows. Williams makes some concessions to this view but returns to his basic interpretation of football hooliganism. In a section not reprinted here, he deals similarly with a point raised by Clarke, that the Leicester Centre fails to analyse the majority of football supporters who are not hooligans. He argues that the actions of the hooligans greatly affect other supporters but that, in any case, the latter are the focus of substantial research at the Centre.

Reading 30 From John Williams, 'Having an away day: English football spectators and the hooligan debate' in John Williams and Stephen Wagg *ed.s, British Football and Social Change: Getting into Europe* (Leicester U.P., a division of Pinter Publishers; 1991) pp. 160–61, 163, 165–67, 169–70, 173, 176–77

You've got to fight, for the right to party

(Beastie Boys)

The party's in Europe

(Cas Pennant, West Ham Supporter)

Introduction

This paper is about English football spectators but, more specifically, it is about hooliganism. For a lot of non-football fans – and even for many who do support the game – hooliganism has become dangerously close to being the national sport's key defining characteristic for the past 25 years. Dalglish may resign, Gazza may even move to Italy, but those in search of 'a row' at football – 'the lads', 'the crews', 'the mobs', 'the top boys' – seem to be a constant fixture 'down at the match'. Their influence has been widespread. In 1989, for example, a number of 'quality' national newspapers in Britain, including the liberal *Guardian*, asked their foreign correspondents to report on how the continent regarded the English after ten years under the Thatcher administration. Were we still the stiff-upper lipped conservative stoics, the doyens of 'fair play' of years gone by? or had the new regime transformed us, in the eyes of our trading partners and competitors, into thrusting and business hungry free marketeers? Neither seemed to be the case. Instead, our near neighbours and fellow Europeans increasingly seemed to associate the English with young hordes of beer-drinking, threatening, thieving, sometimes violent and frequently abusive invaders. In short, a collection of *disruptive* travelling football fans – a serious 'crew', out on continental manoeuvres. Not just the dirty men, but the violent men of Europe, too. They (the continentals) also increasingly blamed the English, a little unfairly, for their own growing hooligan problems, though there seemed little doubt that many young 'city boys' on the continent were getting the message: 'Englishness means trouble'. From Gothenburg to Ghent there sprang up Union Jacks, English football songs and English names for emergent 'hooligan' gangs.

The 'golden years'

There is a considerable amount of evidence that gang violence and hooliganism was quite common in the period before the First World War. A more orderly period followed – in England.

If the early years of the game were notable for their gambling, drinking and the sometimes threatening and violent behaviour of local 'roughs', the inter-war years at football seem, by comparison, to have been considerably more orderly. I have no space here to examine in any detail the peaks and troughs in the history of crowd disorderliness at football matches (see Dunning, Murphy and Williams, 1988, for some discussion on this issue). It seems fairly clear, however, that out of the fairly routine but in the main, by modern standards, relatively small-scale disturbances of the pre-First World War period the game in England – and its audience – gradually, between the wars, became more 'respectable' and less tolerant and expectant of spectator violence. (The situation in Scotland seems much less clear cut. Here, sectarian rivalries, particularly those associated with the major Glasgow clubs, helped to provide greater impetus for the continuation of the violent traditions around the game; see Murray, 1984). In the immediate aftermath of the Second World War, arguably at a time of considerable national consensus of a kind seldom seen before or since (Davies, 1984) and prior to the onset of the increasing privatisation of leisure brought by rising wages and the arrival of television, vast crowds – the largest in the game's history – watched League football matches . . .

Whatever the reasons, 'crowd control' at football for the decade after the war seems to have been largely a case of dealing with the occasional pub fight, or with individual offenders whose inclinations to fight may have had no football-related basis at all (see Holt, 1989: p. 334), or, finally, of dealing with the sorts of problems which were occasionally produced simply by the sheer size of football crowds.

Bad boys, bad boys

The picture of large, and largely orderly, football crowds began slowly to change in England from around the mid-1950s onwards. As some older fans drifted away and amidst a more generalised panic about rising rates of juvenile delinquency and the increasing public and publicised misbehaviour of 'troublesome youth' (Muncie, 1984), young football fans, initially those from the north west, began to attract publicity for their train-wrecking exploits. Football trains, it should be said, had also been attacked and damaged in the 1930s (see Dunning, Murphy and Williams, 1988: p. 109). However, that was a period in which localised teenage youth styles were regularly criticised for their attempts at imitating adult behaviour. In the 1950s, it was the spread of national youth styles, the greater cultural, stylistic and financial independence of working-class youths, and the national media coverage their sometimes disorderly activities drew which especially troubled older genrations and the 'respectable' classes. And, as Hobbs and Robins (1990, p. 17) point out, style travels through the media. The 'unmanageability of youth' became a constant, national media focus in the years which followed, shifting only as, within the changing political, economic and racial contours of British society, youth styles themselves evolved and changed.

> Examples of these new 'youth styles' were 'the Teds' and 'Mods and Rockers'.

Robins and Cohen (1978) argue that the 'youth ends' in north London emerged during the 1966–67 League season. It is perhaps significant, however, that it was on Merseyside in the early 1960s – then a focal point for the rising new British pop cultures – that the first publicised signs in the modern period of the activities of disorderly groups of young supporters were apparent (see Dunning, Williams and Murphy, 1988: pp. 142–45). It was probably in Liverpool, too, that segregation by age at the goal-end terraces received its strongest impetus, drawing as it did upon segregative new pricing policies for 'troublesome' young supporters, but more especially on the introduction by fans of a repertoire of new pop-rooted football songs and chants. Penetrations of the football world by aspects of what was, by 1964, a rapidly expanding teenage leisure industry, had the effect of exacerbating territorial divisions, by age, inside grounds. The new forms of terrace patois – songs, clothes, gestures – were increasingly devised largely by, and for, young fanatics and they were spread by television. Gerry and the Pacemakers' version of 'You'll never walk alone' became the Liverpool FC anthem. Soon, few young goal-end regulars were in danger of 'walking alone', but they did have to be sure of walking – or running – with their 'own kind'. The battle lines were already being laid down for the national struggles over 'who rules' at football; struggles which were to become a near permanent fixture of the sport in England for the next twenty-five years.

This is perhaps the key interpretive paragraph in this extract. It locates post-war hooliganism within the context of working-class communal masculinity.

Sustained by the self-confidence and greater autonomy provided by the new youth cultures and buoyed by the nationalistic excess inspired by the England World Cup success of 1966, 'the lads' began to establish the Saturday afternoon rituals which quickly attracted aspiring 'hard cases' from the housing estates and city neighbourhoods. In the London area, the new recruits were also drawn in from the working-class communities which had been displaced to the suburbs, but the patterns of recruitment were different in different areas, depending upon local traditions and local ecologies. By no means all the young men who joined the ends did so to fight. As Willis points out, the fundamental issue for most young working-class men in urban areas and locations whee violence is an everyday possibility is not some 'cultural obligation' to fight (Hobbs and Robins, 1990: p. 20), but to fight as little as you have to to maintain honour and reputation whilst escaping intimidation and 'being picked on' (Willis, 1990: p. 103). Football, however, provided the kind of adventure and uncertainty and the possible dangers which are sought out by many working-class young men and which transcend conventions and normally approved patterns of behaviour. Crucially, too, for the real 'hard cases' and the 'nutters' who wanted it, terrace rivalries also promised a 'nihilistic grounded aesthetic – the incomprehensible buzz of the momentary disappearance of all meaning' provided by the real fight (Willis, 1990: p. 106). For some the attraction was clearly compulsive, even addictive. As a West Ham ICF 'member' put it: 'When you've run a firm and your adrenalin's gone, know what I mean, and you – and you start (fighting). I mean, it's the best. I mean, 60 quid's worth up yer nose won't, like, top that. Truth, no, it's the truth! I mean sod the coke and the smack, you know. Because the *feeling*, the feeling of doing something like that . . . ' For those less compelled by the 'high' provided by the violence and real pleasure in routing the opposition, there was still the entertainment and pride in having local hard men who nobody messed with easily. Everyone else could at least be there.

In the late 1960s, it was the skinhead who was identified most closely with hooliganism in public perceptions. (Twenty years later, cartoons still depict hooligans as skins.) The stylised hardness of the skins and their heightened celebrations of some of the traditional concerns of working-class youth 'gangs' – their aggressive and often violent masculinity; their community loyalties and collective solidarity; their violent opposition to 'outsiders' and to ruptures in traditional conventions of 'race' and gender – reinforced, and were reinforced by, the emerging terrace orders. When Manchester United fans 'took' east London in May 1967, fighting and trashing in celebration as the north-west club beat West Ham to claim the League Championship, their actions set in motion regional rivalries around football which also later hardened around the politics of style and the masculinised imperatives of conspicuous consumption which took place against the backcloth of a divisive and debilitating economic recession (Redhead, 1987).

Firming it up

The central aim of the early travelling hooligans of the late 1960s and early 1970s was to 'take' the opposing end – literally to fight to occupy the terrace space which had been colonised by the local 'hard core'. At first, these activities, and involvement in them, seemed to demand at least some knowledge of the sport and, more especially, a football-related commitment to the local club. Such strategies initially promised the maximum exhilaration for the invaders and the requisite public humiliation for the vanquished. But they were also usually over pretty quickly, involved little opportunity for any real fighting, and increased the possibilities of arrest. As the police tightened up, the range of match-day activities involved in travelling with 'the lads' spread. Inevitably, the identity of the real fighters and those willing to 'stand' against opponents also became more distinct from that of the rest of the goal end. The 'top boys' set off earlier to matches – sometimes even days earlier – and challenged young men keen to make a name for themselves to survive, strut and, when required, to fight in the action-facilitating locales of unfamiliar, and therefore hostile, towns and cities. Names were adopted by the serious 'crews', or 'firms', frequently taken from their distinctive mode of transport to away games. 'Ordinary' service trains were initially favoured, marking out those men with the connections, 'the bottle' and the cash, from the 'mugs' who favoured the cheaper official football special trains and the inevitable and emasculating police escorts which awaited their arrival at the other end. Later, 'firms' moved on to cars and vans, then back to trains, etc., etc. – whatever seemed right to mess up the police.

The appalled fascination of the media with the named 'firms' only served to heighten the mythologies around them and increase their attractiveness to a growing number of young men whose primary interest seemed to be male comradeship and the possibilities for 'trouble' as much as the football. By the time the World Cup Finals were being staged in Italy, in 1990, 100 young Englishmen could, quite literally, become the centre of attention of the World's media, simply by parading drunkenly up the streets of Cagliari singing the national anthem. If you had been involved, the next day you could read about yourself on the front page of the English tabloids, which had been specially flown in to Sardinia for the occasion. This was fifteen minutes or more of instant fame. Its attractions proved compulsive. For 'the lads', of course, the press coverage was 'all bollocks' but, contradictorily, they studied and collected the reports avidly and danced around for the cameras . . .

Serious hooligan incidents involving English fans in continental Europe began in earnest in 1974 when Spurs fans rioted at a UEFA Cup Final second-leg tie against Feyenoord in Rotterdam. Between that incident and the Heysel tragedy eleven years later, English fans were involved in football disturbances in almost all the major football playing continental countries (see Williams *et al.*, 1989). English-inspired hooliganism abroad is especially significant in the general development of the 'hooligan issue' for a number of reasons. Four seem to be especially important: firstly, as I have already said, such incidents helped to inspire and to shape hooliganism and also hooligan 'crews' on the continent, who routinely came to see the English as the yardstick against which their own performances could be measured. In such circles the English were 'a tough, sometimes outrageous group of people having an exciting time and cocking a snook at everybody' (Ward, 1989: p. 108; also, see Williams and Goldberg, 1990). Secondly, the grave international embarrassment and shame, as well as the physical damage, such incidents on occasions undoubtedly caused increased the determination of a right-wing British government to attempt to legislate hooliganism – and perhaps even the English game itself – away (see Ian Taylor, this volume). Thirdly, English hooliganism abroad served to underscore the links between the traditional territorial properties acted out at football, the sometimes violent excesses of young male fans, and racism. Finally, the English adventures on the continent also played a part in importing into English football culture some of the constituent stylistic features of the much discussed English soccer 'casual'. Let me now say a few things about racism at English football, and then about the rise of the 'casual'.

The race game

According to Holt (1989: p. 343):

> Chauvinism, local and national, lies at the heart of hooliganism, and England fans seem to find in foreigners a convenient target for a vague resentment of Britain's diminished place in the world. Football has become a substitute for patriotism amongst the disaffected, half-educated white working class youth of a nation which, only a generation ago, was respected and feared throughout the world.

These forms of chauvinism also involved racism at football. As Cohen points out (1988: p. 63), racism is not something which is 'tacked on' to English history by virtue of its imperialist phase one of its aberrant moments: it is constitutive of what has become known as the 'British Way of Life'. Cohen's discussion of the 'rough racism' and the 'nationalism of the neighbourhood' which are typical of the rituals enacted through working-class street cultures by young men putting their aggression to work in defining and 'defending' their areas against real or imaginary attack is also useful in understanding the 'selective' operation of racism at football. As Cohen explains, racialised forms of ethnicity produced within working-class culture both supported spontaneous local upsurges of hostility against immigrants and prevented their political exploitation into any larger, more organised, movement (Cohen, 1988: p. 31) . . .

> As more and more groups of supporters found their home team had a black player in it, total racism became more difficult to sustain. However, the National Front and British National Party were very active in the 1980s in trying to promote racism in football.

Signs of the soccer casual

Relating the issue of racism at football ro the rise of the 'casual', Ian Taylor has argued that the shallow, jingoistic, chauvinistic and racist behaviour of some English football fans abroad is the product of the rise of a 'new' hooligan who is, in turn, the result of the emergence of a rampant competitive individualism among a post-war skilled labour aristocracy. These are the young working-class men who have done best out of the deregulation of labour markets brought by the free-market ideologies of Thatcherism. Lacking traditional working-class frameworks of support (neighbourhood, kinship, class institutions), the contemporary anxieties of the new bourgeois worker are revealed in the 'only possible development' available to them: a more intense, nihilistic form of racist, sexist and nationalist paranoia which is also fuelled by the xenophobic ranting of the British tabloid press. Hooliganism enacted by English fans abroad is, according to this view, simply beyond the reach of the pockets of the less skilled or unemployed working-class youth. The apparently high-spending and violent soccer 'casual' is, then, an entirely new departure in the hooligan phenomenon (Taylor, 1987).

I will return, briefly, later to these questions raised by Taylor about who is and who is not now involved in hooliganism at home and abroad. I am sympathetic to some of the points he makes. However, there is some evidence to suggest that in fact the work-less North West has a good claim in arguments concerning the origins of the soccer 'casual', confirming Frith's claim that 'Escape from hard times is a cultural necessity and the harder the times the more fantastic and precarious and desperate a business it becomes' (Frith, 1990: p. 179). By the late 1970s the 'casual' movement was already under way in Liverpool and parts of London. Other provincial towns and cities followed in their wake. Conversely, for the acutely style-conscious, some places have, simply, never caught on.

Wise guys? Hooliganism, spectator behaviour and research

Recent academic debates about the hooligan phenomenon have become almost as lively, and as riddled with masculine posturing, as have been the dust-ups between the rival 'firms'. Some contributions seem to be in danger of becoming a mixture of the slapstick and slapdash. Others offer real insights and real advances. Many have offered well-reasoned critical comments about the approach to the hooligan issue adopted at the Centre for Football Research at Leicester University in the 1980s. I want, briefly, to look at some of these, and in doing so to outline my own views on the weaknesses – as well as the strengths – of the Leicester approach, while considering some of the alternative 'perspectives' which have now been put forward.

The rise of the apparently well-heeled 'casual' and speculation that the 'narcissims of minor difference' of the new youth cultures – an endless 'bricolage of style' (Cohen, 1988: pp. 38–39) – had explored the more traditional rules and rituals of 'community' and 'territoriality' which underpinned the behaviour of young working-class men is one of the reasons why some of the Leicester work on hooliganism has come under attack. I have already said quite a bit about the class origins of the casuals and the continuities involved in their activities and cultural concerns. Indeed, among the various academic positions, I don't think there is too much disagreement on these issues. (More recent research in Scotland confirms that 'all the evidence points to the fact that "football casuals" come, predominantly, from the lower levels of the social scale and are, basically, working class youths'; see Harper, 1990). However, I think Taylor (1987) is probably correct to argue that recent changes in Britain political culture, in the structure of the labour market and in football's developing 'style wars' have contributed to making the firms attractive and accessible to *more* working class men from 'respectable' backgrounds who have money to spend. The more costly and sophisticated demands and attractions of riding with the 'top boys' – media, clothes, Europe, plotting up, messing up the police, etc., etc. – did make associations with hooliganism more fashionable, especially when the activities and utterances of those involved became ever more directed at opposing the pathologising images of 'hooligans' carried and promoted by the media. (However, it should also be said that some working-class achievers have always been involved in hooliganism.) In this sense, Bill Buford's articulate Chelsea 'hooligans', including a Ph.D. student at London University (*Sunday Times*, 17 May 1987); Colin Ward's anti-racist, French-speaking, *Guardian*-reading hooligan guise (Ward, 1989); Hobbs and Robins' (1990) mythologised (and mythical?) schoolteacher member of Arsenal's 'Gooners'; and our own students at Leicester who were still 'involved' in hooliganism despite 'going to college', all have their place in the more recent manifestations of the phenomenon, which have been less straightforwardly 'knee-jerk' responses to violations of territorial rites than sometimes elaborate ploys designed best to engage (and outdress) identified rival firms. In more general terms, Ian Taylor's work is also useful for its determination properly to contextualise developments in football and the hooligan debate in terms of the particular historical and political moments of the game's recent struggles (Taylor, 1989).

The Leicester work on hooliganism, in any event, by no means excludes such cases of young men who have 'got on' but who are not beyond their cultural roots and male friendships networks. The Leicester research has often been mistakenly described as some variant of 'factor analysis' which argues for some simple and direct link, for example, between unemployment or deprivation and hooliganism. Instead, using Suttles' concept of 'ordered segmenation' (Suttles, 1968), the Leicester approach tries to describe the manner in which, under shifting circumstances for each new generation, the structure of lower-working-class communities seems, routinely, to generate specific cultural expectations about the use of violence in public spaces: the production and reproduction in effect of a cultural milieu which, in usually well-prescribed circumstances, demands or rewards physical violence between men (see Dunning, Murphy and Williams, 1988: ch. 9). The flexibilities in this account, particularly with respect to the range of locations, effects and penetrations of such milieux, have, perhaps, sometimes been underplayed in readings which have tried to link the origins of hooliganism in the Leicester work simply with some ideal-type, lower-working class community (see Dunning, Murphy and Williams, 1988; pp. 212–16). This is presumably one of the reasons why Hobbs and Robins ask, only partly, rhetorically whether a key member of West Ham's ICF, a man who once described himself as coming from an 'area where young men are 'born to fight' and who has written about his football adventures, ably milking requests from television for interviews about football violence, can be usefully described as "lower class" (Hobbs and Robins, 1990: p. 8). It is tempting to say one might as well ask the question of another, rather better-known media star who has done reasonably well out of his own business and fighting acumen, Mike Tyson. What is it they say about being able to take the kid out of the street?

David Field: Contemporary Issues in Relation to the Elderly

If old people tend to be somewhat marginalised in society, this is equally true of the scanty coverage of them in introductory sociology texts and syllabuses. This plainly written and informed piece maps out some of the key developments and issues in relation to older people.

Field begins by presenting some demographic data which demonstrates that a significant increase in the number of old people has been occurring in Britain and most other more developed countries. (This increase is also beginning to occur in the developing world and will do so massively in China and India.)

Field then discusses a range of major issues in relation to the elderly. Of the two principal theories which attempt to explain their 'growing absence from social life' – disengagement and exclusion theory – he tends to favour the latter. His discussion of the impact of gender, class and 'race' on old age is brief but useful. He goes on to discuss negative attitudes to the elderly. While Field warns against stereotyping the old as 'a problem', he is clear that old age can bring problems as well as opportunities and fulfilment. His analysis of attitudes towards older people suggests a substantial degree of superficiality, ignorance and negative stereotyping on the part of some members of the general public.

In the best sociological tradition, Field concludes by asking some trenchant questions about the issues under discussion.

Reading 31 From David Field, 'Elderly People in British Society' in *Sociology Review*, Vol. 1 No. 4, April 1992, pp. 16–20

In 1850, less than 5% of the population was aged over 65, whereas today it is 15% with a projected increase to 19% over the next 40 years (see Table 1). It is misleading to treat all people over 65 as a homogeneous group given the wide age span involved, the great variation in physiological and psychological functioning, and the persistence of social class, gender and ethnic differences between people within this category. There are no simple definitions of ageing, but it involves complex physiological changes, changing social circumstances, redefinitions of social identities and changes in psychological functioning. Although the diversity of social circumstances among elderly people needs to be acknowledged and their individuality respected, some generalisations can nevertheless be made about the social and economic position of elderly people in British society. After considering these, this article will go on to discuss some of the other factors which influence the experience of 'being old'.

Demographic trends

I have already noted that Britain is characterised by an ageing population. As can be seen from Table 2, this situation has arisen in the latter half of the century. The main reasons for this change in demographic composition have

Table 1 Percentage of the population aged 65 and over in selected countries

	1980	*2010*	*2030*
Canada	9.51	14.61	22.39
France	13.96	16.26	21.76
Germany	15.51	20.35	25.82
Italy	13.45	17.28	21.92
Japan	9.10	18.62	19.97
UK	14.87	14.61	19.24
USA	11.29	12.79	19.49

Source: OECD 'Ageing populations: the social policy implications', Demographic Change and Public Policy, 1988

been the 'bulge' in the number of births which occurred after the 1914–18 World War and, to a lesser extent, a decline in mortality rates, especially at birth and in the first years of life. Declining mortality has resulted from better nutrition and higher standards of living. At all ages mortality of males is greater than that of females, with the result that in old age females far outnumber males. In the 85 and over age category women presently outnumber men in a ratio of approximately 4:1. This differential is, however, likely to decrease over time because the present generation of elderly people includes disproportionately low numbers of men, reflecting the effect of World War II upon males in the armed services.

Household structure and composition

Most old people (77%) live with their spouse or on their own in their own home but near to other family members. The marital status of elderly people has important consequences for such matters as isolation, sources of immediate help and care, and financial circumstances. Elderly women are more likely than elderly men to be single, widowed or divorced. According to the 1986 General Household Survey (GHS), only about one-fifth of women over the age of 75 are still married, compared with nearly two-thirds of men in this age group. Patterns of household composition vary according to the age, sex and ethnicity of elderly people. The 1981 Census revealed a traditional extended household structure to be typical of New Commonwealth or Pakistan (NCP) headed households, although elderly people from ethnic minorities comprised only 4% of people in NCP households, compared with about 17% in the population as a whole. The GHS found that in 1985 of people aged 65 or over: 43% lived with a spouse only (women 33%); 34% lived alone (women 48%); 7% lived with spouse and others (women 4%); and 12% lived with others (women 15%).

About 5% of old people live in institutions such as old people's homes, or nursing homes, although single people are more likely to do so than those who are married. The proportion of old people in residential care rises with age. There has been a sharp increase in the number of private residential homes since the late 1980s.

A critical issue for the welfare of elderly people is that of how to ensure accommodation appropriate in terms of its size, location (especially with decreasing mobility and transport problems), state of repair, amenities and adaptations (e.g. indoor WC, ramps, etc.), and heating. Roughly 50% of elderly people are owner-occupiers (about the same proportion as in the British population as a whole), although elderly people are much more likely to own their own homes outright than to be buying with a mortgage (46% in 1985). Slightly more older people (40%) are living in private rented residential accommodation than the average, and this accommodation is generally the poorest housing stock, often found in decaying inner-city areas. The 1986 GHS found that amenities and consumer durables were likely to be less well provided in 'elderly households' (especially single person households) than in 'non-elderly' households, although the position of elderly households had improved over the period 1980–85. A study by Plank (1977) of waiting lists for old people's homes revealed that social workers estimated that one-third of the elderly people really needed rehousing, rather than residential care. This still appears to be the case.

Income

Adequate income is critical in enabling elderly people to lead decent, fulfilled and dignified lives in the community. Elderly people are, however, disproportionately represented among those living in or on the margins of poverty in Britain. This is not 'inevitable' but is a reflection of the social and economic arrangements made in respect of income support for elderly people, which contribute to the social construction of poverty and dependency in old age. Some elderly people (but not many elderly women) are in receipt of occupational pensions, although the amount is often small. The main source of income for most elderly people is social security benefits – a national insurance retirement pension and means-tested Income Support. Elderly people may also receive financial help in other ways, e.g. with exemption and remission of health charges, housing costs etc. By comparison with some other countries (e.g. in Europe), the levels of pension in Britain are not generous and, increasingly, people are moving into early retirement as the economic activity rates of elderly people fall. In 1961, 21% of men aged 65 and over were in paid employment, the figure had fallen to 19% in 1971 and was 10% in both 1981 and 1985.

Ageing as role loss

There are two principal social explanations which attempt to explain the growing absence of old people from social life. These explanations point to withdrawal and exclusion respectively. Disengagement theory stresses the voluntary withdrawal of old people from social life, and whilst this may be true for some old people it is an insufficient explanation of the experiences of all old people across the full range of their activities. The 'role loss' explanation stresses that, whether they wish to or not, old people are excluded from wide areas of 'normal life' (e.g. paid work, sport) by social arrangements and social attitudes. Common elements in the transition through old age to death are the loss of roles, difficulties in maintaining reciprocity and independence in social relationships, and decreasing personal autonomy and control over one's life. As we shall see later, an important factor influencing this gradual loss of social connectedness and independence is the old person's health status.

The treatment of the elderly in Britain is one example of what can be termed 'the social construction of age'. In traditional societies, age is constructed differently.

In British society, becoming 'old' is linked to economic and legal definitions associated with pension rights and, especially for men, definitions of economic productivity. Retirement from paid work is frequently a signal to the person involved, and to others associated with them, that they have begun their entry into old age. While many people welcome their retirement from work, it is also true that for many people it is involuntary, unwelcome and unvalued. Entry to old age is unlike many other important status changes, such as graduating or getting married, in a number of ways. It is not generally a valued status, and there are few 'rites of passage' to signal entry into it, especially for those not previously in full-time paid employment. There is little prior socialisation for the role, which is amorphous and unstructured: there are very few social rules for 'being old'.

Entry to old age is defined primarily by an 'emptying out' of roles and activities which is largely irreversible as a result of such things as job loss, the death of a spouse and reduced income. Whereas other status changes typically involve new roles and responsibilities as well as the relinquishing of previous roles and responsibilities, the entry to old age is characterised primarily by the loss of roles, activities and responsibilities, but without the acquisition of new ones. Restrictions imposed by reduced income and/or heath problems may eventually threaten the old person's meaningful integration into their familial and communal social networks as they become less able to reciprocate and become more dependent on unreciprocated support from others. The restriction and loss of social activities may also lead to changes in social identity and an erosion of self-conception. Over time, the cumulative effect is to generate and encourage the loss of independence, particularly where there are financial and health difficulties. This creates problems for old people of retaining their autonomy and control over life.

Gender, class and 'race'

It is also important to be aware of individual and social variations within the broad picture outlined above. In particular, there are clear gender and social class differences. In terms of gender the main differences between men and women are linked to work roles. The current generation of old men are much more likely than the women to have experienced job loss as the first step into old age. Thus women experience greater continuity pre- and post-retirement than men because they are less likely to have been in paid employment, although this may change in the future as more women pursue a work career. Professional and managerial classes are more likely than other groups to work longer past retirement age, perhaps in a part-time capacity, and thus their entry into old age may be more gradual.

Working-class men are more likely to continue with their old life style and leisure patterns, although perhaps 'slowing down' (e.g. getting up later) and 'cutting back' (e.g. doing less gardening) in order to accommodate their changed financial and social status. By contrast, middle-class men are more likely to take up new leisure activities to substitute for paid work.

The gender inequalities which are evident in our society in younger age groups persist into old age, with women more likely to be disadvantaged than men. Although both husbands and wives are likely to be the main lay carers for their sick or disabled spouses, women are more likely than men to do so mainly because they are more likely to be younger than their husbands. They are also more likely to experience the death of their spouse. Such bereavements are one of the main causes of death among old people. After the death of a spouse, men are much more likely than women to remarry. Old women are thus more likely to be caring for another than to be cared for, and are more likely to be living alone than old men. Finally, old women are likely to receive lower levels of pension and other income than men.

Table 2 The over 65's in the UK population

	Numbers (millions)		*% of total population*	
	Aged 65-79	*Aged 80+*	*Over 65*	*Over 80*
1901	1.3 (65–74)	0.5 (75+)	4.7	1.3 (75+)
1921	1.9 (65–74)	0.7 (75+)	5.9	1.5 (75+)
1951	4.8	0.7	10.9	1.4
1971	6.1	1.3	13.4	2.3
1981	6.9	1.6	15.0	2.8
1989	6.9	2.0	15.6	3.5
Males	3.0	0.6	6.3	1.1
Females	3.9	1.4	9.3	2.4
Projected 2001	6.7	2.5	16.0	3.8

Source: Social Trends 1986 (Table 1.1) and 1991 (Table 1.2)

It is difficult to build up a clear picture of the influence of ethnic group membership upon the experience of becoming old. Older people from NCP groups may adhere more strictly to the cultural attitudes and practices of their country of origin and be less than proficient in their use of English. These factors may mean that they have greater difficulty in their use of health and other statutory services than older members of the white majority. One would expect more extensive networks of social support and greater respect for older people among NCP communities. However, with the assimilation of younger members of these communities into the round of British life which has now occurred, some inter-generational tensions and conflicts may arise which have negative consequences for lay care of elderly people in these ethnic minority groups.

Negative attitudes towards old age

Although old age is a status that all of us might expect to reach, negative attitudes about old age and 'the elderly' are common. To use Goffman's terminology, old age is a weakly stigmatised, discreditable status. Old age is not directly and inevitably discrediting for a number of reasons. Most importantly, it is often not immediately apparent how old someone is. In any case definitions of 'old' are indeterminate and so although negative attitudes and stereotypes are prevalent it is often difficult to know who is or is not 'old'. Hence old people who are fit, active and who look young are not stigmatised in the ways in which frail elderly disabled people may be. Indeed, the negative stereotypes of old age seem to be based upon the association between old age, sickness and dependency. Negative stereotyping highlights dependency, sickness and the inability to perform socially. A review by Lehr (1983) of studies of negative attitudes towards old age in industrial societies summarises the evidence as follows:

> Generally the image of the aged, aside from a few positive traits is defined by negative characteristics such as decline and loss of functions and capacities. The aged are perceived as ill, retarded, tired, slow, and inefficient in their thinking; they are seen as asexual, or if even showing sexual interests, as ridiculous.

An account of labelling theory is given in Reading 68.

Such negative, stereotypical attitudes are widespread in British society and are constantly reinforced in the media and everyday conversation. Those who become old will already have internalised these negative stereotypes. It is odd that although we are all candidates for the stigmatising label of 'old and helpless', such negative attitudes persist. Like other stereotypes, stereotypical attitudes of the elderly are global and resistant to change in the face of contradictory evidence. That is, one aspect of the person – age – is taken to subsume and determine the nature of all their other attributes and abilities. Because an old person has difficulty with her walking and eyesight, she or he is also presumed to have difficulty in understanding others, to be unable to make everyday decisions, and to have lost interest in world affairs and their own sexuality. As with other stereotypes the contradictory evidence of able and competent old people who manage their lives successfully is explained away by, for example, claiming they are 'exceptions'.

Most older people do not accept the stereotype of old age as applying to themselves, although there may be self-stigmatisation among some older people. Research shows that old people differentiate between how they look and their chronological age, and that their self-image is often that of being a younger person. Featherstone and Hepworth (1990) talk of the 'Mask of Ageing' to highlight this discrepancy between the 'virtual' identity ascribed by others to old people on the basis of stereotypical responses based upon their appearance, and their 'actual' or self-perceived identity linked to their abilities and 'felt age'.

Not all old people are able to resist the negative label of 'being old', especially if they are dependent upon other people for a range of physical and social support. In such cases, the power of these stereotypical attitudes can be quite coercive and can contribute to the social breakdown of competence. The loss of roles, negative attitudes of others, exclusion from social activities, atrophy of skills and negative self-concepts interact with each other to generate a 'negative feedback loop' as elderly people receive negative messages that they are incompetent and unvalued, and incorporate these messages into their self-concept (Figure 1). In such circumstances the attitudes of others can be said to create social handicaps for the old person and to create a 'self-fulfilling prophecy'.

Figure 1 A cycle of negative feedback

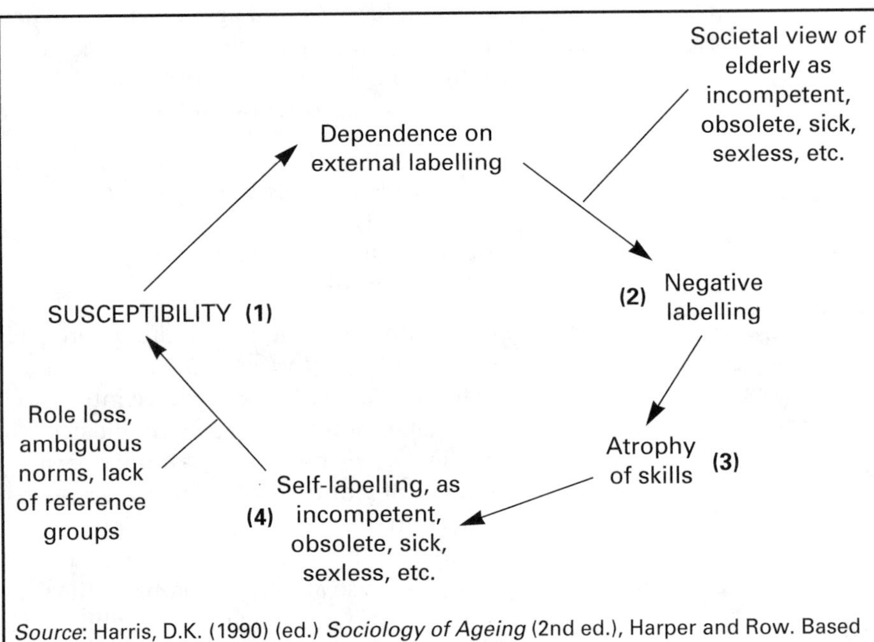

Source: Harris, D.K. (1990) (ed.) *Sociology of Ageing* (2nd ed.), Harper and Row. Based on Kuypers, J. and Bengstone, V.L. (1973) 'Social breakdown and competence: a model of normal ageing', in *Human Development*, 16; pp. 181–201.

The social and psychological impact of ill health and disability

Although many old people remain fit and active until very late in their lives, ill health and activity restriction as a result of disability are common experiences for old people. A distinction is often made between the 'young old' (below 75) who are significantly healthier than the 'old old', especially those over 85. Unlike younger ages, the diseases which particularly characterise old age are degenerative and chronic. That is, they persist over a long period of time, are largely incurable, and typically get worse. The most frequent causes of disability among old people are senile dementia and confusion, arthritis and stroke. The impact of chronic illness and disability is mediated by the nature and extent of the social support old people receive from others, and isolated old people are likely to be more adversely affected by the same level of sickness or disability than those with supportive social networks.

Although there is a clear association between ill health and chronological age, the two are imperfectly related and it is not until after the age of 75 that the association becomes particularly strong. Many old people are not in noticeably worse health than younger adults, and even among those with long-standing disabilities the negative impact upon their quality of life may be relatively minor. As Brocklehurst (1978) puts it, ageing involves 'an increasing frailty within the body, and a slowing of its functions, but none of these changes is in any way disastrous and indeed none is likely to be more than slightly inconvenient'.

Following Brocklehurst we could suggest that there is a four-step progression from impaired health to dependency. First, the effects of ageing lead to background impairment which is not itself disabling. This gradually leads into cumulative multiple pathology and disability which nevertheless does not prevent the old person from functioning independently. Next, a 'precarious balance' is reached where the old person's illness and disability require them to depend increasingly upon the help and support of others. Finally, an acute episode of illness, such as pneumonia or a broken bone, which may require hospitalisation precipitates the breakdown of independence (Figure 2). The act of hospitalisation is often accompanied by a collapse of support from lay carers.

Figure 2 The four-step movement from health to dependency

(1) Background impairment
(2) Cumulative pathology and disability, but retained independence
(3) Dependence upon others to remain at home
(4) Acute illness precipitating loss of independence and movement from own home

Source: Brocklehurst, J. (1978) 'Ageing and health', in D. Hobman (ed.), *The Social Challenge of Ageing*, Croom Helm

Chronic illness and disability have a number of important social and psychological consequences for those who have them in addition to their directly pathological and physiological effects. A number of common disabilities found among old people function to restrict their contact with others and with the wider social environment. For example, arthritis may result in the inability to perform such everyday acts of daily life as dressing oneself, feeding oneself or walking, thus leading old people to depend on the help of others and restricting their capacity to leave their home. The old person may also have less energy to perform such activities, and may therefore restrict them, thereby restricting their range of social activities and social integration with others. Poor vision is another common impairment which interferes with social life through its impact upon recognition of others, ability to read newspapers and transport times and so on. Impaired hearing, another common impairment among old people, similarly functions to restrict social interaction, and in addition the inability of old people to hear what others are saying to them may lead to inappropriate responses and their definition as 'stupid' or 'confused'. Finally, many chronic conditions may have a negative impact on the old person's body image, thereby contributing to a loss of self-esteem.

There is some debate, especially in the USA, about the relationship between ill health and old age. People are living longer, but are these extra years healthy and fulfilling or are they merely additional years of chronic illness, senescence and dependency? The conventional wisdom is that chronic disease becomes more prevalent and disability becomes progressively more severe as one gets older. In this view, medical advances have only prolonged the duration of chronic diseases such as strokes, merely postponing death as a result. An alternative view is that people are living longer because they are fitter, and that serious illness and disability only occur over a very short period of years at the end of the person's life, at whatever age they die. Here medical advances are seen as positively contributing to the quality of an old person's life, for example through hip replacement or cataract surgery. Both of these interpretations seem to have some support from the available British evidence.

The costs of care

Great concern has been expressed about the costs to the NHS and Social Services as a result of the ill health of elderly people. The majority of hospital beds are occupied by people over the age of 65 and during the lifetime of the NHS its expenditure on people 65 and over has risen from 5% to the current level of just above 30%. A common estimate is that the NHS will require an annual increase of 1% in its real income over the rest of the century to keep pace with the additional costs resulting from the increased number of old people in the population. There are also significant costs to local authorities providing statutory social services for old people, and to the families and 'lay carers' of sick and disabled old people. Despite the contributions from the NHS, local authorities and voluntary agencies, the majority of the care and social support provided for sick and disabled elderly people is provided not by the state but by 'informal care' from families and neighbours, especially by women.

It appears to be the case that even quite intensive support schemes to enable very dependent elderly people to remain in their own homes can be cheaper than alternatives in hospital and residential care, and they are preferred by elderly people themselves. Comparative costings are difficult and some important 'costs' are usually left out, for example the material, social and emotional costs of the 'informal carers'. In many areas, however, schemes of this kind – such as home alarm systems, warden controlled sheltered housing, home-help services, meals-on-wheels, and aids and adaptions to the home – are in very short supply.

Concluding comments

It is important not to overemphasise the negative aspects of becoming old. Most old people live in satisfactory physical surroundings, are relatively free from health problems, continue their activities in the home and the community, and maintain a satisfactory balance between the positive social relationships and the inevitable losses which time brings. A study by Bury and Holmes (1991) of those over 90 concludes that 'life after 90 can be compatible with a good quality of life, and is characterised by diversity as well as common problems or needs'.

This potentially long post-retirement period is sometimes referred to as 'the third age'.

When discussing the experience of old age in British society we must remember that people may be classified as elderly from the age of retirement (65 for men, 60 for women) up to 90 years and beyond. This large age span requires us to be sensitive to the wide range of capacities of elderly people and the varied circumstances in which elderly people live their lives. The newly retired and the 'young' elderly (65–74 years) are often not in much poorer health, and their housing conditions and amenities are not greatly inferior to those people in their late 50s and early 60s. Nor do many 65–74 years olds consider themselves to be elderly. For those in the age range 75–84, however, there appears to be a moderate decline in mobility and health, a lower standard of housing and amenities, and a sharp reduction in social contacts outside the home. These trends are accelerated in those over 85. We should also be aware of continuing ethnic, gender and social class inequalities in the material and cultural resources available to old people and in their experiences of ill health and disability. For example, the social class gradient. described by the Black Report and subsequent studies, persists into old age with old people from the Registrar General's social classes IV and V more likely to experience ill health and disability than those from other social class groups.

This brief discussion has covered a wide range of material and raised a number of important issues which you might pursue further. For example, what are the main differences in the ways elderly men and women experience their lives? Are there profound differences between ethnic groups in the ways in which old people and old age are socially constructed? To what extent do legal and social definitions of and provisions for old people create a situation of 'structured dependency' for old people? What evidence is there to support the view that there are widespread negatively held attitudes towards old age and the elderly? What are the implications for the provision of informal care of the elderly of changes in family life resulting from such factors as single parenting, divorce and remarriage, and inter-ethnic marriage? What are the implications for the health services of the increasing numbers of old people in British society? What are the implications of reforms in the health services, especially the move towards 'community care', for the care of old people?

Questions and Issues

Stratification: Sections 3–6

The most relevant readings are indicated in brackets after each question.

1 Compare and contrast Marxist and Weberian perspectives on stratification. (Readings 11–17, 26)

2 To what extent is Marx's analysis of class now 'out of date'? (Section 3, Reading 26)
3 Why do females generally command less power and resources than males? (Section 4, Reading 26)
4 Describe and account for the sexual division of labour in Britain. In what ways has it changed in the post-war period. (Section 4, Reading 16, Reading 26)
5 Discuss the view that the concept of class is more fundamental to the understanding of society than that of ethnicity. (Section 3, Section 5, Reading 86)
6 What is racism? (Section 5, especially Readings 25 and 26, Reading 86)
7 To what extent can contemporary race relations in Britain and Europe be explained in terms of developments in the international division of labour? (Readings 23, 28, 52–54)
8 Describe and explain the relationship between youth subcultures and class in the post-war period. Is this relationship now weaker? (Reading 30, see also my textbook, *A New Introduction to Sociology,* Chapter 10 [Nelson 1992])
9 'Young, working class, female and black' To what extent, and why, is a person of that description likely to be disadvantaged in contemporary Britain? (Readings 12, 16, 19, 20, 26, 35)
10 How useful is the concept of 'life course' in understanding the social situation and experience of a given age group (Section 6, especially, Reading 29)

SECTION 7

FAMILIES AND HOUSEHOLDS

Introduction: Readings 32–35

Figure 1 Household size 1971 and 1991: percentage of households of each size

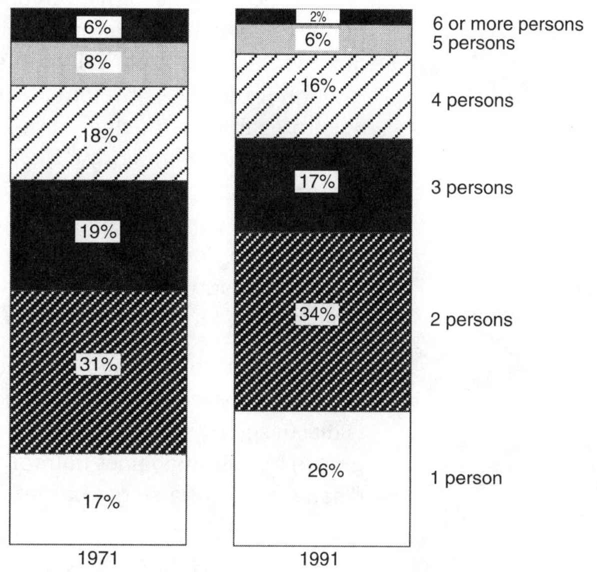

Figure 2 Households and people by type of household*, 1991

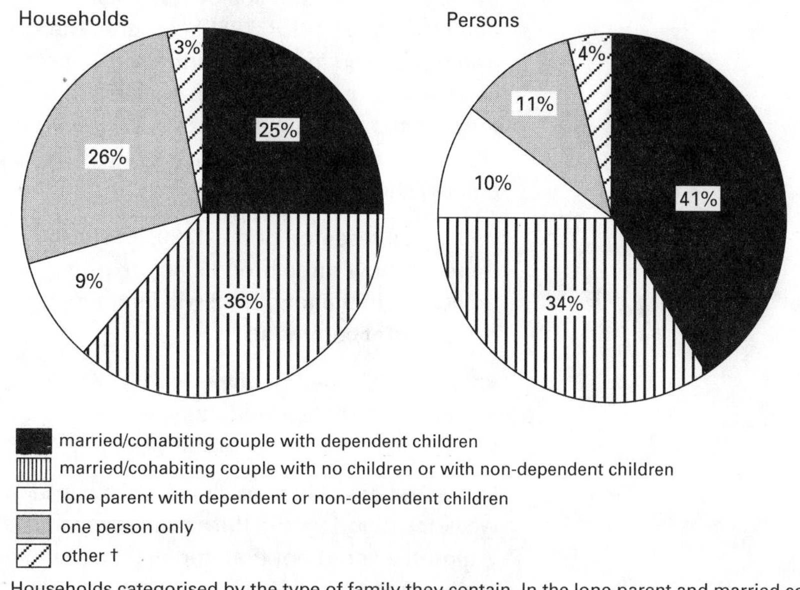

* Households categorised by the type of family they contain. In the lone parent and married couple households, other individuals who were not family members may also have been present.

† 'Other' includes households containing two or more unrelated adults and those containing two or more families.

(From *OPCS Monitor,* September 1992, p. 1 and p. 2)

The data provided at the beginning of this introductory section shows trends in household and family size. While there has been a rapid increase in the number of households with only one or two inhabitants (now 60 per cent), the majority of people still live in households of three or more people. This data provides a useful reference point throughout this section.

This section begins with an overview by Peter Willmott of developments in family and kinship structure. While there has been a tendency for kin to become more widely scattered, Willmott sees no obvious lessening of kinship concern (though for a more problematic view of this issue, see Reading 29). Willmott illustrates that the nuclear family is still part of the direct experience and aspirations of the majority. However, he would concede that there has been a recent increase in the number of people who do not conform to this pattern. The trend to cohabitation and to single parenthood is discussed in 'The Relationship Revolution', summarised in Reading 33. In Reading 34, Faith Robertson Elliot discusses the homosexual family and takes the view that a plurality of family types is now the norm.

The Afro-Caribbean one-parent family is relevant to the issue raised in the previous paragraph, but it is mainly in the context of gender socialisation that it is discussed by Ann Phoenix. What she says about the socialisation of black girls is a caution against uninformed generalisation about the supposed disadvantage of a single-parent upbringing.

32 *Peter Willmott: Nailing some Stereotypes about Family and Kinship*

The work of Peter Willmott and Michael Young on family and kinship is legendary within sociology. Their classic study, *Family and Class in a London Suburb* (RKP, 1960) captured the strong patterns of kinship in traditional working-class communities before these came under pressure from a variety of sources. Although such traditional kinship patterns were weakened through the 1960s, 70s and 80s, Willmott tells us that this 'is not the end of the story'. Kin often did become more widely scattered but did not typically ignore one another as a result.

Willmott's research of the 1980s in North London prompted him to suggest that there are now three broad kinship arrangements in Britain. These are clearly presented in the text, but I will list them here as fractions of the total in order to make a brief comment:

- Local extended family $\frac{1}{8}$
- Dispersed extended family $\frac{1}{2}$
- Attenuated extended family $\frac{3}{8}$

In the first case kin contact is frequent and in the second 'less frequent' (once a week/fortnight). In the third case contact is fairly infrequent. Although Willmott's comment that 'the most striking feature of British Kinship . . . is its resilience' is, as one would expect, sustained by his data, there are worrying aspects to his findings. It is clear that even given the speed of modern communications, the dominant forms of contemporary extended families are not characterised by the sort of routine contact that can *guarantee* help in times of need. The relative increase of the old and, particularly, of the very old as a percentage of the total population, suggests a continuing, if not an increased role for public policy in this area. David Field's analysis of issues in relation to old age (Reading 31) could very usefully be read alongside Willmott's piece.

Reading 32 From Peter Willmott, 'Urban Kinship Past and Present' in *Social Studies Review*, November 1988, pp. 44–46

Thirty-five years ago Michael Young and I uncovered an almost 'tribal' community in the East London district of Bethnal Green. There – only just beyond the boundaries of the City of London – we found that most married people had parents and parents-in-law living near to them, and often other relatives as well. The common pattern was a localised extended family of two or more nuclear families, usually built around the close ties between mothers and daughters, who saw each other every day or nearly every day (Young and Willmott 1957). Other studies done at about the same time or a few years later showed that, although Bethnal Green was perhaps an extreme version of a common working-class pattern, it was not unique. Somewhat similar kinship arrangements were found in Wolverhampton, in a dock community in Liverpool, in Acton (London) and in Swansea. Kinship was likewise an important element in people's lives in the country town of Banbury in 1950 and, despite a series of industrial and population changes in the intervening period, again when the study was repeated in 1967.

The Bethnal Green we described in the 1950s was a place where most residents had lived a long time – over half had been born there and more than half the rest had been there for at least fifteen years, most having been born elsewhere in the East End. Not many lived with kin, but over 90 per cent had some relatives living in the district. As many as a fifth of the married people in our sample with parents alive had their parents living not just nearby but actually in the same street. This was in sharp contrast with the Bethnal Green of a hundred years earlier; research has shown that on three indices – stability of residence, relatives in the household and relatives in the same area – kinship was not much in evidence then. It seems that various subsequent changes in its economy and its housing enabled kinship to thrive in the district by the time of our study. Taking an even longer view of history, Peter Laslett and his colleagues have convincingly demonstrated that in English society *before* the Industrial Revolution, though kinship was no doubt important to many people, it was not as portrayed in the stereotype, where a wide circle of relatives was believed to be a daily presence in the lives of everybody.

A reference to Laslett's explosion of the myth that the extended family was the dominant family form before the industrial revolution.

Today, a new stereotype holds sway: a view that, however it may have been in the past, the research of the 1950s and 1960s was describing a high point of urban kinship that was near the end of its reign. Since then, it is held, a number of changes have broken the old order: high levels of geographical mobility, redevelopment of the inner areas of Britain's cities and industrial towns, changes in the family and marriage, and the increase in the number of wives going out to work (reducing their contacts with their mothers).

There is undoubtedly some truth in this reasoning, and the point can be illustrated by what has happened subsequently in Bethnal Green itself. There, in the late 1950s and 1960s, a large-scale programme of council redevelopment demolished the streets of terraced houses and dispersed families to new towns, to council estates in the outer suburbs or to the new flatted estates elsewhere in London. Recent evidence shows that, as a result, although some close-knit local extended families survived most did not. The same thing has happened in other similar places as well. It all demonstrates the impact that changes in the physical and social environment can have on patterns of kinship residence.

Kinship in the 1980s

But that is not the end of the story. If one looks, in the 1980s, not at the *proximity* of relatives but at *contacts* between them, a different picture comes into focus. A number of recent surveys have shown that between about two-thirds and three-quarters of people – people of all ages, not just the elderly – still see at least one relative at least once a week. I recently completed a study of married people with young children in a North London suburb, a district where as many as a third of the couples had moved in within the previous five years (Willmott 1986). There, the proportion seeing relatives at least weekly was precisely two-thirds. Of those with parents alive, one in ten saw their mother or father or both every day, and nearly two-thirds of living parents and parents-in-law were seen at least once a month. Working-class people saw rather more of their parents and other relatives than middle-class people did, but the differences were not large.

The evidence from that and other recent studies also shows that relatives continue to be the main source of informal support and care, and that again the class differences are not marked. In my North London research, nearly two-thirds of people were helped by relatives, particularly mothers or mothers-in-law, when one of their children was ill; nearly three-quarters were helped with babysitting, again mainly by mothers or mothers-in-law. Four-fifths looked to relatives, mainly parents or parents-in-law, when they needed to borrow money. Surveys of elderly people show that most of the informal help and care they receive comes from relatives, particularly their children or children-in-law.

So, despite a decline in the proportions of people living with or very near to relatives, kinship remains an important force in the lives of most people. Just as the old stereotype of the traditional extended family (pre-Laslett) was wrong in overstating the role of relatives, the new one (post-Bethnal Green) is wrong in understating it. Parents and married children can keep in regular contact partly because they can often arrange their housing so that they live near enough to each other to be able to do so. A small-scale but important study in the Greater London area compared the kinship patterns of people originating from mainly Victorian areas who had stayed in the same district since before they got married with people from similar areas who had moved out. Many of the second group turned out to have remained in close touch with their parents and siblings; they saw as much of them each week as those who had stayed put. This had come about because clusters of relatives – particularly parents and their married children – had moved out to suburban districts where they were within reasonable visiting distance of each other.

Greater mobility has helped give kinship a new face: proximity no longer matters as much as it did. Back in the 1960s a study of kinship in Swansea suggested that, at that time relatives tended to be more scattered than in previous periods (Rosser and Harris 1965). But it also showed that relatively high levels of contact were maintained. In interpreting these results, the researchers were struck by the relevance of the car and they commented that the wider family in the Swansea area might well be described as 'the motorised family'. Car ownership has more than doubled since then. Today the wider family could equally well be called the 'telephonic family'. In 1969 under a third of households in Britain had a phone. By 1984 that was up to nearly four-fifths, and in my North London study it was nine-tenths, with yet again only a small difference between the social classes. People also now more often have relatively spacious homes, where relatives can come to stay.

Not every household has a car, or the kind of public transport that makes relatives accessible; and not everyone has a telephone or a spacious home. Those who do not, and do not have relatives near either, are among the minority for whom kinship is not readily available for companionship or support. On the other hand, some people do still have relatives close at hand. In the North London suburb which I studied, nearly a third of couples had parents or parents-in-law living within ten minutes travelling distance.

Variations in family form

The recent research suggests that there are now three broad kinship arrangements in Britain. And on the basis of the various surveys, a rough estimate can be made of the proportions in each.

The first type is the *local extended family*. Typically two or perhaps three nuclear families in separate households – parents and their married children, typically daughters, with their own children – live near each other. They see each other every day or nearly every day, and they provide mutual aid on a continuing basis. This kind of arrangement probably still applies to something like one in eight of the adult population of Britain. It is more common among working-class families than middle-class, in stable communities than in those marked by residential mobility or redevelopment, and in the north of England, the Midlands, Scotland and Wales rather than in southern England.

The second type, and the one that is now becoming dominant, is the *dispersed extended family*. Like the local extended family, this is composed of two or more nuclear families, again typically made up of parents and their married children, with their children. The big difference is that it is not localised and the meetings are consequently less frequent. Nonetheless,

Figure 1 The changing face of the household in Britain

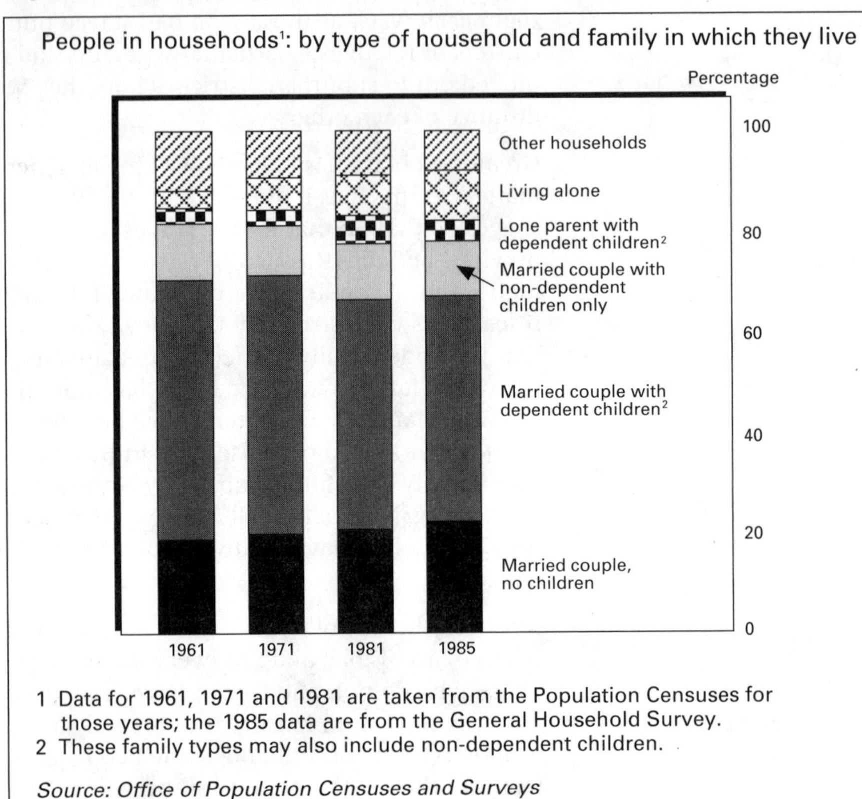

1 Data for 1961, 1971 and 1981 are taken from the Population Censuses for those years; the 1985 data are from the General Household Survey.
2 These family types may also include non-dependent children.

Source: Office of Population Censuses and Surveys

there is still fairly frequent contact, say once a week or once a fortnight, and support is still provided both in emergency and on a regular basis. Such an arrangement depends on cars (or a good public transport service) and on telephones. This pattern is probably more common in middle-class circles than in working-class ones. The evidence on contacts suggests that this second type probably operates for about half the adult population.

On these estimates, this leaves under half the population for whom kinship is less important. Their type of arrangement might be called the *attenuated extended family*. The people concerned include students and other young people, both those who are single and young couples before they have any children of their own. They are at a stage when they are, as they need to be, breaking away from their family of origin – when kinship matters less, and their age peers more, than at any other phase in life.

Of course there are also other people whose kinship is attenuated. Some of them would, as far as one can judge, prefer more contact. They are separated by such things as the needs of their job, or their partner's job, or the workings of the housing markets. At least some of them will say in interviews that they regret the separation. Others, with a smaller or greater degree of consciousness, have chosen not to be near or to maintain contact. Very few of the people of any of these groups have no knowledge of or contact with kin. Most keep in touch with parents, adult children, brothers and sisters by letter or telephone; most do meet them, if only at Christmas, at rites of passage like marriages and funerals, and on one or two other occasions each year. For most, too, relatives provide mutual help, if not on a continuing basis, at least in times of need: parents lend their children money; children go to give help when a parent falls ill; parents, particularly mothers, travel to give their support in illness or at childbirth.

Willmott is clearly of the view that kinship is functional and adaptive and far from moribund and irrelevant.

The most striking feature of British kinship, now and in the past, and in both rural and urban environments, is its resilience. Kinship patterns can be re-established, with continuing contacts and help between parents and adult children in particular, because of an important feature of British – and other Western – kinship systems. In these systems, unlike others, there is usually no emphasis on lineage, on tracing descent over many generations. The range of relatives who matter to most people is, instead, shallow and narrow. People are closest to and care most about those who grew up with them in the same nuclear family. Hence extended family groupings can, as Margaret Stacey (1960) observed in Banbury, grow up in just one generation.

The kinship arrangements that people adopt are, however, not enforced by rules as they are in some societies. This is again a characteristic of British and all Western kinship, and the research by Laslett and his colleagues shows that it applied as strongly in pre-industrial Britain as it does today. It is true that in the past the Poor Law and subsequent legislation imposed certain obligations for maintaining kin outside the immediate family of parents and dependent children. But there were and are no socially recognised precepts about how to behave towards relatives. If a person chooses to see nothing of his or her kin, some other people might think that odd, might even say that it indicates the absence of a proper sense of responsibility – and potential social disapproval of that kind may be part of what keeps some relatives in touch with each other – but the choices can be made.

Yet, although kinship is largely chosen, it not only survives but most of the time flourishes. Sometimes external circumstances work against it, as they did in the Bethnal Green of the 1850s and again in the 1960s and 1970s; sometimes they work to sustain it, as in the Bethnal Green of the immediate post-war years. In our own time kinship has continued, as it still continues, to supply the ties and support that people need. Throughout British history it has proved to be a national resource of great value. This has been possible because of its power to adapt to greater mobility and to the demands and opportunities of an increasingly urbanised world.

David Nicolson Lord (reporting on Duncan Dormor et al., The Relationship Revolution): Will Marriage and the Nuclear Family still be Popular by the Year 2000?

I have chosen to present a newspaper report of *The Relationship Revolution* (1992) rather than include an extract from the original research because the report gives a substantial summary of the research findings in a few clear, but thought-provoking, paragraphs. The trends captured in the report – and apparent in a number of other European countries – strongly challenge the robust picture of neo-conventional marriage and the nuclear family given by Robert Chester in an article printed in the second edition of this Reader (see pp. 106–40). Among the trends referred to in the article, four seem to me to have a particular bearing on the stability of the institutions of marriage and the nuclear family. These are:

1 An increase in co-habitation
2 An increase in children to co-habitees
3 A decrease in the popularity of marriage
4 An increase in the numbers of single-parent families

A particularly controversial aspect of Duncan Dormor's interpretation of his findings is the speculation that a patriarchal society might be giving way to an egalitarian one with both partners sharing household tasks and both in paid part-time work. Here Dormor seems to leave fact for fantasy. What actually seems to be happening is that as the number of single female parents increases, they are typically receiving little help from, let alone enjoying egalitarian task-sharing with, their former male 'partners'. In general, those who look after the children of the growing number of young mothers in part-time work are other women, not ex-partners or other men. Caring for children and most other part-time work done by women is low-paid. These developments are part of a process sometimes referred to as the 'feminisation of labour'. Arguably, it is a process favoured by both capital and Conservative governments.

Reading 33 From David Nicolson Lord, 'Marriage could become irrelevant' in *The Independent*, 10 February 1992, p. 2

Living together before marriage will become near-universal in Europe in the next decade or two, according to a report published today.

Society will be increasingly "matrilineal", with more and more children brought up solely by their mothers. The survey, by the charity One Plus One: Marriage and Partnership Research, says that by 2000 four out of five couples getting married in England and Wales will have lived together before. Currently the figure is a half.

Most people will marry when they want to start a family. If cohabitations remain childless, people will continue to make their commitment explicit through marriage. But once cohabitation becomes a context for childbearing, then marriage "could become irrelevant as an expression of commitment."

> This is the only convoluted paragraph in this article. In essence, it says that currently most (long-term) cohabitees eventually marry but if more start to have families outside of marriage (as in Scandinavia) marriage may become less significant and so less popular (see below).

The report, *The Relationship Revolution*, which surveys the history of marriage in more than 30 European nations since the Second World War, says that while divorce rates are likely to remain stable or even fall, dissolutions of relationships in general will increase. This is because cohabiting unions are less stable than marital ones.

Hence "in countries with high rates of relationship dissolution, a substantial proportion of children will be brought up by mothers alone for much of their childhood. If this trend continues the only indissoluble relationship will be between mothers and their children."

The report's author, Duncan Dormor, said yesterday that evidence showed that children brought up by one parent were adversely affected in terms of educational performance, economic prospects, health and psychological stress.

Dormor's analysis here is interpretation not fact, but it is on an issue of vital importance. Others argue that it is the poverty and isolation of many single parents rather than the absence of the biological father that disadvantages their children.

"Their parents are always their parents for their lifetime so if they lose contact with one of them – and in our society at the moment 85 to 95 per cent of post-divorce children are brought up by their mother – it has a major effect on their life. I think fathering is a different activity than mothering. In terms of creating a better environment for children, two [parents] is better than one."

The report says the rest of Europe may be heading towards the Swedish and Danish model, in which the vast majority of people live together before marriage, nearly half those aged 30 are not expected to marry at all, one in two marriages end in divorce and half of all births occur outside marriage.

The trend towards "young and universal" marriage reached its zenith in the early 1960s. Since then marriage rates have fallen, people's age at marriage has risen, sexual maturity has begun earlier and divorce rates have rocketed. Figures suggest half the women in Sweden and Denmark and a third in much of the rest of Europe may remain unmarried.

People who cohabit are likely to be better educated and non-religious. However, cohabitation is not just "unofficial marriage" but a new relationship entered into for new reasons. An increasing number of "cohabitees" have separate households – which the Dutch call living-apart-together.

Having children is the main reason cohabitees marry, but in Scandinavia this reason appears to be diminishing in strength and there is "strong evidence" that marriage is losing ground to cohabitation. Swedish cohabiting resembles marriage more closely with "greater permanency and childbearing".

The reasons for the decline of marriage, the report adds, are the decline of religion, the growth of working among women, the move from country to city, easier and cheaper divorces and a "reduced willingness to sacrifice opportunities for individual growth and development." Mutual respect heads the list of qualities deemed important in a marriage but since couples expect more of each other, they are also more likely to be disappointed.

Mr Dormor said the apparent new era of difficulty in family relationships might be misleading. It could mark the transition from a patriarchal society to an egalitarian one, in which the standard partnership between a breadwinner and a homemaker was replaced by one in which men and women shared household tasks and both worked part-time.

Faith Robertson Elliot: Alternatives to the Nuclear Family – Overview and the Case of the Homosexual Family

Are there alternative types of family to the nuclear family? Among the suggested alternatives are group or communal living, single-parent families, families of co-habiting couples, and homosexual families. Whether or not these are regarded as alternatives to the nuclear family is a matter of careful definition and consideration. What is clear, however, is that these types of living arrangements widely occur and, therefore, merit sociological consideration.

In the brief opening section to this extract, Faith Robertson Elliot presents some reasons why people might look for alternatives to the nuclear family. Of the various alternatives she considers, I have included some material on the homosexual family (single parenthood is discussed in Reading 35). Two types of homosexual couples/parents are described – male and female (lesbian). Just as there is variety in the nature of nuclear family relations, so there is in homosexual family relations. Robertson Elliot cites the work of Ken Plummer and Donna Tanner to illustrate this.

Like the nuclear family, homosexual families can have problems and tensions. However, Robertson Elliot cites research to show that such families are not doomed to damage children and thus helps to dispel a widespread myth.

Reading 34 From Faith Robertson Elliot, *The Family: Change or Continuity* (Macmillan, 1986), p. 177, 191–94

In some Western societies the belief that 'the family' is oppressive has led to vigorous advocacy of 'alternative life-styles'.

This issue brings us back to the problem of defining 'the family', for if, as we found in Chapter 1 is generally argued, variations in arrangements we think of as 'families' make it difficult to delimit 'the family', then it is difficult to say what constitutes an 'alternative to the family'. For example, is a communal endeavour in which several nuclear families share accommodation and pool resources to be seen as an 'alternative to the family' or as a group of families? Moreover, the definitional problem does not end when we draw a boundary round 'the family', for there is the further problem of drawing boundaries round the 'family alternatives'. For example, is an arrangement in which unrelated young adults share accommodation and pool some resources an alternative to the family? Or merely a non-familial household? Is it to be differentiated from communal endeavours? In other words, how is 'the commune' to be defined? These definitional problems have been lengthily discussed in the sociological literature but have not been resolved.

However, advocates of alternative life-styles, like most conventional people, appear to identify 'the family' with a nuclear family unit based on legal marriage and biological parenting. They then identify as 'alternatives' sexual and parental relationships which break with legal marriage and/or biological parenting. Further, advocates of alternative life-styles appear to be thinking of a specific nuclear family form, namely a unit which is independent of kin and privatised (that is, the conjugal family). The search for a non-privatised arrangement may therefore be part of the alternative life-style endeavour. In addition, the nuclear family may be identified with the sexual division of labour and gender inequality, and some alternative life-style endeavours involve attempts to restructure sexual and parental relationships in ways that will restructure the sexual divison of labour and bring women equality with men.

Same-sex (or homosexual) pairings

Couple interaction

Homosexual couples, like heterosexual couples, show a considerable diversity of relationship styles. We look at Plummer's (1978) classification of male relationships and at Tanner's (1978) classification of female relationships.

> Plummer's categorisation of male homosexual relationships, and Tanner's categorisation of lesbian ones, should dispel any simplistic stereotypes of homosexual couples.

Plummer identifies three types of couple relationships: the homosexual marriage, the boyfriend relationship and the homosexual partnership. The homosexual marriage mirrors conventional heterosexual marriage. Rituals that simulate marriage rituals – the engagement party, the wedding ceremony and honeymoon – may be performed and the relationship itself may be modelled on the traditional heterosexual marriage, with one partner as chief breadwinner and playing the active role in sex while the other is generally subordinate and plays a passive role in sex. The breadwinning partner is usually of higher occupational status than the other. The boyfriend relationship is a relationship in which the couple do not live together. This pattern may be adopted so that each partner maintains autonomy and/or so that the relationship may remain hidden from family and friends. In the homosexual partnership, the partners seek to establish a life-style that is specific to their needs and interests. They therefore reject as a model the heterosexual marriage and traditional gender divisons, and sexual behaviour may not be restricted to stereotyped notions of a male/female partner. They may do everything jointly, including the household chores, and may share their income.

Tanner's small American study of twelve lesbian couples, aged 20–35, is one of the very few studies to report in any depth on the way inwhich lesbian couples arrange their lives. Tanner finds that economic independence was, in general, maintained. Rent and household bills were shared, but furniture was individually bought and owned and bank accounts individually maintained. Eight of the twelve couples had joint hobbies, all entertained together at home and six of the couples went on holidays together. However, they did not attend office functions together and did not in general present themselves to the 'straight' world as a couple. All the relationships, says Tanner, had a strong emotional basis. However, six of the couples had had to deal with extra-couple affairs. As in heterosexual relationships, there was jealousy, insecurity, anxiety in relation to other current or past relationships, quarrels over money and time spent alone, disappointed expectations and even violence.

Finally, Tanner categorises lesbian relationships as traditional-complementary, flexible-nurturing-caretaking and negotiated-egalitarian. The traditional-complementary relationship seems to be similar to the homosexual marriage which Plummer describes for male couples. It is, says Tanner, based on a conventional sex-based divison of labour, with one partner performing a provider role and the other a wife role. The flexible-nurturing-caretaking relationship, says Tanner, may also be characterised by economic dependence in that one of the partners may be younger and may earn less than the other, but there is no stereotyped division of labour and greater reciprocity than in the traditional-complementary relationship. There may sometimes be emotional dependence and couples tend to relate on an adult – child basis. Tanner says that most of the couples in her study fell into this category; she suggests that this type of relationship may feed into idiosyncratic emotional and economic needs in a mutually reinforcing way. In the third type of relationship – the negotiated-egalitarian – couples are of equal economic status and relate on a basis of equality, independence and self-actualisation. Tanner suggests that few negotiated-egalitarian relationships long survive the mutual drive to autonomy.

Parenthood

A homosexual couple cannot, *as a couple*, achieve biological parenthood and like any unmarried couple cannot adopt. Previously married homosexuals may be parents but, although mothers in general tend to be awarded child-custody in preference to fathers, custody is problematic for lesbian mothers and, in the case of homosexual fathers, the prejudice against fathers is reinforced. This prejudice against homosexual parenthood has been justified in terms of presumed risks to the child of aberrant psychosexual development and of stigmatisation and/or rejection by peers.

The prejudice and stigma attached to homosexuality makes homosexual parenthood an emotive issue. However, as is discussed below there is no evidence that children are harmed by being parented by homosexuals.

Even so, divorced lesbian mothers may gain custody of their children where their lesbianism is not known and/or custody not contested. Lesbian women may also achieve parenthood through an unmarried heterosexual relationship, or through artificial insemination, or in rare circumstances through single-person adoption. Some indication of the relative prevalence of each of these pathways to parenthood comes from a study by Golombok *et al.* (1983). These researchers found that in their sample of twenty-seven lesbian mothers, twenty-one had been previously married, four had become pregnant in an unmarried heterosexual relationship, one had adopted a child, and one had adopted one child and conceived a second by artifical insemination.

Studies of lesbian motherhood have shown that co-residing lovers share in housekeeping and child-care responsibilities and are regarded as an aunt, big sister or adult friend by the children (see, for example, Golombok *et al.*, 1983; Kirkpatrick *et al.*, 1981; Lewin and Lyons, 1982). However, lesbian mothers and their lovers do not appear to treat parenthood as a joint enterprise. Lewin and Lyons (1982) provide evidence of conflict between mothers and their lovers over child-rearing, of the partner's jealousy of the mother's children and reluctance to share in parental responsibilities, and of mothers' reluctance to give their partners full co-parental status.

No study finds any evidence that lesbian mothers either direct their children's orientation into lesbianism or encourage behaviour 'inappropriate' to their sex. Moreover, there are indications that children of lesbian mothers have more contact with their fathers than do children of heterosexual lone mothers (Golombok *et al.*, 1983). Furthermore, studies which have compared the psychosocial development of children reared in lesbian-mother households with that of children reared in heterosexual lone-mother households have consistently found no differences between the gender identification and sex-role behaviour of these two groups of children (see, for example, Golombok *et al.*, 1983; Hotvedt and Mandel, 1982; Kirkpatrick *et al.*, 1981). However, this evidence is of limited value. Few of the children studied were post-pubertal. Many would not therefore have had any sophisticated awareness of their mother's sexual orientations. Moreover, it could be argued that to compare the children of lesbian mothers with the children of heterosexual lone-mothers is to compare them with a group which also lacks a male figure in the household and in which children have been shown to be disadvantaged. Finally, in the studies under review, lesbian parenthood generally followed marriage and children's earliest years had been spent in heterosexual households, so their results may not hold for situations in which lesbian motherhood follows a non-cohabiting heterosexual relationship or artifical insemination.

35 *Ann Phoenix: Afro-Caribbean One-Parent Families and Gender Socialisation*

The point of including this extract is not to pursue a theoretical debate about whether the one-parent family in the Afro-Caribbean community is a genuine alternative to the nuclear family. My particular purpose is to explore the ways in which adult gender roles and child gender socialisation are essentially different in such families from those in conventional nucelar families.

The extract begins with an explanation of why family research has often excluded black people and how this has contributed to the 'pathologising' of the black one-parent family. It then examines gender socialisation firstly in relation to two-parent families and secondly in relation to 'families without fathers'. The important point is then made that women of Afro-Caribbean origin are more likely to be in paid employment than white women. This and other factors help to create a sense of independence and power among Afro-Caribbean women. The section on gender differences indicates that this positive role image is passed on to young black females who are, nevertheless, still subject to the influence of images of females as passive and subordinate that are common in Western society.

By dint of empirical investigation and analysis, Phoenix 'depathologises' the black one-parent family. She provides a good example of how sociology can demystify negative stereotypes. But is the Afro-Caribbean single-parent family an alternative to the nuclear family or, in some way, an incomplete or even deviant form of it? It seems sociologically correct to accept the widespread existence of the black one-parent family as a fact and to seek to understand and explain it. Some adults may choose single-parenthood and others become single parents by default. To describe either group as 'deviant' – either morally or statistically – risks giving offence without being sociologically helpful. It is more useful to regard one-parent families as part of a *pluralistic* pattern of family life in which the nuclear family remains predominant, if decreasingly so. Of course, white single-parent families outnumber black single-parent families several times over, and this is a rapidly developing feature of the majority culture which requires much more analysis.

Reading 35 From Ann Phoenix, 'Theories of Gender and Black Families' in Gaby Weiner and Madeleine Arnot *eds., Gender Under Scrutiny: New Inquiries in Education* (Hutchinson in association with the O.U., 1987), pp. 51–52, 52–59

Gender relations and colour

Work on gender is usually reported as if colour and class were not salient to gender relations . . . From this it might be presumed that black people and white people develop gender identities in similar ways. If that were the case colour would be irrelevant to work on gender.

However, the reality of racism means that black people have less access to sources of societal power than white people. Black children and white children therefore have different developmental experiences. There is no evidence that gender relations as described in the literature are not specific to the white people who were the subjects of the research on which the theories were founded. In order to understand why black people are omitted from most work on gender relations it is necessary to consider how black people are generally treated in research and academic literature.

When 'normal' processes are being studied, black people are usually excluded from samples for two sorts of reasons. The first set of reasons is to do with the strict control of the number of variables in studies. This is thought to be necessary if the findings of the study are to be clearly interpreted as being due to the independent variables being investigated. Phrases like 'No blacks or Hispanics were included . . . hence some degree of homogeneity was established . . . ' (Sebald, 1986) are indicative of this set of reasons. This exclusion of black people suggests people are exceptions to the norm, deviant or pathological.

The other set of reasons for the exclusion of black people from research samples are the result of what Jennifer Platt (1985) calls 'samples of opportunity'. Researchers frequently study samples that live conveniently near their university departments, or that are visiting the university for some purpose. These localities are frequently white and middle class. This means that the sampling does not ensure that the final sample is representative of the general population of a town or of the country as a whole. Platt points out that samples of opportunity are not adequate when generalizations are to be made from data. This criticism is even more pertinent when generalizations are to be made from a local study which completely omits a significant section of the population, namely black people.

Whatever the reason for the exclusion of black people from certain research projects, the effect is to underline the common-sense view that black people are different from white people. This differentiation is reinforced by studies of pathological or deviant situations which focus exclusively on black people. So for example there are a number of studies of 'teenage' mothers which include only or predominantly black women (Furstenberg, 1976; Field *et al.*, 1980). This focus is especially significant because when 'normal' mothering and 'normal' child development are being studied black women are excluded in the ways already described. 'Teenage motherhood' is highly socially stigmatized and yet this is one of the areas in which black women are made visible. Black households are included in a similar way when 'father-absence' (another stigmatized category) is being studied . . .

The treatment of women in academic literature has paralleled the treatment of black people described above. Researchers on major social issues have in the past omitted women from their samples but made generalizations about the whole population from the data (see, for example, Willis, 1977). Comparisons have also been made between women's and men's abilities and behaviours in such a way that women are presented as being inferior (see Archer and Lloyd, 1982, for further discussion of this). It is therefore ironic that white feminist writings, which have had significant impact on the way that women are treated in academic (and popular) literature, should themselves also exclude black (and working-class) women and hence help maintain the power differentials between black women and white women (see Carby, 1982; the black women's issue of *Feminist Review*, 1984; Brah and Minhas, 1985; Hooks, 1982 and 1984; and Bhavnani and Coulson, 1986, for discussions of how white feminism has refused to address issues of racism, and hence colluded with racism).

Theories of gender development and 'the family'

Human development does not, of course, occur in a vacuum. It occurs within specific contexts. 'The family' is implicitly given centrality in most theories of normal or optimal child development. In studies of child development parents (predominantly mothers), are usually either observed in interaction with or interviewed about their children. This emphasis on parents only occurs because parents are considered to be (and in this society undeniably are) a major influence on their children. The family therefore is a crucial site for the production of the 'normal' child, who among other things shows appropriate gender behaviour and has the gender identity appropriate to her/his sex.

> Arguably, Phoenix might have continued to put 'normal' in the phrase 'normal family' in brackets. In this section, she argues that simplistic views on two-parent families as 'normal' have contributed to the pathologising of the single-parent family.

The social construction of the normal family which is thought best suited to the production of the normal children described above is a highly specific one. In the 'normal' family, marriage and the having of children are inextricably linked so that marriage entails having children, and the conception of children should necessarily follow marriage (Busfield, 1974).

Once children are born, provision for them is divided between the parents on gender lines.

Fathers are expected to be in a position to make economic provision for their children by having paid employment. By contrast women are expected to stay at home with their children and to be responsible not only for fulfilling their children's basic needs, but also for the ways in which their children develop. This means that mothers need to engage in high quality interactions with their children and to have some knowledge of child development (Urwin, 1985). Mother – child dyads are observed in interaction together as if their homes were isolated from the rest of society. This 'desert-island' approach (Riley, 1983) ignores considerations of how material conditions such as housing and income affect how parents are able to deal with their children. It also has a 'normalizing effect' (Henriques *et al.*, 1984) in that it confirms that it is both right and normal for women and children to be locked up alone with each other all day.

The pervasiveness of this model of the 'normal' family within current dominant ideology means that it is the model implicitly assumed in cultural theories of gender development. (Biologically determinist explanations suggest that gender differences are naturally occurring rather than being subject to environmental influences. They therefore do not require any particular family type for gender development and will not be dealt with here.)

There are three major theories of the processes by which gender development occur. In social-learning theories the child learns gender stereotyped roles through observation and imitation of the same sex parent. In addition parents, by using rewards and punishments, condition children into appropriate gender behaviour. In cognitive-developmental theory (Kohlberg, 1966) the child actively learns that each person throughout life belongs to one of two genders. In psychoanalytic theory it is the awareness of genital sex differences between males and females that eventually leads young children to identify with the same gender parents. (See Sayers, this volume, for discussion of these processes.)

What these three theories have in common is that they assume that children live with both parents. Parents provide the child with the first experiences of what it means to be gendered. So, for example, according to social learning theory parents act as role-models for their children as well as providing them with reinforcement for their gender related behaviour. Similarly, in cognitive-developmental theory parents are an important source of information about gender related behaviours. In psychoanalytic theory children learn gender identification both by observing the behaviour of their parents towards each other, and competing with and identifying with them. This is not to suggest that parents are the only influence on children's gender development. School, other adults and other children, the media, etc. all have an acknowledged role in theories of gender development. The point is that the nuclear family is implicitly included as important in these theories.

The assumed importance of this family type has led to a great deal of research on parental influences on gender development. This research in general has searched for pathological gender development in 'father absent' households (which in reality is frequently synonymous with 'single parent' households), and for the concomitants of normal development, as well as the significance of particular parental behaviours in two parent households.

Many children in western societies do not, however, live in nuclear families. In Britain it is estimated that at any one time 9 per cent of all children under 16 years of age live with their mothers but not with their fathers (New and David, 1985). This percentage represents over 1.25 million children. A large number of children, for some or all of their childhood, do not, therefore, live in the type of family which has been used to construct theories of gender development and which has gained acceptance as the best site for the production and reproduction of gendered subjectivity.

Families without fathers

The occurrence of female headed households is not evenly spread among the population. For a variety of socio-political and historical reasons (including the fact that there are many more black women than black men in the USA) black women of Afro-Caribbean origin in this country, and of African origin in the USA are much more likely not to live with their children's fathers (see Bryan *et al.*, 1985, for discussion of the British situation, and Hooks, 1982; Davis, 1981; and Marable 1983 for the USA). In the USA 50 per cent of black children of African origin live in female headed households. In Britain the comparable figures are 31 per cent for black women of Afro-Caribbean origin compared with 5 per cent for black women of Asian origin and 10 per cent for white women (Brown, 1984). Black children are thus least likely to live in the family grouping considered most suitable for gender development or development in general.

Black women of Afro-Caribbean origin are not the only mothers who are likely to live apart from their children's fathers. In 1985, 65 per cent of births to women who were under 20 years of age were to single women (OPCS, 1986). This percentage is not solely composed of women who do not live with their children's fathers because some of these women will be cohabiting. However it is an indication that in this age group it is now not normative to follow the pattern expected in dominant reproductive ideologies.

Since different family structures are now not uncommon in British society, it is important to gain some understanding of how this diversity affects children's gender development. Research on 'father absence' has concentrated on comparing children who live alone with their mothers with children who live with both parents. The findings of these studies usually show that children who live in households without their fathers are less academically successful, and have more behaviour problems than those who live with both parents (Lamb, 1976; Biller, 1981). These findings are usually attributed to lack of paternal interaction for children of both genders and to boys' lack of a role model to provide sufficient opportunities for social learning. Boys are considered to suffer more than girls from 'father absence'.

By extension the poor educational achievement of black children of Afro-Caribbean descent is frequently blamed on 'father absence' (Scarr *et al.*, 1983; Swann Report, 1985), which is used as a shorthand for inadequate socialization. Similarly, analyses of urban unrest in the popular media give explanations in terms of the pathology of the West Indian family (Lawrence, 1982). Recent reviews of literature in this area have pointed out the unsatisfactory nature of research in this field, and how it fails to take into account such factors as length of father absence, age of children when absence begins, reason for absence etc. as potentially significant (Henshall and McGuire, 1986; Archer and Lloyd, 1982).

Because research on gender development starts from a theoretical position which presumes that fathers are crucial to good child development it fails to give sufficient consideration to precisely how, when, and what it is that fathers actually contribute to the process of child development. Most people would agree that it is desirable that fathers should share the care of their young children. However a study which compares how much modern fathers do with their 1-year-old children compared with thirty years ago suggests that, contrary to popular beliefs, fathers have not started to interact significantly more with their children than their fathers' generation (Lewis, 1984). More research is required on what interactive and non-interactive fathers contribute to their children's gender development.

For black people this lack of research, together with the popular definition of black parents as predominantly 'single parent' helps to both produce and reproduce dominant ideological assumptions about the pathology of black families. It also means that black children are not considered to have received proper gender socialization.

Interest in 'father absence' has meant a concentration on parents and the household as primarily responsible for child outcomes. This excludes social network influences and wider social and political influences on gender identity. Children are not, however, monocultural. It is rare for them to be exposed only to their parents and to stay only in one setting. Television, for example, is an external influence and in addition most children eventually go to school where they meet a variety of people. This approach is therefore not 'ecologically valid', to use Bronfenbrenner's (1977) terms.

Ecologically valid attempts to theorize the process whereby all children acquire gendered subjectivity would require developmental researchers to expand the age range they study beyond the current concentration on the very early years. It would also require that children be studied in interaction with other people as well as their parents, and in more than one setting (for instance, Dunn and Kendrick, 1982, study on siblings and mothers; Tizard and Hughes, 1984, study of young children learning at home and in the nursery school). It must also be remembered that children do not learn about gender in isolation. They learn about it as they simultaneously learn about other social facts in their world, like race and class.

This ethnic comparative data on women in paid employment runs sharply counter to negative stereotypes of women of Afro-Caribbean origin as part of a dependent culture.

So far it has been suggested that the only structural difference between black households which have children in them and similar white households that has been discussed is the greater likelihood that black mothers will be single rather than married or cohabiting. However black women are more likely to be in full-time paid employment than are white women. In 1982, 41 per cent of black women of Afro-Caribbean origin were in paid employment compared with 21 per cent of black women of Asian origin and 21 per cent of white women. If part-time employment and self-employement are included, then 59 per cent of black women of Afro-Caribbean origin were in paid employment compared with 29 per cent of black women of Asian origin and 41 per cent of white women (Brown, 1984).

These figures unfortunately do not tell us how many of these employed women have children, particularly children who are under 5 years of age. However, the Women and Employment Survey showed that 20 per cent of women with pre-school children in Britain work part time, while 7 per cent work full time. 56 per cent of mothers with dependent children are in some form of paid employment (Martin and Roberts, 1984). Thus a substantial proportion of young children receive some care from people other than their mothers. It seems clear that black mothers of Afro-Caribbean origin are more often in paid employment outside the home than are white mothers.

It is thus important to consider issues of ecological validity in research on the acquisition of gender identity. Many children, particularly black ones, are cared for by people other than their mothers. The fact that 'it is almost always women's work to care for and educate children, whether at home . . . ' or elsewhere (New and David, 1985) does not mean that children learn exactly the same things from the different women who look after them. Black women know that their structural circumstances mean that they have no choice but to try to be economically independent (see Bryan *et al.*, 1985). This means that black mothers tend to explicitly teach this to their daughters (Joseph, 1981), while the mothers described by Eichenbaum and Orbach (1985) (who are presumably white), subtly encourage their daughters to be emotionally, rather than economically, independent. Moreover the process of gender development may well be different if there is lack of congruence between mother and caregiver about the way boys and girls are treated and expected to behave, than it would be if they were congruent.

There is no substantial evidence that maternal employment outside the home by itself causes children to hold less gender stereotypic views about women's roles (New and David, 1985). This adds weight to the argument that it is over-simplistic for theories of gender development to implicitly assume that the mother necessarily has a privileged position of influence on gender development. This must be particularly so in families where several individuals share the care of children. These families are currently more likely to be black than to be white. The psychic development of children who grow up in these circumstances remains unexplored in psychoanalytic literature probably because therapists are more likely to see white middle-class rather than black working-class women.

Gender differences

While different processes for the acquisition of gender have been theorized, the structure that facilitates those processes (that is, the nuclear family) is, as discussed above, usually implicitly assumed. In a similar way the content that is to be processed is presumed to be obvious and commonly shared. However, societal divisions of race and class mean not only that the process of gender development is different for different groups of people, but also that gender is differently experienced by black people and white people, by working-class people and middle-class people.

Comparing differences between any two groups tends to polarize them and minimize their similarities. A secondary effect of this is that the two polarized groups appear internally homogeneous. However, there are important within-group differences between women and between men which have relevance for theories of gender development. The effects of racism and what this means for the class position of black people means that black children grow up knowing that black women and black men are in a qualitatively different position from white women and white men.

In western patriarchal societies men gain more educational qualifications than women. Even if educational qualifications are controlled, men obtain proportionally more high status jobs (Archer and Lloyd, 1982). These differences are reflected in family relationships. Governments as well as the rest of society accord men the status of 'heads of households' and provide family benefits on that basis. If there are children in a household, it is women, not men, who bear the weight of societal expectations (which they may or may not share) that they will stay at home, care for and educate those children, giving up any paid employment they have in order to do so.

Since stereotypes usually have political implications and can provide a window on how different groups are perceived in a society, it is useful to consider how women and men are commonly stereotyped. Women are stereotyped as being the complementary opposite of men. They are supposed to be nurturant, passive, weak and non-competitive while men are supposed to be aggressive, active, powerful and competitive – qualities which have frequently been used to justify male dominance of society. This is allegedly the content that girls and boys learn in the process of becoming gendered.

Not surprisingly, however, these stereotypes do not fit all women or all men. In fact descriptions of male and female behaviour and dominant/subordinate positions actually relate only to the situation of those who hold most power within society, the white middle classes. This leaves gender relations between black people and working-class people untheorized and invisible.

In general black people of African origin in the USA and of Afro-Caribbean origin in Britain, gain few educational qualifications (Swann Report, 1985;

Eggleston, Dunn and Anjali, 1984; and Staples, 1985). When they do gain educational qualifications it is more likely to be women rather than men who achieve these (Fuller, 1983; Hare, 1984). Black people (particularly men) are much more likely than white people to be unemployed. When they are employed it is likely to be in the most menial, least-paid jobs (Brown, 1984; Hare, 1984; Staples, 1985). The realities of racism also mean that black men are more likely to be imprisoned than are white men.

Hence, black men are frequently not in a position to support women and children economically. The choice of being supported by a man while staying at home with children is therefore not a realistic one for many black women (Hooks, 1982). This gives an indication of one reason why marriage is less common for black couples than for white couples. While western marriage is often portrayed as being solely the result of romantic love, there still are (and always have been) economic reasons for the contracting of marriage (Gittins, 1986). Where men cannot fulfil an economic role, there is less incentive for marriage . . .

Prior to this passage on the positive gender images black children may receive from within their own community, was some material on negative images of themselves often presented via the media. This has not been included here as the theme is a familiar one.

[I]n contrast with what they learn from the wider society, black children learn more positive gender models from their own social networks. Black women's participation in the labour market means that black children grow up accepting that mothers can also be employed. The fact that black children are more likely than white children to live with other relatives as well as their parent(s) means that they have a wider variety of people to interact with and with whom to develop close relationships.

While there are undoubtedly gender differences between black women and black men (see Hull *et al.*, 1982), the denial of power to black people that results from racism, and the fact that black women and black men occupy different gender positions from white women and white men, mean that the 'dominant/subordinate model' of sexual power relationships is not applicable to black people in the same way it is to white people . . .

This does not mean that black people automatically reject the dominant ideological stereotypes of gender roles. Being subject to the same ideological forces as white people means that many black people accept dominant ideologies of gender (see Staples, 1985). This probably occurs for three reasons. First, because being relatively powerless makes people desire the positions, and so espouse the attitudes of those who are perceived to be more powerful (see Fanon, 1952; and Henriques, 1984). Second, because being at variance with accepted societal practice means that indiviuals are subject to stigmatization. Avowed acceptance of dominant ideology may well be (in Goffman's, 1963, terms) in compensation for the stigma that attaches to individuals who do not fit societal norms. An effort is thus made to reduce the social distance between stigmatized individuals and the rest of society, and hence to remove stigma. The third reason is because the pervasiveness of patriarchal structures means that individual subjectivity cannot help but be affected by them (Thompson, 1977).

It is important to recognize that individuals can simultaneously accept dominant gender stereotypes and actively resist racism because they disagree with the basis on which black people and white people come to occupy different societal positions. It is because black women and white women occupy different structural positions that many young black women actively resist the gender stereotypes that are constructed as 'normal' feminity. So, for example, the passivity and weakness that is meant to elicit a powerful male's protection is redundant for black women (and white working-class women) whose fathers and male peers do not occupy positions of power. It is not surprising then that black female school students and white working-class school students are reported to be more boisterous at school than their white middle-class counterparts, and should be sceptical about the benefits of marriage for them . . .

This 'snippet' on the relationship of race/gender with class (part of a longer section in the original) has been included simply as a reminder of this key relationship. Here is an example of what can be termed one of 'the hidden injuries of class' – the linkage between tyrany and humiliation (an axis of consideration also relevant to race).

Race, class and gender

Because racism operates structurally to maintain black people in a state of relative powerlessness in comparison with white people, most black people are working class. Black children and white working-class children therefore have some common experiences of what it means to be gendered – in particular learning what it means to be excluded from and different from mainstream society. The impact of expriences that give working-class children insight into what it means to be a working-class woman or man is unfortunately not theorized in literature on gender, as the following example from a woman who experienced a working-class childhood makes clear.

> A sense of dislocation can provide a sharp critical faculty in a child . . . Working-class autobiography frequently presents, as a moment of narrative revelation, a child's surprise at the humility of a domestic tyrant witnessed at his work-place, out in the world . . . Beyond the point of initial surprise, none of the literature deals with what happens to children when they come to witness the fracture between social and domestic power . . . (Steedman, 1986, p. 72).

To be a black child, to be a black working-class child, or to be a white, working-class child is to occupy qualitatively different societal positions from white, middle-class children.

Questions and Issues

Families and Households: Section 7

The most relevant readings are indicated in brackets after each question.

1 'Both the extended and nuclear family types are now clearly in decline.' Discuss. (Section 7)
2 What evidence is there that *pluralistic* patterns of family types and couple-partnerships (including marriage) now predominate? (Section 7)
3 Discuss and compare the various types of gender socialisation that occur within families. (Readings 34, 35, 37)

EDUCATION

Introduction: Readings 36–40

This section begins with a brief reading which deals with an old chestnut of the sociology of education: the relationship between class, attainment and occupation. The extract from Bowles and Gintis' 'correspondence principle' is quite theoretical. They argue that, far from providing equality of opportunity, the educational system functions to reproduce the class system. Sue Sharpe's article compares the responses on a range of issues of a group of fourth form female students in 1972 with another group surveyed in 1991. The latter appear to feel more independent, but it is doubtful whether they live in a society which is significantly more 'gender equal'. Feminists are likely to respond with mixed feelings to the changes and continuities that Sharpe notes in her article.

The study of the 'mechanisms' by which schools can contribute to the reproduction of class, gender and racial inequalities has become a major area of the sociology of education. The second edition of this Reader included extracts on labelling in relation to class and gender. Here, the example is of racist labelling by teachers from M. Mac an Ghaill. Stephen Ball has suggested that anti-school subcultures can roughly be divided into 'passive' and 'rejecting' (of school). The Asian 'warriors' described by Mac an Ghaill tend more to the passive, although this tendency is, perhaps, more apparent than real.

The fourth reading in this section deals with the long-running problem of the relative failure of Britain's vocational and technical education and training. Many consider that for all the recent educational reforms, this matter has still not been dealt with adequately.

The final reading is a critical discussion of the 1988 Education Reform Act. It would be difficult to over-estimate the importance of this piece of legislation. It was the basis of the Conservative government's long-term strategy to change the culture of the country by creating an environment of competition and achievement. Some critics of ERA, including David Coulby, are more sceptical of the likely affects.

Stephen Ball's brief introduction to the thought of Michel Foucault in the final section of this Reader (Reading 83) could as well belong here. Foucault sees education as a system of 'power-knowledge' in which both dominant and subordinate groups become encompassed. Foucault does not adopt the Marxist class-based theoretical framework of Althusser and Bourdieu, but his approach appears compatible with theirs and, for that matter, with the more empirical analysis of Bowles and Gintis.

36 Samuel Bowles and Herbert Gintis: The Correspondence Principle

There is a mountain of sociological theory and research which indicates a relationship between social class, educational attainment and the economy. Much of this is accessible to students, at least, in secondary sources. It is not possible to find any single statement which does justice to such a large body of work. For one thing, Marxist and liberal sociologists tend to put different interpretations on the class/education/economy connection. However, Bowles and Gintis exposition of what they term 'the correspondence principle' has impressed many in addition to those who share their Marxist beliefs.

Strictly, the correspondence principle argues that the hierarchical relations and attitudes within the educational system socialise young people for the equally hierarchical social relations of production (i.e. of the economy). The emphasis of this brief passage is on creating a consciousness of acceptance and conformity to 'authority' among the young. Thus, they 'fit into' or 'integrate' with the capitalist system. This analysis is echoed by the French structuralists, Althusser and Bourdieu, and by British theorists of the sociology of knowledge, notably Michael Young. The class basis of Bowles and Gintis' argument is implicit in the extract. It is mainly working-class children that are socialised by the educational system for 'alienated labour'. The children of the bourgeoisie are socialised, often in private schools, for occupations of greater authority and power. In elaborate statistical calculations, Bowles and Gintis attempt to demonstrate that these processes have little to do with innate intelligence and much to do with the reproduction of class (see also Reading 13).

Reading 36 From Samuel Bowles and Herbert Gintis, *Schooling in Capitalist America* (Routledge & Kegan Paul, 1976), pp. 130–31

Our critique of education and other aspects of human development in the United States fully recognizes the necessity of some form of socialization. The critical question is: What for? In the United States the human development experience is dominated by an undemocratic, irrational, and exploitative economic structure. Young people have no recourse from the requirements of the system but a life of poverty, dependence, and economic insecurity. Our critique, not surprisingly, centers on the structure of jobs. In the U.S. economy work has become a fact of life to which individuals must by and large submit and over which they have no control. Like the weather, work "happens" to people. A liberated, participatory, democratic, and creative alternative can hardly be imagined, much less experienced. Work under capitalism is an alienated activity.

i.e. to reproduce a class-based society

To reproduce the social relations of production, the educational system must try to teach people to be properly subordinate and render them sufficiently fragmented in consciousness to preclude their getting together to shape their own material existence. The forms of consciousness and behavior fostered by the educational system must themselves be alienated, in the sense that they conform neither to the dictates of technology in the struggle with nature, nor to the inherent developmental capacities of individuals, but rather to the needs of the capitalist class. It is the prerogatives of capital and the imperatives of profit, not human capacities and technical realities, which render U.S. schooling what it is. This is our charge.

The correspondence principle

> In the social production which men carry on they enter into definite relations which are indispensible and independent of their will; . . . The

sum total of these relations of production constitutes . . . the real foundation on which rise legal and political superstructures, and to which correspond definite forms of social consciousness.

KARL MARX, *Contribution to a Critique of Political Economy*, 1857

Here, the correspondence principle is stated – hierarchical relations in education prepare youth for hierarchical work relations.

The educational system helps integrate youth into the economic system, we believe, through a structural correspondence between its social relations and those of production. The structure of social relations in education not only inures the student to the discipline of the work place, but develops the types of personal demeanor, modes of self-presentation, self-image, and social-class identifications which are the crucial ingredients of job adequacy. Specifically, the social relationships of education – the relationships between administrators and teachers, teachers and students, students and students, and students and their work – replicate the hierarchical division of labor. Hierarchical relations are reflected in the vertical authority lines from administrators to teachers to students. Alienated labor is reflected in the student's lack of control over his or her education, the alienation of the student from the curriculum content, and the motivation of school work through a system of grades and other external rewards rather than the student's integration with either the process (learning) or the outcome (knowledge) of the educational "production process". Fragmentation in work is reflected in the institutionalized and often destructive competition among students through continual and ostensibly meritocratic ranking and evaluation. By attuning young people to a set of social relationships similar to those of the work place, schooling attempts to gear the development of personal needs to its requirements.

37 *Sue Sharpe: 'Just Like a Girl' – The Nineteen Nineties and Nineteen Seventies Compared*

The following piece by Sue Sharpe summarises some of the key findings from her up-dated study to be published by Penguin in 1994. This work was carried out in 1991 and attempts, as far as possible, to replicate her research of 1972 in which she surveyed 249 mainly working-class girls from the fourth forms of four schools in the London borough of Ealing (*Just Like a Girl: How Girls Learn to be Women* [Penguin, 1976]). Both studies contain a sub-sample of girls from black ethnic minority backgrounds.

As well as summarising aspects of the 1991 study, the extract below makes substantial comparisons between the girls from the 1991 and 1972 studies. As Sue Sharpe describes, there is both change and continuity. The girls of the 1990s appear more assertive and independent than their predecessors but, whether they realise it or not, their prospects relative to their male counterparts appear to have changed little.

A distinctive feature of both the 1991 study and its now classic predecessor is the clarity with which we hear the voices of the girls. This is precisely what the author intends and she ensures that their views and meanings are illustrated rather than obscured by the substantial array of statistics generated by her research. The spirit behind the following comments from the 1976 preface remains characteristic of the later study:

> By the time I had completed the research and was getting into complex data analysis I had become increasingly alienated from the work. The warm and living nature of the feelings, ideas and hopes of the girls who had participated had been frozen somehow and lost within long computer sheets covered with endless statistics and calculations. Useful as this type of analysis can be in other contexts, I put it to one side in favour of writing about the girls in a more comprehensive way. I tried to locate their own personal statements within the general situation of girls and women in a way that would be more meaningful. They would then be contributing, not as statistics or as typical examples, but as separate individuals who share patterns of personality and experience through growing up in similar environments and having similar social positions and prospects. (pp. 7–8)

Reading 37 Sue Sharpe, 'Just Like a Girl'

Teenage girls in the early 1990s are 'Thatcher's children'. They have been brought up with a sense of expanding individualism and self enterprise in a period of increasingly severe economic recession. With role models like Madonna and Margaret Thatcher, they have learned that there can be a variety of alternative expressions of femininity. But have their attitudes and expectations significantly changed over the past two decades? For fourteen to fifteen year old girls at school in the beginning of the 1990s, the world of girls in 1972 seemed like a century away. For myself, researching their ideas and hopes at both times, their lives did not appear so far apart. Although there had clearly been many social and economic changes in the intervening two decades, I felt both a sense of difference and yet a strong familiarity about many of their attitudes and expectations.

In 1972, the girls in my research could leave school at fifteen (the last year they were able to do this), and there was a reasonable chance of them getting a job. Teenagers of both sexes looked forward to a fuller landscape of employment opportunities than the relative wasteland of today. Throughout the post-war years, educational policy reports had emphasised equality of educational opportunity regardless of class, gender or race. The comprehensive system of education, hailed as a more equal system of education, did not seem to have provided a solution. In the early Seventies, demands for women's equality were being increasingly raised by a growing women's liberation movement. 'Feminism' had entered the general vocabulary, and the next few years would see both the Sex Discrimination Act and the Equal Pay Act pass successfully through parliament.

The following years witnessed a steady decline in Britain's industrial base. As manufacturing industries disappeared, taking men out of the workforce, service industries expanded, drawing women into the lower paid, lower status and part-time opportunities that opened up in many traditionally female areas of work such as the 'caring' professions. Banking and finance also increased during the Thatcher years. But this expansion was short-lived and the economic recession of the early Eighties recurred and deepened through the remaining years of the decade into the Nineties, with a subsequent contraction in service industries. The impact of this recession was felt in previously secure occupations such as banks and insurance companies, causing unprecedented redundancies. With such high unemployment levels everywhere, reality for young people in Britain in the Nineties is that they can easily spend many years after leaving school with little or no experience of work. The government's intention to provide training schemes for all those leaving school at sixteen or seventeen has fallen far short of its goal. With such bleak prospects, it was not surprising to find that working class girls' attitudes to leaving school and getting a job in 1991 had changed from those of their predecessors. Only a minority of them wanted to leave school at sixteen. The rest looked forward to moving up into the sixth form, or going to a sixth form college or further education college to take GCSEs or A levels. Whatever the nature of their feelings about being at school, they showed an awareness of the paucity of work opportunities and preferred to stay longer in education.

"Well, even if I fail GCSEs this year, I'm going to carry on until I pass. As far as I'm concerned there's no point in leaving without qualifications because you're not going to get a job anyway. So while you're wasting your life at home, you might as well be getting more qualifications for a better job in the future."

Marie

In the Seventies and Eighties ideas and beliefs about equality of opportunities became more commonplace. It might reasonably be assumed that by the early 1990s, girls' job choices would show some change. In my early research, girls from four Ealing schools described job expectations covering about thirty occupations, most of which fell into the general realm of 'women's work'. Significantly, forty percent of these were in some sort of officework. The next most popular jobs were teacher, nurse, shop assistant or bank clerk: these accounted for a quarter of their choices. When receptionist, telephonist, air hostess, hairdresser and children's nurse or nanny were added to these, this range of jobs accounted for three-quarters of their job expectations. Almost twenty years later, girls from the same Ealing schools similarly cited about thirty jobs they expected to go into, and like the generation before them, these were predominantly in 'women's work'. Increased awareness of gender issues and rights, and equality of opportunities, did not seem to be reflected in expanding job expectations. There were, however, some significant differences. For example, the expectation or desire to do officework had shrunk to a fraction of its previous size. Hardly anyone specified wanting to be a secretary or to work in an office, and jobs like receptionist and telephonist were also missing. The disappearance of officework may be explained by several related changes. One is linked to the technological changes that have occurred in the business world, and the way jobs are defined. Secretarial work is now done using word processors and other computing machines, and the relevant lessons taught in school are now called business studies rather than typing and office skills. It also reflects a change in attitude towards careers for girls. Officework was once seen as 'a nice job for a girl', that is, the sort of girl who wants a 'clean, respectable' job until she gets married and gives up full-time work to have children. This criterion has become old-fashioned, and, seeing women actively involved in more exciting work, many young girls declare their intention of avoiding 'a boring office job'. The proportion of girls wanting to work in banking and insurance, however, did show an increase in parallel with the expansion in the financial sector during the past decade.

Unlike previously, these Ealing girls did not expect to become shop assistants or hairdressers, and more surprisingly, no-one specifically wanted to be a nurse, although this desire could be disguised within those who wanted to work in the health services. Working with children, however, which had been a well represented choice in 1972, was even more popular nearly twenty years later. Perhaps being a nursery teacher or nursery nurse, or just generally working with young children represents a realistic and enjoyable job for which working class girls could see a demand, and that would be useful in the future. Unfortunately, this kind of employment is still as low paid and low status as it was in the 1970s. Despite a few men entering this field, it remains a 'caring' job predominantly carried out by women, in keeping with the traditional feminine stereotype. Another popular choice both in the Seventies and the Nineties was working with animals, usually as a veterinary nurse rather than a surgeon. Other jobs named similarly at both times include air hostess, policewoman, beautician, and radiographer. New areas of work mentioned include photography, psychology, psychotherapy, graphic design, conservation, and theatre and media studies, the teaching and training related to which entered the school curriculum in the intervening period. It is not clear at present to what extent these kinds of subjects will be affected by the strictures of the National Curriculum. It was good to see some girls expressing hopes to become car mechanics, engineers, or firefighters, but their fewness in number reflects the slow pace of movement away from the traditional stereotype of women's work.

"Engineering kind of appeals to me, I don't know why . . . I like fiddling around with things at home, electronics kits, and I've been doing a meccano since I was about six. I want to work in telly, backstage, anything fiddling around with cameras or lights. I'm doing that on work experience, I've got eight different engineering jobs in two weeks, all in the BBC . . . I really want to do it. I think it would be a bigger achievement if I got a job, because not many women do it."

Rosie

While work horizons had slightly changed but not significantly broadened, growth was more apparent in girls' personal horizons. They placed a greater stress on equality with men, and on their own needs. I constantly detected an increased expression of assertiveness and confidence, and an emphasis on women's ability to stand on their own feet. They almost unanimously endorsed the importance of having a job or career, and in this respect emphasised being able to support themselves if their marriage or relationship broke down, and not having to depend on, nor be dominated by men. In 1972, girls endorsed their preference to be a girl rather than a boy, and those responding in 1991 were even more emphatic. At neither time, however, did girls find it acceptable to define themselves as 'feminist'. In the early Seventies, this label was attached to the bra-burning image propagated by the media. After more than twenty years of feminist activity and campaigns; the establishment of equal rights legislation; and positive changes in attitudes to women in general, many girls in the 1990s remain reluctant to identify themselves as feminist. The naive association of feminism solely with separatism and a rejection of men, or using the term to define women viewed as too active in promoting women, is still commonplace. They, like many women older than themselves, try to disguise feminist pronouncements by the preface: 'I'm not a feminist but . . . ', and there is a tendency to assume more change than has actually taken place.

"Feminism is still relevant but not so much now. I think things are changing a lot. In my dad's office it used to be the men doing the high-powered jobs and the women doing secretarial work. Now they've got men secretaries, some, and some women. There are still men in the high jobs but there are more women coming in . . . I think it will carry on changing. I hope so, it's a better way to work. I think men are more willing to accept women into the higher jobs . . . I don't think I'd call myself a feminist. I'm not one of those that says 'come on, you should be doing this, you should let women in.' They don't need women now to say there shouldn't be a divide because men've realised it now, everyone is changing. It's a lot better."

Fiona

Girls in the early Nineties recognised various social changes that had already made an impact on the lives of many of their relatives and friends. They assumed that nothing can be taken for granted, especially in employment or marriage. Whether they wished to or not, they were aware that they should stay on at school for as long as they could, because if they left without some qualifications, there might be nothing for them in the world of work. Many rightly assumed that doing A levels would help them in a career, but it was no longer a guarantee of work where there were few or no jobs. On the personal side, their less positive attitudes to marriage acknowledged the current high trend in family breakdown.

"I don't want to get married. I don't see the point in getting married. You could live with someone, then if it broke up then it's easier than going through divorce, half this and half that. Some people think it's traditional and you should do it, but I don't see any point in it. You can make a commitment without marriage."

Lisa

However, while these young women had absorbed some of life's social realities, they remained optimistic about other crucial expectations in which they might be disappointed. For example, they had understandably taken on the ideology of gender equality in education and employment. Many schools have anti-sexist and anti-racist policies and there is general endorsement of equal opportunities. Meanwhile, evidence indicates fewer women than men go to university; women have not made many in-roads into areas of work hitherto thought of as 'men's work'; and they still earn considerably less than men. Girls' hopes in education and employment may therefore be curtailed. Like many of the 1972 girls, they also anticipated combining work and family life, and assumed that future husbands or partners would help equally with housework and childcare. Unfortunately such hopes are difficult to translate into practice. In this respect it is interesting to observe the possibility that some of their own mothers could have been girls who participated in my earlier research, and to speculate on the implications of their current occupations. If we compare their mothers' work to that done by the 1972 girls' mothers, we find that there has been very little change. Each are employed in similar low paid, low status, and often part-time work in areas like cleaning, shopwork, officework, health work and childminding. Without a radical upturn in the economy, employers are unlikely to expand their workforce in the near future nor offer conditions to help women with family commitments. Girls' expectations and aspirations in the Nineties are likely to come up against exactly the same barriers as their predecessors.

The restraining parameters of girl's and women's domestic and working lives have changed little in the last two decades, or they have merely been redrawn slightly differently. But while these constraints remain, girls themselves have changed. Whatever the practical realities of their future lives, they have absorbed assumptions of equality and independence, and the ability to support themselves. Although such concerns can also be seen to reflect the increased emphasis on individualism characterising the Thatcher/Major years, their other concerns remain more altruistic. Like their predecessors, the reasons they gave for choosing a possible job or career tended to endorse non-materialistic values such as helping or meeting people, rather than simply earning money. It is cheering to find that such human values have not been superseded, and that positive aspects of traditional femininity are retained. Perhaps it also reflects an awareness of the contradictory nature of society, which makes it hard for girls to gain access to the economic goals it idealises. On the home front, despite some change in family organisation due to factors like male unemployment, patriarchal values are still endorsed. The 'new man' has been more or less dismissed as a bit of a joke, and few men really share responsibility for home and family, either because they resist doing so, or because the structure of their work prevents this. Boys growing up today are being made increasingly aware of gender equality, but they are unlikely to make it a priority in their own lives. Young women may be more aware and determined about their lives and aspirations, but they look forward to a future in which they are likely to end up juggling work and domestic life like their mothers before them.

38 *M. Mac an Ghaill: An Asian Male Anti-School Group and Racist Stereotyping*

Mac an Ghaill's Book, *Young, Gifted and Black* examines two anti-school peer groups in Kilby school, an all boys 11–16 comprehensive, and also a group of mixed ethnic 'black sisters' in a linked sixth-form college. The two anti-school sub-cultures are made up of Afro-Caribbean and Asian males, respectively. The piece extracted here examines the group of nine Asian students, 'the Warriors'.

Although Mac an Ghaill entitles the relevant chapter of his book, 'The Warriors: Invisible Form of Resistance', it is clear that some of them resist 'overtly as well as "passively"'. What is it 'the Warriors' are 'resisting'? Mac an Ghaill states that 'their shared view of the school was that of a system of hostile authority and meaningless work demands'.

Certainly, there is much in the antagonistic relations between the Warriors and school authority that echoes those of 'the lads' described in Paul Willis' classic *Learning to Labour.* Here, however, there is the added ingredient of racial conflict. Outside of schools, the function of the group in resisting sometimes violent racism is obvious. They clearly perceive racism within schools as more insidious, and, because it is sometimes exercised by legitimate authority – teachers – less easy to combat. Accordingly, their resistance tends to be more subtle and even 'invisible' in the school context.

Like much of the best ethnographic work, Mac an Ghaill's research has an air of authenticity about it. However, it is also open to the type of criticism that such research often attracts. How much 'hard proof' of racism by teachers is there in the extract (not to mention the issue of precise quantification)? To what extent does Mac an Ghaill's empathy with the young Warriors influence their responses? Indeed, how far are their responses a matter of interpretation and opinion, rather than of fact?

I've included a relatively long extract from this book because it contains useful sections on ethnicity and class, gender, and generational relations as well as on inter-ethnic relations.

Reading 38 From M. Mac an Ghaill, 'The Warriors: Invisible Form of Resistance' in *Young, Gifted and Black* (Open University Press, 1988), pp. 111–17, 118–21, 122–24, 125

Introduction

> The Rasta Heads – a male Afro-Caribbean anti-school peer group.

The last chapter was concerned with the visiblity of a sub-cultural group, the Rasta Heads. This chapter examines the 'invisibility' of an Asian male sub-cultural group, the Warriors, and the relationship between these two forms of resistance to schooling. The Warriors developed a specific response to their experience of racism. As pointed out above, at one level they constitute a sub-cultural group which challenges the authority of the school. At another level, the Warriors respond to the teacher expectation of their 'ethnic group' and adopt covert anti-school practices. Also, the teachers working within a culturalist perspective which assumes a class homogeneity of the black community is of central significance in maintaining the teacher stereotype of the 'passivity' of the Asian students. In particular, teachers tend to extend to all Asian students the conformity of the middle-class Asian boys. I hope to demonstrate that an analysis of social background will help to reveal more clearly the students' expectations and achievements at Kilby school. More specifically, I examine the presence of working-class Asian male students in a sub-cultural youth group and their resistance to their experience of racism.

Formation of the Warriors

The Warriors group consisted of nine students: Amerjit, Arshid, Ashwin, Iqbal, Khalid, Kulbinder, Parminder, Raj and Sokhjinder. All of them were born in England. Arshid and Khalid were of Pakistani origin, the parents of the other seven were from India. When the research began, all their fathers were working in non-manual jobs in foundries and factories and five of the boys' mothers were working in local factories. During the research period, four of the boys' fathers were made redundant. The Warriors lived in Kilby, except Sokhjinder who had recently moved with his family to Kingston, a predominantly white area nearby. They all attended local primary schools. Amerjit and Parminder began their secondary school career in the top stream but were demoted to the second stream at the end of the third year. Arshid, Ashwin and Iqbal began and remained in the second stream, and Raj, Sokhjinder, Khalid and Kulbinder in the third stream. All of these students were placed in CSE examination option groups during the fourth year, but Kulbinder was demoted to a non-examination class at the beginning of the fifth year. Parminder gained five grade 1 CSEs and went on to a local sixth form college to take A-level examinations. His increased political consciousness, which developed partly as a result of visits to areas such as Southall, informed his later close identification with, rather than participation in, the group's practices. He maintained that these practices were of political significance but that of more importance was a politically organized response to racism in all its institutional manifestations. Parminder formed a close relationship with Amerjit, the leader of the group.

> The image of the academically high-achieving Asian child can be misleading – especially in relation to those of Bengali or Pakistani origin. Despite Parminder, the Warriors contradict both the academic stereotype and that of the 'passive' Asian pupil.

There were a number of peer groups throughout the school. For the anti-school students, the Warriors were seen as the best organised and toughest group and so were respected and feared. The group projected an image of toughness both to the racists outside the school, and to the teachers and students within. They acted as a model for younger students. For the more conformist boys, the significance of the Warriors was that they caused them trouble either directly by threatening them, or by refusing to cooperate with the teachers and so disrupting their lessons. Due to the teachers' preoccupation with the Rasta Heads, the Warriors as a group were often overlooked, though individual members of the group were regarded as disciplinary problems.

Brake (1980, p. 128) maintains that the findings of research on Asian youth conclude that they are absent from youth culture: 'Asians are rarely found in youth culture . . . and indeed are often absent from formal youth organizations'. Working from within a culturalist perspective, he argues that this absence is the result of the Asian youths' 'strong cultural background' which serves to maintain unity within the community. The Warriors explained their absence in the past from youth sub-cultures in terms of the control exercised by their families.

Iqbal: I think there hasn't been gangs, not so much. It's parents, Asian parents, an' uncles an' everything press their children into education. They maybe beat them, but I used to get really shouted at, but I keep telling 'em education's no good there. They think if ye get CSEs it's good.

Although Afro-Caribbean youth groups emerged earlier and are therefore more visible, Asian youth groups are now developing within schools.

Raj: When the West Indians came down to England they had much more freedom than the Indians. It was basically freedom but the Indians didn't have any, as much social freedom but the West Indians had, so they rebelled first, before the Indians. But now the Indians are rebelling. So we become rude boys and things. We know there en't nothing for us here. But our parents still press us.

Asian boys at Kilby School have identified with various white sub-cultural forms.

Sokhjinder: There are some heavy metal, just a few you know, that I've seen in Kilby. I've seen Teds, Elvis followers, rockers, seen a few punks. There used to be two in this school, Sarwan and Allan, and there's Mods. They wear the odd earring and do their own hair.

Of more significance is the identification by the Warriors with the rude boy sub-cultural form. As is indicated by their choice of name, they wish to project a tough image that challenges the stereotype of the 'passive Asian'. They have adopted from the rude boys an anti-authoritarian attitude, particularly in relation to the police and teachers, the most visible agents of social control which impinge on their lives.

MM: What's the main one for the Warriors?
Ashwin: Most of us are rude boys.
MM: Why rude boys?
Ashwin: I think the main way, the main way why we call ourselves rude boys is 'coz we hate authority and school and the police. We like the music and the people.
Iqbal: Rude boys are tough. They can look after themselves. They go round making trouble, so kids are scared of them.

Studies of white, male anti-school peer groups tend to confirm this.

As was pointed out in the last chapter, the emergence of anti-school peer groups usually occurs during the third year of secondary schooling. The formation of the Warriors group followed this pattern. They claimed that when they first came to Kilby school, they were all conformists. During the third year, attitudes and orientations towards the school began to crystallize. The Warriors group came together as they found boys with a similar response. Their shared view of the school was that of a system of hostile authority and meaningless work demands.

MM: So you were good when you first came here?
Arshid: Only when I came here. I mean most of them in the first year you'll notice, they don't cause trouble and the same in the

second year. But in the third, fourth and fifth year, you get trouble off them.

MM: Well what happens in the third, fourth and fifth year?

Arshid: You just start to grow up, to grow up an' ye know if the teachers push ye round you stand up to them. You start talking back to him.

Ashwin: In the first and second years you don't know teachers that well. But in the third year we began to be better mates and stick together.

The informal group was the means by which the authority of the school was challenged and boredom alleviated. As Willis (1977, p. 23) argues:

> Even though there are no public rules, physical structures, recognised hierarchies or institutional sanctions in the counter-culture, it cannot run on air. It must have a material base, its own infrastructure. This is, of course, the social group. The informal group is the basic unit of this culture, the fundamental and elemental source of all its resistance.

MM: Why go in a gang?

Khalid: It just happened en it?

Kulbinder: For company. You come to school and you look forward to seeing your mates.

Khalid: School is really a meeting place. You come at first to read and learn something, but then you come to see yer friends and talk about what you did the night before and arrange to go places and things. Maybe plan to disrupt a lesson or somethin', and look after yourselves.

The Warriors claimed that their group had no formal rules, but certain behaviour was expected. Perhaps of most importance was the obligation never to inform on group members:

Amerjit: When the riots were on, we thought we'd do our little bit to the collection. And Raj got picked up right an' there was about twenty kids involved. He didn't grass on one. Yer all mates, ye stick together. It's like some really strong organisation like the IRA. They don't grass on each other. They really are, that's what I like to see some strong group like that. Like the coppers were really getting on to Raj, but there was no way he was going to budge. To some people, authority is something good, something you can turn to, but not to us. It doesn't represent that to us. Someone I can turn to is my mates. They just represent something over ye, against ye, trying to split ye up 'coz they know when black people stick together we're strong. Mates always look after each other.

The formation of the Warriors group demonstrates that Asian students can constitute a sub-cultural group which challenges the dominant school culture.

Class and response to racism

Resistance to racism

This research was carried out at a time of increasing violence against black people. A Home Office Report (1981, p. 11) found that:

> The incidence of victimisation was much higher for the ethnic population, particularly the Asians, than for white people. Indeed, the rate for Asians was fifty times that for white people and the rate for blacks was over thirty-six times that for white people.

Similarly, a report by the Commission for Racial Equality (1982, p. 6) detailed the rise in racist attacks:

> In the past year, at least sixteen attacks on black . . . Council house tenants have been reported to the Community Relations Council, including one vendetta last month where fire bombs and stink bombs were posted through an Asian family's front door.

Asians have tended to be seen by racists as an easy target. As a result of these attacks there has emerged a number of youth organizations, most notably the Southall Youth Movement, the Bradford Twelve and the East London Bangladeshi Youth Association, to defend their communities. For example, as *Race Today* (1979, p. 52) reported:

> The election campaign of '79 will be remembered for the extra-parliamentary intervention of the black communities of Britain who have . . . taken to the streets to oppose the presence of the NF in their areas. The demonstrations called by the joint IWAs and SYM [Indian Workers Association and Southall Youth Movement] occupied the streets leading to the town. They were driven there by police equipped with riot shields.

The increase in racist attacks, many of which go unreported to the police, have led many Asians in Kilby to realize that they must organize to defend their community. The following discussion with Mr Swali, the father of Raj, took place on a demonstration to support the Bradford Twelve.

> We have to stick together and support each other. It's this place now, we could be next. There are a lot more attacks now in Kilby. I've seen it get more and more. The police don't care, you phone them and they come two hours too late or not at all. We must defend, protect ourselves.

A similar attitude to organized self-defence is adopted by the Warriors. A central element of their development as a group was their resistance to racism both within and outside the school. The Warriors' most immediate experience of racism was the verbal and physical abuse that they received from white gangs. During the research period, I documented the increasing number of attacks on the boys and their families (see C.R.E., 1988).

MM: When did you become aware of racism?
Kulbinder: I don't really know, it seems like always.

Parminder: You come to experience it everyday. White people look at you in a special way, on buses, in shops, in town and all white places, they look at you. They're kind of suspicious all the time.

Although the harassment of the Asian community in Kilby is not confined to skinheads, they are seen as the most extreme and visible expression of white racism.

Amerjit: I just noticed it for a long time. When yer, I think, when yer in junior school, you kind of don't know anything about racialism. You wouldn't understand what's meant. Ye hear names, but it's when ye get older whites seem to pick on ye, call ye really bad names and smash ye up, especially when there's a gang of whites together, skins and that, an' yer on yer own. They kind of act tough, call ye Paki bastard and smash ye up.

As a result of racists' presence at football matches, most Asian boys never attended local matches, although many of them are keen football supporters. They also knew that this was the location for the distribution of National Front and, more recently, British Movement propaganda.

Kulbinder: A lot of my friends have been attacked on their own an' a lot here. It's getting worse with the National Front and British Movement.

It is this evidence of racist abuse which may explain their absence from school football teams and their involvement in sports like hockey.

The Warriors are aware of the media coverage of 'race' issues. Despite the fact that racist attacks are frequently made on the black community, the media present selected 'black crime', and so create the image of the 'black mugger' waging war against white victims.

Amerjit: The news an' papers an' all right, only talk about when say, when a black person mugs someone. What about the fucking National Front an' the skinheads and a lot of other white people hating us for, for nothing?

Kulbinder: Yeah, an' beating us up, even on the drive, in the park, everywhere. But they only go round in gangs. Twenty white kids got one Indian. I bet the judge would send him away.

On discussing the similarities and differences between black and white people, colour discrimination was felt by the youth to be the main difference.

Amerjit: Colour matters the most, especially if yer talking about being accepted. Like you can go to town or like on our trips out to new places an' no-one knows yer Irish, but they know I'm Indian en it, and you haven't even been born here.

Class and racism

This image of Kilby as a defensive zone and more significantly the adoption of the strategy of community self-defence is not shared by all Asians. Britain means different things to different sectors of the black community. *Race Today* (1976, p. 123) describes it as follows:

> Neither is the Asian community of one mind. A middle-class has developed within . . . For this group, Britain is experienced as quite a different place from those who have nothing to sell but their labour power . . . Until recently, all appeared to be running smoothly. The concentration of attacks from outside had the effect of tearing the veil from the surface, bringing to the fore what the different sections stand for. The middle-class Asians do not want to fight. They prefer appealing to government ministers and the police to calm things down. Pressing on them are the mass of Asian families who have been facing the attacks on the ground. The latter stand for the mobilization of the strength and the power of the community in mass meetings, mass demonstrations and vigilante groups.

> The relationship of class and cultural factors in understanding 'race'/ethnicity is much debated (see Section 5). Mac an Ghaill takes a generally socialist approach but by no means reduces cultural factors to class (see below).

As was shown above, I examined the assumed class homogeneity of the black students at Kilby school. Most of the Asian boys' parents worked in foundries and factories before many of them were recently made redundant. A small group of boys of a non-manual work background attended the school. The latter group were over-represented in the top streams of the school and were not involved in the anti-school sub-culture. Two incidents that occurred during the research period highlighted this relationship between class and anti-school sub-cultural groups. First, the 1981 summer disturbances, in a neighbouring area, which the Warriors described as an opportunity to get even with the police and take advantage of goods. The middle-class students condemned the disturbances. They argued that the police were only doing their job and protecting property, including the supermarkets and factories owned by their families.

Permjit: It was just trouble-makers. They were just out to steal as much as they could.

Sukhdip: The police were around trying to stop trouble.

Vijay: You have to have law and order. We lost a lot of trade immediately after. It had nothing to do with, I mean the riots were not really protests against the police and racialism and all that. They were just, just trouble-makers destroying property in their own area.

The second incident concerned an industrial dispute in December 1982, in which 200 textile workers, mainly Asian women, with the support of the Sikh temples, the Indian Workers Association (GB), the local trades council, the local Labour Party and the Socialist Workers Party, demanded the reinstatement of three workers who were sacked for joining the Transport and General Workers Union, the recognition of their right to strike and the implementation of the Wages Council Act of 1979. The management issued termination notices to the strikers, redundancy notices to those working and threatened to close the factories. The dispute ended with the employees gaining their demands, except the reinstatement of the three sacked workers. As a result of a number of successful industrial actions in the region by Asian workers, the Asian traders responded by forming the Asian Trade Association. This development was described in a *Shakti* article (1983, p. 13) as follows:

> Some years ago it would have been quite easy to blame white racism for grievances of Asian workers . . . Now things have changed. With the rise of a relatively under-developed black bourgeoisie, new tensions have emerged, particularly among Asian workers whose relationship with the management has turned on class lines.

Two students were interviewed concerning their understanding of the strike – Ashwin, one of the Warriors, whose mother worked at the factory involved in the dispute, and Mohan, whose family owns the company:

> Ashwin: My mother prefers to work for Indians. She feels better with the other Indian women, but they just use this really. They show they don't care about them, just, just making lots of money, big cars and all that. I would never work for an Indian man. they don't pay you, like we joke a penny a day. We need the money but you have to strike and stick together if yer gonna get better wages.

Mohan's explanation of the dispute reflected the views of the local Punjabi press, that jealousy was the problem:

> Mohan: It's not about wages like is said. Its trouble-makers who are jealous. There's lots of them in our society. How can it be about wages? If you go to other factories round here they pay less and have less room to work in for the machine. It's like I said to you before, at school you learn too much about workers' rights and nothing, they don't tell you about how difficult it is to have a business. We work a seven day week. White people can't understand. A family business looks after it's own people in our society. With us, they don't feel, they won't get any racial abuse. We don't need unions to tell us. You see it's simple, if wages go up our profits are small, and so you end up closing the factory and anyway look at them on strike, they have lost all that money, so it can't really be about more money.

The response of these two students to the strike reflects the development within the Asian community of a black business class and the organization of workers. This business class has emerged by exploiting the labour of Asian women. Women have increasingly come into the labour market during the 1970s, and it has been the members of the Asian Traders Association who have employed them in the Kilby area. The women's demand for union recognition and the response of the management demonstrates the class and gender divisions between these groups. The class division of the Asian community was reflected in the attitudes and practices of the students at Kilby School. This was demonstrated in the different explanations of racism given by middle-class and working-class Asian students, which reflected those of their parents . . .

Class and teacher racist stereotypes

Parminder was the most politically aware Asian student.

Parminder's political awareness was not representative of the Warriors. they may have offered political explanations of racism, but their resistance to schooling was not informed by an organized political ideology. Parminder had an ambivalent relationship to the Warriors, whom he attempted to organize politically. Then tended to ridicule his beliefs and especially his use of political language, but at the same time he was shown respect as an effective and articulare anti-racist speaker. The dominant ideological response of the Warriors remained within a culturalist perspective. However, Parminder was an important influence on the group's shifting on certain issues beyond the limitations of their position. Of particular significance, was their critical perception of the teacher racially-based stereotypes operating within the school. Once again, we can see in the students' explanations of these stereotypes, the class division of the wider Asian community.

The Warriors suggested that the teacher racist stereotypes were not based upon any real differences in the behaviour of Asians and Afro-Caribbeans. Rather, it was the teachers' classification and labelling processes, to which both groups reacted, which determined teachers' perceptions of students.

MM: Do you think that West Indians cause more trouble than Asians?
Ashwin: No, don't be stupid, that's what teachers think. The Indians cause just as much trouble.
Raj: The West Indians are more obvious some'ow. They're seen more easily.
Iqbal: It's not, it's not that they cause more trouble. Its teachers, they pick on them more.
Raj: They treat them differently. I think they think the West Indians are dumber than us.

They challenged the teacher stereotype of the 'ignorant Afro-Caribbean' by pointing out that it was 'high-ability' Afro-Caribbean students who were involved in the anti-school groups:

MM: Do you think they are more dumber?
Raj: No I don't.
Iqbal: No, because they can do as well as Indian kids, better than a lot of them. The ones who have been in most trouble were the brainy ones, like Kevin and Michael, in the first year they were the brainy ones, really brainy.

These racially-based stereotypes acted as powerful social images and were of central significance to the teachers' perception of their interaction with students. They served to highlight the perceived 'rebelliousness' of Afro-Caribbean students and the perceived 'passivity' of Asians. The Warriors claimed that the Afro-Caribbeans did not cause more trouble for the school authorities, but that they were officially 'seen to'. When an Afro-Caribbean student became a disciplinary problem, it was seen by the teachers as a frequent characteristic of being 'Afro-Caribbean'. Any disruptions caused by Asian students were seen as individual acts of deviancy and did not challenge the teachers' idea of being 'Asian'.

Ashwin: White people, teachers look on Asians as kinda quieter an' think they accept their ideas more, agree with them. They think they won't make trouble. It's things like that.

Iqbal: It's like this, if an Indian does something wrong, like one of us cause trouble they think it's just him. There's something wrong only with him an' all that. But if a West Indian does it, acts bad, they drag him off to the head. They'll really shame him up an' think another bloody West Indian making trouble.

Ashwin: That's what happened with us. But then I think they get scared of the West Indian kids more in the fifth year, Kevin an' all them. An' they think that they make others worse. An' Asian kids are more on, their own. If ye think all West Indian kids are bad ye gonna be scared of them when they get big.

Khalid maintained that these racist stereotypes also operated with authorities outside of school, especially with the police.

Khalid: It's like outside. The police pick on West Indians more. Ye see to them the Asians, they're not so suspicious to them. If they see Kevin an' his lot and if they see us they act differently, more tougher with them.

For the Warriors, the effect of these racist stereotypes, shared by the teachers and the police, was to criminalize the behaviour of Afro-Caribbean youth.

Ashwin's explanation of Afro-Caribbean youth's resistance to schooling questioned another aspect of the racist stereotype adopted by teachers, that of the individualism of Afro-Caribbean youth. Teachers frequently explained Afro-Caribbean students' refusal to cooperate with authority in terms of their inability to work together among themselves. Liberal teachers working with the same stereotype often assumed that this was the effect of slavery. Ashwin's argument challenged this dominant view. He claimed that due to the influence of Rastafari, Afro-Caribbean youth were more aware of racism, and that in the past they were more organized than Asian youth in developing collective techniques to oppose it:

Ashwin: In a West Indian community they have Rastas who tell them things more. It's like if you were an extreme Sikh. The Rastas tell you this society isn't good and you should reject it. They stick together more an' are more aware of what's going on instead of us.

Parminder supported this view, arguing that Afro-Caribbean youth had been at the front of the rebellion in school against racism, but that now Asians were as much involved in rejecting school:

Parminder: I think older Indians weren't so much together, didn't act together enough. Some were like my dad in the union. But the Rastas are really strong, that's why white people are scared of them or try to buy them off like here in Kilby. But Asians have learned, now they are more together all over the country and here. Like the third year gang, they are going to be really bad. The teachers hate them already . . .

One of the central limitations of the culturalist perspective, within which the youth sub-cultures worked, was the emphasis upon cultural differences. However, there tended to be among the working-class groups, like the Rasta Heads and the Warriors, a shared perception and response to racism that was not found among the middle-class Asian students. It is against this background of the class heterogeneous nature of the black community that I locate the resistance to schooling of an Asian male working-class youth sub-cultural group.

Alan Smithers and Pamela Robinson: Academic Success and Vocational Failure in the British Educational System

The following extract from Smithers and Robinson's report on post-compulsory education is highly empirical and has a sharp practical focus. They seek to explain the failure of technical and vocational education in Britain relative to its main international competitors. They find the immediate cause of this failure in the long-established elitism which characterises the British educational system. Currently, this elitism is most substantially (and damagingly) embodied in the narrow-entry system of 'A' levels which

- condemn the majority to 'failure';
- offer in themselves too few technical and/or vocational options; *and*
- reflect a second class status on technical and vocational education.

In the sections from their resport included here, Smithers and Robinson:

1 indicate the anti-vocational/anti-practical history of British education;
2 describe and illustrate aspects of Britain's relative educational under-performance in technical and vocational areas;
3 offer some solutions.

In the context of the relative failure of vocational and technical education in Britain, it is worth noting a very different contribution from Smithers and Robinson's: Martin J. Weiner's, *English Culture and the Decline of the Industrial Spirit* (C.U. Press, 1981). His approach is one of cultural and historcal analysis. His central thesis is that the gentlemanly spirit – rooted in rural England – has always tended ultimately to triumph over the industrial spirit. Once successful, even the great Victorian entrepreneurs wanted nothing more than to send their sons to public schools to be turned into gentlemen. The anti-industrial spirit was passed down into the state system of education where it took a strong hold.

Although controversial, Weiner's thesis plausibly indicates that the 'British disease' of industrial underperformance has its origins in the genteel aspirations of the elite rather than in the militancy of the working class. It is surely more likely that the public schools rather than Working Men's Institutes would dominate the industrial culture of the country.

Reading 39 From Alan Smithers and Pamela Robinson, *Beyond Compulsory Schooling: A Numerical Picture* (The Council for Industry and Higher Education, 1991), pp. 19–20, 39–41, 45–46 by permission of the authors and Patrick Coldstream, Director of the Council for Industry and Higher Education

The extract begins with a brief historical reference to the lack of practical and vocational emphasis characteristic of British education.

The Spens Report (1938) noted that:

> The most salient defect in the new regulations for secondary schools issued in 1904 is that they failed to take note of the comparatively rich experience of secondary curricula of a practical or quasi-vocational type . . . the new regulations were based wholly on the tradition of the grammar schools and public schools.

Spens proposed to remedy this through a differentiated system of secondary education in which there would be Modern Schools, Grammar Schools and Technical High Schools.

The proposal for a tri-partite system was adopted in the 1944 Educational Act, but technical schools never became fully established (at a maximum they took only four per cent of secondary-age pupils) so that the arrangements that emerged essentially set up a simple division in the maintained sector between grammar schools and others.

This sharp split linked to 11+ selection was rejected in 1965 by the Secretary of State, Anthony Crosland, in his circular 10/65 to local authorities directing them to implement 'a comprehensive system', but the purpose of this reorganisation was confused by Harold Wilson's promise as leader of the Labour Party in 1963 that comprehensives would provide "grammar school education for all" Their essential aim was further undermined by failure to rethink the qualifications along with the schools, so that once more practical/technical abilities were neglected.

Much of what was attempted was embarked upon for the best of motives. Because grammar school, academic, not to say classical, education led to so many of the best jobs (and was seen as the best general education), progressive thinkers were determined that no one should be deprived of it.

In short, both the tripartite and comprehensive systems gave low status to technical/vocational education.

The best should be open to all. It was strongly felt that working class youngsters should not be 'fobbed off' with 'mere' vocational education which would limit – for ever – the range of occupational choices open to them. But this conflicted with the aim of developing different kinds of excellence, and it is perhaps fair to suggest that comprehensive schools taken together have never been entirely clear about their purpose. As the Council for Industry and Higher Education has said in another context "sureness of purpose is the essential ingredient of high morale" . . .

Qualifications of workforce

The character of the English education system emerges in the country's workforce. At the graduate level it compares favourably with other countries but, because schools, in effect, dismiss a large proportion of the population as unacademic rather than developing their talents for making things, designing things and working with people, Britain lacks the range and level of developed skills that other countries have at their disposal.

The workforce, as Chart 9.1 shows, seems seriously under-qualified. About two-thirds of the workers lack vocational qualifications compared to only about a quarter in Germany and just over a third in The Netherlands. Only a fifth have vocational qualifications of the level of BTEC National or City and Guilds.

Chart 9.1 Vocational Qualifications of Workforce

Vocational Qualifications	*France (1988)*	*Germany (1989)*	*per cent Netherlands (1985)*	*UK (1988) **
Degree and Higher Diplomas *	14	18	18	17
Intermediate Vocational Qualifications †	33	56	44	20
None §	53	26	38	63

* Degrees, HND, HNC, teaching, nursing and equivalent
† BTEC National, City and Guilds and equivalent
§ General education only (below HE)

Source: Mason, Prais and van Ark (1990) Discussion Paper No. 191, London: NIESR

Detailed studies by the National Institute of Economic and Social Research have demonstrated the consequences for productivity, earning power, workmanship and service; in short many of the things that contribute to the quality of life. In Germany, for example, the technology exists to make and distribute customised kitchen units; these are units tailored to fit the particular shape of a kitchen, an advance on standardised and mass-produced patterns. Attempts to import the technology into this country, however, have failed because workers lack the arithmetic skills required to operate the machinery.

In a study of biscuit-making in The Netherlands, NIESR found that differences in the skill-levels of the workforce had a notable effect on the efficiency of production, with Dutch labour-productivity being about 25 per cent higher. As significant as this is, it is less than the overall Dutch productivity advantages across industry estimated at 45 per cent, probably reflecting the greater scope for using unqualified employees (in loading and packing for example) in automated process industries like biscuit-making. This bears out what NIESR found in comparisons with Germany where Britain seemed at a particular disadvantage when operatives' craft skills were crucial such as in making motor vehicle components, clothes, and wood furniture.

Even the academic track to degree level apparently fails to bring enough people to mathematics, engineering and technology (though it is not clear why the market has not acted to correct this). An analysis of graduate output by country, as in Chart 9.2, suggests that this could, in part, be due to the way those with numerical ability are distributed between engineering and the sciences. While in the UK engineers were only 41 per cent of the aggregated total, in Japan they were 85 per cent and in West Germany 74 per cent.

Surprisingly, perhaps, the higher levels of graduate output in Japan and the United States are mainly in fields such as the social sciences, law and business studies. But it must be remembered that while the UK is struggling to fill the available engineering places, in Japan there are 4.7 applicants for every place and it is the disappointed candidates who turn to business studies. In Britain business studies are often the first choice.

Chart 9.2 Graduate Output by Country

Subject Area	*Per 1000 of Age Cohort*				
	UK (1985)	*France (1981)*	*West Germany (1984)*	*Japan (1985)*	*USA (1985)*
Engineering and Technology	18	20	28	45	25
Science, Maths and Computing	26	33	10	8	27
Medical and Health Related	7	5	13	12	15
Social Sciences, Law, Business Studies	37	58	45	91	87
Arts, Humanities, Education	36	77	37	55	43
Other *	14	9	6	18	33
Total	138	202	139	229	230

* Mass communication and documentation, home economics, service trades, transport and communications, agriculture, forestry, fishing and other not specified.

Source: Annual Statistical Yearbook (1989), Paris: UNESCO

Nevertheless the differences are not as large as is sometimes imagined and it appears that the UK may be producing more science and engineering graduates than Germany. Prais of NIESR has argued that the root of our poor economic performance compared with our industrial competitors lies elsewhere.

Although briefly made, this is a crucial point.

Chart 9.3, adapted from Prais, shows output in engineering in terms of the categories 'doctorate' through to 'craftsman'. It suggests that only at the level of doctorate does the UK compare favourably with the other countries, and particularly in the support levels of technicians and craftsmen it falls seriously behind. This can lead to graduates being deflected to lower level tasks.

Chart 9.3 Qualifications in Engineering and Technology in Selected Countries, 1985

					*thousands**
Level	*UK*	*France*	*Germany*	*Japan*	*USA*
Doctorate	0.7	0.3	1.0	0.3	0.5
Master's degree	2	-	-	5	4
Bachelor's degree	14	15	21	30	19
Technician	29	35	44	27	17
Craftsman	35	92	120	44	na

* Raw numbers for Japan and USA reduced in proportion to UK population, populations of France and West Germany taken as sufficiently similar to UK not to require adjustment.

Source: Prais (1988), National Institute Economic Review, February 76–83

There are reasons, therefore, as we have seen throughout this report, for questioning the efficacy of the present education and training arrangements in enhancing the country's competitiveness, companies' recruitment and individual mastery. It seems important to consider what improvements might be made, and we turn to the possibilities in our final chapter.

Technical and vocational tracks

A widely recognised failing of the English education system is the absence of co-ordinated technical and vocational tracks from school into employment and higher education. A number of reforms have been attempted, but they have tended to be piecemeal and partial, and to have lacked coherence and credibility.

Some of the features of such tracks might be:

- they should be freely chosen; not, as at present, entered after failing academic studies;
- young people in the later years of compulsory schooling should be taught about employment opportunities (rather than just being sent on 'work experience') to help them choose;

- schools and employers should work together so that occupational skills could be developed in occupational contexts;
- education to age 18 should not be compulsory – it is difficult enough to keep some young people there till 16 – but only employers offering approved training should be allowed to recruit young people below the age of 18;
- wage levels for young people should reflect the fact that they are trainees and not fully qualified.

The qualifications they led to would be paramount. They would be sought after only if they led clearly and naturally into employment and further stages of education/training.

> Although widely supported within educational circles, successive Conservative governments have firmly resisted this type of reform of 'A' levels.

The equivalence of the practical/technical track could be established by its too leading to A levels at age 18. These could be among the say five to be studied. Practical/technical options could also comprise part of any diploma that was introduced at 16, or there could be practical/technical GCSEs. In creating GCSEs and A levels in practical/technical subjects care would have to be taken to avoid the 'academic drift' that seems to be besetting technology. Practical/technical A levels could be stepping stones to higher education where they should help with the considrable difficulties in recruitment that the technological subjects are experiencing. A vocational version of the practical track could be created by allowing young people of school age to experience and specialise in the work they might move into.

> It remains to be seen whether the (General) National Qualifications – (G)NVQs – will improve the status of vocational education.

But what would really give impetus to the formation of technical and vocational tracks would be a registration scheme for skilled workers in the way that there is for some professions. If in order to practise as a registered plumber, for example, a person had to demonstrate competence and acquire certain qualifications, then the incentive would be there to acquire those qualifications. Registration schemes of this kind can be introduced only slowly to give current practitioners a chance to qualify, but they would seem worth considering.

It has not been within the scope of this study to make a detailed analysis of educational expenditure, but it looks as if the top part of the ability range receives a disproportionate share of resources. In view of the argument above which shows how the system at present 'creams', is this the distribution of resources we would want? The aim of technical and vocational tracks would be to establish **mainstream** education and training post 16 for all. This would not only have economic benefits but give dignity to many who now look upon themselves as failures.

David Coulby: The 1988 Education Act

The 1988 Education Act was intended to initiate a new era in education and, for better or worse, the signs are that it will do so. Several but not all of the measures introduced by the Act were controversial. There is a wide consensus of support for a National Curriculum and related Assessment – although considerable debate about, respectively, content and format. There is general support, too, for the local management of schools (LMS) which put more managerial autonomy into the hands of school governors and heads at the expense of Local Education Authorities.

The measure aimed at creating an intenal market in education have been much more bitterly contested. An internal market involves the creation of a competitive system within a public service akin to the free market in the private sector. The two measures of the Act which seek to achieve this in education are 'open enrolment' and 'opting out'. 'Open enrolment' requires schools to meet demand for places 'up to the limit of their physical capacity'. It is meant to enable popular ('good'?) schools to expand and to put pressure for improvement or closure on unpopular ('bad'?) schools. As Stuart Maclure comments the aim of open enrolment 'was to increase significantly the power of parents as consumers' (1992:30). The Conservative government expects the exercise of consumer power to improve standards.

'Opting out' allows schools to leave local authority control altogether under certain circumstances. In 1992, John Patten, then Secretary of State, stated that he hoped the majority of schools would eventually become grant maintained i.e. opted out. Such schools are not private or independent because they receive a grant from the central government. However, they are now (1993) largely able to determine their own character and are free to compete for 'customers' as they wish. John Patten's Education Act of 1993 was mainly intended to strengthen the 'free market' aspects of the 1988 Act. It also set up a central mechanism to deal with 'unsatisfactory' schools.

David Coulby deals with a number of themes apparent in the 1988 Act which cut across specific measures These are:

- Popularism
- Privatisation
- Financial control
- Centralisation

Coulby tends to be sharply critical of many aspects of government policy but, given the massive budget devoted to informing the public about the Act, this probably does no more than strike a balance.

Reading 40 From David Coulby: 'The 1988 Education Act and Themes of Government Policy' in D. Coulby and L. Bash *eds., Contradiction and Conflict: The 1988 Education Act in Action* (Cassell Education Ltd., 1991), pp. 1, 4, 4–5, 5–6, 7–11, 11–12, 148–49

The importance of the Act

The 1988 Education Reform Act is a major component of government policy. Along with the legislation on the community charge (poll tax), it is the most important achievement of the third Thatcher government. The ideas and policies behind it were among the main planks of the political platform on which the Conservative Party fought and won the 1987 general election. It brings about the most far-reaching changes to the education system of England and Wales since the 1944 Education Act. Because of the magnitude of these changes which it is bringing about, it probably represents the most important positive government intervention in any area of social policy since Margaret Thatcher became Prime Minister in 1979 . . .

The important strands of government policy of which the Act forms a significant if uneasy part may, at this stage, be summarized under four headings; popularism, privatization, financial control, and centralization. The rest of this chapter examines each of these in turn . . .

Popularism

Margaret Thatcher frequently played the 'nationalist card' during her period in office and identified democracy and capitalism with British nationhood.

Notwithstanding this comment, in 1992 it was announced that the Government intended to set up an enquiry into the functioning of the police force.

Margaret Thatcher's three election successes cannot be explained away as the result of fractures within the political opposition. The policies formulated and adopted by her governments have had considerable popular appeal to people without the wealth and power normally associated with Conservative Party supporters. Among the popular themes which her governments have been able to adopt are notions of nationhood, national role, destiny, heritage and tradition. Within this theme the aspirations of democracy and free-enterprise capitalism have successfully been conflated. Another popularist strand has been the critique and debunking of the self-interest and incompetence of professionals and experts. This critique has been highly selective: it has been applied to teachers, social workers, broadcasters, academics, opticians, ambulance workers and medical doctors, but not to the police, the armed forces or business-people. Indeed this latter group have been seen to carry almost a sacred wisdom and their control over the administration of wide areas of social policy has been encouraged. The 1988 Act itself is an important component of the appeal to popularism and consolidates many of these themes: the traditionalist National Curriculum, lots of tests and assemblies, and attacks on familiar folk-devils such as LEAs, teachers and academics all form part of its attempt to appeal beyond the educational establishment to a broader popular constituency. The power of business-people over other professional groups has become consolidated in the new boards of governors of further education (FE) colleges, polytechnics, higher education colleges and, to a lesser extent, schools. The success of the three Thatcher administrations was derived in no small part from the ability to sense popular feeling and to use this as a basis for policy. This can be seen on the one hand in the sale of council houses or Girobank and on the other in the heightening of controls on trade unions or football supporters. This popularism works in at least two ways: as well as itself providing an apparently inexhaustible supply of electoral support, it also serves to fracture the cohesiveness of any opposition. As each person struggles to find wealth and status in the property-owning, share-owning democracy, any sense of group cohesiveness has been undermined. Groups and individuals are increasingly fractured in their opposition to others, be they black people, trade unionists, youth, the loony left or the educational establishment . . .

In terms of the Act it is tempting to see the most obvious manifestation of popularism in the National Curriculum. Certainly the back-to-basics emphasis, the stress on regular testing and published results, and the momentum to shift the school curriculum back to the familiar safety of the way things were when the parental, or grandparental, generation were at school, all seem to confirm this. The National Curriculum also contains many nationalist elements (explored in Chapter 2) which place it within this familiar government theme.

There are other aspects to the Act which also derive from and strengthen those fractured aspects of popularism. The mechanisms whereby schools can opt out of LEA control encourage the narrow self-interest of a small group of parents even if this is at the expense of the system as a whole. In the city of Bath where the LEA wished to close one secondary school and create a sixthform centre in the interests of rationalization, it was possible for that school (Beechen Cliff) to appeal to sectional parental support in order to opt out of LEA control and thereby evade closure. (This was the case which first tested the opting out legislation in the courts; it is further examined in Chapter 4.) Consequently, the LEA (Avon) could not plan education in the city for fear that the next targeted closure victim would also opt out.

Privatization

Perhaps privatization should not even be categorized separately from popularism. What superficially may be seen as a short-term strategy of selling off centrally held assets in order temporarily to keep down taxes actually has a longer-term popularist result. Margaret Thatcher acknowledged that privatization had led to electoral support and actually linked this to education: 'Just as we gained great support in the last election from people who had acquired their own homes and shares, so we shall secure still further our political base in 1991/92 by giving people a real say in education and housing' (quoted in Chitty, 1989, p. 221). Those who have brought shares in British Telecom and all the succeeding highly publicized privatizations have bought an interest in the continuation of the party in power lest any other party should seek to renationalize these assets. Similar fears inform the voting patterns of those who have been able to purchase their own council houses. Even more fundamentally, some of these people see themselves as having bought an interest in the capitalist system. The share-holding democrats are proud of their involvement with the large corporations and follow their publicity drives and share prices with equal enthusiasm. The growth of sponsorship in sport and cultural activities, not to mention education, along with the re-found global confidence in capitalism which accompanied the rapid political change in Eastern Europe, have served to make the names and interests of the large corporations a source of derived status for those individuals and groups fractured from any other form of cohesiveness. ADT (the initials in this company's title do not stand for anything, but among its main activities is the provision of private security systems and personnel) are sponsoring a city technology college (CTC) in south London. They are also major sponsors of the London Marathon. Completion of the race, commitment to the college, and loyalty to the corporation will be confused for all those who proudly display the corporation's logo on their tee-shirts.

Opting out into grant-maintained status and the various other changes of school structure have led to a more heterogeneous education system. City

The argument here is that although this range of reforms does not privatise the education system, they will have many of the effects of privatisation.

technology colleges and grant-maintained schools (GMSs) provide the structural forms of privatization within the education system. The newly independent colleges and polytechnics with their expensive corporate logos and their happy enthusiasm for managerial language ('strategic plan', 'chief executive', 'bidding', 'cost centres', 'the discipline of the bottom line' and worse) are further proud flagships of privatization. They are structural arrangements which have parallels with those hospitals taking the opportunity to opt out of their area health authorities or current proposals to privatize the prison service or the benefits system. They are obviously important in the way in which they disrupt and damage the pattern of LEA provision.

But in terms of education, privatization also has an important ideological valency not distinct from the theme of popularism. The attack on education carried on by politicians of both major parties since 1976 (Bash and Coulby, 1989, pp. 3–18) has been an attack on state education. By contrast, the Thatcher governments have appealed to the fee-paying sector as an area of excellence and have strengthened this sector by the establishment and expansion of the Assisted Places scheme. The CTCs and GMSs can market themselves as private, as distinct from and superior to the much-derided state education provided by LEAs. Like the independent colleges and polytechnics they are part of that radiant entrepreneurial world of corporate capitalism.

The Assisted Places Scheme provided government funding for certain children to attend private schools who would not otherwise have been able to do so.

Preference given by the government to any form of schooling not maintained by an LEA certainly helps to diversify the forms of institutions and thereby encourage competition between them. It also serves persistently to undermine the state system, as any form of schooling is by definition seen as being preferable to that which the vast majority of the nation's children and young people attend. The argument seems to be that since state schooling cannot be private it cannot be good. Whilst some governors and parents may be persuaded by this to opt out, it does little for the status and morale of teachers and pupils who remain in the persistently denigrated LEA sector.

Financial control

An explicit goal of the Thatcher administrations was to reduce public expenditure. Less explicit is that this ambition seems to apply to all areas of government activity except those concerned with the armed forces or the administration of law and order. Whilst it may be argued that the Thatcher administrations have actually been remarkably unsuccessful in keeping down public spending, the effects of financial stringency on LEAs are becoming more visible. Indeed, this stringency began before the 1979 election. In terms of the pay level of teachers, the physical fabric of many schools and their lack of appropriate books and equipment (see Chapter 8), the inadequency of public spending on education is increasingly noticeable.

The implementation of the 1988 Act has led to increases in public expenditure on education which contradict the government's overall fiscal policy. Chapters 2 and 3 show the ways in which the financing of the

National Curriculum, especially following the impact of the influential Task Group on Assessment and Testing Report (TGAT, 1987) on its implementation, are rapidly growing whilst still remaining inadequate for the job. The cost of the National Curriculum exercise with its cascade of glossy paper and its associated testing mechanisms – running into millions even at the pilot stage – and the as yet unacknowledged implications for systematic nation-wide in-service training (INSET) are beginning to emerge. Similarly, the costs to the public purse of the creation of the CTCs is now proving to be difficult to justify (Chitty, 1989, pp. 223–24). Some of these costs may be met by shifting resources from other areas of expenditure. For instance, the implementation of the National Curriculum will become a priority for the already allocated expenditure of central government resources on INSET. Nevertheless, additional real costs are beginning to mount and this is one of the reasons for the continuing opposition from some sections of the Cabinet to the establishment of a new national testing bureaucracy (see Chapter 3).

The Act not only contradicts this theme of government policy by increasing expenditure on education; it also, in at least one important respect, completely undermines another strand of policy which could have led to savings in education. As mentioned above, the ability of individual schools to opt out of LEA control has paralysed planning and rationalization of schools. The pressure, not least from the Audit Commission, to save money through the reorganization of (especially secondary) schools has thus been undermined. Since government policy on education is to encourage the majority of schools to opt out, this contradiction in financial policy is to be continued and exacerbated.

It may then be speculated that the government's stress on reducing public expenditure is by no means a purely fiscal measure. Not only are the cuts confined to particular areas of government policy, even within an expensive area of social provision such as education, but also the government is happy to contradict its own financial policies provided the ideological and political gains are sufficiently high. For example, it has been claimed by the Opposition spokesperson on education that CTCs are currently receiving eighty times the funding of LEA-maintained schools (Bates, 1990). Similarly generous capital grants to GMS schools, combined with support from local business, can enhance the sense of independence of these schools and gave the pupils and their parents a sense of identification with a differentiated education system. Meanwhile, commercial sponsorship of both CTCs and GMS schools, along with a more general reliance on parents for voluntary contributions towards school equipment and activities, undermines the sense of free and adequate state education as a universal right and endorses the Thatcherite notion of charity as an appropriate form of resourcing for social and educational provision for the non-privileged. Privatization (see pp. 7–9) may be more about gaining votes than saving money, but it also carried for the Thatcher administrations the force of a moral crusade. It is only by considering the move towards centralization in government policy that the nature of the ideological and political gains can be fully understood.

Centralization

The tendency to shift power to Westminster was an ongoing but undeclared policy of the Thatcher administrations. This focus on Westminster control is actually easiest to recognize with regard to relations with other potential power centres. The refusal to offer even limited devolution to Scotland and Wales is one dimension of this. The xenophobic response to the consolidation of the European Community (EC) is another. The Thatcher government was prepared neither to devolve power to regional assemblies nor willingly to play its part in the emergent European state, presumably because it wished as much power and control as possible to remain at Westminster – that is, with itself.

The abolition of the Greater London Council (GLC), the metropolitan councils and, under the 1988 Act, of the Inner London Education Authority (ILEA) are more substantial manifestations of this policy of centralization. Certainly, these abolitions can more readily be seen as the elimination of powerful and prestigious political opposition. But beyond this is the implication that the local state is no longer a valid entity. The creation of the small inner London borough LEAs is only likely to enhance the impression of the lack of viability of the local administration of social policy . . .

The 1988 Act removed from them the control of the higher education colleges and polytechnics. LEA's role in further education had gradually been diminished through the power of the Training Agency. The newly established Training and Enterprise Councils (TECs) have replaced the Training Agency and they have even greater powers and resources in FE decision-making as against LEAs. FE colleges, like the polytechnics before them, may soon be removed from LEA control. The role of the LEAs will be further reduced through the new management arrangements introduced under the Act (see Chapter 7). As increasing numbers of schools opt out into GMS status, the responsibilities of LEAs will diminish further and their resourcing from central government will also be accordingly reduced. It may be that the role of local government in educational provision is being eroded to the point where its only important function will be to monitor the National Curriculum and in particular the testing procedures and results. Any government attempting to lessen the poll tax burden by shifting teacher salaries from local to central government responsibility is likely to exacerbate this trend. The point of erosion of the role of LEAs may still be some years hence, but in the progress towards it there will come a point at which the need for local government itself is questioned. A prefecture system of administrating centrally made policies and decisions may well be seen to be more cost-effective.

Beyond the 1988 Education Act

The aims of an alternative policy would be quite different, in many respects, to those of the 1988 Act. Two broad aims can be suggested. Firstly, responsiveness to overseas economic competition must certainly be acknowledged, but in the concrete terms of encouraging a far greater proportion of each age-cohort into further and higher education, rather than in the abstract terms of 'standards'. It is by fully developing the skills and creativity of its population that the UK is most likely to succeed in international competition. The notion that overseas economic competition justifies a return to a nineteenth-century model of public education is nonsensical. Furthermore, international competition can only be responded to appropriately if it is within the terms of the actual role of the UK in the world system at the end of the twentieth century: that role is as a moderately strong economy gradually finding its place in the major global economy of the EC, and a multicultural, cosmopolitan society reluctantly abandoning arcane, one-nation belief systems. The aim of the education system would be to help the economy and the society to accommodate themselves successfully to these ostensibly uncomfortable roles. To achieve this would necessitate some change to both the structure and the content of education in England and Wales. Secondly, the aim of generating a much higher participation rate in educational success is commensurate with that of eroding the elitism and ethnocentrism which currently informs so much of school knowledge. If these two aims are acknowledged then the structures and content of education which currently enforce a divide between academic and technical knowledge, between education institutions and the workplace, are the ones in particular need of reform.

An alternative educational strategy would attempt to bridge the academic/vocational divide. A more polytechnical education (Castles and Wustenberg, 1979) would ensure that all children came into contact with a range of workplaces throughout their school years. Collaboration between educational institutions and other workplaces would aim to erode mutual ignorance and prejudice. It is necessary to stress that this would have to be a two-way process. Many of the criticisms of education from industry and commerce . . . have been marked by a facile ignorance of the processes of education. Developing knowledge in people from industry and commerce about the conditions of state schooling is as vital as bringing teachers and pupils more closely into contact with the workplace.

Questions and Issues

Education: Section 8

The most relevant readings are included in brackets after each question.

1 To what extent, and in what ways, does the education system contribute to the reproduction of class inequalities? (Readings 36–37)
2 'Education cannot change society.' Discuss this view in relation to gender and 'race'. (Readings 37–38, 40)
3 Discuss the concepts of labelling and stereotyping in the context of education (Reading 38. Textbooks, and the Education Section of the second edition of this book will provide further help for this question.)
4 To what extent do you consider that the educational system is responsible for Britain's economic difficulties? (Readings 36–37, 39–40)
5 What ideological values underlie the Education Reform Act of 1988? (Readings 39–40)

SECTION 9

WORK AND NON-WORK

Introduction: Readings 41–45

This section focuses on some new or relatively new issues in relation to work and non-work. Substantial change is occurring in this central area of social life. The impact of new technology; the shift from manufacturing to the service sector; the increase in long-term unemployment; the new emphasis on consumption; these are all part of a shifting picture.

One attempt to contrast the 'new' in relation to the 'old' is the Fordism/Post-Fordism thesis. Greater flexibility in production and greater variety in consumption are major characteristics of the supposed Post-Fordist world. In a seminal piece, Robin Murray expounds on these themes quite extravagantly. In contrast, Paul Thompson is highly critical of the Fordist/Post-Fordist model, although he does accept some aspects of it. He outlines an alternative 'core theory' of the labour process in capitalist society.

Philip Money's review article is included in this section as a sharp reminder that many of the realities of work and unemployment in Britain are no longer determined here but are features of the global economy in which transnational corporations dominate. The reading describes how white-collar jobs can be exported, apparently even more easily than those in manufacturing. Readings 54 and 55 in Section 12 flesh out the international context of capital and labour. Long-term unemployment in Britain is certainly affected by international factors, although it is in the context of British government policy that Brendan McDonnell discusses it in Reading 44.

The final extract in this section, Reading 45, explores a theme of growing importance, that of consumption and identity. While this area has produced exciting and imaginative analysis, Lunt and Livingstone show that it makes little sense to approach it outside of the context of stratification and inequality.

41 Robin Murray: Fordism and Post-Fordism

The terms Fordism and Post-Fordism are among the most important recently coined in social science. They carry a high content of description and explanation. They describe two distinct types of economic organisation and, beyond that, two distinct social, political and cultural regimes.

Fordism is primarily a form of organising production. It was and is adopted to produce mass goods (or services) for mass consumption. Robin Murray states four principles on which Fordist mass production systems are based:

- products are standardised;
- (some) tasks are mechanised;
- (other) tasks are subject to 'scientific management';
- a flowline assembly system is adopted.

Mass products are consumed on the mass market with potentially massive profits for owners.

Murray goes on to describe other aspects of Post-Fordism: the role of the state, including its economic management and welfare function, collective bargaining, and an overall tendency to centralised and hierarchical organisation. Cultural activities also have a regimented and 'same-like' character.

Post-Fordism sharply contrasts with Fordism in all these areas. Its productive systems are flexible rather than rigid and able to produce more varied and diverse products. In turn, diversity and variety characterise the consumer market.

Under the heading 'Japanisation', Murray then describes the organisation of the labour force into a skilled and well-rewarded 'core' and a less advantaged 'periphery'. In Britain, he partly associates a trend to restructuring labour in this way with Thatcherism. However, he makes it clear that Post-Fordist organisational tendencies have great democratic and participatory potential – if people chose to develop them in that way.

Reading 41 From Robin Murray, 'Fordism and Post-Fordism' in S. Hall and M. Jacques, *eds, New Times and The Changing Face of Politics in the 1990s* (Lawrence and Wishart, 1989), pp. 38–48

During the first two centuries of the industrial revolution the focus of employment shifted from the farm to the factory. It is now shifting once more, from the factory to the office and the shop. A third of Britain's paid labour force now works in offices. A third of the value of national output is in the distribution sector. Meanwhile 2.5 million jobs have been lost in British manufacturing since 1960. If the Ford plants at Halewood and Dagenham represented late industrialism, Centrepoint and Habitat are the symbols of a new age.

The Right portrayed the growth of services as a portent of a post-industrial society with growing individualism, a weakened state and a multiplicity of markets. I want to argue that it reflects a deeper change in the production process. It is one that affects manufacturing and agriculture as well as services, and has implications for the way in which we think about socialist alternatives. I see this as a shift from the dominant form of 20th-century production, known as Fordism, to a new form, post-Fordism.

Fordism is an industrial era whose secret is to be found in the mass production systems pioneered by Henry Ford. These systems were based on four principles from which all else followed:

a) products were standardised; this meant that each part and each task could also be standardised. Unlike craft production – where each part had to be specially designed, made and fitted – for a run of mass-produced cars, the same headlight could be fitted to the same model in the same way.
b) if tasks are the same, then some can be mechanised; thus mass production plants developed special-purpose machinery for each model, much of which could not be switched from product to product.
c) those tasks which remained were subject to scientific management or Taylorism, whereby any task was broken down into its component parts,

redesigned by work-study specialists on time-and-motion principles, who then instructed manual workers on how the job should be done.
d) flowline replaced nodal assembly, so that instead of workers moving to and from the product (the node), the product flowed past the workers.

Ford did not invent these principles. What he did was to combine them in the production of a complex commodity, which undercut craft-made cars as decisively as the handloom weavers had been undercut in the 1830s. Ford's Model T sold for less than a tenth of the price of a craft-built car in the US in 1916, and he took 50 per cent of the market.

This revolutionary production system was to transform sector after sector during the 20th century, from processed food to furniture, clothes, cookers, and even ships after the second world war. The economics came from the scale of production, for although mass production might be more costly to set up because of the purpose-built machinery, once in place the cost of an extra unit was discontinuously cheap.

Many of the structures of Fordism followed from this tension between high fixed costs and low variable ones, and the consequent drive for volume. First, as Ford himself emphasised, mass production presupposes mass consumption. Consumers must be willing to buy standardised products. Mass advertising played a central part in establishing a mass consumption norm. So did the provision of the infrastructure of consumption – housing and roads. To ensure that the road system dominated over rail, General Motors, Standard Oil and Firestone Tyres bought up and then dismantled the electric trolley and transit systems in 44 urban areas.

Second, Fordism was linked to a system of protected national markets, which allowed the mass producers to recoup their fixed costs at home and compete on the basis of marginal costs on the world market, or through the replication of existing models via foreign investment.

Third, mass producers were particularly vulnerable to sudden falls in demand. Ford unsuccessfully tried to offset the effect of the 1930s depression by raising wages. Instalment credit, Keynesian demand and monetary management, and new wage and welfare systems were all more effective in stabilising the markets for mass producers in the postwar period. HP and the dole cheque became as much the symbols of the Fordist age as the tower block and the motorway.

The mass producers not only faced the hazard of changes in consumption. With production concentrated in large factories they were also vulnerable to the new 'mass worker' they had created. Like Taylorism, mass production had taken the skill out of work, it fragmented tasks into a set of repetitive movements, and erected a rigid division between mental and manual labour. It treated human beings as interchangeable parts of a machine, paid according to the job they did rather than who they were.

Taylorism is an hierarchical approach to management, highly compatible with Fordism.

The result was high labour turnover, shopfloor resistance, and strikes. The mass producers in turn sought constant new reservoirs of labour, particularly from groups facing discrimination, from rural areas and from less developed regions abroad. The contractual core of Taylorism – higher wages in return for managerial control of production – still applied, and a system of industrial unions grew up to bargain over these wage levels. In the USA, and to an extent the UK, a national system of wage bargaining developed in the postwar period, centred on high-profile car industry negotiations, that linked wage rises to productivity growth, and then set wage standards for other large-scale producers and the state. It was a system of collective bargaining that has been described as implementing a Keynesian incomes policy without a Keynesian state. As long as the new labour reservoirs could be tapped, it was a system that held together the distinct wage relation of Fordism.

Taylorism was also characteristic of the structure of management and supplier relations. Fordist bureaucracies are fiercely hierarchical, with links between the divisions and departments being made through the centre rather than at the base. Planning is done by specialists; rulebooks and guidelines are issued for lower management to carry out. If you enter a Ford factory in any part of the world, you will find its layout, materials, even the position of its Coca Cola machines, all similar, set up as they are on the basis of a massive construction manual drawn up in Detroit. Managers themselves complain of deskilling and the lack of room for initiative, as do suppliers who are confined to producing blueprints at a low margin price.

These threads – of production and consumption, of the semi-skilled worker and collective bargaining, of a managed national market and centralised organisation – together make up the fabric of Fordism. They have given rise to an economic culture which extends beyond the complex assembly industries, to agriculture, the service industries and parts of the state. It is marked by its commitment to scale and the standard product (whether it is a Mars bar or an episode of *Dallas*); by a competitive strategy based on cost reduction; by authoritarian relations, centralised planning, and a rigid organisation built round exclusive job descriptions.

These structures and their culture are often equated with industrialism, and regarded as an inevitable part of the modern age. I am suggesting that they are linked to a particular form of industrialism, one that developed in the late 19th century and reached its most dynamic expression in the postwar boom. Its impact can be felt not just in the economy, but in politics (in the mass party) and in much broader cultural fields – whether American football, or classical ballet (Diaghilev was a Taylorist in dance), industrial design or modern architecture. The technological *hubris* of this outlook, its Faustian bargain of dictatorship in production in exchange for mass consumption, and above all its destructiveness in the name of progress and the economy of time, all this places Fordism at the centre of modernism.

Why we need to understand these deep structures of Fordism is that they are embedded, too, in traditional socialist economics. Soviet-type planning is the apogee of Fordism. Lenin embraced Taylor and the stopwatch. Soviet industrialisation was centred on the construction of giant plants, the majority of them based on western mass-production technology. So deep is the idea of scale burnt into Soviet economics that there is a hairdresser's in

Moscow with 120 barbers' chairs. The focus of Soviet production is on volume and because of its lack of consumer discipline it has caricatured certain features of western mass production, notably a hoarding of stocks, and inadequate quality control.

In social-democratic thinking state planning has a more modest place. But in the writings of Fabian economists in the 1930s, as in the Morrisonian model of the public corporation, and Labour's postwar policies, we see the same emphasis on centralist planning, scale, Taylorist technology, and hierarchical organisation. The image of planning was the railway timetable, the goal of planning was stable demand and cost-reduction. In the welfare state, the idea of the standard product was given a democratic interpretation as the universal service to meet basic needs, and although in Thatcher's Britain this formulation is still important, it effectively forecloses the issue of varied public services and user choice. The shadow of Fordism haunts us even in the terms in which we oppose it.

The break-up of Fordism

Protests in the 1960s were partly aimed at big 'Fordist-type' bureaucracies.

Fordism as a vision – both left and right – had always been challenged, on the shopfloor, in the political party, the seminar room and the studio. In 1968 this challenge exploded in Europe and the USA. It was a cultural as much as an industrial revolt, attacking the central principles of Fordism, its definitions of work and consumption, its shaping of towns and its overriding of nature.

From that time we can see a fracturing of the foundations of predictability on which Fordism was based. Demand became more volatile and fragmented. Productivity growth fell as the result of workplace resistance. The decline in profit drove down investment. Exchange rates were fluctuating, oil prices rose and in 1974 came the greatest slump the West had had since the 1930s.

The consensus response was a Keynesian one, to restore profitability through a managed increase in demand and an incomes policy. For monetarism the route to profitability went through the weakening of labour, a cut in state spending and a reclaiming of the public sector for private accumulation. Economists and politicians were re-fighting the battles of the last slump. Private capital on the other hand was dealing with the present one. It was using new technology and new production principles to make Fordism flexible, and in doing so stood much of the old culture on its head.

The sociology of consumption has become a major focus of current sociology and postmodern cultural analysis (see Reading 45).

In Britain, the groundwork for the new system was laid not in manufacturing but in retailing. Since the 1950s, retailers had been using computers to transform the distribution system. All mass producers have the problem of forecasting demand. If they produce too little they lose market share. If they produce too much, they are left with stocks, which are costly to hold, or have to be sold at a discount. Retailers face this problem not just for a few products, but for thousands. Their answer has been to develop information and supply systems which allow them to order supplies to coincide with demand. Every evening Sainsbury's receives details of the sales of all 12,000 lines from each of its shops; these are turned into orders for warehouse deliveries for the coming night, and replacement production for the following day. With computerised control of stocks in the shop, transport networks, automatic loading and unloading, Sainsbury's flow-line make-to-order system has conquered the Fordist problem of stocks.

They have also overcome the limits of the mass product. For, in contrast to the discount stores which are confined to a few, fast-selling items, Sainsbury's, like the new wave of high street shops, can handle ranges of products geared to segments of the market. Market niching has become the slogan of the high street. Market researchers break down market by age (youth, young adults, 'grey power'), by household types (dinkies, single-gender couples, one-parent families), by income, occupation, housing and, increasingly, by locality. They analyse 'lifestyles', correlating consumption patterns across commodities, from food to clothing, and health to holidays.

The point of this new anthropology of consumption is to target both product and shops to particular segments. Burton's – once a mass producer with generalised retail outlets – has changed in the 1980s to being a niche market retailer with a team of anthropologists, a group of segmented stores – Top Shop, Top Man, Dorothy Perkins, Principles and Burton's itself – and now has no manufacturing plants of its own. Conran's Storehouse group – Habitat, Heals, Mothercare, Richards and BHS – all geared to different groups, offers not only clothes, but furniture and furnishings, in other words entire lifestyles. At the heart of Conran's organisation in London is what amounts to a factory of 150 designers, with collages of different lifestyles on the wall, Bold Primary, Orchid, mid-Atlantic and the Cottage Garden.

In all these shops the emphasis has shifted from the manufacturer's economies of scale to the retailer's economies of scope. The economies come from offering an integrated range from which customers choose their own basket of products. There is also an economy of innovation, for the modern retail systems allow new product ideas to be tested in practice, through shop sales, and the successful ones then to be ordered for wider distribution. Innovation has become a leading edge of the new competition. Product life has become shorter, for fashion goods and consumer durables.

A centrepiece of this new retailing is design. Designers produce the innovations. They shape the lifestyles. They design the shops, which are described as 'stages' for the act of shopping. There are now 29,000 people working in design consultancies in the UK, which have sales of £1,600 million per annum. They are the engineers of designer capitalism. With market researchers they have steered the high street from being retailers of goods to retailers of style.

These changes are a response to, and a means of shaping, the shift from mass consumption. Instead of keeping up with the Joneses there has been a move to be different from the Joneses. Many of these differences are vertical, intended to confirm status and class. But some are horizontal centred and round group identities, linked to age, or region or ethnicity. In spite of the fact that basic needs are still unmet, the high street does offer a new variety and creativity in consumption which the Left's puritan tradition should also address. Whatever our responses, the revolution in retailing reflects new principles of production, a new pluralism of products and a new importance for innovation. As such it marks a shift to a post-Fordist age.

There have been parallel shifts in manufacturing, not least in response to the retailers' just-in-time system of ordering. In some sectors where the manufacturers are a little more than subcontractors to the retailers, their flexibility has been achieved at the expense of labour. In others, capital itself has suffered, as furniture retailers like MFI squeeze their suppliers, driving down prices, limiting design, and thereby destroying much of the mass-production furniture industry during the downturns.

But the most successful manufacturing regions have been ones which have linked flexible manufacturing systems, with innovative organisation and an emphasis on 'customisation' design and quality. Part of the flexibility has been achieved through new technology, and the introduction of programmable machines which can switch from product to product with little manual resetting and downtime. Benetton's automatic dyeing plant, for example, allows it to change its colours in time with demand. In the car industry, whereas General Motors took nine hours to change the dyes on its presses in the early 1980s, Toyota have lowered the time to two minutes, and have cut the average lot size of body parts from 5,000 to 500 in the process. The line, in short, has become flexible. Instead of using purpose-built machines to make standard products, flexible automation uses general-purpose machines to produce a variety of products.

Japanisation

Manufacturers have also been adopting the retailers' answer to stocks. The pioneer is Toyota which stands to the new era as Ford did to the old. Toyoda, the founder of Toyota, inspired by a visit to an American supermarket, applied the just-in-time system to his component suppliers, ordering on the basis of his daily production plans, and getting the components delivered right beside the line. Most of Toyota's components are still produced on the same say as they are assembled.

Toyoda's prime principle of the elimination of wasteful practices meant going beyond the problem of stocks. His firm has used design and materials technology to simplify complex elements, cutting down the number of parts and operations. It adopted a zero-defect policy, developing machines which stopped automatically, when a fault occurred, as well as statistical quality control techniques. As in retailing, the complex web of processes, inside and outside the plant, were co-ordinated through computers, a process that economists have called systemation (in contrast to automation). The result of these practices is a discontinuous speed-up in what Marx called the circulation of capital. Toyota turns over its materials and products ten times more quickly than western car producers, saving material and energy in the process.

The key point about the Toyota system, however, is not so much that it speeds up the making of a car. It is in order to make these changes that it has adopted quite different methods of labour control and organisation. Toyoda saw that traditional Taylorism did not work. Central management had no access to all the information needed for continuous innovation. Quality could not be achieved with deskilled manual workers. Taylorism wasted what they called 'the gold in workers' heads'.

Toyota, and the Japanese more generally, having broken the industrial unions in the 1950s, have developed a core of multi-skilled workers whose tasks include not only manufacture and maintenance, but the improvement of the products and processes under their control. Each breakdown is seen as a change for improvement. Even hourly-paid workers are trained in statistical techniques and monitoring, and register and interpret statistics to identify deviations from a norm – tasks customarily reserved for management in Fordism. Quality circles are a further way of tapping the ideas of the workforce. In post-Fordism, the worker is designed to act as a computer as well as a machine.

As a consequence the Taylorist contract changes. Workers are no longer interchangeable. They gather experience. The Japanese job-for-life and corporate welfare system provides security. For the firm it secures an asset. Continuous training, payment by seniority, a breakdown of job demarcations, are all part of the Japanese core wage relation. The EETPU's lead in embracing private pension schemes, BUPA, internal flexibility, union-organised training and single-company unions are all consistent with this path of post-Fordist industrial relations.

Not the least of the dangers of this path is that it further hardens the divisions between the core and the peripheral workforce. The cost of employing lifetime workers means an incentive to subcontract all jobs not essential to the core. The other side of the Japanese jobs-for-life is a majority of low-paid, fragmented peripheral workers, facing an underfunded and inadequate welfare state. The duality in the labour market, and in the welfare economy, could be taken as a description of Thatcherism. The point is that neither the EETPU's policy nor that of Mrs Thatcher should read as purely political. There is a material basis to both, rooted in changes in production.

There are parallel changes in corporate organisation. With the revision of Taylorism, a layer of management has been stripped away. Greater central control has allowed the decentralisation of work. Day-to-day autonomy has been given to work groups and plant managers. Teams linking departments horizontally have replaced the rigid verticality of Fordist bureaucracies.

It is only a short step from here to sub-contracting and franchising. This is often simply a means of labour control. But in engineering and light consumer industries, networks and semi-independent firms have often proved more innovative than vertically integrated producers. A mark of post-Fordism is close two-way relations between customer and supplier, and between specialised producers in the same industry. Co-operative competition replaces the competition of the jungle. These new relationships within and between enterprises and on the shopfloor have made least headway in the countries in which Fordism took fullest root, the USA and the UK. Here firms have tried to match continental and Japanese flexibility through automation while retaining Fordist shopfloor, managerial and competitive relations.

Yet in spite of this we can see in this country a culture of post-Fordist capitalism emerging. Consumption has a new place. As for production the keyword is flexibility – of plant and machinery, as of products and labour. Emphasis shifts from scale to scope, and from cost to quality. Organisations are geared to respond to rather than regulate markets. They are seen as frameworks for learning as much as instruments of control. Their hierarchies are flatter and their structures more open. The guerilla force takes over from the standing army. All this has liberated the centre from the tyranny of the immediate. Its task shifts from planning to strategy, and to the promotion of the instruments of post-Fordist control – systems, software, corporate culture and cash.

On the bookshelf, Peters and Waterman replace F.W. Taylor. In the theatre the audience is served lentils by the actors. At home Channel 4 takes its place beside ITV. Majorities are transformed into minorities, as we enter the age of proportional representation. And under the shadow of Chernobyl even Fordism's scientific modernism is being brought to book, as we realise there is more than one way up the technological mountain.

Not all these can be read off from the new production systems. Some are rooted in the popular opposition to Fordism. They represent an alternative version of post-Fordism, which flowered after 1968 in the community movements and the new craft trade unionism of alternative plans. Their organisational forms – networks, work-place democracy, co-operatives, the dissolving of the platform speaker into meetings in the round – have echoes in the new textbooks of management, indeed capital has been quick to take up progressive innovations for its own purposes. There are then many sources and contested versions of post-Fordist culture. What they share is a break with the era of Ford.

Post-Fordism is being introduced under the sway of the market and in accordance with the requirements of capital accumulation. It validates only what can command a place in the market; it cuts the labour force in two, and leaves large numbers without any work at all. Its prodigious productivity gains are ploughed back into yet further accumulation and the quickening consumption of symbols in the postmodern market place. In the UK, Thatcherism has strengthened the prevailing wind of the commodity economy, liberating the power of private purses and so fragmenting the social sphere.

To judge from Kamata's celebrated account, working for Toyota is hardly a step forward from working for Ford. As one British worker in a Japanese factory in the North-East of England put it, 'they want us to live for work, i.e. Japanisation is far from 'utopia' – for the workforce.

whereas we want to work to live'. Japanisation has no place in any modern *News From Nowhere*.

Yet post-Fordism has shaken the kaleidoscope of the economy, and exposed an old politics. We have to respond to its challenges and draw lessons from its systems.

Paul Thompson: A Critical Review of the Fordist/Post-Fordist Model and an Alternative 'Core Theory' of the Labour Process

The simple and sweeping description and explanation of Fordist/Post-Fordist theory is highly seductive. Precisely for this reason it begs for cool and, if necessary, complex analysis. This may be a case where an elegant theory needs to be cut to size by a brutal gang of facts. There has certainly been no lack of challenge to the Fordist/Post-Fordist model of the development and regulation of capitalist society. In the reading below, Paul Thompson first critically reviews the theory and then outlines an alternative 'core theory.' Thompson's approach reflects the 'labour process' theory of Harry Braverman (*Labour and Monopoly Capital*, 1974). Braverman argued that most service sector labour, like most manual labour, had been 'deskilled' and 'degraded' in order that capitalist management could achieve greater control over the labour process. As the extract below makes clear, Thompson agrees with Braverman that in capitalist society labour process should be understood in terms of the relations between capital and labour (a matter which those adopting a Fordist/Post-Fordist approach tend to assume rather than explore). However, Thompson describes himself as 'post-Braverman' in that, as well as requiring updating, the accuracy of some of Braverman's deskilling analysis is open to question.

Whereas Thompson can build on Braverman, he finds the empirical evidence and theoretical arguments against the Fordist/Post-Fordist approach to be highly damaging to the theory. The extract begins with three criticisms of the analysis:

1 The dichotomy between mass production and specialisation is too crude.
2 There needs to be greater caution in analysing the extent and role of flexible technology.
3 The idea that mass markets are saturated has been 'vastly overstated.'

All this prompts Thompson to conclude about Fordism/Post-Fordism that it 'could be in principle that the general model is unworkable'.

However, Thompson does not wholly dismiss Fordism/Post-Fordism. For instance, he does consider that at the descriptive level there is substantial truth in the core/periphery view of what is happening to the labour force. What the Fordist/Post-Fordist perspective fails to do is to relate labour control to the fundamental nature of capitalist production. In contrast, in the second part of this extract, Braverman does sketch out how labour process theory can be so related. He indicates six elements of such a 'core theory' (of which numbers 3 to 6 appear as 1 to 4 in the extract). These are:

1 A general theory of capitalism
2 An account of the production process and its components in historically specific capitalist economies
3 An analysis of the role of labour and the capital–labour relations (in generating surplus value)
4 An analysis of the logic of accumulation of profit which forces capital constantly to revolutionise the production process
5 An analysis of the control of labour (much of the first part of this extract is about this matter)
6 An analysis which recognises that in capitalist society the relation between capital and labour is based on structured antagonism, i.e. that it is in the interests of capital to make a profit out of labour (in that sense, to 'exploit' it), but that it is in the interests of labour to achieve higher wages.

Throughout this book, there have been examples of radical thinking of the left going beyond the legacy of Marx. Significantly, this is also true of Paul Thompson, one of the major analysts of the labour process in capitalist society. For reasons he briefly explains at the conclusion of this extract, Thompson does not consider his formulation of labour process theory as 'incompatible' with Marxist social theory, but does see it as 'separable' from it. This implies that a radical sociology of work does not equate with a Marxist sociology of work.

Reading 42 From Paul Thompson, *The Nature of Work: An Introduction to Debates on the Labour Process* (Macmillan, 1989), pp. 224–29, 241–46

A powerful case has been made that changes in work organisation necessitate a major theoretical shift. But how valid is the analysis? Unfortunately there is every indication that it is based on very shaky foundations. The basic dichotomy between mass production and flexible specialisation is seen by many commentators as crude and ill-considered (Williams *et al.*, 1987; Smith, 1987; Wood, 1988a; Pollert, 1988; Walker, 1988). It neglects the significance of process and batch variations and repeats the myth of the dominance of the assembly line. Mass production itself is defined in a very narrow way, when in practice it is not necessarily inflexible and using dedicated equipment to produce in a standardised way. Flow lines can now cater for considerable diversification and multi-model lines. Indeed, many of the Japanese advances have been made within such a framework. Even the standard version of Fordism 'still represents a powerful model of transfer, specialisation and work integration at the level of the factory' (Walker, 1988: 17). Hyman (1988) notes the irony that sectors of the British economy were shifting to a Fordist model of product planning and labour control just as flexible specialisation was supposed to be taking root as a global trend in the 1970s.

Caution should also be used in discussion of flexible technology. Advanced programmable machinery remains an extremely expensive investment, especially for the small firms who are to be at the leading edge of customised production. It is necessary to break the idea of any necessary link between flexibility and advanced manufacturing technology. The latter is not always flexible or used for this purpose. Emphasis is as likely to be on co-ordination of the labour process, quality and routeing (Wood, 1988a: 9).

JIT – just in time – a flexible production technique.

Again, many Japanese companies have achieved flexibility through methods of organising production such as JIT, without always having the most sophisticated technology.

Finally, the idea that mass markets are saturated is also vastly overstated (Williams *et al.*, 1987; Pollert, 1988). Many industries, including those covering most consumer goods, continue to sell to mass markets, while products such as colour televisions and videos are commonly produced on the basis of families of interrelated models. If we turn to the concept of flexible specialisation itself, we find it is 'very elusive' beyond reference to shorter production runs and less rigid technologies (Berggren, 1988). Williams *et al.* (1987) show clearly the standard of evidence used by Piore and Sabel to be often poor or non-existent. Of course, there are the regions such as those of the 'Third Italy' mentioned earlier. However, their analysis also highlights some sectors of the engineering industry at the expense of the more Fordist ones (Murray, 1987). Nor is it correct to generalise about the existence of craft labour. Such work is undertaken by a minority, mainly men, and coexists with semi-skilled assembly work carried out by women and heavy forging and foundry tasks done by southern Italian and North African workers.

These are areas in Italy in which production organised on 'post Fordist' lines occurs.

It could be that in principle the general model is unworkable, but the description of what is happening to the work of the 'core, flexible employee' is correct. Multiskilling is clearly a reality for a growing proportion of manufacturing employees, but evidence shows that it bears little resemblance to a renewed craft labour. Case studies of flexible manufacturing systems show that Tayloristic criteria still underpin work design (Charles, 1987), while Shaiken *et al.'s* examination of the work process under flexible production showed that:

> Managers in the plants we studied introduced new technology guided by a vision of the automated factory, or continuous process plant, not nineteenth century craft production. They attempted to remove planning responsibility and autonomy from the shop floor more often than they tried to combine flexible technology with broadly skilled workers.
>
> (Shaiken *et al.*, 1986: 18)

What *is* taking place is flexibility across a range of what were previously demarcated skills or tasks. The result, in Hyman's (1988) words, is an expanded portfolio of competences. Many jobs remain short-cycle and are enlarged simply by adding on extra tasks, whether it be maintenance or those that have been previously routinised or fragmented. Despite the uplifting language, that is very much the message of what flexibility means from conventional sources such as *Business Week* (1983) and the National Economic Development Council (1986).

'Quality of Work Life' (QWL) refers to those initiatives promoting more employee involvement in the work process and/or participation in management.

As for QWL initiatives, they undoubtedly indicate a movement towards greater engagement with the co-operation, knowledge and tacit skills of the workforce. But again they should be kept in perspective. QWL is a highly constrained form of empowerment that is far removed from either of the traditional agendas of industrial democracy or job enrichment. These constraints arise from the subordination of participation within management decision-making processes, efficiency criteria and power relations that have remained largely untouched (Giordano, 1988; Hyman, 1988). Certainly, the delegation to workgroups of some immediate and localised production decisions, such as those on the monitoring of product quality, can happily coexist within managerial structures of directive control.

This kind of emphasis is consistent with evidence about Japan. The intellectual skills referred to by some commentators neglect the fact that the scope and depth of the multitude of jobs are often so routinised that they could be picked up easily by other workers (Kumazawa and Yamada, 1988: 27–8). One of the lessons learned by Western companies is that the required skills are as much *behavioural* as technical (Sayer, 1986). Among core workers the competitive individualism induced by the manpower policies of large firms creates an effective form of self-regulation. However, this is reinforced by high levels of supervision and assessment, making parallels with a system of responsible autonomy limited (Wood, 1988b: 18). It has been established (Littler, 1982) that lack of enthusiasm for the rigid separation of conception and execution meant that Taylorism was never deployed as a comprehensive control system. However, in those aspects which were taken up – chiefly work study and design – visiting production managers have found extensive and effective use (Berggren, 1988). The emphasis on 'scientific' selection and recruitment suggests an extension of part of the Taylorist agenda underutilised in the West. Even workers' involvement in industrial engineering can be seen as an internalisation of Taylorist techniques (Sayer, 1986).

Returning to Western business, there remains the area of changes in the broader employment relationship. A new set of multiskilled core workers is clearly going to have a level of job security. However, there is a tendency for Piore and Sabel to 'extract only the better aspects of the overall situation of workers' (Walker, 1988: 32), for there are costs, not least those that come from the effort intensification arising from added tasks and responsibilities. Additionally, new techniques such as JIT rely on continual and controlled pressure (Turnbull, 1987). This is graphically illustrated in Slaughter's (1988) account of 'management by stress' at the GM NUMMI plant. Line breakdowns and stoppages are encouraged so that operators' weaknesses can be identified in order to fine-tune and stretch them further. The casualities of intense work pace, excessive workloads, and limited cover for absentees and injuries are well documented for Japan, Britain and the USA (Kamata, 1982; *Daily Telegraph*, 1987; Moberg, 1988). In this context the degree of emphasis on collaboration by flexible specialisation writers can be questioned. A level of co-operation is built into the capitalist labour process and may be enhanced by new management methods. But the current interpretation is not only an abstraction from the inherent tensions in the capital-labour relation but even from the normal conflicts of interests between professional and occupational groups.

In discussing the costs of flexibility, it is also legitimate to ask *which* workers are we talking about? Women remain largely invisible within the flexible specialisation analysis (Jenson, 1988). While there can be no simple equation that core equals male and periphery equals female (Walby, 1988), if we acknowledge the gendering of flexibility, the consequences may be less benign in labour market terms. The major growth area for female labour has been in the clerical and service sectors, yet the latter curiously does not figure in the flexible specialisation picture of economic trends (Hyman, 1988). Certainly the emphasis on factories of the future seems to set aside the service (and manufacturing) sweatshops of the present. Though some models overestimate the number and novelty of peripheral workers, the flexibility debate has understated the costs of exclusion from the core, and the casualisation of conditions and loss of legal protection involved.

The fundamental problem of the flexibility discourse is its conflation of description, futurological prediction, prescription and even post-hoc rationalisation (Pollert, 1988; Hyman, 1988). Wood (1988a) has acidly described it as moving from Bravermania to Cybermania! It may be a new analysis, but it is the same old romance of automation – a well-travelled route reproducing a deterministic vision of technological trajectories in which choices are frozen (Smith, 1987). The new ingredient is a fashionable nod in the direction of the sovereignty of markets and the consumer. Parallels with mistakes made at certain stages and by some contributors to the labour process debate abound. These include: an indealised view of craft work; unproblematic readings of skill; over-rationalistic conceptions of management strategy (towards flexibility); and the presentation of changes in work organisation as if they were complete historical breaks.

I would argue that the labour process debate has learned from those mistakes. Whether the discussion of flexibility does the same we can only judge over time. It will be a pity if the two paradigms do get locked into mutually destructive combat. The problem may not be as simple as 'holding different parts of the elephant' (Walker, 1988; 18), but real changes have taken place. Multiskilling and quality circles *are* partial breaks with Taylorism; this emphasises the theme of earlier chapters that scientific management has never been a whole or coherent package. In fact it is possible to reinterpret changes in production as a form of *flexible Taylorism*, as Berggren does in his analysis of the Swedish motor industry. Others may prefer to stick with neo-Fordism. Ultimately the label is less important than the recognition that no qualitative break has been made in the organisation of the capitalist labour process: 'the new solutions ride on the back of the old' (Williams, 1988: 7). The general idea of flexibility has always been central to notions of the elasticity of labour power in the extraction of surplus value (Pollert, 1988: 4). But the nature and significance of flexibility vary according to their context in time, sector, nation and choices of actors in the labour process . . .

The core theory

In this chapter I have argued that the specific ideas of Braverman and his co-thinkers on concrete issues such as skill or control do not constitute *the* labour process theory. Given that consequent debate and research has considerably advanced our knowledge in these and other areas, they do not even represent an 'orthodoxy'. But empirical work and theorising on such issues are, in any case, not the basis of a *core* theory. This must work at a different level of analysis. Underlying many of the disagreements we have examined has been a seeming denial that a certain level of abstraction concerning the dynamics of the capitalist labour process is a necessary starting point and framework for empirical investigation. One aspect of this is expressed by Coombs: 'What is needed therefore is an account of the production process and its components in historically specific capitalist economies, not in "capitalism in general"' (1985: 144).

My argument would be that the two are not incompatible. Without them, the trend in the debate has been inexorably towards the accumulation of a plant particularism deliberately eschewing any broader theoretical foundation. Burrell comments that many of the critics are wedded to an empiricist approach in which reality, in the form of 'facts', renders itself up in a non-problematic way to the observer. Case studies are used as a method of falsification to produce counterfactual evidence to 'grand theory'. This is not new in British industrial social science: 'the labour process approach is merely the latest integral target for the empiricist attack, which in opposition draws strength and gains greater legitimacy for its own tired, contingent produce' (Burrell, 1987: 9). This may be an over-harsh judgement, but the problem of loss of theoretical direction is a real one.

If we examine the major formative theoretical inputs from Braverman, Richard Edwards, Friedman, Burawoy and others, we do find a core, albeit a different one from that commonly discussed. This concerns what Littler refers to as 'the central indeterminacy of labour potential' (1982b: 31). The social relations which workers enter into to produce useful things becomes a capitalist labour process when the capacity to work is utilised as a means of producing value. This rests on the capacity of capital to transform labour power into labour for profitable production, and therefore on the unique characteristics of labour as a commodity. There are four crucial things which follow from this and which form further elements of the core theory.

First, as the labour process generates the surplus, and is a central part of both man's experience in acting on the world and reproducing the economy, the role of labour and the capital-labour relation is privileged as a focus for analysis. There is no assumption that the privileging of the capital-labour relation has any specific significance for analysing other social relations outside production. We are referring to privileging *for* an analysis of production, not privilege *over* any other form of sphere of analysis. Put another way, the problem of 'privileging' one part of the circuit arises only if the analyst assumes that this one part determines what happens in others (Edwards, 1989). This notion of a 'relative autonomy' of the labour process will be returned to later.

The above framework necessarily involves relations of exploitation, though it need not and should not involve a labour theory of value (see Hodgson, 1984; Wright, 1985). Exploitation does not depend on the notion of labour alone creating value, not to mention socially necessary labour time determining the value of a commoditiy in exchange. Rather, it rests on the appropriation of the surplus labour by capital, based on its ownership and control of the means of production, and the separation of direct producers from those means. As Burawoy (1985) notes, one consequence is that the standpoint of the direct producer is central to a critique of capitalism. But there is another part of the opening statement about 'man acting on the world' that needs extending. As 'human labour is the irreplaceable centrepiece of social production' (Walker, 1988: 1), workers' skills and creative capacities can never be altogether eliminated from the production process.

Second, there is a logic of accumulation which forces capital constantly to revolutionise the production process. This arises from the competition between units of capital and the antagonism between capital and labour that is unique to capitalism as a mode of production. In contrast to the earlier arguments of Cohen, this logic of accumulation has no determinative link with or 'impacts' upon any specific feature of the labour process such as use of skills. The three specific features identified by the Brighton Labour Process Group (1977) – the division between intellectual and manual labour, hierarchical control, deskilling/fragmentation – are not inviolable laws. At any given point capital may reskill, recombine tasks, or widen workers' discretion and responsibility. However, the accumulation processes that compel capital to transform the conditions under which work takes place and cheapen the costs of production, sets limits to the use of workers' creative capacities and constrains attempts to dispense with hierarchical relations.

The third point follows from the above. There is a control imperative. Market mechanisms alone cannot regulate the labour process. As Littler observes, 'To translate legal ownership into real possession, the employer must erect structures of control over labour' (1982b: 31). Marx's notion of the transition from formal to real subordination is unhelpful if defined in terms of specific historical periods or as a finished process. It is only useful to the extent that it highlights capital's continual need to realise control in the context of the pressures to revolutionise the labour process and secure value.

Recognising the control imperative specifies nothing about the nature, specificity or level of control mechanisms. Nor is it necessarily linked to managerial strategy, which is an analytically distinct question. At a minimum the imperative refers to workers and work being under the *general* directive control of capital, with the effect that the workforce is subordinate to the defined aims of the enterprise (Edwards, 1986). General control is distinct from *immediate* control over work processes such as line speeds or manning, which are merely 'open' to control. Capital can cede elements of control in these areas by intent or accommodation to rival power, without weakening their overall direction of the labour process. None of these points need in any way be taken as a dismissal or exclusion of control mechanisms that originate outside the workplace, such as those that derive from patriarchal relations.

Fourth, the social relation between capital and labour is based on 'structured antagonism' (Edwards, 1986). Exploitation, the struggle to transform labour power into labour, the requirement for capital to seek some control over the conditions of work and maximise their side of the wage-effort exchange – all these factors create a variety of forms of conflict and resistance. Edwards uses the term structured antagonism partly to make clear that it is not necessarily manifested in visible conflict. However, it is in this area that the most substantial modification to the existing theory must be made, particularly in the light of the orthodoxy of Marx and Braverman. A great degree of consensus has developed among more recent writers concerning the significance of the contradictory nature of the capital-labour relation, or 'its two-fold nature', as Cressey and MacInnes (1980) put it. Precisely because capital has continually to revolutionise production and labour's role within it, it cannot rely wholly on control or coercion. At some level, workers' co-operation, productive powers, and consent must be engaged and mobilised.

This is not primarily a question of material inducements, or even general ideological persuasion. Co-operation and the generation of consent are systematically built into the capitalist labour process, as Burawoy made clear in Chapter 6. I have summed this dual relation elsewhere:

> . . . workers are compelled into acts of resistance while actively participating in the workings of the capitalist labour process. Conflict and cooperation are not entirely separate phenomena, one inherent in capitalist production, the other externally induced false consciousness. They are produced, in part, by the same process. The result is a continuum of possible and overlapping worker responses, from resistance, to accommodation on temporary common objectives, to compliance with the greater power of capital, and consent to production practices.
>
> (Thompson and Bannon, 1985: 98–9)

Cressey and MacInnes add the point that at the same time as workers have an interest in resistance to subordination, they are partially tied to the interests of the unit of capital that employs them. This recognition of the complex interplay of antagonism and co-operation provides a definite advance on the control versus resistance model which tended to see each acting on the other, rather than each containing contradictory elements (Edwards, 1986: 42).

The core theory framework works at a level of abstraction that can help make intelligible the general structure of relations between capital and labour in the workplace. It can enable broad trends to be identified pertaining to specific dimensions of those relations. However, the form, content and historical development of changes in the labour process have to be established empirically, rather than 'read off' from any general categories. There are no specific imperatives in the spheres of control, skill or indeed anything else.

An additional and equally important role is that of setting boundaries and points of intersection with other theoretical frameworks, and analyses of other social relations. On the former count, like Edwards, I regard a core theory of the labour process as materialist, as drawing heavily on some Marxist categories, but not in itself Marxist. This is not because of the need to reject any specific element of the 'package' such as the labour theory of value. Rather it is *because* Marxism is a total theory in which the labour process plays a crucial role in generating the class struggle and class consciousness necessary for revolutionary change. Such a development may be regarded as desirable, depending on your viewpoint. But there are simply no necessary theoretical or empirical links between conflict and exploitation at work and those wider social transformations. The kind of analysis of the labour process outlined above cannot provide a predictive theory concerning the behaviour of employers and workers based on identifiable sets of interests generated within production. I am not arguing that support for labour process theory is *incompatible* with a general belief in Marxist social theory; merely that the two are *separable*.

Philip Money (Reviewing Robert Reich): Exporting White–Collar Jobs to Where Labour is Cheap

We are now all familiar with the process by which transnational firms export manufacturing jobs to locations where labour is cheap and compliant. Less well-known is the growing extent to which this is also happening to jobs in the service sector. Yet it is easier to convey information around the globe than manufactured goods, and the practice of exporting service work is likely to grow.

This would seem to be bad news for Britain. In the 1980s, the expansion of the service sector was touted as the alternative to manufacture and as a new basis of economic prosperity. For perhaps a century, clerical or other service-sector work has been regarded as secure and desirable by many working-class and lower middle-class people. Such jobs were lost in unprecedented numbers during the recession of the 1990s. The following review article gives some indication why many may not reappear.

Reading 43 From Philip Money, 'White collar jobs flow from Britain as data processors are lured by cheaper labour' in *Guardian*, 25 August 1992, p. 11

All eight firms on a Home Office shortlist of companies to transfer criminal records to the police national computer are foreign.

Although several domestic firms claim they can do the job, a Home Office survey found "that for reasons of economy it may be necessary to undertake the data for conversion in the Far East".

The Home Office has yet to make a decision, but it is believed one of the leading contenders for the contract is the Kansas-based Saztec which would export the work to its office in Manila, although the company has a data processing facility in Scotland.

Saztec has already won other data processing contracts from the Home Office, the Treasury, the Cabinet Office Library, and the Royal Botanic Gardens.

This is part of a trend that was widely foreshadowed in the early 1980s – the transfer of significant number of "back office" white-collar jobs from developed countries to offshore locations where costs are less, working regulations more relaxed and unions non-existent.

Communications with company head offices are, in many cases, instantaneous via satellite or fibre optic link.

The trend mirrors manufacturing, where firms such as General Motors moved to Mexico closing Detroit plants.

The predicted large-scale transfer of white-collar jobs off-shore has yet to happen but recent advances in technology and the nature of the sector give cause for concern. So far the biggest changes have taken place in data processing.

Professor Robert Reich, of Harvard's John F. Kennedy School of Government, said in his book The work of Nations: "The foot soldiers of the information economy are the hordes of data processors stationed in back offices at computer terminals linked to worldwide information banks."

Data processing has established a firm foothold in areas such as the Caribbean, the Philippines and to some extent Ireland with its relatively low wages. Yet the skills of such workers are often equal to or better than workers in the US and the UK. Staff turnover, however, is typically 1 or 2 per cent compared with 35 per cent in America.

Saztec says that its 800 Filipino workers are among the best-paid in the country, earning an average of 3,600 pesos (£75) a month. This compares with the 2,600 peso (£54) salary of a doctor, but is only a fifth of salaries at Kansas head office.

The emphasis on accuracy is achieved through the military-organisation of staff, "with a military command structure, discipline, ranks and strict attendance rules'. There is nil staff turnover.

Although Saztec does not specify the workload which its Manila "back office" can handle, other data processing firms based in the Philippines claim to be able to process up to 700 million keystrokes a month. In the Caribbean, the selling point is the high technology infrastructure of "teleports" or "digiports".

These facilities, such as the one recently established in Jamaica, provide sophisticated infrastructure such as satellite links for the exclusive use of foreign data processing firms. There are also generous tax breaks.

In the beginning, the long turnaround time needed for data to be processed in the Caribbean rendered the local industry an adjunct to its American competitors. Raw data had to be flown in by plane, processed and the completed computer disks or tapes flown back to clients. Now most data is transmitted instantaneously.

According to a recent report by the UN's International Labour Organisation, Jamaican "digiport" workers enjoy conditions similar to those in America, but the crucial difference is that most Jamaican data entry workers earn less than $1 (50p) an hour, compared with up to $12(£6) for a similar worker in the US. This allows the Jamaican industry to boast of cost savings of up to 40 per cent over a similar job done in America.

One of the highest profile companies to be involved in the Caribbean is American Airlines, which in 1983 sacked 200 workers at its data processing office in Tulsa, Oklahoma and moved to Barbados.

By 1990 the airline employed more than 1,000 data processors in Barbados and the Dominican Republic to enter names and flight numbers from used airline tickets. The tickets are flown in daily, processed and sent via satellite to a computer bank in Dallas.

One argument against concern over the shift of clerical jobs to Third World countries is that they are positions which few people in the First World want to do anyway. This overlooks the growing complexity of jobs which can be done in "back offices."

Carl Clarke, the minister of trade industry and commerce in Barbados, said in recent years there had "been a shift to the higher value-added type of processing activities", such as the assessment of claims for insurance companies, the design and manufacture of computer software, technical support services for computer software companies and most recently, telephone marketing and phone-based mail order.

A good example of the trend is Ireland, which in the 1970s concentrated on data processing to lure companies from Britain and America. Ireland has relatively low wages, a young, well-educated workforce, lucrative tax incentives for foreign companies, and excellent telecommunications. Wright Investors Services, based in Shannon, provides its American clients with sophisticated financial analysis of companies from all around the world. The firm, whose head office is in Bridgeport, Connecticut was established in the late 1980s and employs 85 analysts.

Peter Donovan, the company's president, drew the comparison between $20,000 (£10,000) the Irish analysts earn and the $45,000 (£22,500) in America.

In Belfast, the eight staff of Dataprep Services do the typing for the Prudential's top executives based at its City of London headquarters and for the London offices of charity, Business in the Community. The work is fed down a telephone line at 1.6 times normal speed, recorded, and electronically slowed at the Belfast end. The material is typed and then transmitted back to the client.

Steve Harvey, one of the Dataprep's founders, said: "The potential is huge. We easily foresee employing at least 50 people within five years".

Brendan McDonnell: Unemployment and Economic Policy

In September 1992, unemployment went above ten per cent of the workforce and was still rapidly rising. It had been still higher in the early 1980s and, even during the short-lived boom of the late 1980s, it was at historically high levels. Unemployment has become a major rather than a marginal issue in our national life and it has certainly begun to attract more interest from sociologists.

I have selected this extract because it contains a useful descriptive outline of some of the major aspects of unemployment, notably in relation to duration, region, age and gender. Perhaps the most significant 'new factor' about unemployment (apart from sheer scale) is that the long-term unemployed are an increasing proportion of the total number of the unemployed. This reflects the fact that more of the unemployed are able and willing to work, but their skills have become obsolete (or perhaps have been rendered so by government policy).

This passage does not provide a full discussion of all the major causes of the 'new unemployment'. On the contrary, its analytical sections are severely critical of government policy (although the opinions of government advisors are quite fully cited).

Reading 44 From Brendan McDonnell: 'The UK: Engineered Mass Unemployment' in F. Gaffikin and M. Morrissey *eds., The New Unemployed: Joblessness and Poverty in the Market Economy* (Zed Books, 1992), pp. 146–50, 158–60

Unemployment

Figure 7.8 UK Unemployment 1980–91, totals and rates

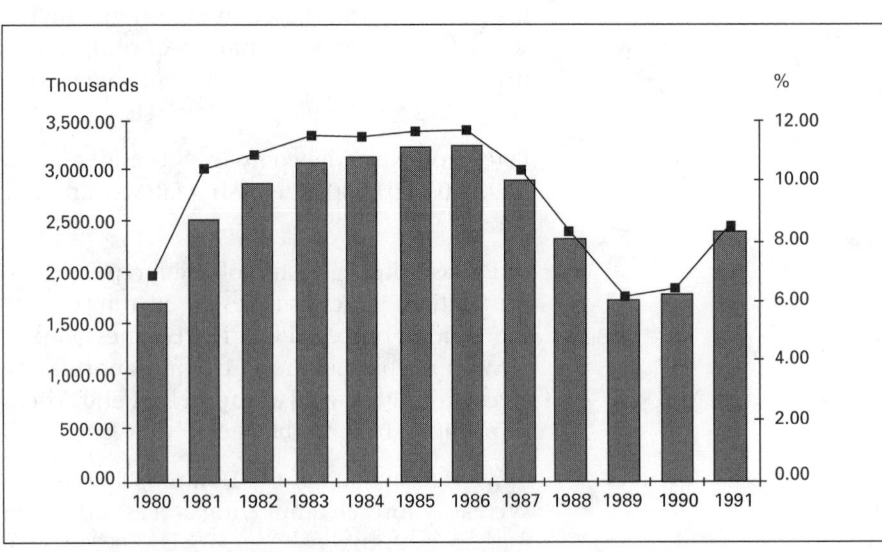

Source: DFP, *Monthly Economic Report,* October 1991.

Unemployment rose sharply as the recession struck between 1979–81, thereafter it continued to rise steadily until 1986, despite the fact that the recovery was well under-way by 1983. Having peaked at 3.3 million in 1986, unemployment fell steadily to 1.6 million in 1989, still well above its 1979 level. However, with the onset of the second major recession in a decade, in the latter half of 1990, unemployment is again on the rise and is forecast to continue to do so into the second half of 1993, when it is expected to rise once again to over 3 million.

With the Conservative party's continued emphasis on inflation as the number one economic priority, unemployment is set to remain at historically high levels. In recognition of the fact that the 'natural rate' of unemployment will have to remain high to achieve an acceptable level of inflation, part of the policy emphasis has been to redefine the way unemployment is calculated. Since 1979 there have been some 29 changes, making comparisons over the period difficult.

Duration

As well as aggregate changes in unemployment there have been significant changes in the composition of the unemployed since 1979. The growth and persistence of the problem is most obvious in the figures for the long-term unemployed. In 1979 the percentage of the total unemployed who were jobless for more than one year was 25 per cent; by 1988 it had increased to 41 per cent.

The duration of unemployment has always been a contentious political issue as the longer unemployment continues, the greater is the cost both to the individuals concerned and to the state. Indeed the Conservative government, as part of a process of redefining unemployment, sought to view the problem as being largely confined to long-term unemployment.

Therefore, much debate has focused on the reasons for prolonged periods of unemployment. Writers like Minford have pointed to the level of benefits acting as a disincentive, arguing that unemployment support operates like a minimum out-of-work income available indefinitely. Those in the low-paid category, who have lost their jobs could become long-term unemployed because it will not pay them to lower their wage expectations sufficiently to get a new job. McCormick refers to the fact that a 'large fraction of the very long-term unemployed in Britain's depressed areas are former 'career successes', having previously held well-paid, long lasting skilled manual jobs, from which they were made redundant'. The process of de-industrialisation and the restructuring of British industry, which accelerated in the 1980s, resulted in mis-matches between skills and location of people to fill new jobs. Those skilled manual workers from traditional industries, located mainly in the north, were therefore more prone to long bouts of unemployment.

Government responses have been based on notions of labour inflexibilities among the long-term unemployed, assuming the problem to be that of demotivation and lack of skills. Policy has focused on tightening eligibility for benefits and schemes to retain and remotivate the long-term unemployed. However, as Daniels notes, while the characteristics of the unemployed have a strong influence upon who among them are successful in being recruited for the jobs available, it is the general level of demand in the economy that determines the numbers of those jobs.

Regions

As referred to earlier, the structural changes in employment over the eighties has meant that there have been regional differences in the distribution of unemployment. One of the most visible aspects of the 1979–81 recession has been the widening of the north-south divide. The severity of this disparity is best reflected by regional differences in unemployment rates, which have been greater during the 1980s than at any other time since the depression of the 1930s. The north lost over 1.4 million jobs between 1979 and 1986, a drop of employment of 12 per cent compared to a job loss of only 168,000 in the south, a fall of less than 2 per cent. Even with the growth of employment since 1983 regional disparities have failed to narrow, with most of the growth occurring in the southern regions. Since 1979 the region with the highest rate of unemployment has continually suffered approximately twice as much unemployment as the region with the lowest rate. Regional policy had begun to close the regional gaps prior to 1979 but this has largely been reversed during the 1980s.

The lack of growth in the north has been explained by the industrial and labour force composition of the region, rather than any disadvantages of the region as a location. McCormick comments that the widening differences between aggregate north-south unemployment rates are indicative of 'the worsening unemployment circumstances of both manual workers relative to non-manual and of former manufacturing employees relative to those in the service sector, together with the higher proportion of manuals and manufacturing that happen to be present in the North'. While the north-south divide is a major economic problem, it is important to acknowledge that unemployment blackspots exist in all parts of the UK, even in regions of generally low unemployment. Inner city areas, in particular tend to have highest unemployment whereas the suburbs and smaller towns tend to have lower rates.

> It is the case that the South East – previously an area of low unemployment – was badly hit in the recession of the early 1990s.

Age and gender

Males have consistently been over-represented among the unemployed, this trend was accelerated after 1980 when male unemployment really took-off and continued to remain high relative to female unemployment throughout the 1980s. The slower rise among females can be explained by the way unemployment is counted and in the changing structure of the labour market. Following changes to the unemployment measure after 1982, many females seeking work, particularly married women, were excluded from the register as they were no longer entitled to benefit. The biggest shake-out of employment occurred in the male-dominated manufacturing industries, while the growth service industries tended to recruit females into part-time lower paid jobs.

Figure 7.9 Unemployment by Gender 1978–79

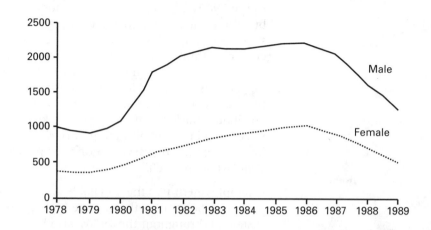

Source: Employment Gazette 1991

Age is a major factor in determining what happens to people after they become unemployed. Older workers have been consistently over-represented among the unemployed; it generally takes them longer to find jobs and these are usually inferior to their previous employment. In the 1980s, this trend continued, but most striking was the increase in youth or young adult unemployment. Despite a range of special measures, prolonged unemployment among young people became considerably more prevalent in the early 1980s.

Figure 7.10 Unemployment Rates by Age 1986–89

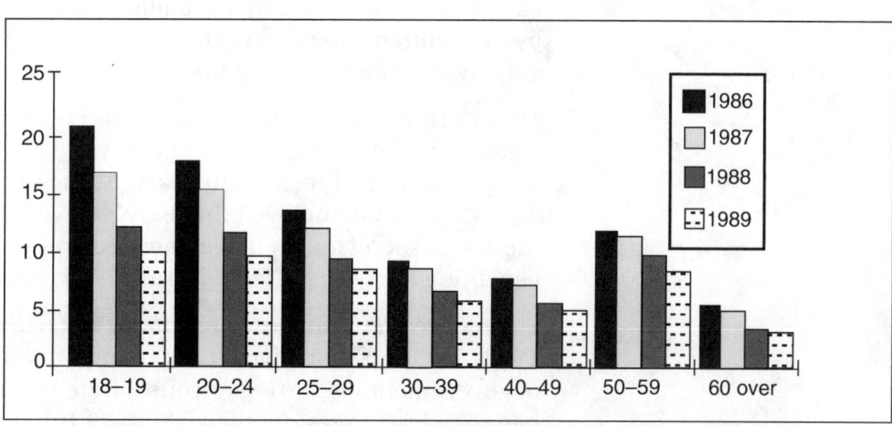

Overview

In the 1980s, high unemployment not only became politically acceptable, but also came to be used as a deliberate instrument of economic policy. The stagflation and industrial unrest of the late 1970s produced a sea-change in economic thinking and in public perceptions about economic priorities. The pursuit of full employment objectives through demand-led growth were no longer considered viable or even desirable. The Tories successfully propagated an anti-inflationary, monetarist alternative. It was accepted that an all out attack on inflation was the key economic priority and that the price would have to be a temporary rise in unemployment. However, the implementation of a severe monetary policy on top of a deep recession in 1980–81 simply deflated the economy and caused unemployment to soar.

Unemployment was the inevitable and wholly predictable result of a deliberate policy of deflation. The high levels of unemployment, which were sustained throughout the 1980s, also helped to fulfil other economic policy objectives, namely dampening wage inflation and weakening the power of trade unions. This, it was claimed, was essential to create the conditions for sustained non-inflationary growth.

Having successfully ditched full employment as a primary economic objective, the government then sought to off-load the responsibility for reducing unemployment onto the unemployed themselves – blaming the victim. As the economy began to recover in the second half of the 1980s, but unemployment continued to remain stubbornly high, the focus on supply-side policies intensified. The long-term unemployed in particular had to be coerced, remotivated and retrained back into employment. Undoubtedly, while increasing the competitiveness of the unemployed will enhance their employment potential, it is only through sustained demand-led growth that the overall size of the unemployed pool can be reduced. The jobs that had been created in the consumer-led boom of the late 1980s were primarily in the service sector, were low-paid and part-time. These were concentrated not in areas of highest unemployment, but in the south and east of the country. Many were filled not by the registered unemployed, but by new entrants to the workforce such as women returners; thus overall employment increased but unemployment still remained high.

The effects of the past 12 years of market-led economy policy has been to create levels of unemployment far beyond anything envisaged or considered acceptable in the previous 30 years. At the same time, unemployment as an issue and the unemployed themselves have largely become marginalised, as the Tories successfully pursued an electoral strategy which concentrated on benefiting the better off two-thirds of the population.

The recovery and supposed economic miracle of the second half of the 1980s has been short-lived. Lack of investment and the 'hands off' approach of government, preferring to concentrate on enterprise rather than industry, has done little to restore the viability of Britain's manufacturing sector. Struggling to recover from the decimation of the early 1980s, British manufacturing is once again threatened by crippling interest rates and an overvalued exchange rate. Dis-investment and the abandonment of regional policy meant that regions outside the southeast benefited little from the late 1980s boom. In the midst of the second recession in a decade, unemployment is set to climb back to the levels of the mid-1980s.

Forecasters predict high unemployment is set to remain a permanent feature of the 1990s.

Peter K. Lunt and Sonia M. Livingstone: Consumption and Identity

It is sometimes said that the wealthier societies have moved into an age of consumerism in which identity is increasingly expressed through consumer and leisure activity rather than productive or work activity. Without accepting such a simplistic dichotomy (what we consume surely depends on what we earn), Lunt and Livingstone do consider that a change in emphasis from a preoccupation with work to consumption has occurred.

I am aware that the few pages I have selected to represent some of Lunt and Livingstone's arguments tend to give rather an abstract and condensed picture of what is, in fact, quite a concrete piece of research. Their conclusions (included here) rest mainly on questionnaire data from 279 respondents, ranged in age from 18 to 82 years, 62 per cent of whom were women and 38 per cent men. Although Lunt and Livingstone use the term 'mass consumption' to refer to the consumption of the vast majority, the whole point of their analysis is that 'late modern' society is characterised by a great variety of patterns of consumption by means of which individuals and groups do express their various identities. However, they do not consider that consumption is unharnessed freedom and they stress the variety of constraints, pressures and they even 'dangers' in consumer activity in a capitalist society.

Lunt and Livingstone give an indication of the necessary theoretical scope of the study of consumption. The good news is that the study of consumption is also fun – or can be. In their book, *Common Culture*, Paul Willis *et al.*, stress that consumption can be a creative (even, paradoxically, a productive) activity, and analysing the meaning of patterns of consumption can be equally stimulating. It may even be that some current theory of consumption is almost too extravagantly speculative. For instance, Zygmunt Bauman may exaggerate when he argues that consumption 'offers freedom to people who in other areas of their life find only constraints' (1988). He describes those who are able to participate substantially in consumption as 'the seduced' and those who are not as 'the repressed'. The former are happily connected to capitalist society through the consumer market whereas the latter are subject to isolation and surveillance often in decaying inner-city sites.

A variety of images of the consumer stalk the pages of current sociological literature. Mike Featherstone refers to the 'heroic' consumer of the late twentieth century dedicatedly creating a well-staged life-style out of a plethora of consumer-commodities. We also come across the insatiable 'dreamy consumer' (Campbell, 1987) as well as the more familiar, supposedly rational, consumer of classical economics. However, any adequate theory of consumption needs to embody the hierarchical and inegaliterian aspects of consumption as well as its expressive side.

Reading 45 From Peter K. Lunt and Sonia M. Livingstone, *Mass Consumption and Personal Identity* (Open University Press, 1992), pp. 24–25, 166–71

Mass consumption and personal identity

The material conditions of consumer society constitute the context within which people work out their identities. People's involvement with material culture is such that mass consumption infiltrates everyday life not only at the levels of economic processes, social activities and household structures, but also at the level of meaningful psychological experience – affecting the construction of identities, the formation of relationships, the framing of events. The social psychological research which we present in the following chapters demonstrates, on the one hand, how people 'manage' the pressures of modern consumerism and, on the other, how personal identity is fundamentally social, for modern consumer culture creates the need to have, to discover, an identity. Processes of identity formation as we understand them in contemporary society . . . are intimately bound up with changing material conditions. As Giddens (1991) has pointed out, the modern condition entails both opportunities and dangers for the individual. The material conditions within which and in response to which we form our identities are not benign. They both afford possibilities for personal development and they threaten that development – increased freedoms go hand in hand with increased responsibilities.

Giddens implies that we have moved away from traditional forms of relationship, forms which were stable, uncontestable and faithfully reproduced from one generation to the next, offering little opportunity for personal development but a high degree of security. However, we need not argue that the possibilities for personal development under modern consumption are new in order to argue for its significance. Indeed it is a myth of modern consumerism that only the new is significant, putting pressure on research to claim new forms of social relationship. Rather, we can argue for evolving forms, transformations, breaks and continuities which are significant in their meanings and their social effects.

The focus of our enquiry into mass consumption and personal identity is the way in which the response of ordinary people to their economic circumstances involves the negotiation of personal identities in terms of needs, rights and responsibilities in everyday economic affairs. The construction of personal identities draws on conventionally given class, gender, cultural and generational identities as well as on individual biographical and family experience. The identities which result and are reflected in people's feelings of security, their notions of their needs and desires, their feelings of pleasure and involvement, their moral judgements, and explanations for social and economic processes, their response to social influence and the way they conduct their social relationships. They give meaning to everyday economic activities and experiences. These diverse aspects of personal identity are constructed through responding to the challenge, opportunities and problems which modern consumer culture presents to the individual . . .

People are continually guided by moral and social issues in their economic choices. Their decisions to save, to spend, their orientation to shopping and possessions are all tied into a complex set of beliefs about their place in the economy, the 'proper' way in which to handle their finances and the relation between everyday economic activity and broader social concerns. However, people's conceptions of their place in the social and economic order are not fixed. Rather, people engage with lifestyle representations and expectations which are changing and often in conflict – addressing contradictions between the ways of different generations or different cultures or, within their own time and place, between the ways which are normative and those which are alternative or which resist social pressures. Economic practices are more than decision-based economic behaviours. Being involved in material culture is a way of locating oneself in a changing social and moral order.

Consumerism is popularly represented through two discourses, the regressive and the progressive. Together, these constitute a debate in society about the development of sociopsychological identities in terms of individuals' rights, responsibilities and resources within material culture. Many people endorse the dominant representation of recent and dramatic change, believing that we are moving away from old forms of social organization, with old moralities, towards the age of consumerism. Hence they express concern about advertising, financial organizations and the availability of credit. The widespread faith in progress tempers their otherwise gloomy vision. In short, people experience a contradiction between the desire to embrace the opportunities of modern consumer society and the fear of inevitable loss involved in the new social order. New developments – credit cards, shopping centres, compact disc players – are regarded with ambivalence.

It is popularly believed that since the end of the Second World War the material conditions of ordinary people have improved and that people are increasingly involved in consumer culture. This may be accounted for in terms of the strenuous efforts of retailers and manufacturers and a complementary relaxing of legislation restricting the availability of credit to ordinary people. These market and financial changes are themselves dependent on economic changes which reflect the move away from an economy rooted in mass production to a more consumer-led economy. In terms of personal identity, these changes are seen to increase both personal freedom and personal responsibility. Time and again, the contradictions of previous times being hard but secure, limited but moral, oppressive but authentic, emerged in our discussions.

Such representations and beliefs affect many aspects of everyday life, especially when socially shared: saying is doing, and increasingly, what happens between people is action in the form of talk (Goffman, 1981, Moscovici, 1984). These representations of change affect personal and social relationships, influencing domestic identities and the relationship between expertise and the laity (Livingstone and Lunt, 1992). The banks, like other institutions such as the mass media, have changed their position in relation to their client groups or audiences, shifting responsibility onto the ordinary person, moving from a discourse of duty to one of choice. The ways in which people can officially borrow money are an example. Before the era of the credit card, if someone wanted to borrow in an agreed way, they had to apply to the bank for a loan in person, and legislation dictated that for durable goods the purchaser had to put down a proportion of the price before they could be given a loan. If credit was unavailable through these official means, then people turned to unofficial forms of credit. The credit card changed this: the client is free to 'spend' the allowed credit wherever and whenever they choose. He or she is also vulnerable to the temptation to spend, relatively unconstrained by having to possess, negotiate or account for the money. Underlying these changes are legislative changes reducing restrictions on borrowing and the change in orientation of financial institutions to extend their relations with business to their relations with lay people.

In fact, the consumer boom of the late 1980s persuaded the banks to tighten up on credit.

The discussions in which people are engaged – about social change, the role of the individual, and the nature of the economy – are, in part, the means by which these changes, roles and forms are made meaningful and by which resources and opportunities are negotiated in relation to duties and responsibilities (Fraser, 1989; Moore, in press). Notions of proper economic conduct and the place of material concerns in everyday life are constructed through such discussions. The looking back which is so much a part of the debate about personal responsibility in the face of increasing economic opportunity is not simply a form of nostalgia (Robertson, 1991) but is used to make sense of present events – setting up a contrast in order to conduct a debate. There are no right and wrong answers here, only a series of temporary positions adopted on the issue of how to spend, what to value, and so on. At different times and for different purposes, certain arguments are ruled in or ruled out, but they may be brought back later or used in different combinations for different effects. The discussions are rhetorical, concerned with opinions, and the oppositions between opportunity and danger, freedom and responsibility, pleasure and the moral order, form the dynamic around which this debate is played out (Mason, 1989; Billig, 1991).

The discussions are an attempt to locate the material world in a meaningful, human context. But this debate is not only a personal one; it is also a public debate, one which exercises the mass media and the major political parties. In 1991, both the Labour and Conservative parties produced citizens' charters which attempt to formalize the new relations between the active consumer and the state. While ordinary people are ambivalent about the opportunities and dangers of increased involvement in consumer culture, there is a parallel ambivalence for those in power giving up aspects of their control. We will attempt here to sketch the social contexts of this ambivalence.

Habermas (1984), among others, has examined changes in the institutionalization of societies in the modern period. He argues that the breakdown of broad religious world views at the beginning of the modern period involved the construction of expertise in the areas of science, politics and morals. The growing specialization of institutional control in society has always been linked to expertise, and the financial sector is no exception. In their turn, the experts manage the laity, determining the rights, resources and responsibilities – indeed, the identities – of ordinary people. As part of the development of the late modern period, identity has become a matter for public debate, as we saw continually in our discussions and interviews. The characterization of public influence on political processes has moved from the elite contribution of the café society to representation in the mass media, for mass consumption (Thompson, 1990)

The segmentation and specialization of modern life meant that important aspects of experience were seen as the legitimate domain of experts. For example, aesthetics was limited to high art, detached from everyday life, which was involved with the purely functional forms of mass-produced goods. Debates on the place of the citizen consumer have challenged the separation between different domains, different questions, which is central to modernism: science (concerned with truth), morality (concerned with norms and value) and art (Concerned with aesthetics and taste). These separated elements of culture are being placed together (Holub, 1991), their boundaries are threatened (Featherstone, 1991). We have seen that people do regard recent times as characterized by an overwhelming diversity of goods, with new and exciting possibilities of involvement in consumer culture. At the same time, we have seen that people do have a sense of loss of the old life and of loss of continuity with the present and the future.

The authors consider that 'faith in experts' and certainty based on accepted 'codes' has been eroded by an increase in personal control and responsibility.

The passive role dictated by modernity for the ordinary person, that of receiving meanings articulated by experts in the fields of science, morality and art, is made palatable by the simplicity of living life according to established codes.

Mulgan (1991) suggest that governments are giving up central control over these questions because of three broad influences: the collapse of communism, the green movement and the development of consumer-led economies. In their different ways, these movements all involve questions about the balance between individual and state responsibility. For example, the green movement asks individuals to challenge the separation of local and global by taking responsibility for the global in their domestic consumption practices. The development of consumer-led economies depends upon a growing involvement in consumption and its associated values by ordinary people. These two developments are in many ways opposed. The picture of responsibility in the green movement requires a constraint which would hinder the development of consumerism. The changing political order cross-cuts this debate by increasing involvement through citizenship. Citizenship is linked to national movements, thus opposing global ecological considerations, and it links to personal identity through engagement in political action rather than through consumption.

These developments and debates pose a challenge to existing political parties to formulate a balance between these apparently contradictory forms of social participation (national/global, political protest/consumer involvement, technological/ environmental).

There are also problems with all these movements: the individual may be given more and more responsibility without the resources or power to act effectively (Mulgan, 1991). For example, the consumer is given the responsibility for generating wealth in the economy, for protecting the global environment and for the political and moral welfare of the community. But despite the implicit claims of much popular culture, it seems unlikely that people have the resources and power to manage this responsibility. Thus there are basic questions to be answered about how much power actually goes along with the new responsibilities given to ordinary people. Is the centre slimming itself down by contracting out various responsibilities while retaining strategic control at the centre? (Mulgan, 1991). This problem is reflected in people's ambivalence about their involvement in consumer culture and their fears about the direction and future of consumerism and their experienced lack of control over it.

Giddens (1991) discusses the notion of identity in late capitalism in terms of a movement away from the various forms of emancipatory politics towards what he terms 'life politics'. While emancipatory politics in its various forms was concerned with releasing people from the constraints of traditional social positions by dissolving fixed positions and hierarchies, life politics 'is a politics of self-actualisation in a reflexively organised environment, where that reflexivity links self and body to systems of global scope' (Giddens, 1991, p. 214). Protest movements were an attempt to reveal the invasion and exploitation of daily life by social and political agencies. Life politics goes beyond this to encompass a level of involvement in social and political life of the ordinary person which enables them to challenge not through protest but through taking control of the shape of their own lives in the negotiation of their personal identities – the personal is political. As it has become possible to construct personal identities, so identity has become a social issue and a topic for public debate.

At the centre of the developments of late capitalism is the individual with personal rights, responsibilities and resources. The individual has choice to make which will influence economic, social and political life on a broad scale. The problem for the individual is to construct an authentic sense of identity in an unsupportive context, and to come to terms with the consequences of their choices. This is a social task, for it is conducted between individuals, groups and institutions, and because it concerns meanings, social representations and political ideologies. This struggle to construct a sense of identity by the citizen in the late twentieth century, is itself dependent on the negotiation of views of truth, beauty and morality.

If there has been a freeing of the individual to establish their 'own' identity through involvement in a consumer culture, then the question of what constitutes self becomes problematic. If it becomes possible to construct ourselves, the it becomes possible to reconstruct ourselves or to construct diverse selves. How then do people maintain a sense of stability, of continuity across time and place? How do people negotiate their place in the reproduction of existing forms of social relationship if everything is transitory and open to reconstruction? This was a fundamental problem for people which emerged in our work on generations, where generational differences were constructed in relation to perceptions of changes in material conditions. People attempted to impose a notion of continuity by seeing life as a trade-off between security and freedom. They felt that the financial institutions and governments had given up too much responsibility, that the individual has too much opportunity, more than they can handle: the individual has greater freedom of choice through involvement in consumer culture but is also more vulnerable. There was a strong feeling that society was veering from one extreme to another when what was required was a more thoroughly worked-out relation between individual and institutional responsibility . . .

The people we have talked to during our research for this book are engaged in a debate concerning the nature of identity in consumer culture. The dynamic of the debate is a natural milieu for them, there is no resolution offered, merely layers of discourse which play with a series of oppositions concerning tradition and modernity, freedom and determinism, opportunity and danger. Big issues played out in a domestic setting.

Questions and Issues

Work and Non-Work: Section 9

The most relevant readings are included in brackets after each question.

1 To what extent is Britain now in a post–Fordist age as far as the organisation of the economy and work are concerned? (Readings 41–42, especially, and also 43, 52)
2 Discuss the concepts of international capital and the international division of labour in relation to the British economy and workforce. (Readings 41–43, 52–53, 84)
3 Describe and explain the importance of employment in contemporary British society. (Readings 46–47, 68–69)
4 To what extent would you say people's identities are now defined more by their patterns of consumption and life-styles rather than by their relationship to the means of production? (Section 9, especially Readings 31, 47, 68–69)

SECTION 10

ORGANISATIONS

Introduction: Readings 46–48

There is a fresh and pragmatic air about David Beetham's discussion of bureaucracy and other organisational forms. He sees the main approaches to organisational analysis 'as each emphasising an essential aspect of organizational efficiency' rather than as perspectives engaged in a battle to the intellectual death.

The reading from Walter Powell will introduce many readers to fresh territory. He discusses three types of organisational forms: markets, hierarchies and networks. Most of the extract is concerned with markets and networks. It could be argued that markets and networks are sometimes too insufficiently institutionalised to be considered as forms of organisation. However, they are certainly intended to coordinate human activity which is the main purpose of organisations. Further, these two concepts deal with areas of social activity which sociology urgently needs to address.

After two theoretically wide-ranging passages, it may seem incongruous to include a brief, descriptive report on workers' participation. However, organisational democracy remains very much on the agenda in Europe, if not in England. Perhaps, after all, we have something to learn in this respect.

David Beetham: Bureaucracy – Weber and Variations

David Beetham describes and criticises Weber's model of bureaucracy and then presents what he sees *not* as alternatives to bureaucracy but as variations of bureaucracy. The models of organisations which he presents are:

- Classical (or Mechanistic) Bureaucracy
- Human Relations
- Cybernetic or Information Models
- Organizations as Association of Experts

In my view, the strength of Beetham's approach is that instead of seeing the second, third and fourth of these conceptions of organisations as wholesale alternatives to bureaucracy, he regards them as variations and possible improvements on Weber's perhaps too rigid model. Let us look briefly at Beetham's approach to the four organisational models.

He reduces Weber's definition of bureaucracy to four summary points. According to Weber, bureaucracy is characterised by:

1 Hierarchy (of Authority)
2 Continuity (of Office Holders)
3 Impersonality (Rules not Favouritism guide Transactions)
4 Expertise (based on Merit and Training)

While appearing to accept the necessity of bureaucracy in a 'mass industrial society', Beetham is critical of several aspects of Weber's model. He introduces differing organisational perspectives as ways of modifying Weber's original model according to circumstances.

Confusingly, Beetham sometimes uses various terms to refer to a given organisational form. For the sake of clarity, I have labelled the relevant section in the text 'Human Relations Model'; 'Information Systems Model'; and 'Organisations as Associations of Experts'. The Human Relations Model presents members of organisations as having personal needs and expectations. They are not merely functional units. The Information Systems Model emphasises the need for 'information flow', that is decision making should not simply be from the top downwards. The concept of organisations as Associations of Experts stresses that authority can be based on professional and other expertise, and that this is of a different kind from bureaucratic authority.

A reading of the 'Japanisation' section of the extract from Robin Murray (Reading 41) will show that Japanese manufacturing reflects the insights offered by the above conceptions of organisation to a much greater extent than traditional bureaucratic (or Fordist) types of organisation.

Reading 46 From David Beetham 'Bureaucracy' (Open University Press, 1987), as reprinted in Grahame Thompson *et al., eds., Markets, Hierarchies and Networks: The Coordination of Social Life* (Sage Publications, 1991) pp.128–36

The purpose of this chapter is to explore the models of bureaucracy developed within different academic disciplines. What is a model for? People who talk about 'models' in social science often confuse three quite different purposes which the construction of a model can serve: to provide *definitional* test; to set a *normative* standard; to develop an *explanatory* framework. A definitional model of bureaucracy will be concerned to specify the criteria which determine what is to count as a bureaucracy, and what is not. It answer the question: how do we recognize a bureaucracy when we see one? A normative model seeks to prescribe what are the necessary conditions for organizational efficiency or effectiveness, and to explore how far bureaucracy (either in general or in particular) is able to satisfy these conditions. It answers the question: how efficient are bureaucracies? An explanatory model aims to provide a framework for explaining the way bureaucracies function in practice, and why they have the consequences they do for the formation and execution of policy. It answers the question: why do bureaucracies function as they do?

Now of course these different questions are interrelated. To answer the question about bureaucratic efficiency, we need to know how bureaucracies actually work; and a typical reason for finding out why bureaucracies function as they do, is to discover how they might be made more efficient, and what are the major limitations or obstacles to making them. But the fact that the three types of question – definitional, normative and explanatory – are interrelated, does not make them the same question, and we need first of all to distinguish them in order to understand their interconnection. Those writers who *define* bureaucracy as organizational efficiency or inefficiency are confusing two different questions that need to be kept apart. And a similar mistake is made by those who assume that a normative model of 'rational' decision-making will suffice to explain how decision-making actually takes place; or, conversely, who believe that what actually occurs somehow sets the standard for what is attainable. In order to avoid this kind of confusion, the first part of the present chapter will concentrate on the question of bureaucratic efficiency, and the later part on explanatory models of bureaucratic functioning; in this way we shall also come to understand their interconnection more clearly.

Max Weber himself developed the 'ideal type' which is a form of model – his ideal type of bureaucracy being a major example.

But why do we need models at all? The reason is that societies are enormously complex, and present formidable problems to those who seek to understand them. The characteristic method of social science is to construct simplified conceptions or models of social life to help define, evaluate or explain this complexity. Of course the world as it is will not exactly match the models we construct. In practice it may be difficult to say whether a particular organization meets the definitional criteria for a bureaucracy; in some respects it may, in others it may not. It will be a matter of degree. In practice we may find that the general principles of organizational efficiency need modification to take account of actual variations in organizational purpose and context. And an explanatory model may require considerable elaboration in order to accommodate the complexity of social reality. But we can only grasp the complexity at all by starting with simplification, and by representing the complexity as so many variations around, or modifications of, or deviations from, the simplification we have constructed. Naturally, if the deviations become too great, we shall need to revise or even abandon our model. In this way the world of actual practice imposes its own discipline upon the flights of intellectual speculation, and provides the decisive test of more or less useful model building. But to abandon model-building itself is to become bogged sown in a morass of descriptive detail, or in interminable lists of principles to meet every possible contingency, such as clog up much of the writing on organization theory.

In this chapter, then, we shall explore the models of bureaucracy developed within the academic disciplines of sociology and political economy. In doing so we shall find that they differ, not only in terms of their particular focus of interest (social, economic or political), but also in terms of their distinctive method of simplification or model construction. The aim will be to clarify these differences, and to assess whether they are mutually conflicting or complementary; whether, that is to say, they embody antithetical approaches between which we have to choose, or whether they can be integrated into a larger and more comprehensive theory of bureaucracy.

Bureaucracy and administrative efficiency

The sociology of organization

What do the Vatican and General Motors, NASA and the British Health Service have in common? Organizational sociology sets itself the task of answering such questions, through an exploration of the most general features common to organizations in all sectors of modern society, and by theorizing about the conditions for organizational efficiency, regardless of whether the institution concerned is public or private, sacred or secular, devoted to profit or to preaching, to saving life or to ending it. In doing so it takes its starting point from the work of Max Weber, who was among the first to develop a generalizable theory of organization applicable across modern society. Weber's answer to the above question would have been simple: they are all bureaucracies.

In his definition of bureaucracy, Weber sought to identify the most basic features common to modern systems of large-scale administration. He distinguished ten or eleven of these, but they can be reduced for convenience to four main features. Bureaucratic administration, according to Weber, is characterized by: hierarchy (each official has a clearly defined competence within a hierachical division of labour, and is answerable for its performance to a superior); continuity (the office constitutes a full-time salaried occupation, with a career structure that offers the prospect of regular advancement); impersonality (the work is conducted according to prescribed rules, without arbitrariness or favouritism, and a written record is kept of each transaction); expertise (officials are selected according to merit, are trained for their function, and control access to the knowledge stored in the files). Together these features constitute Weber's definitional model of bureaucracy: the criteria that a system of administration has to meet for it to be properly called 'bureaucratic'.

But what exactly is 'administration' or a 'system of administration'? At its simplest, administration can be understood as the coordination and execution of policy, and a system of administration as an arrangement of offices concerned with translating policy into directives to be executed at the front line of an organization (shop floor, coal face, battlefield and so on). That is to say, not everyone who works in a bureaucratic organization is a bureaucrat. As administrators, bureaucrats have to be distinguished from 'chiefs' above, and 'front-line workers' below. Let us consider each of these in turn.

In his discussion of bureaucracy, Weber drew a sharp distinction between an administrative staff and the association or corporate group which employs it. A corporate group is a voluntary or compulsory association of people (anything from a nation down to a trade union, company, political party, university and so on) which either directly or indirectly elects a leadership or governing body to manage its affairs (cabinet, committee, board, council). The governing body in turn employs an administrative staff to carry out its polices. This administrative staff, if constituted according to the criteria listed above, will be called a bureaucracy. It is important, therefore, to distinguish between a bureaucracy and the governing body which employs it. The members of each differ crucially in the nature of their position, function and responsibility. Members of a governing body are typically elected and may work only part-time; their function is the broadest formulation of policy and rules for the association, and the provision of the necessary funds for its administration; their responsibility is outwards to the association as a whole (electorate, shareholders, members). Members of a bureaucracy, in contrast, are always appointed from above, and are responsible to the governing body for the execution of its policy and the administration of its funds. Although this distinction may sometimes be blurred in practice, it is vital in principle.

If at the upper end of an organization the distinction between bureaucrats and 'chiefs' or 'leaders' is relatively clear, drawing a sharp boundary at the lower end is more problematic. According to Weber, the essential characteristic of a bureaucrat is the exercise of authority within a bureau. Production workers neither exercise authority nor work in a bureau. Secretaries or typists are employed in a bureau, and their work is essential to the basic bureaucratic activity of maintaining the files. But they do not exercise authority; they are 'office workers', not 'officials'. On the other hand, many staff working in government offices at the bottom of its employment hierarchy exercise authority over a relevant public if not over other workers (social security officials, customs officers and so on). To exclude such archetypically bureaucratic figures from the ranks of a bureaucracy would be paradoxical indeed. So the boundary line cannot simply be drawn above 'front-line workers', as I suggested initially. It depends on the nature of the organization. In a private industry, bureaucratic authority will be coterminous with management; in a government agency, it may extend right down to those who staff the counter, and who comprise an essential part of the administration of policy and the exercise of authority.

Boundaries constitute a problem for any concept, and insistence on precision in all circumstances can become mere pedantry. Provided we are clear that bureaucrats are by definition both subject to higher authority and involved in exercising authority themselves, then we can call those organizations bureaucratic whose administration is arranged according to the principles of Weber's model, even though not everyone working within them, either at the top or bottom of the hierarchy, is necessarily to be counted a 'bureaucrat'.

So far we have been concerned with Weber's definitional model of bureaucracy, with the criteria a system of administration must meet if it is to count as bureaucratic. Many organizational sociologists have accepted Weber's definition because it is clear, precise and generalizable. But Weber also claimed much more controversially, that the closer an organization approximated to his model, the more efficient it was likely to be; and that it was the superior efficiency of bureaucratic administration that accounted for its general expansion within modern society. In other words, Weber believed that the defining characteristics of bureaucracy were *also* necessary conditions for administrative or organizational efficiency; in effect, that his definitional model served as a normative model as well. 'Experience tends to show,' he wrote, 'that the purely bureaucratic type of administrative organization is, from a purely technical point of view, capable of attaining the highest degree of efficiency [. . .] it is superior to any other form in precision, in stability, in the stringency of its discipline, and in its reliability.' And in another passage he wrote: 'the fully developed bureaucratic mechanism compares with other organizations exactly as does the machine with the non-mechanical modes of production.'

How did Weber justify this claim? There are two things to note about it at the outset. First, when he insisted on the superiority of bureaucracy, his standard of comparison was not some absolute ideal, but the forms of administration known to past history: by unpaid volunteers, local notables, collegial bodies or kinship networks. To adapt Weber's own analogy, the internal combustion engine may appear wasteful when compared with some ideal of maximum energy utilization, but it is vastly superior to a horse. Secondly, by 'efficiency' Weber meant not one single characteristic, but a complex of values which included quality of performance (for example speed, predictability), expansion of scope and cost-effectiveness of operation. These were in his view the characteristics required of an administrative system which had to meet the complex and large-scale administrative needs of a mass industrial society, rather than those of a localized economy geared to the rhythms of nature and the political requirements of a narrow elite.

If we examine the different elements of Weber's bureaucratic model, we can see how each could contribute to meeting these criteria of efficiency. The central feature of bureaucracy is the systematic division of labour, whereby complex administrative problems are broken down into manageable and repetitive tasks, each the province of a particular 'office', and then coordinated under a centralized hierarchy of command. The mechanical analogy is here quite precise; the subdivision of a complex set of movements into their constituent elements, and their reassembly into a coordinated process, achieves an enormous expansion of scope, precision and cost-effectiveness of operation. Other aspects of bureaucracy contribute to the same end. Its impersonality ensures that there is no favouritism either in the selection of personnel, who are appointed according to merit, or in administrative action, which is kept free from the unpredictability of personal connections. Its rule-governed character enables a bureaucracy to deal with large numbers of cases in a uniform manner, by means of categorization, while systematic procedures for changing the rules free the administration from the inflexibility of tradition ('the way things have always been done'). For Weber, the contrast with traditional forms of administration offered not only an essential point of comparison, but a means of identifying features of bureaucracy that would otherwise be taken for granted. Thus the separation of the official from ownership of the means of administration ensured that the operation as a whole was freed from the financial limitations of the private household, and that the individual was rendered dependent upon the organization for his or her livelihood, and thus amenable to its discipline. Such factors secured an enormous expansion in administrative capacity and predictability in comparison with the non-bureaucratic systems of the past.

Robert Merton (1937) pointed out that 'ritualism' – a mindless repetition of rule-governed routine – can be dysfunctional to bureaucracy.

Weber's claim that the defining criteria of bureaucracy also constitute a model of administrative efficiency is one that has been widely challenged by subsequent sociologists. Their studies of how organizations actually work in practice suggest that adherence to bureaucratic norms can hamper efficiency as much as promote it. This is because the principles of bureaucratic organization, so they argue, are more ambiguous than Weber realized, producing significant 'dysfunctional' effects, which become more accentuated the more rigorously the principles are applied. Each, that is to say, has its distinctively pathological manifestation. Adherence to rules can become inflexibility and 'red tape'. Impersonality produces bureaucratic indifference and insensitivity. Hierarchy discourages individual responsibility and initiative. Officialdom in general promotes 'officiousness', 'officialese' and similar pathologies. Max Weber, it is argued, failed to recognize the ambivalent character of bureaucracy, partly because studies of organization were in their infancy in the early decades of the century. But it was also because his ideas were unduly influenced by the examples of the Prussian army and the Taylorian system of scientific management. The model of machine-like discipline that they both offered obscured key dimensions of organizations, an understanding of which is necessary to secure their efficient operation.

Here Beetham begins to discuss what are usually considered as alternative organisational forms to bureaucracy, but which he presents as modifications of it.

What are these dimensions? They can best be grasped by counterposing to Weber's essentially mechanistic model alternative conceptions of organization developed by later sociologists. One alternative is the idea of an organization as a social system or network of interpersonal relations. Weber's model of organizational efficiency assumes that all aspects of the individual personality which are not relevant to the strict performance of his or her duties will be cast off as the individual enters the organization, or suppressed through effective socialization. If this were so, then a complete account of an organization could be given by providing a formal definition of the duties of each office, and of the relation between them; efficiency, in turn, would be a matter of securing a rational division of tasks at every level. In practice, however, people's personalities are never so totally subsumed into their roles, They come to the organization as individuals, with personal needs and expectations for which they seek satisfaction: from social intercourse at the work place; from the exercise of skill and a measure of control over the work process; from being treated 'as people' rather than as the impersonal occupants of a role. And the manner of their social interaction at work can be crucial to the effectiveness of their performance. Any authority which ignores these factors or tries to suppress them is likely to meet with resistance. People can be compelled to work upon command, but not to work efficiently or with commitment. That requires their active cooperation, which is as much a matter of informal negotiation as of authoritative command.

Human Relations Model

Information Systems Model

A different perspective on organizations is to see them as communications systems, in which the efficient transmission and processing of information is necessary to effective decision-taking. Arguably, Weber's concept of administration put too much emphasis on the execution of policy, to the exclusion of policy formation and review, both of which require effective mechanisms for collecting and processing information within the organization. There are good reasons for believing that a strictly hierarchical structure is not the most appropriate for these tasks. One is that its direction of emphasis is from the top downwards, whereas the transmission of information also requires effective channels of communication upwards from the 'grass roots' of the organization. Admittedly, it is always possible for those at the top of a hierarchy to construct separate institutional arrangements for monitoring performance outside the normal structures of policy execution. But this produces wasteful duplication, and in any case those know most about the adequacy of a policy who are responsible for actually administering it. A further defect of hierarchies is that they are constructed in a pyramidal fashion, narrowing as they approach the summit. Again, while this may be an effective structure for subdividing tasks and processing instructions downwards, it creates potentially enormous problems of overload or blockage in processing information in the opposite direction. Hierarchical systems suffer from too much information as much as from too little; or, rather, it is information in the wrong place, and it requires sophisticated procedures for sifting as well as transmitting it, if it is to be useful to policy formation and review. This is the argument for decentralized types of organization, in which the responsibility for decision-making is pushed downwards to the point where the information is available to make them.

Association of Experts Model

A similar conclusion can be reached from a different conception of organizations, which emphasizes the role of specialist expertise within them. Such a conception typically draws a contract between two forms of authority, which, it is argued, Weber did not adequately distinguish. The first is bureaucratic authority, which derives from the occupation of a position or office within a hierarchical structure, and from the powers that reside in the office. The second is the authority which derives from expertise, which resides in the individual as 'an authority', not in the position he or she occupies. Now Weber would no doubt have said that the two tend to coincide, and that the occupants of a bureaucratic office typically develop their own administrative or managerial expertise. However, this overlooks the fact that most administrators are involved in supervising people with expertise which they do not themselves possess: financial technical or professional. For these subordinate experts there can be considerable conflict between obedience to the instructions of a superior or the rules of the organization, and obedience to the requirements or principles of their profession. The one involves an externally imposed discipline, the other one that is internal to the nature of the specialism itself. The conclusion is then drawn that the most effective form of organization for experts is not a bureaucratic hierarchy, but a lateral network, whose discipline is maintained by loyalty to the organization as a whole, rather than to the narrowly defined duties of a specific office.

Each of these three alternative conceptions corresponds to a different historical phase in the study of organizations since Weber's time: to a shift from the 'scientific management' to the 'human relations' school; from mechanical to cybernetic or information models; from organization as hierarchies to organizations as associations of experts. Each has its corresponding prescriptions for organizational efficiency. It follows from the Weberian conception of bureaucracy as a hierarchy of offices that efficiency is to be attained by a rational division of labour, and a clear definition of competences. For those who see organizations as a system of interpersonal relations, efficiency becomes a matter of motivating subordinates within arrangements involving mutual give and take. For those to whom organizations are a communications system, efficiency is to be achieved by the effective sifting and transmission of information, and by locating decisions where such information is most readily available. For those, finally, to whom organization is a matter of the effective application of expertise to essentially technical problems, efficiency means finding arrangements under which experts are best able to exercise their distinctively professional capacities.

Each of these conceptions has in its time been presented as the final truth. It would be more plausible, however, to see them, not as mutually exclusive alternatives, either to the Weberian model or to one another, but as each emphasizing an essential aspect of organizational reality, all of which need taking into account and which together necessitate a modification in the strictly bureaucratic conception of organizational efficiency, rather than its outright replacement. Common to them all is the recognition that authority cannot be just a matter of the assertion of official powers vested in a formal hierarchy or a particular position. This is because subordinates possess their own powers, which reside in informal social networks, in the control of information, or in their own expertise. If the characteristic power of superiors is to initiate, the power of subordinates can be used to modify, delay or obstruct those initiatives. It is the ability to harness such powers to serve the goals of the organization, rather than merely the convenience of those who possess them, that constitutes the exercise of authority in its widest sense. From a sociological standpoint, success in this is not primarily a matter of individual personality, but of how the organization itself is structured. Too monolithic a hierarchy will produce a mentality of 'work to rule'; too decentralized a structure without corresponding means of monitoring or influencing performance will produce a 'work to convenience'. Each represents a distinctive form of bureaucratic inertia; in extreme circumstances they can occur simultaneously.

The conclusion that organizations are a combination of formal and informal relations, and that they need to balance the competing requirements of authority and initiative, of command and communication, seem merely platitudinous. Indeed, it is precisely because general conclusions about organizational efficiency have the quality of platitude that many recent sociologists would argue against generalizing about the matter at all, in abstraction from the particular contexts in which organizations have to operate. There is no 'one best way', they would argue, no universally applicable principles of organizational efficiency. This does not mean that anything goes, or that the question can be reduced to hunch or intuition; but that the criteria for effective operation will vary systematically with the purposes, technology and environment of the organization. On this view, it is the task of theory, not to produce a list of abstract generalizations, that are true everywhere, but to discover which types of organization are most appropriate to which particular kinds of context.

Walter W. Powell: Three Types of Organisational Forms – Markets, Hierarchies and Networks

It may be that the three concepts explored in this extract could provide the means for a shake-up in what can seem to be stale teaching about organisations. Of the types of organisations discussed by Powell, the most familiar is 'hierarchy', and this concept requires no further introduction from me. The term 'network' appears less frequently in introductory literature despite its routine use in academic organisational analysis. It helps to think of networks as roughly synonymous with organic organisational structures. Networks function through relationships of mutual trust and benefit rather than through rules and routine. An example of industrial networking occurs in parts of the Japanese motor industry where manufacturers and suppliers cluster together in an interdependent relationship which both excludes competitors (the market) and avoids bureaucracy (hierarchy). At a more homely level, a group of parents who form a baby-sitting circle for their mutual convenience is a network.

It may surprise some readers to see 'markets' cited as a key from of organisation. In fact, exchange between individuals and groups is a primary form of organisation (even though, until recently, it has tended to be neglected in sociology). In the contemporary world, share, financial and commodity markets operate in a global context, and transactions within them can greatly affect other aspects of social life.

In this extract, rather more attention is given to networks than to the other two types of organisational form dealt with here. This reflects Powell's intention to make the case that networks are a thriving type of economic organisation. Although Powell's analysis is directed at economic organisation, in the case of hierarchies and networks it can be generally applied to organisation in other contexts.

Reading 47 From Walter W. Powell: 'Research in Organizational Behaviour' 12 (1990), adapted and reprinted in Grahame Thompson *et al.*, eds., *Markets, Hierarchies and Networks: The Coordination of Social Life* (Sage Publications, 1991), pp. 268–74

My aim is to identify a coherent set of factors that make it meaningful to talk about networks as a distinctive form of coordinating economic activity. We can then employ these ideas to generate arguments about the frequency, durability and limitations of networks.

When the items exchanged between buyers and sellers possess qualities that are not easily measured, and the relations are so long-term and recurrent that it is difficult to speak of the parties as separate entities, can we still regard this as a market exchange? When the entangling of obligation and reputation reaches a point that the actions of the parties are interdependent, but there is no common ownership or legal framework, do we not need a new conceptual tool kit to describe and analyse this relationship?

Surely this patterned exchange looks more like a marriage than a one-night stand, but there is no marriage license, no common household, no pooling of assets. In the language I employ below, such an arrangement is neither a market transaction nor a hierarchical governance structure, but a separate, different mode of exchange, one with its own logic, a network.

Table 1 Stylized comparison of forms of economic organization

	Forms		
Key features	*Market*	*Hierarchy*	*Network*
Normative basis	Contract – Property rights	Employment relationship	Complementary strengths
Means of communication	Prices	Routines	Relational
Methods of conflict resolution	Haggling – resort to courts for enforcement	Administrative fiat – supervision	Norm of reciprocity – reputational concerns
Degree of flexibility	High	Low	Medium
Amount of commitment among the parties	Low	Medium to high	Medium to high
Tone or climate	Precision and/or Suspicion	Formal, bureaucratic	Open-ended, mutual benefits
Actor preferences or choices	Independent	Dependent	Interdependent
Mixing of forms	Repeat transactions (Geertz, 1978)	Informal organization (Dalton, 1957)	Status hierarchies
	Contracts as hierarchical Documents (Stinchcombe, 1985)	Market-like features: profit centres transfer pricing (Eccles, 1985)	Multiple partners Formal rules

In practice, most organizations are of 'mixed' form rather than of one 'pure' type. Here an indication is given of likely mixes.

Many firms are no longer structured like medieval kingdoms, walled off and protected from hostile forces. Instead, we find companies involved in an intricate latticework of collaborative ventures with other firms, most of whom are ostensibly competitors. The dense ties that bind the auto and biotechnology industries cannot be easily explained by saying these firms are engaged in market transactions for some factors of production, or by suggesting that the biotechnology business is embedded in the international community of science. At what point is it more accurate to characterize these alliances as networks rather than as joint ventures among hierarchical firms?

We need fresh insights into these kinds of arrangement. Whether they are new forms of exchange that have recently emerged or age-old practices that have gained new prominence they are not satisfactorily explained by existing approaches. Markets, hierarchies and networks are pieces of a larger puzzle that is the economy. The properties of the parts of this system are defined by the kinds of interaction that take place among them. The behaviour and interests of individual actors are shaped by these patterns of interaction. Stylized models of markets, hierarchies and networks are not perfectly descriptive of economic reality, but they enable us to make progress in understanding the extraordinary diversity of economic arrangements found in the industrial world today.

Table 1 represents a first cut at summarizing some of the key differences between markets, hierarchies and networks. In market transactions the benefits to be exchanged are clearly specified, no trust is required, and agreements are bolstered by the power of legal sanction. Network forms of exchange, however entail indefinite, sequential transactions within the context of a general pattern of interaction. Sanctions are typically normative rather than legal. The value of the goods to be exchanged in markets is much more important than the relationship itself; when relations do matter, they are frequently defined as if they were commodities. In hierarchies, communication occurs in the context of the employment contract. Relationships matter and previous interactions shape current ones, but the patterns and context of intra-organizational exchange are most strongly shaped by one's position within the formal hierarchical structure of authority.

The philosophy that undergirds exchange also contrasts sharply across forms. In markets the standard strategy is to drive the hardest possible bargain in the immediate exchange. In networks, the preferred option is often one of creating indebtedness and reliance over the long haul. Each approach thus devalues the other: prosperous market traders would be viewed as petty and untrustworthy shysters in networks, while successful participants in networks who carried those practices into competitive markets would be viewed as naive and foolish. Within hierarchies, communication and exchange is shaped by concerns with career mobility – in this sense, exchange is bound up with considerations of personal advancement. At the same time, intra-organizational communication takes place among parties who generally know one another, have a history of previous interactions, and possess a good deal of firm-specific knowledge, so there is considerable interdependence among the parties. In a market context it is clear to everyone concerned when a debt has been discharged, but such matters are not nearly as obvious in networks or hierarchies.

Markets, as described by economic theory, are a spontaneous coordination mechanism that imparts rationality and consistency to the self-interested actions of individuals and firms. [. . .]

The market is open to all comers, but while it brings people together it does not establish strong bonds of altruistic attachments, The participants in a market transaction are free of any future commitments. The stereotypical competitive market is the paradigm of individually self-interested, non-cooperative, unconstrained social interaction. As such, markets have powerful incentive effects for they are the arena in which each party can fulfil its own internally defined needs and goals.

Sociology students may find some of the material on economic markets somewhat technical. However, even a 'gloss' of market theory is useful.

Markets offer choice, flexibility and opportunity. They are a remarkable device for fast, simple communication. No one need rely on someone else for direction, prices alone determine production and exchange. Because individual behavior is not dictated by a supervising agent, no organ of systemwide governance or control is necessary. Markets are a form of non-coercive organization, they have coordinating but not integrative effects. As Hayek (1945) suggested, market coordination is the result of human actions but not of human design.

Prices are a simplifying mechanism, consequently they are unsuccessful at capturing the intricacies of idiosyncratic, complex and dynamic exchange. As a result, markets are a poor device for learning and the transfer of technological know-how. In a stylized perfect market, information is freely available, alternative buyers or sellers are easy to come by, and there are no carry-over effects from one transaction to another. But as exchanges become more frequent and complex, the costs of conducting and monitoring them increase, giving rise to the need for other methods of structuring exchange.

Organization, or hierarchy, arises when the boundaries of a firm expand to internalize transactions and resource flows that were previously conducted in the marketplace. The visible hand of management supplants the invisible hand of the market in coordinating supply and demand. Within a hierarchy, individual employees operate under a regime of administrative procedures and work roles defined by higher-level supervisors. Management divides up tasks and positions and establishes an authoritative system of order. Because tasks are often quite specialized, work activities are highly interdependent. The large vertically integrated form is thus an eminently social institution, with its own routines, expectations and detailed knowledge.

A hierarchical structure – clear departmental boundaries, clean lines of authority, detailed reporting mechanism, and formal decision-making procedures – is particularly well-suited for mass production and distribution. The requirements of high volume, high-speed operations demand the constant attention of a managerial team. The strength of hierarchical organization, then is its reliability – its capacity for producing large numbers of goods or services of a given quality repeatedly – and its accountability – its ability to document how resources have been used (DiMaggio and Powell, 1983; Hannan and Freeman, 1984). But when hierarchical forms are confronted by sharp fluctuations in demand and unanticipated changes, their liabilities are exposed.

Networks are 'lighter on their feet' than hierarchies. In networks modes of resource allocation, transactions occur neither through discrete exchanges nor by administrative fiat, but through networks of individuals engaged in reciprocal, preferential, mutually supportive actions. Networks can be complex: they involve neither the explicit criteria of the market, nor the familiar paternalism of the hierarchy. A basic assumption of network relationships is that one party is dependent on resources controlled by another, and that there are gains to be had by the pooling of resources. In essence, the parties to a network agree to forgo the right to pursue their own interests at the expense of others.

In network forms of resource allocation, individuals' units exist not by themselves, but in relation to other units. These relationships take considerable effort to establish and sustain, thus they constrain both partners' ability to adapt to changing circumstances. As networks evolve, it becomes more economically sensible to exercise voice rather than exit. Benefits and burdens come to be shared. Expectations are not frozen, but change as circumstances dictate. A mutual orientation – knowledge which the parties assume each has about the other and upon which they draw in communication and problem solving – is established. In short, complementarity and accommodation are the cornerstones of successful production networks. As MacNeil (1985) has suggested, the 'entangling strings' of reputations, friendship, interdependence and altruism become integral parts of the relationship.

> It is worth adding here for consideration that the following five attributes are often associated with networks: solidarity, altruism, loyalty, reciprocity, trust.

Networks are particularly apt for circumstances in which there is need for efficient, reliable information. The most useful information is rarely that which flows down the formal chain of command in an organization, or that which can be inferred from shifting price signals. Rather, it is that which is obtained from someone whom you have dealt with in the past and found to be reliable. You trust best information that comes from someone you know well. Kaneko and Imai (1987) suggest that information passed through networks is 'thicker' than information obtained in the market, and 'freer' than that communicated in a hierarchy. Networks, then, are especially useful for the exchange of commodities whose value is not easily measured. Such qualitative matters as know-how, technological capability, a particular approach or style of production, a spirit of innovation or experimentation, or a philosophy of zero defects are very hard to place a price tag on. They are not easily traded in markets nor communicated through a corporate hierarchy. The open-ended, relational features of networks with their relative absence of explicit *quid pro quo* behavior, greatly enhance the ability to transmit and learn new knowledge and skills.

Reciprocity is central discussions of network forms of organization. Unfortunately it is a rather ambiguous concept, used in different ways by various social science disciplines. One key point of contention concerns whether reciprocity entails exchanges of roughly equivalent value in a strictly delimited sequence or whether it involves a much less precise definition of equivalence, one that emphasizes indebtedness and obligation. Game theoretic treatments of reciprocity by scholars in political science and economics tend to emphasize equivalence. Axelrod (1984) stresses that reciprocal action implies returning ill for ill as well as good for good. As Keohane (1986) notes, the literature in international relations 'emphatically' associates reciprocity with equivalence of benefits. As a result, these scholars take a view of reciprocity that is entirely consistent with the pursuit of self-interest.

Sociological and anthropological analyses of reciprocity are commonly couched in the language of indebtedness. In this view, a measure of imbalance sustains the partnership, compelling another meeting (Sahlins, 1972). Obligation is a means through which parties remain connected to one another. Calling attention to the need for equivalence might well undermine and devalue the relationship. To be sure, sociologists have long emphasized that reciprocity implies conditional action (Gouldner, 1960). The question is whether there is a relatively immediate assessment on whether 'the books are kept open', in the interests of continuing satisfactory results. This perspective also takes a different tack on the issue of self-interest. In his classic work *The Gift*, Marcel Mauss (1967), attempted to show that the obligations to give, to receive, and to return were not to be understood simply with respect to rational calculations, but fundamentally in terms of underlying cultural tenets that provide objects with their meaning significance, and provide a basis for understanding the implications of their passage from one person to another. Anthropological and sociological approaches, then, tend to focus more on the normative standards that sustain exchange; game theoretic treatments emphasize how individual interests are enhanced through cooperation.

Social scientists do agree, however, that reciprocity is enhanced by taking a long-term perspective. Security and stability encourage the search for new ways of accomplishing tasks, promote learning and the exchange of information, and engender trust. Axelrod's (1984) notion of 'the shadow of the future – the more the immediate payoff facing players is shaped by future expectations – points to a broadened conception of self-interest. Cooperation thus emerges out of mutual interests and behavior based on standards that no one individual can determine alone. Trust is thereby generated. Trust is, as Arrow (1974) has noted, a remarkably efficient lubricant to economic exchange. In trusting another party, one treats as certain those aspects of life which modernity rendered uncertain (Luhmann, 1979). Trust reduces complex realities far more quickly and economically than prediction, authority or bargaining.

It is inaccurate, however, to characterize networks solely in terms of collaboration and concord. Each point of contact in a network can be source of conflict as well as harmony. Recall that the term alliance comes from the literature of international relations where it describes relations among nation states in an anarchic world. Keohane (1986) has stressed that processes of reciprocity or cooperation in no way 'insulate practitioners from considerations of power'. Networks also commonly involve aspects of dependency and particularism. By establishing enduring patterns of repeat trading, networks restrict access. Opportunities are thus foreclosed to newcomers, either intentionally or more subtly through such barriers as unwritten rules or informal codes of conduct. In practice, subcontracting networks and research partnerships influence who competes with whom, thereby dictating the adoption of a particular technology and making it much harder for unaffiliated parties to join the fray. As a result of these inherent complications, most potential partners approach the idea of participation in a network with trepidation. All of the parties to network forms of exchange have lost some of their ability to dictate their own future and are increasingly dependent on the activities of others.

Mary Brasier: Workers' Participation

In Britain, during the 1980s, management was greatly strengthened and the unions were weakened. The notion of workers' participation in the running of industry was scarcely mentioned and seemed to belong to a bygone age. However, the situation is very different in some other parts of Europe. In fact, it is in the more economically prosperous parts of Europe, such as the Scandinavian countries and Germany, that workers' participation in industry tends to be most strongly established. In contrast, British Conservative governments have argued that workers' participation and the various rights secured in the Social Charter (also referred to in this article), do not suit British industrial relations. On the other hand, it may be that workers' participation would contribute positively to industrial productivity and dynamism here, as it appears to do elsewhere.

Reading 48 From Mary Brasier: 'Workers on Board' in *Guardian*, 9 November, 1990, p. 24

Four times a year three union officials, three shopfloor representatives from local factories, an Audi employee and a white-collar worker meet in the boardroom at Volkswagen's headquarters in Wolfsburg Southern Germany. They are part of the supervisory board of the car-maker which elects and watches over management. One of the items on their forthcoming agenda is likely to be a proposal to introduce a similar role for workers in the company's overseas operations.

If Volkswagen management agrees, it will be the first step towards introducing – across the European Community – a form of worker participation or *Mitbestimmung* which has been at the heart of German industrial relations since the war.

IG Metall, the metalworkers' union and the largest union in the country, is leading the drive to introduce worker participation outside Germany. It is close to agreeing a contract with Volkswagen which would set up structures in the company's foreign operations to ensure workers access to information about the company.

According to Ortwin Witzel at Volkswagen: "IG Metall and the works council would like to extend their influence in Belgium and Spain to the same level as in Germany".

Parallel moves by other German unions aimed at securing representation at European level for workers are increasing pressure on other EC countries that do not give the shopfloor access to the boardroom to improve industrial democracy.

"We are now in a situation where it is urgent," explains Reinhard Reibsch at IG Chimie, Germany's biggest chemical union. "In the chemical industry a lot of companies do decide on a European scale whether to close a plant. We do not want to export the German system of participation, but we do want consultation and information for workers' representatives in all countries. This law was created for the national level and we now have an international level of decision-making."

He believes plans from the European Commission to change company law after the Single Market to introduce new forms of participation will not be enough to give representation to workers in subsidiary plants. "The EC regulations will only work where there is one company, not where companies are producing in different countries of the community," he says. "We need to create a new type of participation at European level."

The German proposals are still a long way from imposing the kind of two-tier board system which is compulsory in Germany itself and gives workers the right to half the seats on the company's board. But moves by German unions will be viewed with some alarm in Britain where employers have always resisted suggestions for shopfloor participation at boardroom level, In the 1970s the Bullock proposals for worker directors failed in the face of massive political and industrial opposition.

Despite its protestation of enthusiasm for Europe this week, the Confederation of British Industry remains opposed to the reality of this form of integration at its own back door.

In his closing speech to the CBI conference on Tuesday, director general John Banham launched an attack on the Social Charter, which also contains proposals for harmonising worker rights, as akin to the delusion that "Karl Marx lives on".

EC proposals offer companies the choice of adopting two-tier boards and workers' councils – the classic ingredients of the *Mitbestimmung*, or a looser form of consultation procedure which is the soft option designed to appeal to British industry.

Volkswagen's actions will not directly affect the UK, where it has no assembly lines, but the resistance by German workers to any suggestion of compromising their power in a Single European market could force the issue in Britain where employers would prefer the least radical alternatives.

Yet, *Mitbestimmung* has worked well for German industry. Enshrined in law since 1976, it obliges companies with more than 2,000 workers to have a supervisory board on which half the members are worker representatives elected mainly from the shopfloor but also from executive ranks every four years.

According to Dieter Wienke at the Confederation of German Employers Federation, the system has changed management style in Germany in the last 14 years. "You have to see the social implications of management decisions . . . There are some problems of course, but in practice it functions well. We were not in favour of this act and most companies are not, but it works."

The occasions on which the supervisory board, with its balance of workers and shareholder representatives clashes with the management board, which has the final say are limited by behind-the-scene manoeuvring to ensure that at the meeting consensus can be achieved. The main drawback of the system is that decision-making is slower.

If there is deadlock, the chairman of the supervisory board, who is from the shareholder side, has a casting vote.

Dieter Von Herz at Continental tyre-makers, based on Hanover, says that in the last 14 years the casting vote has only been used once. "*Mitbestimmung* makes no sense if you use the double voting right. The philosophy and practice in German industry is that every chairman of the *Aussichtsrat* (supervisory board) wants to avoid using it. Co-determination has really forced both sides to understand the other side better," he says.

Continental may also have discovered a further benefit of having workers in the boardroom. Siegfried Schiller is a specialist rubber worker at Continental who has stepped into the spotlight of Europe's most acrimonious takeover battle. He is head of the works council of Continental and he could prove an effective defence against rival tyre-maker Pirelli, whose overtures seeking a merger of the two companies are turning increasingly into an all-out attack.

Faced with increased interest from acquisition-hungry foreign firms, insistence on workers' rights might allow German industry to throw a barrier in the path of predators. It could prove a selling point as Germany, under the EC umbrella, tries to sell its model of boardroom democracy to sceptics like the UK.

Questions and Issues

Organisations: Section 10

The most relevant readings appear in brackets after each question.

1. How would you relate organisational theory to the Fordist/Post-Fordist model? (Section 10 and Readings 41–42)
2. 'Bureaucracy is the most efficient and fair form of large-scale organisation.' Discuss. (Section 10 and Readings 41–42)
3. 'Business will never be democratic'. Discuss. (Section 10 and Readings 41–42, 55)
4. To what extent do you consider that markets, hierarchies and networks operate in a complementary rather a conflicting manner? (Section 10, especially Reading 47)

URBANISATION AND COMMUNITY

Introduction: Readings 49–51

This section and the next closely complement each other. Both examine the forces which help to create, or which disrupt or destroy, communities and societies. The 'over-determining' or contextual forces in which development or decline takes place are economic, but the role of political power is also a significant factor. There is a sense, too, in which individuals and groups invest their own meanings in, and contribute to, the change of social environments. These themes are signalled in the opening reading from Philip Cooke in which he searches for the most suitable term to indicate 'social activity that is focused on place.'

The extract from Paul Harrison's book on Hackney provides vivid empirical demonstration of some of the theoretical points made by Cooke and also adds further theoretical perspective. He describes people engaging with circumstances and problems seldom substantially of their own making. Further discussion of one of the problems associated with the inner city – certain categories of crime – is discussed in Reading 72. The underclass debate has particular relevance to the inner city and is also discussed in Reading 72.

Anthony D. King's piece provides a detailed framework for investigating the colonial city within the world economic system and goes on to review the development of theoretical perspectives on the role of contemporary cities in the world system.

Philip Cooke: The Concepts of Locale, Locality and Community

In this extract, Cooke argues the case against the use of the term 'community' as a catch-all concept to describe 'social activity that is focused on place'.

In the first paragraph he records three main objections against the word community as an adequate description of such activity:

1 It is 'inward-looking with regard to place' (given that much that affects places comes from outside of them).
2 It over-stresses stability (at the expense of conflict).
3 It over-stresses continuity (at the expense of change).

Cooke finds Anthony Giddens' use of the term 'locale' as a alternative to community wholly unconvincing – it is even vaguer in meaning than community. He presents his objections to the term locale in a crisp paragraph.

He then goes on to advocate and explain the use of the term 'locality' as a better concept than community to describe 'social activity that is focused on place'. However, he rejects Savage's use of the term which seems to describe localities as simply the product of structural or external forces (say, national government or big business investment) and insists that the concept should also include what he calls the 'pro-active' participation of individuals and groups in a given place. He strongly associates the right to such participation with the modern concept of citizenship – by which it is established in law.

Reading 49 From Philip Cooke, 'Locality, Economic Restructuring and World Development' in Philip Cooke *ed., The Changing Face of Urban Britain: Localities* (Unwin Hyman, 1989), pp. 10–12

Locale, locality and community

There is a gap in the social science literature when it comes to a concept dealing with the sphere of social activity that is focused upon place, that is not only reactive or inward-looking with regard to place, and that is not limited in its scope by a primary stress on stability and continuity. Community is inadequate because it fails to satisfy the second and third conditions. Also, it fails to satisfy the first condition in that it is not strictly denotative of place. It is by no means unusual to speak of community aspatially as in the idea of communities of interest or 'community without propinquity' (Webber, 1964). Community is, therefore, too broad in its spatial reach and too narrow in its social connotations, especially in respect of its external content. 'Locality' is a strong candidate for filling the gap.

Before considering the adequacy of *locality* to the task in hand it is worth briefly considering the value of the apparently cognate concept of *locale* recently introduced by Giddens (1984). As Giddens puts it,

> Locales refer to the use of space to provide the *settings* of interaction, the settings of interaction in turn being essential to specifying its contextuality . . . Locales may range from a room in a house, a street corner, the shop floor of a factory, towns and cities, to the territorially demarcated areas occupied by nation-states (Giddens, 1984, p. 118).

There are three reasons for rejecting the notion of locale as a candidate to fill the gap. The first of these is that it is even looser than community in its spatial scope. For, although there are such appellations as the 'community of nations' and, even more formally, the European Community, even common usage seldom extends its application to the scale of the room. The second reason for rejecting locale is that it reproduces the passive connotations of community in the way it refers to setting and context for action rather than as a constituting element in action. Finally, unlike even the inadequate notion of community embodied in the work of earlier theorists of community, locale lacks any specific social meaning. It remains primarily a synonym for space – a particularly old-fashioned one, since it stands for a space which can be *occupied* by socio-political entities such as the nation state.

A better conceptualization, offered by Savage et al. (1987), sees locality as the product of the interactions of supralocal structures. These may, it is proposed, give rise to local specificity, but this never goes as far as to warrant the designation 'local culture' though it does merit the appellation 'locality'. However this approach is too restrictive in its structural determination. It shares with community and locale a blind spot with respect to the active, potentially effective power embodied within both the concept of locality and the practices of its members. If locality is reduced to the interactive outcome of common structural determinations it becomes impossible to explain local variations between otherwise similarly constituted places. Yet we know that historical and contemporary social practices of an innovative character emerge in specific localities, sometimes in more than one more or less simultaneously.

Historical examples would include the ways in which industrial districts such as Sheffield, Stoke-on-Trent, Limoges, Lyons and Bradford emerged either singularly or sometimes in parallel as localities displaying particular productive specialisms. Outside the industrial sphere, the development of localities with particular aesthetic specialisms such as Salzburg for opera, Cannes for film appreciation and Nashville for country and western music cannot readily be explained without considerable reference to local initiatives of a collective kind. Returning to industry and the highly contemporary period new specialisms are being forged in small towns such as Treviso in Italy where clothing production is dominated by, but by no means limited to, the activities of the Benetton company. Meanwhile, Boston in Massachusetts has become an important software and high technology centre and Cambridge (UK) is blossoming as a research and development complex in industrial science and engineering.

Such examples probably have to be understood in terms that include but move beyond the purely structural. Each is a clear illustration of local mobilization by a few or many individuals and groups taking full advantage of what may be called *pro-active capacity*. What this means is rather straightforward. In sovereign nation states there are two main levels at which collective identification is actively expressed. The first is the national level: individuals are officially accorded a nationality with which as subjects they identify to a greater or lesser degree. The second is the local level where individuals work and live their everyday lives for the most part. At both these levels individuals of the appropriate age have democratic rights and freedoms of expression. Furthermore, the existence of such rights implies, in practice, the existence of the two levels. One of the key attributes of sovereignty is the right to *name* localities, a fact made visible whenever the control of territory is transferred as, for example, when colonizing powers annexe it or when emergent nations win independence. Membership of a locality by birth, or by residence for a qualifying period, admits the individual to the citizenship bestowed on 'nationals' of the soveriegn power.

Citizenship is thus a precondition for participation in the range of affairs that may take place in the territory of the nation state. Those lacking citizenship and residing in an alien nation state lack many of the instruments of pro-activity such as welfare or electoral rights, though they may possess certain economic rights. Such groups constitute and fall back upon what is more accurately called their community than their locality, though it is not unreasonable to consider such a community as existing in a particular locale.

Thus the discussion of the status and meaning of locality returns us to the point of departure. Citizenship as a means of social participation implies the existence of the modern nation state, an institution which became generalized only from the period when cultural modernity and industrial capitalism became dominant social paradigms. The modern nation state is one in which citizenship applies at both the local and the central levels. Both levels are key means for social mobilization and political intervention. For individuals who are *subjects* of the sovereign power of the nation state their citizenship rights are exchanged for their allegiance. Citizen subjects obtain civil, political and social rights (Marshall, 1977) in exchange for certain obligations such as those involving obedience to the law, including acceptance of military conscription in time of war. As Turner (1986) puts it: 'To be a citizen is to be a person with political rights involving liberty and protection in return for one's loyalty to the state' (Turner, 1986, pp. 106–7).

That the state can enforce this relationship is the result of modern methods of surveillance (Giddens, 1984) such as the various certificates, licences and numbers by means of which the modern state *locates* individuals in their localities.

In conclusion, locality is a concept attaching to a process characteristic of modernity, namely the extension, following political struggle, of civil, political and social rights of citizenship to individuals. Locality is the space within which the larger part of most citizens' daily working and consuming lives is lived. It is the base for a large measure of individual and social mobilization to activate, extend or defend those rights, not simply in the political sphere but more generally in the areas of cultural, economic and social life. Locality is thus a base from which subjects can exercise their capacity for pro-activity by making effective individual and collective interventions within and beyond that base. A significant measure of the context for exercising pro-activity is provided by the existence of structural factors which help define the social, political and economic composition of locality. But the variation between similarly endowed localities can only be fully understood in terms of the interaction between external and internal processes spurred, in societies dominated by capitalist social relations, by the imperatives of collective and individual competition and the quest for innovation.

Paul Harrison: What Happens in the Inner City Can Happen Anywhere – Hackney as an Example

In sociological terms, the inner city is not a fixed physical entity with unchanging characteristics. On the contrary, it is a dynamic process of economic, social and cultural activities – or lack of activity. Paul Harrison examines Hackney as an example, although he refers to many other inner-city areas. Even though it has long been a predominantly working-class area, Hackney has not always been characterised by those negative factors – economic decline, environmental blight, population exodus, social 'problems' – widely (though not always correctly) associated with inner cities. As recently as the early 1970s, the average wage in Hackney was above the national average. The significance of this is that the nature of capitalist economic development is such that areas – urban or otherwise – which prosper today may decline tomorrow and vice-versa. Harrison makes this point repeatedly throughout his book.

This extract divides into two parts. The first describes three factors which tend to define inner-city areas with multiple problems. These are:

1 areas of older industry
2 areas of particularly bad housing
3 areas of above-average numbers of less-skilled manual workers.

The second part of the extract skilfully links global and national economic and political developments with economic and social problems in Hackney. It becomes quite clear that a sizeable proportion of Hackney's population has become 'trapped' (although Harrison does not use the word) into poverty: jobs are lost, and the means to travel to where there might be jobs are not available. After reading Harrison, it becomes difficult to blame the poor as a group for their poverty.

Reading 50 From Paul Harrison, *Inside the Inner City: Life Under the Cutting Edge* (Penguin, 1985), pp. 21, 22–24, 47–49

If you stand where the kites fly on the summit of Parliament Hill in Hampstead, on a clear day you will see, about half-way between the spire of St Michael's church in Highgate and the steel-and-glass skyscrapers of the City of London, the six immense tower blocks of Nightingale Estate. They stand, in two ranks of three, almost in the centre of Hackney. It is less than four miles from Hampstead and Highgate in space, but if social distances were measured in miles it would be half-way round the globe. The gulf between the inner city and the desirable neighbourhood is a measure of the wide gap between wealth and poverty in Britain.

> While this is overwhelmingly true, there are 'enclaves' of Hackney which have become 'gentrified', i.e. occupied mainly by middle-class people.

The inner city is the social antipodes of middle-class Britain, a universe apart, an alien world devoid of almost every feature of an ideal environment. It is the place where all our social ills come together, the place where all our sins are paid for.

The inner city is now, and is likely to remain, Britain's most dramatic and intractable social problem. For here are concentrated the worst housing, the highest unemployment, the greatest density of poor people, the highest crime rates and, more recently, the most serious threat posed to established law and order since the Second World War. And yet it is not a peculiar, exceptional problem. For all the deprivations found concentrated in the inner city are widespread throughout the country, strongly present in the peripheral northern and Celtic regions, and in scattered pockets almost everywhere. The inner city is therefore a microcosm of deprivation, of economic decline and of social disintegration in Britain today. It is not only a particular sort of place on the map, but a symbol and summation of the dark side of a whole society . . .

There is no clear definition and no definitive listing of inner-city areas, but a useful pointer is the list of authorities that receive funds under the various urban programmes. They include many inner London boroughs: Brent, Islington, Hackney, Newham and Tower Hamlets in the north and east, Hammersmith and Ealing in the west, Lambeth, Lewisham, Southwark, Greenwich and Wandsworth south of the river. Outside London they were, until 1980 at least, largely concentrated in a few (though heavily populated) areas: Clydeside, Tyneside, south-east Lancashire, South and West Yorkshire, the West Midlands, urban South Wales and urban Northern Ireland.

Three closely related factors define most of the problems of these areas. The first is that they are areas of older industry: clothing and textiles, shipbuilding, docking, and, more recently, steel, cars and refining. They are often areas of former prosperity, now upstaged by changes in the pattern of world trade, in technology or in transport. The gradual decline in competitiveness of these industries is paralleled by a gradual shedding of labour and a relative decline in wage rates – and hence rising unemployment and falling incomes among residents. Often firms in these places have been bought up by larger companies or multinationals, or absorbed into vast nationalized monopolies, so that the destinies of local people and communities are increasingly controlled from outside. What determines their prosperity or misery is an impersonal calculus of profit or rationalization pursued regardless of social costs.

Second, these are areas of particularly bad housing, a mixture of old Victorian terraces, often built specifically to house manual workers and now reaching the end of their useful life, and more modern council housing, frequently of the worst possible design; an environment short of parks and access to countryside, full of dereliction and dehumanized concrete, places as if infected by a peculiar physical disease of blight, like a wall patched with mould or a heath scarred by fire.

Third, these are areas with higher-than-average concentrations of manual workers, low-skilled, unskilled, or de-skilled as the industries they worked in have declined; areas of high unemployment and low incomes, where people are effectively stranded by their poverty, unable to travel to work outside the area, unable to afford private housing or to qualify for council housing elsewhere. People, like the places they live in, who were exploited for as long as there was profit in doing so and then abandoned to survive as best they could. The cheap housing in these areas also draws in other disadvantaged groups with low income or little capital: immigrants, single parents, the mentally and physically handicapped. At the same time the gradual decline of the area pushes out those with freedom to move – with savings, skills or educational qualifications.

The concentration of so many disadvantaged people in a single area produces other effects: local government poor in resources and sometimes in the quality of staffing; a poor health service, since doctors cannot find decent accommodation or much in the way of private practice; a low level of educational attainment due primarily to poor home backgrounds and the low average ability in schools; and, finally, high levels of crime, vandalism and family breakdown, and, wherever communities of divergent cultures live together, conflicts based on religion or race.

It is important not to consider the inner cities as unusual or isolated phenomena. The bulk of poverty, of bad housing, of declining industry, is in fact found outside the inner cities. The poor, wherever they live, carry their own inner city round with them, like snails their shells, and every urban area has some district of some size – even if it is only a single housing estate – that shares the interacting problems of concentrated poverty, unemployment, bad housing and crime of the larger inner city areas.

Conversely, a varying, often large proportion of those who live in local authorities commonly termed as 'inner city areas' are not seriously deprived. Every such authority has its more desirable streets and neighbourhoods, and Hackney is no exception. The inner city proper is invariably a more limited zone than the local authority boundary. Its irregular frontiers would in fact coincide with the location of disadvantaged people in sub-standard housing. Thus the inner city is less a precise geographical location than a mode of existence – more diffuse in some places, more concentrated in others – of the poor and disadvantaged. That is what makes it so hard to change, for it is not a surface wound that can be treated locally with a plaster, but the symptom of nationwide processes that created, and segregate, poverty.

As Harrison goes on to discuss, it is international as well as nationwide processes that profoundly affect the inner city.

The inner city in the world economy

The inner city, like the depressed regions, is the inevitable result of the unplanned, destructive way in which the British economy adjusts to changes in the global economy. The most radical change in the international division of labour over the past decade and a half has been the entry of developing countries on to the manufacturing stage hitherto hogged by the developed countries. It began with goods such as clothing and footwear; they require a lot of labour to produce, and labour is much cheaper in the Third World. But the process has continued, extending to the production of more complex consumer durables and processed materials, from assembled electrical products and cars to textiles, ships and steel. The newly industrializing countries like Hong Kong, Singapore, Taiwan, Mexico, Brazil and Argentina are emerging as competitors over a wide range of traditional British industries.

The more progressive and adaptable developed countries, such as Japan, West Germany and the United States, have shifted their economies into the kinds of activities in which the Third World cannot yet compete – those that require a high level of capital investment and a highly skilled, well-educated workforce: the production of capital goods, communications equipment and computers, and the more sophisticated consumer products. Britain, too, is making the shift, but not as smoothly, swiftly or completely. She thus finds herself caught in the middle and squeezed at both ends, undercut by cheaper Third World wages in labour-intensive industries, outmanoeuvred by higher levels of investment and applied technology in her developed-country competitors. The blame for our lag is widely spread: among financiers who prefer oil, property or foreign countries for investment, managers who do not modernize fast enough, workers who resist improvements in productivity, educationists who cling tenaciously to academic ideals, politicians who have been unable or unwilling to involve government in the forward planning of the economy.

This recession lasted into the early 1980s and was followed by another in the late 1980s/early 1990s.

At the end of the seventies, deep world recession arrived on the scene to complicate matters. To some observers it is merely the second hiccup in post-war expansion produced by a wave of oil-price rises. To others it is a far more sinister affair, a repeat of the Great Depression, the downturn of the fourth Kondratiev wave of long-term expansion and contraction since the first beginnings of capitalism (named after the Soviet economist who postulated such waves back in 1919). But this recession was more complicated. Inflation, the symptom of the intensified scramble of competing social groups for more pie and of the unwillingness of governments to control the share-out, had come to stay. The conventional ways of combating recession by increasing government borrowing and spending seemed only to stoke inflation. Keynes fell out of fashion, Friedman came in. And so recession was deepened by deflation, high interest rates, public-spending cuts. Conservatives in Britain and America hoped to compensate by cutting taxes, but growing budget deficits forced Thatcher and Reagan to renege on their promises, except for the rich. The overall result was a steep decrease in world and British demand, and a further increase in the severity of competition.

Some British companies adjusted successfully to the new cut-throat environment, though their 'success' has meant shedding labour and shutting down uneconomic factories. Others adjusted negatively, without investing, simply by pushing workers harder and paying them less in real terms. Others still, in the hardest-pressed industries, simply closed down and recovered what cash they could from the sale of their premises and equipment. Organized labour, especially the manual working class, was hammered in the process. In the expansive fifties and sixties union strength had grown considerably, and unions were able to increase real wages and reduce the share of profits. One of the attractions for Conservatives of monetarist deflation was that it reversed these trends; deep recession clobbered the unions and cut real wages.

All of these processes had a particularly destructive impact on the depressed regions and the inner cities. For these were often the sites of prosperity in earlier phases of industrialization, and have more than their share of industries now being upstaged by the Third World. They have many antiquated, badly sited premises that are incapable of adaptation to new modes of production and new channels of transport. To these problems the inner city adds others: clogged roads, high crime rates, a less disciplined workforce, and frequently, especially in London, high rates and rents to boot. As the new competitive climate made more industries and premises uneconomic, a new generation of depressed areas and inner cities began to develop.

But the process of adjustment is not only a problem for communities; it is above all a problem for people. It is not only machinery and factories that become outmoded, it is also trades and skills. With the new microchip technologies, economic adjustment is progressively destroying manual and low-grade clerical jobs and marginalizing increasing numbers of workers, not only the unskilled, but also the de-skilled who cannot find local openings for their skills, and those with skills that are no longer highly prized, such as tailoring. It has not been common British practice to care overmuch about those people whom economic change has left standing – to guarantee them retraining, further education or new jobs. In recession, far from expanding to meet the greater need, our education and restraining systems contracted. A sub-proletariat has been produced and is growing in numbers: under-educated, unskilled or de-skilled, unemployed and increasingly unemployable, and dangerously concentrated in poor regions and inner cities.

Anthony D. King: Colonial Cities and Contemporary Cities in the One World System

This reading is made up of two extracts from Anthony King's book, *Urbanism, Colonialism, and the World-Economy.* The first provides a framework for analysing the colonial cities within the European world empires. As the diagram makes clear, what King seeks to do is to indicate the pattern of relationships between colonial cities – say, Calcutta, Lagos, Dublin – with various other levels right up to the world-economic system. Most of this outline is clear, although inevitably in so brief a space some points are sparsely illustrated (you may think of some examples yourself).

History provides insight for understanding the present. The point of King's historical schema is that it is on the blueprint of the past that contemporary cities can best be understood. The old global empires may have gone, but the major cities of the world are linked – economically, socially and culturally – in a world system. A main point in the second extract, however, is that sometimes the dominant flow of influence, particularly economic, is into rather than out of European metropolitan areas. The case of the Japanese in Britain is an obvious example.

King goes on to describe how an appreciation that cities, including Western cities, are *not* distinct social/political/economic entities but part of a capitalist world system has gradually transformed 'urban' sociology in Britain and Europe. The city is now perceived and analysed as the ever-changing focal point of wider processes, particularly economic production and consumption, but also of cultural ideas and style. However, as Philip Cooke argues (Reading 49), people do respond to, mediate and change the impact of these processes.

Reading 51 From Anthony King, *Urbanism, Colonialism, and the World-Economy* (Routledge, 1990), pp. 22–27, 69, 70, 71

Frameworks for analysis

What insights can be derived from studying colonial cities? The answer depends on one's perspective: studying the colonial city is not about developing a model but about understanding processes on a global scale. From a 'development' viewpoint, it provides the context for testing theories of dependence, or the emergence of global capitalism. It is a laboratory for testing hypotheses: for geographers, on the cultural variable in spatial change; for anthropologists, on the 'Westernization' of material culture; for sociologists, it poses questions about the degree of universality (and transferability) in institutions or social processes that the 'artificial' establishment of colonial societies provides an ideal laboratory to investigate; for architects or planners, it demonstrates the distinction between notions of a 'cultural order' and the 'rational professionalism' of the Western capitalist city.

My own interest is concerned with these and other issues: what can we understand about a society by examining its physical and spatial environment? And conversely, what can we understand about the physical and spatial environment (the buildings, the architecture, and the spatial structure of the city) by examining the society in which they exist (King, 1980). To answer these questions, however, we first need to know the functions of the city, the form and working of its institutions and organizations, the distribution of power between different groups, and something of their values, behaviour, and activities. And where this chapter perhaps emphasizes the physical and spatial dimensions of the city, it is clear that an understanding of this, as all other aspects, requires a thorough knowledge of the economic and political history of each city, including the social relations of production.

Whatever our perspective, some kind of framework is necessary within which to examine and compare a variety of colonial cities at different historical times. Urbanism, to quote Harvey again, 'is not just the history of a particular city but the history of a system of cities' (Harvey, 1973: 250). It is, indeed, even more than this, for the system exists at various levels. Which of these levels we choose to examine, and the order we accord to them, will depend on the problem to be investigated.

1. The city in relation to the colonised society or territory (see Figure 2.1).
Here we can consider the existing indigenous economic, social, political, and cultural forms or local conditions (resources, climate, and environment) that contribute to the distinctive character of the colonial city: the Indian contribution to Calcutta, the African contribution to Lagos; the effect of the environment on settlement patterns or emerging culture. At this level, the city can be viewed as a spearhead of economic, political, and cultural penetration, following which the structural organization, or reorganization, of the colonized society or territory takes place. Such organization includes the reorientation of trade and transport; reordering the urban hierarchy and establishing a new system of towns; the emergence of new occupations and systems of stratification; the creation of new bases of political power, the growth of new elites; the promotion of cultural change, in religion, education, science, language –

including 'Westernization' – and resistance in the politics of cultural nationalism; the direction or redirection of the economy to a metropolitan and world system and through this, the development of a labour market in the colonized society that affect both the colonial city as well as rural areas, with consequent agricultural decline; demographic change, particularly migration, with tensions between city and rural areas, between (where they exist) 'traditional' and 'modern' cities, and involving the break-up of kinship and tribal structures with consequent social disorganization, or the distinctive social, ethnic, or racial composition of the city.

2. The city and the metropolitan power.
At this level are considered those factors that influence the colonial society and city itself: switches in capital investment from domestic to overseas; booms and slumps affecting emigration; ideological changes, or shifts in political power in the metropole motivating people to the colonies; changes in metropolitan colonial policies, particularly as they impact urban and regional development (Dossal, 1989); colonial policies affecting indigenous and colonial subjects; metropolitan attitudes in regard to indigenous cultures, including racial, social, or legal issues, etc.

Figure 2.1 Framework for investigating aspects of the colonial city

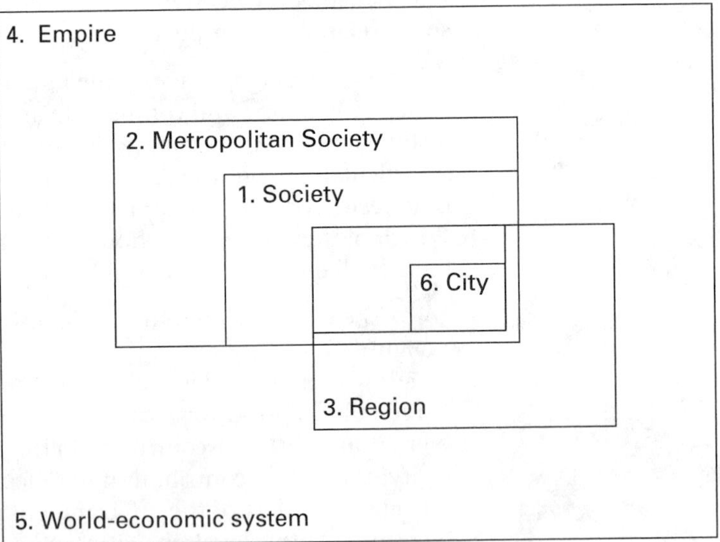

Colonial cities also provide insights into the metropolitan society, its institutions and culture in a way that an examination of metropolitan society alone does not permit. Metropolitan institutions, lifted out of their social, cultural, historical, and, not least, environmental context, and transplanted to colonized – often 'tropical' – lands, can be seen, if not like 'flies in aspic', nevertheless in a new light. Together, they form an interacting urban system (Chapter 7), which also has a hierarchy with the

Imperial capital at its head (Christopher, 1988, points out that in 1931, London was five times larger than the next largest city in the imperial hierarchy – Calcutta). Some institutional forms and functions are shared by all the cities in the hierarchy (e.g. certain legislative, administrative, or judicial instruments, professional practices, language, bureaucratic procedures); others are confined to the metropolis (political decision-making at the highest level, principal banking and financial functions, cultural accumulation in museums, or cultural constitution in universities, libraries, or research institutes); other institutions and practices are confined to the colonies (e.g. indentured labour, slavery, particular forms of land tenure, racial segregation by residence, etc.). Functionaries (colonial governors, inspectors of police, engineers, missionaries, and educators) move between the city and the metropolitan power as well as within the colonial urban system itself.

Within the historic British Colonial Empire, for example, there are elements common to London, Madras, Cape Town, Nairobi, Kingston, Halifax, and Gibraltar. This is the appropriate level to examine movements of labour, capital, images, ideas, or goods. It provides the framework within which people and ideas move (e.g. from Britain, via India, to South Africa or Australia) or to understand particular cultural phenomena (the 'Bengal Room' in the 'Victoria Hotel' in 'Vancouver', 'British Columbia', Canada) . . .

3. The city in the region.
This level might be represented by one geographic continent, either in whole or in part (India, South America, and West Africa) or a larger area (South-East Asia and the Caribbean). Here, different colonial and local powers are operating; in the analysis of the form and function of the city, its demographic composition, the manner of the incorporation of labour, the development of trading relations, or the effects on the colonial city of rivalries between competing colonial powers, this is a significant level of analysis (Basu, 1985).

4. The city as part of empire.
Within the empires – Dutch, Spanish, British, French, etc., understood as economic, political, social, and cultural systems, are different cities. Some of these are 'colonial' in the sense considered here (e.g. Kingston); others are metropolitan (London, Liverpool, and Bristol); others subsequently become independent (e.g. Adelaide).

5. The city and the world system.
Viewed in this context, the colonial city provides an additional key to unravel the complexities of an increasingly evident world-economy. Within this framework, between the 1950s and 1980s, the city (e.g. Hong Kong, Singapore, Jakarta) has been conceptually transformed from the colonial city to the Third-World city to the world city (Redfield and Singer, 1954; Dwyer, 1974; Drakakis-Smith, 1987; Friedmann, 1986). In this framework, we can consider the role of the colonial city in incorporating the colonial state into the world-economy, or the effects on the city of global developments (e.g. demand for colonial products, capital

circulation and investment, long wave periods of expansion and decline in the world economy, wars, etc.).

6. The colonial city *per se*.

These various frameworks, implying different sources of structural influence on the city and its relation to others, do not preclude analysis of the internal dynamics of the city itself, nor of the role of particular agents or municipal politics. Moreover, the frameworks and the phenomena to which they relate are obviously interconnected. Yet because of its distinctive role in incorporating the colonized economy into that of the metropole, in linking one (and often more than one) culture with another, and embodying the characteristic power structure inherent in colonialism, the colonial city has distinctive functions and features, as well as organizations and institutions and these are often represented in the physical and spatial form of the city. The most widespread of these is 'economic dualism' (Santos, 1975), and the 'dual city' in which this was expressed (though these must be understood as interdependent and not separate entities); another is cultural pluralism where race combines with other criteria of stratification (occupation, wealth, and religion) to produce a distinct ecology. The consciousness of race, and racial conflict with which it is often associated, is perhaps the major urban manifestation of colonialism.

Given the emphasis in this, and other readings in this volume, on the city as part of a wider system, it is worth reiterating that city dwellers can actively participate in the structuring of their own lives.

British and other metropolitan cities in the world system

. . . It is common knowledge that the economy of the country [Britain] in general and of her cities in particular depend today on fluctuations in a capitalist economic system that operates on a global scale. The economic fortunes of Tyneside depend on decisions taken in Tokyo just as those of urban Scotland are affected by policies made in corporate headquarters in New York. As a contributor commented at the 1982 World Congress of Sociology in Mexico City, Germany's largest industrial city is São Paulo, Brazil. As a place of production, consumption, administration, or culture, the city is embedded in a global economy . . .

Urban studies and development theory

Two different, though frequently overlapping areas of discourse have, from the late 1960s, undergone massive changes: the first in urban sociology, subsequently and alternatively identified as urban political economy or neo-Marxist structural approaches, and the second, development theory, as it moved through theories of social change, modernization, dependency, world systems, and the internationalization of capital . . .

From a given Marxist perspective, urbanism was viewed as the particular geographic form and spatial patterning of relationships taken by a particular mode of production and the process of capital accumulation. According to this viewpoint (and drawing on Hill, 1977), this required: fixed investment of part of the surplus product in new means of production; the production and distribution of articles of consumption to sustain and reproduce the labour force; stimulation of an effective demand for the surplus product produced; and additional capital formation through ever-increasing product innovation, market innovation, and economic expansion: 'the capitalist city is a production site, a locale for the reproduction of the labour force, a market for the circulation of commodities and realisation of profit, and a control centre for these complex relationships' (Hill, 1977: 41; see also Hill, 1984).

A useful overview of the state of the art about this time was provided by Walton (1976) who brought out the problematic concerning the nature of 'the urban', the need to understand urban forms by reference to changing modes of production, with the central feature of the contemporary (capitalist) city being the growing concentration of the means of collective consumption and the organization of production and consumption. As Smith summed up much of this work in 1980, 'urbanisation is often confused with capitalism. The effects of capitalist economic development often are mistaken for effects of urbanisation' (Smith, 1980: 235). It was not that this conclusion was especially new; rather that a decade of research had helped to forge the theoretical tools with which the processes could be understood. The absence of commitment to an orthodox Marxist position was not an impediment to appreciating the significance of these developments, nor did others forget the history of pre-capitalist urbanization (see especially, 'Introduction' in Abu-Lughod and Hay, 1977; Friedmann and Wolff, 1976; Walton, 1979).

Yet despite the international context in which the 'new urban studies' were undertaken, much of the work was, till quite recently, as Walton pointed out in 1976 (p. 307), *intra*-national in focus; nor did these or more conventional urban studies add up to a more coherent theory of urbanization (Friedmann and Wolff, 1982). Little had been done to extend the analysis 'to cross national urban hierarchies or world urban systems despite the fact that the fundamental process of concern is clearly, in Amin's (1974) words, one of 'accumulation on a world scale' (Walton, 1976). (The reference is to S. Amin (1974) *Accumulation on a World Scale.*) . . .

See Reading 84.

It is with the development of the world political-economy approach to urbanization, welding together the perspectives of the two fields outlined previously, including notions of the world-system (Wallerstein, 1974; 1979; 1984) that more promising developments have taken place. Where previously:

> development research guided by the modernisation perspective tended to concentrate exclusively on problems internal to Third World countries . . . more recent theoetical literature redefined the concept of development as a process embedded in the structure of the world economy and having consequences for both advanced and backward societies. Hence, the study of development should not be limited to underdeveloped countries but it should include, as a primary concern, structures and process in the international system.
>
> (Portes and Walton, 1981: 3)

From this research, two early concepts or ideas have stood up well over the years, first, Castell's notion of dependent urbanization, and second, in the context of capital accumulation on a global scale, ideas stimulated by Harvey's oft-quoted paragraph:

> the geographical pattern in the circulation of surplus can be conceived only as a moment in a process. In terms of that moment, particular cities attain positions with respect to the circulation of surplus which, at the next moment are changed. Urbanism, is a general phenomenon, should not be viewed as the history of particular cities, but as the history of the system of cities within, between, and around which the surplus circulates . . . the history of particular cities is best understood in terms of the circulation of surplus value at a moment of history within a system of cities.
>
> (Harvey, 1973: 250)

Whilst originally, Castell's notion of dependent urbanization implied that urbanization took place in the colonial or neocolonial society but the industrialization, which was historically associated with urbanization in modern societies, occurred in the metropolitan (Castells, 1977: 47–9), in more recent years, it has become evident that it is metropolitan urbanization that is equally dependent.

Questions and Issues

Urbanisation and Community: Section 11

The most relevant readings appear in brackets after each question.

1 Why is the concept of community such a problematic one within sociology? Discuss what alternative terms might usefully replace it. (Section 11, especially Reading 49)
2 Why are inner urban areas associated with social problems? (Readings 50, 66–67, 71, 73)
3 Discuss the relationship between Britain's national and regional economies and social structures and the capitalist world system. (Section 11, especially Readings 50–51)

DEVELOPMENT AND UNDERDEVELOPMENT

Introduction: Readings 52–54

As in the second edition of this reader, the 'development' section opens with a piece by Robin Cohen which overviews some of the main theories of development/underdevelopment. The presence of modernisation theory in that extract and its absence from this one indicates Cohen's own preference for working within a radical conflict framework of analysis, and perhaps his judgement that such an approach has now been established as more relevant than modernisation theory. In this reading, Cohen critically describes how the new international division of labour theory (NIDL) has built upon the underdevelopment theory of Gunder Frank and the capitalist world-system perspective of Immannuel Wallerstein. The latter attempts to lay to rest the notion that the nineteenth century modernisation paradigm of change has much relevance to the world at the approach of the twenty-first century.

The extract from Ward and Cross links very well with the previous reading from Cohen. They discuss – what so far have been – mainly negative effects of economic globalisation on Britain's black minority population.

John Clark examines development at the level at which it most matters: the everyday life of the poor. He provides some very useful definitional analysis of poverty and development. His fundamental point, however, is that development is something done *by* people not *to* them: it is not merely about resources, but *empowerment.*

I have not included here an extract on the make-up and role of what may be an emerging 'transnational capitalist class', nor have I included a reading on the various groups, such as the Green movement and international labour, which seek to influence or control its activities. However, an introductory discussion of this important issue is presented in my *A New Introduction to Sociology* (Nelson 1992), see especially p.486.

Robin Cohen: International Capital and Labour – Development and Underdevelopment

It is evident that the flow of international capital and economic investment has much to do with development and underdevelopment. (The latter occurs when foreign investment impedes or reverses the development of an economy.) Here, Cohen reviews several theories about this process and concentrates particularly on 'the new international division of labour' theory (NIDL) originally associated with a number of German scholars.

Cohen begins by suggesting that Gunder Frank's influential 'metropole-satellite' model of development/underdevelopment is insufficiently complex. In particular, he cites Warren's telling criticism of Frank that some previously underdeveloped economies have later shown the capacity to develop. In quite a condensed paragraph, Cohen then refers to a number of disparate theorists who generally take the view that the pattern of global development/underdevelopment is increasingly 'uneven', complex and unpredictable.

The NIDL theorists have built on criticism of Frank's model and regard international capital as highly flexible and adaptable in its use of global labour. Despite important differences, Cohen finds the NIDL approach useful and describes it in detail. Particularly interesting are the figures he cites for the foreign investment of British companies – which dwarf their domestic investment: British capital can thrive while 'the nation' struggles.

From Robin Cohen, *Contested Domains: Debates in International Labour Studies* (Zed Books, 1991), pp. 123–28

Reading 52

In essence what we people in the Western Hemisphere really need is a more efficient division of labour among us. The division of labour is one of the tried and true economic principles that will be as valid in 1976 as it was in 1776 when it was first spelled out by Adam Smith ... The less developed countries would also gain. With abundant supplies of labour and wage levels well below those of the US, they could export processed food, textiles, apparel, footwear and other light manufactures.

– Rockefeller 1963: 102–3

Capital today has two ways available to it of reconstructing the industrial army: on the one hand the intensification of capital exports and the systematic suffocation of investments at home, i.e. sending capital where there is still excess labour-power, instead of bringing labour-power to excess capital; on the other, the intensification of automation, or in other words the concentration of investments to set free as much living labour as possible.

– Mandel 1978: 182

When the leading living capitalist and the leading living Trotskyist agree on the best prescription for the survival of capitalism, albeit in somewhat different language, it is perhaps time for the rest of us to defer to their joint wisdom. Certainly, there is no doubt that the processes anticipated by Rockefeller and suggested by Mandel have become part of our contemporary world economy. The casual traveller to the four 'golden economies' of Asia – Hong Kong, Taiwan, Singapore and Korea – cannot fail to be impressed by the sudden evidence of modernity and industrialisation. Even using the appellation 'Third World' of such places sounds absurd, particularly when one is conscious of the transformation of great sections of the old industrial boom cities – like Cleveland, Detroit, Birmingham or Liverpool – into depressed slums and economic wastelands. Clearly, an economic transformation of some magnitude is taking place, as investment patterns alter and industrial plant becomes spatially redistributed.

Readings 23 and 50–51 further discuss the role of Britain's regions and cities in the world system.

The global shifts in the location of manufacturing enterprises have been recognised in a number of largely discrete academic debates which still require more synoptic vision to bring them together. One line of argument has stemmed from a critique of Latin American dependency (or 'underdevelopment') theory, which, in the popularised versions offered in Frank's early works (1967, 1969), came to dominate much thinking about the non-European and non-North American countries. The model Frank suggests as characteristic of relations between rich and poor countries is a chain of 'metropole-satellite' connections with the stronger partner being parasitic on the weaker. As Roxborough (1979: 45) notices, the image is graphically rendered by Swift's verse:

So, naturalists observe, a flea
Hath smaller fleas that on him prey;
And these have smaller fleas to bite 'em,
And so proceed ad infinitum.

The problem with this model is that it allows very little room for alterations in the fleas' existing preying order. It is difficult to explain how, for example, Brazil became more powerful than Portugal, or the US than its former coloniser, Britain. Class relations within and between countries also remain obscure because the theory largely relies on aggregate trade and investment data which intrinsically cannot illuminate some of the social structural relationships that were held fundamental to the exercise.

With respect to the growth of industrialisation in Third World countries, the left-wing economist Warren (1980: 166, 193–8) denounces dependency theory as 'nationalist mythology', arguing that 'it may be that the greater the previous experience of imperialist penetration, the greater the subsequent ability to respond to the world market'. He shows statistically that the growth rates of many of the less developed countries compared favourably to those of the developed market exonomies in the period 1960–73. Though Frank (1981: 96–101) subsequently sought to derogate the extent and meaning of this development in less developed countries, the substance of Warren's critique stands – in that any student of development has to recognise a more complex picture of growth at different, and in terms of dependency theory unpredictable, points in the global economy.

Recognition of tendencies towards the uneven distribution of global development sites in the contemporary period also comes from those working with a 'world system' perspective (Hopkins 1977, 1979; Wallerstein 1979) who allow switches in fortune between peripheral and 'semi-peripheral' states; from those who see the multinationals as leading a new phase of capital accumulation and expanding their global reach (Barnet & Müller 1974; Hymer 1979); and from those who seek to rework the classical Marxist texts on imperialism despite the force of Warren's (1980: 114–15) acid comment that, 'the quality of post-war literature has naturally suffered from ascribing rising significance to a phenomenon of declining importance'. (But, for exceptional accounts see Amin 1974; and Magdoff 1978.) More recently, a thriving and self-critical group of 'urban and regional' scholars have prefigured a 'political economy of space' that attempts to contextualise the new class and economic relations arising from the redistribution of production sites (Castells 1977; Harloe 1977; Harloe & Lebas 1981). On the side of the world from which capital and jobs appear to be departing, more alarmist and in tone nationalist studies talk of the 'collapse of work' or the 'deindustrialisation' of the US (Jenkins & Sherman 1979; Bluestone & Harrison 1982).

Some of the threads of these debates, though by no means all, are woven together in the work of a number of German scholars who coined the expression 'the new international division of labour' (NIDL) (Fröbel et al. 1980; Ernst 1980). Without overt intellectual debt, the NIDL theorists basically followed the line of analysis suggested by Warren's critique of dependency theory and, to a lesser degree, by the depiction of 'peripheral capitalism' suggested by Amin (1974). Taking over the vocabulary of world systems theory, they argued that industrial capital from the core was moving to the periphery as 'world-market factories' were established producing manufactured goods destined *for export.* The strategy of export-oriented manufacturing from newly-industrialising countries (NICs) was also adopted as an alternative to import-substitution strategies of development, which were held to have failed Third World countries. The movement of capital away from the core industrial countries was, in turn, necessitated by the difficulties in securing and realising high profits – as industrial conflict, the increased reproduction costs and the growing organisation of migrant communities prevented the attainment of high levels of exploitation. These difficulties were particularly evident in European countries, where, at the beginning of the 1970s, the initial economic advantages that accrued to employers by importing large numbers of migrant workers rapidly began to erode. On the one hand, many Third World countries had large supplies of cheap, unorganised labour. The oversupply of labour-power had occurred with the commoditisation of agriculture (accelerated by technological innovations like the 'green revolution'). As the rural poor were pushed off the land, unemployment, underemployment and, for some, the process of full proletarianisation had resulted. The NIDL theorists further observed that technical and managerial developments in the labour process now allowed the effective use of peripheral labour-power. The increasingly minute division of labour permitted the reorganisation of unskilled and semi-skilled tasks. With a minimal level of training, levels of productivity soon matched or exceeded metropolitan levels.

The movement of manufacturing capital to parts of the periphery was also accelerated by an investment climate made more attractive by government policies. A number of governments in the Third World passed laws restricting the organisation and bargaining power of the unions. They provided freedom from planning and environmental controls, poor and therefore cheap health and safety standards, permission to repatriate profits without restriction, tax holidays and in some cases, like Singapore, a powerful paternal state, which appeared to guarantee political stability. At the level of transport and communications, international facilities had dramatically improved in the form of containerised shipping, cheap air cargo, and computer, telex and satellite links. Especially in the case of low-bulk, high-value goods, with a high value added at the point of production, it was often no longer necessary for the site of production to be near the end-market. Examples of goods of this kind include electrical or electronic goods, toys, shoes and clothes – virtually the same list Rockefeller had identified in the early 1960s. Finally, the world-market factories could be staffed predominantly by young women, who were particularly prone to exploitation given the difficulties of organising a group characteristically under patriarchal dominance and with a limited commitment to life-time wage labour. (See Fröbel et al. 1980; Elson & Pearson 1981; Henderson & Cohen 1982; Henderson 1985.)

See Cohen, Reading 23.

In short, it looks very much as if metropolitan employers, having been frustrated in their countries in fully exploiting imported migrant labour, had alighted on another cohort of exploitable workers in the periphery, whom they would now be able to deploy directly rather than by importing their labour-power. Moreover, it was a labour force that presented few of the demands for social and political rights that even the South African government and companies are slowly having to recognise. The empirical demonstration of the thesis was supported by some convincing data (Fröbel et al. 1980: 275, 276–90) from Federal Germany. After 1959, when restrictions on German companies investing abroad were lifted, a steep increase in the amount of direct foreign investment began to occur – from DM 3,291 million in 1961, to DM 19,932 million in 1971, to DM 47,048 million in 1976. However, this investment did not, in general, represent a net expansion of German capitalist development on a world scale, but rather the integration of new sites and the relocation of certain manufacturing processes previously reserved for domestic manufacturing. Within Germany, this was bound to have consequences for the number of jobs available. A small rise over the period 1967 to 1973 was followed by a sudden drop of nearly a million jobs over the next three years. However, this loss of domestic jobs coincided with an *increase* in turnover and profit for key German firms. Simultaneously, an estimate for the number of jobs created abroad by German manufacturing firms by 1976 was 1.5 million. Fröbel and his colleagues (ibid. 287) are properly cautious in saying that these figures alone 'do not allow us to deduce the extent to which employment abroad has replaced employment in Germany', but the inference is none the less there for all to read. By the pattern of imports of manufactured goods, by the statements of the companies themselves and through an examination of the free production zones in Third World countries, we are led ineluctably to the conclusion that capital has migrated in search of its own comparative advantage, especially in respect of labour-power costs, and at the expense of domestic and imported workers, whose job chances have been correspondingly diminished.

The picture presented by the NIDL theorists seemed to confirm observable reality in the NICs and also presented a far superior explanation for industrial decline in the old centres than that currently preferred by 'monetarists' and right-wing demagogues. Consequently, part of the work undertaken by Henderson and this author (1982) on international restructuring was a replication study using the British data. Again, the basic contours of the German experience were evident. As is shown in Table 8.1, if the rate of overseas investment by British capital is compared to the rate of investment within Britain (as measured by net domestic fixed capital formation), 'overseas' starts at three times the rate of 'domestic' investment and accelerates to nearly four times the rate towards the end of the period surveyed.

Again, although it is difficult to separate out the many factors producing unemployment (including government policy, automation, the loss of international competitiveness and underinvestment), there is some evidence to suggest that in Britain, as in Germany, key firms are adding to their payroll overseas and cutting their workforce in Britain. Thus, an ILO report (1981: 82), surveying the operations of 118 major British firms, shows that over the period 1971–5, they added 150,000 employees to their payrolls abroad compared to only 80,000 in the UK. As the study concludes, 'employment-wise they were clearly growing much faster abroad than at home, both in absolute and relative terms'. The US also reveals a similar picture. Bluestone & Harrison find that between 1968 and 1976 there was a loss of approximately 15 million jobs as a result of plant closures. The closures partly resulted from technological changes but managers also saw the transfer of production abroad as an attractive alternative to production at home, for risk was diversified, greater control over labour was achieved and they could take advantage of large international wage differentials (see Nash & Fernandez-Kelly 1983: ix).

Table 8.1 Domestic and Foreign Investment from Britain, 1969–80

Year	*Domestic (£ mil)*	*Overseas (£ mil)*
1969	4,233	13,950
1970	4,754	14,400
1971	4,911	15,180
1972	5,488	19,170
1973	6,859	19,500
1974	7,906	19,224
1975	9,603	23,415
1976	9,844	30,401
1977	9,628	30,573
1978	10,908	35,328
1979	11,483	41,024
1980	11,483	48,439

Source: Henderson & Cohen (1982) citing Government Blue and Pink Books

Although impressed with the NIDL theory, Cohen has significant reservations about it and it is fair, at least, to indicate these. However, for an adequate analysis the reader will have to refer to Cohen's book.

From the discussion and data so far presented, it would seem that NIDL theory provides a major key to understanding some of the processes of capital accumulation in the modern world order. While not wishing to deny its powerful explanatory value and the important contribution made by the NIDL theorists, there are none the less some major limitations and omissions that inhere in the theory. I will concentrate my critique of NIDL theory on three aspects, taking the opportunity also to develop some alternative formulations. First, *conceptual problems* – where I shall argue that the variety of meanings attaching to the phrase 'division of labour' makes it

> It is worth saying that on the first point, the term 'division of labour' is confusing because it is sometimes used to refer to the occupational division of labour and sometimes to the division of labour by gender and/or race.

difficult to understand what precise phenomena are under investigation. This uncertainty can in turn lead to differing political and practical conclusions for those committed to the theory. Second, *historical gaps* – where I maintain that NIDL theorists have ignored or misconceived the historical evolution and successive phases of the international division of labour. And third, *empirical omissions* – where I shall show that NIDL theory tends to concentrate attention exclusively on the growth of the manufacturing sector in the periphery at the expense of other growth points in the global economy, which are better reflected by measuring movements of labour, rather than movements of capital.

Robert Ward and Malcolm Cross: The Effects of Economic Globalisation on the Employment of Black Minorities in Britain

There is relatively little accessible material which relates the position of Britain's black minorities in the employment market to wider developments in the national and international economy. Ward and Cross's article, from which the extract below is taken, fills the gap. The extract makes a number of points in quite a condensed way, and it may help to provide a skeletal plan to guide the reader through it.

The extract begins with an outline summary of the differential patterns of employment and unemployment among Britain's ethnic minorities. It includes information on gender differences.

The section entitled 'interpretation' refers briefly to the influence of racial discrimination on employment patterns, but concentrates on several 'features of the socio-economic environment' which also affect the employment market situation of black people. These are:

1 Economic globalisation
2 Increased product differentiation
3 The decline of labour intensive production.

Ward and Cross then raise the question of 'how economic minorities might respond to their increasingly marginal economic position'. They discuss:

1 The impact of the new jobs that have been created
2 The issue of qualifications and training
3 The role of the public sector in providing employment
4 The role of self-employment.

Generally, their conclusions on these matters are not heartening for black people. They go on to relate these points to the pattern of ethnic minority employment outlined in the opening section of the extract. Differences between black ethnic groups and between the sexes strongly indicate that patterns of employment are affected by other factors in addition to racial discrimination.

Reading 53 From Robert Ward and Malcolm Cross, 'Race, Employment and Economic Change' in Philip Cohen *ed., Poor Britain* (Open University Press, 1991), pp. 124–32

The extract begins with a summary of the main differences in the pattern of ethnic employment.

1 *Area of settlement*

Continuing concentration in industrial regions and in areas of original settlement.

2 *Unemployment*

Substantially higher unemployment for all ethnic minorities than for Whites in all regions and areas;
Substantial inter-ethnic differences: Indians best placed, followed by West Indians, the Pakistanis and Bangladeshis.

3 *Level of employment*

No clear, overall White: ethnic minority differences;
Indians and Whites more concentrated in higher level positions;
West Indians and Pakistanis and Bangladeshis in lower level positions.

4 *Gender differences*

(i) *Unemployment*: Men better off among Indians, Pakistanis and Bangladeshis, women better off among West Indians

(ii) *Area of settlement:* Indian women worst off in dispersed locations, no difference among Whites and West Indians

(iii) *Level of employment*: Female employment levels more closely matched across ethnic minority groups; highest concentration of *male* higher level position among Indians, of *female* higher level positions among Pakistanis and Bangladeshis; no substantial gender difference in employment level of Indians/Whites, but among West Indians and Pakistanis/Bangladeshis employment level of men is substantially lower than among women.

Interpretation

The systematic racial disadvantage which has accompanied ethnic minorities from the New Commonwealth since their arrival in Britain in the 1950s and 1960s is still clearly in evidence (Smith, 1977; Brown, 1984; Brown and Gay, 1985). But the pattern of ethnic differentiation set out above contains features which suggest that the crude tendency to discriminate on racial grounds against those from South Asia and the Caribbean is heavily mediated by features of the socio-economic environment. In looking for an interpretation of the pattern that racial disadvantage now takes, we begin by reviewing some of the main features of global economic change over recent decades in order to identify significant developments in industry structures and in opportunities and demand for paid work.

However, international labour is widely used, in 'cheap' service sector work (see Reading 52).

The large-scale immigration of the 1950s and early 1960s from the Caribbean and South Asia marked the last phase in the increasingly global search for labour by employers in Western economies seeking to maintain their established industrial dominance by economies of scale and traditional, labour-intensive production methods. However, their competitiveness in many global markets was already being undermined by the rise of large firms in the Far East enjoying substantial cost advantages and extending their focus from domestic to international markets. This process has continued as newer forces in global manufacturing, notably Japan, have faced increasing competition in turn from other industrialising economies.

The impact of fierce global competition on Western manufacturing concerns has varied. Some industries, such as motor-cycle manufacturing in Britain, went into terminal decline before any effective way of responding to the new competition could be developed. In some cases, including other sectors of the engineering industry, the main response has been to close down plants in North West Europe and switch investment to low wage economies further afield. A system of global quotas was devised to protect the competitive position of textile firms in Western industrial economies and allow time for restructuring to face changing competitive trends. Increasingly complex joint ventures have been initiated with global competitors designed to buy some of the benefits of their competitive strength.

Underlying many of the adjustments made by Western firms has been a recognition of the changing pattern of demand for their products. At the time of New Commonwealth immigration to Britain there was still a large demand for basic goods and services of a traditional kind sold on price. The philosophy 'pile it high and sell it cheap' was still common currency in many areas of retailing, notably clothing and food. However, this recipe for commercial success was under threat from two sources. First, it was precisely the goods with 'commodity' characteristics which exhibited a stable demand and were sold on price which were most vulnerable to foreign competitors with substantial labour cost advantages. Secondly, the steady growth in disposable income was enabling a long-term trend to become established away from standard products to more differentiated goods and services. Fashion, shown in the more rapid recycling of styles covering an ever wider range of garments, and the development of specialized products for particular uses transformed consumer behaviour. Demand grew, but for products with a distinctive and increasingly international fashionality. Grocery supermarket retailing facilitated similar trends in the food industry: less generic goods and more diverse, specialized items sourced increasingly from abroad.

Thus the combined effect of growing international competition and a sharp increase in the differentiation of demand was to question the future competitiveness of many traditional domestic products. Smaller, more flexible firms emerged in response to the growing influence of fashion. Italian design increased its hold on consumers, and retailers reacted by switching orders abroad. Where British design or British capital continued to support manufacturing, it was more and more through off-shore production. All these factors had a serious effect on the competitiveness of British industry and hence on the market position of labour.

Furthermore, the impact of the restructuring of product features and locations of production on the labour force in Britain was matched by the transformation of processes. The most successful industry sectors in the new conditions of international competition tended to be those based on proprietary knowledge (such as pharmaceuticals) or capital intensive production of highly differentiated goods (such as high quality cars). There was little scope for traditional, labour intensive operations in the new business environment.

The impact of these trends on the labour market position of migrants from the Caribbean and South Asia, together with their children, can easily be appreciated. In some sectors, notably textiles, they had provided the labour force to keep traditional sectors using labour intensive methods competitive, not least by operating the night shift to allow more effective use of capital equipment. But in many instances the economies they provided were insufficient to allow the survival of the business. In other sectors, such as car assembly, the labour force had become more multi-racial but the deteriorating position of labour led to, often successful, attempts to reclaim jobs for White workers. In particular, the 'lads of dads' could still be offered prior access to jobs on the grounds of family connections in the firm and local residence (Lee and Wrench, 1983).

This transformation in the shape of British industry competing in international markets gathered pace in the 1970s, leading to the massive shake out of firms in the first four years of the Thatcher government of 1979 and the huge rise in unemployment. In some sectors, ethnic minorities were concentrated among those losing their jobs. In other cases, employment in sectors where Black labour had been on the increase became much less accessible.

Before returning to the distinctive features of the employment situation of Caribbeans and South Asians in Britain to see how far this interpretation of broad economic processes of change can be used to support the picture shown, it is useful to consider briefly four additional points concerning how ethnic minorities might respond to their increasingly marginal economic position: what opportunities have newly created jobs offered, how far can education and training provide entry to jobs in the new economic context, what potential is there in the public sector to provide economic opportunities and how far can an ethnic business sector provide an alternative economic ladder? It is beyond the scope of this chapter to deal with these topics in detail but it is useful to consider their role in constructing a framework to interpret the economic situation of ethnic minorities.

First, while millions of jobs have been lost to the UK economy in recent years, it can be argued that millions of new jobs have likewise been created. However, it is crucial, in assessing their potential for providing new economic opportunities for ethnic minorities, to consider the nature of the employment created. To begin with, many of the new jobs have required advanced knowledge, frequently supported by formal qualifications, which are outside the reach of those made redundant. In many cases, again, even when the level of knowledge or experience required makes them accessible to the casualties of economic contraction in the 1980s, the firms creating employment are located in areas well away from the centres of industrial concentration where ethnic minorities have settled. Of the jobs created in urban-industrial areas, however, many consist of part-time employment unsuited to the needs of ethnic minorities. In practice, the choice of many of those entering the job market or looking for work in mid career in industrial areas without advanced formal qualifications is between unemployment or accepting low wage work in one of the new service industries which are not facing international competition and can make intensive use of cheap labour to deliver their services.

Reading 39 discusses training in greater detail.

Secondly, there are opportunities for those still at school or entering the labour force to acquire the education, training and qualifications needed to bid for the high quality employment being created. Indeed, the high level of students among those aged 16–24 years of an ethnic minority background suggests that this opportunity is being seized. For example, the proportion of West Indians (18 per cent) in this group classified as students in the Labour Force Survey is almost half as high again as the figure for Whites (13 per cent), while the proportions of Indians (32 per cent) and Pakistanis and Bangladeshis (30 per cent) are three times as high (Department of Employment, 1988). Interestingly, among Whites there is no significant gender difference in the proportion of students, among Asians males are very much more likely to be students and among West Indians females are somewhat more likely to be students. However, there is a far from automatic correlation between student status and eventual employment in a high level position. Among those in post-school training schemes, too, there are many factors which mediate this relationship, not least the concentration of White school leavers in the category of training most likely to be offered good quality work and the tendency noted in studies to associate ethnic minority school leavers with the need for corrective training in attitudes (Cross, 1987). Thus, while ethnic minority school leavers have much to gain from pursuing higher and further education or vocational training, the return to these investments in human capital, whether through features of the education/training or of the subsequent selection process, may fall short of expectation.

Thirdly, given the readiness of public bodies, notably local authorities, to declare themselves equal opportunity employers, it may be argued that there are relatively better opportunities for ethnic minorities in public sector employment. In the USA, for example, Blacks have been over-represented in public sector jobs while remaining under-represented in the private sector (Bailey and Waldinger, 1988). Indeed, there are many examples of local authorities who have taken action to increase the proportion from ethnic minorities among their employees. However, there is little to suggest that this is having a significant impact on their employment prospects. Vacancies only occur when staff are being replaced or new jobs created and, given pressures on the public sector in recent years, there have in all probability been insufficient vacancies, especially in high level positions, to have a noticeable effect, even assuming the availability of qualified ethnic minority candidates and an absence of racial bias in recruitment. In practice, informal processes which serve to maintain the employment of particular ethnic or social groups operate in the public as well as the private sector.

Finally, self-employment has in recent years been enthusiastically supported as an avenue of economic opportunity open to those unable to find paid work. Furthermore, there is a widespread assumption that this is an area where Asians in particular have a natural advantage. However, both these views are highly misleading unless they are put within context. For example, in 1977, fifteen years after the end of unrestricted immigration from the New Commonwealth, the rate of self-employment among household heads from India and Pakistan was no higher than for the general population (National Dwelling and Household Survey, quoted in Ward, 1987b, p. 160). Similarly, in the USA, the business participation rate among Asian Indians has been much lower than that for many European ancestry groups (ibid, p. 163). It was only after the recession of the late 1970s/early 1980s that Asian business achieved any statistical significance in Britain, and much of it has been accurately portrayed by Aldrich and his colleagues (1982, 1984) as a precarious attempt to make a living less rewarding than paid employment. Admittedly, Indians in Britain show a high level of self-employment and a level of unemployment only half as high again as that of Whites. Yet Pakistanis and Bangladeshis have the highest rate of self-employment of all minorities identified in the Labour Force Survey (23 per cent) and also the highest unemployment rate (31 per cent, compared to 10 per cent for Whites) (Department of Employment, 1988, pp. 167,177). While Asian business, therefore, has allowed many to avoid unemployment, there are very many others for whom it has not provided an economic livelihood, either in the form of business ownership or a job in an ethnic firm. Finally, levels of self-employment among Asians in Britain are above average, among West Indians they are below average.

Thus, the lesson to be drawn from the pattern of ethnic business is that, as with small businesses in general, it is only successful in particular contexts which favour its development. The networks of interdependent Asian firms in the clothing trade show some of the success characteristics of their counterparts in industrial districts in Italy (Werbner, 1984; Bamford, 1987; Ward, 1987a). But much Asian business disguises the continuing reality of economic disadvantage.

Application

The interpretation of economic change and its impact on ethnic minority communities fits well with the pattern of ethnic differentiation described above.

First, the continuing concentration of ethnic minorities in the industrial regions and areas of original settlement where they have borne the brunt of economic retrenchment can be interpreted in terms of a lack of qualification for many of the jobs being created elsewhere, restricted access to such jobs where they were competing with local Whites, difficulties in moving house to new areas and a preference for seeking whatever economic livelihood could be obtained from a base within the ethnic community.

Secondly, the substantially higher unemployment experienced by all ethnic minorities in all regions and areas shows the universality of racial disadvantage at work in the general response to the restructuring of employment. While there are highly significant inter-ethnic differentials in the level of unemployment which suggest that particular communities have adopted distinctive methods of coping with economic crisis, the single clearest differentiating factor in the economic position of West Indians and Asians compared to Whites is the higher level of unemployment among a population of migrants (with their children) who came to Britain to find work. It is hard to avoid seeing, in this pattern, the systematic racial bias shown in detailed studies of racial discrimination in employment (Smith, 1977; Brown, 1984; Brown and Gay, 1985). However, the distinctive position of all ethnic minorities identified shows that racial disadvantage is very unevenly experienced and is highly contingent on factors specific to particular groups and locations. In particular, the gulf between unemployment levels among Indians and Pakistanis/Bangladeshis shows the dangers of defining a generalized 'Asian' orientation to ways of making a living and shows the continuing significance of class and class-related differences in coming to terms with the realities of economic processes in Britain (Nowikowski, 1984).

Thirdly, in contrast to the overall differences in unemployment rates, ethnic differences in level of employment are much less clear-cut. This, together with the pattern of inter-ethnic differences, suggests that within the place of employment, opportunities depend far more on socio-economic and other distinctions than the quest for a job.

> It is worth stressing the extent to which the gender factor further complicates the complex pattern of ethnic employment.

Finally, the greatest complexity is found when gender is brought into the analysis, giving further support to the view that the experience of racial disadvantage is heavily conditioned by factors internal to particular ethnic minorities. The lesser impact of unemployment on men among Asians may reflect the gender-specific path of ethnic business development. Among those from the Caribbean, the fact that women suffer less from unemployment may be related to their greater involvement in education, but both may reflect more basic features of economic opportunity structures. Further interesting inter-ethnic differences are found when gender is combined with area of residence. The higher level of unemployment among Indian women in dispersed locations suggests that a considerable proportion of their jobs are generated within Indian communities and related business networks. The fact that Afro-Caribbeans are much less affected by unemployment away from established centres of the ethnic community points to a much more individualistic method of obtaining employment which is more successful in low concentration areas, in part no doubt a function of differences in qualifications.

Again, the closer match between the levels of employment among women in different ethnic groups raises interesting questions about gender-specific dimensions of the impact of racial disadvantage. Gender based differences between ethnic groups also call for explanation. The above average level of employment among Pakistani/Bangladeshi women presumably reflects the tendency for women of lower social status not to be economically active.

But the same phenomenon among Afro-Caribbeans occurs despite a high level of labour force participation among women.

Conclusion

This chapter has sought to describe and interpret the reality of paid work among the ethnic minority population in Britain in terms of a broad overview of economic processes over recent decades. It has been outside the scope of the chapter to review the large body of detailed analysis concerning ethnic differentiation in particular types of employment. Our concern has been much more to demonstrate the essential inter-relatedness of different contributing factors. The statistical pattern of racial disadvantage in employment is strongly suggestive of the continuing existence of racial discrimination as confirmed elsewhere. Its impact, however, depends upon a number of contextual factors. Among these, the types (and quantities) of jobs created compared to those lost are clearly of great importance. This gives rise to *socio-economic* explanations which emphasize the polarization of employment into high-level knowledge based jobs beyond the reach of many of those from ethnic minorities in the labour market and low pay, low skill jobs in the service economy. The implications of this approach are, as Cross (1989) has observed, to concentrate on better education and training and more effective welfare support as ways of reducing the impact of racial disadvantage in employment.

There is a separate approach, however, which focuses on the *spatial effects* of economic change and the locational distribution of employment. This emphasis, too, is given support by the statistical pattern set out above. The implications of this line of analysis are quite different, away from welfare support which ties the poor into areas where their prospects are worst towards the encouragement of geographical mobility to areas of employment growth. This is not a blandishment to ethnic minorities to get on their bikes; rather it is a recognition that state sponsored support, such as employment training, might be more closely tied to real job prospects.

Both these approaches need to be complemented by a recognition of the dynamics of *ethnic differentiation*. All ethnic minorities were not in the same employment position from the outset, and the process of economic restructuring has tended to make their paths diverge still more. It is too early to say whether the division within the 'Asian' communities between Indians and Pakistani/Bangladeshis is one which will narrow in time, as educational performance data suggest, or whether Afro-Caribbeans and some poor Asians share the same economic fate. Some have argued for the former view, which generates the prospect that the employment future for those of Caribbean origin in the UK is of critical importance (Cross and Johnson 1988). It is not inconceivable that we may be witnessing the development of an urban 'underclass' at precisely the same time that economic fortunes overall are improving (Wilson, 1987).

What is undoubtedly true is that attempts to devise policies which are effective in reducing racial disadvantage in employment need to pay close attention to the internal dynamics within particular ethnic communities (and sub-communities), and to gaining an understanding of the socio-economic and spatial effects of economic change, as well as to more direct policies of combating racial discrimination.

John Clark: Poverty, Democracy and Just Development

There may seem a certain 'inevitability' about the capitalist world system as described in various of its aspects in the previous readings in this section. This is even more so after the collapse of 'the official opposition' of the Marxist Communist bloc. In fact, there has long been substantial, non-Marxist but radical criticism of many aspects of global capitalism. The following extract from John Clark may be considered as representative of this broad tradition. Certainly, his concern with economic and political democracy and participation reflects a strong current of opinion among voluntary organisations involved in development.

Clark writes in a straightforward way, and I will merely pick out one or two of his main points for emphasis here. Perhaps most prominent in his broad approach to poverty is his emphasis on the powerlessness of the poor. This theme is continued when he discusses the meaning of development: it means 'enabling people to achieve their aspirations'. To do this, people must not only be adequately fed and housed (which, of course, they must be), but they must also be empowered in ways that enable them to define and to gain what they want for themselves. Clark concludes by spelling out in more detail what he considers to be the meaning of *just* development.

Reading 54 From John Clark, *Democratizing Development: The Role of Voluntary Organisations* (Earthscan Publications, 1991), pp. 19–22, 23–25, 26–30

What is poverty?

The principal objective of development must be the eradication of poverty and its underlying causes. This necessitates an understanding of what these causes are.

Poverty concerns income and assets but it is about much else besides. It concerns health, life expectancy, diet, shelter, education, security, access to vital resources, and other aspects of living standards. It is also a relative concept. The poverty of the single mother in London is the splendour of her peer in Calcutta. Both, however, are denied options routinely open to those more fortunate. There is no single measurement because of the diversity of the variables. A number of attempts have been made to calculate Physical Quality of Life Indices or Wealth Indices (the most scholarly of which is that of UNRIST), but these are usually flawed because the statistics that are available from most developing countries are unreliable or out of date. If the purpose of quantifying living standards is to improve policies then figures which are more than two or three years out of date are almost useless.

The most useful rough and ready indicator of poverty (advocated by the United Nation's Children Fund, UNICEF) is the Under-5 Mortality Rate

(U5MR) because the statistics are relatively reliable and regularly available, and because of its close relationship to all the other poverty variables.

Even these figures are usually only available on a national basis, and assessments of poverty in particular regions of a country or among specific classes usually have to be determined by one-off surveys of child mortality or malnutrition.

It is sobering that, in spite of the abundance of statistics about all aspects of development, so little is known about the human condition. It is difficult to say with certainty who is poor, and are they getting poorer; who is hungry, and are they getting hungrier. For example, the World Bank's flagship, the annual *World Development Report* (WDR), contained statistical annexes with a total of some 334 columns of data in 1988. None of these indicated malnutrition rates for any age group. None indicated prevalence of T.B., diarrhoea or other diseases of poverty. None indicated the proportions of the populations who have access to safe drinking water. The report did, however, contain a table showing household expenditure on motor cars. Throughout the 185 pages of text the issue of poverty is not raised (except for half a page revealing it to be on the increase) until the very last page when the reader is reminded that "reducing poverty remains the ultimate challenge of development policy". (Similarly, the 1989 report all but ignores the issue of poverty, but the 1990 report is an exception. For the first time in ten years the report's chief concentration is on poverty issues.)

A compelling analysis of the causes of poverty is offered by Robert Chambers. He describes an interlocking web of five factors each of which feeds off and exacerbates the others. The factors are poverty itself, physical weakness, isolation, vulnerability, and powerlessness. To Chambers's list two others factors should be added: environmental damage and gender discrimination.

Isolation means lack of contact, not just in a physical sense, through living in a remote area, but also in a social sense, through ostracism or illiteracy.

Vulnerability can be due to natural disasters, to exploitation, to physical incapacity or to social conventions (e.g. the dowry system which bankrupts many families with large numbers of daughters in countries such as Bangladesh).

Powerlessness also relates to exploitation and comprises three categories:

1 Powerlessness to prevent the elite trapping all or most of the benefits of a development advance; for example, agricultural extension services favouring the larger farmers, credit schemes benefiting the already wealthy, food aid being siphoned off by government officials, and so on. This phenomenon has been powerfully described by BRAC, a Bangladesh voluntary organisation.

2 Powerlessness to prevent robbery, deception, blackmail or violence.

3 Powerlessness to negotiate – an absence of bargaining power.

This description of poverty accords closely to surveys of poor people's own attitude towards their situation. (Sadly, few such studies have been made.) For example a survey of poor people in two villages in India produced the following criteria of poverty:

more than one family member working as an attached labourer;
residing on patron's land;
marketing produce just through patron;
members seasonally out-migrating for jobs;
selling more than 80 per cent of their marketed produce immediately post-harvest;
cash purchases during the slack festival season;
adults skipping one meal a day during the summer months;
women and children not wearing shoes regularly;
only housing made of mud;
animals and people living in same dwelling.

Similarly, a survey in Sierra Leone of poor farmers' perception of their biggest problems yields the following issues:

How to buy food at reasonable prices in the dry season;
how to get credit to build up herds;
animal and human health;
injustice from the forest department;
dealing with the "modern world".

It is clear that a lack of opportunity for self-determination and a vulnerability to risk are perceived by the poor as most important, but these factors are often ignored by outside agencies. Sometimes, in fact, these problems can be compounded. Diversity is the strategy adopted by the poor in the face of adversity, yet so many officially funded development schemes seek to lock poor farmers into monoculture. Other schemes increase the authority of officials or merchants over the poor.

If aid is to attack deprivation then it needs to act on all of the interlocking and underlying causes. Attending to the easier factors while ignoring others builds unsustainability into the design of the programmes at the outset. Hence nutrition and health projects to combat physical weakness; roads and education to combat isolation; disaster preparedness and crop insurance to combat vulnerability; and income generation to combat poverty must be combined with the redistribution of assets; freedom of political and trade union association; legislation to assure human rights; programmes to elevate the status (as well as income) of women, and environmental protection.

The World Health Organisation estimates that perhaps 10 to 20 per cent of the population of the Third World (excluding China) falls into this category. It would cost $13 billion to lift them out of poverty (about a quarter of the total Aid budget).

In most developing countries the majority of the population would be poor by Northern standards, but perhaps only a small proportion are so poor as to be physically at risk. The World Bank has commissioned a major academic study of the problem of extreme poverty. The conclusions of this study were that the "extreme poor" should be seen as a distinct social group – one that suffers from, or is prone to, malnutrition – and that the World Bank should launch a major initiative to safeguard the "food security" of this group . . .

What is development?

The orthodox economist might define development as the achievement of economic growth and hence improved living standards. It is achieved by improving the use made of a country's human, natural and institutional resources. The Gross National Product (GNP) provides the obvious measurement of progress according to this definition. But this narrow definition offers little to the poor. Decades of experience have shown that economic growth does not by itself lead to improved living standards for the majority. Improving the application of human resources can be brought about through trampling on human rights. The natural-resource base can be depleted for short-term profit – "environmental borrowing". Improving the effectiveness of institutions can be achieved through turning them away from the services that the local populations want of them.

The signal failure of development has been its inability to remedy the problem of hunger. In 1974 political leaders from across the world came together for the first ever World Food Conference. Shaken by the starvation that had plagued Ethiopia and other African countries the previous year, the politicians spent several days analysing the causes of hunger and what could be done to prevent future suffering. Announcing the Conference's conclusions at the close, Henry Kissinger, then US Secretary of State, asserted the common commitment to a new approach which would mean that, within a decade, hunger would be abolished and that no child need go to bed hungry at night.

With cruel irony the tenth anniversary of that conference was marked by the worst famine that Africa had ever seen. The world's public was generous, but it was not content to donate cash. It was a time to demand change. The pop-stars of Band Aid and those who "ran for the world" in Sport Aid demanded action to "change the world", to dismantle the political barriers that had obstructed international action, to cut through the red tape of European Commission bureaucracy that was hampering governmental relief efforts, and so make the surplus food mountains of Europe available to the starving of Africa. And some of the major charities called on their supporters not just to give more, but also to lobby their governments in the North for action to end the debt crisis, to make official aid more relevant to the poor and to improve terms of trade for the developing countries.

Official statistics revealed that, in spite of all the fine rhetoric, the number of people who faced the daily threat of starvation actually rose over the decade which was to see the end of hunger. World Bank estimates of "food insecurity" put the number at 700 million. It also became apparent that the prospects for reversing the trend were reducing as the wealth gap between nations widened. The threat of recession at the start of the 1980s had to a large extent been avoided, but this had been achieved by pursuing policies which created a more hostile economic environment for the Third World. The governments of developing countries in turn had pursued policies which protected their elites from the ravages of recession, but which loaded the burden of austerity on to the poorer groups. The wealth of Marcos, of Mobutu and others grew to dizzy heights while the poor became poorer . . .

Development is in crisis, and the clamour for a new approach is growing, a new approach based on a broader definition of development.

At its broadest, "development" means quite simply "improving the society". Since the society comprises no more than the people it is made up of, development therefore means "enabling people to achieve their aspirations". This may appear a rather tautological argument, but it has three virtues. Firstly, it indicates the fundamental necessity to build any development model on a foundation of democratic processes. How else can we judge what people's aspirations are? Secondly, it reveals the need to make political choices – it goes without saying that it is impossible to satisfy *all* the ambitions of *all* the people *all* of the time. Choices must be made by those who wield the power about which groups' aspirations are to be prioritized. And thirdly, it speaks of "enabling" rather than "providing" – hinting that true development is done *by* people not *to* people, that development might be co-ordinated by the governments and official aid agencies in their provision of institutions, infrastructure, services and support, but that it is *achieved* by the people themselves.

Development is not a commodity to be weighed or measured by GNP statistics. It is a process of change that enables people to take charge of their own destinies and realize their full potential. It requires building up in the people the confidence, skills, assets and freedoms necessary to achieve this goal.

Just development

"Just development" is about attacking the web of forces which cause poverty. This demands that equity, democracy and social justice be paramount objectives, alongside the need for economic growth. It must enable the weaker members of society to improve their situation by providing the social services they need and by enabling them to acquire the assets and to improve the productivity of those assets. It must combat vulnerability and isolation. It must ensure the sustainable use of natural resources and combat exploitation, particularly the oppression of women. And it must make the institutions of society accountable to the people.

A developing country has three principal assets. It has its economic resources – such as its investments, infrastructure and foreign exchange reserves, its natural resources and its human resources. Unless the country nurtures and uses each one of those assets to full potential then it will fall behind. Any country, for example, which is obliged to drain its economic resources in order to service its debts will inevitably turn to plundering its natural resources and its human resources.

Just development, therefore, comprises the following ingredients, some of which are more familiar to orthodox development thinking than the others:

Development of infrastructure

Early official aid strategies concentrated on infrastructure in the belief that roads, railways, ports, telecommunications, power stations and similar schemes would open up the country to future trade and prosperity. Such hopes have rarely born fruit. Infrastructure may make development *possible* but it doesn't make development. Conversely, development, poverty alleviation and famine relief are severely hampered where infrastructure is weak or unreliable. In rural areas there is usually a marked correlation between vulnerability to hunger and proximity to roads or other communications channels. Just development, therefore, must concentrate infrastructural development on the needs of the most vulnerable areas.

Economic growth

Though sometimes overlooked by voluntary organizations, economic growth is vital for financing the improvements in the quality of life desired by the people. But it is only one component of development, as walls are only one component of a building. A house without windows or doors becomes a prison, so too a society based solely on growth becomes an economic machine.

Poverty alleviation

People are the most precious resource of any country. There is little prospect for any country which allows its people to remain hungry, sick or ill-educated. The provision of health care, schooling, good nutrition and safe water may initially be expensive welfare measures, but in the long run, by improving the strength of the workforce, they are a wise use of resources. As Winston Churchill once said "There is no finer investment for any community than putting milk into babies".

Equity

While some governments and official aid agencies have recognized the importance of poverty alleviation, few pay more than lip service to the concept of equity. The former, though important in terms of human capital, is generally seen as the compassionate action of a civilized regime with funds to spare. The latter implies a shift in the development model so as to invest in the poorer members of society through the redistribution of wealth and incomes. The former is a strategy of investing the surplus resources a nation generates into human capital. The latter is a strategy of generating surplus in a different way.

Equity is not charity. It should be pursued because the nation as a whole runs more efficiently and becomes better off when its productive assets are broadly distributed. Countries as politically diverse as China, Japan, Cuba, South Korea and Finland have demonstrated this. In particular the land reform programmes of the South East Asian examples have proved to be remarkably strong foundations for rapid social and economic improvements. The success of these countries and the other so called "Tigers" of the region (though their human rights records may leave much to be desired) is usually ascribed to their pursuit of "export-led growth" though it would be more accurate to describe their strategy as "equity-led growth".

Gender equity is also of critical importance. In most countries women comprise at least half the workforce. Any development strategy which fails to recognize this is guilty of denying this sector the chance to achieve its full potential. This is not only bad for women, it is bad for the country. Similar arguments can be made about the need for equity between nations. It is desirable from a moral stand point, but it is necessary if we are to achieve an economically healthy and a politically stable world.

Natural-resource base protection

Just development must attend to future generations and to the health of the planet, not just to immediate needs. Hence it is essential that the natural-resource base is used wisely and sustainably. To achieve growth by the depletion of non-renewable resources is as artificial as the achievement of short-term government spending plans by the printing of money. Both are forms of borrowing from the future. The latter, as is well known, leads to economic inflation. The former leads to "environmental inflation". It creates a legacy of environmental debt, which is a debt that cannot be written off.

Environmentalism and economic growth are not natural enemies. To replace environmentally unfriendly products and lifestyles will be costly and so growth – if it is the right kind – is important. In a production process there are two sources of "value added" – labour and nature. The right kind of growth is that which maximizes the former contribution and ensures that the latter is derived at a sustainable rate.

Democracy

In any geographic region, those countries where people are more free to speak out, to associate in political parties or trade unions, where there is a free press, where governments are open and freely elected, and where institutions of the state are publicly accountable tend to fare better and to have more contented populations. The rapid transformations in Eastern Europe, Latin America and elsewhere illustrate this. Governance is improved by strong civil society.

The Soviet Union has distinguished between political democracy (Glasnost) and economic democracy (Perestroika). It has been more energetic in pursuing the former, but by 1990 realized the unsustainability of political changes without parallel economic reforms. In many African countries, conversely, there have been major economic reforms, often urged by IMF/World Bank structural adjustment programmes, but without political liberalization. The World Bank has observed that African countries such as Botswana and Mauritius which *are* democratic are also more economically successful.

Just development calls for an effective partnership of the government and the people, and this is only possible through the achievement of democracy in its broadest sense.

Social justice

For a sustainable and trusting partnership between governments and the people to be possible, full human rights must be guaranteed. Social justice also demands the eradication of all forms of discrimination, whether on grounds of race, creed, tribe or sex. A country where social justice is impaired is a country divided. Its human assets will not be used to their full potential. Factionalism will lead to wasteful tension and fighting. And offended parties will resent and perhaps seek to undermine the state.

The DEPENDS approach

The ingredients of just development combine to make the acronym DEPENDS:

Development of infrastructure
Economic growth
Poverty alleviation
Equity
Natural-resource base protection
Democracy
Social justice.

The DEPENDS approach is as appropriate for governments, for the World Bank and for other official aid agencies as it is for NGOs, and it is even more important that they adhere to it. Of course subscribing to a formula of words in itself is useless. Development agencies should objectively assess whether their actions match up to those words.

Questions and Issues

Development and Underdevelopment: Section 12

The most relevant readings appear in brackets after each question.

1 Describe and explain the relationship between international capital and labour. (Section 12, especially Reading 52; Section 11, Reading 51)
2 To what extent is Britain part of a capitalist world system? (Section 12, Reading 84)
3 Who most benefits from development? What might be involved in democratic development? (Section 12, especially Reading 54)

POLITICAL SOCIOLOGY

Introduction: Readings 55–60

Who rules Britain? An easy answer might be to say that 'the people do' – because they have the right to give or take away the power to govern by means of the vote. But important though this power is, it is not the same as actually ruling the country year by year, decade by decade. In the opening reading in this section, John Scott reviews several theories of who rules Britain. His own answer to this question is that no single class rules Britain but that the upper class dominates government. To maintain this dominance, however, it must work in coalition with other social groups forming a 'power bloc'. Members of the power bloc may change according to circumstances.

The second reading, from Antonio Gramsci, is in the Marxist tradition of challenge to capitalist political and ideological dominance. In it, he discusses his influential concept of hegemony (political/ideological dominance). In recent years, the British Labour party has failed to break the stranglehold of Conservative hegemony. In Reading 57, I analyse Labour's 'identity crisis'. Bryan Turner's discussion of the concept of citizenship – touted as, potentially, the 'big idea' of the 1990s – examines and develops social democratic citizenship theory as opposed to the consumerist approach of John Major. (It might be useful to read Turner's piece alongside Paul Wilding's section on citizenship in Reading 67.)

In Reading 53, Ralph Miliband discusses the 'new' social movements, particularly the women's movement and the black liberation movement. Alberto Melucci takes the view that the new movements go beyond class politics and are harbingers of new politics for a new era. Ralph Miliband disagrees. He takes the view that only a class-based political movement can fundamentally change capitalist society and that to be an effective part of this transformation the new social movements must work within this larger force.

There is no overall assessment of Thatcherism in this section. However, Paul Wilding's 'The British Welfare State: Thatcherism's Enduring Legacy' is extensively reproduced in the next section (Reading 66). It is wide-ranging and is a good starting point for reviewing 'the Thatcher effect'.

In the final reading in this section, Charles Murray highlights a major contemporary issue: the enormous social disparity between the wealthy and the poor. It is Murray's sombre analysis that impresses, rather than his conservative package of solutions.

John Scott: Britain – Ruling Class, Political Elite or Power Bloc?

The issue discussed in this reading is whether the economically very wealthy are also politically a ruling class. Very usefully, Scott begins by summarising both Marxist ruling class theory and various forms of elite theory. He then attempts to establish whether there is a British upper class and, having done so, whether it is also a ruling class. In giving evidence for the existence of an upper class, he presents substantial economic but limited cultural data. In establishing that a wealthy and unified upper class exists, Scott refutes the managerial position of Dahrendorf.

But is the upper class also a ruling class? Scott concludes that it is not – largely because 'there is not a perfect association between membership in the upper class and membership in the political elite'. However, he makes the important point that the upper class is very well placed to achieve political dominance provided that it allies itself with other social groups. These alliances constitute a 'power bloc' – a term Scott finds more accurate in the British political context than either 'ruling class' or 'elite'.

Reading 55 From John Scott, 'Does Britain Still Have a Ruling Class?' in *Social Studies Review*, Vol. 2, No. 1, September 1986, pp. 2–7

The Marxist position

The classic formulation of the concept of a ruling class comes, of course, from Karl Marx. The orthodox Marxist position has maintained that the division of society into opposed social classes involves a fusion of economic and political power in the hands of the bourgeoisie and the exploitation and oppression of the proletariat. Bourgeoisie and proletariat – the capitalist and the working classes – are mutually antagonistic social groupings, and the working class can improve its situation only by building up its own power base outside the formal structures of society. Collective organisation, class consciousness and political leadership are the bases of working-class power and will ensure the revolutionary overthrow of the capitalist class and the wholesale transformation of society.

The bourgeoisie, for its part, has a dual power base. It is the economically dominant class, having powers of ownership and control over the means of production; and it is the politically dominant class, monopolising the levers of power within the state. The modern state, whether liberal or authoritarian, is not a neutral instrument of administration, but a tool of class dominance. In the conflict between bourgeoisie and proletariat the state becomes the 'executive committee' of the bourgeoisie, acting at the behest and in the interest of the capitalist class as a whole. The position of the bourgeoisie as a ruling class is reinforced further by its dominance in the cultural sphere, which ensures that the prevailing ideas are mere ideological expressions of its interests and function to legitimate and obscure its power (Marx and Engels 1848).

The Italian and German theoretical traditions

The mainstream of research within the social sciences, however, has rejected this straightforward equation of economic and political power. Researchers have drawn heavily on the Italian and German theoretical traditions which have emphasised the analytical independence of the two sources of power and which introduced the concept of 'elite' to understand the collective organisation of political power.

The Italian writers Mosca and Pareto were key figures in the 'neo-Machiavellian' tradition of political analysis, which stressed the importance of political sovereignty as the essential bulwark against social dislocation. The late achievement of independence and political unification in Italy highlighted this question in a practical way, and led political theorists to attempt to theorise the mechanisms of power in a sovereign state. Mosca and Pareto argued for the inevitability of minority rule, the former using the phrase 'ruling class' to refer to any politically dominant minority. Pareto sought to distance himself from the Marxist phraseology completely, and referred instead to the existence of elites. The active, organised minority in any society constitutes the elite and is able to rule over the disorganised majority which constitutes the 'mass'. The opposition of elite and mass, and the continual 'circulation of elites', is the social dynamic of political behaviour.

In Germany also historians and philosophers were concerned to theorise and legitimate the power of a centralised nation state, reflecting once more the late achievement of political unification in Germany. Weber was closely involved, both intellectually and politically, in these debates, and his analyses of party and bureaucracy in the modern state were allied with a concern to counter the Marxist conflation of political and economic power. The phenomena of class, status and party, Weber argued, were analytically distinct, their interrelationships in particular historical settings being a matter for empirical determination. Weber's stress on the autonomy of party politics is furthered in the work of his student Robert Michels, who became an influential figure in Italian thought after his move to that country. Michels formulated the famous 'iron law of oligarchy', which holds that any politically organised group will find itself headed by a small minority: the need for effective action buttresses the power of the leadership, which thereby becomes detached from the mass of its supporters.

The ideas behind the 'elitist' tradition

What are the core ideas of this 'elitist' tradition of social thought? Pareto originally attempted to base his idea of the elite on natural inequalities. The 'Pareto curve' – still widely used in economics – was an attempt to measure mathematically the distribution of innate skills and abilities, and Pareto argued that such phenomena as the distribution of income and wealth would follow a similar curve. Those who were found at the top end of each distribution could be regarded as the 'elites' of their respective areas, and there would be a close association between each of the hierarchies. Political power, Pareto felt, should be found in the hands of that segment of the overall elite – the governing elite – which actually undertakes an important part in the activity of government. Pareto recognised, however, that the actual governing elite in a society may not be drawn exclusively from those at the top of the hierarchies of ability and advantage, and he was led to formulate a more general model of political rulership which had a more adequate sociological basis.

Elite dominance for Pareto was rooted in organisational ability and the factors which later writers have termed 'the three C's' – consciousness, cohesion and conspiracy – and power was vested in whoever could achieve these conditions. Pareto argued that the inevitability of elite rule was founded in the requirement for organisational ability which lay at the heart of the state. Elite rule is a constant fact of history despite the replacement of one elite by another in the succession of historical periods. Pareto recognised two types of political leaders, which he termed 'lions' and 'foxes'. Lions excel in force and coercion, and Pareto claimed that they embody a deep-rooted instinct or sentiment for stability and order. Foxes, on the other hand, embody sentiments of imagination and creativity and excel in cunning and manipulation. The skills of both lions and foxes enter into political rule, though the balance between them will vary from one situation to another. Any particular elite, therefore, will have a predominance of one or the other type of leader. But whatever their origin and particular skills, elites are liable to see their power weakening in the course of their rule. As they succumb to the privileges of office, elites become less effective and so more liable to infiltration by 'foxes' or overthrow by 'lions'. In this way, Pareto argued for the continued 'circulation of elites'.

Ruling class or political elite?

Many of the details of this model of the political process have been rejected, or simply forgotten, by later researchers, but the critique of democracy to which it led has remained a powerful influence. Pareto and Michels agreed that democracy was little more than a sham. In a liberal democracy all the large parliamentary parties formed parts of the political elite, and the most that resulted from an election was a shift in the composition of the elite. The elite itself persisted as a force separate from the masses to whom it was nominally responsible. Mosca was more favourably disposed towards democracy than was Pareto, the teacher and follower of Mussolini, and he felt that the degree of popular influence possible in a democratic regime was an important advance over other forms of elite rule. It is perhaps in this view that the origins of the modern 'elitist theory of democracy' are to be found.

This theory of democracy prevailed amongst American writers of the 'pluralist' school, who argued that democratic politics involves the competition for dominance among a plurality of competing elites – organised labour, business groups, political parties, voluntary associations, pressure groups, and so on. According to this view, the modern democratic state is simply the neutral arena within which these elite groups compete, and the mechanisms of popular election and lobbying ensure that no one elite is able to dominate the exercise of political power. This political pluralism is seen as incompatible with the concept of a ruling class, not least because it is assumed that the class structure no longer corresponds to the classic Marxian picture – if needed it ever did. Pluralists hold that modern societies are continuous stratification hierarchies, in which each status level merges imperceptibly into its neighbours. Furthermore, each stratum is able to form a plurality of interest groups and so is able to enter into the democratic competition to determine the composition of the elite.

This view of the stratification system and its associated theory of democracy has been rejected by a number of important researchers, for whom the concept of 'elite' nevertheless remains a leading idea. Mills (1956) and Domhoff (1967) argue that there remains a fundamental class division between the wealthy and propertied owners and controllers of large-scale businesses, on the one hand, and the middle and working classes on the other. The propertied class, furthermore, follows a privileged and exclusive pattern of schooling, has a high level of intermarriage, and is virtually closed to recruitment from outsiders. This class is able to dominate politics, so forming a power elite; and Mills argues that the terminology of 'economic class' and 'power elite' is preferable to the Marxist conflation of the two in the concept of the ruling class. The power elite brings together the economic leadership and the political and military leadership, though all members of the power elite share a common class origin and social background.

The key issues to have emerged in the debate over the ruling class, therefore, concern (a) whether or not a propertied upper class still exists, and (b) whether politics is dominated by such a class. In order to answer the question 'Does Britain still have a ruling class?' the evidence on each of these areas must be reviewed.

The development of the upper class in Britain

Although there is widespread agreement that Britain did once have a sharply defined upper class, many researchers have argued that the twentieth century has seen its demise. This upper class was formed in the late nineteenth and early twentieth century from the landed, commercial and manufacturing classes of earlier periods, but it was unable to sustain its position in the face of the economic trends of the twentieth century. I intend to argue against this view, and so will initially outline the development of the propertied classes in Britain.

Early capitalist development in Britain led to the formation of two distinct classes of landowners in the sixteenth century, the landed magnates and the landed gentry. The magnates were the dominant force in land-ownership, owning large estates which frequently spread over two or more counties. Their orientation towards their land was predominantly as *rentiers*, as capitalist landowners living on the rental income from their land. The farmers who rented this land from them and the independent gentry of small landowners were dependent on and subordinate to the magnates, but by the eighteenth century the division between magnates and gentry had become far less sharp and the two groups comprised segments within a unified class of landed rentiers.

For much of the nineteenth century the 'upper class' was virtually coterminous with the 'landed class'. But economic dominance was not exclusively a feature of land ownership. The capitalist development which transformed 'feudal' landholders into landed rentiers was initiated and implemented by commercial capitalist interests centred on market trading and international finance. The merchant 'bourgeoisie', which had crystallised as a distinct and important class by the fifteenth and sixteenth centuries, controlled the import and export trade, and ensured that domestic production became increasingly oriented to the market system. By the eighteenth century, this class of merchants and financiers held a strong position in the commercial centres of London, Bristol, Glasgow and Liverpool, and showed a high degree of internal specialisation.

In London especially, merchants were divided into East and West India merchants and into specialisation by commodity – spice, tea, cloth, bullion, and so on – and there were, in addition, specialist bankers who dealt with landowners and provincial merchants. Some of the provincial merchants were involved in the provision of finance to the industrial undertakings which produced the goods in which they traded, but the owners of the numerous manufacturing enterprises spawned in the industrial revolution depended mainly on the capital provided by their own families. Thus, nineteenth century Britain had three relatively distinct upper classes – landed, commercial and manufacturing – each of which was sharply divided from the classes below them. But this objective economic division was not reflected directly in popular images of class. Landed antipathy to trade and industry, and the obviously superior wealth of some of the largest landowners, led the manufacturing and commercial classes to perceive themselves, and to be perceived by others, as 'middle class'. These wealthy and powerful 'middle classes', however, were clearly demarcated by wealth and lifestyle from the lower middle class of shopkeepers, artisans, and clerks, and their generally privileged position makes it realistic to regard them, economically speaking, as 'upper class'.

This was reflected in the slow fusion of land, commerce, and manufacturing which took place in the later part of the nineteenth century. As the scale of manufacturing industry increased, leading to demands for capital which could not normally be met by the manufacturers themselves, so links between the London financiers and the manufacturers were established and strengthened. At the same time, the depression in agricultural rentals in the last third of the century reduced the incomes of many landowners and forced them to raise mortgages through their bankers or to sell parts of their estates. This closer integration of land and commerce was furthered by the increased involvement of many landowners in mining, railways, and urban development, and a number were recruited as directors of the large joint stock companies formed at the turn of the century. By the early years of the twentieth century it was possible to speak of a unified upper class with its roots in the increasingly intertwined areas of land, commerce and manufacturing.

The managerialist position

It has been widely accepted, even amongst those responsible for shaping the Labour Party's views on equality, that this 'business class' lost its power during the 1940s and 1950s. Partly as a result of the policies of the postwar Labour Government and partly because of internal changes in business, their control over the levers of economic power had crumbled. Most importantly, it was claimed that there had been a transfer of power from owners to managers, from the upper class to the new middle classes. As a result, the wealthy families lost their function in the system of production and faced a continuous and effective attack upon their wealth. The upper classes had become simply irrelevant.

In a previous article (Scott 1986) I argued that this managerialist position could not be sustained. The managerialist case rests upon inadequate evidence and faulty theory. In advanced capitalist societies there has been a move away from personal and family ownership of business to more impersonal structures of ownership. The transfer of shares from private individuals to financial intermediaries – pension funds, insurance companies and banks – has led to a 'depersonalisation' of property.

In Britain this has involved the emergence of 'control through a constellation of interests' in many of the largest business enterprises. The large financial intermediaries comprise a dominant bloc of shareholders, but their interests are too diverse to allow them to pursue a common policy. The directors and managers cannot ignore their interests – as the managerialists assume – but neither are they the mere tools of the financial intermediaries. The board of directors is, therefore, the focus of corporate control. It is the arena in which shareholders, lenders, and executives come together to exercise control over the strategy to be pursued by the enterprise. A key question in considering the survival of a capitalist upper class in Britain, therefore, is the source of recruitment to company boards. Are those who actually shape the policies of the business world drawn from the world of the propertyless 'new middle class' or from surviving wealthy families? And if they come from wealthy families, what is the connection between their personal wealth and the impersonal structure of corporate property?

An economically privileged upper class

Although the majority of directors are salaried employees, this does not mean that they are *merely* salaried employees. Research has shown that there are two sources of privilege and power which buttress their position and serve to differentiate them from the mass of salaried 'middle-class' managers. First, they are participants in the exercise of control and, as such, are able to determine their own conditions of employment. While they do not always have personal ownership of the company for which they work, or even a substantial percentage holding in its capital, the mechanisms through which they are recruited and dismissed and through which their pay and fringe benefits are determined are different from those regulating other forms of work.

Second, the majority of directors are indeed substantial shareholders and, therefore, have an additional source of income. While their percentage holding in any particular company may be very small, the monetary value of shares held is considerable and directors tend to hold shares in a wide range of companies. Top corporate 'management' and the large personal shareholders are one and the same group. The shareholdings of directors give them an interest in the success of the business system as a whole: their general financial interests are identical to those of the financial intermediaries, and their shareholdings are often managed on a day-to-day basis by bank investment departments. There is, therefore, a fusion of interest between directors and the structure of depersonalised property.

But not all directors correspond to this pattern; some are, in fact, the kind of entrepreneurial capitalists which the managerialist thesis claimed has disappeared. Over a half of the top 250 enterprises in Britain have dominant shareholders with majority or minority control, and in almost a half of these the dominant shareholder is an individual or a family. Many companies bearing a family name are still today under the direct ownership and control of that family: Baring and Rothschild in banking, Laing and McAlpine in construction, Sainsbury and W.H. Smith in retailing, and Guinness and Whitbread in brewing, to name but a few. And in many cases where control through a constellation of interests exists, founding families and individuals are to be found on the boards of directors and as substantial shareholders. This is the case, for example, in Cadbury Schweppes (the Cadbury family), Marks and Spencer (the Marks and Sieff families), and General Electric (Lord Weinstock).

Top corporate decisions, therefore, are taken by a group of directors with significant shareholding interests, often with controlling blocks of shares, and with interests which are closely allied with those of the financial intermediaries. Directors and top executives are the beneficiaries of the structure of impersonal share ownership, and through their membership of the boards of banks and insurance companies are actively involved in taking decisions about the use of this impersonal 'institutional' share ownership. Top directors are tied together through the 'interlocking directorships' which are created whenever one person sits on two or more boards. Through these interlocking directorships a web of connections is created which ties together a large number of enterprises and casts the 'multiple directors' in a key role as coordinators of the business system as a whole. Their power and influence spreads from individual enterprises through major sectors of the economy.

Top business controllers today, therefore, continue to show many of the characteristics of the prewar business class which earlier commentators believed had disappeared. While there may have been a shift in the balance between personal and impersonal possession since the 1930s, there has been no demise of the upper class as an economic force. One indication of its continued wealth is, perhaps, the continued importance of business enterprises as a source of personal fortunes. Millionaires dying in the 1970s and 1980s included, amongst many others, Viscount Rothermere (*Daily Mail* newspapers), who left £4.1 million; Sir Cyril Kleinwort (Kleinwort's bank), who left £2.4 million; Frederick Colman (Reckitt and Colman), who left £2.3 million; and Alan Pilkington (Pilkington's Glass), who left £1.5 million. As Figure 1 shows, the overall concentration of wealth is still such that 1% of the adult population owns 23% of the national wealth.

Figure 1 The distribution of wealth in Britain (1980)

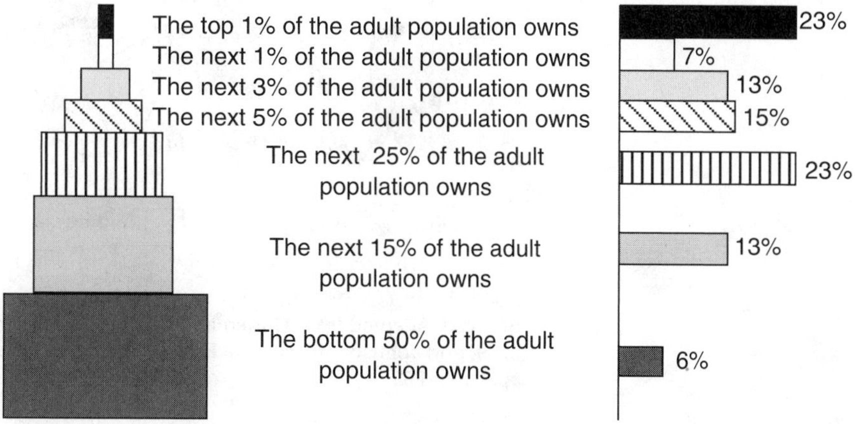

The top 1% of the adult population owns 23%
The next 1% of the adult population owns 7%
The next 3% of the adult population owns 13%
The next 5% of the adult population owns 15%
The next 25% of the adult population owns 23%
The next 15% of the adult population owns 13%
The bottom 50% of the adult population owns 6%

Source: Adapted from Stanworth P., 'Elites and Privilege', in Abrams, P. and Brown, R. (eds), *UK Society,* Weidenfeld and Nicholson, 1984.

The development of political rule in Britain

Britain, then, still has an economically privileged *upper class* with substantial wealth and control over the levers of economic power. But does it still have a *ruling class*? That is to say, are those who make up the political 'elite' still recruited predominantly from this upper class? Research on the social composition of the political elite has shown the way in which the landed magnates and financiers who dominated eighteenth century politics were gradually joined in the late nineteenth century by the leading manufacturers. On this basis, writers such as Guttsman (1963) and Sampson (1982) made the further claim that the twentieth century has seen the rise of the middle classes to power. Just as the managers are supposed to have replaced the capitalists in the business enterprise, so the managerial and professional middle classes as a whole are supposed to have usurped the political power formerly held by the upper class.

Figure 2 is typical of the results produced by such research and it is clear that the proportion of titled and landed aristocrats in the political elite declined as the proportion of 'middle-class' politicians increased. But it is important to note that the category of 'middle class' was used by the researchers to include all those with business, administrative, or professional positions: it includes both the upper class *and* the salaried middle classes. Thus, the apparently increasing middle-class composition of the cabinet – and other sections of the 'elite' – masks any continuity that may be present in its upper-class composition. As I have shown, 'aristocracy' and 'upper class' are not identical terms, and the declining salience of the hereditary peerage does not, in itself, indicate the demise of upper-class rule.

Figure 2 Class composition of cabinet (1868–1970)

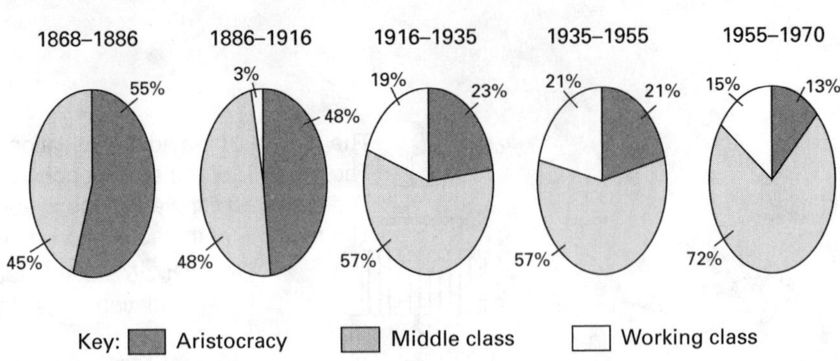

Sources: Adapted from Guttsman, W., *The British Political Elite*, McGibbon and Kee, 1963, p. 79, and Johnson, R. W. 'The British Political Elite', *European Journal of Sociology*, 1973, pp. 50 and 52.

Figure 3 Public school background (1939–70)

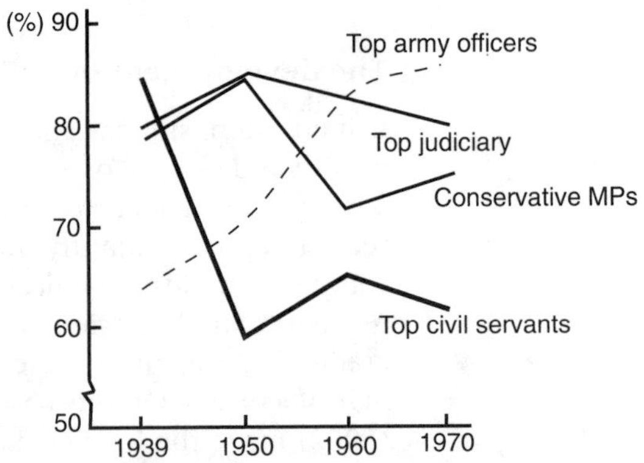

Sources: Adapted from Boyd. D., *Elites and their Education* NFER, 1973. Ch. 5: and Johnson, R. W., *op cit.* pp. 40 and 42.
Note: The '1939' figures for Conservative MPs relate to the period 1918–35, and the '1960' figures relate to 1959.

The most sophisticated attempt to use the elite concept to study upper-class power in Britain is to be found in the work of Miliband (1969), who follows the same line of argument as Mills and Domhoff. The various parts of the 'state elite' – cabinet, parliament, judiciary, civil service and military – are recruited disproportionately from among the economically dominant upper class. This similarity of economic background is reinforced by the fact that they had studied at a small number of major public schools and at Oxford and Cambridge Universities. Figure 3 shows clearly that annual fluctuations in the numbers recruited from public schools vary around continuing high levels. Indeed, the top army officers showed a rising trend in public-school recruitment. It is these very same schools which supply the directors of many of Britain's largest enterprises; about three-quarters of the directors of large financial and industrial enterprises attended a public school, and about a half attended Oxford or Cambridge. The upper class and the political elite show a similarity of social background and are, in many cases, the same people.

But there is not a perfect association between membership in the upper class and membership in the political elite: not all capitalists are politically active, and not all leading holders of political power are drawn from a business background. This fact makes it difficult to sustain the conventional Marxist view of the 'ruling class'. The state cannot be simply the executive committee of the capitalist class if some of its members are drawn from outside that class. Mills was correct, therefore, in rejecting the concept of 'ruling class' because it posited a simple correspondence between political and economic power. In this sense, Britain does not have a ruling class. But is the alternative 'elite' framework any more viable? It has been shown that elite research produces significant results only if related to the prevailing structure of class relations. The classical views of Pareto and Mosca fail to do this – indeed, their very *raison d'être* was the rejection of class analysis. To continue to use the terminology of elite theory, as even such a sophisticated writer as Miliband has done, is to run the risk of having research findings interpreted in the light of the arguments of the classic elite writers. This would result in a misunderstanding of the dynamics of political power in Britain today.

The 'power bloc'

Neither 'ruling class' nor 'elite' can be used as adequate descriptions of the British political structure. Historical patterns of class dominance must be understood in terms of the particular alliance of classes and sections of classes which constitute the 'power bloc'. A power bloc is an informal coalition of social groups, often under the leadership of one group, which actually holds the levers of political power in a society. An upper class may succeed in forming a power bloc in which it holds a dominant position if it is able to guarantee certain concessions to its partners. A dominant class must, therefore, accommodate itself to the interests of the other classes on whose support it depends. In such circumstances it is not necessary for *all* members of the upper class to be equally active in politics and so the composition of key political positions will show a relatively mixed social background. Of course, such power blocs are generally built in a less deliberate way than this definition implies: power blocs emerge as the partly unintended result of *ad hoc* and implicit agreements.

British society in the twentieth century has been ruled by just such a power bloc, headed by the upper-class members of the 'establishment' and having its political expression in the Conservative Party. Over the course of the century the cohesion of the power bloc has weakened, but it remains the basis of upper-class political dominance. To paraphrase the Marxist writer, Karl Kautsky: Britain has an upper class that dominates government, but it does not have a ruling class.

Antonio Gramsci: Ideological Hegemony and Unifying Theory and Practice

Brief though this extract is, I hesitate to include a reading which, in translation at least, is at times obscure. The justification is, however, a strong one. Although he died in 1937, Gramsci's writing had a great influence on the revival of Marxist thought which ran from the early 1960s to the late 1980s. His work inspired a new flexibility in Marxist thinking and helped the left to address a number of issues central to its survival. Despite his efforts, it is open to question as to how effectively the Marxist left has survived.

This extract begins by addressing a problem which has haunted Marxism perhaps more than any other creed: the chasm between intellectuals and the masses. Gramsci goes on to introduce the concept for which he is perhaps most celebrated, that of 'hegemony'. Hegemony is a 'field' of political–ideological influence or force. It involves the use of systems of communication, such as education and the media, in order to achieve ideological influence.

Gramsci advocates the eventual unity of theory and practice. An aspect of this is closing the gap between the intellectual elite and the mass of workers. Arguably, socialism did for a time substantially breach this gap for many working-class people to whom it appealed as a 'philosophy of praxis'. The problems experienced by the Labour Party both in transmitting its message and deciding what its message is suggests that this is less the case now (see next Reading 57). More fundamentally, however, it may be that Gramsci's notion of a total unity of theory and practice belongs more to the realm of religion than politics. In this life, there is always likely to be a distance between what 'is' and what 'ought to be'.

Reading 56 From Antonio Gramsci, 'Culture and Ideological Hegemony' in Jeffrey C. Alexander and Steven Seidman *eds., Culture and Society: Contemporary Debates* (Cambridge University Press, 1990), pp. 52, 53–54

> Gramsci used the term 'organic intellectuals' to describe intellectuals whose thought closely reflected the interests of the working class.

One could only have had cultural stability and an organic quality of thought if there had existed the same unity between the intellectuals and the simple as there should be between theory and practice. That is, if the intellectuals had been organically the intellectuals of those masses, and if they had worked out and made coherent the principles and the problems raised by the masses in their practical activity, thus constituting a cultural and social bloc. The question posed here was the one we have already referred to, namely this: Is a philosophical movement properly so called when it is devoted to creating a specialised culture among restricted intellectual groups, or rather when, and only when, in the process of elaborating a form of thought superior to "common sense" and coherent on a scientific plane, it never forgets to remain in contact with the "simple" and indeed finds in this contact the source of the problems it sets out to study and to resolve? Only by this contact does a philosophy become "historical", purify itself of intellectualistic elements of an individual character, and become "life". . . .

The active man-in-the-mass has a practical activity, but has no clear theoretical consciousness of his practical activity, which nonetheless involves understanding the world in so far as it transforms it. His theoretical consciousness can indeed be historically in opposition to his activity. One might almost say that he has two theoretical consciousnesses (or one contradictory consciousness): one which is implicit in his activity and which in reality unites him with all his fellow-workers in the practical transformation of the real world; and one, superficially explicit or verbal, which he has inherited from the past and uncritically absorbed. But this verbal conception is not without consequences. It holds together a specific social group, it influences moral conduct and the direction of will, with varying efficacy but often powerfully enough to produce a situation in which the contradictory state of consciousness does not permit of any action, any decision, or any choice, and produces a condition of moral and political passivity. Critical understanding of self takes place therefore through a struggle of political 'hegemonies' and of opposing directions, first in the ethical field and then in that of politics proper, in order to arrive at the working out at a higher level of one's own conception of reality. Consciousness of being part of a particular hegemonic force (that is to say, political consciousness) is the first stage towards a further progressive self-consciousness in which theory and practice will finally be one. Thus the unity of theory and practice is not just a matter of mechanical fact, but a part of the historical process, whose elementary and primitive phase is to be found in the sense of being "different" and "apart", in an instinctive feeling of independence, and which progresses to the level of real possession of a single and coherent conception of the world. This is why it must be stressed that the political development of the concept of hegemony represents a great philosophical advance as well as a politico-practical one. For it necessarily supposes an intellectual unity and an ethic in conformity with a conception of reality that has gone beyond common sense and has become, if only within narrow limits, a critical conception.

This 'second' consciousness is akin to what Marx regarded as 'false' consciousness. It is the product of socialisation into capitalist society and leads people to conform to it.

In essence, the hegemonic struggle is between conformist and revolutionary political consciousness.

Mike O'Donnell: What's Left for Labour?

It is less important to summarise the following reading than to alert the reader to its precise genre. It is, in fact, a hybrid – part political science and part committed political 'journalism'. Roughly, the first two thirds of the reading analyse fairly dispassionately the electoral predicament of the Labour party. This is done largely in terms of an 'identity crisis' which I suggest the party has been experiencing for some time. The next part of the article discusses some of the attempted solutions to this crisis offered by various Labour politicians and thinkers. This section ends with a discussion of the concept of community currently (1993) espoused strongly by Tony Blair. The concluding part of the article is largely my own contribution to the debate under discussion. As such, the reader is forwarned against possible subjectivity.

Reading 57 Mike O'Donnell 'Electoral Defeat and Labour's Identity Crisis'

I well remember as a first year university student joining the throngs in Trafalgar Square who variously welcomed or lamented Labour's election victory of October 1964. Labour held office for 11 of the next 15 years to 1979, but has not governed since. Why this is so has been extensively discussed. The reasons cited for failure in four elections since 1979 are endless: the numerical decline of the working class; the Party's links with the Unions; widespread disenchantment with socialism; the leadership's failure to achieve electoral appeal; the Party's internal divisions – and so the list goes on. I do not intend to add to this discussion here. Rather, I will explore the crisis of identity that may have contributed to Labour's defeats, and which has certainly been exacerbated by them.

Historically, Labour's main identity has been that of a Socialist Party, although it has perhaps never been quite clear *how* socialist. Nevertheless, Clause 1V of the Party's constitution famously commits it to 'the common ownership of the means of production, distribution and exchange'. It does not require much argument to demonstrate that such a programme would have minimal electoral appeal today in the unlikely event of it being taken seriously by the Labour leadership. In fact, Labour's main period of nationalisation was 1945 to 1950 – almost half a century ago. Relatively little nationalisation occurred under Harold Wilson. To the extent that socialisation means nationalisation, the Labour Party has not been socialist for a long time.

However, in recent years Labour has not worn its other identity – that of a liberal reformist or social democratic party – with total comfort either. Reforming liberalism involves the protection and extension of basic rights and commitment to equal opportunities. It was the Wilson years that represent Labour's highest achievement in the area of liberal reform. The Divorce Law Reform Act and the Abortion Act were seen as extensions of personal choice and freedom and bore the influence of a politician who at heart, has always been a liberal, Roy Jenkins. The introduction of a national system of comprehensive schools and the continued expansion of the higher education sector were conceived of in terms of extending equal opportunity and not, in more socialist terms, of securing greater equality of outcome. There was relatively little redistribution of income and wealth during these year's of Labour government (other than through pension and life insurance schemes).

Despite the recent difficulties of the British Labour Party, internationally social democracy remains a highly viable political philosophy and programme. Elsewhere in Europe, social democratic parties have been regularly voted in and out of office during the last twenty years. It is part of the achievement of Mrs Thatcher that she managed to taint the moderate Wilson and Callaghan governments with being both 'socialist' and 'liberal' (which was presented as 'permissive'). The Labour Party was associated both with socialist egaliterianism (the Party of high taxes and wasteful bureaucracy) and with 'sixties permissiveness' (the 'break-up' of *the* family, the increase in youth crime and violence). Thus, Labour's two main ideological reference points – socialism and liberalism – were turned against the Party and were used as a two-thonged whip with which to beat it.

In the early 1980s, the Labour Party argued over whether it should revert to socialism or retain its established social democratic or liberal identity. While the traditional socialists certainly lost this argument and were marginalised in the Party, it is something of an overstatement to say that the social democrats won it. It is true that the Kinnock–Hattersley axis was broadly social democratic, but what emerged from the troubles of the early 80s was not a new and vibrant reformism, but an emphasis on managerial style and image which seemed to aspire to neutrality in terms of ideological content. The aim appeared to be to create an impression of competence and to raise public confidence in the Party's ability to govern which Mrs Thatcher had so effectively undermined. This concern with image and presentation at the expense of content conceded the ideological high ground to Thatcherism. The Labour Party seemed constantly to be reactive rather than proactive in relation to ideas during the Kinnock period of leadership. In retrospect, his time as leader looks like an exercise in damage limitation.

Whatever the contribution of ideas to winning elections, Mrs Thatcher had plenty of them. Not only did she have a 'big' idea, but she had a full supporting cast as well. The 'big' idea was, of course, the free market which was based on nineteenth century classical liberalism and opposed to the reformist liberalism referred to above. Economic freedom was linked with personal freedom and popular democracy. Not only was the promise of personal riches on offer, but also the prospect of 'power to the people' at the expense of state bureaucracy, local government, and self-serving professionals. Most galling, perhaps, for the Left was that Tory populism had far more vitality and appeal than democratic socialism. The Left had to watch an orgy of inegaliterianism take place blessed by the popular will.

Against the background of recurrent electoral defeats, there has been a steady stream of attempts by Labour politicians to redefine the ideology of the Party. If there is a common theme in the writings and speeches of Hattersley, Blair, Brown, Blackstone and others at the Institute for Policy Research, and more latterly, John Smith, it is the attempt to link individual freedom with the provision of social resources and support. Thatcherism and its offspring, Majorism, are seen as unable to deliver on their promise of individual freedom because they fail to provide the means to achieve it. The failure of their governments to nurture the education and health systems and to ensure adequate investment in training and industry hamper individual freedom. Worse than that – Tory individualism – in the form of market mania – is seen as undermining the fairness and efficiency of both the public and private areas of society. Competitive individualism, economic decline, and social fragmentation are seen as the Conservative legacy and, crucially, the three are seen as highly related.

The new Labour ideologists have quitely dropped the traditional socialist view that equality is the core value to be pursued, although they are all concerned to achieve a fairer society. Only Hattersley tries to keep the theme of equality central to his thinking and even he sees equality mainly as a precondition of freedom. The reasons for Labour's shift in emphasis from equality to individual freedom are not hard to seek and can only be briefly indicated here. First, the brute fact seems to be that individualism has more appeal to the electorate than equality. The logic of this may be rooted in real socio-economic developments. Greater affluence and more efficient technology inevitably allow people to differentiate themselves more and to express themselves more diversely. Second, few in the contemporary Labour Party themselves believe in equality in traditional socialist terms. Certainly, there is little belief in nationalisation to achieve common ownership of the economy and not much more in equality of outcome, i.e. equality of access to material and cultural resources (as opposed to equal opportunity). Third, fairly or otherwise, socialism and Marxism have inevitably been tainted with the debacle of Eastern European communism.

Labour's new ideological tack of linking individual freedom with social opportunity may not be the all-conquering 'big idea' that some are hoping for. However, it is a plausible riposte to the most fundamental Thatcherite fallacy that society does not exist. Indeed, there may be more mileage in this direction than has yet been appreciated. In the aftermath of the social chaos and decay precipitated by Thatcherism, the phrase 'restoration of community' commends itself as an ideological slogan. Tony Blair, in particular, has begun to adopt it as such. The strengthening of community – local and national – would require a programme massive in imagination and construction. An adequate system of preschooling, education and training systems which care for as well as enable all participants, the revitalisation of industry, a halt and then a reversal of the steady rise in crime, the implementation of the social chapter, and the restructuring of welfare might require as many as four terms in office to achieve. Framing such a programme within the concept of a restoration of community as well as within that of enhancing individual freedom has ideological coherence and might also have electoral appeal.

It is perhaps irrelevant to worry over whether such a programme is socialist or not. As well as an effective and convincing programme, Labour needs to find a rhetoric and language which people believe meaningful and to which they respond. The language of the old Left does not meet these requirements. A language is needed that effectively challenges the meanings of competitive individualism, acquisitiveness, and nationalism evoked by Thatcherism. 'Individual freedom', 'social opportunity' and 'community' may be words to move people. I would suggest that 'enpowerment' might be another.

The fundamental failure of socialism was in its failure to redistribute power rather than resources. If people genuinely have power, they themselves will ensure a fairer distribution of resources. Labour's emerging ideology and programme will come to little if it fails to devolve power. To achieve this will require radical institutional change. Two key measures are the adoption of a Bill of Rights as a bulwark against the erosion of liberties and the implementation of democratic participation in the running of industry. Initially, the latter could follow the German or Swedish model and ultimately perhaps might develop along more radical lines. Ways must also be found to open up other areas of British life to democratic participation and accountability, and the current cult of managerial elitism and feather-nesting should be stopped. The country's institutional system requires a democratic overhaul. Ironically, Thatcherites have done more damage to certain traditional centres of power than has the Left. If the reform or even abolition of the country's antiquated monarchy and House of Lords is on the agenda, it is due mainly to the activities of the Tory press. It would be paradoxical indeed if the country were to be led towards republicanism by the *Sun* rather than by the Labour party! Instead of leading the assault on the deferential and conservative culture of Britain, the Labour party itself reflects these attitudes. The Party needs to adopt policies which will open up public life to women and ethnic minorities on an equal basis. This may mean imposing targets and quotas.

Finally, there are signs that the Labour party is redefining itself positively in European and international terms. In particular, Gordon Brown has seen real progressive potential in the economic and social programmes emanating from Brussels. Further, a Europe united is a far stronger antidote to dangerous nationalism than a Europe divided. The mantle of chauvinism fits better the Right of the Conservative party. In principle, a party of the Left should reflect wider ideals of cooperation and common humanity. This applies especially to the global dimension where, of course, the greatest challenges lie. If the Labour party drops its concern with achieving 'the right image' and instead develops and expresses with conviction policies about the global environment, world hunger, and nuclear proliferation and militarisation, as well as a coherent domestic programme, it may well find that principle and popularity can run together. All this may not amount to a single 'big idea' but perhaps it is naive to think in such terms. What is important is that an alternative road is being opened up for Labour which should enable it to avoid the Party's previous mistakes and establish a healthy distance from Thatcher/Majorism.

References

Blackstone, T., Cornford, J., Hewitt, P., and Miliband, D., *Next Left; An Agenda for the 1990s* (IPPR, 1992).
Field, F., 'Finding Labour's Lost Domain' in *Guardian*, 3.2.93.
Straw, J., *Policy and Ideology* (Blackburn Labour Party, 1993)
Smith, J. *et al.*, with a foreword by Tony Blair, *Reclaiming the Ground* (Spire, 1993).

58 Bryan S. Turner: T. H. Marshall's Theory of Citizenship – and Beyond

In two articles in the journal, *Sociology*, Bryan Turner sought to develop further the concept of citizenship and apply it to contemporary political and social thought. In the first of the two pieces – from which an extract is given here – he critically presents T. H. Marshall's seminal theory of citizenship.

Marshall saw three key elements constituting the rights of a citizen: the civil, the political and the social. Each of these has tended to develop during a particular historical period, and this is well presented in the extract. Marshall regarded the development of citizenship as a bulwark against the insecurities that the economic free market, characteristic of capitalist society, can bring. Marshall saw the social rights of citizenship – primarily embodied in the welfare state – as the latest accretion of citizenship in Britain. Turner comments that the pressure put on the welfare state under Thatcher and Major demonstrates that social rights cannot be taken for granted as a permanent and universally accepted feature of British society (of course, there are many parts of the world where they are barely established at all).

In order to understand the section of the extract in which Turner makes his own contribution to citizenship theory, it will be useful to list the four points which he considers must be addressed if a general theory of citizenship is to be formulated successfully. (These appear in his second piece, not included here.) They are:

1 the rights and obligations of citizenship, i.e. the *content* of citizenship in relation to law, politics, welfare, education, culture etc;
2 the differences in the *type* of citizenship as it varies historically and between societies, e.g. whether citizenship is passive or active (see below);
3 the *social conditions* under which citizenship expands or contracts;
4 the *effects* that the type of citizenship in a given society has on that society.

Whereas Marshall addressed particularly the first of the above points, Turner concentrates mainly on the second. He explores two related themes:

1 situations in which citizenship comes from 'above' or 'below';
2 the relationship of citizenship to private (individual and family) and public (political) life.

Turner raises as many questions about citizenship as he provides answers. However, in an unequal and insecure world no issue is more crucial than to establish a conceptual and practical basis for citizen's rights. If some of Turner's considerations are demanding, the relevance and urgency of his message should be clear.

Reading 58 From Bryan S. Turner, 'Outline of A Theory of Citizenship' in *Sociology* Vol. 24, No. 2, May 1990, pp. 191–92, 206–9, 211–12, 212–13

While Marshall's analysis of citizenship is well known, it will be valuable here to outline briefly the three dimensions of citizenship which he considered in his original work. Marshall, whose intellectual roots were in the liberal tradition of James Mill and J.S. Mill, elaborated a specifically social version of the individualistic ideas of English liberalism. One theoretical and moral weakness of the liberal tradition was its failure to address directly the problem of social inequality in relationship to individual freedoms (Laski 1962). At the heart of Marshall's account of citizenship lies the contradiction between the formal political equality of the franchise and the persistence of extensive social and economic inequality, ultimately rooted in the character of the capitalist market place and the existence of private property. Marshall proposed the extension of citizenship as the principal political means for resolving, or at least containing, those contradictions.

The initial idea for his theory of citizenship was developed in 'Citizenship and social class' in 1949 (Marshall 1963). It was further developed in *Social Policy* (Marshall 1965), where he addressed the question of the evolution of welfare policies in Britain between approximately 1890 and 1945 as a specific example of the growth of social rights. However, his famous contribution to the analysis of social policy contained no explicit statement of his theory of social citizenship. Finally, he proposed a theory of capitalist society as a 'hyphenated society' in *The Right to Welfare and Other Essays* (Marshall 1981) in which there are inevitable tensions between a capitalist economy, a welfare state and the requirements of the modern state. Marshall was thus primarily concerned with the social-welfare history of Britain between the eighteenth and twentieth centuries in terms of the growth of citizenship as expressed in three dimensions namely, the civil, the political and the social.

Marshall argued that in the eighteenth century there had been a significant development of civil rights which were mainly targeted at the legal status and civil rights of individuals; and these rights were to be defended through a system of formal law courts. Civil rights were concerned with such basic issues as the freedom of speech, rights to a fair trial and equal access to the legal system. Secondly, Marshall noted an important growth in political rights in the nineteenth century as an outcome of working-class struggle for political equality in terms of greater access to the parliamentary process. In this area, political citizenship required the development of electoral rights and wider access to political institutions for the articulation of interests. In the British case, this involved the emergence of political rights which were associated with the secret ballot box, the creation of new political parties and the expansion of the franchise. Finally, he drew attention in the twentieth century to the expansion of social rights which were the basis of claims to welfare and which established entitlements to social security in periods of unemployment, sickness and distress. Thus, corresponding to the three basic areans of social rights (the civil, political and the social), we find three central institutions of contemporary society (the law courts, parliament and the welfare system). Marshall's final theorisation of this issue conceptualised capitalism as a dynamic system in which the constant clash between citizenship and social class determined the character of political and social life. These tensions were summarized in his notion of the hyphenated society, that is a social system in which there were perpetual tensions between the need for economic profitability, the taxation requirements of the modern state and the rights of citizens to welfare provision . . .

A typology of citizenship

. . . [C]omparisons between different histories of citizenship in Europe suggest a model of citizenship development in terms of two dimensions. The first dimension is the passive-active contrast depending on whether citizenship grew from above or below. In the German tradition, citizenship stands in a passive relationship to the state because it is primarily an effect of state action. It is important to note that this distinction is in fact fundamental to the western tradition and can be located in medieval political philosophy, where there were two opposed views of citizenship. In the descending view, the king is all powerful and the subject is the recipient of privileges. In the ascending view, a free man was a citizen, an active bearer of rights. In the northern city-states of Italy, the Roman law facilitated the adoption of a populist notion of citizenship; the result was that the *populo* came to be regarded as an aggregate of citizens who possessed some degree of autonomous sovereignty (Ullmann 1975). The second dimension is the tension between a private realm of the individual and the family in relationship to the public arena of political action. In the German case, an emphasis on the private (the family, religion, and individual ethical development) was combined with a view of the state as the only source of public authority. This typology allows us to contrast Germany with other historical trajectories.

The contrast between the English and the German traditions of political participation would appear to be very considerable. It was Weber of course who drew attention to the historically important contrast between constitutional law in the Roman continental system and the English judge-made law within the common law tradition. Weber argued that continental constitutionalism provided better safeguards for the individual, but he underestimated the importance of the common-law tradition in providing precisely a *common* basis for rights. The struggle against the absolutist state in England had lead to the execution of the king, an expansion of parliamentary authority, the defence of the English common-law tradition and the assertion of individual religious rights. Of course, it has long been held that the English tradition of individual rights in fact supported an unequal and rigid class structure. Effective social rights resided in individual rights to property, thereby excluding the majority of the population from real social and political participation (Macpherson 1962). The absence of a land army and the state's dependence on a navy, the early de-militarisation of the English aristocracy and the incorporation of the urban merchants into the elite contributed to English gradualism (Anderson 1974). After the demobilisation of the new model army, two royal guard units were retained for primarily ceremonial duties. The British army was not modernised until the late nineteenth century. The monarch could no longer intimidate parliament (Downing 1988:28). A more important point is that the constitutional settlement of 1688 created the British citizen as the British subject, that is a legal personality whose indelible social rights are constituted by a monarch sitting in parliament. The notion of citizen-as-subject indicates clearly the relatively extensive notion of social rights but also the passive character of British civil institutions. The defeat of

> Turner describes British citizenship as 'passive' in that historically and legally it is 'subject' to the monarch sitting in parliament. Thus, in Britain, it is not the people who are sovereign but the monarch in parliament.

absolutism in the settlement of 1688 left behind a core of insitutions (the Crown, the Church, the House of Lords and traditional attitudes about the family and private life) which continued to dominate British life until the destructive force of the First and Second World Wars brought British culture eventually and reluctantly into the modern world.

By contrast with both the English and German cases, the French conception of citizenship was the consequence of a long historical struggle to break the legal and political monopoly of a court society within a social system which was rigidly divided in terms of estates. The very violence of this social transformation resulted in a highly articulate conception of active citizenship in the revolutionary struggles of the eighteenth century. The old myth that the king represented, combined and integrated the multiplicity of orders, groups and estates had become transparent during the political conflicts of the eighteenth century. Revolutionary political theories, acting against the absolutist conception of sovereignty, followed Rousseau in conceptualising society as a collection of individuals whose existence would be represented through the general will in popular parliamentary institutions. What bound Frenchmen together into a common nation was again the concept of citizenship (Baker 1987). Frenchmen had ceased to be merely subjects of the sovereign and had become instead common citizens of a national entity. There are therefore two parallel movements whereby a state is transformed into a nation at the same time that subjects are transformed into citizens (Lindsay 1943). The differences between the French and English revolutionary traditions may be summarised in two contrasted views of citizenship by Rousseau and Burke (Nisbet 1986). For Rousseau in *The Social Contract* the viability of citizenship required the destruction of all particular intervening institutions which separated the citizen from the state. By contrast, Burke in *Reflections on the Revolution in France* in 1790 argued that the essence of citizenship was the continuity of local groups, particular institutions and regional associations between the sovereign power of the general will and the individual. For Burke an organised civil society must have hierarchy, order, regulation and constraint; its hierarchical character precluded the very possibility of 'the rights of man' (Macpherson 1980).

Turner describes the origins of French citizenship as more 'active' as the French people *did* break with the monarchy and became themselves sovereign.

Finally, the American case represents another variation on the history of western citizenship. The American example shared with the French a strong rejection of centralised power, adopting also the discourse of the rights of man and privileges of independent citizens. The Boston Tea Party was a symbolically significant expression of the idea 'no taxation without representation'. The radical nature of the 'democratic revolution' in America struck observers like Alexis de Tocqueville with great force; he came to regard America as the first macro-experiment in democracy in modern history. For de Tocqueville, the democratic foundation of the nation was explained by the absence of aristocracy, the frontier, and the exclusion of an established church. Although there was a radical tradition of citizenship expressed in the idea of an independent militia, American democracy nevertheless continued to exist alongside a divisive racist and exploitative South. In addition America's welfare state was late to develop and provided very inadequate forms of social citizenship and participation for the majority of the population. This weak tradition of citizenship in welfare terms has been explained by the very strength of American individualism, and by the checks and balances of the federal system; American citizenship was expressed in terms of localism versus centralism, thereby limiting the development of a genuinely national programme of welfare rights. To some extent the dominance of individualism and the value of personal success have meant that the 'public arena' is typically understood in terms of individual involvement in local voluntary associations. Americans 'have difficulty relating this ideal image to the large-scale forces and institutions shaping their lives' (Bellah *et al.* 1985:199). The political is seen as morally suspect. This cultural analysis of American individualism would not therefore contradict Mann's analysis. On the contrary, they may be regarded as complementary. In America, the articulation of sectional interests through democratic institutions constrains the emergence of class-based politics.

The point of this historical sketch has been partly to provide a critique of the monolithic and unified conception of citizenship in Marshall and partly to offer a sociological model of citizenship along two axes, namely public and private definitions of moral activity in terms of the creation of a public space of political activity, and active and passive forms of citizenship in terms of whether the citizen is conceptualised as merely a subject of an absolute authority or as an active political agent.

We can now indicate how this ideal-typical construction might now be applied to specific cases:

Note The diagram reads both down and across. Thus, English and German citizenship is seen as 'passive' (down) and French and English citizenship as having a strong public dimension.

Citizenship

Below	Above		
Revolutionary French tradition	Passive English case	+	public space
American liberalism	German fascism	–	

Here Turner makes some generalisations about the relationship between 'below'/'above' democracy and 'public'/'private' space.

In France, a revolutionary conception of active citizenship was combined with an attack on the private space of the family, religion and privacy. In a passive democracy, citizenship is handed down from above and the citizen appears as a mere subject (the English case under the seventeenth century settlement). In a liberal democratic solution, positive democracy emphasises participation, but this is often contained by a continuing emphasis on privacy and the sacredness of individual opinion. In plebiscitary democracy, the individual citizen is submerged in the sacredness of the state which permits minimal participation in terms of the election of leaders, while again family life is given priority in the arena of personal ethical development

(Maier 1988). While revolutionary democracy may collapse into totalitarianism, plebiscitary democracy degenerates into fascism (Lefort 1988). In totalitarian democracy, the 'state, in pushing egalitarianism to the extreme, closes off the private sphere from influencing the course of political affairs' (Prager 1985:187).

. . . [T]he globalization of citizenship

While the notion of citizenship continues to provide a normative basis for the defence of the welfare state, certain crucial changes in the organisation of global systems have rendered some aspects of the notion of citizenship redundant and obsolete. The contemporary world is structured by two contradictory social processes. On the one hand, there are powerful pressures towards regional autonomy and localism and, on the other, there is a stronger notion of globalism and global political responsibilities. The concept of citizenship is therefore still in a process of change and development. We do not possess the conceptual apparatus to express the idea of global membership, and in this context a specifically national identity appears anachronistic. Indeed the uncertainty of the global context may produce strong political reactions asserting the normative authority of the local and the national over the global and international (Robertson and Lechner 1985; Robertson 1987).

Global environmental problems and poverty are the background against which Turner suggests the need to develop a concept of world citizenship (the *rights* pertaining to which would require practical implementation).

The analysis of citizenship has in recent years become a pressing theoretical issue, given the problems which face the welfare state in a period of economic recession. However, the problem of citizenship is in fact not confined merely to a question of the normative basis of welfare provision; its province is global. It includes, on the one hand, the international consequences of peristroika and glasnost in the Soveit Union, and, on the other, the implications of medical technology for the definition of what will count as a human subject/citizen. While Marshall's aim in formulating a theory of citizenship was by contrast rather modest in its focus (to understand the tensions in Britain between capitalism and social rights), his statement of the issues has proved to be extremely fruitful in sociology and political science.

The limitations of Marshall's approach, however, are equally obvious. His framework is now widely regarded as evolutionary, analytically vague and ethnocentric . . .

Recent ethnic conflict in Europe – particularly in what was Yugoslavia – have over-ridden the more unifying power of common citizenhip. One might add to Turner's comments on ethnicity and citizenship that there remain unresolved issues in relation to gender and citizenship.

In this article I have been concerned with two dimensions . . . namely the private/public division in western cultures, and the issue of passive and active versions of citizenship. However, any further development of the theory of citizenship will have to deal more fundamentally with societies in which the struggle over citizenship necessarily involves problems of national identity and state formation in a context of multiculturalism and ethnic pluralism. The societies on which this article has largely concentrated – France, Germany, England, the Netherlands and colonial America – were *relatively* homogeneous in ethnic terms during their period of national formation. With the exception of North America, these societies had no internal problem of aboriginality . . . but ethnic migration has been critical (indeed crucial) in other contexts such as in South Africa, the Middle East, Australia and New Zealand (Turner 1986b:64–84). We may in conclusion indicate two possible lines of theoretical development of the (western) notion of citizenship. The first would be the conditions under which citizenship can be formed in societies which are, as it were, constituted by the problems of ethnic complexity (such as Brazil), and the second would be an analysis of the problems which face the development of global citizenship as the political counter-part of the world economy.

Ralph Miliband: New Social Movements and the 'Primacy' of Labour

This extract from Ralph Miliband's *Divided Societies: Class Struggle in Contemporary Capitalism*, examines the relationship between the labour movement and new social movements such as the women's and black movements.

A Marxist himself, Miliband is aware of the wide support for social movements (such as feminism and anti-racism) among people who may not often be Marxist, but who are often more or less radical. He is at pains to recognise that the social movements express powerful feelings and address real grievances. However, he is uncompromising on one point – that of the 'primacy' of the labour movement. By this he means that the labour movement is essential to 'revolutionary' change because it arises out of the conflict between capital and labour at the core of the capitalist system i.e. in productive relations. He emphatically states that the social movements cannot fundamentally change the capitalist system 'without labour movements being organised as political forces'. Elsewhere in his book, he contends view that feminism, anti-racism and other social movements can be most effective as part of a wider socialist movement.

Many critics disagree with the 'primacy' of labour thesis. For instance, for Alberto Melucci what is 'new' about the new social movements is that they arise away from productive relations and outside of labour politics. He would regard Miliband as stuck in the 'old' politics despite the latter's efforts at bridge-building. He rejects the concept of an historic, collective agency of change and sees the new movements as relationships of individuals which are constantly being redefined (see *Nomads of the Present*; Hutchinson Radius, 1989).

Reading 59 From Ralph Miliband, *Divided Societies: Class Struggle in Contemporary Capitalism* (Oxford University Press, 1991), pp. 95, 110–14

New social movements encompass a great diversity of causes and concerns. The most notable are feminism, anti-racism, ecology, peace and disarmament, student movements, and sexual liberation. To these may be added liberation theology and the movements and currents of thought and action associated with it. Of course, the cause and concerns associated with one new social movement are not exclusive to it: there is a great deal of ideological sharing between them.

A preliminary point needs to be made regarding any comparison between new social movements and labour movements. This is that the notion of the 'primacy' of the latter as agencies of radical change does not, in itself, at all require a devaluation of the importance of new social movements. It is unfortunately true that Marxists and others on the 'traditional' Left have often given the impression that they viewed the strivings and struggles of these movements as of no great consequence, or as an unwelcome 'diversion', at best, from the 'real' struggle . . .

'Primacy' does not mean domination or absorption. Nor certainly does it devalue the work of new social movements, whose support labour movements would undoubtedly require in the advancement of their transformative endeavours. This support is not only a matter of additional numbers – even though new social movements can activate constituencies which labour movements are unable to reach. It is also a matter of the contribution which new social movements can make – and have in fact already made – to the enrichment of the theory and practices of labour movements. For there can surely be no question that new social movements are the bearers of many ideas and practices which must form part of any emancipatory project worthy of the name, but which labour movements have traditionally tended to neglect or which, in some countries, they have opposed.

To speak thus, however, is to assume certain affinities and possibilities of co-operation and alliance between labour movements on the one hand and new social movements on the other. It is an assumption which many people in new social movements have questioned not least because labour movements themselves have exhibited many of the deformations and vices against which feminists, black people and others are struggling. But much here depends on what are throught to be the reasons for these deformations and vices.

In this section, Miliband seeks to explain why the labour movement itself has often been sexist or racist – the very kinds of problems which concern the 'new' social movements.

Among these reasons, a central place needs to be accorded to the context in which deformations and vices occur. That context exercises a very strong pull in the direction of sectionalism, fragmentation, competition, and struggle among workers themselves, and also in the direction of discrimination and closure exercised against vulnerable minorities. Throughout the history of capitalism, workers have sought to improve their bargaining position *vis-à-vis* employers by preventing the access of women, black people, Catholics, Irishmen, or whoever, to their occupations. The roots of such discrimination lie in the attempt to protect jobs and conditions; and the divisions and fragmentations and hostilities this causes are frequently encouraged or even fostered by employers. Discrimination is then rationalized by ideological constructs and racist or sexist stereotypes according to which women are unsuited to particular forms of work, black people are stupid, Irishmen are shiftless, and so on; and these constructs acquire a life of their own and become an autonomous part of the culture. To ignore this economic dimension in the history of racist or sexist discrimination is to leave a crucial facet of reality out of account.

It is nevertheless true that a great deal of oppression, discrimination, aggression, and violence exercised by white men, whether workers or bourgeois, against women, black people, ethnic minorities, gays and lesbians, cannot be traced back in any plausible way to direct or even indirect economic pressures. A different explanation is required, and must be sought, I would argue, in traditional ideological prejudices and positions, nurtured over many generations, and reinforced by the multiple alienations, frustrations, and anxieties generated by societies whose dynamic is ruthless competition and frantic acquisition, and whose ethos constitutes a permanent denial, in practice, of co-operation, fellowship, and solidarity. Such societies provide a fertile ground for the festering of the 'injuries of class' and for the development of pathological deformantions: mechanisms of legitimation for these deformations readily come into play and designate victims as themselves responsible for the sufferings inflicted upon them, and for diverse social ills.

Feminists and others rightly point out that pre-capitalist societies were similarly deformed, and that Communist societies are also afflicted by racism and sexism. From this, it is but a small step to the claim that such phenomena are trans-historical, and rooted in human nature, or in male nature, rather than in social processes susceptible to drastic attentuation and to eventual extirpation. But this ignores the fact that pre-capitalist societies were also class societies marked by domination and exploitation, with their own 'injuries of class'. As for Communist societies, the circumstances in which they came into being, their economic, social, and political conditions, and the circumstances in which they have developed as Communist regimes have made them exceedingly prone to the perpetuation of deformations which they have inherited and are formally pledged to eliminate, and which are deeply rooted in their tradition and culture.

In short, explanations for enduring evils such as sexism and racism must be sought in the social context in which they occur. To seek them outside that context, and to invoke for their explanation trans-historical and supposedly immutable traits of human nature or male nature is to retreat from rational analysis.

Here Miliband argues that 'such phenomena' as racism and sexism cannot be 'generic' or part of 'human nature' because there are many examples of co-operation between members of different 'races' and between the sexes.

The case against 'generic' explanations (or rather pseudo-explanations) for such phenomena as racism and sexism is reinforced by much historical experience. The point bears repeating: there have been innumerable instances everywhere of workers, male and female, white and black, Catholic and Protestant, Muslim and Jewish, acting together in struggle and achieving a high, if temporary, level of solidarity.

The pulls against the maintenance of solidarity are very strong, but they have been proved again and again not to be insuperable. Workers divided by gender, race, ethnicity, and religion *have* come together in trade unions and parties and other organizations of labour movements, and have found common ground and solidarity in common struggles against employers and the state.

A crucial responsibility in this area, too, falls upon trade unions and political parties of the Left; and the record on this score is not quite as bleak as is often suggested. It is true that the history of trade unionism is spattered with instances of prejudice and discrimination, much more virulent in some countries (for instance, the United States, not to speak of South Africa) than in others, but nowhere negligible. But given the economic context in which trade unions operate, and the sexism and racism which pervade the culture of all societies, the remarkable thing is not that trade unionists should have been affected by these prejudices but that the organizations of which they are members should, in country after country, have been in the forefront of the opposition to racial and gender disrcimination. Nor are the labour movements worst affected by such evils frozen in immutable positions: it is enough for instance to compare the level of racism prevalent in American trade unions before World War II with its level in more recent times to see that however slow and limited progress may be, it does occur.

As for labour and socialist parties, they have, from their very beginnings, been among the most consistent forces opposing the prejudices prevalent in their societies. It was the leader of the German Social Democratic Party, August Bebel, who published in 1878 one of the major feminist texts of the nineteenth century, *Women and Socialism*, which became the essential statement on the subject for party members and others; and Angela Weir and Elizabeth Wilson note that 'the German SPD had a women's movement with 175,000 members in 1914 and had introduced the first motion calling for the enfranchisement of women in the Reichstag in 1895. The SPD was formally committed to creches for working mothers, equal pay for equal work, the education of women, relaxation of the abortion laws and availability of contraceptives.

At different levels of commitment, the same story can be repeated for all parties of the Left everywhere. In terms of formal commitment at least, and often in practice as well, parties of the Left have proved to be the staunch supporters of many of the causes and concerns which move the new social movements and it is worth adding that Communist parties in particular, for all their great shortcomings and failings, have been in the vanguard of the struggle against oppression and discrimination in their societies, often in exceptionally harsh and dangerous conditions – for instance, in the southern states of the United States (or in the North for that matter) and in South Africa. The policies and strategies of Communist parties might often be mistaken; but this does not diminish the reality of the commitment of their members to a vision of human emancipation which knows no boundaries of gender or race. Much the same vision has inspired socialists everywhere.

Against this, feminists and members of racial or ethnic minorities are well entitled to point to lapses, in practice, from formal party commitments, or to practices which belie the commitments; and members of new social movements in general may well argue that the issues which concern them are not granted an adequate place in the range of concerns of the parties of the Left. But however justified these grievances may be, the failings to which they point are clearly not irremediable; and they do not preclude, given some flexibility, the waging of common struggles over mutually agreed policies and aims. Suspicions, disagreements, and rivalries will endure; but they need not be crippling.

It must, however, be said that labour movements will remain at the core of the struggle for radical reform and revolutionary change in advanced capitalist societies. New social movements may doubt this, or deny it. But all conservative forces in these societies do not doubt it. For them, the main antagonist, as always, remains organized labour and the socialist Left: it is they who must above all be contained, repelled, and, if need be, crushed. It is to these ends that class struggle from above is mainly directed; and it is to the ways in which this struggle is conducted that I now turn.

Charles Murray: Would it Matter if the Very Rich 'Forgot About' the Poor?

Somewhere in this book I have been keen to include a reading which forcefully presents the view that in rich societies the wealthy and the comfortable majority may choose to 'forget about' the poorest ten or twenty per cent of society. Charles Murray discusses this possibility in relation to the 'top' and 'bottom' groups in American society but his analysis could be broadly applied to any wealthy society. This piece appears in the political sociology section but it could equally come under other headings – including deviance and urbanisation. Whether seen in terms of crime or housing and job development, the linking notion is that the rich and the powerful – and perhaps even the moderately comfortable – may 'spin off' the poor and powerless leaving them to their own devices with perhaps a minimum degree of surveillance and social control.

This kind of thesis is all the more convincing perhaps when it is articulated by a conservative critic. Charles Murray has been fiercely attacked for his 'reactionary' analysis of the so-called 'underclass' (see Reading 16), but here he manifests a sensitive, conservative conscience about this group. Many may find his 'solutions' flimsy, but there is no doubt that he puts his finger on a serious and dangerous social development.

Reading 60 From Charles Murray: 'An American caste system' in *The Independent*, Monday 22 July 1991

It makes sense to be a little schizophrenic about the American future. Much is positive, whether one thinks about the future personally or politically, but there is a dark side looming.

The dark side flows from a prediction that in itself seems innocuous: as national wealth grows in the coming years, so will the proportion of people who are rich. To get an overall idea of the trend to date, consider that, as of the end of the Korean War, using constant 1988 dollars, fewer than one family in 50,000 had an income of $100,000 or more. By 1989, almost four families per *hundred* had an income that great. This is a phenomenally large change.

The number of the rich will tend to grow more rapidly in the coming years. Several factors lead to this conclusion, principally the increasing monetary value of cognitive skills, meaning a combination of ability and training for complex mental work. This trend has been in evidence for some time. In 1980, for example, a male college graduate made about 30 per cent more than a male high-school graduate. By 1988, he made about 60 per cent more. The comparison with people who didn't even graduate from high school is starker yet.

In coming years, the price for first-rate cognitive skills will skyrocket, for reasons involving the nature of changes in technology (constantly more complex at the leading edge), politics (constantly creating more complicated laws with more complicated loopholes), and the size of the stakes (when a percentage point of market share is worth hundreds of millions of dollars, then the people who can help you get that extra percentage point are worth very large incomes). Meanwhile, real wages for low-skill jobs will increase slowly if at all, and efforts to increase wages artificially (by raising the minimum wage, for example) will backfire because the demand for low-skill labour is becoming more elastic as alternatives to human labour become numerous and affordable.

The net result is that the rich are going to constitute a major chunk of the population in the relatively near future, and this group will increasingly be the most talented. Why be depressed by this prospect, which in many ways sounds like a good thing? Because I fear its potential for producing something very like a caste society, with the implication of utter social separation.

Briefly, I am trying to envision what happens when 10 or 20 per cent of the population has enough income to bypass the social institutions it doesn't like in ways that only the top fraction of 1 per cent used to be able do to. Robert Reich, the liberal Harvard economist, has called it the "secession of the successful". A simple example is the way that the fax, modem and Federal Express has already made the US Postal Service nearly irrelevant to the way some segments of American society communicate. A more portentous example is the mass exodus from state schools among urban élites.

I sympathise with many of the reasons why people with money take these steps. For almost three decades now, government has failed miserably to perform its basic functions, from preserving order in public spaces to dispensing justice to providing decent education in its schools. But the reasonableness of the motives does not diminish the danger of the potential consequences.

As this American caste system takes shape, American conservatism is going to have to wrestle with its soul. Is conservatism going to follow the Latin-American model, where to be conservative means to preserve the mansions on the hills above the slums? Or is it going to remain true to its American heritage, where the thing-to-be-conserved has not been primarily money or privilege but a distinctively American way of self-government and limited government?

All the forces that I can discern will tend to push American-conservatism toward the Latin-American model. For example: conservatives are now being joined by defectors from urban liberalism who have been mugged – sometimes figuratively, often literally. These new conservatives' political agenda is weighted heavily toward taking care of number one, using big government to do so whenever it suits their purposes. More broadly, the culture of the urban underclass, increasingly violent and bizarre, fosters alienation. As each new social experiment fails to diminish the size of the underclass, our increasing national wealth will make it tempting to bypass the problem by treating the inner city as an urban analogue of the Indian reservation.

This temptation will be augmented by the increasing power of people at the upper end of the income scale to use government for their own ends. If the rich constitute 10 to 20 per cent of the population, their political power will be so immense as to transform the power equation. The left has been complaining for years that the rich have too much power. They ain't seen nothing yet.

It will be sadly ironic if the politics of caste are called 'conservative', for the greatest bulwarks against the power of privilege are some good old-fashioned American conservative principles. Enforce strict equality for individuals before the law. Prohibit the state from favouring groups, including rich and influential groups. Decentralise government authority to the smallest possible unit. None of these principles is a panacea, for the forces that will tend to produce an American caste system are powerful and complex. But these classic conservative principles are more needed than ever, at a time when the seductions for conservatives to abandon them are increasing.

Questions and Issues

Political Sociology: Section 13

The most relevant readings appear in brackets after each question.

1 Who rules Britain? How is the power and authority of the ruling group legitimised? (Readings 55–56)

2 'For over a quarter of a century, socially, politically, and ideologically, the foundation of the Labour Party's support has been eroded.' Critically discuss this view. (Readings 56–59, 66)

3 Describe and explain the main theories of citizenship. What is their relevance to contemporary British politics and society. (Readings 16, 58–59, 84)

4 Critically discuss the view that the new social movements address the main current 'problems' of society more relevantly and dynamically than the labour movement. (Readings 59, 65, 66)

HEALTH, WELFARE AND POVERTY

Introduction: Readings 61–66

The first reading by Peter Townsend and his colleagues sets the context for the rest. It argues that a purely 'medical' or scientific approach to health is inadequate. In their view, social and environmental factors affect health, and policy ought to reflect this. They are implicitly critical of the individualistic solutions to health problems advocated by the Conservative health ministers of the late 1980s and early 90s (see Readings 65 and 66).

Rob Mears analyses a wide range of issues relating to health inequalities. He is critical of aspects of both the traditional welfare state approach to achieving health equality and of individualistic approaches. In his conclusion, he attempts to move beyond polarised solutions. Sonja Hunt deals in detail with an important issue raised by Mears: the death, injury and pollution caused by private cars. Yet, as she points out, the proliferation of private cars is not widely 'constructed' as a major social problem.

A key area of the sociology of health is the quality of interpersonal interaction between patients and doctors. Agnes Miles examines research findings on two gender-related aspects of interaction: firstly, whether or not doctors treat male and female patients differently, and secondly, patients' views of doctors. Although some stereotyping and simplistic assumptions occur on both sides, matters are often more complex than might be anticipated. Reading 9 provides a further illustration of a more qualitative approach to health issues.

Tom Hulley and John Clarke address the issue of why many people, including some of the poor themselves, blame the individual for his or her own poverty and disadvantage rather than looking for explanations in wider social, economic or political circumstances. The essence of their answer is that people tend to accept dominant ideologies about the causes of social problems. While this is not an original conclusion, the details of their analysis produce fresh insight through an effective synthesis of interactionist and post structuralist concepts.

61 Peter Townsend, Peter Phillimore and Alastair Beattie: The Medical and Social Models of Health

The first section of this extract critically appraises the medical (or 'machine') model of health and introduces the social model of health which is strongly preferred by the authors. While they accept that the scientific basis of the medical model has led to real progress in medical practice, they maintain that only a model of health rooted in an understanding of the social factors which condition people's lives can provide a basis for a radical improvement in the general level of health. The effect of social class inequalities will be fundamental to such a model, and they make a case for a definition of class that is more widely based than simply on a person's occupation.

In the second section, the authors apply their argument to contemporary society, particularly Britain. Rather cleverly, they link government complaints about the lack of a clear connection between official health expenditure (in-put) and improved health (out-put) with their own scheme for a wider, more 'social model of health'. They find substantial support for their sort of approach in the work of the Centre for Health Studies at Yale University and in the 'Black Report' on 'Inequalities in Health' in the United Kingdom.

Reading 61 From Peter Townsend, Peter Phillimore and Alastair Beattie, *Health and Deprivation* (Croom Helm, 1988), pp. 6–9, 9–14, 16–17

Concepts and models of health

. . . [W]hat must we understand by 'health'? In rich countries the concept of health has come under fierce scrutiny in the late twentieth century. Part of this has been due to a reaction against what has been perceived to be the dehumanising effects of medical ideology and technology when carried to extremes – as in features of the modern practice of chemotherapy, surgery and obstetrics (see, for example, Powles, 1973; Illich, 1975; Navarro, 1976; Ehrenreich, 1978; Stark, 1982). Medicine is felt to be too narrowly concerned with diseases, rather than with people. Another aspect of the scrutiny of health stems from a different reaction – against the artificial, clamorous and manufactured nature of modern urban life. The search for 'the good life' has become as important as the critique of medicine in changing attitudes to health and preparing people to consider different perspectives.

Scientifically there are two alternative modes of explanation. These were reviewed in the Black Report (1980, pp. 5–9). Firstly, there is the medical model. This is an engineering approach to health, built originally upon the Cartesian philosophy of the body conceived and controlled as a machine, and dealing essentially with the cure of diseases in individuals. We mean that the idea is carefully structured in terms of cure rather than prevention, disease rather than the promotion of health and welfare, and the examination and treatment of individual rather than of social conditions – whether of couples, friends, families, groups, communities or populations. The curious fact here is that in trying to escape the social and political controversies which are necessarily involved in, say, pursuing unremittingly the reasons for differences in rates of mortality or morbidity between populations, or promoting the health and wellbeing of unemployed groups, or families living in poverty, or the population as a whole, the professional servant of medicine has accepted a circumspection of the scope of his or her work and a set of values which permits more than three-quarters of his or her potential scientific expertise and work to be drawn off and reconstituted as areas of political and bureaucratic responsibility. The restricted definition of responsibility for health has implications of which everyone should become aware. The development of knowledge to enlarge health is constrained. Some major social causes of ill-health and death are underestimated or ignored; and faith in the capacity of human beings to control the problems of life and liberate their potentialities is needlessly diminished.

Here ideology (the medical model) is linked to practice which reflects and reinforces the medical model.

The medical model is of course embodied in organisations and in the everyday analysis of fresh events. Ideas and meanings are not just disembodied abstractions; they are reflected in practice and structures. This means that priority is given in the allocation of resources to the prestigious departments of the practice of acute medicine, to specialised hospital treatment rather than general practice, and to casualty treatment instead of screening, prevention and health education. The use of the word 'ancillary' to denote someone whose work is defined to fit in with, but is clearly of lesser status than, that of medicine itself, is significant. Therefore the particular forms of the organisation and practice of health care in Britain and in other countries reinforces the meaning of health central to the medical model. This is liable to be forgotten: even the critics of medicine will constantly be presented with examples of the re-affirmation of its principles which seem to deny any alternative.

Two qualifications have to be made to this summary representation of the medical model. One is that it is not unambiguously consistent and clear-cut. The social is accommodated to the medicalised meaning of health. There are specialities which introduce the social aspects of health, like psychiatry, paediatrics and social medicine or epidemiology, but there is a degree of necessary intellectual subordination or self-imposed submission. Thus, for example, epidemiology itself has generally been interpreted restrictedly as the study of the distribution of disease as the aggregate of individual phenomena (McMahon and Pugh, 1970; and see the critical discussion of Paterson, 1982). In addition, some critics of medicine, who have argued that most of the decline in premature mortality in the nineteenth and twentieth centuries has been due to social changes like improvements in diet and living standards generally (in particular McKeown, 1976; but see also Winter, 1977 and 1981 for a valuable historical illustration), have sought more to call attention to the complementary features of an 'environmentalist' approach than to reconstitute medicine within an alternative model of health. The same is true of certain penetrating evaluations of medical care – using social factors, including class as a form of standardisation (for example Charlton *et al.*, 1983). They do not situate medicine as just one of the social institutions in an alternative model which seeks to explain the distribution of health. There are other ways in which medicine cannot be said to be 'monolithic'. There are forms of fringe medicine, like osteopathy, which are acceptable to many in the medical profession as well as to the public, as well as those forms which are unacceptable. Moreover, some conceptions of preventive action – albeit narrow or limited, and particularly when related to individual conditions or behaviour, such as check-ups or education about the risks of smoking or eating a diet heavy in cholesterol – are approved if not universally pursued.

Another qualification is equally important. Criticism of the medical 'model' which has developed must not be interpreted as cavalier rejection or disregard of certain benefits it has to offer. The challenge is in pursuing the larger questions about health to which medicine can offer only a partial or fragmented answer. Specialised features of medicine must therefore be

In the remainder of this paragraph, the authors present the basic case for a social rather than a medical model of health (although there are aspects of the medical model which they consider worth presenting).

incorporated into a larger model, parts of which are currently ill-developed. Certainly they are far less developed than some justly admired and honourable technologies and procedures of medicine. In contradistinction the social model of health takes as its basis the fact that human behaviour is ultimately social in its origin and determination, and depends upon social organisation and convention to encourage or restrain. People perform roles, have relationships and observe customs which are socially defined (including those which are made compulsory in an authoritarian state) and this provides the means both of identity and activity. This is not to say that people conform greyly to a uniform pattern: there are divergencies of age, background, environment and stage of family development which permit wide variation in personality and behaviour within any social structure, but the 'social' is what provides the necessary framework for observed health. It defines the pattern of daily life, diet, shelter, work and form of reproduction, upbringing and care; and it defines the variations between communities in adjoining areas as well as between cultures or nations. The vitality, endurance and freedom from disease, disability and stress – of individuals as much as of groups – can only be defined, explained and enhanced in that context.

. . . The definition of health adopted upon the foundation of the World Health Organization is often quoted as a modern illustration of the social model of health as an alternative to the medical model. In fact it represents a rather lame compromise. The WHO defined health as 'a state of complete physical, mental and social well-being and not merely the absence of disease or infirmity'. (This theme was confirmed in the Alma-Ata declaration – Alma-Ata, 1978.) In fact, while emphasising positive in contrast to negative aspects of health, this definition conveys a curiously passive, steady-state idea of 'well-being' instead of one grounded in more active fulfilment – whether of productive work or useful and satisfying social roles and relationships. The definition implicitly favours an individual rather than a social orientation towards health, which may be said to perpetuate the wrong order of priorities in understanding and gaining control over the phenomenon. A more thoroughgoing social and dynamic conceptualisation has to be sought.

What are the implications of adopting a social model of health? Trained personnel would continue to work within the traditional practices of medicine but more of them would begin to work on prevention, on the early stages of disease and on recovery and rehabilitation. Of course it is not only 'health' but the social context of health which requires clarification to develop better theory to explain the distribution of health. We say 'social context' because the two traditions of research which we have identified – those of inequalities of health by area and by class – are imperfect representations of the population variations experienced in social structure and organisation and need to be better synthesised. Although some points will be discussed in ensuing chapters, certain introductory comments are required.

Here, the important point is made that what may appear as problems of geography or environment, invariably reflect underlying social inequalities.

A 'social' model of health must reflect the pervasive characteristics of social institutions and state organisation. This means that society and not location must be treated as providing the causal mainspring of any local variations which may be observed in, say, health. Indeed some characteristics of 'location' are themselves socially rather than naturalistically derived – such as form of industry, enclosure and non-enclosure, waterways and roadways, afforestation or deforestation, vegetation and housing – and some of these features will ultimately be related to the history and present configuration of the ownership and price of land. So while there will be 'naturalistic' elements like climate or rock and land formation, many of them will have been adapted, reconstituted or overlaid by human use and will relate to, if not strictly conform with, social structure. The same points apply to the development of a concept of 'environment' to explain some of the effects of location upon health. Our necessary implication is that the *social* factors which themselves lie behind geographical, area or environmental variations in the distribution of health require identification.

A second necessary step is to accept that social class must not be regarded as just another social indicator, like employment status, tenure, race or overcrowding, but as *the* social concept which is fundamental to the explanation of the distribution of health – to which the listed indicators are secondarily related. In key respects this is a matter for scientific judgement (on the basis of empirical observation, experiment, statistical correlation, and theoretical consistency and integrity) and not mere ideology. As such, class must not be unnecessarily restricted to one aspect of social life, like occupation, but must be defined (operationally as well as in general principle) as a total reflection of differences in rank in economic and social position. This explains the Black Report's insistence on reinterpreting the usage of 'social' class in many commentaries on health as 'occupational' class (Black Report, 1980, p. 18).

The Registrar General has traditionally used an occupational classification as a basis for defining social class. A specific occupation may indeed denote, within narrow limits, what a person's earnings are likely to be, and therefore what income he or she and the household are likely to have, and the kind of home and the area they are likely to live in, as well as the amount of wealth they are likely to possess, the education they are likely to have had and even the kinds of customs and leisure activities they are likely to pursue. This is why in many studies of the past, occupational categorisation has 'worked' so well. It is because occupational status has borne an approximate correspondence, albeit a rough one, with class structure that explains its widespread use. However, that does not presuppose either that social class should be reduced to occupational status or that occupational status continues to be as good a proxy for social class as formerly. Both require contemporary attention. People's social class is fundamental to the opportunities in, and experience of, life. This can be demonstrated at each of the stages of pre-natal development, infancy, childhood, education, occupational career, marriage, child-rearing, post-family maturity and retirement.

The fact that it is more difficult to categorise people by social class than, say, by race or age does not mean that it is any less important or fundamental. Neither is the problem just one of methodological procedure – of finding how a population can be ranked in relation to an amalgam of resources, status, power situation and disposition – it is in obtaining the necessary information in the first place; it is in appreciating that there are interests in society which are not particularly keen that such categorisations should be made, because questions would inevitably be raised about positions of wealth, power and privilege. Thus, it is difficult, for example, to take inherited wealth and the advantages of certain physical resources into account as factors in children's development and later recruitment to the grade as well as kind of jobs held. Perhaps the single most important component of 'class' which social scientists need to address is income – or a wider definition of income to include wealth and resources in kind, including fringe benefits (Townsend, 1979, Chapter 6). There is evidence that when successively more comprehensive and exact definitions of income are applied to a survey population, correlations with ill-health and disability are markedly more significant (ibid., p. 1176).

The contemporary case for a fresh approach

The need for a theory of health has become increasingly recognised in recent years and this study illustrates that need. Dissatisfaction with the cohesion of health care policies has been expressed independently, by bodies appointed by the British Government and by the DHSS itself. To different observers the failure to reduce inequalities in health, and the evident failure both to define and apply clear priorities which at a time of scarce resources utilise them economically, have become better recognised both by those in administrative control of services and by those studying or using them. Internationally there has been evidence of increasing percentages of Gross National Product being swallowed up by health care expenditure without any evident correlation between expenditure and health (Abel-Smith, 1967; Simanis, 1973; Abel-Smith, 1979; OECD, 1985). There have been calls for a more wide-ranging and fundamental approach to research (Alma-Ata, 1978), and research centres and institutes have been set up to proselytise an interdisciplinary approach (see the review by Stacey, 1980; also, Centre for Health Studies, Yale University, 1977).

In Britain the Department of Health has become sensitive to criticisms of its understanding as well as its direction of policy. The House of Commons Social Services Committee (House of Commons, 1980, paras 23–24) put the point comprehensively in its Third Report in 1980:

> We would wish to emphasise, however, that the case for improving the Department's capacity to monitor the services for which it is accountable to Parliament does not rest solely on the need to assess the effects of expenditure changes on efficiency. The point has much wider implications. Our concern is to be able to assess the government's plans in terms of their effects on explicit policy aims. Our underlying question is:

> what is the NHS trying to do, and what is the relationship between expenditure plans and the government's policy objectives?

The Committee went on to deplore the lack of information about the likely effects of the Government's expenditure plans on its priorities and argues powerfully for a more effective system for both setting and monitoring priorities. In particular the Committee felt that inputs of resources explained little or nothing about the value of outputs of services to patients (House of Commons, 1980, paras 23–24). In a White Paper attemtping to answer the criticisms, the Department admitted that

> information on final outputs – the benefit accruing to the individual or the community as a result of services provided – is more difficult to come by: mortality and morbidity rates partially fill this role, but even with these the full extent of the causal link between input and output is uncertain (UK Government, 1980, p. 8).

This book – especially its three-fold representation of 'health' in terms of measures of delayed development as well as of mortality and disablement – is intended to make some contribution to meeting criticisms of this kind.

How are more effective policies to be developed? – or, in the language of both the DHSS and its recent critics, how is the causal link between 'input' and 'output' to be supplied? Recent overseas and UK sources can be quoted to illustrate what work might be done. When making the case for a multi-disciplinary centre to study health at Yale University the proponents stated:

This quotation provides a particularly powerful statement of support for a social model of health.

> By far the greatest proportion of resources devoted to recent research on ill-health by social, bio-medical, and public health scientists alike, has been allocated to the development of detection, diagnostic and curative techniques, the study of medical-care delivery, and the examination of preventive measures directed towards the alteration of individual behaviour (for example, Breslow and Wilner, 1977). While much research obviously remains to be done along these lines, there has been underestimation of both the social obstructions to health that lie beyond the competence of medicine alone to remedy, and the avenues to health open through social programmes far removed from medical care and from efforts to alter individual behaviour (Centre for Health Studies, Yale University, 1977, p. 2).

The group at Yale University went on to explain the alternative, or more comprehensive, approach. Because the kind of case made by the group is poorly understood and recognised, perhaps it deserves to be illustrated at some length. The connection between food and social institutions, for example, was carefully established.

> If dietary factors are implicated as proximate risks for colon cancer or for heart disease, they must be understood in combination with other social factors, for example, perhaps, a life-style requiring quick, high energy foods, the vulnerability of consumers to food advertising, the use of chemical feeds for market livestock, the use of chemical additives in foods,

> the availability of only certain types of foods in the market place, and the structure of the . . . food industry (ibid, p. 8).

All were clearly implicated not only in understanding cause, but also in developing policy . . .

In the United Kingdom, perhaps the best illustration of this approach is the Report of the Working Group in Inequalities in Health, under the chairmanship of Sir Douglas Black (frequently referred to as the Black Report). The Working Group devoted a chapter of its 1980 report to the need for addtional information and research for the development of better theory. This immediately followed its analysis of the causes of inequalities in health. The Working Group accepted that cultural and genetic factors played an important role but concluded that 'material deprivation' was the predominant factor in explaining inequalities. Too little, however, was known about its form and impact and the Working Group therefore proposed that there were two very important means of developing our knowledge. One was through the longitudinal approach, and the three longitudinal health surveys provide examples (1946, 1958 and 1970 cohorts – see for example Douglas, 1951; Douglas and Walker, 1966; Davie *et al.*, 1972; Colley *et al.*, 1973; Douglas and Gear, 1976; Wadsworth and Morris, 1978; Butler, 1977; Butler and Osborne, 1985). Another approach using the longitudinal method is provided by following up a small percentage of census data (see, for example, Fox and Leon, 1985).

The other means of developing knowledge recommended in the Black Report was

> the way in which economic, social and environmental variables interact within small geographical areas. Such a study would be limited to a small number of such areas, selected on the basis of social condition or health data. It would involve collection of detailed economic, social, environmental and occupational data, as well as data on the health, ill-health and mortality of the population. Such a study, we believe, would also permit far more detailed appreciation of the health effects of social and economic policies (without the need to assume the independence of such policies) than is possible from aggregate level data (Black Report, 1980, p. 223).

The Working Group also called for the development on indicators of area social conditions and health – especially for use in resource allocation, and for further research into health hazards in relation to occupational conditions and work. These lend themselves to research in small areas and might be said to reinforce the case for choosing to undertake a study of the interation of social factors implicated in ill-health. In particular, the Working Group called for further work to be undertaken into the use of occupational class as an indicator: it called both for the development of a composite indicator of family class (amalgamating the occupations of husband, wife and their respective fathers) and research to distinguish the direct and indirect association between occupation and health. Too little was known about the conditions and amenities of work, as distinct from the specific

This is a practical example of the more sophisticated understanding of class called for earlier in this extract.

hazards of certain industrial conditions (for a detailed review of one aspect of the relationship between occupations and health, see Harrington, 1978).

What are the administrative and political implications of adopting a social model of health? Trained personnel would continue to work within the traditional practices of medicine but more of them would begin to work on prevention, the early stages of disease, and recovery and rehabilitation. More emphasis would necessarily be given to relief from pain, discomfort, stress and boredom, but also to education for health and participation in local and national measures to deal with common family and community problems and promote new modes of organisation. A 'health' policy would represent a version of existing housing, environmental health, safety at work, anti-pollution and public protection services in which priorities were more clearly established. Health personnel would work in a greater variety of social contexts. At the present time neither local nor national policies constitute concerted strategies which are related to operational information about the health of the population and which seek to co-ordinate the work of different administrative departments. Whether that can be achieved will depend on the capacity of the social and medical sciences to provide a social model of health to transform the nature of health care much as Newton and his successors transformed the nature of physics in the eighteenth century.

Rob Mears: Debates about Health Inequalities

Rob Mears' analysis of health inequalities, brings specialist expertise to an area of growing interest to sociology students.

Mears begins with a useful review of the health and welfare reforms of the Beveridge era and observes that in health, as in other areas, these reforms did not noticeably decrease inequalities between social groups (although they did provide vital protection for the needy). Perhaps, this is not surprising in view of debate both about what precisely health equality might mean in practice and whether, in any case, it is a feasible goal of the welfare state. The Black Report published in the early 1980s suggested a shift in policy to improving social and economic conditions to achieve greater health equality rather than relying mainly on health and welfare reform. However, the Conservative administrations preferred more individualistic explanations and solutions to health issues, and the Black Report was shelved.

In his conclusion, Robert Mears argues that social structural and individual approaches to health issues are not necessarily incompatible. However, if this indicates a possible new approach to health policy, there remains much work to be done on the issue of effective implementation.

Reading 62 Rob Mears, 'Debates about Health Inequalities'

Introduction

A starting point for a specifically sociological interest in the welfare of populations is the recognition that health and illness are not randomly distributed. Both official statistics on disease and death and the work of epidemiologists have revealed the systematic ways in which life expectancy and the risks of disease or disability are associated with social class.

The existence of a link between social position and life expectancy is long established and official statistics continue to show a close relationship between social class, measured by occupation, and health status, measured by life expectancy. What is not so easily established is the precise nature of the causal relationship, its meaning and what policy implications flow from demonstrating an association between class and health. Although there are problems in arriving at a definition of 'health' that goes beyond life expectancy, and problems with measuring 'health', there is a broad consensus that, whatever measures or indicators are used, there exist significant inequalities between social classes. Whether these differences are getting wider or remaining relatively stable over time is a source of considerable controversy, as is the vexed question of what, if anything, ought to be done about health inequalities.

Health and welfare reforms in the UK

In Britain in the 1940s the Beveridge Report identified the five great evils that were to be tackled by the post Second World War Welfare State: want, ignorance, idleness, squalor and disease. Publicly funded health and welfare provision would ensure basic minimum living standards and these would start to tackle the 'great evils' by providing pensions and benefits, free education, full employment, public housing and free comprehensive health care.

The optimism of the early years of the Welfare State was such that there was a widespread belief that the costs of the Health Service would gradually decrease. The hoped-for eradication of ignorance, poverty and urban squalor would lead to a mopping up of the pool of disease and the demand for health services would diminish. Within a few years it was realised that such optimistic visions were unrealistic. Far from decreasing, the demand for medical care continued to grow, and this is a feature of health care systems in all advanced societies regardless of particular funding mechanisms.

The introduction of the NHS in 1948 was seen by many as the answer to health inequalities between social classes. It was believed that free comprehensive health care, covering preventive as well as curative services, would enormously benefit the lower classes. A National Health Service funded from taxation, free at the point of delivery, covering all stages of the life cycle and all conditions would put an end to the financial obstacles that stood in the way of the poor receiving expert medical attention. By removing the financial burden the poorer classes would have access to the best services without fear of the financial consequences. Given this wider access to the 'best that money can buy' it is easy to understand why there were optimistic expectations about improving life expectancy and health for all.

Also, because 'free' health care was part of a welfare package that included child health screening, free education, old age pensions, unemployment and sickness pay and other benefits, it was assumed that the long term redistributive impact of the Welfare State would reduce differences between social classes and this would be reflected in reduced inequalities of life expectancy and health status. In other words, one of the aims of the newly created health and welfare system was to reduce inequalities, and as such the Welfare State had a specifically redistributive intent. Although there was no assumption that the Welfare State would create equality, it was widely assumed that some kind of redistribution from the rich to the poor was to be achieved through taxation and public spending. Because of these assumptions there was a widespread expectation that social class differences in life expectancy would diminish. However, contrary to expectations, it became evident in many countries that differences between social groups have in fact been increasing since the 1930s.

What does equality of health mean?

Social scientific analysis of health usually involves a distinction between inputs (e.g. expenditure on buildings, personnel, services etc.) outputs (e.g. number of consultations, operations, prescriptions etc.) and outcomes (e.g. length and quality of life). Although more doctors may mean more people treated, there is no straightforward assumption that more resources devoted to health services necessarily buys better health. Inevitably social scientists have asked sceptical questions about the rather tenuous link between what is invested in health services and the state of public health. If the aim is to equalise outcomes by reducing, say, the inequalities in death rates, this will almost certainly mean the pursuit of social and economic policies that are well outside the scope of health services.

Even within the health service, the equality of input has several different meanings. Firstly, there is equality of care, based on the assumption that all who suffer from the same condition should get roughly similar treatment. The only criterion which should influence decisions about treatment is medical need. As a result all should receive similar quality of care from their doctors, nurses and other health professionals. Needless to say, this is very difficult to measure and creates the greatest potential controversy, especially if it is suggested that health professionals may actually treat people differently depending on their social class.

There is also a geographic dimension to equality. This focuses on the spatial distribution of doctors, hospital beds, specialist services etc, to ensure some rough degree of fairness between regions and localities. In 1948 there was an explicit commitment to iron out the geographical inequalities in the distribution of medical services at the inception of the NHS. Evidence of marked regional differences in health spending led to the 1976 report of the Resource Allocation Working Party (RAWP) The Working Party devised a formula for calculating the distribution of resources to each region of Britain. As a result there has been a gradual and continuing shift in resources away from the relatively well provided areas to the relatively underfunded regions.

Linked to the geographical distribution of resources is the issue of access to health services. One aim of equality might be that the distribution of services should not disadvantage particular groups. For example, car ownership, access to public transport, private telephones, paid time off work, etc will all have some impact on the costs to individuals of seeing the doctor. Even if equality to access could be guaranteed it would not necessarily lead to equal utilisation. Whether or not a particular service is used will depend partly on expectations, attitudes and beliefs about health, illness and the medical profession. Researchers have interpreted access and utilisation data to argue both for and against the claim that middle class people make more effective use of the health service. This raises the whole question of the extent to which the health and welfare services benefit particular social groups or classes at the expense of others.

The debate about redistribution

The idea that the British Welfare State would have a redistributive impact in favour of poorer people has certainly been questioned. Richard Titmuss was an early sceptic and recent work by others has tended to confirm the view that far from benefitting the poorer sections of the population, state welfare spending has tended to benefit members of the middle class. As both consumers of welfare services and as suppliers of professional services, the middle classes have been net beneficiaries of any 'redistribution'. Only expenditure on council housing favours the poor while State spending on all post 16 education, mortgage subsidies, and the health service represents a shift of resources in the direction of the better off (Goodin & Le Grand).

Not only does welfare spending give middle class people access to health care, education, housing, transport and so on, it also benefits them as providers. Employment as professionals and administrators within the health, welfare and education sectors is a major source of job opportunities for the middle class and their children. As public sector employment has grown it is the middle classes who benefitted from the creation of skilled and relatively highly paid employment. Even though it may fly in the face of 'common sense', it appears that any redistribution brought about by the Welfare State has tended to advantage the middle class.

A considerable body of research has gone into debating whether or not manual workers benefit from the NHS relative to non-manual workers. Some of this research has suggested that access to and utilisation of health services is skewed in favour of non-manual workers and their families. This covers a wide range of things from the geographic distribution of health centres to the amount of time the GP devotes to consultation with patients from different social classes. The social class gradient in terms of taking advantage of preventive services is particularly marked.

At a more detailed level, sociological research has shown that middle class patients were more likely to be known to their GP and that on average middle class patients had longer consultations and elicit more information from their doctors. It seems reasonable to speculate that educated, middle class people, armed with information about their condition and about the range of treatments or services on offer may well be able to get more favourable treatment.

Some research suggests that there is 'underutilisation' of the health service by the poorest sections of the population. Julian Tudor Hart has described the operation of an 'inverse care law' for health in which those who need health care most receive least. The 'inverse care law' stands as an indictment of the NHS because its founding principles stressed equality as one of its main aims.

Evidence of health inequalities

Towards the end of the 1974–1979 Labour Government the Secretary of State for Health established a Working Party under the Chairmanship of Sir Douglas Black, President of the Royal College of Physicians, to examine patterns of health inequalities. One of the aims of the Working Party was to establish the extent to which differentials based on social class were being narrowed or were becoming more pronounced.

The main finding of the 'Black Report' was that, "despite more than thirty years of a National Health Service expressly committed to offering equal care for all, there remains a marked class gradient in standards of health." (Townsend & Davidson p. 15). The Working Party discovered that whilst life expectancy has improved for all social groups since the end of the Second World War, the differences between social classes, as measured by the Registrar Generals classification of occupations, have been preserved and in some cases widened. The Report comments, "The lack of improvement, and in some respects deterioration of the health experience of the unskilled and semi-skilled manual classes (Classes V and VI), relative to Class I, throughout the 1960s and early 1970s is striking. Despite the decline in the rate of infant mortality – in each class, the difference between the lowest class (IV and V combined) and the highest (I and II combined) actually increased between 1959–63 and 1970–72". (p. 206).

The Report claimed that death rates for both women and men before retirement are two and a half times as great in social class V as in social class I. These striking differences in death rates can be seen across the age range – at birth, childhood, and middle age. For almost all causes of death – infectious and parasitic diseases, cancers, heart and vascular diseases, congenital abnormalities through to accidents, poisonings and violence, there are twice as many deaths of children in social class V than in social class I.

According to a recent review of the data, even the 'diseases of affluence' have disproportionately affected non-manual men:

> The new epidemics have not affected all sections of society equally. Proportionately, more early deaths have occurred . . . among unskilled than professional workers. Young men, aged 25–44, in unskilled occupations have four times the risk of dying from lung cancer, stomach cancer, ischaemic heart disease and stroke than young men in professional occupations. For accidents, the relative risk is threefold. In

> childhood an overall relative risk of three for accidents and violence conceals differences of tenfold or more for deaths from falls, fires and drowning. (Power *et al*, p. 1)

Debates about health inequalities have tended to focus on life expectancy (mortality data), although the occupational class gradient is just as marked in the case of morbidity. However, morbidity data are more difficult to analyse as they are open to all the problems of interpretation, emphasis and meaning to which sociologists subject all official statistics. Can we assume that GP consultations tell us very much about the distribution or frequency of illness, or that hospital discharge figures tell us much about 'cure'? Nevertheless, sociologists can make use of such statistics, as well as data generated by the General Household Survey and reports of service use provided by the Department of Health. Evidence about life expectancy is being supplemented by more research interest in assessing the quality of life. Consequently, there is more interest in trying to devise useful measures of sickness and health, disability and handicap. For the first time the 1991 Census asked about chronic illness in an attempt to assess the extent of handicap and disability in the country. Once we move away from relatively objective measures, such as GP visits or hospital admissions, to more subjective self-assessment of health, it is important to understand what different people mean when they make judgements about their health.

Defining 'health'

Health can have a range of different meanings for individuals, and age, social class, gender, ethnicity, sub-culture and family beliefs will all play a part in shaping individual evaluations of what it means to be 'healthy'. Sociological research has been influential in alerting health professionals to the fact that they cannot assume shared meanings and assumptions between themselves and the people they care for, or that there is one unified set of beliefs and values about what it means to be healthy or ill.

Social class differences are evident from people's judgements of their own health. For example, in a study of the health beliefs and practices of a sample of lower working class women, Blaxter shows how a chronic health record did not prevent many women from describing their health as 'good'. Even when they suffered from chronic bronchitis, varicose veins, asthma and other serious and persistent complaints, the women did not think of themselves as 'ill'. The norms of what constituted 'good health' were conspicuously low compared to the expectations and standards of women in other social classes. For the women in this study, to be 'unhealthy' meant that you were in hospital or completely unable to carry on with normal tasks and responsibilities such as housework. They regarded many of their conditions as inevitable and probably untreatable. There were frequent references to the fact that certain conditions were to be expected at their age. The evidence of an 'accelerated' – life pattern, early marriage, early motherhood, early grandmotherhood, early widowhood – led to an acceptance of deteriorating conditions as an inevitable part of the ageing process. One woman of forty seven defined herself as 'healthy', yet she suffered from a painful and swollen leg and arthritis. Another of the same age attributed regular bouts of dizziness to advancing years. These women described themselves as 'healthy' as long as the problems they encountered were seen as 'normal for people like us'.

This example highlights the significance of subjective evaluations of health. The structure and pattern of our lives can shape our beliefs about normal health which in turn plays a part in determining what we do about it. The most common response to feeling ill is to buy medicines over the counter from chemist shops or maybe from 'alternative' therapists. Community health surveys have revealed the extent of much 'unofficial' sickness. Only when we make use of the formal health care system do we become part of the official morbidity data which sociologists draw on to make sense of the relationship between health and class.

Explanations of health inequalities

After reviewing the available evidence, the Black Report outlined four different explanations for health inequalities between social classes. One explanation, that the Report dismisses, is the claim that class differences are not real but are an artefact of the way data are interpreted. The changing size and composition of social classes make comparison over time invalid. The gap between Social Class I and V may be widening, but the unskilled manual working class is shrinking as a proportion of the whole population. The gap between classes has been offset by the fall in the relative size of the poorest classes. Consequently, the data tends to exaggerate the extent of inequalities and play down improvements in the health of the whole population.

Another approach to the issue of social class inequalities in health is described as natural and social selection. The Black Report, rather confusingly, conflates the Darwinian notion of genetic or biological inheritance with the process of social selection. Inequalities, it is claimed, might reflect genetic inheritance and the causal link is reversed – it is not class that determines health but social position is a consequence of biological inheritance. Social selection refers to the likelihood that those in better health are more able to climb the social ladder while the least healthy drift downwards. Furthermore, the advantages are reinforced over time because healthier individuals tend to choose each other as partners.

Of more interest to sociologists were those explanations which focused on the circumstances and way of life of different social groups. Cultural/behavioural explanations emphasise the part played by individual behaviour and their cultures in accounting for health and life expectancy. Such explanations focus on individual behaviour, and the choices, consumption patterns and lifestyles adopted by people, and the ways in which these are reinforced and reproduced in particular groups or sub-cultures. Those who choose 'unhealthy' lifestyles are presumed to be ignorant of the consequences of their actions and are the obvious targets for health education campaigns. If they persist in their pathological behaviour they have no one to blame but themselves. Tobacco consumption is an obvious example here.

While acknowledging the importance of 'unhealthy lifestyles', the Black Report favoured a materialist perspective on health inequalities. This emphasises the part played by economic and socio-structural forces in the reproduction of good or poor health. Such explanations focus almost exclusively on wealth distribution, working conditions, the quality of housing, the adequacy of income and the effects of poverty. Just as the 1960s witnessed the "rediscovery" of poverty by academics, so social scientists seemed to be rediscovering the link between poverty and disease that had so concerned nineteenth century reformers.

As a result of this preference for materialist explanations, the Black Report concentrated on recommendations for social reform, and in particular the need to redistribute real disposable income to those groups who have the poorest health.What the Report called the "Wider Strategy' can be summed up thus: "While the health care services can play a significant part in reducing inequalities in health, measures to reduce differences in material standards of living at work, in the home and in everyday social and community life are of even greater importance . . . we have in mind . . . a marked relative improvement in the living standards of the poorest people" (p. 173).

The Report argued for a comprehensive anti-poverty strategy with particular emphasis on policies directed at families with young children incorporating improved nutrition, pre-school education, day care etc. The recommendations for improved working conditions, more spending on housing and more adequate disability allowances, flow from the priority they accorded to structural or material factors. Most of the academic and political debate has concentrated not on the policy recommendations but on the competing explanations of health inequalities.

Responses to the Black Report

The initial response of the Department of Health was to ignore the Report and to make its contents the subject of as little public comment as possible. After a year of political controversy it was eventually published in 1982. In a foreword to the Report the Conservative Minister made clear that, against a background of Government attempts to reduce public expenditure there was no question of the recommendations of the Report being implemented.

What was controversial about the Report was its claim that the health gap between the higher and lower occupational groupings, far from getting narrower, was actually getting wider. In the academic world the Black Report triggered off an intense and lively debate centring largely around the competing explanations, the interpretation of mortality data and the extent to which the policy recommendations could be linked to the analysis (see Carr-Hill). Some argued against the Report's findings claiming that "A preliminary analysis of changes in specific disease categories shows that those which contributed most to mortality among the poor (infectious and respiratory diseases) have sharply declined in importance, suggesting that there may have been a decline in health inequality between poor and rich." (Illsley and Le Grand cited in D. Green Ed.)

Furthermore, the Black Report was criticised for its assertion that materialist or structuralist explanations explained health inequalities and that rival explanations could be brushed aside. Some commentators also argued that the policy recommendations advanced in the Black Report did not necessarily flow from their analysis. Scriven argued that "It is not clear from the report that the assumptions upon which they based their recommendations were based upon any evidence . . . Social class is at best an ambiguous measure . . . Until the causal relationships are better understood any interventions which have the goal of improving health will be mere 'shots in the dark'." (Scriven, p. 247). The reliance on Registrar General's classification of occupations led others to claim that the term 'social class' disguised as much as it revealed. "As the Black Report pointed out (only subsequently to ignore its own reservations), there are serious problems about social class as a tool of analysis: problems which range from the classification of married women under their husband's occupation to the fact that there can be wide variations in resources relevant to health (housing, education, income) within any social class." (Klein, p. 10).

The appeal of individualistic explanations

Materialist or structural explanations go against 'common-sense' understanding because most people in our culture tend to think of life chances in terms of *individual* decisions and freely chosen lifestyles. As Hurd comments,

Hurd's argument closely parallels that of Hulley and Clarke presented in the second part of Reading 65.

> In Western Industrial societies the ethic of individualism has led to a concentration on the position and activities of the individual and to individualistic explanations. People have not perceived the regularities in the patterns of social behaviour but only the individual differences . . . in this respect . . . a sociological way of thinking is not the normal way of thinking in our society. On the contrary most people think individualistically. The emphasis upon an individual's responsibility for his or her actions is elevated into an explanation of social phenomena . . . it is one of the main claims of sociology that these social phenomena cannot be explained in individualistic terms, but only by recognizing the impersonal forces which are brought into play when large numbers of men and women interact with each other. (p. 6)

In the case of health inequalities it is easy to see the political appeal of individualist explanations. Not only do they divert attention away from social trends in the distribution of health *and* wealth, they can also contribute to a climate in which the 'victims' are to blame for their own plight. This approach is attractive to some powerful groups because it locates the origin of ill health in individual behaviour and as such is useful in diverting attention away from the structural threats to health such as long term unemployment, poor housing, poverty etc. Politically it may be preferable to concentrate instead on blaming people for their ignorance, self-indulgence or fecklessness. This approach also appeals to some health educators because it perpetuates the assumption that many aspects of health and illness are within the control of individuals if only they would heed the correct messages.

Individual/cultural explanations are not only part of commonsense thinking, they are also consistent with the dominant modes of analysis in medicine. Health professionals have a limited exposure to sociological theories and concepts. The emphasis in medical and traditional nurse training on individual pathology and the individual professional/patient relationship tends to reinforce a belief in the individual as the prime unit of analysis. Biomedicine with its focus on individual pathology, reinforces such an approach.

An important tradition in sociology is the emphasis on the constraints which limit people's lives. Even a decision about whether or not to smoke tobacco is tied up with locations in the social system. From Durkheim onwards sociologists have been trying to understand how different social structures produce different forms of personal behaviour. Apparently 'individual' decisions about consumption patterns are rooted in social structure, "Decisions to smoke or not to smoke, to drink excessively, sensibly or not at all, are undoubtedly at one level purely individual decisions. But it is a very long time since Durkheim argued that even that most individual of acts, suicide, was socially structured." (Bechofer, p. 14).

Competing approaches to understanding the causes of ill health are clear in the following extracts. The first comes from Government pronouncements on the desirability of disease prevention. The clear message is that responsibility for good or poor health lies with the individual.

> Much of the responsibility for ensuring his (*sic*) own good health lies with the individual. We can all influence others by our own actions. In particular parents can set their children a good example of healthy living. We can all help to influence the communities in which we live and work as much by our example as by our efforts . . . Much ill-health in Britain today arises from over-indulgence and unwise behaviour. Not surprisingly, the greatest potential and perhaps the greatest problem for preventive medicine now lies in changing behaviour and attitudes of health. The individual can do much to help himself, his family and the community by accepting more personal responsibility for his own health and well-being. (*Prevention and Health* HMSO 1977, p. 39)

In contrast, Nicky Hart argued that the most effective measures to prevent ill-health in contemporary society would probably not involve medical expertise at all and would not involve exhortations to individuals to change their lives. She argued that most doctors would agree that their actions have a relatively limited impact on the health of people. Instead she advocates

See also Reading 64.

> . . . measures such as the following: re-routing of heavy traffic away from the most densely populated residential areas, which also happen to be working class neighbourhoods; free milk and high quality food at school; more aggressive legislation to prevent industrial accidents and diseases; a

> complete ban on smoking in public places; greater stability of employment and income in the economy; the removal of economic sanctions for sickness amongst manual workers and so on. Together such measures would represent an attack on the structure of inequality in Britain. (Illsley).

This argument is part of an emerging conventional wisdom that investment in medical services may have very little impact on the health of populations. The determinants of good health, particularly in the early years may well be quality of accommodation, heat, space, range and quality of food, quality of parenting, leisure and access to and utilisation of preventive measures.

Conclusions

The debate about the origins of health inequalities has tended to polarise. There are those who favour materialistic explanations, which leads them to focus on the need for structural change, and those who prefer cultural explanations, which leads them to concentrate on changing individual behaviour. What is the way out of this dilemma? Maybe it is mistaken to assume that a choice must be made between these alternatives. The problem lies partly in the terminology and concepts used by the protagonists. A false dichotomy is erected by counterposing 'structure' and 'culture'. Lessons can be learnt from similar debates in the sociology of education about the explanations for educational 'underachievement'. These also tended to polarise into those who concentrated on material inequalities and those who focused on the values and beliefs of middle and working class homes and sub-cultures. Some of the best sociological work transcends this distinction between individual and structure, and material versus cultural explanations, to show how they are interdependent.

Ultimately decisions about how to respond to data on health inequalities depends on ideological, moral and political allegiances. Explanations at the level of the 'individual' or 'society' are not necessarily mutually exclusive. Similarly, advocating policy initiatives at the level of the 'individual' does not preclude action at a structural level. For example, Government Ministers may lecture the elderly about the benefits of wearing woolly hats indoors as a preventive measure against hypothermia in the winter. However, advice of this sort is not necessarily an alternative to providing more generous state retirement pensions or subsidising fuel costs.

As we all live longer social scientists are asking questions about the "quality of life", as well as its quantity. For example, there is more interest in measuring the quality of care and degrees of handicap or mobility among people with chronic conditions. Such information draws attention to the distribution of welfare services, the adequacy of income maintenace for the sick and the elderly, problems of access and mobility. All of these raise issues of resource distribution between particular groups and classes. Sociologists may not be able to resolve any of these debates but research can highlight the consequences, intended and unintended, of particular policy options.

The political Left and Right opt for explanations that are more likely to accord with their views on the benefits or disadvantages of public spending and redistributive health and welfare policies. For the political Right the issue is of opposition to publicly funded health and welfare on the grounds of inefficiency and inequity as well as the acceptance of inequality as inevitable and 'fair'. If the operation of the free market has consequences that are undesirable then these are justifiable and they should not be ameliorated by social policy, especially if this entails public spending.

Others argue that intervention must be based on a careful appraisal of its likely impact. They claim that the underlying causal mechanisms of health and illness must be properly understood to ensure that any intervention would have the desired outcome. There are very complex interrelationships between economic circumstances, behaviour, genetic inheritance, health service use and individual health. It is certainly not self evident where in this cycle the most effective intervention might be made. Blane argues that "there is no easy answer to changing inequalities in health, which have complex, multi-causal explanations, rooted in the general nature, conditions and styles of living of the different social classes." Nevertheless he goes on to argue that a reduction in health inequalities "depends on major social changes both in work and outside work, as well as clearly organized and concerted efforts by central government and individual citizens to attack directly the sources of inequality." (Blane, p. 123).

In conclusion, social scientists are interested in the pattern of health inequalities for several reasons. From the perspective of applied social science, policy makers and planners need to know about trends in public health in order to distribute resources and target particular groups or services. It is also important to understand trends in health status in order to anticipate demand so that social science can contribute to the effective planning of services for the future. Because health services are part of a wider Welfare State, the gap between the health of different social groups is an important indicator of the effectiveness of welfare services and a way of measuring the achievements of the Welfare State.

Sociologists are interested in the general pattern of inequalities in society. When Weber described the distribution of "life chances" between social classes he could not have been thinking quite so literally about life expectancy. An average difference of 7 years in life expectancy between men in social classes I and V represents a powerful and telling illustration of the extent of inequalities. Consequently, understanding the trends in life expectancy between social classes is one crucial way of knowing whether and to what extent we are moving in the direction of a 'classless society'.

References

Bechofer, F., 'Individuals Politics and Society: A Dilemma for Public Health Research' in Claudia Martin and David McQueen, *ed.s, Readings for a New Public Health* (Edinburgh University Press, 1989).

Blane, D., 'Inequality and social class' in Donald L. Patrick and Graham Scambler, *ed.s, Sociology as Applied to Medicine* (Bailliere Tindall, 1982).

Blaxter, M. and Patterson, E., *Mothers and Daughters: a Three Generational Study of Health Attitudes and Behaviour* (Heineman Educational Books, 1982).

Goodin, R. E., and Le Grand, J., *Not Only the Poor: The Middle Classes and the Welfare State* (Allen and Unwin, 1987).

Hurd, G., *ed., Human Societies* (Routledge, 1974).

Illsley, R., *Professional or Public Health* (Kings Fund, 1980).

Klein, R., 'Acceptable Inequalities' in D. Green, *ed., Acceptable Inequalities* (IEA London, 1988).

Power, C., Manor, O., and Fox, J., *Health and Class: The Early Years* (Chapman and Hall, 1991).

Scriven, E., 'Comments on Inequalities in Health: The Report of a Research Working Group' *Political Quarterly,* Vol. 1, Part 2 (1981).

Townsend, P. and Davidson, N., *Inequalities in Health* (Pelican, 1982).

Agnes Miles: Gender and Treatment, and Patients' Views of Doctors

This extract summarises research on the doctor–patient relationship from the perspective of gender. It does this from the points of view of both doctor and patient. First, do doctors tend to treat females and males differently? The answer here is more complex than might be expected, and Miles's summary of the research needs to be picked through carefully. There is some evidence that – for the same medical complaint – females are more likely than males to be diagnosed as psychosomatic or as influenced by emotional factors. On the matter of prescription patterns, there is evidence that women are more likely to be prescribed tranquillisers and to stay on them for longer than men. On the other hand, the view that these patterns can be explained by crude stereotyping is, at least, complicated by Verbrugge and Sterner's evidence showing that women receive more medical care than men.

Two significant points which emerge from the second part of the extract – patients' views of doctors – are worth highlighting. First, it is the high prestige in which the medical profession is still held that tends to incline some patients towards a favourable view of how doctors are treating them. They assume they are 'getting the best' (perhaps even when they are not). Second, patients' judgements of the quality of their treatment seems to be positively affected to the extent that they have a personal relationship with their doctor built up over time. The gender dimension of the discussion is maintained in the second section.

Reading 63 From Agnes Miles, *Women, Health and Medicine* (Open University Press, 1991), pp. 158–64

Do doctors treat female and male patients differently?

As discussed, doctors, of both sexes, employ their personal values and views of the world in categorizing their patients and the question arises as to whether systematic differences are to be found in doctors' methods of treating patients, according to the gender thereof. Treatment for the psychological problems of female patients has been much debated, the argument going that doctors are inclined to regard a variety of complaints made by women as emotional or psychological in origin, not to be taken too seriously, while similar complaints from men are given greater weight and are more thoroughly investigated. Central to this argument is the stereotypical view, widely held in Western society, of women as weak and unstable, given to complaining and exaggerating their discomforts. This view is prevalent among men and accepted by many women and it would be surprising if doctors (mostly male) did not share the views of the society of which they are a part (Leeson and Gray, 1978). If doctors think that women patients tend to maximize their discomfort and complain unduly, they may dismiss their problems lightly, thus providing inferior medical care.

This issue is contentious and difficult to resolve, partly because the evidence is contradictory and partly because the implications are unclear. In an influential study, Lennane and Lennane (1973), noted that doctors systematically dismissed or minimized certain female complaints. They were able to show that when women complained of severe pains during menstruation, of nausea and other symptoms in pregnancy and of unusually severe pain in childbirth, doctors often attributed these complaints to emotional or 'psychogenic' causes in the women concerned. The researchers argued that in spite of strong evidence of an organic basis of the complaints, the doctors regarded the women as having psychological problems and overstating the pain. The Lennanes were of the opinion that this treatment indicated a deeply rooted sex bias on the part of the doctors, who did not take women's pains seriously, and did not adequately investigate their causes.

Differential treatment given to male and female patients for similar complaints was noted by Bernstein and Kane (1981). They studied the attitudes of physicians towards female and male patients by using simulated cases (vignettes of patients' complaints and ways of presenting their problems to the doctor). The results showed that doctors responded differently to female and male patients, as depicted, some 25 per cent thinking that women were likely to make excessive demands on the time of physicians. Women's complaints were judged more likely to be influenced by emotional factors and were identified as psychosomatic more frequently than were men's complaints of a similar nature. Bernstein and Kane detected no difference as between male and female doctors, but very few of the doctors were female (225 male, and 28 female, doctors participated in the study).

Not only this study, and some others based on simulated cases, but some of those in which researchers were able to record real consultations, confirmed the case for differential treatment. Thus, Wallen *et al.* (1979) tape-recorded 336 consultations between U.S. male doctors and their patients, their analysis showing that these doctors were more likely to attribute psychological causes to the illnesses of female than of male patients, and so were more pessimistic in their prognoses: they regarded female patients as emotionally unstable and difficult to treat. Armitage *et al.* (1979) found that U.S. male patients received more services for comparable conditions.

The above-quoted researchers put one side of the argument, but other evidence suggests that the reality is more complex. Also using the simulation technique, McCranie *et al.* (1978) observed no gender bias. These researchers presented doctors with vignettes of patients complaining of chronic headaches or chronic abdominal pain, accompanied by some usual additional symptoms (these cases being selected because they could be indicative of either psychological or organic illness) and asked the doctors how they would handle these problems. The results of this study showed that while the doctors predominantly favoured organic explanations in making their initial diagnoses, they were not more inclined to diagnose women's symptoms as indicating psychological illness than they were those of men.

More influential have been the studies carried out by Lois Verbrugge and her colleagues who examined data from the National Ambulatory Medical Care Survey in the United States. They selected a number of common complaints (e.g. chest pain, back pain, headache, fatigue, dizziness) and studied the medical responses to patients who consulted doctors for these complaints (Verbrugge and Steiner, 1981). Their analysis revealed a systematic, but somewhat unexpected, difference in doctors' treatment of male and female patients: in about 30–40 per cent of the services and dispositions studied, gender differences occurred showing that women received more medical care. They noted that gender differences persisted even when patients' age, seriousness of problem and diagnosis were controlled. Women received more extensive services – more laboratory tests, blood-pressure checks, prescriptions and return appointments.

This finding tends to pose problems for any simplistic judgement that doctors tend to stereotype women in the medical context – as the following discussion indicates.

Not only are research results rather contradictory, but the interpretations that may be placed on gender-based differences in treatment are unclear. The core of the difficulty is that receiving increased medical attention may be seen as an advantage or as a disadvantage. On the one hand, it can be argued that it is in the patient's interest to receive a thorough medical investigation of problems, because such will lead to a better chance of treatment and cure, while dismissing complaints and neglecting to investigate them may well bring more pain and worse problems. On the other hand, more medical care for patients can be seen adversely: lives of patients may be 'over-medicalized', laboratory investigations may serve the doctors' interests as much, if not more, than those of the patients, and medical technology can be over-employed. Moreover, the use of medical intervention and technology is more easily effected on powerless, compliant sections of society such as female patients, and it has been suggested that intervention may be used as a form of punishment for complaining women.

Both interpretations have been put forward. Thus Lois Verbrugge argued that more tests and treatments are used on women who are easily intimidated and are seen as unduly complaining, while Armitage argued that doctors provide more treatment and care for men because they take their complaints more seriously and regard their return to work as more important.

It is also possible that the gender of the patient triggers a response in the doctor which results in a particular method of treatment. In this respect, differences in the prescribing of tranquillizers for women and for men has received much attention. It is certainly the case that female patients receive more prescriptions for tranquillizers than do male patients, but interpreting the prescribing habits of doctors is notoriously difficult. Ruth Copperstock and colleagues (1978, 1979) studied sex differences in the use of psychotropic drugs in Ontario, Canada. Her studies were based on computerized records of a prescription agency of prescriptions dispensed during certain time periods. She found that a consistently higher proportion of women than men received tranquillizers and that women went on using them for longer periods than did men. Cooperstock argued that this pattern was connected with doctors' differential perceptions of women and men, i.e. because women are expected to present them with many emotional and 'ill-defined' symptoms doctors prescribe tranquillizers for them more readily and without much thought as to alternatives.

Other studies showed similar patterns, for example, that amongst elderly institutionalized patients, women were given more tranquillizers than the men, even when symptoms were controlled (Milliren, 1977).

Patients' views of doctors

How do people in general, and women in particular, view the medical services? What are their attitudes to, and how satisfied are they with, the services they receive? These questions can be asked at different levels of abstraction. First, at a general level, views about medicine as an institution, about the medical profession and about the organization and delivery of medical services, can be ascertained. Second, levels of satisfaction with particular kinds of doctors (e.g. gynaecologists, GPs, hospital consultants) can be explored; and third, at a much more specific level, patients' views concerning individual medical practitioners, particular consultations and episodes of treatment, can be collected. Researchers variously have attempted to collect information on these issues, general and specific, which are interrelated, general attitudes to the institutions of medicine influencing specific views on doctors and consultations, and personal experience with individual doctors in turn colouring attitudes to the medical profession and to medical care.

Studies tend to find that at a general level, people have a great regard for Western medicine and medical practitioners. There is an inherent and strong belief in the achievements and accuracy of medicine and considerable deference is accorded to doctors. Even when asked about particular services, such as child health or primary care, the most frequent findings are of general satisfaction from the majority of those asked. It is only when considering relationships with individual doctors, and particular consultations or illness episodes, that criticisms and dissatisfaction emerge.

It has been argued that belief in Western biomedicine has weakened as a result of the publicity concerning medical disasters such as thalidomide, and about the side effects and harmfulness of drugs which previously promised safe solutions to problems (e.g. the contraceptive pill and tranquillizers). Certainly there are indications that drug solutions to problems are becoming less popular, that 'natural' remedies are more sought after, and that 'alternative' medicine has gained ground in recent years. However, it is likely that so far only a minority of, mainly middle-class, people have turned away from traditional medicine and then only in areas where medical knowledge has manifestly failed to provide a solution. Otherwise mainstream thinking continues to adhere as strongly as ever to traditional medicine.

Collecting information about patients' satisfaction with medical services and medical practitioners is beset with methodological problems. Ann Cartwright and her colleagues conducted two interview surveys in England & Wales and found that the majority of people said that they were 'satisfied', or 'very satisfied' with their general practitioners – 91 per cent in the second survey (Cartwright, 1967; Cartwright and Anderson, 1981). Indeed, when people were asked if there were qualities which they thought general practitioners should have, but their doctors had not, three-quarters of the sample could not think of anything to say. It may well be, though, that people who are asked such questions may not have thought about the issues, or may not like to appear critical of doctors. They may have been conditioned to accept medical services in an uncritical spirit and this may well be true of those respondents who habitually feel themselves powerless on encountering the dominance of the medical profession.

Unlike findings in large surveys, small-scale studies which explore patients' views in greater depth, in concrete situations, tend to find a great deal of dissatisfaction with medical services and with individual doctors, and find also that patients are able to say a great deal concerning their reasons for dissatisfaction (Stimson and Webb, 1975; Cornwell, 1984). Moreover, studies exploring the range of patients' feelings about their doctors, report that such feelings fluctuate according to particular experiences and encounters. Ongoing relationships with doctors are seldom straightforward; a person may like some things about a doctor and dislike others and this complexity of likes and dislikes rarely constitutes an end product which can be called 'satisfaction' or 'dissatisfaction'.

Past researchers did not always systematically distinguish between female and male patients' responses to doctors and although it is likely that responses of both are complex there may well be gender differences. However, their feelings about doctors may well be more important to women, most of whom meet doctors more frequently during their lifetime than do men and who more often consult doctors with emotional problems. It is easier to establish patterns of satisfaction and reasons for fluctuations in feelings where relationships between doctors and patients are long-term and regular, rather than being based on the occasional meeting. Thus, the doctor–patient relationship of women who see their general practitioners frequently, who regularly meet their obstetrician during pregnancy, or who are having on-going treatment by their psychiatrists, are of special interest.

What characteristics do women like and dislike in their doctors? The individual doctor's personality, manners and interpersonal skills matter a great deal; indeed, Ann Cartwright found that when asked about the qualities they appreciate in doctors, the majority of respondents say something concerning the ways in which their doctors look after them (Cartwright, 1967). Women, especially, want a doctor to be accessible (i.e. readily available when wanted), approachable (i.e. can be consulted with all sorts of problems), understanding, sympathetic, considerate and not patronizing (Cartwright and Anderson, 1981; Miles, 1988). Home visits also score when patients consider their doctors' manner of looking after them.

This interesting gender difference is also seen to have a generational dimension (see next paragraph).

In Britain, where the 'family doctor' has traditionally been a provider of medical care on a long-term basis, many women like an on-going personal relationship with one doctor, who knows the whole family. Studies note that women, more than men, hold it to be important to maintain a warm, personal relationship with their family doctor; they want the doctor to be a friend, whom they can trust, rather than someone who appears a cool, distant, scientific expert with whom the relationship can only be business-like (Cartwright, 1967; Miles, 1988; Roberts, 1985).

In their study of three generations of Scottish women, Blaxter and Patterson (1982) noted some changes between generations; more of the older women than the younger ones valued the friendly 'family doctor', and a long-term relationship with one general practitioner, and disliked impersonal service. However, for both older and younger women, the doctor's manner of looking after patients was of the utmost importance.

According to Blaxter and Patterson (1982, pp. 164–165):

> For younger mothers, the distinguishing feature of good or bad medical practice was willingness to make house calls. A 'good' doctor was one who came promptly. 'I 'phone back of nine she's here by ten. I never have to wait', and a 'bad' doctor was one who was 'not that ready to come in', or 'takes too long to arrive'.

And (pp. 166–167):

> The amount of time the doctor had to spare for a consultation was a salient feature of service for both generations. Grandmothers, particularly, defined a 'good' doctor as one who could offer his time, and a 'bad' doctor as one who 'has the prescription written out before you've even spoken!'

Patients are not necessarily able to distinguish between the effects of the doctor's personality and manners on the quality of service, and the effects of the structure on that service. Impersonal care, meeting a large number of 'faceless' doctors, the 'conveyor belt' system of seeing patients, are frequent complaints in antenatal care, but these feelings of depersonalization derive as much from the service structure as from the way doctors behave. Thus, women may see many different doctors during pregnancy (Oakley, 1981), and even if each of them is warm and friendly (and the possibility is that some are not) the women experience lack of continuity and the lack of a personal interest in them, factors which may effect their view of doctors.

. . . The prestige of medical knowledge and the medical profession is high even if individual doctors are criticized; moreover, the service provided tends to be accepted as not only 'satisfactory', but the only possible service, (where awareness of alternatives is lacking). Commenting on the high proportion of people in her survey who expressed satisfaction with general practitioners, Ann Cartwright took this to be a sign not so much of a positive feeling that everything was well, but of a passive, rather apathetic acceptance of the *status quo* (Cartwright, 1967). There is also an inclination in many people to keep to the 'known' and well-tried, rather than to opt for an 'unknown' service. As Santayana remarked, habit is stronger than reason.

A good illustration of such conformist attitudes is given in a study of women's responses to antenatal care in Scotland, carried out by Maureen Porter and Sally Macintyre. Women's views concerning two types of antenatal care were explored: for women with pregnancies deemed to be 'unproblematic' and where the medical expectation was that the birth would be 'uncomplicated', there were fewer routine visits; more care was provided by GPs and midwives and less by obstetricians, and women were not undressed and palpated at each visit. By contrast, women who were deemed to have 'problematic' pregnancies were seen as often as obstetricians and GPs thought necessary (Porter and Macintyre, 1984). Overall satisfaction and the particular likes and dislikes of women were elicited in interviews. Not surprisingly, in view of previous research, it was found that the majority of women expressed overall satisfaction with the care they received. It was more surprising to find that as between GP surgeries and hospital an almost identical proportion of women, 84 per cent and 83 per cent, respectively, expressed satisfaction (Table 6.1).

In the view of the researchers (Porter and Macintyre, 1984, p. 1198), the

> data suggests that pregnant women – and the same may be true of other health service users – are fairly uncritical and assume that whatever care they are receiving has been well thought out and is probably the best there is. These women tended to accept and be satisfied with whatever care arrangements they experienced and to prefer them to alternative possibilities. They were conservative in the sense of saying that 'what is, must be best'.

Table 6.1 Overall satisfaction and usual place of care: percentage of women

Overall satisfaction	*Usual place of care*	
	GP (n = 164)	*Hospital (n = 42)*
Dissatisfied	1	5
Mixed feelings	15	12
Satisfied	84	83

Source: Porter and Macintyre, 1984

Similar 'conservative' sentiments were noted by Ann Cartwright in relation to childbirth arrangements (Cartwright, 1979). However, Porter and Macintyre argued that 'whether it is because of conservatism, deference or politeness that women express preferences for familiar systems of care' such sentiments should not be 'construed as indicating "real" levels of satisfaction' (Porter and Macintyre, 1984, p. 1200). Indeed, women in Aberdeen, where the study was conducted, when interviewed about their likes and dislikes concerning antenatal care, mentioned a number of things about hospital provision that they wished were different; they wanted shorter waiting times, more continuity of care, and a less impersonal atmosphere.

Sonja M. Hunt: The Cost of the Car

The cost of a car usually refers to how much it would cost to purchase one. Here, it is the *social* cost of the car which is at issue. Apart from its practical uses, the car is one of the main consumer status symbols of our time. Generally, we prefer not to think that we should use our cars less or that there should be fewer cars. Yet, the social and individual cost of cars is enormously high. Sonja Hunt charts this cost in ghastly detail. Thousands of children are killed or maimed by cars every year. Even in this area, it is the children of the lower social classes that suffer most. Hunt also examines the damage to health and the environment caused by waste emissions from cars. This, too, we seem prepared to accept rather than seriously restrict our use of cars.

In a modern mobile society, the only alternative to the blanket use of private cars is the provision of more public transport. In a section not included here, this is precisely what Hunt argues for.

Reading 64

From Sonja M. Hunt, 'The Public Health Implications of Private Cars' in C. J. Martin and D.V. McQueen *eds., Readings for a New Public Health* (Edinburgh University Press, 1989), pp. 100–4, 105, 106, 107–8

Conservative government policy tended to stress individual responsibility in the aetiology or cause of disease (and of health).

The current vogue for targeting individual behaviour as a major factor in the aetiology of disease and disability can be seen as an interesting example of the creation of social problems and the manipulation of public awareness. Primarily four types of behaviour receive a disproportionate amount of attention. These are smoking, dietary habits, exercise and alcohol consumption. Why these four should have been 'chosen' in preference to other, perhaps more pertinent, human activities is, of course, related to the fact that powerful groups, whether medical, educational or commercial have the capacity to influence the flow of information and debate on matters affecting the public health. Directing attention to some issues rather than others can be seen as part of the social construction of 'problems' whereby certain groups have the power to act collectively to define a problem and then initiate attempts to relieve, change or eliminate the problem (Kitsuse and Spector, 1975).

The implications of private car ownership for the public health have thus largely escaped serious attention, principally because there have been few people with any interest in raising it as an issue. This may be related to the fact that those people with the power to do so are themselves likely to have a 'lifestyle' in which the motor car plays a prominent role. There are political and economic reasons too. The road lobby is very powerful and enormous amounts of revenue are raised from taxes on petrol. The attention given to car driving as a major hazard to the public health can be judged by the fact that the World Health Organisation document on Health Promotion devotes 12 lines to it (WHO, 1982). These concentrate solely on alcohol, drugs and seat-belt use. This comparative lack of interest not only creates the impression that hazards associated with motor cars are trivial relative to, say, lack of exercise, but simultaneously conveys the idea that it is a few irresponsible 'maniacs' who tank up themselves as well as their vehicles, drive carelessly and refuse to wear seat belts who are to blame for any hazards associated with cars. Thus attention is diverted from the enormous impact of car use on disease, death, disability, quality of life, the integrity of the environment, social intercourse, social inequalities and from the huge financial cost to the public purse.

Every private car should carry a government health warning.

Car driving kills or maims over 40,000 people every year in Britain

In 1982, there were 71,586 fatal or serious road accidents in Great Britain, the vast majority of which involved private cars. Of the surviving victims over half will have some permanent disability or disfigurement. . . . [T]he major proportion of incidents on the road are not accidents at all, but the foreseeable outcome of a combination of speed, carelessness, insensitivity, poor judgement, aggressive behaviour and egocentricity, sometimes aggravated by alcohol.

Although road accidents come fourth in the list of major causes of death, after lung, colon and breast cancer, they approximate lung cancer as the primary cause of years of life expectancy lost (Thunhurst, 1983). The peak years for the diagnosis of lung cancer are between ages 64 and 75, for coronary heart disease it is 55 to 64 years and for stroke it is over 75. By contrast, motor vehicle accidents are commonest in the under 40s and as a cause of death in children they approximate that of malignant neoplasms. In the City of Manchester, between 1980–1984, 35 per cent of all pedestrians and 28 per cent of all cyclists killed or seriously injured were children (Manchester City Council, 1986). In Britain, as a whole, pedestrian child fatalities in the age group 10–14 years has increased by 38 per cent in the last 10 years (TRRL, 1986) . . .

In total there are about one and a half million *reported* 'accidents' on the roads every year in Britain, and last year there were about 12 million world-wide. The number of deaths resulting from these 'accidents', at around 6,000, is undoubtedly an underestimate . . .

Most accidents to children occur in deprived urban areas where there is little play space. Boys in Social Class V are seven times more likely to be in an accident than those in Social Class I. Interestingly enough, the responsibility for this has usually been placed upon the child or upon his mother. The former for lack of road sense, impulsive behaviour or carelessness and the latter for lack of control or stress (Brown and Harris, 1978). Thus ameliorative measures have focused upon safety education for the children, or counselling and parental education for the mothers; a wonderful example of those who 'own' a problem trying to place responsibility for it onto less powerful groups, getting them to acknowledge the problem as belonging to them and urging them to change *their* behaviour accordingly (Gusfield, 1975).

Recent studies have shown that, in fact, children spend relatively small amounts of time in impulsive activities such as ball games; rather, for most of the time, they simply stand around or walk about (Chapman *et al.*, 1980). The association between stress in mothers and road accidents involving their children is probably an artefact of living in disadvantaged circumstances. Children from the lower social classes are less likely to have gardens or other play space and, therefore, spend more time in the streets. The real vulnerability of the children stems from their frequent daily exposure to risky situations, not their behaviour (Chapman *et al.*, 1980). Cars and other vehicles are allowed to pass through crowded urban streets which may even be widened and have obstacles removed to ensure traffic flow, leading to increased speed. Nicholas Ridley said in 1986, 'The motorist should not be hampered by petty rules and unnecessary restrictions of his liberty'. Is it an 'unnecessary restriction of liberty' to require that motorists drive slowly in urban areas if this will save the lives of several hundred children every year?

Studies of driving in urban areas have shown that no allowances are made by drivers for the presence of a child at the kerb (Chapman *et al.*, 1980). Most motorists maintain or increase speed, rarely do they slow down or move over to the crown of the road in anticipation. The 'jumping' of designated pedestrian crossing areas is not uncommon. Many drivers seem to assume that a car has the right to unimpeded progress.

It has been suggested, ironically enough, that measures pertaining to driver safety, for example seat-belts, padded fascia, better braking, improved acceleration, have resulted in increased accidents to other road users. Protecting car drivers from the consequences of their own follies can encourage careless driving and certainly faster driving (Adams, 1984) . . .

About 8 per cent of people involved in road accidents end up with permanent disabilities, including brain damage. World-wide, this means about one and a half million individuals, who, since they are mainly young, constitute a long-term drain on the energy, emotions and resources of their loved ones as well as on health and social services . . .

Public health economists have paid little attention to cost factors associated with motor vehicle accidents. In Scotland the estimated cost of *one* fatal accident is over £160,000 and last year the cost of all road accidents was in excess of £200 million. In Great Britain the total cost was £2,370 million (Plowden and Hillman, 1984).

Measures taken to reduce the burden of road accidents have generally focused on the convenience of the motorist and are designed to cause maximum inconvenience to others. Feeble old ladies and women with prams must struggle up steps and over bridges or scurry through stinking underpasses. Children unlucky enough to have no garden must confine themselves to the indoors or play at their peril. All such measures ignore the evidence that the main aetiological factor in deaths and injuries from road accidents is car driving itself.

Driving can damage your health and your environment

In towns and cities the foul and pestilent congregation of vapours which make up what is known as 'air' contains a large measure of car exhaust emissions. The most abundant of these is carbon monoxide, which is released in highly localised concentrations, especially in urban areas. High levels of this gas can hang in the air for extended periods of time. Levels as high as 100 parts per million (ppm) have been recorded at rush hours, reaching 350 ppm at peak times (Walker, 1975). These levels are sufficient to cause headache, lassitude and dizziness in normal people, since carbon monoxide interferes with the ability of the blood to carry oxygen due to its combination with haemoglobin. For susceptible people, for example, those who suffer from anaemia, have low haemoglobin levels, smokers and cardiovascular patients, the effects may be serious. Carbon monoxide at commonly occurring levels has been linked to aggravation of angina pectoris, atherosclerosis and stroke and has been implicated in poor survival rates from myocardial infarction (Goldsmith and Aronow, 1975).

Internal combustion also results in elevated levels of hydrocarbons. Photochemical oxidation creates derivatives from hydrocarbons which become secondary pollutants producing photochemical smog composed of ozone and other toxins. These cause eye irritation and plant damage, but the main problem is that they augment the effects of sulphur dioxide and nitrogen oxides (Duffus, 1980). Sulphur oxides are produced in comparatively small amounts by the combustion of fuel oil but the amount produced by cars adds to the output from industry and is a major cause of 'acid rain' through the oxidation of sulphates. Respiratory problems and eye irritation can be triggered by the inhalation of sulphur oxides at concentrations as low as 1.6 ppm. When concentrations of 5 ppm lasting for one hour occur, serious problems with respiration can ensue . . .

Many of the substances created by the internal combustion engine have a synergistic effect, so that whilst the impact of any single chemical may be relatively small, combinations of two or more, may have serious implications. There has been a growth of interest in vehicle emissions as a cause of lung, and possibly other, cancers. Robinson (1979) plotted the increase in cases of lung cancer in Australia between 1920 and 1972. Overall the percentage increase was 2,810 per cent. During the same period the increase in motor car use was 2,840 per cent, whilst tobacco use, for example, rose by only 69 per cent.

There is also some evidence that those who service and maintain cars such as garage hands, may be at risk from a variety of cancers (Theml, 1986). Although petrol engines have become cleaner over the years and total emissions are less, the increase in sheer volume of traffic has offset this and car use now accounts for a greater percentage of air and land pollution than it did 20 years ago (Ryan, 1980) . . .

Conclusion

Far from being regarded as anti-social, the private car has been elevated to a status symbol, a cause for pride, a target of devotion. Even people who are aware of the problems associated with car ownership will plead that a car is a necessity rather as others might argue that they need a cigarette or a drink to help them cope with the exigencies of daily life.

The encouragement of car ownership is just as much a product of powerful lobbies as is smoking or alcohol use. Industrial societies subsidise motorists to a large extent (Bouladon, 1975). The car and oil industry, motoring organisations and road contractors exert their influence in the interests of private profit at enormous cost to the public purse. The drain on the public sector is not due solely to the cost of accidents and disability, hours lost at work or health services provided, but includes noise, vibration, congestion, damage to buildings, loss of time, waste of space, high energy consumption, pollution and inconvenience to others, especially those already at a disadvantage by virtue of age, sex or infirmity. In addition to the cost of 'accidents', congestion alone is estimated to cost the country £3,000 million in lost time and wasted fuel (GMCP, 1987).

The risks to life, limb and environment associated with cars are either ignored or treated as an acceptable price to pay (acceptable to motorists that is). Yet the number of people who will be killed on the roads between now and 1990 will far exceed the projected number of AIDS victims, and the number of people disabled for life will be many times greater; yet the resources and time devoted to this serious public health problem are far, far fewer. We have reached the ludicruous situation in Britain where the success of transport policy is measured by the number of vehicles that can travel at high speed to the detriment of everything else, a criterion comparable to measuring the success of health policy by the number of people who pass through hospitals.

Tom Hulley and John Clarke: The Social Construction of Social Problems – Ideologies and Discourses

This extract brings together in a reasonably accessible way two different theoretical traditions in relation to social problems. The first is social interactionist or labelling theory – as presented by Howard Becker – and the second is discourse theory associated with Michael Foucault's post structuralism (although this is not specifically referred to in this text).

However, the extract begins with a distinction between individual and structural explanations of social problems. Individual explanations 'blame' the individual whereas structural explanations find the prime causes of a 'problem' within social circumstances. In this way, poverty can be seen either as the result of a personal defect, such as laziness, or as the result of social structural change, such as the decline of a given industry. Hulley and Clarke seek to explain why many people (in their view mistakenly) tend to explain social 'problems' in individual terms. Essentially, people do this because they regard conformity to the predominant ideas and forms of behaviour in a society as 'normal' and non-conformity as 'abnormal' or 'deviant'. Thus, in a racist society many may regard the behaviour of members of given minority cultures as 'odd', 'strange', 'deviant', 'not like us'. In short, they see it as a 'problem'. To give another example, in a patriarchal society, people may see a woman who is depressed, bored and/or exhausted by domestic work as 'a bad wife' or 'a bad mother' or as in need of help – again, the problem is individualised. In explaining how individual explanations of problems are constructed within given social and ideological contexts, Hulley and Clarke make the case that structural interpretations of social problems actually explain much more about their origins, causes and nature. It is worth asking yourself whether or not you agree with them on this matter.

It is worth pointing out that this extract can be read almost as two separate pieces. Approximately the first half deals with the social construction of social problems and is quite simple. The second half relates this approach to the concepts of ideology and discourse (and so to structural theory). The latter is demanding but very rewarding reading. I have indicated the end of the first half and the beginning of the second in the text.

Reading 65 From Tom Hulley and John Clarke, 'Social Problems: Social Construction and Social Causation' in Martin Loney *et al., eds., The State or the Market* (Sage Publications, 1991), pp. 10–11, 12, 14–19

There is a simple, but valuable, distinction between two ways of approaching the explanation of social problems. On the one hand, there are claims that problems arise from the defects of particular individuals. On the other, they are seen as the result of particular patterns of social organization. There are, of course, intermediate explanations which try to merge these individual and structural approaches in differing combinations. We shall return to these later but this basic distinction between individual and structural approaches provides the most useful starting point.

One very familiar example of a social problem – poverty – illustrates the significance of this basic distinction. We can see that some people are visibly badly dressed, poorly housed, undernourished, short of money and generally worse off than others. We can add to this figures detailing the different sources and levels of income which enable us to define who the poorest members of our society are. But identifying poverty is not the same as explaining it. 'Why', we may innocently enquire, 'do some people have less money?'

Structural explanations of this condition would focus on the social patterns involved in the distribution of wealth and income. The inequalities in this distribution would be explained by reference to the way in which society, and particularly, the economy, is organized. The individual character or behaviour of poor people would not be a feature of this analysis. By contrast, individualist explanations would focus on the shortcomings of those individuals who fail to do as well as others. They point to defects in the character, personality or behaviour of individuals which have impaired their chances to progress in life.

Although we have distinguished these two approaches to the explanation of social problems, it is important to note that one of them – the individualist approach – is both more familiar and more popular. Whatever social problem is being discussed, there is a strong likelihood that the explanations which first spring to mind will be ones which start from the defects of individuals. This predominance of individualist explanations is true both in the social sciences and in what we might call 'everyday' accounts of social problems: what 'everybody knows' about poverty, unemployment, crime, and so on. This leaning towards individualism produces two problems for the study of social problems within the social sciences. The first is that introducing structural explanations of social problems runs 'against the grain' of what is commonly understood or taken for granted. This mismatch between structural explanations and the individualist tendency of everyday accounts of social problems is what underpins the criticism that 'social scientists make excuses for' whoever is seen as the problem. Individualist explanations keep a tidy fit between the cause of a social problem (individual defects) and the pressure to identify someone as responsible/guilty/at fault. The second problem which the predominance of individualist explanations raises is that of how to account for this dominance and to explore its consequences for social problems. These questions are also associated with criticisms levelled at social scientists; that they are disruptive, radical or critics of the status quo by asking difficult questions about what is 'taken for granted' by members of a society.

On precisely this theme was Charles Wright-Mills famous call for sociologists to seek to relate 'personal troubles' (the individual level) with 'public issues' (the structural level).

Leaving such criticisms aside for the moment, let us look further at the individualist or defect explanations of social problems. We said earlier that such explanations were more popular in the social sciences themselves as well as in everyday accounts. Indeed, whole branches of sociology, psychology and criminology have devoted themselves to the search for the defects which cause social problems. We might define this as the attempt to discover the 'X' factor; the thing which distinguishes 'normal' people from those (the 'deviant') who are the cause of social problems: what is it that makes some people become poor/commit crimes/use drugs/get divorced when most people do not? Even if we just take one of those problems – why do some people commit crimes? – the list of possible candidates for the 'X' factor is enormous. There is something different about their upbringing, their mental processes, their relationship with their parents, their absorption of morality, the area in which they live or their biology . . .

. . . In the early 1960s, however, an American sociologist raised a fundamental challenge to this view of how to go about explaining deviance. In *Outsiders* (1963), Howard Becker argued that rather than deviance being the property of an act, it was in fact a 'label' – a social definition – attached to the act by others:

> Social groups create deviance by making the rules whose infraction constitutes deviance and by applying those rules to particular people and labelling them as outsiders. From this point of view, deviance is *not* a quality of the act the person commits but rather a consequence of the application by others of rules or sanctions to an 'offender'. The deviant is one to whom that label has successfully been applied; deviant behaviour is behaviour that people so label. [Becker, 1963: 9]

See previous editions of this Reader for a substantial extract from Becker's influential *Social Problems: A Modern Approach* (John Wiley, 1966)

It is this process of social definition or social construction which is Becker's major contribution to the study of social problems. It opens up a series of questions for the social sciences to consider:

1 What conditions come to be defined as social problems? (For example, the maltreatment of children took place long before *child abuse* was defined as a social problem.)
2 Who defines them? Which individuals or groups have the power or authority to identify conditions as social problems?
3 How are they defined? What are the causes or explanations advanced for the problem being defined?
4 What are the social consequences of these definitions? Responses to a social problem are shaped by definitions of its cause; for example, explanations which put low intelligence as a cause of criminality led to arguments that the breeding of future generations of people with low intelligence should be restricted.

These questions concern the social *construction* of social problems, rather than their social *causation*. In British society, the process of constructing social problems tends to have a number of common features. First, social problems are identified with deviant or abnormal *minorities*, who are contrasted with an assumed normal majority. Attempts to define social problems in ways which challenge this abnormal minority/normal majority construction of problems are likely to be resisted very strongly. For example, in the social construction of drug-taking as a social problem, definitions of drug-taking which argued that most British adults were drug users (including use of alcohol, tobacco, tranquillizers, sleeping pills, and so on) were marginalized in favour of definitions of the drug problem as confined to a deviant minority who took 'illegal' drugs.

Secondly, the distinction between normal and deviant tends to fit with individualist 'defect' explanations of the problem: deviants have the 'X' factor which separates them from the normal majority. In this process, our view of the 'normal' is as important as the explanation for why some are deviant. What is identified as normal is a whole bundle of expectations about how people will live their lives in our society. 'We' grow up in families, go to school, get qualifications, get jobs, fall in love, get married, buy a house, have children, look after them, send them to school, and so on. Although many people's lives do not, in fact, fit these expectations, they nevertheless persist as an ideal of what normal life is like, against which we measure 'deviants'.

Thirdly, these expectations – these 'norms' – are social. That is, they are specific to a particular society (Britain) at a particular point in its history (the late twentieth century). Other societies have different patterns of expectations – about families, gender roles within families and the nature of work. Our own society has had different expectations at other points in its history. For example, the expectation that it is normal to buy a house is relatively recent. For earlier generations it was a privilege restricted to the comparatively wealthy. Equally, think how norms about bringing up children have changed since the Victorian expectation that 'children should be seen and not heard'. In spite of norms being socially and historically specific, the particular pattern of norms is equated in most societies with the 'natural' way of doing things. The dominant view of normal life often assumes that it fits with a natural (or God-given) order. This view denies that norms are *chosen* and also ignores important variations between cultures and through time.

In Britain ideas of family life play a central role in this cluster of normal/natural ideas about social behaviour and social problems. Indeed, the idea of the family provides a point at which our views of what is normal and what is natural meet. The family is seen as the natural institution through which people grow and develop, where they learn social identities, acquire values and learn how to behave properly. These ideas of family life interlock with other patterns of social expectations about what is normal and natural – in particular, expectations about gender and age. At its simplest, this network of ideas assumes that women will care for children and make a home while men take responsibility for earning the material necessities, making essential decisions and offering protection to the other members of the family. Families begin with a heterosexual couple who provide the stable base from which to produce and bring up children. Children remain in the household until they reach adulthood, moving from a state of dependence towards increasing independence. These elements form the core of what has been called 'familial ideology' and are also the basis of 'traditional morality' in Britain.

Most of the remainder of this extract is devoted to explaining why people 'construct' social problems in a given way. The concepts of ideology and discourse are central to this theoretical explanation.

The links between these patterns of ideas and the processes of defining social problems are sketched in Figure 3, showing how familial ideology connects to the identification of differences between the normal and deviant, and how deviance is likely to be identified as the result of a 'defect' (that is, those causing social problems lack something which makes the rest of 'us' normal).

Societies are not static, and the precise pattern of prevailing or dominant social norms is liable to change. For example, the rising numbers of divorces and remarriages may come to be accepted as part of 'normal' family life (rather than the presumption of lifelong partnerships). But their acceptance is not just a matter of whether they are 'statistically normal' (whether the majority of marriages end in separation or divorce) but it is also a matter of ideological conflict about what should be treated as normal. This process of determining what is commonly accepted as normal shows that norms are chosen rather than natural. During the 1980s in Britain, for example, proponents of traditional morality have been trying to promote a return to the 'old certainties' (the security of proper family life, in particular) in the face of what they see as a 'liberalization' of moral values (easier divorces, more single-parent families, and so on). Ideological conflict tends to be important in affecting where the line between 'normal' and 'deviant' is drawn but the fundamental principle of distinguishing between the two remains central to the processes of constructing social problems and still tends to produce a view of defiance as the result of an individual defect.

Figure 3 The social construction of social problems

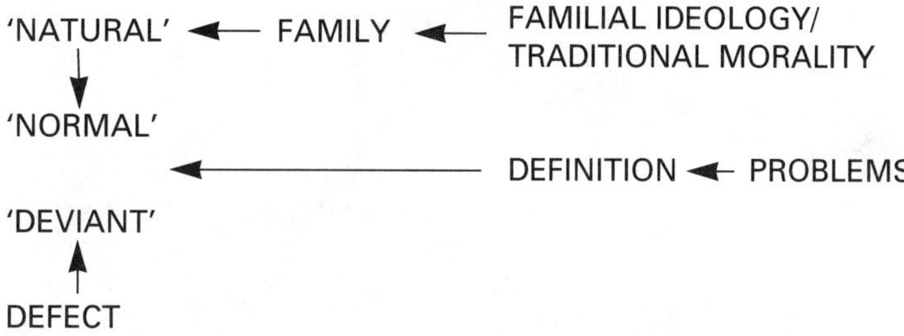

Figure 4 traces this line of connection between deviance and defect, as well as adding two new elements to the original Figure 3: ideology/discourse and intervention. Our views of the distinction between normal and deviant are underpinned by the prevailing ideologies and discourses which produce definitions of the normal and acceptable and which present explanations of the abnormal and deviant. By ideologies and discourses, we refer to sets of interlinked beliefs which provide ways of mapping and defining reality. As 'social maps' they lead to particular courses of action by providing ways of orienting ourselves to the world in which we live – like maps they identify the best routes to take and which behaviours are not allowed: the 'no entry' signs for disapproved behaviour. Although there are more complex arguments, for us the most important distinction between ideologies and discourses lies in their 'global' and 'local' qualities. By ideologies we tend to refer to wide-ranging systems of ideas which link individuals, social institutions like the family, gender roles, politics and the shape of the overall society and its place in the world. To follow the map analogy, ideologies are maps of the overall structure which allow us to place ourselves and discern the main lines of connection to everywhere else. Discourses are more 'local' – the detailed maps of a particular aspect of the society. They are associated with specialized knowledge or expertise and tend to be the province of 'experts'. The rest of us know such maps are there and the experts (doctors, lawyers, social workers and so on) can be consulted if needed. Although such 'maps' are more local, they have important consequences for the wider social ideologies because of the authority that accompanies 'expertise'. Wider social ideologies draw on such specific discourses in framing the images of the society (for example in our notions of the rule of law, health, mental health and the like). At the same time, discourses tend to embody the main dimensions of dominant social ideologies and then work them out in more complex detail (for example, the medical profession's production of knowledge about 'normal' and 'abnormal' sexuality).

Figure 4 Social construction and social intervention

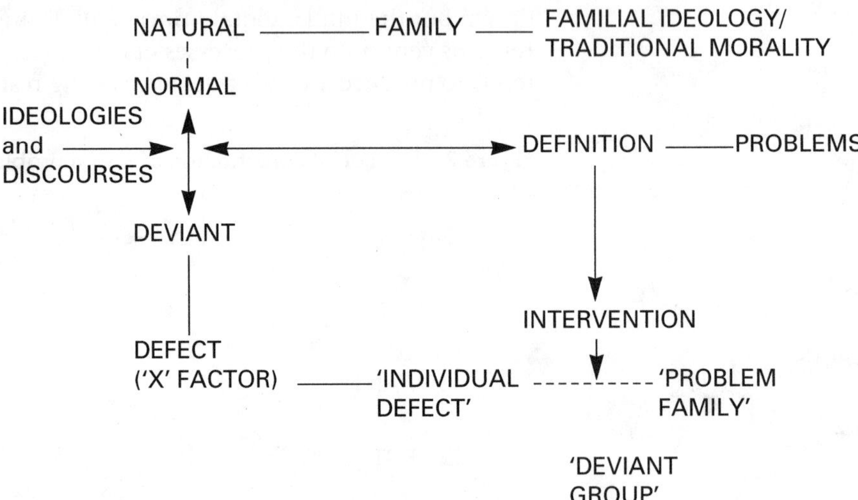

Two other things need to be said about ideology and discourse. Both are not stable or fixed. In most societies a dominant ideology can be identified as well as resistances to it from other ideological positions. In modern British society, the dominant ideology is a *hybrid* created out of the acceptance of patriarchal and capitalist relations; liberal-democratic government; and a particular set of values derived mainly from Judaeo-Christian tradition. Extending this 'hybrid' analogy, the ideology changes over time but different 'strains' retain the same key elements. It is challenged by subordinate ideologies, which may be non-patriarchal, non-capitalist and alternative in other ways. Often these challenges are partial, so Marxist ideology may be seen to resist capitalist and religious ideas, but not patriarchal ones. Discourses, at a 'local' level, can work as forms of resistance to parts of the dominant ideology and thus may influence partial change. More often, discourses serve to contain resistance within a limited area. For example, feminist discourses on health, the family and education may have successfully amended parts of the dominant ideology without replacing any key elements.

> Here, the authors confront 'head-on' the relative basis of 'normality' (or 'commonsense'), well aware that 'normality' is regarded by many as the rock-solid basis of their (and others') lives.

The most consistent area of resistance to dominant ideology concerns the definition of what is seen as normal. For example, violence against women in the home was until recently not identified publicly as a social problem. It was viewed, perversely enough, as a 'private' matter – taking place and to be settled 'behind closed doors'. This definition dominated both in general ideology and in the relevant discourse – the law – embodied in the workings of the police and the courts, who were reluctant to 'interfere in private matters'. This definition has been challenged by women's groups, who argue that the exercise of male power through violence is an issue of public concern no matter where it takes place. Such challenges have affected general social ideologies (to some extent) and the expert discourses of the law (to some extent). What emerges, though, is the avoidance or suppression of challenges which claim that this problem has its roots in structural conditions (male power) rather than in defective individuals. Thus, domestic violence, while accepted as a social problem, is linked back to 'defect' theory, identifying the defect in the aggressor (a few bad apples who cannot control themselves) or, more perniciously, finding defects in the victims (women who 'invite' violence).

This leads to the second feature of dominant ideologies and discourses, which is the way in which they are organized around the opposition of normal and deviant. This distinction is a major principle around which the maps are drawn and even though what counts as a problem may shift, the attempt is made to map all problems around this opposition, resulting in the identification of deviance with defect. The effect of this mapping of the social world might be summarized as 'in spite of a few bad apples, the vast majority of people are normal, thank goodness'. This process can effectively marginalize or discredit resistance. So even at a personal level, people who do not or cannot fulfil normal expectations may accept blame and feel guilty. This has been well expressed by women who have taken the exceptional and 'abnormal' step of leaving the family. They felt that staying would have been more damaging to their families and themselves. They suffered greatly because of normal expectations but showed how their 'deviancy' helped create better family relations (Parkin, 1990). By contrast, respectable, law-abiding men who have killed their partners, demonstrate how 'normality' can be a cause of destructive interpersonal actions (Smith, 1989). Normality imposes a personal surrender to intolerable pressures while resistance is perceived as deviance. The imposition of normality can be seen to cause violence and breakdown. This might explain, in part, why certain groups are more frequently labelled as having 'psychiatric' problems. The incidence of mental health problems among women, certain groups of Black men, unemployed people and disabled people is greater than for the whole population.

Such examples suggest that the importance of ideology and discourse is not restricted to the way they 'map' the world but that these maps lead to practical consequences. How problems are defined, and who defines them, affect what response will be made to the problem. In the example of domestic violence, the dominant definition of it as a 'private matter' ensured that no intervention took place. As the definition has shifted, so have the responses. Its definition as a criminal act brings such violence into the realm of possible intervention by the police and courts, who prosecute some offenders. Where it is defined as a failure in the interpersonal relations between the particular couple, it may become the focus for intervention by a counsellor aimed at helping the couple to 'cope' with 'their' problem. For some women's groups it became the focus of mutual self-help, establishing refuges and support networks to create the chance for women to escape direct violence. All of these tend to operate at the level of the individual, in spite of the attempts to define such violence as a structural problem involving power differentials between men and women adn the exercise of violence within such unequal relations. On the ground established by the distinction between normal and deviant and the linkage between deviance and individual defect, intervention tends to be directed towards particular 'cases' – individuals, families, groups who are identified as having a defect, rather than at structural conditions. In the same way, the disadvantages of ethnic groups as a consequence of racism throughout the social structure can be constructed as the result of cultural, educational or even biological defects.

We can see that ideologies or discourses are both systems of ideas and have real consequences for people's lives.

Paul Wilding: Thatcherism and the Welfare State

As Paul Wilding points out, it is too early to offer anything more than provisional assessments of the Thatcherite changes to the welfare state. However, his own effort is thought-provoking and, in my view, remarkably fair. He covers the following ten areas:

- The challenge to collectivism
- The promotion of private provision
- The 'cuts'
- The new managerialism
- Greater social division
- The attack on local government
- The mixed economy of welfare
- The rights of citizenship
- The regulatory state
- The impact on the Labour Party.

It would be a mistake to associate Thatcherism merely with Mrs Thatcher. Wilding's own working definition of Thatcherism is 'the ideas and policies of the Thatcher governments'. The flow of new ideas and policies that characterised Thatcherism was fed by a variety of advisors, think-tanks and ideologically-minded politicans. Many aspects of Thatcherism continued under John Major, although the severe recession of the early 1990s provoked powerful demands for a different approach.

Reading 66 From Paul Wilding, 'The British Welfare State: Thatcherism's enduring legacy' in *Policy and Politics*, Vol. 20 No. 3, 1992, pp. 201–3, 204, 205–7, 207–10, 210–11

The 1980s were the decade of Thatcherism. They were years when major changes were made, and attempted, in public and social policies. They were also years dominated by the ideology to which Mrs Thatcher gave her name. This paper is an exercise in analysis and prophecy. It attempts to anticipate the probable enduring impact of Thatcherism on the British welfare state and foresees ten enduring legacies.

Much has been written about Thatcherism and the British welfare state. There have been analyses of the impact of the policies of the Thatcher governments in particular areas of policy – for example, Forrest and Murie on the sale of council houses (Forrest and Murie, 1988). There have been surveys of the Thatcher years – for example, Johnson's *Reconstructing the Welfare State* (Johnson, 1990). But there has been no attempt at an interim overall assessment of the likely enduring legacy of the Thatcher governments. Obviously, it is too early for anything more than a tentative, high risk, back-covering essay. This paper takes the risk and sets out the legacies judged likely to be enduring.

As the raw material for an assessment, we have the ideas and policies of the three Thatcher governments. There are many problems, however, in making judgments. Hugo Young stresses that in every sphere – economy, society, government – 'the effect was ambiguous' (Young, 1989, p. 532). Kavanagh and Seldon stress what they describe as the 'unevenness' of the Thatcher 'revolution'. They speak of the impact as 'tangential, major, insignificant or catalytic, depending on the subject under review, or indeed the predilections of the author' (Kavanagh and Seldon, 1989, p. vi).

There are other problems too. We don't know how far the *potential* of the radical legislation of 1988–90 will be realised. We don't know the length, breadth, height or depth of the late 1980s and early 1990s recession. We don't know the extent to which a Conservative Party led by John Major will follow in the Thatcher wake. We don't know the long-term impact of the economic and social changes of the 1980s which made manual workers a minority of voters at the April 1992 election and which will mean, in future, shareholders outnumber trade union members in the polling booths (Crewe, 1988, pp. 29–30).

Having made all those desirable and academically necessary reservations, my argument is that Thatcherism has left a very significant legacy, much of which is likely to endure. I pick out ten legacies which I see as the significant ones.

The challenge to collectivism

I One of Thatcherism's enduring legacies will surely be the powerful ideological and practical challenge which it has mounted to collectivism. Collectivist approaches to welfare provision are grounded in two beliefs – the virtue and necessity of social rather than individual responsibility for substantial areas of life and the practicality of efficient and effective provision by government.

These sustaining beliefs had never been unchallenged, but they had never been challenged so broadly, consistently and fundamentally. Thatcherism asserted the necessity and superiority of individual responsibility and the actual, or potentially damaging, nature of wider social responsibility. It insisted on the inevitable inefficiency and ineffectiveness of monopolistic provision of goods and services outside the disciplinary framework of the market.

The challenges were no longer from idiosyncratic mavericks who could easily be waved aside. They were coming from people in the highest places, able to put their ideas into practice.

The welfare state is, above all, an experiment in collectivist politics. Thatcherism pronounced it to be an experiment that had failed. Market failure was seen as less likely and less damaging than government failure (Marquand, 1988, p. 75).

Thatcherism has questioned, and substantially damaged, the credibility of the two basic instruments of collectivist welfare policy – bureaucracy and professions. They are billed as self-interested, self-serving, inefficient and ineffective. Nicholas Deakin sees the general acceptance of the case against large welfare bureaucracies as 'among the New Right's most striking intellectual achievements in this whole area of policy' (Deakin, 1987, p. 177). If we have doubts about welfare bureaucracies, we must be sceptics about collectivism and about the whole traditional welfare state enterprise.

There has been a full-frontal challenge to the collectivist mode as an efficient, effective and desirable approach to resolving the problem of industrial society. Certainly there has been no general rolling back of the state in central areas of social policy – though there has in more peripheral areas such as regulation of the labour market. What we have seen is a firm challenge to the principle, scope and instruments of collective provision.

That challenge has had an important impact on those committed to welfare state-type policies. We are all less statist than in the past. We are all much more dubious about bureaucracy as an effective instrument. We are all more sceptical about the skills and disinterestedness of the professions. Thatcherism did not initiate the challenge to collectivism, but gave it force, weight, ideological legitimacy and a new respectability. Supporters of state welfare will never look to collectivist answers with quite the same simple enthusiasm as before – and that is a sea change in opinion with enduring implications.

The promotion of private provision

II A second legacy likely to be lasting is the promotion of markets and the private provision of welfare. Markets can be extended via the development of private provision or thorugh the development of internal markets within public services. Privatisation can embrace a range of policies – reductions in state services which force individuals to make private provision, reduction of state subsidy or state regulation, an increase in charges which places more of the cost of a service on individuals or aid and subsidy to the private sector. The Thatcher governments have moved on all these fronts.

The 1980s were notable for the active promotion of the market mechanism and the virtues of private provision. While no major area of welfare was totally privatised or opened to market forces, there was a considerable expansion in market-oriented policies in all the main services.

There has been a more than doubling of the number of people covered by private health insurance with tax concessions to the low paid and to elderly people. There has been a considerable expansion in private hospital beds. Consultants' contracts were altered in 1981 to allow those in full-time employment with the National Health Service to engage in private practice. Charges for prescriptions increased by 1,425% between 1979–90 in an effort to 'privatise' drug costs. Charges for dental examinations and eye tests were introduced in 1989.

There has been aid and comfort to the private sector in education via the Assisted Place Scheme which was offering over 33,000 places by 1990–91 at a cost of some £62m. A larger share of the cost of supporting students in higher education was placed on parents as the assumed parental contribution doubled in real terms from 1980–87 (Glennerster and Low, 1990, p. 39).

There were also massive subsidies to the extension of private home ownership via the discounts offered to council house tenants buying their houses. The cost of mortgage tax relief more than doubled in real terms in the 1980s. To encourage people to quit the state earnings-related pension scheme after 1988, taxpayers had to pay out an initial £2bn with the prospect of an ultimate bill of up to £5.9bn (*Guardian*, 2 May 1991). In the field of personal social services, Johnson argues that 'privatisation lies at the heart of the proposals' in the National Health Service and Community Care Act 1990 (Johnson, 1990, p. 185). In the field of private residential care for elderly people, there was an enormous expansion fuelled by Income Support payments costing £1.3bn a year by 1991 (*Guardian*, 18 February 1991).

Through the 1980s there was firm pressure on the public sector to contract out public services, culminating in the Local Government Act 1988 which compelled local authorities to put particular services out to tender. The National Health Service was also being compelled to contract out services such as cleaning, catering, laundry and portering.

Another strand in this market enterprise has been the development of quasi-competitive markets within state services. The clearest example of this is in the National Health Service under the 1990 Act where different elements within the Service will buy and sell services to and from each other. In education, schools are also entering a new, competitive environment in which they compete for pupils via published annual reports, examination results and open enrolment.

Riddell speaks of privatisation as 'the most striking policy innovation since 1979' (Riddell, 1989, p. 87). Peter Jenkins, however, writing in 1987, judges that 'the greatest failure of the Thatcher Revolution has been in the application of market economics to the Welfare State' (Jenkins, 1987, p. 329).

What we have seen is a gradualist but sustained approach to extend private provision and market principles. There has been no large-scale attempt to re-commodify welfare goods – apart from housing, which has always been a very mixed economy – but private provision is now much more firmly established within all the major areas of welfare and market values and mechanisms have thrust deep into the former collectivist strongholds of health and education.

At one level, Jenkins is right. To the casual observer, not much has changed since 1979. In reality, a great deal has changed. The private sector has grown and there have been massive injections of public money to support this development. Private provision has been expanded in ways which would now be very difficult to roll back and the value and validity of the market mechanism – duly domesticated and regulated – seems widely accepted.

The 'cuts'

III A third enduring legacy will be 'the cuts' – placed firmly in inverted commas to emphasise the complexity and contestability of the concept. At one level, there were no cuts. Total social welfare expenditure increased in real terms every year between 1979–80 and 1987–88 (Le Grand, 1990, p. 341). The real issue is whether increases in expenditure matched increases in need and whether they were sufficient to maintain standards. Increased resources and declining services may sound paradoxical but may represent reality.

Le Grand and his colleagues show that though expenditure on the National Health Service continued to increase after 1979, it was at a much slower rate than in the years 1974–79. Real expenditure increased under Labour at an average annual growth rate twice as high as under the Conservatives. If volume expenditure is used, the rate of increase under Labour was four times as high. These lower rates of increase in expenditure were accompanied by more rapid increases in need calculated according to the Department of Health's index. What has happened is that growth in resources has not matched the growth in need and demand (Le Grand *et al.*, 1990, p. 97 *et seq*). It is the same story in personal social services (House of Commons, 1990, Para. 57 *et seq*).

In some areas there has been no increase in resources but sharp cuts – housing is the best example. In other areas there have been overall increases in expenditure – social security for example – but the government has sought to restrain expenditure by nicks, chips and slices in relation to different elements of the current and future programme, while leaving the basic framework intact.

My purpose here is simply to illustrate the complexity of the issue of cuts and to make the argument that whether what has happened is properly described as expenditure restraint or cuts, the legacy will be enduring. It will be enduring because of the practical, political and economic difficulties involved in making them good. A couple of years of restraint or cuts can be restored. A dozen years of such policies cannot. The costs – economic and political – are just too great. The legacy is a new lower base-line of expenditure and a new lower level of service provision . . .

The new managerialism

IV One undeniable and certainly enduring legacy of Thatcherism is a new managerialism, a new stress on efficient and effective management in the public sector, on clarity of objectives and value for money. Pre-1979, shamefully little concern was given to the economy, efficiency and effectiveness of social policies. Eleven years of Thatcherism have changed that.

There were cuts to encourage greater efficiency. There was privatisation to introduce the greater efficiency which private ownership and the market mechanism were thought bound to bring. There were the Audit Commission, Rayner Scrutinies, the Financial Management Initiative. There was the Griffiths Review of the Management of the National Health Service recording 'institutionalised stagnation', a lack of clarity of objectives, an inability to assess effectiveness, and a lack of ability to control costs (DHSS, 1983). The Griffiths Review of Community Care followed a few years later with a sharp and elegant indictment of a policy which in nearly 30 years had moved little beyond aspiration and lacked the basic elements to ensure that desired intentions were translated into action (DHSS, 1988).

The 'rise of management' in the NHS (and also in education) has been at the expense of professionals. My own assessment of the new managerialism is less positive than Wilding's. This is partly because they themselves threaten a new bureaucracy and because they frequently grant themselves huge salary increases.

There has been a host of specific and particular initiatives – the institutionalisation of general management in the National Health Service at unit, district and regional level, staff appraisal, the development of performance indicators, a stress on Quality Assurance, short-term contracts for managers, performance-related pay, the installation of private sector managers in the public sector, the decentralisation of budgets so head teachers, general practitioners and social services staff are all budget holders. There has been a profuse development of guidelines and procedures to try to institutionalise best practice.

There are both positive and negative outcomes of this drive for better management. Obvious positives are the questions now clearly and firmly inscribed on every manager's heart. What am I trying to achieve? What is it costing to do what I'm doing? What are the outcomes?

The negatives are less obvious but are important. There is the risk that what counts is what can be easily measured. Because costs are almost always more easily measured than benefits, the drive for efficiency, in fact, becomes an exercise in cost-cutting. A broader issue is the relevance of the ideas of the new managerialism to the public sector, Pollitt, for example, raises critical and sceptical questions about the ways in which the public sector differs from the private (Pollitt, 1990, Ch. 5). What is plain is that more is required for managing the complexities of the health or personal social services than simple, general 'management' skills. Nevertheless, the achievement is a new critical, evaluative questioning of the aims, organisation, effectiveness and efficiency of welfare services, which will certainly outlive Thatcherism. 'The prize for undeniable achievement', Peter Hennessy argues, 'must be awarded for improved public service management' (Hennessy, 1989, p. 114).

Greater social division

Although this section makes a crucial point, I have substantially shortened it. The point is covered in Readings 65 and 16.

V A fifth probably enduring legacy of the Thatcher years is greater social division. The fact of such increased division is widely accepted across the political spectrum. 'If the poor did not become poorer in an absolute sense', says Samuel Brittan, 'there was certainly a major relative shift against them in the distribution of income and wealth' (Brittan, 1989, p. 2). 'The existence of growing divisions within Britain', Riddell insists, 'is indisputable' (Riddell, 1989, p. 149). Hugo Young's verdict is that 'ten years commitment to this cause [inequality] etched itself deep into the social fabric' (Young, 1989, p. 535). Alan Walker writes of the evidence building up 'to the overwhelming conclusion that Britain is a much more sharply divided society in 1987 than it was just eight years earlier' (Walker, 1987, p. 130).

What is the nature of the change and why is such a legacy likely to be enduring? There is an ideological change sharply expressed by Kenneth Baker to the 1987 Conservative Party Conference. 'The pursuit of egalitarianism', he assured enthusiastic delegates, 'is over' (quoted in Johnson, 1990, p. 126). For the first time since 1945, there was a clear and explicit abandonment of the belief that public policy should, in some vague and faltering way, be concerned with promoting equality. Equality became a bad word in the dominant vocabulary of politics. Even socialism, which had always been said to be about equality, made a significant change of emphasis. Equality ceased to be an end and was downgraded to the status of a mere means to the greater end of freedom (Field, 1981; Hattersley, 1987) . . .

The legacy of increased social division is likely to be enduring for five main reasons – the sharpness and depth of the divisions, the extent of the redistribution required substantially to reduce them, the way in which those at the bottom of this more divided society have become politically marginalised, the new ideological justification offered for wider inequality, and the way in which the disadvantages of the disadvantaged are likely to be perpetuated by the new emergent world of internal markets in the social services. Those on the wrong side of the division are no longer – if they ever were – the stuff of politics. More people have been persuaded that social ills – such as poverty – are inevitable, that ills such as unemployment are no longer as painful as in the past and that, in any case, there is little government can do about them (Taylor-Gooby, 1990, p. 8). People have been baptised in a new realism – a powerful conservative force.

The attack on local government

VI A sixth enduring legacy of Thatcherism will be a discredited and dowgraded local government system. In the ten years after 1979, some fifty separate Acts of Parliament were passed aimed at reducing the independence of local authorities. Ken Young sees Mrs Thatcher's confrontation with local government as 'the most prolonged and . . . arguably the most significant' of all her various struggles (Young, 1989,

p. 124). What makes it so significant is the sheer scale of the change which it marks in British political institutions. Local authorities have lost powers, duties, independence and the right to raise revenue at a level they and their electors consider appropriate. Young sees the removal of the right to make decisions about the revenue to be raised as 'an undoubted violation of any principle of local self government' (Young, 1989, p. 125).

During the 1980s, local authorities were compelled to sell housing. They almost lost their historic house-building function, and in 1988 the government sought to supersede the local authority as landlord. The 1988 Education Reform Act marked a massive transfer of power from Local Education Authorities to the Department of Education and Science. Jack Straw, Labour Party spokesperson on education, calculated that the Act gave the Secretary of State 415 new powers (Johnson, 1990, p. 125). From the other end, Local Education Authorities were weakened by the opportunity offered to schools to opt out of LEA control and seek grant-maintained status. Local management meant that LEAs lost financial control of individual schools. The LEA no longer planned and managed a system of education as it had in the past.

The Local Government Act 1988 marked a further assault on the power of local authorities. Henceforward they were compelled to put a range of services out to tender – a step towards the dream outlined by Nicholas Ridley – Secretary of State for the Environment towards the end of Mrs Thatcher's time as Prime Minister and one of her strongest supporters. He said that he looked forward to the day when local councils would only meet once a year – for lunch and to check all the contracts were in order.

In 1990, the National Health Service and Community Care Act firmly established in statute the idea of the *enabling* local authority – an idea hinted at from the mid-1980s. The essence of the idea is that the local authority moves from being the key provider of key services to being the body which organises, supervises, regulates and funds the provision of such services by other competing bodies – a total change of function and major loss of status. These proposals for changes in the approach to community care took so long to emerge in legislative form, it seems, because of the drive initiated by Mrs Thatcher to find an alternative to the local authority even for this enabling role.

These are simply the key landmarks in a consistent policy of what Lord Jenkins of Hillhead, ex-Labour Cabinet Minister, founder of the Social Democratic Party, calls 'civic degradation' (quoted in Riddell, 1989, p. 177). There are other elements – the removal of control of Polytechnics and Colleges of Higher Education, the bypassing of local authorities by the creation of alternative bodies – Urban Development Corporations and Housing Action Trusts, for example – the abolition of the Greater London Council and the Metropolitan Counties.

The aims of the Thatcher governments have been plain – to reduce the financial independence of local government, to limit its role and functions, to squeeze it from the top – central government – and from the bottom – consumers, and from either side by voluntary and private provision. Is this degradation permanent? The answer is 'probably'. Nearly all governments find the independence of local authorities an irritation or worse. All oppositions complain about the way central government treats local government – but when in power they do little to reverse the policies about which they complained with such passion when in opposition.

If the legislation of 1988–90 is carried through to its logical conclusion, the welfare state in the 1990s, Le Grand points out, will be one where local authorities will not own or operate schools, houses or residential care institutions (Le Grand, 1990, p. 351). A fourth Conservative government is probably required to make those changes irrevocable, but the revolution is well under way.

The mixed economy of welfare

VII A seventh enduring legacy of Mrs Thatcher's years will be the new force given to the concepts 'the mixed economy of welfare' or 'welfare pluralism'. It was not an idea invented by Thatcherism, but it was an idea which Thatcherism took up, colonised and propagated. Its fundamental strength is that it expresses the simple truth. Welfare is, and has always been, a mixed economy of formal and informal, public and private, voluntary and family provision.

What Thatcherism did was to take this fact, give it a particular ideological twist, and promote this interpretation as aspiration and policy. Welfare pluralism as ideology can mean very different things. For some, it expresses the aspiration to develop non-statutory services which complement public provision because there are certain things which the non-statutory sector can do better than the statutory. For other people, it means supplementing public services because they always fall short of what is required. For others, welfare pluralism is the idea, and the fact, which makes it both possible and legitimate to work towards the replacement of state welfare as the dominant mode of provision. Thatcherism used welfare pluralism in this latter way as a stick with which to beat state provision, and as the reality which gave legitimacy to such an assault.

Webb and Wistow describe one of the important developments of the decade beginning in the mid-1970s as being 'the collapse of the pure doctrine of state welfare' (Webb and Wistow, 1982, p. 57). It is a good example of how to reveal truth by exaggeration – there never was a pure doctrine of state welfare but it did collapse in the late 1970s and 1980s.

Thatcherism abhorred public monopoly. Hence it sought to encourage alternative sources of welfare. It promoted the private sector through public subsidies, tax breaks, the opening up of services to private contractors, the vigorous encouragement of commercial sponsorship and by incorporating it in public policy – for example, Norman Fowler's 'twin pillars' approach in the reform of social security in the mid-1980s which sought a new partnership between the state and private sectors.

The voluntary sector was similarly favoured. From very early on in the first Thatcher government, there were ministerial eulogies – for example, Patrick Jenkins' speech as Secretary of State to the Directors of Social Services in September 1980 and Mrs Thatcher's famous address to the WRVS in February 1981 (quoted in Webb and Wistow, 1982, pp. 92–3). A considerable expansion of direct financial support from central and local government followed (Knapp, 1989, pp. 239, 241) . . .

The government's aim was both to assert and promote the significance of private and voluntary welfare provision, even if that meant substantial injections of public money at a time of tight restraint on expenditure on traditional services.

The Thatcher governments also discovered and eulogised the informal sector and particularly the carer – those individuals, largely women, who devoted themselves to caring for frail and dependent elderly people. They were the pillars of family care – though the government preferred to describe it as 'community care'. Their labours saved the long-suffering taxpayers many billions of pounds. They were living embodiments of the great virtues and value (particularly to others!) of individual and family responsibility. They illustrated – when the respective contibutions were compared – how relatively trivial was the contribution of state-provided services to human well-being. It was easy to shift the emphasis from 'relatively trivial' to 'essentially unimportant'.

That welfare is a mixed economy is a statement of simple reality. Recognition of that reality should clearly inform policy. In the 1980s it did much more than that. It was used to justify and legitimate a reduced role for public provision and an expanded role for the non-statutory sector – private, voluntary and family. Private and voluntary welfare have become more firmly embedded in government policies. They are central to the development, for example, of the enabling local authority. Emphasis on the actual, and socially desirable, key role of the family helps to give legitimacy to the reduction of public services.

Thatcherism took up and used the fact of the mixed economy for ideological and political purposes. The private sector has grown and it has become more important in overall policy. Similarly, the voluntary sector has expanded – sometimes in a gadarene-like rush. Some elements have become dangerously dependent on government funds – and have suffered and perished as government priorities changed. It has become more important to government – and the converse is equally true.

Private and voluntary welfare have both become key elements in government policy. There are three reasons why this new stress on the mixed economy of welfare is likely to be lasting – welfare *is* a mixed economy, public opinion is supportive of a mixed economy, and the intricacy and complexity of the relationship which has been created and the practical difficulties involved in unpicking it.

The rights of citizenship

This section provides many examples of the curtailment of the rights of social citizenship under Thatcherism. As such, it is an excellent complement to Bryan Turner's more theoretical piece on citizenship (Reading 58).

VIII Another enduring legacy of Thatcherism is likely to be the attempt at a redefinition of the rights of citizenship. 'A central goal', says Gamble, 'has been to discredit the social democratic concept of universal citizenship rights, guaranteed and enforced through public agencies, and to replace it with a concept of citizenship rights achieved through property ownership and participation in markets' (Gamble, 1988, p. 16).

Citizenship has always been a balancing of rights and obligations. Arguably, the welfare state has been too much concerned with rights and too little concerned with obligations. What Thatcherism has sought to do is to redress the balance and to redefine citizenship 'using the language of obligation and responsibility' (Lister, 1990, p. 20). But 'behind the eulogy to the private citizen, and her or his responsibilities', says Lister, 'the public citizen and the public rights of citizenship are being buried' (Lister, 1990, p. 68).

The assertion of citizenship rights in the welfare state was an attempt to modify the inequalities and inequities inherent in capitalism. The Thatcher governments nourished no such aims because, for them, inequality was the fuel and motor of economic growth. Citizenship rights can blur and blunt the market disciplines which are essential to the achievement of the society which will ultimately guarantee to all citizens their real rights – as consumers.

The Thatcher governments have sought to challenge the idea of universal provision of free services as a right for all citizens as the basic method of approaching welfare. In social security, for example, since the 1986 Act, says Lister 'Means tested benefits are now explicitly presented as the fulcrum of the system' (Lister, 1989, p. 117). The principle of free services has been eroded by the extension and increase of charges for some services – prescriptions, dental checkup, eye tests, for example.

An adequate income – adequate according to the norms of a particular society – is a fundamental right of citizenship. The increase in poverty since 1979 – for example the increased numbers of people with incomes below basic social security – marks an increase in people lacking this very basic right. A test of this right might be how provision is organised for the poorest and most vulnerable. In 1986, the Social Fund was created as the last resort element in the British social security system to provide loans and grants on strict condtions to the very poorest. The National Audit Office's report on the Social Fund's operation in 1989–90 shows the Fund operating in a way which seemed to deny basic citizenship rights. One-third of all applications from these people in the direst need were refused. 40% of applicants were refused budgeting loans. There was a clear lack of consistency and equity between offices. Provisions were introduced in the Social Security Act 1990 to allow the Secretary of State to issue directions requiring local social security offices to treat their budgets as an over-riding constraint when considering applications (National Audit Office, 1991).

The increase in homelessness – one million households involving three million people were registered by local authorities in the 1980s – and a further one million were refused registration – shows a large group of people without, perhaps, the most basic citizenship rights – shelter.

Some groups of claimants – young people for example – have lost the right to social security benefits. Others can only claim benefits at reduced rates. Social Fund applicants have lost any independent right of appeal. Increasingly onerous and stigmatizing conditions are placed on the recipients of unemployment benefit. They must be immediately available for work. They must be actively seeking work. After three months on benefit they are not able to refuse work outside their usual occupation or place of residence and low wages will not be considered a satisfactory reason for refusing a job.

To a degree, such conditions represent the responsibility side of cititzenship but they can be – and seemingly are – used in ways which deny people full citizenship. Such an approach is consistent with the view expressed by the *Sunday Times* that 'Social stigma is an essential ingredient of social order and must, slowly and cumulatively, be restored' (quoted in Lister, 1990, p. 26). Stigma and rights of citizenship fit ill together.

Another assumed, but never formally accepted, right of citizenship has been, perhaps, mortally wounded in the 1980s – the right to work. The stress on responsibility rather than rights has not been seen as extending to enabling people to be economically self-supporting and productive. The right to work has been attacked by declarations that there is nothing government can do about unemployment, by explicitly giving it a lower priority than other issues, and by the partially successful re-education of the electorate not seriously to care about unemployment (Young, 1989, p. 502).

The social rights of citizenship have been established slowly in Britain over more than a century. They remain fragile, however, because of the challenge they supposedly pose to the economy and economic 'needs'. They are easily reduced, rationalised and rewritten over time by what look like minor changes in policies or the coverage of services, or by changes in the small print of regulations, or by the withdrawal of resources. Once eroded, restoration is not easy.

The rights of citizenship are a political artefact – created out of political action and only sustained by it. Thatcherism is a rejection of politics as a method of improving the world. In an environment of hostility to politics, where economic growth is seen as the most important engine of welfare, social rights must suffer.

The regulatory state

IX Another legacy of Thatcherism is likely to be the regulatory state. What we saw in the 1980s was not a simple rolling back of the state but a more complex pattern of government activity. This is Glennerster's argument – that what we see again and again – in housing, education and health and personal social services – is an elaboration of the forms of government intervention rather than a simple retreat (Glennerster, 1989, pp. 109–10).

All the ways in which the Thatcher governments have sought to break the mould of traditional forms of provision depend on government playing a powerful role in regulating the new pattern of welfare – a free economy but a strong state. The Education Reform Act means a whole range of new kinds of regulation to implement the National Curriculum and a pattern of national testing at given ages, to control opting out, to govern local management and parental involvement, to set the pattern for charges for extra curricular activities and so on. This is more not less government!

The same is equally true of other areas of social policy. There is to be more inspection and regulation – even if less public provision. In personal social services, the Government's Social Services Inspectorate is to have a new status and a new authority. Local inspectorates are to be created in each Social Services Department. Private residential homes must be regulated and inspected. Contracts made with voluntary and private sector bodies for the provision of services must be supervised.

The welfare state encapsulated a very simple – even simplistic – model of welfare, publicly funded and publicly provided. It was easy to organise and control. Deviation from that model increases complexity because of the government's ambivalence towards the more mixed economy it wishes to establish. It believes in the model but faith stops short of confidence that the new pattern of provision can be trusted to deliver appropriate services – without a measure of state regulation. It accepts – implicitly if not explicitly – the potential defects of market provision in some areas. The result is an expansion of regulation, inspection, supervision, guidelines. A new form of regulatory welfare state rises phoenix-like from the ashes of the old collectivist provider state.

In so far as all political parties accept the reality of the mixed economy of welfare and the virtues and value of markets and a more plural system, the regulatory state is here to stay.

The impact on the Labour Party

X The final enduring legacy of Thatcherism's impact on the welfare state lies in its impact on the Labour Party. 'A major shift in policy', Gamble writes, 'becomes permanent when the opposition parties adopt it as their own' (Gamble, 1988, p. 219). The Labour Party has certainly not adopted all Mrs Thatcher's policies, but it has moved significantly and substantially. It has accepted – albeit reluctantly – the sale of council houses, it has accepted the National Curriculum, it has accepted a more mixed economy of welfare. It talks of 'market socialism' and accepts the value in appropriate circumstances of the market mechanism. 'It is in this notion of market socialism', says Tomlinson, 'that the effect of the New Right on the left's economic arguments is most notable in recent years' (Tomlinson, 1990, p. 34). Labour has been forced to retreat from any arguments about the virtue and value of high rates of taxation to achieve collective goals. High taxes are seen to be undesirable in principle, irrespective of what they are used for. Equality is not an end, merely a means to greater freedom.

Labour has moved, compelled to fight on the issues which Mrs Thatcher has established as the key ones. She has set the agenda. 'Arguably', Hugo Young writes, 'the new model Labour Party was one of her most important creations' (*The Thatcher Legacy*, 1990, p. 6) . . .

Conclusion

The essential legacy of Thatcherism does not lie in the wholesale restructuring of the welfare state. Rather, it lies in its contribution to attitudes, ideas and approaches – which does not make it less considerable.

The conventional wisdom about the inevitability and the appropriateness of collective action has been challenged. Markets in welfare have been actively promoted. Significant 'cuts' in areas hitherto deemed politically sacrosanct have been made. A new, sharper approach to the management of social services has been pressed on the world of welfare. Inequality has been positively promoted as a virtue and a more divided society has resulted. Local government has been systematically shorn of powers, rights and duties so that it is little more than an enabling outpost of a more centralised state. The mixed economy of welfare has been promoted and accepted. Fact has become policy in a way which sustains both the critique of collectivism and the promotion of markets. The rights of citizenship have been curtailed. Responsibilities have replaced rights as the password. Citizens have become consumers with all the loss of rights which that means. While government may provide less, the forms of regulatory government involvement have expanded and extended its reach. Collectivism may be sick but the regulatory state is in rude health. And, lastly, the influence of Thatcherism has permeated the opposition. The Labour Party has trimmed its sails to the agenda set by Thatcherism.

Much of what has happened in the 1980s will endure. The welfare state was ripe for change and Mrs Thatcher's governments seized a ripening time. Even if there was no initial strategy, there was a commitment which evolved into a strategy in the third term, when the really radical proposals took shape. The changes, though, have been too numerous and too economical for any new government to be able easily to restore the old order, even if it wished to do so.

At the deepest level, however, Thatcherism has failed totally. Mrs Thatcher always saw her basic aim as being to change the hearts and minds of men and women. Seen in that light, Thatcherism has to be regarded, in Ivor Crewe's words, as 'a crusade that failed' (*Guardian*, 30 November 1989). She inspired the converted but she was unable, in Skidelsky's judgement, 'to create a larger constituency of understanding. She failed as an educator' (Guardian, 21 December 1990). The opinion poll evidence is unequivocal. Through the 1980s, opinion moved remorselessly against Thatcherism and became ever more firmly committed to the social democratic heresy of higher taxes and better services (Taylor-Gooby, 1990, p. 2). In spite of the

Thatcher governments' crusading approach 'remarkably few of its injunctions about the good and proper life', Young concludes, 'appear to have impinged on the British mind' (Young, 1989, p. 529). That is important but certainly does not weaken the argument that Thatcherism will leave an enduring legacy. Governments take account of public opinion but often only to ignore it if they judge the issue to be one which will only have a limited impact on actual voting behaviour. Opinions about welfare seem to fall in that category.

Thatcherism's enduring legacy will be twofold. Firstly, it is in challenging the conventional wisdom and opening issues for debate. Many sacred cows have lost their odour of sanctity. Secondly, there are the many actual institutional changes – the deposit of 11 years of creeping Thatcherism. The undoing of so much minor change, even if cumulative in its impact, is not the kind of task to which succeeding governments feel called. Because of Thatcherism, the future of welfare will be very different.

Questions and Issues

Health, Welfare and Poverty: Section 14

The most relevant readings appear in brackets after each question.

1 Describe and account for the relationship between social class and health inequalities. (Section 14, especially Readings 61–62, 65)
2 Explain and illustrate what is meant by the 'social construction of health'. (Readings 61–65)
3 'Social problems are what people think they are'. Discuss. (Readings 62, 64–65)
4 Who, if anyone, is to blame for poverty? (Readings 62, 65)
5 What is meant by the 'new poverty' and 'dependency culture'? (Readings 16, 44, 62, 65)
6 Why, by most measures, did the poor become relatively poorer and the rich richer under Thatcherism? (Readings 66–67)

SECTION 15

DEVIANCE

Introduction: Readings 67–72

The first reading in this section is a classic from Howard Becker presenting the concept of labelling. Few single concepts have been more influential in sociology. Labelling theory develops the insight that 'social reality' is largely defined by the powerful. Much of the rest of this section is about 'nitty-gritty' issues of crime, but for readers who want to pursue the question of how deviance and social 'problems' come to be defined, Reading 66 will be helpful.

Most of the readings in this section are about the kinds of crime to which the majority are most at risk – for instance, street crime and domestic violence. It is particularly useful, therefore, to precede these readings with an overview of crime from Duncan Campbell which illustrates that crime can be big business as well as petty and personal.

The next two readings deal with a currently influential approach to crime – the left realist. Both 'right' and 'left' realism claim to be concerned with seeking solutions to crime which have the support and even the involvement of victims or potential victims of crime. However, 'right' solutions tend to the individualistic and 'left' solutions to the communal (particularly, involving multi-agency approaches, i.e. joint action by public and private organisations). The left realist approach involves considerable community involvement in researching crime, particularly through the medium of the victim survey. Reading 70 specifically examines the experience of female victims of crime.

Reading 71 is made up of two short articles which have a different emphasis on, if not distinctly different views about, the relationship between poverty and crime. Bob Holman has little doubt that poverty can have a degrading effect and tends to be associated with certain types of criminal activity. In contrast, Richard Kinsey draws on social survey data to suggest that in a number of significant respects the stereotypes of the law-abiding middle class and the more criminally-prone poor is misleading. Both write about a particular area of Scotland, and although their debate is more widely relevant, their empirical data may not be. In reading 72, Alison Uttley discusses the growing phenomenon of the surveillance of everyday life.

Howard S. Becker: Deviance and Labelling

Whereas Durkheim describes deviance in terms of breaking society's rules, Becker defines it as the public 'labelling' of an individual as a rule-breaker or deviant, whether or not she/he actually performed the act of which she/he is accused. In defining deviance in this way, Becker draws attention to the power of society and, particularly, of law enforcement agencies such as the courts or police to make labels 'stick'. He also stresses the consequences of labelling in terms of social stigmatisation and loss of personal esteem and opportunity. Both these points are apparent in the extract from Malinowski's research in the Trobriand Islands quoted by Becker. It is only when the youth is publicly labelled as a sexual deviant that he is fully regarded as such, and only then do the consequences of 'being a deviant' come into operation. Although Becker is certainly not a Marxist, his anlaysis is quite compatible with the view that the wealthy and powerful can frequently avoid unwanted labels, whereas the less well off and powerless find this more difficult to do. Both interactionists and modern Marxists, therefore, go beyond Durkheim's primary concern with rules and rule-breaking to issues of power, control and enforcement.

Reading 67 From Howard S. Becker, *Outsiders: Studies in the Sociology of Deviance* (Collier Macmillan, 1966), pp. 8–12

The sociological view I have just discussed defines deviance as the infraction of some agreed-upon rule. It then goes on to ask who breaks rules, and to search for the factors in their personalities and life situations that might account for the infractions. This assumes that those who have broken a rule constitute a homogeneous category, because they have committed the same deviant act.

Such an assumption seems to me to ignore the central fact about deviance: it is created by society. I do not mean this in the way it is ordinarily understood, in which the causes of deviance are located in the social situation of the deviant or in 'social factors' which prompt his action. I mean, rather, that *social groups create deviance by making the rules whose infraction constitutes deviance,* and by applying those rules to particular people and labeling them as outsiders. From this point of view, deviance is *not* a quality of the act the person commits, but rather a consequence of the application by others of rules and sanctions to an 'offender'. The deviant is one to whom that label has successfully been applied; deviant behavior is behavior that people so label.

Since deviance is, among other things, a consequence of the responses of others to a person's act, students of deviance cannot assume that they are dealing with a homogeneous category when they study people who have been labeled deviant. That is, they cannot assume that these people have actually committed a deviant act or broken some rule, because the process of labeling may not be infallible; some people may be labeled deviant who in fact have not broken a rule. Furthermore, they cannot assume that the category of those labeled deviant will contain all those who actually have broken a rule, for many offenders may escape apprehension and thus fail to be included in the population of 'deviants' they study. Insofar as the category lacks homogeneity and fails to include all the cases that belong to it, one cannot reasonably expect to find common factors of personality or life situation that will account for the supposed deviance.

What, then, do people who have been labeled deviant have in common? At the least, they share the label and the experience of being labeled as outsiders. I will begin my analysis with this basic similarity and view deviance as the product of a transaction that takes place between some social group and one who is viewed by that group as a rule-breaker. I will be less concerned with the personal and social characteristics of deviants than with the process by which they come to be thought of as outsiders and their reactions to that judgement.

Malinowski discovered the usefulness of this view for understanding the nature of deviance many years ago, in his study of the Trobriand Islands:

> One day an outbreak of wailing and a great commotion told me that a death had occurred somewhere in the neighborhood. I was informed that Kima'i, a young lad of my acquaintance, of sixteen or so, had fallen from a coco-nut palm and killed himself . . . I found that another youth had been severely wounded by some mysterius coincidence. And at the funeral there was obviously a general feeling of hostility between the village where the boy died and that into which his body was carried for burial.
>
> Only much later was I able to discover the real meaning of these events. The boy had committed suicide. The truth was that he had broken the rules of exogamy, the partner in his crime being his maternal cousin, the daughter of his mother's sister. This had been known and generally disapproved of but nothing was done until the girl's discarded lover, who had wanted to marry her and who felt personally injured, took the initiative. This rival threatened first to use black magic against the guilty youth, but this had not much effect. Then one evening he insulted the culprit in public – accusing him in the hearing of the whole community of incest and hurling at him certain expressions intolerable to a native.
>
> For this there was only one remedy; only one means of escape remained to the unfortunate youth. Next morning he put on festive attire and ornamentation, climbed a coco-nut palm and addressed the community, speaking from among the palm leaves and bidding them farewell. He explained the reasons for his desperate deed and also launched forth a veiled accusation against the man who had driven him to his death, upon which it became the duty of his clansmen to avenge him. Then he wailed aloud, as is the custom, jumped from a palm some sixty feet high and was killed on the spot. There followed a fight within the village in which the rival was wounded; and the quarrel was repeated during the funeral . . .
>
> If you were to inquire into the matter among the Trobrianders, you would find . . . that the natives show horror at the idea of violating the rules of exogamy and that they believe that sores, disease and even death might follow clan incest. This is the ideal of native law and in moral matters it is easy and pleasant strictly to adhere to the ideal – when judging the conduct of others or expressing an opinion about conduct in general.
>
> When it comes to the application of morality and ideals to real life, however, things take on a different complexion. In the case described it was obvious that the facts would not tally with the ideal of conduct. Public opinion was neither outraged by the knowledge of the crime to any extent, nor did it react directly – it had to be mobilised by a public statement of the crime and by insults being hurled at the culprit by an interested party. Even then he had to carry out the punishment himself . . . Probing further into the matter and collecting concrete information, I found that the breach of exogamy – as regards intercourse and not

> marriage – is by no means a rare occurrence, and public opinion is lenient, though decidedly hypocritical. If the affair is carried on *sub rosa* with a certain amount of decorum, and if no one in particular stirs up trouble – 'public opinion' will gossip, but not demand any harsh punishment. If, on the contrary, scandal breaks out – everyone turns against the guilty pair and by ostracism and insults one or the other may be driven to suicide.

Whether an act is deviant, then, depends on how other people react to it. You can commit clan incest and suffer from no more than gossip as long as no one makes a public accusation . . .

Duncan Campbell: The Business of Crime

Given that crime is so often associated with the 'lower' class rather than the rich and 'respectable', it is very useful to have a description of crime as the multi-billion pound industry that it is. Duncan Campbell provides this.

Of course, sociologists have long been aware both of 'white-collar' crime and of the crimes of political and business elites. The opportunities and rewards available to the latter for committing crime can be substantial and dwarf those available to the lower-class criminal. Research also shows that middle and, especially, upper-class people are less likely to be prosecuted for the crime they commit and tend to receive shorter sentences if, and when, they are tried and found guilty. Thus, the top executives found guilty in the Guiness share-support trial received short sentences despite the billions of pounds involved. One of them, Ernest Saunders, had his five-year sentence commuted because he was apparently suffering from Alzheimer's disease. He subsequently took up a well-paid post in industry. The wealthy often have better means available to avoid getting caught. Ironically, Robert Maxwell was able to use the libel laws very effectively in this regard.

Campbell is less concerned to trace which groups commit what crime than to describe the various types and financial value of criminal activity. Read with a sociological eye, however, it is a simple matter to deduce that some types of crime involve not only professional criminals, but other professional and business people.

Reading 68 From Duncan Campbell, 'Crime Becomes Boom Industry' in *Guardian,* August 17 1992, pp. 1–2, 24

Professional crime is now the fourth largest industry in Britain and the country's fastest-growing business.

A Guardian survey, using research from government and private sector sources, indicates that professional crime now has an annual turnover of around £14 billion. This is higher than ICI, British Aerospace, Hanson and BAT and surpassed only by BP, Shell and Unilever.

While professional crime has not yet reached the pre-eminence it enjoys in, say, Colombia, Bolivia or Italy, it is now one of the major money-making businesses.

Crime also now employs, either as active criminals or in the law enforcement agencies, courts, prisons and probation services, more than 420,000 people.

More than twice as many people now gain employment in the criminal area, whether legal or illegal, as in the textile industry. In employment terms, crime is the equivalent of the energy and water industry (408,000) and not far short of banking (585,000).

The survey, compiled by the Guardian from figures from the Home Office, the Association of British Insurers, Customs and Excise, the British Retailers Consortium, the Serious Fraud Office, the Department of Employment and other public and private bodies, shows that criminal proceeds have never been higher.

Drugs, fraud and shop theft account for the largest portion of criminal enterprises. Proceeds from drugs and fraud now total at least £8 billion. Both those areas are expanding rapidly, as is car crime.

The estimates do not include the black economy areas of tax fiddling and the sums do not include the costs of administering the criminal justice system – the cost of policing last year, for instance, was £4.67 billion. The figures are an estimate of what people make from crime.

Last month, the newly formed National Criminal Intelligence Service said that it had already identified about 50 top earning criminals, all making at least six figure sums a year.

There are believed to be a few hundred other criminals at this level of earning. Below them is the increasing number of people who, as the recession deepens, now routinely make a living from drugs, fraud, armed robbery, burglary, car theft, arson and shoplifting. Crime has risen by 32 per cent under the present government.

New "recession" and "Euro" crimes have emerged as big money-earners: arson is on the increase as businesses fold and fiddles on Euro grants and subsidies are providing a multi-million pound living for the more sophisticated end of the criminal market in Britain and Europe.

Yesterday Tony Mullet, the Director of the NCIS, said: "While crimes like fraud and drug dealing are not highly visible, their effects on society are pernicious".

The NCIS respresents the first serious attempt at a national strategy "to target the top level of criminals whose activities cause financial and personal harm out of all proportion to their numbers", added Mr Mullet, previously the Chief Constable of West Mercia. He stressed that estimating illicit earnings and the numbers of those involved in serious organised crime remained an inexact science but he believed that NCIS could have an impact on such crime.

Making crime pay, to the tune of £14 bn

Crime is often described as a growth industry, the people who profit from it are called professional criminals. But how big an industry is it? And how much do criminals actually make out of crime?

The Guardian has collated information from a number of sources in what is believed to be the first comprehensive attempt to examine how much is made from crime in the United Kingdom.

The figures inevitably include estimates and guesstimates. We have made use of the data available from police, Home Office, insurers, businesses, banks and professional criminals.

The conclusion is that professional crime now has a turnover of around £14 billion. This places it fourth in the league table of companies below BP, (£41.2 billion) Shell, (£29.7 billion) and Unilever, (£23.1 billion) but above BAT, (£13.8 billion) British Telecom, ICI, British Aerospace, British Gas, Grand Met, Sainsbury and Hanson.

It affords employment for 130,000 police officers, 50,000 civilian staff, 34,200 prison officers, 7,000 probation officers, 10,000 staff in magistrates courts, 2,000 in crown courts, 175,000 security industry personnel, 1,200 barristers, those of the 69,000 solicitors doing criminal practice, and of course, the professional criminals themselves. A number of these help to make up the 45,000 prison population. In addition, there are the ones that have never been caught.

The National Criminal Intelligence Service computer will have room for 25,000 names when it is up and running.

Tony Mullet, director of the service, said this summer that 50 top criminals had been targeted, men earning at least £100,000 a year from crime. There are probably in addition "some hundreds", including drug dealers and bank robbers, making similar good livings.

All this makes crime one of Britain's largest employers with around 420,000 on either official or unofficial payrolls.

To put it in context, here are other industries and their workforces:

Retail distribution	2,119,000
Education	1,766,000
Hotel and Catering	1,134,000
Construction	843,000
Banking	585,000
Food, drink, tobacco	495,000
Crime	420,000
Energy/water	408,000
Textile industry	175,000

Below we look at how crime has become the fastest-growing, recession-proof business.

Arson:

Increases at time of recession. A mixture of known criminals torching properties for a fee, often as little as £1,000, and people whose businesses are failing and who see arson as a chance to claim insurance. The latter are often caught. Last year commercial fire damage cost £774.6 million and domestic £243.5 million. The Association of British Insurers reckons that 40 per cent of the total is arson, giving a total of £407.2 million.

Drugs:

For a number of years it has been guesstimated that Customs seize around 10 per cent of the drugs in this country. Both Customs and NCIS, who took over intelligence gathering on drugs this year, stress that the 10 per cent figure should not be seen as the official one. A Customs spokesman reckons that the percentage seized could be anything between 10 and 25 per cent but "even that is a wild stab in the dark."

There are two additional yardsticks which are used in calculating drugs money: the Home Office register of heroin addicts, which shows an annual growth, and the street price of the drugs. If drug prices rise dramatically it is a fair indicator that there is a shortage. This happened in the 1980s in the cannabis market after a 50 ton seizure but street prices remain steady at present.

The 1991 seizures by Customs and Excise show that the market is stable and growing.

	Kilos	*Value*
Cocaine	1,061	£138m
Heroin	356	£40m
Cannabis	22,500	£63m
Synthetic	473	£33m
Total		£274m

Using the 10 per cent figure this would suggest that the drugs trade is worth £2.74 billion.

VAT fraud:

Customs had 59 major cases of VAT fraud that they pursued last year with a total value of £19 million. This does not include "compounding" which would take the total up to around double.

There are two main VAT fraud methods – suppressing sales and declaring less trade or "input frauds", false invoicing using bogus companies. Many former armed robbers moved into the simple VAT fraud of buying gold abroad, often in Holland, and flying or shipping it into Britain where it was resold, avoiding VAT. It was a simple money-maker with the added advantage that no violence was needed.

Estimate: £38 million.

CAP frauds:

One estimate has it that Common Agricultural Policy frauds cost the EC citizen £20 per head per wage erarner, although Customs suggest this is "guessing in the wind".

Frauds involve claims for bogus subsidies, the misappropriation of grants and false declarations of container loads. It is of growing concern to Interpol. In 1991, £40 million was traced in an area described by MEP John Tomlinson as "the greatest incentive to crime in Europe".

UK estimate: £500 million.

Plastic card fraud:

£165.6 million a year (according to the Association for Payment Clearing Services). Les Agar, head of South Yorkshire drug squad: "Studies of drug activity have convinced us of the strong link between the fastest growing categories of crime such as cheque and credit card fraud and increasing use of drugs. These are problems which feed on each other."

Banks are notoriously cagey about the amounts lost, partly because they do not wish to disturb customers and alarm shareholders by revealing the sums lost by what many security experts feel is their overactive promotion of cards.

There are plans to introduce personalised cards which would have the photos of the owner on them and would make crime more difficult but progress on this has been slow.

Car crime:

A car is stolen in Britain every two minutes and a total of 575,000 were stolen between October 1990 and September 1991.

A further 889,000 cars were broken into and had valuables removed, car radios being the most popular target, with 400,000 stolen. One in five cars are stolen from public car parks. Home Office figures suggest that 27 per cent of cars that go missing are stolen for profit and 8 per cent for insurance fraud, the remainder being joyriders. The crime is one of the major growth areas as was recognised when four men were jailed for a total of 24 years in June at Southwark crown court for running what police believed was a multi-million car ringing racket.

Total: £626 million.

Extortion:

One of the largest attempted extortions of recent years was carried out by Rodney Witchelow, jailed for 17 years attempting to extract £500,000 from pet food and baby food companies. There have been a series of imitators, who cause irritation and lose money for the company but rarely make money for themselves. The Met reported a wave of copycat attempts after the screening of a documentary on contamination/extortion. Estimates of what is paid out are less than £100,000.

Fraud:

The most serious and complex frauds are investigated by the Serious Fraud Office, who in the last financial year had investigated cases involving the theft of £5.3 billion. An SFO spokeswoman said these varied from "a one man band taking the money because he wants to buy a yacht to people carrying out fraud to keep a company going".

The SFO only investigate frauds of £5 million upwards or ones that are highly complex or in the public interest to pursue. Local fraud squads attached to individual police forces investigate lesser fraud, with the Metropolitan Police fraud squad the major investigator. They liaise with the SFO on borderline cases. The 1991/92 Met fraud figure was £47.2 million. Provincial forces have their own fraud squads. Total fraud likely to be around £5.3 billion.

Armed robbery and theft from commercial property:

Armed robbers are still the main "faces" in criminal circles, the underworld's equivalent of Lloyd's names. Younger, more reckless, robbers have entered the field, with London remaining the armed robbery capital. There were 1,618 armed robberies in London last year compared with 1,291 the year before. This is half the national total and yielded nearly £8 million.

There are many hidden areas of theft. The brewing trade, for instance, loses £10 million a year from aluminium beer kegs which are stolen and smelted down. Aluminium is worth £1,000 a ton. Bernard Buckley of the Joint Brewers Association says: "It's massive".

The current estimate for the total of theft, which includes armed robberies, from businesses, offices, factories and industrial estates is: £316.6 million.

Burglary:

Shows no signs of abating. Ranges from the skilled country house burglar who specialises in disconnecting burglar alarms – "we love to see an alarm on an outside wall because then we know exactly what we have to do", says one – to the local teenager breaking in via the bathroom window.

Total last year: £590.7 million.

Shop theft:

This remains a growth area of crime, whether carried out by specialised teams – gangs of Australians and Colombians have won reputations for sophisticated operations – or schoolchildren. There were 289,700 shop theft offences in the last year to the end of March.

Research is being conducted on behalf of the British Retailers Consortium which represents 90 per cent of all retailers.

They believe that the Home Office estimate of £2.5 billion lost annually in shop theft, which includes instore pilfering and break-ins, is a great under-estimate as many shoplifters are dealt with by a caution. A likelier minimum total would be £3.2 billion.

Street crime:

The last Home Office estimate (1990) had £13 million as the figure for muggings and pickpocket thefts. Sums involved may be small but mugging is a crime that causes most concern to the victim.

Blackmail and kidnapping

The most successful blackmail cases are never reported. They tend to be carried out by full time and "one-off" criminals who come across usually sexually embarrassing material.

Police acknowledge that some victims would rather pay than face scandal or ridicule.

Kidnap is a growth crime. There is an increasing trend for criminals to take an employee of a bank or supermarket hostage and demand a ransom from their companies or relatives.

Police believe some cases are never reported for fear of reprisals.

Some of those involved are "amateurs", like bankrupt businessman John Warrington jailed last year for 15 years for kidnapping a woman and demanding £500,000. Others are pros.

There were nine kidnappings in London last year, compared with two the year before and a spate in Kent and Essex.

Compiled with assistance from: Home Office, Customs and Excise, British Retailers' Consortium, National Criminal Intelligence Service, Association of British Insurers, Serious Fraud Office, British Security Industry Association, Bar Council, Law Society, Department of Employment, Institute for the Study and Treatment of Delinquency, Victim Support.

Jock Young: Left Realism, Crime and the Social Survey

The mood to engage more directly with the 'realities' of crime has affected thinkers of the Left as well as of the Right. Here Jock Young crisply states the motivations behind the development of a left realist approach to crime. The roots of left realism lie in a simple desire to reduce the amount of suffering experienced by working-class (and, of course, other) people as a result of crime. This involves an attack on crude Marxist romantic and other left idealist approaches to crime which see it as some sort of attack on the capitalist system. In contrast, left realists see much crime as an attack on working-class people or their property which needs to be reduced or, if possible, stopped.

The left realist approach, including its preferred research methodology – the victim survey – is democratic. Here, Young argues that a properly designed victim survey is perhaps the only way to achieve adequate data about the experience and opinions of victims (see Reading 70). Their opinions should provide an essential in-put into policy. Left realists also argue that members of local communities must themselves be involved in crime prevention and, in this respect, there is a developing consensus with right realists.

Reading 69 From Jock Young, 'Left Realism and the Priorities of Crime Control' in K. Stenson and D. Cowell *eds.*, *The Politics of Crime Control* (Sage Publications, 1991), pp. 146–49

Left Realism in criminology is a social democratic approach to the analysis of crime and the development of effective policies of crime control. At the heart of this approach is the recognition that crime is now a very real source of suffering for the poor and the vulnerable, particularly in the inner cities. Ironically, for too long it has been the parties of the Right that have gained most benefit from this at the ballot box. They have claimed, with some justification, that the liberals and the Left have cared more for the offender than for the victim. This has provided a rationale for right-wing administrations expanding the budgets of the crime control industry, without adequately ensuring that citizens get value for the public money so spent, while simultaneously reducing spending on other public services. At the same time they have shown scant interest in investigating the deeper causes of crime and tackling those socioeconomic conditions which help to provide fertile soil for the growth of crime; in fact their policies seem almost designed to promote it. Furthermore, when their policies clearly fail to halt the rising tide of crime, as in Britain, they are not above making tactical shifts in claiming that the problems have been exaggerated and that since there is little the police and justice systems can do in any case, it is better for citizens to do more to protect themselves!

Yet, for too long, many voices on the Left have found the kinds of crime which cause greatest public alarm to be an embarrassment, since most of these crimes occur within poor neighbourhoods and involve both poor victims and assailants. It is difficult to romanticize this type of crime as some kind of disguised attack on the privileged. The response by the Left has often been to shift attention away to the anti-social behaviour of the powerful and to the discriminatory and stigmatizing behaviour of the agencies of control. This position, in effect, denies the external reality of crime and tends to reduce it to a set of labels imposed on the behaviour of the allegedly powerless (Young, 1986).

A social democratic approach to crime must avoid the mistakes of those on the Right and the Left and, using empirical research, take care to discover the experiences and concerns of ordinary citizens. Through this, it should encourage the move towards more accountable strategies of crime prevention and control, in which fairness and non-discrimination should be founding principles. This may help to build up confidence among the poor in reformed official agencies. Only by developing a genuine partnership between official agencies and the public can real progress be made towards a more civilized way of life. Left Realism offers the hope that something *can* be done about crime.

In this chapter I will first outline the structure of realist theory, in particular, the role of surveys and the linkages between four key factors: the police and other agencies of control; the public; the offender and the victim. Then I will examine the role of the agencies involved in crime control.

Britain, like most advanced industrial countries, has faced a seemingly inexorable rise in crime since the Second World War, and this is in spite of better living standards and a vast increase in expenditure on police, judiciary and prisons.

Some crime control measures work, some do not, and some are simply counter-productive, but precious little research is available to sort out the wheat from the chaff. This is extraordinary, given the vast amount spent on crime control in Britain. In 1988, for example, £3500 million went to the police force, £698 million to the prisons and £1000 million to the criminal justice system. In the private sector, £1000 million was spent on security equipment alone, while local authorities spent as much again on crime-related areas.

Yet this expenditure seems to have little effect on the rise in crime, and more research is urgently needed. At present, policy decisions can only be based on the last 15 years of substantiated findings. We need, for example, to know the success rate of relatively new crime control measures, such as the neighbourhood watch schemes, and how this differs between, say, inner-city areas and the suburbs.

A consensus exists as to the need for a multi-agency approach to crime control. Partly, this comes from the obvious fact that crime has always been controlled through the family, through schools, and by the police. But it also, more importantly, stems from how all of society can co-operate in preventing crime; every crime control agency or social institution needs support from the others.

A further reason why research needs to be updated is that the public's attitude must be gauged. Many crimes, such as attacks against members of ethnic minorities or cases of domestic violence, are under-reported, because the victims feel that the police will not treat them sympathetically. Only some very probing social surveys can reveal what the public expect from crime control agencies and, until this is done, effective policies cannot be made.

Obviously the task of any crime control policy is to reduce crime in general. In this, it is like a community health project: success cannot be measured by how much a well-off person can jump the queue for care, but how such indicators as reduction of infant mortality and increased life expectancy for adults reflect the effectiveness of the service.

Both crime and ill-health, while being universal problems, affect some sectors of society more than others. Therefore we must target our resources in order to reduce the general rate of crime. Unfortunately – and this had always been a problem with welfare provision in Britain – resources have been distributed more to those people with political muscle and social power, rather than to those in most need. The history of the National Health Service and state educational provisions are adequate evidence. Crime control has parallel problems.

The survey and the citizen

For Left Realism, the social survey is a democratic instrument (Painter *et al.*, 1989; Jones *et al.*, 1986, 1987; Crawford *et al.*, 1990): it gives a detailed picture of consumer demand and satisfaction. Without such research, policy makers have little to go on. Many crimes are unreported and the aggregate statistics for the whole country do not give enough information. Rates of crime and types of crime will obviously vary between inner-city, suburban and rural areas, so without local surveys there is no basis for appropriate crime control measures.

Unless the views of the public are made clear in this way, experts and politicians will advise and act on their own. For example, crimes against women – from harassment to rape or murder – are often ignored because of under-reporting by victims. This is ascribed to 'irrationality' on the part of women, yet it seems rational, if a woman is attacked by her partner, that she will not report it for fear of further violence.

Generalized national research produces figures of little worth. More invidiously, it allows politicans to talk of irrational fears of crime when compared to the average risk rate of the 'average' citizen. The 1982 British Crime Survey showed that the risk of experiencing robbery in England and Wales was once every five centuries; an assault resulting in injury once every century; a burglary once every 50 years. But 'irrational' fears are not so, for people who live in circumstances where there is a high risk of being a victim of crime.

The left realist approach to crime control sees social surveys as crucial. Without them, we cannot know the 'lived reality' of people at risk, which in turn affects key policy decisions such as the role and effectiveness of beat policing or neighbourhood watch schemes. However while research can help in the direction and prioritization of crime control, its results cannot provide us with a blueprint. The process of moving from input to policing involves four stages: identification of problems, assessment of priorities, application of principles, and ascertaining possibilities.

The victimization survey accurately provides a map of the problems of an area. Although based on public input, it delivers what any individual member of the public is ignorant of: that is how private problems are publicly distributed. In this task, it shows which social groups within the population face the greatest risk rates and geographically pinpoints where these occurrences are most frequent. In this it directs crime intervention initiatives towards those people and places which are most at risk. It therefore reveals the concealed crime rate and it ascertains its social and spatial focus. But it goes beyond this, for risk rates alone, however delineated, do not measure the true impact of crime and hence the actual patterning of crime as a social problem. To do this we must advance beyond the one-dimensional approach of aggregate risk rates and place crime in its social context. The myth of the equal victim underscores much of conventional victimology with its notion that victims are, as it were, equal billiard balls, and the risk rate merely involves the calculation of the chances of an offending billiard ball impacting upon them. People are, of course, not equal; they are more, or less, vulnerable, depending on their place in society.

First of all, at certain parts of the social structure, we have a compounding of social problems. If we were to draw a map of the city outlining areas of high infant mortality, bad housing, unemployment, poor nutrition, etc, we would find that all these maps would coincide and that futher, the outline traced would correspond to those areas of high criminal victimization (Clarke, 1980). And those suffering from street crime would also suffer most from white-collar and corporate crime (Lea and Young, 1984).

The first of these two aspects is illustrated in the next extract (Reading 70, from the Islington Crime Survey carried out by Jock Young, among others).

Further, this compounding of social problems occurs against those who are more or less vulnerable because of their position in the social structure. That is, people who have least power socially suffer most from crime. Most relevant here are the social relationships of age, class, gender and race. Realist analysis, by focusing on the combination of these fundamental social relationships, allows us to note the extraordinary differences between social groups as to both the impact of crime and the focus of policing . . .

T. Jones, B. MacLean and J. Young: Female Victims of Crime

The most commonly used official measure of crime is crime recorded by the police. Victim surveys provide another measure of crime. In most categories of crime, the number claiming to be victims is higher than that recorded by the police.

In addition to providing an alternative or supplementary measure of crime, victim surveys can provide data on people's experiences of and attitudes towards crime. The Islington Crime Survey sought substantial information of this kind from female victims. Two areas are considered in the extract below: avoidance behaviours by women and the impact of sexual and domestic assault on women. Fear of becoming victim to certain types of crime means women tend to adapt their behaviour to reduce the risk of crime more than men. The extract includes an examination of some ethnic and age dimensions of these behaviours. The section on sexual and domestic assault is included for its stark information about brutal types of crime which even today may often remain hidden.

Reading 70 From T. Jones, B. MacLean and J. Young, *The Islington Crime Survey* (Gower, 1986), pp. 167–175, 178

Avoidance behaviours

A number of questions were asked on the interview schedule which attempted to measure the kinds of precautions which people take in order to reduce their risk of victimization. Table 4.8 presents the questions and the gender differences measured by them:

Table 4.8 Avoidance behaviour (by gender[1])

	Never		*Occasionally*		*Often*		*Always*	
Question	*Male*	*Female*	*Male*	*Female*	*Male*	*Female*	*Male*	*Female*
Avoid going out after dark	73.5	29.2	12.6	17.1	7.0	16.9	6.9	36.7
Avoid certain types of people	52.2	32.6	32.9	31.3	10.3	22.9	4.7	13.2
Avoid certain streets or areas	61.6	36.0	21.9	24.4	11.9	22.3	4.6	16.1
Go out with someone else instead of alone	73.4	27.3	13.5	20.3	9.2	29.1	3.9	23.3
Avoid using buses or trains	85.5	59.9	9.4	21.9	3.4	11.6	1.8	6.8
Use a car rather than walk	81.1	55.5	7.7	14.3	5.7	16.5	5.5	13.7

[1] Expressed as percentages of respondents

Base: All respondents weighted n= 9386

Table 4.8 clearly illustrates that there are substantial differences between men and women in terms of the precautions which they take simply to avoid the possibility of crime. 37% of all women never go out after dark whereas only 7% of all men avoid going out after dark simply as a

DCS, BCS and MCS (below) refer to other crime victim surveys. The British Crime Survey is national in scope.

precaution against crime. The differences are all quite high for each of the indicators of avoidance behaviour investigated by the survey. These gender differences, by way of comparison, are also observed by the 1984 DCS, although its treatment of the first BCS data is sketchy in relation to gender. The overall percentage for items 3 and 4 above are reported in the second BCS as 41% of women avoid certain streets or areas *after dark* usually or always, and half the women went out with someone rather than alone usually or always (Hough and Mayhew, 1985, p. 40).

These figures do not lend themselves to a proper comparison of the two survey's findings. The MCS found that 96% of the men under thirty, 93% of the men between the ages of 30 and 49, and 77% of older men never avoided going out after dark as a precaution against crime. Women on the other hand reported that 19% under 30, 21% between the ages of 30 and 49 and 46% of older women always avoided going out after dark as a precaution against crime (Kinsey, 1984, p. 91).

For purposes of simplicity of analysis and presentation of data, all of the measures or questions asked on the survey regarding avoidance behaviour were collapsed into one composite measure which we called the scale of avoidance behaviour. From this composite measure we determined which groups of people were either low, medium or high on the scale of avoidance behaviour, and we were then able to break this down by a number of key variables. Table 4.9 breaks down the scale scores for avoidance behaviour by gender, in order to grasp an overall difference between men and women in terms of this type of behaviour:

Table 4.9 Avoidance scale scores (by gender[1])

Avoidance	*Men*	*Women*
High	3.4	20.2
Medium	36.1	64.2
Low	60.5	15.6

[1] Expressed as percentages in each category

Base: All respondents weighted n= 9386

As can be predicted from the previous information, the differences between men and women are high and indicate that women are forced to take the responsibility for their own safety themselves much more seriusly than do men. The difficulty with Table 4.9, however, is that it does not make allowances for the variations which occur across age and race which were observed in the tables in the previous section on perceptions of risk. In order to control for the variables of race and age, Table 4.10 gives the break down of avoidance behaviour as measured by the scale by race, age, and by gender.

Table 4.10 illustrates some very important relationships which must be further elaborated. There can be little doubt that women are much more likely than men to avoid potentially threatening situations, and the differences between men and women seem to reduce as age is increased. As people get older they tend to take more precautions regardless of gender or of race. The only exception to this general trend is that of black males who almost never avoid specific situations and in the medium avoidance category the middle age black males are a higher percentage than older males. There are, however, some very substantial differences between women of different race. 18% of all white women, 34% of all black women and 44% of all Asian women almost always avoid specific situations as a precaution against crime. By way of comparison, it must be remembered from Chapter 2 that while women were more likely than men to be victims of personal crimes, such as theft from person, assault and sexual assault, it was clearly black women, generally, who were more at risk than white women, except for sexual assault in which white women were more at risk, and theft and assault where white women were more at risk in the youngest age category. As can be seen from Table 4.10 it is the youngest age group of white females who are the least likely to avoid specific situations and are, therefore, the most at risk.

It is difficult to speculate what impact less avoidance behaviour displayed by black women would have on their victimization rates. It may well be that by

Table 4.10 Avoidance behaviour (by age, race and gender[1])

	Low		*Medium*		*High*	
	Males	*Females*	*Males*	*Females*	*Males*	*Females*
White						
16–24	69.0	15.3	29.9	69.8	1.1	14.9
25–44	72.9	16.1	26.3	64.3	0.8	19.6
45+	51.6	16.2	42.7	65.5	5.7	18.3
Total	61.9	16.0	34.9	65.8	3.2	18.2
Black						
16–24	60.9	16.9	39.1	53.5	0.0	29.6
25–44	56.8	12.1	43.2	60.3	0.0	27.6
45+	56.3	9.5	43.8	42.9	0.0	47.6
Total	57.6	13.1	42.4	53.3	0.0	33.6
Asian						
16–24	45.5	14.3	45.5	54.3	9.1	31.4
25–44	40.4	14.7	53.2	44.1	6.4	41.2
45+	30.8	13.3	53.8	26.7	15.4	60.0
Total	38.0	14.1	51.5	41.5	10.5	44.4
Other						
16–24	77.8	11.1	22.2	66.7	0.0	22.2
25–44	44.4	11.1	48.1	63.0	7.4	25.9
45+	69.2	7.7	7.7	61.5	23.1	30.8
Total	58.9	9.8	27.9	63.2	13.2	27.0

[1] Expressed as percentages in each category

Base: All respondents weighted n= 9386

avoiding situations they are avoiding a certain level of victimization. On the other hand, they may well be exposing themselves to more victimization by staying in during the evenings and avoiding strangers, in that it may well be acquaintances which are victimizing them. In either event, it is clear from Table 4.10 that women generally, and particularly older and black women, feel it is necessary to restrict their behaviour and avoid certain situations as a precaution against crime. *In this sense, the Islington Crime Survey helps to illustrate that a "curfew on women" appears to be implicitly operative.*

As suggested earlier, however, simple avoidance behaviours may not be a successful strategy in that there appears to be a level of aggression directed at women from people whom they know. Furthermore, as the above data suggest, avoidance behaviour increases with age when the actual risks of criminal victimization decrease with age. It was shown in Chapter 2 that the risk curve for women reaches a peak in the younger years, and this finding corresponds to all the known resaearch of this kind. While some writers such as Hough and Mayhew (1983, 1985) and Maxfield (1984) suggest that this is an anomaly, we feel that the level of violence to which women are subjected during their younger years (in part a consequence of less avoidance behaviour comparatively) makes them more cautious with age. Furthermore, in a sexist society younger women are perceived as sexual objects and are more subject to forms of sexual harassment accumulating over time. This point will be further explored in the final section.

It seems a double gender injustice that females are much more likely to be victims of male violence than vice-versa and that some often feel their own freedom of movement is constricted as well.

There can be little doubt that many women experience violent criminal victimization when younger, and they learn that not only is violence an unpleasant experience to say the least, but it is something about which little satisfactory institutional support is available leaving the responsibility to women to take their own precautions. This will be explored in the next section. We feel that the differentiation as portrayed by the BCS between risk and avoidance is due to two reasons. The first is that the BCS is only concerned with occurrences in the previous year. If a woman, for example, were the victim of rape three years ago it may be safe to assume that the experience had an effect on her both in terms of victimization and increased avoidance behaviour. While the BCS would not capture the case of rape, they would capture the fear and avoidance behaviours, leading the authors to the conclusion that these were out of proportion to risk. A second reason is that where the BCS focusses on the individual, we focus on the household. In this manner we can actually relate people's fear and avoidance with other householders' experiences. Unlike the BCS which assumes that people live in isolation and are not affected by the experiences of other family members, we are concerned with the social impact of crime on the entire household. For example, if two sisters living together had the experience of one of them being sexually assaulted, and it was the one who was not that was interviewed by the BCS, then they may conclude that the respondent's fear was out of proportion to risk. We, on the other hand, would have captured the incident and established the relationship between fear and avoidance and the incident of the sexual assault for the other sister.

In order to examine more closely the nature of some offences directed at women, the following section will briefly focus on the level of aggression that the female respondents of our sample experienced in the last year for the two most common criminal victimizations directed at women specifically – sexual assault and domestic assault.

The impact of sexual and domestic assault

Unlike other surveys the ICS revealed a high proportion of sexual and domestic assaults. The following two examples selected from the descriptions of offences given by respondents will help to illustrate some of the more violent incidents to which women were subjected.

1 Domestic assault, white female
"My husband and I are separated now. I asked him to leave. It was stupid, we started arguing, it was to do with cards and women. He became very angry and lost his tempter, he started hitting me and throwing things about, kicking the dog. He punched me down the stairs, I was quite badly hurt. He only ever gets like that towards me, he says, because he loves me. He's polite and nice to other people, that's why they never suspect any trouble and he takes it out on me."

2 Sexual assault, white female
"I was collecting up empty glasses in the bar just after closing, when a drunken lout, seeing that I had both hands loaded up with a pile of glasses, grabbed me from behind, and pushed his hand inside my bra and grabbing hold of [my breast] very hard. He then bit into my neck at the back, as I was calling for my husband who was in the other bar. He then moved is hand and pinched [me] between his nails. His other hand at the same time reached around the other way pulling up my skirt and clasping [me]. He pulled up sharply which stretched the knickers tightly through my crotch until the elastic snapped and they tore through. All the while he was biting into my neck harder and harder against the bone at the back just above the shoulder blade and pinching my breast. He then dug his nails and fingers into my vagina, and then it was over as suddenly as it started when my husband arrived from the other bar and pulled him off.

I'd say that all this happened in the space of about twenty seconds or less. I remember the whole thing so vividly and I was thinking absolutely clearly – wide awake and I knew that with 12 or more glasses piled inside each other in both hands, that if I tried to struggle or pull away I would most likely have tripped and fallen forwards onto the glasses causing myself a very nasty injury."

These two examples show that there is a very real level of violence to which some women are subject and that to make the attempts to avoid them from happening, or to be frightened that they may occur, is not an unrealistic response.

In virtually all of the measured occurrences of sexual assault and domestic violence the victim could give information about the assailant, with only 5% of the victims of sexual assault being unable to do so. All of the victims of domestic violence claimed to have known their assailant before, which is hardly surprising due to the definition of domestic violence, while 18% of the rape/attempted victims and 25% of the sexual assault victims knew their assailants. This figure seems low since it is a common assertion in the literature that very few sexual assaults are committed by strangers. It is quite probable that the ICS was more successful in capturing cases of unknown assailants than it was in discovering cases in which the assailants were known. Nevertheless, out data indicate that most of the cases of sexual assault which we found involved assailants that were unknown to the victim.

It is worth reminding the reader that the following data refer to an inner-urban area – they are not a firm basis for wider generalisations.

In order better to illustrate the level of violence used and the type of injury sustained we have partitioned out the data for the offences of domestic assault, rape/attempted and sexual assault. Because of the low number of actual rape or attempted rape cases, generalisation from these data is not warranted. Table 4.11 is the types of violence used by offence:

Table 4.11 Type of violence used (by offence[1])

	Domestic Violence	*Rape Attempted*[2]	*Sexual Assault*
Grabbed/Punched	74.5%	73.3%	67.7%
Punched/Slapped	92.1%	83.4%	14.3%
Kicked	56.9%	46.2%	4.5%
Weapon used	19.7%	24.7%	–
Raped	–	26.3%	–
Attempted rape	.7%	73.7%	–
Sexually assaulted	2.2%	–	100%
Other	5.5%	–	14.1%

[1] Multiple responses asked of respondent.

[2] Indicates other types of violence in combination with the rape or attempted rape (this applies to all subsequent tables).

Base: All victims weighted data

From Table 4.11 it can be seen that a substantial level of violence is used on all offences but particularly domestic violence. Even more dramatic is that the level of physically injurious violence seems higher for domestic assault than it is for rape/attempted since in all categories, except for the use of a weapon where the difference is slight, the proportion of cases reporting a specific form of violence is higher than for rape. In the cases where other forms of violence were reported, the interviewers recorded such things as strangulation, cigarette burns, pinched and bitten, stabbed in the face with a cigarette, spat at, hair pulled and head-butted.

It is clear from Table 4.11 that a high level of violence is directed at women in the commission of these offences, but in order to determine what injuries are sustained from these assaults Table 4.12 breaks down type of injury by type of offence.

From Table 4.12 it can be seen that at minimum nearly all respondents reported bruises. Surprisingly, almost 10% of all domestic assaults resulted in broken bones, indicating that while the survey under-estimates domestic violence, it is probably the most serious cases which have been disclosed to interviewers, so that generalization to all cases of domestic violence may not be warrented. Nevertheless, there appears to be sufficient violence in the cases disclosed to warrant concern. Other types of injury recorded by the interviewers included, sprained ankle, sprained wrist, sore breast, loss of hair, burns, bite marks, dizziness, bloody nose, tooth knocked out, bruised vocal chords, damaged back, broken vein in ear, bumps on head, "internal damage", concussion and partial loss of hearing.

Weapons were used in 22% of the cases of domestic assault on female respondents, and on 52% of the victims of rape/attempted. There were no weapons used in any of the cases of sexual assault uncovered by the survey. Use of weapons in domestic violence was restricted to whites and blacks. It would appear that white males are much more likely than black males to use weapons in domestic disputes since of the cases in which weapons were used 76% were white and 18% were black, with the balance falling into the residual category. Table 4.13 illustrates the type of weapon used by the three offences and the frequency of cases in which each weapon type was reported:

Table 4.12 Injury sustained (by offence[1])

	Domestic Violence	*Rape Attempted*	*Sexual Assault*
Bruises/Black eyes	96.3%	100%	86.5%
Scratches	62.2%	19%	56.0%
Cuts	45.0%	19%	13.5%
Broken bones	9.8%	–	–
Other	15.2%	25%	48.9%

[1] Multiple answers asked of respondent

Base: All victims – weighted data

Table 4.13 Type of weapon (by offence[1])

Percentage of Cases in which Weapon was Used			
Weapon	*Domestic Violence*	*Rape Attempted*	*Sexual Assault*
Bottle or glass	32.6%	46.2%	–
Knife or scissors	21.2%	28.0%	–
Stick, club or blunt object	28.3%	–	–
Firearm	–	–	–
Other	17.0%	25.8%	–

[1] Refers to female respondents only

. . . By way of summary to this section, it is very obvious from the data generated from the ICS that there is a considerable level of criminal violence used against women in the forms of domestic assault, rape/attempted and sexual assault. The most frequent and the most harmful in terms of obvious physical injury was observed for domestic violence. Psychological effects were most frequent in rape cases. Institutional responses were judged to be unsatisfactory on all cases of sexual crimes, and the impact that all of the offences produced for the victims was strikingly severe. There can be little doubt that many women face a significant level of criminal violence, especially in their younger years, so that it is not surprising, in fact, it should be expected that older women display a fear of leaving their homes during the evening. The anomaly is that due to the levels of domestic violence, women, in using avoidance behaviour as a precaution against crime, may be subjecting themselves to risks of domestic violence.

The Poverty and Crime Debate: Some Evidence from Scotland

71.1 Bob Holman: The Real Links between Poverty and Certain Types of Crime

The debate about the causes of crime intensified as the crime rate – notably crimes against property – soared throughout the 80s and early 90s. Bob Holman's article on the links between poverty and crime should be read in the wider context of this still inconclusive debate. First, Holman would be the first to agree that certain types of crime tend to be associated more with the upper and middle classes. These include all sorts of financial and business fraud and theft. Second, Holman is at extreme pains not to blame all the poor for the crime that a minority of them commit. He sees collective social injustice, not the supposed moral or cultural inadequacy of the poor, as the main factor conducive towards crime. (Again, the majority of the poor do not commit crime so there can be no simple link of cause and effect between poverty and crime.) Holman sharply rejects Charles Murray's 'underclass' explanation of the high rate of certain crimes among the poor which is based on a view of their cultural inadequacy.

The five links Holman makes between social deprivation and crime are realistic and tangible. They are:

1 young people are bored;
2 drugs are readily available;
3 desperation – in the face of poverty;
4 the opportunity is there;
5 the culture of inequality.

In effect, he implies, that better education and training, more jobs, and a fairer social policy would reduce both poverty and crime.

Reading 71.1 From Bob Holman, 'Poverty is First among Crimes' in *Guardian*, 24 June 1992, p. 21

Nine o'clock on a Sunday morning. A trembling woman comes to our flat to phone the police. She had been woken by smoke and discovered a room ablaze from a burning missile thrown through a window. The previous evening a gang had attacked her partner outside the chippie, leaving him with 44 stitches.

The police interpreted the fire as a warning from the gang not to give evidence against them. Within hours, the family had been moved away to a bed and breakfast establishment. Soon they will be transferred to another flat. The children, who had been so happy in our clubs and the local schools, will face yet more upheavals.

When the agency for which I work held its AGM in the crowded Tenants' Association flat, next door flowers were piled high in a close where, a few days before, a teenager had been brutually stabbed to death. It is the paradox of terrible crimes in the midst of many good people.

Another neighbour, a member of the committee of the agency which employs me, obtained a job as a security guard at £1.90 an hour. She was alone in a disused building when five raiders burst in. While two held knives at her throat, the others made off with the gas cooker.

A mother, having just left her child at the creche run by the local community association, was knocked to the ground by two men who made off with her purse. The next day, the Salvation Army captain tells me that yet again his old van has been stolen. He grins: "They didn't get far this time. It broke down."

These crimes occurred within a few days in one district of Easterhouse, a peripheral Glasgow estate where unemployment is high and where 64 per cent of schoolchildren receive clothing grants – that is, they come from families with very low incomes. The apparent connection between crime and poverty is dismissed by John Major, who attributes illegal behaviour to individual wickedness, and by the Education Secretary, John Patten, who blames parents.

More surprising, Melanie Phillips, drawing upon the Scottish Crime Survey, asserts that "it seems to knock down the claim that crime inevitably rises when deprivation is rising" (Guardian, March 20). She holds that decreasing crime rates in Scotland should persuade English police to look north for solutions.

I agree that the English can learn from the Scottish. However, from where I live, the claims about a decreasing crime rate and a lack of connection with social deprivation must be challenged.

Many if not most crimes in our locality are not reported. People whose flats are screwed are rarely insured. The detection rate for such crimes is low, so why bother to call in the police? Sometimes the victims know the perpetrators but are too frightened to complain.

Whatever the recorded figures for Scotland as a whole, those in Strathclyde, which contains much of the country's urban population, are very different. Breaking down the 1991 Strathclyde figures between its police divisions serves to establish the links with social deprivation. D Division includes a large commuter area, villages, part of the city shopping centre and Easterhouse. Over the division, 39,012 crimes and offences were recorded in 1991, that is an average of 0.2 crimes per person. In Easterhouse, the average was double that. There is a connection between social deprivation and crime.

In establishing the connection, there is a danger of providing ammunition for the underclass school. New-right gurus, led by Charles Murray, claim British inner cities and peripheral estates are being taken over by a growing underclass of feckless young men, who refuse to work, and irresponsible lone mothers, who fail to bring their children up properly. This argument suggests that, supported by welfare benefits, they seek pleasure in drugs and further income from crime. He cites places like Easterhouse as examples of underclass "communities without fathers [where] the kids tend to run wild" and so become the next generation of criminals.

The underclass explanation of social problems has been gleefully accepted by politicians on the right to argue that social security benefits should be cut so as to drive the unemployed into low-paid jobs, that welfare should be transferred to a private market which can create those jobs, and that social workers should be more ready to coerce the young "barbarians", as Murray calls them, into acceptable life styles. The underclass proponents thus link poverty and crime in order not to reduce poverty but in order to attack the deprived.

If Murray lived in Easterhouse he would have learnt these lessons. Young people may be unemployed but not from choice: most want desperately to work and even compete to deliver newspapers or cut grass. Most children, over 70 per cent, live with two parents. Most residents, including lone parents, care deeply about family and community life. After all, they are the ones who suffer from local crime.

Consequently, many take counter action, like the father who has never known employment but works four evenings a week in youth clubs so that children have an alternative to the street. He is not unusual. Easterhouse has more than 200 community groups. It is not being over-run by an underclass. That is a myth. The reality is of a majority of ordinary and decent citizens who yet find themselves in the midst of crime and vandalism.

If an underclass is not the explanation, why is social deprivation and crime connected? A partial answer is that poverty and inequality generate circumstances which facilitate rather than deter crime. Firstly, many young people are just bored. Few go on to higher education. Few go on to real jobs. Teenagers with no Income Support and older ones on poverty incomes hang about the streets and shops. A minority turn to crime, but a minority can commit many offences.

Second, drugs are readily available. The drug barons do not stay in Easterhouse, they arrange the delivery knowing that some bored young people will be easy prey. Their consequent drug abuse does not make them members of an underclass any more than it does university students who partake. It does make them criminals both as takers of illegal drugs, with ecstasy and heroin on the increase, and as petty dealers.

Next, desperation: poverty has now reached depths unknown to me in my previous 30 years in welfare work. The removal of Single Payment grants for essential items like cookers and fires has driven some Income Support recipients to the Social Fund for loans they can hardly afford. Others turn to charity. In one week our local Salvation Army captain gave away 41 second hand beds and, with stocks exhausted, then supplied mattresses for children to sleep on. In desperation, a few will shoplift or steal.

The opportunity is there. Easterhouse buildings make crime easy. Security doors on tenement blocks are often broken. Once inside the close, a housebreaker is hidden. With one in four flats abandoned, empty rooms offer easy passage to occupied dwellings via thin walls or through the lofts.

Finally, there is the culture of inequality. On television and in popular papers, residents can perceive and resent the inequality of our society. These inequalities may not excuse crimes but they do throw light on why a sense of injustice makes them more likely.

Crime cannot be attributed to the birth, in poverty-stricken areas, of a new breed called the underclass. Rather, social deprivations generate a futility which makes some prey to drug exploiters; a desperation which compels others to take advantage of the many means of stealing; and a sense of grievance which both can incorporate to justify their actions.

The police take a number of initiatives, but they do require extra personnel, for one of the most effective deterrents to crime is the probability of being caught. But in conditions of great poverty they can deal only with the symptoms not the cause of crime.

Nor can responsibility be foisted on to the local community. Residents are already involved in anti-drug projects. Their credit unions lessen the need to approach loan sharks. Food co-ops provide cheaper products for members. Youth clubs ensure outlets for some youngsters. Community action deserves greater resources. But it can only alleviate not redress social deprivations. Something more fundamental is required. Crime prevention can best be tackled by poverty prevention.

Dr Holman is a neighbourhood worker in Easterhouse.

71.2 *Richard Kinsey: No Evidence of a Causal Link between Poverty and Crime*

Although he is polite about it, Richard Kinsey clearly has substantial reservations about the very explicit way that Bob Holman links poverty and certain types of crime. Kinsey gives a very different picture of the Easterhouse estate from Holman. The basis of their evidence is also very different. Holman draws from direct observation and personal experience and Kinsey from a large-scale social survey.

According to Kinsey's research, the proportion of criminals and victims among the middle and working classes is not very different – if self-report and victim surveys rather than official statistics are taken as the basis of evidence. Although Kinsey's research was carried out in Scotland and the findings are explained partly with reference to Scottish factors, it may well be that his main conclusions would apply to England as well.

Reading 71.2 From Richard Kinsey, 'Idle Chatter of Underclasses and Welfare Junkies' in *Guardian*, 24 June 1992, p. 21

Mention crime and most people think of deprivation. After a decade of rising police statistics, trouble in the inner cities and widening divisions in wealth and opportunity, it is not surprising. Add in the magic words "underclass' and "dependency culture" and then political right shares common purpose with the left – the search for the missing link between poverty and crime.

Whether in terms of the "incentives to failure" of post-war welfarism – hence Dan Quayle blaming sixties liberals for Los Angeles – for the structural inequalities of class, race and patriarchy, the problem of the "high crime rate area" is taken for granted. Blame or sympathy comes afterwards.

Almost irrespective of crime, it seems every city and every town has its "bad area". Profoundly disquieting no doubt, but for many I suspect it's as much a source of comfort as of alarm – crime and delinquency are not a problem in "our area" or for "our children". In part, I'm sure, this is why our study of young people in Edinburgh seems to have upset so many people.

Some of the findings were fairly brutal. From a sample of more than a thousand schoolchildren aged 11 to 15, a third of 14- and 15-year-old girls had been victims of indecent exposure or had been sexually propositioned or molested in public by adult men. But what caused the stir was that the men concerned showed no respect for social class or residential area. All young people – from the most deprived to the most affluent areas of the city – were equally at risk.

Much the same can be said of the reaction to our findings on offending. Seven out of 10 young people questioned told us they had recently – albeit occasionally – committed an offence. Usually these were petty offences: shoplifting, vandalism, graffiti. Only rarely were they involved in car theft, housebreaking or robbery but, as with victimisation, the pattern of offending crossed the boundaries of social class and neighbourhood without discrimination. But, again, people seem almost unhappy when the notion of a "hard core, delinquent underclass" evaporates.

There are persistent offenders, just as there are pockets of high crime and violence. But to focus attention exclusively on either can distort far more than it reveals. In his article on Easterhouse – an area "notorious" for having some of the highest levels of multiple deprivation in western Europe – Bob Holman provides a graphic catalogue of some recent and horrifying incidents. But Bob would be the last to suggest that a teenager will die every few days or that all areas of Easterhouse are torn apart by violent crime.

A survey last year for the Safe Easterhouse Initiative found that 27 per cent of residents felt their particular area was a bad place to live, of whom around a quarter put forward problems of crime as their main reason for disliking the area (i.e. 6 per cent of all Easterhouse residents). At the same time, many more people said that what was good about Easterhouse was "it was quiet and there was no trouble".

There is much more that can be done to address specific problems of crime – such as door entry systems – and public money could and would make a real difference. But crude stereotypes of high crime rate areas can be as damaging as crime itself – ask any school leaver from Easterhouse trying to get a job.

In this context, the findings from the British Crime Survey (BCS), Scotland, 1988 are important. Thus, while 6 per cent of households in the poorest council estates in Scotland had been vandalised and 8 per cent broken into, so too had 4 per cent and 7 per cent in the affluent suburbs. Similarly, with violence. While a quarter of young men with household incomes under £10,000 had been the victim of some form of violent crime in the past year, so too had 50 per cent of those with higher incomes.

This is not to say that the problem of crime and poverty are not linked. They are – but what really counts is not so much the *incidence* of crime but its *impact*. For example, when the BCS asked victims about the effects of crime, only 2 per cent of those with household incomes over £20,000 described emotional reactions lasting over a month – in comparison with 20 per cent of those with incomes under £10,000.

Indeed – compounding and compounded by other, far deeper problems of poverty – even the most trivial offence can take on a different dimension. At the end of a lousy day, a vandalised phone box says it all. Crime is the last straw.

But more than this the findings from BCS, as well as the survey of young people, clearly question any direct *causal* connection between poverty and offending. Despite the fact that poverty is ground into Scottish culture – recent figures suggest 42 per cent of children under five are living in poverty in comparison with 32 per cent in England and Wales – crime north of the border has shown a remarkable capacity to buck the English trends and to confound conventional wisdom.

Thus, in comparison with 1981, the 1988 BCS showed household crime in Scotland had remained unchanged, while personal offences fell by 12 per cent. In England and Wales, personal offences rose by 3 per cent, while household offences leapt 22 per cent.

In particular, rates of assault, robbery and personal theft were all *lower* in Scotland. (Of all personal offences, only non-violent thefts from the person were – very slightly – higher in Scotland.) Similarly car thefts – up 28 per cent in England and Wales – fell by 7 per cent in Scotland. Thefts from cars in Scotland rose slightly but only by 8 per cent in comparison with 54 per cent south of the border. And perhaps most surprising, vandalism in Scotland fell by 25 per cent to a rate of 1,073 offences per 10,000 households, in comparison with 1,521 in England and Wales.

Twenty years on from the introduction of the Children's Hearing System and the broad decriminalisation of juvenile justice in Scotland, the findings on vandalism and car crime – typically offences committed by the young – are striking. In Scotland, we were largely spared experiments with the short, sharp shock and punitive responses to juvenile crime, leaving lay panels to concentrate on the welfare of the child and the family rather than deterrance and retribution.

The panels have had a mixed reception. There are those who remain at best ambivalent – the panels are "too soft on crime" – while others call for their extension to include 16- to 21-year-olds. But in the light of the Scottish findings, nobody can argue that sparing the rod has been a failure.

Similarly, there is little evidence from the survey that the Scottish police have been unduly hampered by their much more restricted powers. (Unlike the English police, who can hold suspects for up to 96 hours of questioning, their Scottish counterparts are strictly limited to six hours.)

Nor does it seem that greater "political control" has interfered with policing north of the border. (In Scotland, membership of the police authorities is exclusively a matter for local government unlike in England and Wales where a third of the membership is made up from the unelected magistracy.) Indeed, the survey showed the Scots to be considerably more ready to report crime to the police, perhaps suggesting greater confidence in the criminal justice system.

But such differences in the law, the juvenile justice system and political structure are easily forgotten. Again, we come back to stereotype. Would anyone have noticed if Scotland's crime rates had been *higher* than England's? I doubt it.

The image of schemes such as Easterhouse have penetrated deep into the collective consciousness. But then people also forget that the Gorbals is long gone and that Scottish cities have a history which not only marks them out – culturally and architecturally – from their English counterparts but which may be as important as the difference in policy and politics.

Edinburgh for example, has been described as the most residentially segregated city in Britain. Not far down the road from Glasgow's

Easterhouse, Bearsden has one of the highest concentrations of graduates and professionals in the United Kingdom. Throughout urban Scotland, starting in the thirties through to the seventies, Scotland's working class was decanted in tens if not hundreds of thousands to peripheral schemes the size of many English towns.

Easterhouse has a population rivalling Dover. In Edinburgh, more people live in Craigmillar than in Falmouth, while in Pilton the population is twice that of Mr Major's home town of Huntingdon. And these are only some of the many. The contrast with the small council estates and inner cities of England could not be more marked.

It has often been said that, in England, as relative deprivation intensified and the disparities in wealth accelerated throughout the eighties, so crime – especially property crime – went up. In areas of London, where gentrification meant affluence living next door to poverty, immediate need went hand in hand with opportunities for crime.

In Scotland, though absolute levels of deprivation were the same – if not worse – the physical isolation of the peripheral schemes guaranteed that the opportunities were fewer and the injustice less glaring. The recipe which has led to higher crime and urban disorders throughout English towns was missing.

At one level, the lesson of what Malcolm Rifkind has called Scotland's "residential apartheid" seems simple. Reduce the opportunities for crime – which *must* mean increasing other opportunities – and crime will fall. But that is by no means the whole story.

For while the Scottish housing schemes may be physically and socially marginalised and while the market – and the social disorganisation and dislocation that accompanies developments like Canary Wharf – shows little interest in them, the communities remain strong and stable. The survey in Easterhouse showed the mean length of residence was 20 years. As a result, perhaps, in the face of genuine problems, the cultural resilience and the means of collective, practical support remains intact, giving the lie to any ideological chatter about the "underclass" and "welfare junkies".

Alison Uttley: Surveillance and Crime: Where do We Draw the Line

This brief reading requires little introduction, except perhaps to signal the growing importance of the issue under discussion. Modern technology means that we can be, and often are, watched and even filmed without being aware of it or without ever being informed it has happened. This raises important ethical issues. Is general surveillance acceptable in order that the minority who break the law can be caught more easily? The video-camera has introduced massive – if initially unintentional – surveillance of behaviour during sporting events. How do you think it has worked in that context? Is there any justification for using surveillance in the private realm? Apart from possible invasion of privacy, could data from surveillance have other negative aspects – for instance, could it be used for blackmail? Whatever the answer to these questions, it is urgent that we develop the debate.

Reading 72 From Alison Uttley, 'Who's looking at you, kid?' in *Times Higher Education Supplement* 30 April, 1993, p. 48

Today's camera lenses may be no bigger than a pinhead: useful if you want to observe unawares the meanderings of a population. If you're lucky, you might even catch someone committing a crime.

The right to privacy versus a greater human good is not a philosophical dilemma the police and security services take seriously. Last week they announced that high street surveillance had been so successful at reducing street crime that closed circuit television systems were to be installed in a further 10 to 15 towns next year. They encountered little opposition, but if they were expecting any, the police couldn't have made the announcement at a better time. Pictures from commercially installed cameras were splashed across every newspaper in the land recently showing James Bulger being led to his death from a shopping centre. And arrests were made after a video outside Harrods showed two men walking by 30 minutes before a bomb went off in a nearby litter bin. Two such high profile and emotive cases were bound to increase public acceptance of surveillance.

The misuse of surveillance equipment sent shivers down spines before Orwell's *1984* was published, and even those who have not read the chilling tale hardly require much imagination to picture the ease with which an entrapment can be made. The technology has become so sophisticated that if the authorities want to conceal a camera, they can do so with great ease. Informed consent is apparently not an issue. Do people behave differently if they suspect they are being watched? Are they less likely to attend meetings or demonstrations? Won't criminals move elsewhere, causing a shift rather than a reduction in street crime?

Supporters of public surveillance argue there is no real difference between a television camera and a watching policeman or security guard. In any case, they say, in a public place one has voluntarily given up one's privacy.

Andrew Belsey, director of the Centre for Applied Ethics at the University of Wales, says that in isolation, high street cameras pose a small threat, outweighed by the benefits of crime prevention. However, the trend is part of a more serious threat. "I think we may be drifting into a surveillance society without any public discussion."

The assistant chief constable of South Wales last week outlined a remarkable idea which to the suspicious-minded might appear to confirm this. In an attempt to help the estimated one in 10 women who are victims of domestic violence prove their case, he advocated covert video and audio surveillance in the home.

The equipment would be controlled by the woman, who would allow police to install cameras in the home – without the partner's knowledge. She would attempt to get evidence without his knowledge or consent. The start of a slippery slope, or do the ends justify the means?

Police forces, local authorities and businesses spend about £300 million a year on video security equipment. Professor Belsey says it is important to distinguish between public surveillance in the street and private security in shops, banks, filling stations and so on where organisations have the right to protect property. None the less, the dangers were being overlooked. "I am quite prepared to believe a lot of information is collected and illegally accessed by our security services," he says. The sophistication with which marketing organisations build dossiers on individuals' lifestyles showed how easy it is to track movements and spending patterns through credit card organisations.

"I am worried that while people are only too happy to accept the benefits of using plastic money, they have not thought through the consequences," he says. "There needs to be much more public awareness."

But not everyone accepts that there is a threat to civil liberty. David Feldman, professor of law at Birmingham University, says video surveillance is not a civil liberty issue. "There cannot be any invasion of privacy in a high street because that is in the public domain," he says. "I am not sure that I agree that there is any legitimate expectation of not being surveyed in a public place, particularly for legitimate ends like crime prevention."

Achieving a balance between two legitimate interests – crime prevention and individual privacy is a matter for political judgement Professor Feldman says, but more worrying is the vagueness of guidelines covering the use of the material. "I am not convinced there are sufficient procedural guidelines to ensure confidentiality is preserved," Professor Feldman says.

In addition, he says, there is the threat of misinterpretation of video evidence. In the James Bulger murder, for instance, the first arrest was of an innocent boy. "This is not a matter of invasion of privacy, it is a matter of interpretation of evidential material," Professor Feldman says. "You can't say people are being entrapped or induced to commit crime because of video surveillance but one must consider that lives can be ruined."

Video evidence could also reduce chances of a fair trial, he adds. "What we must decide is whether this is outweighed by the greater public good."

Concern over the lack of guidelines for using surveillance information are echoed by Ian Leigh of Newcastle University's law school. In a forthcoming book examining security and intelligence in the United Kingdom, Canada and Australia, (published later this year by Oxford University Press) Mr Leigh and Newcastle colleague Laurence Lustgarten will explain how controls over surveillance are too weak. "A low level of authorisation is needed," Leigh says. "Yet clearly if cameras are recording events this is an intrusive activity."

Visual surveillance in a public place may be authorised by a chief superintendant, or if no recording is to take place, by an inspector.

Only a small proportion of surveillance practices is regulated Mr Leigh says and where rules exist, they are lax. "The security agencies are left to roam free," he adds. "And even when supervision exists it is undertaken primarily by other organs of the state which work closely with the security bodies, rather than by an external and politically independent body. Any such limited external review as does exist takes place long after operations are carried out."

Liberty (the National Council for Civil Liberties), also says it is concerned about the explosive growth in video surveillance because of the absence of any controlling legislation. "Like most police operations, video surveillance is not subject to any real accountability at either local or national level," Liberty says. Apart from privacy, Liberty's main concern is that video surveillance may increasingly be seen as a method of controlling public order. "Video surveillance could be used to harass and intimidate people who pose no genuine threat to society."

Professor Belsey agrees that to claim that the law-abiding have nothing to fear is not good enough. "This is another example of a small number of people changing the way everyone else lives," he says.

Questions and Issues

Deviance: Section 15

The most relevant readings appear in brackets after each question.

1 'Deviant behaviour is behaviour that people so label.' Which groups are most likely to be labelled deviant in Britain, and why? (Section 15)

2 Describe and critically discuss left realist analysis of crime and crime prevention. (Readings 69–70)

3 What are the causes and consequences of male criminal violence towards females? (Readings 22, 70)

4 What, if any, is the relationship between poverty and crime? (Readings 66, 67–68, 71)

SECTION 16

RELIGION

Introduction: Readings 73–76

The sociology of religion is about the relationship between religion and society or, put another way, it is about religion as part of society. This is a large perspective, but it does exclude from consideration the nature of religious truth and the relative claims to truth of the various religions (except in so far as these have social effects). The sociology of religion can be approached from both macro and more inter-personal perspectives.

The first reading, from Gregor McLennan, illustrates how ideology and, in particular, religious ideology can function to 'legitimize' or 'delegitimize' the dominant social order. He also refers to other functional effects of religious ideology. Reading 74, from Marx and Engels, eloquently illustrates their analysis of the way that religion can serve the interests of the dominant class and ideologically delude the subordinate class.

The reading from Ernest Gellner introduces the issue of secularisation and considers how the religion, Islam appears to challenge the liberal values that underlie Western secularisation (see also Reading 27). I have decided not to select readings which rehearse the arguments for and against the secularisation thesis as there is no difficulty in gaining access to material on this issue. Gellner takes the view that secularisation has generally occurred but sees Islam as a large and challenging exception.

Eileen Barker's book, *The Making of a Moonie*, is characterised by an awareness of the importance of personal and inter-personal meaning and communication in the sociological intepretation of religion. She is equally aware of the relevance of social context in influencing religious choice. In this extract, she reminds us of the personal idealism that can underlie religious motivation and, to that extent, introduces a more subjective element than is apparent in the first two readings in this section.

Gregor McLennan: Ideology – Definition and Roles

This is as clear an introduction to the key concept of ideology as I have come across. As such it should be very useful to students in understanding ideology in relation to, for instance, religion, the media and education.

The extract contains much detailed material but is quite schematic and contains two short summaries. There is no need for extensive summary here. What may be useful is to repeat, for convenient reference, the definition of ideology which the extract works towards:

> Ideologies are sets of ideas, assumptions and images by which people make sense of society, which give a clear social identity, and which serve in some way to legitimize relations of power in society.

A basic understanding of ideology in these terms is an essential part of sociology, including, the sociology of religion. Religious belief systems may legitimise an existing social order or they may challenge it. McLennan gives examples of each in this extract.

Reading 73 From Gregor McLennan, The Power of Ideology, Unit 17, D103 (Open University Press, 1991), pp. 111–14

The meaning of 'ideology'

What, then, do we mean by the term 'ideology'? When first coined by French thinkers in the late eighteenth century, 'ideology' was intended to refer to the scientific study – the 'ology' – of ideas, in much the same way as 'psychology' was to be the scientific study of the 'human mind', and 'sociology' was to be the scientific study of society generally. Gradually, however, it has become more usual to see 'ideology' as referring not so much to the *study* of beliefs and ideas in society, as to the beliefs and ideas being studied. Thus, ideology came to be regarded not as a scientific discipline in itself, but rather as a specific type of belief system within society, to be examined as such by the social scientist.

> Nowadays, the study of ideology means the study of beliefs and ideas in society – what they are, why they are believed, and what their effects are.

You should note here that already we have gone beyond the possibility that ideology simply refers to any and every kind of 'idea' or 'belief'. After all, people have beliefs about lots of things which may or may not be about society and which they may or may not share with others. However, to regard ideas and beliefs as specifically 'ideological' requires a minimum of three conditions:

1 that those ideas are indeed *shared* by a significant *number* of people;
2 that they form some kind of coherently related *system*; and
3 that they connect in some way to the nature of *power* within society.

To start with, then, we can say that ideologies are systems of collective, widely-held ideas and beliefs concerning the nature of society and its dominant power structures.

The case of religion is instructive in clarifying this distinction between ideas and ideologies. On the one hand, religions involve ideas and beliefs about gods, spirituality and salvation. Religious doctrines in this sense are not necessarily about society and could perhaps be regarded purely as a matter of theological truth and individual faith. Put that way, it would appear that religious ideas should not be thought of as ideological. On the other hand, most religions also involve definite notions of rightful authority, moral conduct, of the good society, of heaven on earth, and so on. Religions often carry implications about whether a particular type of hierarchy of *social* power is legitimate or not. Put that way, religion *can* be regarded as ideological in some respects.

Take Catholicism as an example. In medieval times, it could be argued, Catholicism served to reflect and support the typical threefold social hierarchy of feudal lord, priest and peasant in that everything on earth was believed to have a fixed and unalterable place in a divinely ordained order. Given that doctrine, the idea of rebelling against the worldly order of the day was treated as a sin as well as a crime. Today, by contrast, Catholicism in some South American countries is labelled 'liberation theology' because it holds that there is absolutely *no* theological justification for social and political inequality. Quite the opposite. So the priest is in this case united with the peasant *against* the landlords rather than being in league with them as in medieval times. In both these cases, religion plays a distinct ideological role, though the ideological contents of the two Catholic outlooks point in radically different directions, the one serving to sustain the social order of its time, the other attempting to challenge it.

Looking at religion from the point of view of ideology is interesting partly because its ostensible subject matter is usually spirtual rather than socio-political in any direct sense. Many other belief systems, though, do have a very direct link with issues of social structure and political power. In particular, ideas concerning equality or inequality, social justice, freedom and progress are classic grounds for ideological contestation. Such ideas are either about whether the *present* state of society – the social order – is right and good; or they are about how some *future* social order would greatly improve the human condition.

Ideologies, in other words, serve either to sustain or to undermine the *legitimacy*, the rightfulness, of a socio-political order. Ideas which are both widely held and tend to support the prevailing social order are sometimes referred to as *dominant ideologies*. Ideas that strive to undermine the dominant order, or which propose alternatives to existing society (which may sometimes be 'utopian' alternatives) can be designated as *counter-ideologies*. In this unit, I shall concentrate, for convenience, on the nature of dominant ideologies, though from time to time I shall bring in how counter-ideologies differ from these in important respects.

The idea of a socio-political order as used to describe the context of ideology is itself quite broad. It certainly includes the various short-term 'regimes' of particular political parties, monarchs or leaders. But equally importantly, it also refers to the longer-term, deeper-lying economic, social and moral bases upon which politics in the narrow sense operate. Whether a society is basically capitalist or socialist, whether it is liberal or not, whether it is democratic or authoritarian, whether it is culturally 'western', or white, or male-dominated: all these sorts of issues can validly be included in the notion of a social order. When a political regime or social order is legitimate, this means that it is generally accepted and endorsed as fair, appropriate or right in the minds of its people. When it is considered illegitimate, it has little moral support of a popular kind.

Summary

- Ideologies are collective beliefs which help to legitimize or delegitimize a social order.
- Ideologies encourage us to view the social world in a particular light, and by adopting an ideological framework certain consequences follow about how we *live*.
- Ideologies are in a sense always about *power*, even where their belief-content is ostensibly to do with something else (such as God, or masculinity, or the national character).

What ideologies do

In developing a proper definition of ideology in this way, to say what ideologies *are* involves beginning to ascertain what they *do* in society. So, for example, to say that ideologies are collective beliefs about society is useful, but only up to a point. A better analytical purchase is gained when we add that what these ideological beliefs do is to sustain or challenge prevailing social orders. Our definition of ideology, in other words, will tend to be closely bound up with what we think the *point* of ideology is; that is, with its potential social *role* or function.

In terms of my previous note, this section examines the 'effects' of ideology.

It is worth elaborating on this by considering some of the ways in which dominant ideologies sustain a social order. To see the social world through the lens or frame of an ideology is to put things in a certain perspective, to perceive social life according to relatively stable values, assumptions and images. At this point, I want to emphasize that the components of ideologies are not only 'ideas' as such. Often they take the form of fairly vague background assumptions, prejudices and inclinations. But these ideological assumptions are in practice no less potent or coherent for being imprecise. So one role of ideologies is simply that they give shape to people's perceptions and values: they help them make sense of society.

Reading 65 provides some practical examples of ideology used in this sense.

A second and related role of ideologies is that they perhaps fulfil a general human need to feel psychologically 'at home' in an awesome, infinite universe. Ideologies in that sense provide some local answers to the metaphysical puzzle of 'the meaning of life'. They deliver a definite sense of social order and sometimes cosmic order. Ideologies thus serve to link theory and practice closely together: through *identifying* as individuals with their values and perspectives, we can come to see ourselves as having a definite place and purpose within the larger scheme of things.

This 'function' of ideology has been stressed by Talcot Parsons.

A third general role of (dominant) ideologies is that they can help to secure social integration, so enabling societies to 'hang together' over time in a viable way. Virtually all known societies have contained serious differences of wealth and power, talent and education amongst their members. How, then, have they managed to avoid continually breaking apart? One answer is that ideologies provide a potent reservoir of beliefs and values out of which a kind of social glue or cement can be made and used to mend the cracks of internal social division and conflict, thus preventing social disintegration.

In particular, Durkheim emphasised the ideological role of religion in strengthening 'social solidarity' – i.e. as a kind of 'social cement'.

A fourth possible way in which ideologies sustain a prevailing social order is that they serve the particular interests of dominant groups or ruling classes (thus the term 'dominant' ideology). For example, it has often been asserted that liberal ideas of the free market and competitive 'winner-takes-all' attitudes are simply ideologies which further the specific interests of the capitalist class. Similarly, the 'vanguard' role of the proletariat as highlighted in Soviet Communist doctrine prior to the 1980s was arguably little more than an ideological cover for the self-interest of Party bosses in state socialist societies. So the ultimate purpose of ideology from this point of view is to gain widespread social acceptance of beliefs which in the end serve the interests not of the masses at all, but rather of particular élites.

Marx himself often used this approach to ideology to attack 'capitalist' or 'liberal' ideology.

Summary

We have identified four possible social roles or functions of dominant ideologies. Ideologies:

1 help us make sense of society from within a particular framework of meaning;
2 provide metaphysical security and a sense of social identity;
3 act as a 'social cement' in circumstances of social division;
4 serve the material interests of ruling groups.

Counter-ideologies also fulfil these roles to an extent, but clearly they are less concerned about cementing the *existing* order than presenting an alternative order. Also, counter-ideologies attempt to serve the interests of subordinate groups, not ruling groups.

There are some important things to note at this stage about these social roles that are played by ideology. First of all, although each role has its own distinctive emphasis, these roles are often compatible with one another. You could accept some or all of them to some extent. You could accept, for example, that ideology acts as a social cement, then go on to argue that it does so by serving privileged social interests. (This combines roles 3 and 4.) Or you could hold that the larger part of making sense of society (role 1) is really about feeling personally 'at home' in the world (role 2).

The second thing about the list of roles is that it is by no means complete. You could add to it. You might, perhaps, want to say that ideologies are the means by which powerful *individuals* get the *masses* in society to endorse their dictatorial tendencies. Or, if you were a psychoanalyst, you might want to argue that ideological attachments are social reflections of deep-seated, psycho-sexual conflicts within individuals.

A third point to emphasize is that we are talking of *possible* social roles for ideology, not proven roles. Indeed, it is seldom the case that any particular role is wholly fulfilled. Take the view that ideology furthers the interests of dominant groups. Such a role is unlikely to be totally realized within any given society, and moreover there will probably be quite significant variation in its embodiment in different societies. What we are getting at here is that whilst it is tempting to think in terms of the single, definitive function of ideology, it might be better to think of its potential *roles* in the plural. Although there is a tendency to speak of *ideology*, in general and in the singular, it is sometimes more appropriate to think about ideolog*ies*, in the plural. It is not wholly improper to talk of ideology in general and its main social roles; the point is simply that we must be careful not to overgeneralize . . .

From the points made so far, we can now put forward a 'baseline' conception of ideology:

Ideologies are sets of ideas, assumptions and images by which people make sense of society, which give a clear social identity, and which serve in some way to legitimise relations of power in society.

Karl Marx: Religion as Ideology – 'The Opium of the People'

Marx is here claiming that 'the oppressed' seek in religion what they do not get in 'this world' – namely, some kind of fulfilment and content. Controversially (see below), Marx regards pursuit of fulfilment through religion as 'illusory' – a kind of spiritual opium.

Marx agrees that the majority are 'alienated' but urges a different solution. People must analyse ('unmask') the causes of their problems that relate to this world and act politically to change matters.

It is quite possible to accept Marx's argument that the oppressed should tackle their oppression in this world without taking the view that religion is always 'illusory'. Some religious people do deal fully with the causes of oppression in 'the here and now', others do not. Perhaps a fair revision of Marx would be that only for the latter group is religion 'illusory' in this given respect.

Despite the previous paragraph, this passage from Marx contains the essence of Marxist humanism – that social justice and, within realistic limits, the fulfilment of human potential should be sought in this world – that we should 'cull the living flower'.

Reading 74 From K. Marx and F. Engels, 'On Religion' reprinted in R. Bocock and K. Thompson, *eds., Religion and Ideology* (Manchester University Press, 1985), pp. 11–12

Religious distress is at the same time the *expression* of real distress and the *protest* against real distress. Religion is the sigh of the oppressed creature, the heart of a heartless world, just as it is the spirit of a spiritless situation. It is the *opium* of the people.

The abolition of religion as the *illusory* happiness of the people is required for their *real* happiness. The demand to give up the illusions about its condition is the *demand to give up a condition which needs illusions*. The criticism of religion is therefore *in embryo the criticism of the vale of woe*, the *halo* of which is religion.

Criticism has plucked the imaginary flowers from the chain not so that man will wear the chain without any fantasy or consolation but so that he will shake off the chain and cull the living flower. The criticism of religion disillusions man to make him think and act and shape his reality like a man who has been disillusioned and has come to reason, so that he will revolve round himself and therefore round his true sun. Religion is only the illusory sun which revolves round man as long as he does not revolve round himself.

The task of history, therefore, once the *world beyond the truth h*as disappeared, is to establish the *truth of this world*. The immediate *task of philosophy*, which is at the service of history, once the *saintly form* of human self-alienation has been unmasked, is to unmask self-alienation in its *unholy forms*. Thus the criticism of heaven turns into the criticism of the earth, the *criticism of religion* into the *criticism of right* and the *criticism of theology* into the *criticism of politics* [. . .]

The philosophers have only *interpreted* the world, in various ways; the point, however, is to *change* it.

Ernest Gellner: Secularisation and the Exception – Islam

This extract from Ernest Gellner begins with a brief summary of the secularisation thesis. Notwithstanding the contrary views of such critics as David Martin, Gellner strongly argues that the 'modern' world is overwhelmingly a secular one. The apparent exception of the United States is characterised by the practice of a 'social' religion rather than a genuinely spiritual culture, according to Gellner.

The real exception to secularisation is Islam. Whereas the 'third world' in general has regarded secularisation as part of modernisation and the price of riches, Islam has resisted this trend. The Islamic exception raises a host of fascinating questions, some of which Gellner plays with. Could the Islamic countries become successful modern economies while remaining true to Islam? Gellner does not see why not. Could Islam seriously challenge the hegemony of the secular West? Is the relationship between secularisation and modern technological and economic development necessarily as close as has often been assumed?

Gellner describes Islam as 'fundamentalist' in that it denies the distinction between the religious and the secular. Religion should rule the whole of life and so there is no room for the secular. In contrast, it is an essential feature of Western modernity that no single version of religious truth is allowed to control secular life. Pluralism prevails.

Reading 75 From Ernest Gellner, *Postmodernism, Reason and Religion* (Routledge, 1992), pp. 4–7, 18–22

The realm of Islam presents an interesting picture in the modern world. Sociologists have long entertained, and frequently endorsed, the theory of secularization. It runs as follows: the scientific-industrial society, religious faith and observance decline. One can give intellectualist reasons for this: the doctrines of religion are in conflict with those of science, which in turn are endowed with enormous prestige, and which constitute the basis of modern technology, and thereby also of modern economy. Therefore, religious faith declines. Its prestige goes down as the prestige of its rival rises.

Alternatively, one may give structural reasons: religion is linked to the celebration of the community, and in the atomized world of modern mass society, there is little community to celebrate, other than possibly the national state – and that state has found its own new ritual and set of values in nationalism. So the erosion of community life is reflected in the loss of faith, and the diminished appeal of ritual.

There are many variants of this theory. What matters is that, by and large, the secularization thesis does hold. Some political regimes are overtly associated with secularist, anti-religious ideologies; others are officially dissociated from religion, and practise secularism more by default than by active affirmation. But few states are formally associated with religion, or of they are, the link is loose, and not taken too seriously. Religious observance and participation are low. When they are higher, the content of the religion is often visibly social rather than transcendent: formal doctrine is ignored, and participation treated as a celebration of community not of conviction. Religious issues are seldom prominent. Where community survives, it seems to prefer to celebrate itself almost directly, without seeing itself through the prism of faith.

During the age of emergence of the world religions, stress shifted from lived ritual to transcendent doctrine, and it looks as if now the wheel has come full circle, and that where religion contains some vigour, it does so by becoming civic once again. In North America, religious attendance is high, but religion celebrates a shared cult of the American way of life, rather than insisting on distinctions of theology or church organization, as once it did. Apparent exceptions to the trend towards secularization turn out on examination to be special cases, explicable by special circumstances, as when a church is used as a counter-organization against an oppressive state committed to a secular belief-system. It is possible to disagree about the extent, homogeneity or irreversibility of this trend, and, unquestionably, secularization does assume many quite different forms; but, by and large, it would seem reasonable to say that it is real.

But there is one very real, dramatic and conspicuous exception to all this: Islam. To say that secularization prevails in Islam is not contentious. It is simply false. Islam is as strong now as it was a century ago. In some ways, it is probably much stronger.

At the end of the Middle Ages, the Old World contained four major civilizations. Of these, three are now, in one measure or another, secularized. Christian doctrine is bowdlerized by its own theologians, and deep, literal conviction is not conspicuous by its presence. In the Sinic World, a secular faith has become formally established and its religious predecessors disavowed. In the Indian World, a state and the élite are neutral *vis-à-vis* what is a pervasive folk religion, even if practices such as astrology continue to be widespread. But in one of the four civilizations, the Islamic, the situation is altogether different.

The 'secular faith' referred to here is Communism.

Why should one particular religion be so markedly secularization-resistant? This is an important question. Whether the answer which will be offered is the correct one, I do not know, and I doubt whether anyone else does either: historical interpretations are difficult to establish. It happens to be the best I can offer; it may provide some illumination, whether or not it contains all the truth. If it provokes a better alternative theory, I shall be well satisfied.

As is made clear later in this extract, Gellner considers that Islam is highly compatible with or, in Weber's terms, 'congruent with' modernisation.

Islam is a founded religion, claiming to complete and round off the Abrahamic tradition and its Prophets, and to do so with finality. Muhammad is the *Seal* of the Prophets. Earlier versions of the divine revelation, in keeping of the two Abrahamic religions, are held by Muslims to have become distorted by their adherents.

The faith is based on the divine Message received by the Prophet Muhammad in the seventh century. The events which occurred during the first few generations of Muslims are recorded and vividly present to the consciousness of Muslims, and provide the basis for the division of Islam into three sects: the majoritarian Sunnis, the Shi'ites and the Kharejites. The Kharejites are the least numerous.

The central doctrines of Islam contain an emphatic and severe monotheism, the view that the Message received by the Prophet is so to speak terminal, and that it contains both faith and morals – or, in other words, it is both doctrine and law, and that no genuine further augmentation is to be countenanced. The points of doctrine and points of law are not separated, and Muslim learned scholars are best described as theologians/jurists. There is no canon law, but simply divine law as such, applicable to the community of believers, rather than to the organization and members of some specialized agency.

The fact that, in this way, legislation is pre-empted by the deity has profound implications for Muslim life. It does not merely mean that a fundamentalist may have difficulties in accepting modern law and legislative practices; it also means that a certain kind of separation of powers was built into Muslim society from the very start, or very nearly from the start. This version of the separation of powers did not need to wait for some Englightenment doctrine concerning the desirability of a pluralist social order and of the internal balance of independent institutions. It subordinates the executive to the (divine) legislature and, in actual practice, turns the theologians/lawyers into the monitors of political rectitude – whether or not they always have the power to enforce their verdicts. The principle that 'the community will not agree on error' may endow communal consensus, rather than the political centre, with a kind of legislative authority. Within this communal consensus, the voice of the learned is liable to possess special weight. After all, the community must heed an already existing law and it is natural to respect the opinion of those better informed . . .

To continue the argument: in Islam, we see a pre-industrial faith, a founded, doctrinal, world religion in the proper sense, which, at any rate for the time being, totally and effectively defies the secularization thesis. So far, there is no indication that it will succumb to secularization in the future either, though of course it is always dangerous to indulge in prophecy. The reasons which have made this achievement possible seem to be the following: all 'under-developed' countries tend to face a certain dilemma. (By 'under-developed' countries I mean any society affected by a deep economic-military inferiority, such as it can only remedy by reforming itself fundamentally. France was under-developed in the eighteenth century, and Germany at the beginning of the nineteenth.) The dilemma such countries face is: should we emulate those whom we wish to equal in power (thereby spurning our own tradition), or should we, on the contrary, affirm the values of our own tradition, even at the price of material weakness? This issue was most poignantly recorded in Russian literature of the nineteenth century in the form of the debate between Westernization and Populism/Slavophilism.

It is painful to spurn one's own tradition, but it is also painful to remain weak. Few under-developed countries have escaped this dilemma, and they have handled it in diverse ways. But what is interesting, and crucial for our argument, is that Islam is ideally placed to escape it.

The trauma of the Western impact (appearing in diverse Muslim countries at different points of time, stretching from the late eighteenth to the twentieth centuries) did not, amongst Muslim thinkers, provoke that intense polarization between Westernizers and Populists, *à la Russe*. Muslims seldom idealise their own folk tradition; they leave vicarious populism to Europeans imbued with the T. E. Lawrence syndrome. The situation provoked a quite different reaction. The urge to reform, ever present in Islam, acquired a new vigour and intensity. No doubt it also acquired some new themes and additional motivation: why has the West overtaken us, why is it such a menace to us?

The distinction between 'high' and 'folk' or popular Islam is crucial to Gellner's argument.

But the dominant and persuasive answer recommended neither emulation of the West, nor idealisation of some folk virtue and wisdom. It commended a *return* to, or a more rigorous observance of, *High* Islam. Admittedly this was linked to the historically perhaps questionable assumptiion that High Islam had once dominated and pervaded the whole of society, and also that it was identical with *early* Islam, with the teaching and practice of the Prophet and His Companions. This is questionable; but what is certainly true is that High Islam constituted a perfectly genuine local tradition, and one long established, even if it has not succeeded in pervading the entire society, and whether or not it is really identical with the practice of the first generation(s) of Muslims.

So self-correction did not need to go outside the society, nor seek pristine virtue in its social depths: it could find it in its own perfectly genuine and real Higher Culture, which has indeed only been practised by a minority in the past, but which had been recognized (though not implemented) as a valid norm by the rest of society. Now, seemingly under the impact of a moral impulse and in response to preaching, but in fact as a result of profound and pervasive changes in social organization, it could at long last be practised by *all*. Self-reform in the light of modern requirements could be presented as a *return* to the genuinely local ideal, a moral home-coming, rather than a self-repudiation.

It is this vision which has now conquered the Muslim world. As an ideology of self-rectification, of purification, of recovery, it has a number of very considerable and striking advantages. It does not appeal to an *alien* model; it appeals to a model which has unquestionable, deep, genuine local roots. It may or may not really be identical with the real practice of the first generations of Muslims; but it *does* correspond to what so to speak normative, respected individuals and classes had preached and practised for a very long time. A man who turns to Reformist Islam does not, like a Westernizer in nineteenth-century Russia, thereby convey his contempt for his own ancestors and tradition. On the contrary, he re-affirms what he considers the best elements in the local culture, and which were genuinely present. And a man who turns to Reformist Islam is also close to 'the people', to what countless petty bourgeois actually practise, and to what many peasants aspire to practise, without at the same time committing himself to any implausible, far-fetched idealization of peasant or shepherd life as such. At the same time, whilst it is truly local, and genuinely resonates throughout the whole of society, this reformist ideal is also severely demanding, and unambiguously condemns and reprobates that folk culture which can, with some show of plausibility, be blamed for 'backwardness', and for the humiliation imposed by the West. High Islam had always opposed the ecstatic, undisciplined, personality-oriented variant of Islam. Now it could oppose it and be reinforced with some new arguments: it was *this* that had held us back! Not only have we so slid back from the shining example set us by the Prophet and the early Muslims, but in so doing we also made it easy for the infidel to humble us. The colonialists had exploited, or indeed encouraged and fomented, the worst streaks in our own culture. In this way the old impulse towards self-reformation and purification blends with reactive nationalism: it is indeed exceedingly hard to separate the two.

Weberian sociology leads us to expect a certain congruence between a modern economy and its associated beliefs and culture. The modern mode of production is claimed, above all, to be 'rational'. It is orderly, sensitive to cost-effectiveness, thrifty rather than addicted to display, much given to the division of labour and the use of a free market. It requires those who operate it to be sensitive to the notion of obligation and the fulfilment of contract, to be work-oriented, disciplined, and not too addicted to economically irrelevant political and religious patronage networks, nor to dissipate too much of their energy in festivals or display. If this is indeed what a modern economy demands, and, above all, if this is what is required by the process of *construction* of a modern economy (and perhaps also of a modern polity), then Reformist Islam would seem to be custom-made for the needs of the hour. In fact, given the congruence between what Weberian sociology would lead one to expect, and what is offered by High and Reformist Islam, there is a bit of a puzzle concerning why Muslim economic performance is not rather more distinguished than it actually is. The economies of Muslim developing countries are not catastrophic, but they are not brilliant either, which is what the preceding argument might have led one to expect. Given the distorting effect of oil wealth, it is of course not easy to pass a definitive judgement.

But, whatever the state of the economy, there cannot be much doubt about the present situation in the ideological sphere. In the West, we have become habituated to a certain picture, according to which puritan zeal had accompanied the early stages of the emergence of a modern economy, but in which its culmination was eventually marked by a very widespread religious likewarmness and secularization. The sober thrifty work-oriented spirit, which helps amass wealth, is then undermined by the seductions brought along by that which it has achieved. The virtue inculcated by puritanism leads to a prosperity which subverts that virtue itself, as John Wesley had noted with regret.

In the world of Islam, we encounter quite a different situation. Though long endowed with a commercial bourgeoisie and significant urbanization, this civilization failed to engender industrialism; but once industrialism and its various accompaniments had been thrust upon it, and it had experienced not only the resulting disturbance but also some of its benefits, it turned, not at all to secularization, but rather to a vehement affirmation of the puritan version of its own tradition. Perhaps this virtue has not yet been rewarded by a really generalized affluence, but there is little to indicate that a widespread affluence would erode religious commitment. Even the unearned oil-fall wealth has not had this effect.

As with all hypotheses about the future a caveat of 'wait and see' is required.

Things may yet change in the future. But on the evidence available so far, the world of Islam demonstrates that it is possible to run a modern, or at any rate modernizing, economy, reasonably permeated by the appropriate technological, educational, organization principles, and combine it with a strong, pervasive, powerfully internalized Muslim conviction and identification. A puritan and scripturalist world religion does not seem necessarily doomed to erosion by modern conditions. It may on the contrary be favoured by them.

Eileen Barker: The Young and Religious Sects – What Makes a Young Person Become a Moonie?

Since the 1960s a series of religious sects or 'cults' have appeared which have proved particularly attractive to young people. These include the Children of God, the Divine Light Mission, Scientology, Transcendental Meditation, and the Unification Church (or 'Moonies' – after their leader Sun Myung Moon).

Eileen Barker's research is into the Moonies, but her questions about the sect and probably her answers have wider relevance to other new religious movements (NRMs). The key questions she asks are: 'under what circumstances will young educated westerners follow a man from Korea, accept a set of beliefs, adopt a style of life and perform actions which seem strange, wrong and unnatural to their parents, their friends and to most of the rest of society – and what are the consequences of such a phenomenon?' (p. 16). Barker is aware of the accusation of brainwashing against the sect and looked closely into this matter.

The extract below summarises the four variables she considered in assessing the extent to which choice or coercion explain why someone joins the Moonies. The four variables are:

1 the social context inwhich the decision whether or not to join the Unification Church is reached (including the 'brainwashing' issue);
2 the individual's predispositions (interest, values, hopes and fears);
3 the individual's understanding of the attraction (or otherwise) of the Unification Church;
4 the individual's past experience and expectations of society.

(*Note*: the above is roughly the order in which the variables appear in the extract, although the discussion of them involves considerable overlap.)

Barker's conclusions about the relative importance of the above variables are highly interesting. She seldom finds that simple brainwashing is the main explanation for why an individual joins the church (variable 1). Indeed, the 'typical' recruit tends to be idealistic and intelligent rather than a naive dupe (variable 2). Such people tend to be attracted to the ideals of the church (variable 3) and repelled by society's materialism (variable 4). Interestingly, it is similarly idealistic and intelligent young people who were found to be attracted to the American New Left in the 1960s (O'Donnell, unpublished PhD thesis, Keele University, 1974).

Barker's comments on society's failure to provide adequate outlets for the idealism and intelligence of many young people are sobering. They are even more relevant in the 1990s when the spectre of unemployment hangs over the educated as well as the uneducated.

Reading 76 From Eileen Barker, *The Making of a Moonie: Choice or Brainwashing*?' (Basil Blackwell, 1984), pp. 232–35, 238–40, 242–44, 247–51, 255.

'What conclusions have you come to?' is a question I have been asked on countless occasions by those (including the Moonies themselves) who have heard that I was studying the Unification Church. I have never quite known how to respond. I have, of course, come to many conclusions, but it is difficult to produce one, or even half a dozen, which could sum up the entire research – or even that part of it which is concerned with the recruitment. Quite often, when it is learned that I have myself been through the 'brainwashing process', the initial question is supplemented with: 'Have you ever felt that you want to join?' The answer to that (to the Moonies' chagrin) is a simple one: 'No, not for an instant; I have always found the movement eminently resistible.' But this is a personal response, and it does not follow that I might not feel that I can understand how others could find themselves wanting to join. Indeed, I suppose that if I were pushed to provide a single conclusion to this part of my study, it would be that I believe it *is* possible to increase our understanding of why certain people become Moonies. Having said that, however, I would also want to insist that no single explanation can be given and, indeed, that any single explanation would be *wrong*. It is necessary to consider a large number of data, not all of which might, by themselves, seem very important, but which, when taken together, can build up a general (possibly an unavoidably *too* general) and rather complicated picture. In this final chapter I try to sketch the outlines of a picture which emerges from the details presented in the earlier chapters.

One cannot, however, order and generalize data without some sort of 'organizing principle', and here, as throughout the rest of the book, I have been guided by an attempt to assess the relative importance and interaction of the four variables which . . . were isolated in chapter 5 as those which would be most significant in deciding the manner and extent to which coercion rather than choice might be responsible for the particular outcome.

Put less abstractly, the questions that are being addressed are: to what extent does someone become a Moonie because he decides, in the light of his predispositions and past experiences, that the beliefs and practices of the Unification Church are 'better' than those of the 'outside' society? How far do his experiences of the outside society constitute a 'push' towards the Unification alternative? How far does the Unification alternative present an attractive 'pull' away from other alternatives? and to what extent is the immediate (Unification) environment responsible for *reinterpreting* the person's predispositions and experiences so that he is aware only of what the Unificationists themselves want him to be aware of and thus will recognize only one possible future – being a Moonie?

Variable 1

Starting with what is probably the most contentious of the four variables, it is clear that the Unification environment has played an important role in the recruitment of the majority of the members in the West. Unlike most of the other new religions, the Moonies usually try to persuade their potential recruits to attend residential courses. While this practice may in itself cut down the number of people who are willing to learn about the movement, it does mean that those who attend will be in a carefully controlled situation which can exert a considerable influence on some of the guests.

There is no evidence that any kind of physical coercion is used by the Moonies, or that the diet or workshop activities seriously impair the biological functionings of the guests to the extent that they would be judged incapable of behaving 'normally' were they in another *social* environment at that time. There is, however, plenty of reason to believe that the Moonies will do their best to influence their guests' perception of the situation in which they now find themselves. Some of the guests' memories are more likely to be evoked than others; hopes and fears and, sometimes, feelings of guilt may be played upon; care is taken to find out what 'resonates' with each individual; options are painted in terms most favourable to the Unification Church's alternative; less attractive aspects of the movement are suppressed or, occasionally, denied; in some places, most particularly in California, there has been little opportunity for potential recruits to be exposed to a countervailing influence; and, most significant of all, the experience of a loving, caring community within the Unification environment can foster feelings of personal involvement with individuals, which then developed into feelings of trust and commitment and loyalty to the group – feelings which may encourage the guest to accept, more readily than he would otherwise, the world from a Unification perspective.

But it is also obvious that the Unification environment is not irresistible. Conversion to the movement is the result of a (limited) number of *individual* experiences; it is not the result of a mass-induced hypnosis. The fact that most people who are subjected to the Moonies' attempts to recruit them are perfectly capable of refusing to join the movement rules out those explanations which rely totally on Unification techniques of coercion for an explanation of recruitment to the movement. It also rules out any suggestion that the alternative which the Moonies offer is irresistible – even when it is presented within a Unification context. It points, instead, to the conclusion that the personalities and previous experiences which guests 'bring with them' must play a significant role. This leads us on to the question: in what ways do those who join the movement differ from those who do not?

Variable 2

In chapter 5 I explained how, although we certainly have to examine individual cases if we want to find out what goes into the making of a Moonie, and although we have to recognize that no two cases are ever identical, looking only at the individual Moonie (or ex-Moonie) cannot help us to decide on the type or degree of coercion or choice that may be involved in Unification recruitment. I described how, by means of comparative analysis, it was possible to detect some interesting differences between the bundles of characteristics to be found in five different groups of people: (1) those who became Moonies; (2) those who joined, but then left within a day or two or, at the most, a few weeks; (3) those who went to a workshop, but did not join; (4) a 'non-exposed' control group of a similar age and from a similar background to the Moonies; and (5) the population as whole.

If we look at the population as a whole, it is clear that only a very small proportion has shown any favourable interest in the proselytizing efforts of the Moonies. Those who have responded have tended to be overwhelmingly between the ages of 18 and 28, predominantly male, disproportionately middle-class and usually unmarried. By way of contrast, those who have become Home-Church or Associate members have shared many of the characteristics of that section of the population which is affiliated to the more conventional churches – that is, they have tended to be older, female, of a slightly lower-class (although still disporportionately middle-class) and, frequently, married.

Plenty of reasons have been put forward to explain why young adults will do things which seem to their elders (and some of their peers) to be wrong-headed, irresponsible, incomprehensible, bizarre or insane. Youth is a time for idealism, rebellion and experimentation. If one happens to come from the advantaged middle classes, one can afford the luxury of denying onself luxuries while following idealistic pursuits. Enjoying the health of youth and unencumbered by immediate responsibilities, one can disclaim material interests – at least until one has 'matured' sufficiently to abandon extravagant fantasies, settle down, accept and probably uphold the pursuits and values of conventional society.

Such observations undoubtedly have a considerable amount of truth in them, and they can help us to understand why those who commit themselves to full-time membership of the Unification Church are liable to be drawn from a particular age range, but by themselves these genralizations are far too sweeping and could apply to many periods throughout history. We might want to ask whether there are more specific features of contemporary society which could be providing a more specific push towards a movement like the Unification Church. Furthermore, such generalizations do not help us to explain why some of these young people should become Moonies while others become Anglicans, Maoists, freedom fighters, punks, glue-sniffers, football hooligans or explorers of the upper reaches of the Amazon. We have seen that not all young people flock to find out what the Unification Church has to offer – in fact, the majority of them express an extreme distaste not merely for the movement as it has been publicized, but also for many of the beliefs and practices which it embodies. How do some of these young people come to see it in a different light?

Variable 3

The assumption that the Unification alternative is universally repugnant to anyone in his right mind has been partly responsible for questions about recruitment to take the form: 'How could *anyone* become a Moonie?' and for the reply to be that no one in his right mind *could* become a Moonie. The fact that there *are* Moonies has then been explained in one of two ways, the simplest explanation being that the person was not in his right mind because he had been subjected to an irresistible technique such as brainwashing or mind-control. I have argued, however, that this leads to another question: how (once he has come into contact with the movement) could anyone *not* become a Moonie? The fact that there are those who do resist the Unification techniques would seem to lead to a second explanation: that those who become Moonies cannot really be said to be in their right minds because they are particularly passive, pathetic or suggestible people. But the evidence suggests that, although a few Moonies might fall into this category, the majority do not; indeed, it seems that, while some such people may be drawn to the workshop, it is precisely those whom one might have expected to be the most vulnerable to persuasion who turn out to be non-joiners, with the few who do agree to join deciding to leave within a very short space of time. It would seem, then, that there is at least a prima-facie case for assuming that although the Unification alternative is not attractive to the majority of young people, it can hold an attraction for some people who appear to be 'in their right minds' . . .

[T]he Unification Church is unlikely to appeal to people who are interested primarily in making money or 'getting on' in a competitive rat race; it offers a 'higher' ideal than the materialism of modern society – it offers a religious ideal. But it is not the sort of religion which offers its followers a method of withdrawing from this world in order to meditate upon the Beyond or to glimpse their own inner godliness through mystical experiences; nor is it the sort of religion which enjoins its members to await their rewards in the next world. It is a religion which promises to change this world, for everyone, so that it is a better world – indeed, the best of all possible worlds, the sort of world which God intended there to be when He first created the Garden of Eden. Exactly what the Kingdom will be like in detail may be left to the individual to imagine, but it is known that cruelty, uncetainty and compromise will disappear; everyone will know what is true and good in accordance with God's divine Principle; and everyone will know where he or she stands. It will be a world in which a loving, caring God has a loving, caring relationship with each individual, and in which each individual will also find him or herself as an integral part of a God-centred family into which children, unencumbered by original sin, will be born the inheritors of the New Age.

Whatever the details, the means to achieve the goal are, it is believed, known by God – and by the Messiah who came to reveal God's Principle and to act as the perfect example for the less-than-perfect disciples. And while the goal may in some ways seem abstract, the means most certainly are not. Not only is each individual given spiritual guidance, but he is also set tasks of a highly practical nature. It is possible for Moonies to *see* what they are achieving as they pursue their individual goals, and in so far as thses intermediate goals take the form of fund-raising or recruiting new members, it is even possible to calculate the successes and failures of each day's work. The strict organization and the discipline mean that everyone knows exactly what he should be trying to achieve, and that he is part of a larger, unified whole. But the organization is not presented as an impersonal, bureaucratic machine run by interchangeable little cogs; it is seen as a devoted Family of brothers and sisters who are lovingly cared for by 'True Parents'. The concept of indemnity implies that the more arduous his labour, the more the sacrificial Moonie will have accomplished – but the sacrifice is not for ever. The promise is that it need not be long before those who accept the challenge to fulfil their responsibility can enjoy the results of their contribution to the building of the Kingdom.

The non-Moonie option

Variable 4

Turning now to the *non*-Unification alternative, one can draw a distinction between specific 'pushes' which affect a particular individual and more general feelings of discontent which can affect a wide range of individuals. Colin provides an example of someone who was experiencing a relatively specific push. He had been taking drugs and was deeply involved with a girl who wanted to marry him. He saw the Unification Church as an undreamed-of haven of peace:

> I could feel the prison doors just closing on me and I could see a really miserable life ahead of me. I used to think, if I've got these things bothering me, why don't other people have these things bothering them? Not knowing everybody has these kind of difficulties in life, nobody exposes them or talks to each other about them, so everybody lives in their own little world, never really getting to known anyone. You find this even with married couples. . . .
>
> I remember after the weekend I just cried – I felt such a happiness inside me like I hadn't felt all my life. And for the first time in my life I saw a real direction and a real hope for mankind, I really did.

Colin's situation was not unique, but the evidence suggests that the typical Moonie is no more likely than his peers to have found himself in a particularly harrowing situation. Far more common are cases in which the society in which the potential recruits found themselves was not posing any immediate threat so much as forming a general backcloth of disillusionment and discontent. It was this backcloth against which the Unification alternative would be judged and which could result in the sort of direct comparison that could lead a Moonie to declare: 'The bad society around me showed me that the Family life was the right way.'

What, then, are some of these more general experiences of society which the potential recruit takes with him to the Unification workshop? I shall not attempt to represent an account of society 'as it really is'. One would naturally expect Moonies' descriptions to be affected by their current membership of the movement, but what follows is not meant to be a picture of the 'outside' society as it is defined by the Unification Church. What we are concerned with here is an attempt to understand the social environment as it could have impinged upon the consciousness to the potential convert *before* he met the movement, and which other people would also recognize, even if they would not choose the Unification Church as a viable alternative. The description is drawn not only from the Moonies' accounts of their non-Unification lives but also from the direct and indirect responses of the control group and other non-Moonies to whom I have talked. It is a selective description in that it focuses on those aspects of society which could contribute a push towards (rather than a pull from) the alternative offered by the Unification Church for the sorts of people whose more immediate experiences of society were considered in the previous chapter.

In caricature, the potential recruit can see the non-Unification world as a divisive, turbulent, chaotic society, characterized by racial intolerance, injustice, cut-throat competition and lack of direction – a society which seems to be out of control and heading for imminent disaster. He can see an immoral (possibly amoral) society which no longer recognizes absolute values and standards; everything is relative to the utilitarian interests and desires of a pleasure-seeking, money-grubbing, power-hungry population; the pathetic eyes of skeletal children stare accusingly out of Oxfam posters – which are placed, with Kafkaesque humour, beside glossy advertisements for colour television sets, luxurious automobiles and exotic wines. It is a secular society which dismisses religious questions and spiritual quests as irrelevant vestiges of a pre-scientific age, or confines them to the ivory tower of theological colleges; in so far as the traditional Churches still function, they are (sparsely) populated by hypocritical or apathetic congregations and clergy who consider the occasional token ritual to be sufficient energy to offer unto God. . . .

Disillusionment with society is scarcely a new phenomenon. Glancing briefly at recent history, Western society has observed a series of rejections by vocal sections of its middle-class youth. During the late 1960s it was the 'imperialistic bourgeois structure of capitalism' which was a primary focus of dissent; students in America, in Europe and, for slightly different reasons, in Japan declared that the structure of society must be changed. When the structure seemed remarkably resilient in the face of demos and vindictive rhetoric, the attempt to change it was replaced by an attempt to reject it altogether. Flower children and hippies dropped out of society and into the new counter-culture.

In contrast to the materialistic, dehumanizing, quantifying rat race, the counter-culture was supposed to allow everyone to develop and fulfil him or herself as a unique individual, in his or her own right, at his or her own level. Everyone could do his or her own thing, unencumbered by the standards of others; everyone could be equal; everyone could achieve everything. But while the counter-culture offered a haven from the rat race for some, for many of those who had been brought up in an achievement-oriented society it offered only a temporary respite during the initial honeymoon of rejection. Lack of direction and a life bereft of goals or purpose still faced those who continued to find themselves seeking a challenge and wanting to *do* something. The individual became bogged down in the vast expanses of anything or nothing which seemed to be his or her sole existential choices. Within the open, unstructured counter-culture, realities and relationships were quickly created, but with no social pressures to reinforce them or hold them together, they crumbled under minor assault. Disillusionment and frustration awaited those who still wanted to know who they were and where they stood in an environment which had chosen to defy definitions and boundaries, and in which sincerity rested upon the rejection of absolute truths. The freedom of spontaneity had become the insecurity of antinomianism. So long as infinity was the only limit for both the means and the goal, nothing was obtainable. There were no benchmarks which allowed one to know whether one had got anywhere. The liberated individual was alone. He was unable to plug into anything with which to pull his lonely, unattached spirit up by its sagging bootstraps.

In theory young people find themselves in a society of opportunity. All have an equal chance to climb the ladder of the achieving society or to enjoy the permissive society in which anything goes. The world is their oyster. But in practice only a few can prise open the oyster and find anything of value inside. In the competitive, claustrophobic rat race, pearls are few and far between; in the agoraphobic counter-culture, all can have as many pearls as they please – but, as a result, pearls have become worthless.

The Moonie option

Barker continues to discuss Variables 3 and 4 in this section

By way of contrast, the alternative which the Unification Church offers is one which seems both to recognize and to provide an explanation for the evils of the contemporary world. By making sense of the past, it offers hope for the future; it offers a clear direction, a clear leadership which knows what to do and how to do it. It is, paradoxically, a movement which offers freedom from directionless choices.

It offers a religious community within which God is at the centre of everyday life; God is a living Being with whom each individual can have a personal relationship. It is not only a community in which each individual can feel the comfort of a loving God – it is also one which gives each individual the chance of comforting *Him*. It offers a loving, caring environment which gives its members not only warmth and affection but also a chance to love and sacrifice themselves for others. It is, paradoxically, a community which gives by taking.

The Unification Church offers the potential recruit the chance to be part of a Family of like-minded people who care about the state of the world, who accept and live by high moral standards, who are dedicated to restoring

God's Kingdom of Heaven on earth. It offers him the opportunity to *belong*; it offers him the opportunity to *do* something that is of value and thus the opportunity to *be* of value.

This can be pretty heady stuff for some of those who are experiencing an aching vacuum for 'something'. I have already suggested that the potential Moonie is not the sort of person who will accept anything, but it is not difficult to see how the Unification Church might appeal to someone who is idealistic and who has enjoyed the security of a sheltered family life; someone for whom the big decisions may have been taken, but who is, none the less, an achiever – so long as he has a clear idea of what it is that he has to achieve; someone who has a strong sense of service, duty and responsibility but can find no outlet for his desire to contribute; someone whose belief that everything in the world *could* be all right had been held for a longer time than that of his more cynical friends whose illusions had been shattered at an earlier age and with whom he now has some difficulty in finding much in common; someone for whom religious questions are important and who is receptive to religious answers . . .

Those who feel that the Moonies are wasting their lives might, for example, want to recognize the difficulty that young people have in finding an occupation which they feel is worth while and in which they are contributing something of value to others. Most of us do not believe that there are easy answers to the problems of contemporary society, but that does not mean that there are not many ways in which the energy and idealism of youth may not be tapped, with advantages both to the individuals concerned and to the wider society. Of course, some opportunities do exist, and many young people do make a positive contribution to the welfare of others and society in general, but there are many more who are frustrated, feel helpless and hopeless and suffer from a lack of direction and an absence of meaning in their lives. Traditionally, religion has offered direction and meaning in the lives of believers, and indeed it still does for large numbers of people. Traditional religion has, however, frequently tended to become bureaucratized and ritualized, and new religions have emerged throughout the course of history to offer their followers a surer, more immediate promise of salvation than the often stagnant institutionalized religions can – especially in times of rapid social change. If they wish to keep their flock, the more orthodox Churches might do worse than try to be slightly more open to discussion about religious questions at a personal level with adolescents. It is not only to those who become Moonies that members of the clergy can appear to be either too remote to approach – or too trendy to be taking either God or religion seriously.

But this is no place to dwell upon the gaps generated by either society in general or the traditional religions in particular. The task I have set myself in this book is confined to addressing the question of why someone will take up the Unification alternative and, as so many people seem to accept that to do so must be the result of brainwashing, my analysis has focused on the evidence and arguments which could support or question such a possibility.

What then are my conclusions? Has my study led me to believe that people join the Unification Church as the result of irresistible brainwashing techniques or as the result of a rational, calculated choice? As will doubtless be clear to anyone who has read thus far, the short reply to such a question is that I do not find either answer satisfactory, but that the evidence would seem to suggest that the answer lies considerably nearer the rational-choice pole of the continuum than it does to the irresistible-brainwashing pole . . .

In this book I have tried to give some justification for the approach that I have taken. I do believe that by comparing the Moonie bundles of characteristics with those of non-joiners and the control group, we have, on the one hand, been able to question whether some of the factors whch others have assumed must have been important were in fact all that important, and, on the other hand, we have been able to isolate significant influences which the Moonies might not deny as part of their background but certainly would not use as part of their own explanation. It is, moreover, possible to see how the sorts of explanation which the Moonies give correspond to the kinds of explanation one might expect from people with their sorts of bundles – that is, their own explanations are not all that strange considering the sort of people that they are. For example, the following quotation succinctly epitomizes the kind of response that the Unification Church can elicit from, in this case, a religiously oriented 'doer' with a social conscience: 'I felt that I had been challenged. If you believe it's true, it demands a commitment to action because of what it's saying about the world today and how God's working in the world today.' . . .

Given the enormous diversity to be found between Moonies and between Unification practices according to time and place, it is no doubt foolhardy to attempt too specific a final summary of my conclusions, but it does seem that if one were to gauge the relative influence of the four variables in the recruitment of a large number of Moonies . . . one would find the largest cluster of cases (well over half) around a point at which the four variables were fairly evenly balanced (what I called a situation of 'non-conscious fit') . . .

Questions and Issues

Religion: Section 16

The most relevant readings appear in brackets after each question.

1 Explain and illustrate what is meant by describing religion as 'ideology'. (Section 16, especially Readings 73–74)
2 Discuss the extent to which religion and the media fulfil similar roles in relation to society? (Readings 73–74, 77–78)
3 Critically assess the view that there is fundamental cultural and ideological conflict between 'the West' and Islam. (Readings 28 and 75. A fuller response will require reference to other sources.)
4 What makes a young person become a Moonie? (Readings 8, 76)

THE SOCIOLOGY OF THE MEDIA

Introduction: Readings 77–80

The sociology of the media grows as does the presence of the media in everyday life. Few, if any, areas of sociology raise more fundamental questions. Does the media enhance or decrease or even threaten our freedom? Does it stimulate our intelligence and capacity for creativity and pleasure or turn us into 'cultural dopes'. Who owns the media and does it matter? Should we – like classical scientists – still be researching the 'effects' of the media or rather examining how audiences interpret the media? Are there different answers to all these questions for different individuals and groups? To the last question, the answer is surely 'yes' which indicates an appropriately cautious approach to the theories presented below.

In making this selection of readings, I have sought to provide examples which effectively represent current theoretical developments and concerns. Those who are unfamiliar with the sociology of the media may find it helpful to read the relevant chapter of *A New Introduction to Sociology* (Nelson, 1992), the companion textbook to this Reader. There, media debates are heavily sign-posted in terms of familiar sociological perspectives. In these readings, the sign posts are slightly less obvious. It may be useful to pick them out in relation to each reading, always remembering that these days sociologists seem increasingly uncomfortable with the simple labels others pin on them.

James Curran discusses several organisational models of the media. In particular, he examines the extent to which each model is more or less democratic. He finds liberal, Marxist and Communist models lacking in this respect. He explores a number of practical democratic alternatives all of which combine the free market with an element of public involvement and interest. At this point, the reader may find it helpful to refer to a reading in the second edition of this Reader (p. 717). Here Peter Golding and Graham Murdock discuss conglomerates and the media, especially in relation to new communications' technology.

The next two readings mark a sharp change from macro theory to a more micro level of concern with audience participation in and interpretation of the media. Fiske's analysis of 'Women in Quiz Shows' is not untypical of this emerging area of research. Such research stresses the active involvement of audience members, and represents almost the opposite of the 'hyperdermic needle' model of the 'mass media' in which the audience is presented as 'injected' with 'ideological dope'. Silverstone's piece examines some of the more general methodological and theoretical implications of this approach.

Simon Cottle's wide-ranging coverage of the sociology of the news examines again in this particular context many of the key issues which were raised in the preceding extracts. Essentially, however, it is an up-to-date and highly informed critical presentation of theoretical trends in the sociology of news.

James Curran: A Critique of Liberal and Marxist/Communist Perspectives on the Media – and a Radical Democratic Alternative

After succinctly summarising the classic liberal perspective on the media, Curran describes what he refers to as the radical democratic approach. Both perspectives argue that the media should represent a range and balance of interests. However, adopting the radical democratic approach, Curran contends that in practice capitalism and patriarchy have limited diversity and distorted balance in liberal democracies. He argues that, in contrast, a radical democratic approach must find ways of achieving a genuine balance of media involvement and output including (in the more radical 'strand' favoured by Curran) representation of interests critical of the powerful.

In his analysis of traditional approaches to the left to the media, Curran distinguishes between Marxist and communist perspectives. The former is a critique of the media in capitalist society – which is seen as the ideological 'opiate of the masses' – and the latter is a system of state control supposedly operated in the cause of enlightening the working classes. Curran provides an excellent diagram (reproduced on p. 461) which compares and contrasts the four perspectives he deals with in his article. As far as the Marxist perspective is concerned, he considers that it substantially underestimates the degree of freedom (relative autonomy) possible in capitalist society. He sees the communist media under Stalin as highly repressive.

Curran emphasises that the key characteristic of the media, as envisaged by the radical democratic perspective, is that it would *in practice* 'enable the full range of political and economic interests to be represented in the public domain'. Reassuringly, in terms of the claimed practicality of the radical democratic perspective, Curran is able to cite examples of where it actually (if partially) operates. These are:

1 a centrally controlled market economy, e.g. the BBC
2 a mandated market economy, e.g. the Dutch Broadcasting System
3 a regulated market economy, e.g. the Swedish Press System
4 a regulated mixed economy of public, civic and market sectors, e.g. as currently debated in Poland [at this time, then, this remains a hypothetical example].

These examples are clearly explained in the text. The first one is particularly interesting as it concerns the BBC.

It is worth noting that in his contribution to the construction of a radical democratic perspective on the media, Curran uses elements from both the liberal and Marxist perspectives. This represents the pragmatic spirit of reconstruction typical among radical sociologists since the demise of Marxist communism.

Reading 77 James Curran, 'Rethinking the media as public sphere' in P. Dahlgren and C. Sparks *eds.*, *Communication and Citizenship* (Routledge, 1991), pp. 29–31, 34–8, 46–52

Liberal and radical approaches

According to classical liberal theory, the public sphere (or, in more traditional terminology, 'public forum') is the space between government and society in which private individuals exercise formal and informal control over the state: formal control through the election of governments and informal control through the pressure of public opinion. The media are central to this process. They distribute the information necessary for citizens to make an informed choice at election time; they facilitate the formation of public opinion by providing an independent forum of debate; and they enable the people to shape the conduct of government by articulating their views. The media are thus the principal institutions of the public sphere or, in the rhetoric of nineteenth-century liberalism, 'the fourth estate of the realm'.

Underlying the traditionalist version of this theory is a simplistic view of society as an aggregation og individuals, and of government as 'the seat of power'. The key social relationship that needs to be policed by an ever-vigilant media is therefore the nexus between individuals and the state. Indeed, in some presentations of liberal theory, the media are on permanent guard duty patrolling against the abuse of executive power and safeguarding individual liberty.

However, one problem with this approach is that it fails to take adequate account of the way in which power is exercised through capitalist and patriarchal structures, and consequently does not consider how the media relate to wider social cleavages in society. It also ignores the way in which interests have become organized and collectivized, and so does not address the question of how the media function in relation to modern systems of representation in liberal democracies. Consequently, it has nothing useful to say about the way in which the media can invigorate the structures of liberal democracy.

The starting-point of the radical democratic approach is that the role of the media goes beyond that defined by classic liberalism. The media are a battleground between contending forces. How they respond to and mediate this conflict affects the balance of social forces and, ultimately, the distribution of rewards in society.

A basic requirement of a democratic media system should be, therefore, that it represents all significant interests in society. It should facilitate their participation in the public domain, enable them to contribute to public debate and have an input in the framing of public policy. The media should also facilitate the functioning of representative organizations, and expose their internal processes to public scrutiny and the play of public opinion. In short, a central role of the media should be defined as *assisting the equitable negotiation or arbitration of competing interests through democratic processes.*

Table 1.1 Alternative perspectives of the media

	Liberal	*Marxist critique*	*Communist*	*Radical democratic*
Public sphere	Public space	Class domination	—	Public arena of contest
Political role of media	Check on government	Agency of class control	Further societal objectives	Representation/ counterpoise
Media system	Free market	Capitalist	Public ownership	Controlled market
Journalistic norm	Disinterested	Subaltern	Didactic	Adversarial
Entertainment	Distraction/ gratification	Opiate	Enlightenment	Society communing with itself
Reform	Self-regulation	Unreformable	Liberalization	Public intervention

However, there is a basic ambiguity within the radical democratic tradition. The less radical strand argues that the media should reflect the prevailing balance of forces in society: a 'representative' media system is tacitly defined in terms of existing structures of power. This has led to the construction of broadcasting systems which, in different ways, have sought to reflect the balance of social or political forces in society. In Sweden, this has taken the form of incorporating representative popular movements into the command structure of broadcasting; in Germany and Finland, a system of making broadcasting appointments informed in part by the principle of proportional political representation; in the Netherlands, allocating airtime and technical facilities to representative organizations; and, in Britain and elsewhere, imposing a public tury on broadcasting to maintain a political balance between the major political parties.

But there is another strand within the radical democratic tradition which believes that the media should be a 'countervailing' agency (though within a framework that ensures representation of all interests). This is sometimes articulated in politically neutral, ethical terms: the media should expose wrongdoing, correct injustice, subject to critical public scrutiny the exercise of power (whether this be by trade unions or business corporations). Alternatively, it is formulated in more overtly radical terms: the media should seek to redress the imbalance of power in society. Crucially, this means *broadening access to the public domain* in societies where elites have privileged access to it. It also means compensating for the inferior resources and skills of subordinate groups in advocating and rationalizing their interests by comparison with dominant groups. Although this formulation can be made to sound elitist and opposed to a 'representative' media system, it has an underlying rationale. Since no 'actually existing' liberal democracy is a polyarchy in which power is evenly diffused or in perfect equipoise, it is legitimate for the media to function as an equilibrating force.

> Here Curran makes clear his own commitment to what might be termed a 'strong' version of the radical approach.

The radical approach also differs from the traditional liberal one in the way it conceptualizes the role of the media in modern democracies. In traditional liberal theory, the media are conceived primarily as vertical channels of communication between private citizens and government: they inform individual choice at election time, and they influence governments by articulating the collective view of private citizens. In contrast, radical revisionism advances a more sophisticated perspective in which the media are viewed as a complex articulation of vertical, horizontal and diagonal channels of communication between individuals, groups and power structures. This takes account of the fact that individual interests are safeguarded and advanced in modern liberal democracies partly through collective organizations like political parties and pressure groups, and at a strategic level through the construction and recomposition of alliances and coalitions. The role of the media is to facilitate this intricate system of representation, and democratize it by exposing intra-organizational decision-making to public disclosure and debate . . .

The radical approach attempts to blend 'liberal' individualism with 'socialist' collectivism (without, however, too much concern for labels).

The divergence between liberal and radical approaches is even more marked when it comes to a debate about how the media should be organized. This is something that will be discussed more fully later. It is sufficient, here, to signal one important difference. Traditional liberals believe that the media should be based on the free market since this guarantees the media's independence from the state. Radical democrats usually argue, on the other hand, that the free market can never be an adequate basis for organizing the media because it results in a system skewed in favour of dominant class interests.

The crucial modifications to the 'free market' inherent in the radical approach are presented below.

Radical democratic and traditional Marxist/Communist perspectives

Although the radical democratic approach owes a considerable debt to marxism, it can be differentiated from it both in terms of stalinist practice in the Soviet Union and also in terms of traditional marxist critiques of the media in western liberal democracies.

The radical democratic concept of a public sphere as a public space in which private individuals and organized interests seek to influence the allocation of resources and regulate social relations has no place in a traditional communist conception of society. This assumes that the common ownership of the means of production has removed structural conflicts, and created the conditions in which the common interests of society can be realized through the application of the scientific precepts of marxist-leninist analysis. The Communist Party as the custodian of scientific materialism has 'a leading role' – a euphemism for exclusive political monopoly – in co-ordinating the different elements of society in the realization of its common interests. The role of the media is defined within this framework: it educates people in the tenets of marxist-leninism; it aids the co-ordination and mobilization of the people in the tasks that need to be fulfilled; even media entertainment has an educational role in providing models for emulation and instruction and is expected not to subvert official definitions of Soviet society. Only one element of traditional communist theory of the media – the stress on its function as a safeguard against bureaucratic distortions of the state – allows it a free-wheeling, campaigning role. But the way in which the media was controlled before *glasnost* generally ensured that this remit was interpreted narrowly.

Admittedly, the functioning of the Soviet media before Gorbachev was at times more restricted in theory than in actual pracitce (thus reversing the pattern of the west where the media has long been more restricted in practice than in theory). When there were tensions and disagreements within the higher echelons of the Communist Party, the Soviet media expressed to some extent a diversity of viewpoint. This was particularly true of the early period of Soviet history, when the Soviet press was also organized and conceptualized in a more pluralistic way than it was to be later. But the communist conception of the media that took hold in the Soviet Union before the Gorbachev regime was deeply authoritarian; and the actual practice of the Soviet media was stunted by the underdevelopment of a civil society independent of the state. Even after negotiating the rapids of cold war scholarship, it is clear that the traditional communist approach is far removed from the radical democratic perspective that has been outlined.

The marxist critique of the media in the west cannot be readily reproduced as a single set of ideas since Marx himself never formulated a fully fledged analysis of the capitalist press, and subsequent marxist interpretations have taken a number of divergent forms. But traditional marxism offers an understanding of the capitalist media that is at odds with the radical democratic approach. According to old-style marxism, the liberal concept of the public sphere is a chimera, disguising the reality of bourgeois domination. The media are agencies of class control since they are owned by the bourgeoisie or are subject to its ideological hegemony. Indeed, the media should be viewed as an ideological apparatus of the state – the ideational counterpart to the repressive apparatus of the police, judiciary and armed forces through which the ruling order is ultimately sustained. The view that the media can be 'reformed' is dismissed as naïve. Significant changes in the media can only be effected through the socialist transformation of society.

This is opposed by a radical democratic view which offers a different understanding of the relationship of the media to power structures in society. Radical democrats usually argue that journalists have sometimes a considerable degree of day-to-day autonomy, particularly in broadcasting corporations which have won a measure of autonomy from government and in commercial media with dispersed shareholdings, where there is no dominant owner. This relative autonomy enables journalists to respond to a variety of influences – a change in the general climate of opinion, a shift in the milieux in which journalists move, the recomposition of accredited sources (due to, for example, a change of government), the emergence of new market trends calling for a competitive response . . .

This is not to adopt uncritically liberal pluralist arguments. The media systems in most liberal democracies are not representative. On the contrary, most under-represent subordinate interests and are canted more towards the right than their publics. This reflects the prevalence of capitalist media ownership, and consequent influence on personnel recruitment and promotion, market distortions limiting real choice, media dependence on powerful groups and institutions as news sources and the unequal distribution of resources within society for the articulation and generalization of social interests. But the radical democratic approach believes that the media can be reorganized in a way that will make them more representative or progressive. One way in which this can be done is to secure democratic consent for their reform through the state.

The third route

The two main approaches to organizing the media – the free-market liberal and collectivist-statist strategies – each have drawbacks. Yet they can be combined in ways that minimize their defects and capitalize on their strengths.

One central deficiency of the market approach is that it produces an unrepresentative media system. The high level of capitalization in most sectors of the modern media restricts market entry to powerful capitalist interests. It also shields them from competition save from other capitalist entrepreneurs and large corporations. In Britain, for example, the establishment costs of a new national daily are at least £20 million; for a local cable TV station around £40 million; for a substantial commercial TV regional franchise well in excess of £100 million; and for a satellite TV service over £500 million. Only in marginal sectors of the media – low-circulation magazines, local free sheets and local community radio stations – are entry costs still relatively modest.

The second, related problem is that most media markets are distorted due to the large economies of scale that are an especially pronounced feature of the communications industries. A small number of 'majors' have long dominated the film and music production industries. Newspaper chains overshadow the press in most liberal democracies. Only in television has state action in some countries restricted the development of private monopoly power, but even in this sector things are changing fast. Government privatization policies and the commercial exploitation of the new TV industries are promoting the development of dominant TV companies.

The character of media oligopoly has also changed. Dominant producer companies in different sectors of the media have merged to produce multi-media conglomerates. These have expanded on a global scale, and in many cases have become linked through cross-ownership to core sectors of finance and industrial capital. Their growth poses a problem for two reasons. It has increased the power of an unrepresentative capitalist elite, symbolized by Murdoch and Berlusconi, to control the distribution of information and ideas on an unprecedented scale. Second, their rise has been accompanied by an erosion of the competitive processes which in a limited but still important way made them publicly accountable.

The third major defect of the market system is that it tends to lead to a narrowing in the ideological and cultural diversity of the media. This is not merely the by-product of market distortions – restricted market entry and global concentration of ownership – but is built into the 'normal' processes of media markets. Intense competition between a limited number of producers encourages common denominator provision for the mass market. This is particularly true of TV due to the peculiarities of the medium. Television can achieve higher sales in terms of larger ratings at minimum extra cost, which reinforces the economic advantages of targeting the middle market. Some TV companies are also funded entirely by advertising, which is less sensitive to intensities of consumer preference than direct consumer payments. This also encourages the production of bland programmes with a universal appeal to an undifferentiated, mass audience.

In short, the free-market approach has three central flaws. It excludes broad social interests from participating in the control of the main media. It leads to concentration of media ownership. And it promotes cultural uniformity, particularly in TV output. These shortcomings should be viewed in terms of what a democratic society should require of its media. At the very least, an adequate media system should enable the full range of political and economic interests to be represented in the public domain, and find expression in popular fiction. A market-based media system, in modern conditions, is incapable of delivering this.

The advantage of the collectivist approach is that it can enable interests with limited financial resource – which are excluded in a market-driven system – to have a share in the control of the media. It can also prevent control of the media from falling into the hands of an unrepresentative, capitalist elite. And through collective arrangements, it can also ensure that media output is pluralistic and diverse.

But the potential promise of collective provision has often been contradicted by its actual practice. This is partly because collective provision through the state can result in state control, as is illustrated notoriously by the stalinist experience. A multi-tiered system of control was evolved in the Soviet Union – based on formal legal censorship, control over the material production and distribution of communications, control over senior appointments, indoctrination in journalism schools and, more indirectly, control over the flow of information – which turned the media into an instrument of the state and the Communist Party.

The collectivist approach proved more successful in European countries with a tradition of liberal democracy. Even so, a number of problems recurred. State pressure was sometimes brought to bear on broadcasters, through control over appointments, public funding and the allocation of franchises. Even when the direct abuse of state power was minimized, effective control over broadcasting was exercised, to a lesser or greater extent, by a professional elite integrated into the hierarchy of power. Their domination was legitimized in some countries by a paternalistic definition of public-service broadcasting which emphasized the leadership role of cultural bureaucrats in educating and informing the masses. This led to insensitivity and lack of responsiveness to the diversity of public taste, particularly in situations where there was no effective competition.

These defects in the functioning of the collectivist approach draw attention to the positive aspects of the market mechanism. A market-based system does not guarantee the autonomy of the media from the state since the same interests that dominate the media can also dominate the state. But it does minimize the exercise of state leverage through control of funding and appointments. Similarly, the processes of the free market do not ensure, as we have seen, that the media mirror the ideological and cultural diversity of the public. But when competition is not deformed by oligopoly and restricted entry, it does result in greater responsiveness to audience preferences.

The question then becomes how can one combine collectivist and market approaches in a synthesis that incorporates the strengths of both. To judge from the European experience, there are four alternative answers to this question (though each has a number of different variations).

One model is the *centrally controlled market economy*. Its underlying rationale is that the terms of and rules by which competition is conducted should be centrally determined according to the public interest. One example of this approach is provided by the British TV system, in which free-market competition is tempered in a number of ways. The largest organization, the BBC, is publicly owned and is expected to set quality standards since it is run for the public good rather than private gain. The other main players in the system – ranging from a regionally based commercial network (Channel 3), a public trust corporation (Channel 4), local TV stations (cable TV) and a national commercial consortium (B Sky B) – are differentiated in organizational terms in order to promote choice. The principal TV channels are also funded mainly by different sources of revenue (licence fee, advertising and subscriptions) in order to avoid the uniformity induced by direct competition. And all TV channels are subject to content controls, though with varying degrees of stringency and policed in different ways.

The full complexity of the system need not be described here. Built into its design are a number of central objectives: quality defined in terms of a negotiation between elite norms and audience ratings; diversity defined in terms of a mix of different types of programme rather than of values; and political representation defined in terms of Westminster consensus rather than popular dissensus. However, these objectives can be changed and modifications can be made in the system to achieve this. Thus, a number of reforms have been proposed which would strengthen broadcasters' autonomy from politicians, and extend the ideological and cultural range of programme output. Indeed, one of the advantages of the centrally controlled approach is that systemic modifications can be effected relatively easily: the disadvantage is that this facility can be abused.

An alternative approach represented by the Dutch broadcasting system takes the form of a *mandated market economy*. Both airtime and the use of publicly owned production facilities, with technical staff, are allocated in the Netherlands to different groups on the basis of the size of their membership defined by the sale of their programme guides. This results in a plurality of organizations from commercial groups like TROS to VARA (with close links to the Labour Party) and the NCRV (a conservative, protestant organization), each providing a comprehensive package of services. None of these groups, unlike the central news service, is required to adopt a bi-partisan approach. The intention is to produce a broadcasting system that reflects a wide spectrum of political opinion and cultural values. But although the concept behind this system is seductive, it is not without problems.

Broadcasting organizations which lost audiences to TROS began to imitate its commercial entertainment formula, thereby weakening the diversity of the broadcasting system as a whole. The relatively high level of Dutch audiences attracted to cable TV, with a heavy diet of US programmes, also indicates a certain level of consumer dissatisfaction with Dutch broadcasting.

The third approach is the *regulated market economy*, represented by the Swedish press system. The thinking behind this is that the market should be reformed so that it functions in practice in the way it is supposed to in theory. Its most important feature is that it lowers barriers to market entry. The Press Subsidies Board provides cheap loans to under-resourced groups enabling them to launch new papers if they come up with a viable project. The Board has acted as a midwife to seventeen new newspapers between 1976 and 1984, most of which have survived. The second important feature of the system is that it tries to reconstitute the competitive market as a level playing field in which all participants have an equal prospect of success. Since market leaders have the dual advantage of greater economies of scale and, usually, a disproportionately large share of advertising, low-circulation papers receive compensation in the form of selective aid. The introduction of this subsidy scheme has reversed the trend towards local press monopoly.

A number of safeguards are built into the system in order to prevent political favouritism in the allocation of grants. The Press Subsidies Board is composed of representatives from all the political parties. The bulk of its subsidies – over 70 per cent in 1986 – is allocated to low-circulation papers, with less than 50 per cent penetration of households in their area, according to automatically functioning criteria fixed in relation to circulation and volume of newsprint, irrespective of editorial policy. Beneficiaries from the subsidy scheme include publications from the marxist left to the radical right: the paper which has the largest subsidy is the independent Conservative *Svenska Dagbladet*, which has been a consistent critic of successive Social Democratic governments. The subsidy scheme is funded by a tax on media advertising.

The twin precepts on which the Swedish press system is based – the facilitation of market entry and the equalization of competitive relationships – could be extended to broadcasting, even though spectrum scarcity prevents the creation of a full broadcasting market. Indeed, this is already in the wind. In 1989 the European Commission issued a directive calling for member countries to introduce a system whereby broadcasting organizations are required to commission a proportion of programmes from independent companies. Although the directive set no date, this policy has already been adopted in some countries. Market entry could be further facilitated, it has been argued, by establishing the broadcasting equivalent of the Swedish Press Subsidies Board, which would assist the funding of under-resourced groups, with viable projects, to complete in the radio or TV sectors.

A policy of market equalization is also being considered in a European context. The ability of national agencies to shape the ecology of broadcasting systems so that they are a democratic expression of the societies they serve is threatened, it is maintained, by economies of scale in the global TV market. US programmes are sold for foreign transmission at a fraction of their original cost, and at a price that is much lower than the cost of making original programmes in Europe. The threat posed by cheap US syndication to national broadcast systems has been blocked hitherto by official and unofficial quotas limiting the import of American programmes. But this protectionism is being breached by the emergence of satellite TV enterprises which transmit quota-breaking US programmes across national borders. This has prompted the call for satellite TV to be brought within the ambit of a regulated market economy through the auspices of the Council of Europe and European Commission. So far, both bodies have proposed an undefined limitation on non-European imported programmes to be policed by national agencies at the point of up-link to satellite TV delivery systems. This lack of definition ensures, however, that it will have no practical effect.

The fourth approach arises from the current debate in Poland about how broadcasting shuld be reorganized, with similar discussions occurring elsewhere within social democratic parties. It takes the form of a proposal for a regulated mixed economy, composed of *public, civic and market sectors*. One version of this proposal entails having a major, publicly owned sector committed to public-service goals, including the provision of mixed, quality programmes and politically balanced reporting. The market sector would be subject to minimum controls, and would be established through the sale of franchises to commercial companies which would also pay an annual spectrum fee. This would help fund, in turn, a civic sector whose role would be to extend the ideological range and cultural diversity of the system. The civic sector would have assigned frequencies and an Enterprise Board which would help fund new and innovatory forms of ownership and control, including employee ownership, subscribers with voting rights, consumer co-ops and stations linked to organized groups. The Enterprise Board would function not as a traditional regulatory body, policing programme content, but as an enabling agency assisting financially the emergence of new voices in the broadcasting system.

These four approaches represent alternative responses to the question of how a media system can be constructed that enables divergent interests to be fully represented in the public domain. They all have one thing in common: they marry a collectivist approach to market processes. They thus represent an attempt to define a third route which is superior to failed market and collectivist policies. Their aim is to recreate the media as a public sphere in a form that is relatively autonomous from both government and the market.

John Fiske: What Women do in Quiz Shows – and What it Means

Since the mid-1980s, a growing body of work has examined media audiences not as passive recipients of media ideology, but as active individuals and groups who make their own interpretation of the media. John Fiske is generally considered to take quite a strong view of the extent to which people can and do make sense of the media in terms of their own everyday experience.

In this extract, Fiske examines the meanings and interpretations female participants and audiences 'get out of' three popular quiz shows: *The New Price is Right*; *Family Feud*; and *Perfect Match*. Each programme allows him to examine, respectively, the themes of consumerism, family and romance – through the eyes of the women. Fiske leaves us in no doubt that he sees these programmes as reinforcers of capitalism and patriarchy, but equally, he stresses that the mainly female participants in them find the space and freedom to exercise skill and judgement, to have fun, and to assert themselves. Sometimes the fun and assertion can be at the expense of 'piggish men' or domestic drudgery – so sometimes a glimpse of a bigger freedom appears in the activities of the female participants.

Or is Fiske kidding himself? Is he perhaps romanticising the audience as some of his critics have suggested (Silverman, 1990)? Although Fiske pays more attention to audience/participants' meanings than most of the theorists he criticises, it is still arguable that he is reading his own radical interpretations into what are actually quite conventional understandings on the part of the women. In fairness, however, he is emphatic that what the women do is shaped in a context predetermined by more powerful others.

Reading 78 From John Fiske, 'Women and Quiz Shows: Consumerism, Patriarchy and Resisting Pleasures' in M. E. Brown *ed.*, *Television and Women's Culture* (Sage Publications, 1990), pp. 134–37, 138–40, 140–41

US television has broadcast over 330 different quiz and game shows, most of them in day time, most of them aimed at women. In Australia and the UK, a day's television without a quiz show of some sort is rare, and frequently at least one example of the genre rates in the top ten program. The role of game shows in women's culture is problematic, and in this chapter I wish to explore the questions of how far they bear the forces that subordinate women, and to what extent they enable these forces to be opposed, evaded or negotiated.

Quiz shows, along with soap opera, are often considered as one of the lowest forms of television. The fact that low critical standing coincides with their appeal to women should alert us to the possibility that the reasons for denigrating them should be sought not in the shows themselves, nor in their role in women's culture, but rather in the disciplinary power of patriarchy to devalue anything that resists, threatens, or evades its power. It is the function of this book to interrogate patriarchy, so let us take quiz shows seriously; let us posit that they can play active, pleasurable roles in women's culture and investigate what those roles and pleasures might be.

> In the present context, the terms 'semoitic features or discourses' can be regarded as synonyms for 'themes' (i.e. themes present in the programmes).

The approach I wish to take is to follow some of the main lines of argument attacking quiz shows, and suggest that their error lies not in their analysis of the semiotic features of quiz shows, but in their evaluation of the roles such meanings play in women's culture. I wish to concentrate on three of these semiotic features or discourses common throughout the genre and discuss each with reference to one particular show. These discourses are those of consumerism, the family, and romance.

Woman as consumer

Quiz shows are a cultural product of consumer capitalism. They foreground commodities, they blur the distinctions between themselves and the commercials embedded in them and the rewards that they offer are those of the commodity system. In short, they relentlessly address and position the women as housewife and consumer. But in the consumerist, capitalist society in which we live, the *only* cultural resources are those provided by the system and those social forces that govern it. This is as true of language and systems of representation as it is of commodities. A whole range of recent cultural theories, particularly ideological and feminist, have argued with great sophistication and persuasiveness how the interests of the dominant are served by the systems they control. But these theories need to be mitigated, if not contradicted, by studies focusing on *how* the subordinate make use of these systems. The art of everyday life, according to Michel de Certeau, is the art of making do: people make do with what they have, and if all they have are centrally provided resources, the point at issue becomes what people might do with them, rather than what they might do to people.

Without such an emphasis, it becomes difficult, if not impossible to conceive of subordinated groups, such as various groups of women, having any culture of their own: they would become merged into the mass so feared by the Frankfurt school. There is no 'authentic' folk culture for the subordinate to draw upon: 'high' culture is available and of interest to a minority only (within which women have difficulty in establishing a place for themselves) and no alternatives exist. Women's oral culture, or gossip, makes use of a language deeply inscribed with patriarchal values, but uses it in a feminine way. Similarly I would argue that women can use commodities (and quiz shows as cultural commodities) in ways that negate or evade the economic and gender power of the system that produces and distributes them.

The New Price is Right is the consumerist quiz show par excellence. The contestants are nearly all women, and the knowledge required is what our society treats as 'women's' knowledge: that of the prices and comparative values of commodities. The show consists of a variety of games and competitions in which the winner is the one who best judges commodity prices and values; who is, in other words, the best shopper. But if all the show does is to reproduce and repeat women's role in domestic labour, why, we must ask ourselves, should they find it popular and pleasurable? If women are the shoppers for the family in real life, why should they choose to fill their leisure with more of the same?

While recognising that the show clearly addresses women as consumers, we must also recognise the differences between the conditions of consumption on the show, and those of consumption in domestic labour, for it is in the differences that the pleasures lie for women.

The notion of the quiz 'as carnival' – when the 'normal' order can be mocked and reversed – is central to Fiske's analysis of the quiz.

The most obvious of these is the difference between the public and the private. Consumption in everyday life is essentially a private affair. Its skills go largely unrecognised and unapplauded. This lack of social acclaim for women's knowledge and labour is part of the strategy to silence them under patriarchy. *The New Price is Right* is characterised by noise, cheering and applause; the studio audience's enthusiasm verges on hysteria, the successes of the consumer contestants are wildly applauded. There is a strong element of the carnivalesque here, and for Bakhtin, the carnival was the occasion when the repressions of everyday life could be lifted, when the voices of the oppressed could be heard at full volume, when society admitted to pleasures which it ordinarily repressed and denied. The essence of carnival was the inversion of the rules of everyday life, necessitated by the need to maintain the oppression of a populace that would otherwise refuse to submit to this social discipline. So the forces of carnival are opposed to those which work to repress and control the everyday life of the subordinate.

Two main forms of liberation are expressed in the game-show audience's enthusiasm: the first is to give public, noisy acclaim to skills that are ordinarily silenced; the second is simply to be 'noisy' in public; to escape from demure respectability, from the confines of good sense that patriarchy has constructed as necessary qualities for 'the feminine'.

Women, particularly those from the lower socio-economic groups who form the core of the show's audience, are subordinated economically as well as socio-politically. This economic subordination takes two forms: the limited amount of money available to women and the ownership of that money. For women fulfilling the traditional feminine role of unwaged domestic labour, the money is the husband's. Earning and providing for the family is socially linked to masculinity, while spending and managing that money therefore becomes the feminine. In *The New Price is Right*, money is replaced by knowledge: masculine money by feminine knowledge. The show symbolically liberates women from their economic constraints and in so doing liberates them from their husbands' economic power (one of the many ways patriarchy has contructed and subordinated the feminine) . . .

Closely allied to the discourse of consumption is that of the family. The woman as consumer and the woman as family nurturer are overlapping roles. As its name suggests, *Family Feud* situates the woman firmly within the family. The game is played between two families of four and consists of guessing which were the most common answers given to a question by a random sample of a hundred people. The winner is the person (or family) who best understands or empathises with what other people are thinking. It is a democratic form of knowledge in that it depends upon majority belief rather than factual truth; it is inclusive rather than exclusive, for it does not distinguish clearly between those who possess it and those who do not; and its distribution throughout society lies outside the control of those with social power. This is a bottom-up knowledge, not a top-down one. It is also an 'interior', domestic form of knowledge and is thus a particularly feminine one. If the knowledge used in *The New Price is Right* is that developed by women to manage the economic resources of the family, the knowledge used in *Family Feud* has been developed to manage the family's emotional resources. It is knowledge of people, and how they are thinking and feeling that enables women to manage and smooth relationships within the family.

Though the families are of both sexes, females predominate, and the role of leader or spokesperson is almost invariably a woman. Adult men are comparatively uncommon contestants, though boys and younger men appear fairly frequently within the families. Women's leadership roles, normally confined to the domestic sphere, here become public: they speak for their families in a way that has traditionally been the role of the male. *Family Feud* may appear to offer fewer and more muted resistive pleasures than *The New Price is Right*, fewer opportunities to escape the repressive discipline of patriarchy, but the contradictions are still there within it.

Women and romance

Perfect Match, however, is a different matter entirely. It has arguably the most progressive gender politics of all quiz or game shows, and deserves its success as the ratings hit of the mid 1980s on Australian television.

The game consists of a 'wooer' of either sex choosing a date from three members of the opposite sex. Each has to answer the same three questions asked by the wooer, who can hear, but not see, the dates. The studio audience and, of course, the viewer, can both see and hear. The date chosen by such 'human knowledge' is then compared to the wooer's 'perfect match' who is selected 'scientifically' by a computer. If the human knowledge and scientific knowledge coincide, that is if the wooer chooses his or her scientifically 'perfect' match, the couple win extra prizes. But their main prize is always a date, usually on a short luxurious holiday. The central segment of the show consists of a previously matched couple returning to tell of their experiences on their date, both 'live' together in the studio, and separately on tape as they were each interviewed immediately afterwards.

The progressiveness of this show lies in a number of features which tend to minimise the differences between male and female sexuality. These differences have been established during the development of patriarchal capitalism and the nuclear family which it produced in order to naturalise patriarchal power (see below).

The structure of each show equalises the genders, for each show has two games, in one of which a woman chooses from three men and in the other, the sexes are reversed. The responsibility for initiating the relationship, the open control of the process of romantic choice and the more passive role of being selected are explicitly shared equally between the genders.

More importantly, perhaps, feminine sexuality is freed from the responsibility and respectability of marriage. Women, like men, are expected to find pleasure in their sexuality and no longer have to justify this pleasure as cementing a marital relationship, or at least a relationship in which marriage is the object. Women can 'rage' and find pleasure on their dates and in their social life in a way that has been traditionally defined as exclusively part of masculine sexuality. Women are free to enjoy it in a way that is almost never shown unjudgmentally elsewhere on television. (In TV dramas, women enjoying their own sexuality for the pleasure and control it can offer them are generally punished in the narrative.)

Of course, this 'liberation' from the discipline of patriarchal definitions of sexual differences is never complete, and, indeed, the show would not be popular if it were so. The traditional forms of patriarchal control are there to remind us what is being evaded: the title sequence has all the trimmings of traditional romance – soft focus, hearts, pinks and blues, romantic music – but they are so exaggerated as to parody traditional romantic values. Parody is a subversive form, for it exposes and mocks the essential features of its object. Here its object is the patriarchal conventions of the romance narrative. The growth of the romance genre throughout the nineteenth century paralleled the growth of the nuclear patriarchal family and the redefinition of feminine sexuality to fit within it, so the parody of that which is to be escaped from is a powerful part of the progressive gender politics of the show . . .

Women's culture within patriarchy

I have concentrated in this chapter on the meanings that quiz shows might have for their women fans, and attempted to account to some extent for their popularity with women by means other than the 'cultural dope' theory. Women are not cultural dopes. They are not complicit in, nor do they find pleasure in, their subordination under patriarchy. Of course, women's responses to this subordination may range from the oppositional to the (fairly) comfortably accommodating. In this chapter I have made oppositional readings of quiz shows which can be made by any among the subordinate against the thrust of dominant ideology and social power. It is important to stress that these are the tactics of those among the subordinate who choose not to oppose the repressive system head on but make guerilla raids upon it and seek out its weak points, the places where it can be turned against itself. Subordinated groups have to make do with what they have, and what they have is what the dominant system provides. The art of everyday culture is the art of making do, an art at which women excel through many generations of oppression, and from whom other subordinated groups have much to learn.

> Do you agree with Fiske that the 'oppositional readings' or understandings of quiz shows presented above 'might' be made by women participants/ viewers?

The study of the popular culture of subordinated groups (and *all* popular culture is the culture of the subordinate, even if it may use the cultural commodities of the dominant as its raw material) should direct itself to the tactics of 'making do'. Of course quiz shows are not radical texts. They do not attack or subvert patriarchal commodity capitalism with revolutionary zeal. Indeed, like all cultural commodities, they bear the ideology of the system that promotes and distributes them . . .

Roger Silverstone: Some Key Issues in Developing a New Audience-based Method of Researching Television

This reading is just a small extract (the conclusion) from a much longer article on audience research methodology and objectives by Roger Silverstone. What follows here, however, provides a succinct if dense summary of the research approach he advocates. Above all, he seeks a methodology which does justice to what viewers make of television as well as to the commercial, ideological and artistic forces behind television. The approach he advocates is ethnography – specifically observation and in-depth interviews. As Silverstone observes, a considerable body of television research of this kind already exists, including that of John Fiske author of the previous extract. Silverstone draws together and extends into a coherent theoretical agenda a variety of insights variously shared by others.

In a part of his article which is not included here, Silverstone argues that an anthropological approach to television must analyse television as technology (including how people use and adapt it); as consumption (i.e. in cultural terms) and as a form of 'rhetoric' (the meanings 'put into' and taken from television).

Anthropology is the direct study of people's everyday lives. Anthropologists invariably use ethnographic methods. An anthropology of the television audiences would be based primarily on the use of television by individuals in households. It is an approach founded on the premise that to understand the place of television in society the household context in which people watch (or half-watch or ignore) television must be understood as well as the intentions and control of owners and producers of television (see Reading 80).

Silverstone suggests three aspects of such research: description, dynamics and consequences. 'Description' is self-evidently necessary. 'Dynamics' refers to the issue of audience passivity/activity (exemplified in Reading 78). 'Consequences' refers to how individuals and groups are affected by and change as a result of television. In principle, Silverstone does seem to outline an agenda for research which reflects current understanding of the medium.

Reading 79 From Roger Silverstone, 'Television and Everyday Life: Towards an Anthropology of the Television Audience' in M. Ferguson *ed., Public Communication: The New Imperatives* (Sage Publications, 1990), pp. 186–89

Towards an anthropology of the television audience

Television as 'text' and television as technology are united by their construction, their recontextualization, within the practices of our daily lives – behind and beyond the closed doors of our houses – in our display of goods and cultural competences, both in private and in public. If we are to make sense of the significance of these activities, which after all, are the primary ones for any understanding of the dynamics of the pervasiveness and power of the mass media in contemporary culture, then we have to take seriously the varied and detailed ways in which they are undertaken.

This is the basis for the case for an anthropology of the television audience, and for a commitment to ethnography as an empirical method.

The starting-point for any such study is the household or the family, for it is here that the primary involvement with television is created, and where the primary articulation of meanings is undertaken. The household or family, itself embedded in a wider social and cultural environment, provides through its patterns of daily interaction, through its own internal system of relationships, and its own culture of legitimation and identity formation, a laboratory for the naturalistic investigation of the consumption and production of meaning (Anderson, 1988).

(i.e. the way people watch television reflects household dynamics, e.g. who controls the remote control?)

The empirical questions raised are many and various. Significantly, they revolve around three sets of issues. First, *description*: we need to know about the different patterns of consumption in different families and households in different areas at different stages of their life cycles. We can hardly hope to ask more sophisticated questions of the processes of consumption and reception, or provide more enlightened suggestions for policy, until we have some knowledge of the what and the how and the who of audience involvement with their television in the context defined by their involvements with other technologies and other things and people.

Such a requirement in turn suggests another: an ethnographic approach to family and household use of television. Observation and detailed and specific interviewing, at least as a first step, must ground any attempt to understand the embedded practices of the audience in the domestic setting. In short, we need to provide substance to the notion of the embedded audience by a consideration of the particular patterns of family and household life. This is a problem of the place of the household or family in the wider context of society, culture and technology – a problem which suggests the need for an integration of ethnography and political economy (Marcus and Fischer, 1986: 85) – but it is also a problem of the dynamics of the household and the family itself as the specificity of social and cultural and technology relations are negotiated within its own domestic space and time.

Second, *dynamics*: we need to understand the differences between the active and the passive viewer and to define these terms (or reject them entirely) within a context of the differential practices of different individuals, and in relation to different family and household 'techno-cultures' (Giner, 1985). We ought to be in a position to distinguish both within families and households and comparatively between families and households the various kinds of relationships that audiences generate with television and other communication and information technologies, beginning, for example, with the distinction between primary and secondary viewing or between referentiality and poeticality (Katz and Liebes, 1985). We also need to know who is involved and in what kinds of ways with television and to identify gender-, age- and class-based differences where they occur and where they seem to be significant.

A frequently raised issue in this context is who in a household decides 'what's on' – a problem sometimes resolved by having two or more televisions in the house (which itself has consequences for household interaction – see Silverstone's third point).

The argument that new technologies based on the computer and telephone are interactive in a way that the older ones based on the television and the video are not, needs to be tested against such assessments as I have suggested in relation to the activities surrounding the television set. We also, finally, need a sense of changing patterns of use, particularly in so far as technological developments are offering a more complex and varied communication culture to the domestic consumer, who in turn is being offered more choices and more encouragement to make them. 'More choice' is itself a problematic notion in this context.

Third, *consequences*: there is a whole series of questions to be asked about the consequences, both for individuals within the household or family and for the household and in particular for the family as a whole, of their involvement with television. These are important questions, of course, having major implications for policies, not just for the future of television but also for the future of the family.

The key issues, I would suggest, revolve around questions of isolation and integration. What are the consequences of differential involvement with television for individual and family identity and social and cultural involvement? How does the differential pattern of use and consumption affect the boundary around the household? This question itself fragments into a number of separate but necessarily interrelated further questions: questions to do with the separation of the public and the private; the existence or absence of different networks (social, technical or informational) along which different family or household members might find routes to the community; the links between home and school, home and work, home and leisure opportunities, and the question of to what extent they are affected by the household's use of television and an increasingly wide range of television-based services.

It has also been suggested that the incorporation of television (and of television-based technologies and services) into the household is likely not to be without consequence also for the daily lives of family members, for their material and moral identities. The use of television and video can integrate or separate not just the family as a whole from its neighbours or wider society, but can integrate or separate the individuals within the family, as age and gender groups form and re-form around particular activities that centre on the use of the screen or screens in the family home (Lull, 1980a and b; Morley, 1986). Here the questions have to do with the placing of the television in the micro-geography of the home (cf. Palmer, 1986), its articulation with other information and communication technologies, its role in defining age and gender identities, its significance as an aemliorator or prompter of conflict.

In making such sweeping suggestins and in framing them, as I have done here within the triangle of technology, consumption and rhetoric, I am not for one moment suggesting that research has to start from scratch. There is a wealth of literature and work already undertaken to draw upon, and I have referred to some of it. The key challenge lies in our ability to construct the audience as both a social and a semiological (a cultural) phenomenon, and in our ability to recognize the relationship between viewers and the television set as one powerfully mediated by the determinacies and indeterminacies of everyday life – by the audience's daily involvement with its daily medium. This is certainly not a new idea, but it is one which we have barely begun to take seriously.

80 *Simon Cottle: Sociological Perspectives on the News – A Critical Review*

In a piece written especially for this volume, Simon Cottle provides an authoritative summary of the main theories and related research about the news. He concentrates on contemporary theoretical developments, but makes appropriate reference to established approaches. Indeed, he very usefully shows that the sociology of the news is not simply a matter of 'one damn theory after another', but that real progress has been made in furthering our cumulative understanding of how the news is 'made' and how audiences interpret it and are affected by it. In his conclusion, he goes further and offers some suggestions as to what direction the sociology of the news (and media) might take next, given its present position.

Cottle begins by arguing that the processes of *selection* and *framing* inevitably involved in collecting and producing the news mean that the news can never be objective in any absolute sense. However, he does not believe that this means journalists should not seek to be impartial and represent a range of opinion. Cottle then goes on to discuss a number of key issues drawing on theoretical perspectives as appropriate.

The section titled 'Proprietorial control and media conspiracy' discusses what are sometimes termed 'left' and 'right' conspiracy theories of the news media. The former suggests that proprietors such as Rupert Murdoch or the late Robert Maxwell control the media, and the latter that media radicals manipulate the news to their own political inclination. While recognising that in given instances either of these explanations *might* be applicable, Cottle finds them both inadequate as substantial general theories of the news. More subtle and convincing is the 'political economy' approach which analyses news in the context of 'commercial constraints'. Thus, the economics of the capitalist market (economy) are seen as structuring the content and bias (politics) of the news.

The news is processed through complex organisational systems before it reaches us. The section entitled 'Contexts and contacts – organisational studies' examines these processes. A key point made in this section is that members of elite groups tend to have a much more significant in-put into the news than others (a perspective which seems highly compatible with the political economy approach). The section 'Communicators and their culture – journalist studies' switches emphasis from the role of organisations to that of journalists themselves. Under critical scrutiny, it becomes clear that the ideal of journalistic objectivity – often considered fundamental to a liberal society and routinely adopted by journalists – is besieged from several directions (some of them indicated above).

The final section is 'Culture as control, contest and ritual – culturalist studies'. Marxist interpretations which, with varying degrees of subtlety, see the news media as a force for ideological conformity are presented; so too is the liberal view that the news media is a vibrant part of a democratic culture. A trend in current thinking is to analyse the news as ritual (as well as ideology). For instance, it is obvious that watching the royal broadcast on Christmas Day has an element of family and national ritual about it. Cottle draws attention to the implications of some initial analysis of the ritualistic aspects of watching the news.

Reading 80 Simon Cottle, 'Behind the Headlines: The Sociology of News'

It is frequently said that the news is 'biased'. Considering the deluge of news daily pouring from local and national newspapers, proliferating radio stations, ever increasing TV news bulletins and programmes punctuating night and day schedules, not to mention those cable and satellite TV news channels beaming in from Europe and beyond, and all soon to be augmented by a fifth UK terrestrial channel, it is perhaps unsurprising that news can, on occasion, provoke distrust or disbelief. Given the bombardment of messages daily being communicated to millions of people in this country, as in most others throughout the globe, surely it would be more surprising if news portrayals were to escape entirely without criticism or dissent. This is all the more so when considering those constituencies of interest, differentiated by class, culture, gender, age and other important dimensions of social experience and life chances, but who all, nonetheless, go under the umbrella terms of 'audiences', or even 'public opinion'. Media sociologists as much as anybody else of course, are not exceptions here, often preferring a particular agenda of news interests and informing point of view in relation to news events. Where most media sociologists may differ from others in their criticisms of the news media however, and it is here that for the most part the distinctive contribution of media sociology to an understanding of news can be found, concerns firstly a general unease with the simple assertions of 'news bias', and secondly, the kinds of explanation that are offered when accounting for the types and forms of news that are currently available to us.

Bias and the media

This reading seeks to review something of the distinctive contribution of media sociology to an understanding of news. It goes behind the headlines and beyond simple, if frequently rehearsed, 'commonsense' positions on the news media in an attempt to throw light on what remains a daily outpouring of news images, ideas and agendas of concern flooding into people's daily lives. To take the issue of news 'bias' first. Though the charge is often heard, less often is an indication forthcoming of what exactly 'unbiased' news would be like. Typically, the person making the allegation has assumed that their own perception and understanding of the events in question are beyond dispute, that they have in other words an objective understanding. Given what we know about the social nature of perception, informed by differing social experiences and mediated by language – itself a social construct capable of sustaining different social viewpoints – such simplicities rarely stand up to much scrutiny. Certainly as the news events in question become more complicated and informed by competing social and/or political viewpoints, so claims to objectivity become increasingly tenuous. This is so for at least two basic reasons.

First, in order to select certain 'newsworthy' events from the daily flux, and not others, is to already have made certain judgements, whether conscious or not about their relative importance. In other words, whatever news is or should be, it cannot simply be taken to be an objective record or mirror image of 'what's out there'. If selections, of necessity, must be made so too must they involve acts of interpretation. Journalists, just like the rest of us, must constantly strive to make sense of news happenings, that is, place events within some sort of framework of understanding before they can effectively communicate these to others. The act of interpretation is therefore unavoidable and informs the process of news selection and story telling throughout. It is these twin interpretative processes, involving both the *selection* of news and its subsequent *framing* within a news story, that calls into question those claims of both professional journalists and their critics who argue that news is, or should be, simply the objective recording of reality. Interestingly, the journalistic tendency to refer to 'news stories' should itself alert us to those news processes involving the active imposition of a narrative or fictional form upon news events.

If journalists cannot meet such impossible demands of 'objectivity', what about 'impartiality', typically taken to be the faithful reporting of newsworthy events and opinions without prejudice, political favour or informing vested interest? Here journalists frequently do recognise that news is rarely a simple event, but is typically informed by conflicting accounts of, and prescriptions towards, such events. This distinction is crucial and opens the way for a more complex and discursive understanding of the news journalists' craft in which notions of 'balance' come to the fore. The news journalist may now be seen as less concerned with objective recording, than with the impartial presenting of competing accounts and social viewpoints informing and organising news stories. At this point it is perhaps worth drawing a distinction between the British press and broadcasting, given the known political partisanship, and tabloid excesses, found across the pages of the newspapers. Nonetheless, even when confining our remarks to broadcasting and those more 'respectable' organs of the press, problems remain.

First, how do journalists decide exactly whose voices and viewpoints should inform a news story, and by omission those that should not? Typically seeking to 'balance' a news story by finding representative voices from 'both sides', the multiple viewpoints informing many conflicts frequently become lost from view or forced into simple oppositions, as was recently documented in my news production study of a leading news story (Cottle, 1991). Second, is it really the case that journalists do not have a form of vested interest? The vested professional interest of telling a 'good' news story perhaps, maximising upon the news values of conflict, deviance and drama. Here too it seems, journalist claims to 'impartiality' are not entirely secure.

To take just one illustration to demonstrate the points above, throughout the 1980s and early 1990s inner city disorders were selected for headline news treatment while those more enduring problems of urban deprivation, disadvantage and discrimination found concentrated in inner city locales went largely unreported. News selections, in other words, involved important omissions and silences as well as those prominences of 'riot' portrayal and aftermath. Also, the typical news framing of inner city disorders as outbursts of 'criminal rioting' orchestrated by 'criminals and/or political extremists' in contrast, say, to either the spontaneous 'cry for help' from 'the poor and dispossessed', or first stirrings of 'proto-political rebellion' informing the 'uprisings of the oppressed', indicated that the news media, via the language and images used, were actively and unavoidably emgaged in social processes of interpretation (Tumber, 1982; Murdock, 1984; Cottle, 1993a). To take one example from my own research into the reporting of the 1985 Handsworth/Lozells disorders, if one looks at the 251 'social actors' gaining news access across one full year of 153 news reports by a leading TV company, only on two occasions were the voices of black youths presented, with the police finding access on 73, and leading government politicians on 51, occasions (Cottle, 1993). It can be suggested that such relative 'silences' were, and are, important to the extent that the field of conflicting social viewpoints in relation to these important events have found differing opportunity to 'put their case' in their bid for wider public understanding. Issues of 'impartiality' as well as 'objectivity' it would seem are not beyond critical scrutiny, notwithstanding journalist claims to the contrary.

It can be argued, then, that news is necessarily selective, partial and involves acts of social interpretation which may, or may not, correspond to the array of possible social viewpoints found elsewhere. This, it hardly needs to be said, is not necessarily the same as suggesting that journalists and/or their proprietors are responsible for deliberately distorting or 'biasing' the news. Unfortunately it is exactly this position which continues to inform many accounts of the news media, whether from the political right or political left. The contributions from media sociology however, discussed below, suggest that such accounts fall short of an adequate explanation of the daily operations of the news media. It is to a review of these various levels of sociological insight and explanation, that the discussion now turns.

Proprietorial control and media conspiracy?

If questions of news 'bias' appear to be more complicated than either news critics or professional journalists sometimes allow, so too are the array of explanations that have sought to account for the forms, silences and saliences of available news. Perhaps the most commonly heard, though least satisfactory explanation, concerns the notion of a media conspiracy and/or understanding of proprietorial manipulation and control. To take the notion of proprietorial control first. It has long been argued that 'The class which has the means of material production at its disposal, has control at the same time over the means of mental production' (Marx 1876:64). This class-based view of 'mental production' has often been interpreted in fairly direct terms, with the control secured through ownership of the mass media seen as the means by which owners further their economic interests and class-based politics. Now, clearly, it is only necessary to think of the known interventions of a Rupert Murdoch or late Robert Maxwell, dictating headlines and authoring articles promoting related business interests, to concede that proprietorial involvement confers considerable opportunity in this regard.

However, when considering the spectrum of news forms, including the tabloids and the broadsheets, both independent and public broadcasting, as well as the massive density of news disseminated on a daily basis, such an explanation, at best, appears rather slim. Such an instrumental account of media control and manipulation also forgets to inquire into those various constraints and pressures that confront even the biggest media tycoon. Here reference can be made to the constant battle fought in the marketplace of competition for audiences, readerships and advertisers, and hence the need to appeal to customer interests; the numerous news businesses included within international media conglomerates which practically prohibit individual 'hands on' intervention on a daily basis; the constraints imposed by shareholders and boards of directors keen to maximise investments and profitability; and finally, the professional conduct and practices of the journalists themselves who may well seek to resist, albeit with varying degrees of success, 'unprofessional' proprietorial interference. None of this is to suggest that proprietorship does not, in some circumstances, confer the possibility of unwelcome control and personal intervention; it is to suggest, however, that such an explanation of news forms remains undeveloped and incapable of accounting for the routine operations of the different news mediums.

What then of conspiracies, the second of our popular arguments concerning the news media? This is an explanation that has come into vogue in recent years, with senior Conservative politicians alleging a left wing bias in such unlikely institutions as the BBC, though such claims are not unheard within left accounts of the media, only here it tends to be media moguls working at the behest of powerful establishment and state interests. A conspiracy, of course, is inherently difficult to prove, which may well go some way in accounting for the resilience of this form of explanation. A conspiracy involves, at the very least, a covert meeting in which like-minded people consciously decide to pursue a hidden plan in concert. Once again, it can be conceded that, in certain circumstances and in relation to particular news events, such is not beyond the bounds of possibility.

However, a number of objections can be raised which considerably qualify the usefulness of such an account as a general explanation of the operations and forms of the news media. These include: the complexity and multiple sites of news production and dissemination, and those numerous people involved, all presenting immense difficulties to conspiratorial intent and organisation; the competing and conflicting interests found within even the upper echelons of a class-based society and state institutions which militate against the development of a monolithic view of either class or state interests; the rapidity of news production and dissemination, with incoming news despatched before attempts at conspiratorial control can be organised; the professional journalist ethos keen to bolster its claim to be a public guardian and watchdog; finally, in recent years at least, attempts to curb, censor and control 'controversial' broadcasts (of which there have been many) have tended to assume an overt character, generating considerable public debate and disquiet. Once again, notions of conspiracy though intrinsically difficult to debunk, and impossible to rule out in entirety, appear to offer little as a general explanation for the operations of the news media. What then, have media sociologists proposed as a way of accounting for the news media?

Commercial constraints – studies in political economy

If forms of conspiracy and ownership control theories advance explanations where news content is seen to be directly influenced by the deliberate interventions of owners and others, political economy approaches have questioned the explanatory reliance upon intentional and politically motivated behaviour. A leading exponent of this approach has argued for instance, 'The pivotal concept here is not power but determination. Structural analysis looks beyond intentional action to examine the limits to choice and the pressures on decision making' (Murdock, 1982:124). In other words, it is maintained that it is not necessary to seek out politically motivated interventions into the news process by owners and others to explain prevailing forms of news coverage. Rather, it is simply necessary to attend to the structural dynamics and constraints that surround media industries within a competitive economy.

Situated within the marketplace, media industries just like any other form of business enterprise, are compelled to make profits if they are to survive. The search for increased profits via reduced costs and increased sales involves two main economic forces, often international in scope: forces of economic centralisation (the tendency to swallow up competitors), and forces of conglomeration (the tendency to swallow up related industries and enterprises). This resultant lack of media diversity in turn tends to lead to the production of standardised, predictable and politically 'safe' media products (whether newspapers, television programmes, films or records etc.) all aimed at mass audiences. Moreover, the increasingly prohibitive costs of market entry deter the growth of new, and innovative, media industries resulting in a further constriction of available media forms, and the effective silencing of alternative or oppositional political voices within the mass market. The economic necessity to pursue large audiences and advertising revenue ensures that those who do manage to gain a foothold in the market quickly succumb to producing prevailing media products.

If the largest audience/readership is found within that broad band of opinion referred to as the political consensus, then on this account such an audience will be reflected in the types of news and other programming fare it receives. Or, to put it another way, those interests and opinions of minority groups and alternative points of view which lie outside such a broad consensus, will find little representation within the mass media. Such is the influence of the marketplace, even public service broadcasters are forced to reproduce those commercial successes found in the independent sector, given their pursuit of audience ratings. Moreover, the political economy approach has not been confined to the operations of national news media: for example, one leading exponent has used the approach to document current trends of a more global nature. Here market forces are said to have led to an increasing commodification and control of information, which in turn reinforces and perpetuates a form of global inequality.

> . . . what has been and continues to be a condition of global media domination by a powerful market economy can now be seen to represent only the initial, elementary stage of a far more comprehensive and cultural hegemony. (Schiller, 1985:11)

In summary, the political economy approach identifies the general, and impersonal, forces of the market rather than the politically motivated behaviour of individual media bosses as crucial to an understanding of the news media, and mass media in general. Though such an approach provides a necessary starting point for understanding the operations of the news media, is it sufficient? Here it is possible to raise the following qualifying remarks. There is a tendency, perhaps, to assume market forces will inevitably and irresistibly lead to bland consensus products across news and entertainment fields. This appears to have been overplayed and fails to recognise the way in which market forces may also encourage niche marketing and the targeting of particular consumer and other interest groups. Similarly, the spectrum of news outlets though often discussed as if producing essentially similar products, each delivering standardised news in comparable styles, underestimates the extent to which limited, but important, forms of diversity characterise the existing spectrum of news forms. When combined with a once prevalent, but now largely discredited notion, of a 'dominant ideology', this approach has also tended to assume powerful media effects, simultaneously failing to interrogate the complexities and forms of the news media in any detail, and ignoring actual instances of audience media use and consumption. In short, the political economy approach has sometimes been asked to do too much work by its exponents in accounting for not only forms of media fare, but also the maintenance of social order, via the imposition of a dominant ideology. This said, the approach continues to provide a broad and necessary underpinning to any serious account of the news media and their news agencies, now operating within an increasingly international marketplace.

Contexts and contacts – organisational studies

Between the impersonal forces of the market place and the final news product there remains a complex of institutional and professional journalist practices, for the most part bureaucratically organised. With their sights fixed on such news production contexts, a number of studies have developed a further area of sociological news inquiry. News, as many commentators have observed, doesn't just happen, it is produced. That is, the news watched on the TV or read in the morning daily is the result of a whole series of decisions and practical operations involving countless professionals. As a news editor of a daily newspaper a pressing concern would be, no doubt, to ensure that news stories are routinely filed by reporters and that they cover the areas of news deemed of interest to a defined audience, all in general agreement with a news policy. Clearly, this requires a degree of bureaucratic organisation where routines and time-schedules ensure that a newspaper is in fact produced day in and day out, on time and to the specified requirements. A divison of labour between production staff and specialist reporters is thus required with the creation of predictable news beats to cover designated types, and pages, of news. One means of 'taming the news environment', then, is to seek to plan in advance a number of 'diary' news stories. These may include notified official visits, important press conferences, the routine supply of court reports and so on, all of which can be guaranteed to be available on the day of publication. Such bureaucratic responses by journalists and news teams have been said to colour the type of news that we get.

> News is a peculiar form of knowledge: its character derives very much from the sources and contexts of production. With few exceptions, those sources and contexts are bureaucratic, and news is the result of an organised response to routine bureaucratic problems. (Rock, 1981: 64)

This argument can be taken further, with bureaucratic routines and the 'perishability' of news stories seen to exercise a profound, if unintended consequence, on the communication of meaning.

> Production is so organised that its basic dynamics emphasise the perishability of stories ... It is always today's developments which occupy the foreground. The corollary of this point is that there is an inherent tendency for the news to be framed in a discontinuous and ahistorical way, and this implies a truncation of context, and therefore a reduction of meaningfulness. (Schlesinger, 1987:47)

Far from the conscious or deliberate interventions of media owners, or even the unintended yet real effects of a form of economic logic, the news now appears to have an ideological form – to the extent that history and social process disappear from news accounts, leaving isolated 'events' – and this is thought to reflect the manner in which news production is organised. Moreover, if news organisation and production can be found to impact upon the form of news stories, it has also been found to critically influence those 'who get on', an important issue first raised above when discussing journalist claims to impartiality.

In a bid to routinise and therefore control the news production process news organisations tend to maintain close contact with those agencies and institutions that are likely to provide a continual flow of news stories.

Observing the activities of crime reporters, who could perhaps more accurately be termed 'police reporters' given the perceived reliance of journalists upon police information and insights, Steve Chibnall observes how such reporters increasingly become drawn into the world of the police and their particular frameworks of understanding.

> It is in fact a complex process of socialization by which the journalists frame of reference, methods of working and personal system of perceptions and understandings are brought into line with the expectations of his sources. (Chibnall, 1981:88)

A similar form of incremental identification has been noted in a study of journalists assigned to military units during the reporting of the Falklands War.

> The enmeshing, the identification, the whole process of involvement had nothing to do with each individual's private views, feelings about the war, or the attitudes of his organization. The dynamics of the situation were so powerful they overwhelmed all this. (Morrison and Tumber, 1988:99)

Studies such as these have indicated that journalist reliance upon routine source institutions effectively serves to reproduce the voices of the powerful. This position has forcefully been argued by Stuart Hall when he states 'broadcasters and their institutions mediate – hold the pass, command the communicative channels – between the elites of power (social, economic, political, cultural) and the mass audience' (Hall, 1975:124). This is not simply the outcome of a response to 'tame the news environment' however but also follows, paradoxically, upon the professional journalist's claim to impartiality. This is so since it is precisely those social, political or military elites who command the authority and knowledge to comment authoritatively on events, and who, in turn, can lend a semblance of impartiality to the journalist, now seen to merely report the comments of others. In consequence, it is suggested the elites of society via the news media are granted an opportunity to become the nation's 'primary definers' (Hall *et al.* 1978:58). It is they who tell us how to interpret and respond to certain events, whether inner city riots, the latest rise in street crime statistics, or the military events in the Falklands.

The insights from these studies of news organisation and production are considerable, and go a long way in complementing the general insights derived from the political economy approach. However if political economy approaches can be accused, on occasion, of reducing everything to the impersonal logic of the market place, perhaps a similar criticism can be extended to some of these studies. Only here the generalising tendency concerns the patterns of news access and general contours of news subjects reported, to even the truncated character of news itself (ahistorical, decontextualised etc) which are now all taken to reflect those bureaucratic responses to the daily pressures of news production. The question that can be posed to such studies is, what role have the journalists in this general shaping of news? Do they simply give expression to the impersonal bureaucratic imperative, or can they actively shape the news, perhaps in line with other forms of influence?

Communicators and their culture – journalist studies

An obvious place to begin accounting for the forms and patterns of news coverage might be considered to be the journalists who actually produce the news. Can we account for the news by inquiring into the social and educational backgrounds, political values or other general journalist characteristics along lines, say, of age, gender or ethnicity? The short answer appears to be that while such characteristics may well inform the knowledge base drawn upon by journalists and thus enhance forms of news reporting, such differences are generally of secondary importance when considered in relation to processes of journalist training and professional socialisation. While some studies have noted the general 'middle-class' background of journalists, frequently political attitudes and values have not been found to reflect one particular political stance (Elliott, 1977; Janowitz, 1975). The interesting question arises, if differences of political attitude can be found within the newsroom, how can we account for the remarkable uniformity of news product that is daily produced?

In this regard a much cited early 'gate-keeper' study fails to provide much insight. David Manning White observed a news editor selecting and rejecting possible news stories from the incoming stories filed by a press agency. This editor thus acted as a crucial decision point, literally acting as a form of gate, through which a minority of successful stories passed, while the majority fell into the waste bin. Observing this particular 'gate-keeper', it was noted how such processes were 'highly subjective' and 'reliant upon value-judgements based on the gate-keepers own set of experiences, attitudes and expectations' (White, 1964:165). Interesting as this study is, the fact that remarkable patterns and continuities of news coverage and content can be discerned within the news media suggests that such decisions have been informed by professional, and not simply, personal judgements.

A number of researchers have now observed, for instance, how the professional training and socialisation of journalists effectively 'oils the wheels' of production and permits the production of a standardised product while minimising the degree of conflict and disagreement within the newsroom (Breed, 1955; Sigelman, 1973; Soloski, 1989).

> Both news professionalism and news policy are used to minimise conflict within the news organisation. That is, professional norms and a news organisation's news policies are accepted by journalists, and only in rare instances are either professional norms of news policies a point of disagreement among the staff of the news organisation. Like a game, professional norms and news policies are rules that everyone has learned to play by; only rarely are these rules made explicit, and only rarely are the rules called into question. (Soloski, 1989:218)

Interestingly, to return briefly to our initial discussion of news 'bias' and concerns of 'objectivity', not only have such studies observed how professional judgements and values smooth the daily workings of journalists with their colleagues and superiors within the news organisation, but so too may the adoption of professional claims to 'objectivity' be considered as a means of avoiding conflict with external critics:

> To journalists, like social scientists, the term objectivity stands as a bulwark between themselves and the critics. Attacked for a controversial presentation of the 'facts', newspapers invoke their objectivity almost the way a Mediterranean peasant might wear a clove of garlic around this neck to ward of evil spirits. (Tuchman, 1972:660)

The sociological approaches to the study of news discussed so far have clearly advanced considerably on our 'commonsense' accounts above. Whether addressing those impersonal operations of the marketplace identified by political economists, the organisational and bureaucratic responses to news production observed in a number of news production studies, or interactional considerations found to inform journalist-colleague, journalist-public, or even journalist-source contacts discussed above, each has arguably made an important contribution to our understanding of news and the news making process. One last area of study requires discussion however, and this concerns those broad range of studies, here termed culturalist studies, in which journalists are thought to give cultural expression not only to a set of professional news values, but also to those wider social relations and competing interests thought to organise society at any point in time.

Culture as control, contest and ritual – culturalist studies

It has frequently been observed that news appears to be informed by recurring news values. In a now classic statement, Johan Galtung and Mari Ruge, for instance, discern that for a news story to be selected it should exhibit one or more of the following: the *frequency* of time-span taken by the news event should correspond to the publication cycle of the news media, thus a murder or a battle are more likely to be reported than social trends or the history of a war; the size of an event must be such that it rises above established news *thresholds*; the news event should be *unambiguous*, that is, it must be relatively clear; it must be *meaningful* which involves both cultural proximity and relevance to the news audience; it should be *consonant* or confirm audience values and expectations; be unpredictable or *unexpected;* ideally offer a degree of *continuity*, that is, be a running story, and contribute to the *composition* or mix of news stories; as well as make reference to *elite nations and elite persons* and include aspects of *personalisation* and *negativity* (Galtung and Ruge, 1981: 52–61).

In such ways as these, news is seen as expressing general, if nationally resonate, cultural values. Others have suggested, however, that news values may serve more particular ideological interests and needs by selecting and interpreting events in accordance with dominant social interests. The influential series of *Bad News* studies by the Glasgow University Media Group are representative of such an informing position:

> . . . television news is a cultural artefact; it is a sequence of socially manufactured messages, which carry many of the culturally dominant assumptions of our society. From the accents of the newscasters to the vocabulary of camera angles; from who gets on and what questions get asked, via selection of stories to presentation of bulletins, the news is a highly mediated product. (Glasgow University Media Group, 1976:9)

If such studies imply that news broadcasts advance a dominant ideology, other studies have suggested that though offering a 'preferred reading' news is open to negotiated forms of interpretation (Morley, 1980; Hartley, 1982; Philo, 1990). The writings of Stuart Hall, developing upon Antonio Gramsci's idea of 'hegemony', have tended to indicate that rather than news simply advancing a dominant ideology, news broadcasts provide a degree of internal contestation and negotiation where wider social and political interests seek to establish a hegemonic dominance. This involves a continual contest, at the level of cultural engagement, to win over social and political viewpoints to a particular interpretation of events. Given the conflicts and divisions that characterise society as a whole however, this is a struggle which must be constantly fought and is rarely fully accomplished. Such culturalist studies as these then, see news as a key site in the dissemination and negotiation of ideology. Not all culturalist approaches to news however regard news as principally a mechanism of ideological control and contest.

Philip Elliott has drawn an important distinction between ritual and ideology arguing that:

> . . . ritual cannot simply be reduced to the rational. It draws on what is customary, familiar and traditional in the culture. It tries to add spiritual and emotional communion to any sense of political unity, though from any single point of view it may not work. (Elliott, 1980:146)

If culturalist approaches to news have tended to operate within a Marxist and neo-Marxist framework of analysis, Elliott appears to have recognised the importance of Durkheimian insights concerned with those bonds of social solidarity expressed and reinforced through collective forms of worship and ritual. One need only ponder those patriotic news appeals unleashed in times of national disaster and war, or the symbolic and emotional appeals of royal weddings and so on, to realise that news can and does 'work' at the level of emotional appeal as much as rational dissemination of information. News may well, in other words, provide a ritualised performance in which the symbolic bonds of collectivity find repeated expression and affirmation. Indeed, for some commentators at least, rather than interpreting the historical development of national broadcasting in which news plays a prominent part, in terms of ideological processes, the development of broadcasting is thought to have contributed to processes of 'democratic deepening' and 'brought into being a radically new kind of public – one commensurate with the whole of society . . . Particular publics were replaced by the general public . . . the fundamental democratic thrust of broadcasting . . . lay in the new access to virtually the whole spectrum of public life' (Scannell and Cardiff 1991:14).

Clearly, there is much room here for argument and discussion, not to mention further research. What is more clear, is that culturalist informed studies of news are now legion and have generated many incisive readings of current and past news forms. The detailed attention devoted to the analysis of news programmes, approached as 'texts' in need of cultural interpretation, has also increased recognition of the different forms of news, both popular and serious, and the different manner in which each appeals to different audiences. A recent study of the way in which different TV news forms, from breakfast TV to main channel evening broadcasts, and from regional TV news to Channel 4 news have each differently 'mediated' environmental issues according to established programme-audience appeals is revealing in this respect (Cottle, 1993b). Studies of the distinctive appeals and popular pleasures afforded by the tabloids are also beginning to appear, once again correcting the earlier impression that news forms are all essentially similar.

The creative explosion of interest in cultural studies has also generated a number of more recent avenues of news research which are worth briefly mentioning. If news can usefully be approached as a form of ritual engagement with the wider society and its preoccupations, others have also suggested that the family and domestic contexts in which news is consumed may also reveal much about those temporal daily routines and spatially located behaviours and relationships that characterise modern society (Lodziak, 1987; Morley and Silverstone, 1990). News, in such studies, is likely to be regarded as just one television moment within a domestic TV viewing milieux. This work has only just begun, though interesting findings along lines of gender difference and domestic news consumption have already been suggested. This in turn points to the increased interest in audiences as active, discerning and differentiated along a number of dimensions which are thought to influence the way these different 'interpretative communities' make sense of or 'decode' news programmes. Such studies inevitably qualify previous, albeit largely implicit, notions of the audience as 'passive dopes' who unconsciously receive a deadly dose of dominant ideology (see Morley, 1980; Wren-Lewis, 1985; Philo, 1990).

Culturalist studies of news have tended to approach news as more or less directly informed by, and expressive of, those wider cultural values, social interests and political divisions that characterise society as a whole. Herein lies its strength, recovering those wider if contested meanings current within a society at a particular point in time. Such studies have tended to lack a theory of 'mediation' however. To what extent news is purposefully produced by journalists in accordance with, say, professional codes and conventions or personal political allegiances, or in pursuit of maximum audience ratings and advertising receipts, or perhaps in line with organisational routines and bureaucratic imperatives, or even, on occasion, in accordance with proprietorial intervention, tends to remain undisclosed and unexamined. In such accounts, the practical realities of news making and the specific and particular ways in which news production 'mediates' this wider culture remain unexplored and undertheorised. Its contribution to our understanding of news, however, remains considerable.

Conclusion

This study has reviewed a number of approaches to the study of news and their respective contributions to an understanding of the news making process and influences upon the news product. Clearly each has much to offer, and all improve on the simple charges of 'news bias' and those typical explanations of 'media conspiracy' and 'ownership control'. Indeed, the idea of 'news bias' was said to be misleading and generally unhelpful in critical commentaries on the news media. This was so because the simple idea of news 'bias' has tended to assume, given the right conditions, that news objectivity is in fact obtainable and therefore fails to grasp the manner in which 'reality' is always subject to social processes of interpretation – including the 'reality' of the news critic. That said, it does not follow that news has no responsibility to report fairly and faithfully those events and happenings which are socially thought to be of importance, or represent the competing and often conflicting views which inform most new stories. It is in these more socially proximate or relative terms that the adequacy, or otherwise, of the news can begin to be critically appraised.

However, interesting and insightful it may be, no critical perspective can wholly explain such forms of news portrayal. Here a number of approaches to the study of news have been outlined, including those approaches of political economy, organisational and production studies, journalist studies, and culturalist studies, with each seeking to go behind the headlines and explain exactly why news should assume the forms that it does. These have frequently been anchored in different positions of social theory, and yet each has provided invaluable insights and levels of explanation. Theories, it can be suggested, provide a useful way of focussing or 'spot lighting' areas of research interest and inquiry by posing certain questions; implicitly however they may well displace other avenues of fruitful investigation. Given the multi-faceted nature of news and its deeply embedded presence within modern society and daily life it may be unrealistic to suppose that any one approach to the study of news could provide comprehensive understanding and analysis. That said, those different approaches outlined above have together, despite the inevitable tensions that remain between them, contributed enormously to our understanding of news and the news making process. No doubt the sociology of news will continue to develop these, and other, explanations and insights so long as the daily deluge continues.

References

Breed, W., 'Social Control in the Newsroom' in *Social Forces* 33 (1955), pp. 326–35.

Chibnall, S., 'The Production of Knowledge By Crime Reporters' in S. Cohen, and J. Young, *ed.s, The Manufacture of News* (Constable, 1981).

Cottle, S., 'Reporting the Rushdie Affair: A Case Study in the Orchestration of Public Opinion' *Race and Class* Vol. 32, No. 4 (1991), pp. 45–64.

Cottle, S., *TV News, Urban Conflict and the Inner City* (Leicester University Press, 1993a).

Cottle, S., 'Mediating the Environment: Modalities of TV News' in A. Hansen, *ed., The Mass Media and the Environment* (Leicester University Press, 1993b).

Elliott, P., 'Media Organizations and Occupations: an Overview' in J. Curran *et al., ed.s, Mass Communication and Society* (Edward Arnold, 1977).

Elliott, P., 'Press Performance as Political Ritual' in H. Christian, *ed., The Sociology of Journalism and the Press,* Sociological Review Monograph No. 29 (University of Keele, 1980).

Galtung, J., and Ruge, M., 'Structuring and Selecting News' in S. Cohen and J. Young, *ed.s, The Manufacture of News* (Constable, 1981).

Glasgow University Media Group, *Bad News* (RKP, 1976).

Hall, S., 'The "Structured Communication" of Events' in *Getting The Message Across* (Paris: UNESCO, 1975).

Hall, S. *et al., Policing the Crisis* (Hutchinson, 1978).

Hartley, J., *Understanding News* (Methuen, 1982).

Janowitz, M., 'Professional Models in Journalism: The Gatekeeper and the Advocate' in *Journalism Quarterly* Vol. 52 (1975).

Lewis, J., 'Decoding Television News' in P. Drummond and R. Paterson, *ed.s, Television in Transition* (BFI Publishing, 1985).

Lodziak, C., *The Power of Television* (Frances Pinter, 1987).

Marx, K., *The German Ideology* (Lawrence and Wishart, 1976).

Morley, D., *The Nationwide Audience* (British Film Institute, 1980).

Morley, D., and Silverstone, R., 'Domestic Communication – Technologies and Meanings' in *Media, Culture and Society* Vol. 12. No. 1 (1990), pp. 31–56.

Morrison, D.E. and Tumber, H., *Journalists at War* (Sage Publications).

Murdock, G., 'Large Corporations and the Control of the Communications Industries' in M. Gurevitch *et al., Culture, Society and The Media* (Methuen, 1982).

Murdock, G., 'Reporting the Riots: Images and Impacts' in J. Benyon, *ed., Scarman and After* (Oxford: Pergamon, 1984).

Philo, G., *Seeing and Believing* (Routledge, 1990).

Rock, P., 'News as Eternal Recurrence' in S. Cohen and J. Young, *ed.s, The Manufacture of News* (Constable, 1981).

Scannell, P., and Cardiff, D., *A Social History of Broadcasting* Vol. 1 (Blackwell, 1991).

Schiller, H., 'Electronic Information Flows: New Basis for Global Domination?' in P. Drummond and R. Paterson, *ed.s., Television in Transition* (BFI Publishing, 1985).

Schlesinger, P., *Putting 'Reality' Together* (Methuen, 1987).

Sigelman, L., 'Reporting the News: An Organisational Analysis' in *American Journal of Sociology* 48 (1973), pp. 132–51.

Soloski, J., 'News Reporting and Professionalism: Some Constraints on the Reporting of News' in *Media Culture and Society* Vol. 11 (1989), pp. 207–28.

Tuchman, G., 'Objectivity as Strategic Ritual: An Examination of Newsmen's Notions of Objectivity' in *American Journal of Sociology* 77, (1972), pp. 660–79.

Tumber, H., *Television and the Riots*, Broadcasting Research Unit, (British Film Institute, 1982).

White, D. M., 'The "Gatekeeper": A Case Study in the Selection of News' in L. A. Dexter and D. M. White, *ed.s, People, Society and Mass Communication* (Free Press, 1964), pp. 160–72. (First printed 1950).

Questions and Issues

The Sociology of the Media: Section 17

The most relevant readings appear in brackets after each question.

1 How 'objective' and 'balanced' is the news in Britain? (Readings 77, 80)
2 Discuss the view that the wealth, power and control of the media conglomerates makes a democratic media virtually impossible. (Readings 77, 80)
3 To what extent have traditional perspectives on the media failed to understand the experience of media audiences? (Readings 78, 79)
4 To what extent does the media tend to reinforce the status quo? (Section 17)

THEORY – CURRENT DEVELOPMENTS

Introduction: Readings 81–86

Where is sociological theory going? The answer to this question is that it is moving in a variety of directions rather than towards the dominance of any single theory. It seems to be the case, however, that the view of sociology as a number of competing perspectives, as it had been widely perceived over the last quarter of a century or so, is now on the wane. 'The perspectives approach' has not been replaced by a single unified paradigm as I once suspected it might be ('Limited Perspectives', Vol. 9 No. 3, *Social Science Teacher*, 1979). In Kuhn's terms, sociology would still have to be regarded as 'pre-paradigmatic' (Reading 81). However, it is arguable that sociology is maturing as a discipline, and certainly being practised more widely in a professional way, without precisely developing through the stages Kuhn describes in relation to natural science. For sociology, maturity may lie in part in the acceptance of diverse approaches.

The traditional structural perspectives of Functionalism and Marxism and the established interpretive perspectives of symbolic interactionism (Reading 87) and ethnomethodology have not, of course, disappeared. However, they now tend to be employed less exclusively and, one might almost say, less 'monotheistically' (Reading 86). Part of the impact of postmodernism and poststructuralism on sociology has been to shake 'belief' in the aspirations of structural or 'grand' theory (Readings 82, 83 and 86) to be totally explanatory. Perhaps the most impressive of current developments is the various attempts theoretically to link agency and structure. Anthony Giddens theory of 'structuration' is a notable contribution in this direction. Michel Foucault's concept of 'power-knowledge' embodies the compelling notion that powerful ideas generate their own normative structures within which, if the individual is not alert, subjectivity itself can be formed and captured (Reading 83).

Some have found in postmodernism and poststructuralism not so much an attempt to collapse the separation of the subjective from the objective, but a romantic and self-indulgent immersion in relativism and subjectivity (Ernest Gellner, *Postmodernism, Reason and Religion* [Routledge, 1992]). This does not seem to me to be quite fair, although it is easy to see how less vigorous applications of the new approaches might result in an ill-disciplined, 'do your own thing' trendiness. The extract from Erving Goffman is included as a reminder that vigorous attempts to link the various levels of social experience have long been a part of sociology (Reading 85).

If there is an increasing attempt to accommodate growing social diversity within sociology, there is also an urgent awareness that the macro frame of reference has also been changing in recent years. It is increasingly difficult to understand British society without adopting European and global perspectives. Immanuel Wallerstein puts the case for a sociology which is intrinsically global in nature (Reading 84). My own contribution, concluding this section, attempts to overview and comment on some of the above themes (Reading 86).

Thomas S. Kuhn: Scientific Paradigms

Thomas Kuhn's famous essay, *The Structure of Scientific Revolutions*, is of interest to social scientists for two major reasons. First, he forces them to reconsider their assumptions about science itself – assumptions which they may carry over into social science. Second, Kuhn's notion of the paradigm described below has been very influential within social science.

Kuhn's comments on the nature of science and how scientific knowledge changes (by 'revolutions') has, perhaps, particular implications for positivists. The major meaning of paradigm (it has a second meaning with which we need not concern ourselves) is that 'it stands for the entire constellation of beliefs, values, techniques, and so on shared by members of a given community'. By 'community' Kuhn means the leading specialists in a given scientific area. His central point is that these beliefs and so on affect both the process of scientific inquiry and the way scientists 'see things' (an example is given below). This is a far cry from the positivist's confident claim that science is the objective pursuit of factually verifiable knowledge. Equally, the concept of paradigm challenges models of sociological theory/methods based on the view that sociology is exclusively concerned with establishing relationships between social facts.

The last point brings us to the second way in which Kuhn's concept of paradigm has been influential within sociology. He suggests that, at any given time, a particular scientific discipline tends to be dominated by a given paradigm. This is certainly not currently the case within sociology, and possibly never has been. Apart from the positivist/interpretist division, positivism itself is internally divided into Functionalism and various forms of conflict theory including Marxism (not all varieties of which are positivist, however). Likewise, interpretists are divided into symbolic interactionists and ethnomethodologists, although by no means all interpretists consider the two approaches to be logically exclusive. Arguably, then, sociology is characterised by several competing paradigms, and some consider that this detracts from its claims to be a science or, at least, a mature science. These are controversial observations and I discuss them further in the concluding reading to this section.

In what follows, Kuhn's initial presentation of his theory of paradigms is probably easier to understand than the examples he concludes with. However, some examples must be included as the theory stands or falls by them.

Reading 81 From Thomas S. Kuhn, *The Structure of Scientific Revolutions* (University of Chicago Press, 1970), pp. 10–11, 111, 114–17.

The route to normal science

In this essay, 'normal science' means research firmly based upon one or more past scientific achievements, achievements that some particular scientific community acknowledges for a time as supplying the foundation for its further practice. Today such achievements are recounted, though seldom in their original form, by science textbooks, elementary and advanced. These textbooks expound the body of accepted theory, illustrate many or all of its successful applications, and compare these applications with exemplary observations and experiments. Before such books became popular early in the nineteenth century (and until even more recently in the newly matured sciences), many of the famous classics of science fulfilled a similar function. Aristotle's *Physica,* Ptolemy's *Almagest,* Newton's *Principia* and *Opticks,* Franklin's *Electricity,* Lavoisier's *Chemistry,* and Lyell's *Geology* – these and many other works served for a time implicitly to define the legitimate problems and methods of a research field for succeeding generations of practitioners. They were able to do so because they shared two essential characteristics. Their achievement was sufficiently unprecedented to attract an enduring group of adherents away from competing modes of scientific activity. Simultaneously, it was sufficiently open-ended to leave all sorts of problems for the redefined group of practitioners to resolve.

Achievements that share these two characteristics I shall henceforth refer to as 'paradigms', a term that relates closely to 'normal science'. By choosing it, I mean to suggest that some accepted examples of actual scientific practice – examples which include law, theory, application, and instrumentation together – provide models from which spring particular coherent traditions of scientific research. These are the traditions which the historian describes under such rubrics as 'Ptolemaic astronomy' (or 'Copernican'), 'Aristotelian dynamics' (or 'Newtonian'), 'corpuscular optics' (or 'wave optics'), and so on. The study of paradigms, including many that are far more specialised than those named illustratively above, is what mainly prepares the student for membership in the particular scientific community with which he will later practice. Because he there joins men who learned the bases of their field from the same concrete models, his subsequent practice will seldom evoke overt disagreement over fundamentals. Men whose research is based on shared paradigms are committed to the same rules and standards for scientific practice. That commitment and the apparent consensus it produces are prerequisites for normal science, i.e., for the genesis and continuation of a particular research tradition . . .

Revolutions as changes of world view

Examining the record of past research from the vantage of contemporary historiography, the historian of science may be tempted to exclaim that when paradigms change, the world itself changes with them. Led by a new paradigm, scientists adopt new instruments and look in new places. Even more important, during revolutions scientists see new and different things when looking with familiar instruments in places they have looked before. It is rather as if the professional community had been suddenly transported to another planet where familiar objects are seen in a different light and are joined by unfamiliar ones as well. Of course, nothing of quite that sort does occur: there is no geographical transplantation; outside the laboratory everyday affairs usually continue as before. Nevertheless, paradigm changes do cause scientists to see the world of their research-engagement differently. In so far as their only recourse to that world is through what they see and do, we may want to say that after a revolution scientists are responding to a different world . . .

In the sciences, therefore, if perceptual switches accompany paradigm changes, we may not expect scientists to attest to these changes directly. Looking at the moon, the convert to Copernicanism does not say, 'I used to see a planet, but now I see a satellite'. That locution would imply a sense in which the Ptolemaic system had once been correct. Instead, a convert to the new astronomy says, 'I once took the moon to be (or saw the moon as) a planet, but I was mistaken'. That sort of statement does recur in the aftermath of scientific revolutions. If it ordinarily disguises a shift of scientific vision or some other mental transformation with the same effect, we may not expect direct testimony about that shift. Rather we must look for indirect and behavioral evidence that the scientist with a new paradigm sees differently from the way he had seen before.

Let us then return to the data and ask what sorts of transformations in the scientist's world the historian who believes in such changes can discover. Sir William Herschel's discovery of Uranus provides a first example and one that closely parallels the anomalous card experiment. On at least seventeen different occasions between 1690 and 1781, a number of astronomers, including several of Europe's most eminent observers, had seen a star in positions that we now suppose must have been occupied at the time by Uranus. One of the best observers in this group had actually seen the star on four successive nights in 1769 without noting the motion that could have suggested another identification. Herschel, when he first observed the same object twelve years later, did so with a much improved telescope of his own manufacture. As a result, he was able to notice an apparent disk-size that was at least unusual for stars. Something was awry, and he therefore postponed identification pending further scrutiny. The scrutiny disclosed Uranus' motion among the stars, and Herschel therefore announced that he had seen a new comet! Only several months later, after fruitless attempts to fit the observed motion to a cometary orbit, did Lexell suggest that the orbit was probably planetary. When that suggestion was accepted, there were several fewer stars and one more planet in the world of the professional astronomer. A celestial body that had been observed off and on for almost a century was seen differently after 1781 because, like an anomalous playing card, it could no longer be fitted to the perceptual categories (star or comet) provided by the paradigm that had previously prevailed.

The shift of vision that enabled astronomers to see Uranus, the planet, does not, however, seem to have affected only the perception of that previously observed object. Its consequences were more far-reaching. Probably, though the evidence is equivocal, the minor paradigm change forced by Herschel helped to prepare astronomers for the rapid discovery, after 1801, of the numerous minor planets or asteroids. Because of their small size, these did not display the anomalous magnification that had alerted Herschel. Nevertheless, astronomers prepared to find additional planets were able, with standard instruments, to identify twenty of them in the first fifty years of the nineteenth century. The history of astronomy provides many other examples of paradigm-induced changes in scientific perception, some of them even less equivocal. Can it conceivably be an accident, for example, that Western astronomers first saw change in the previously immutable heavens during the half-century after Copernicus' new paradigm was first proposed? The Chinese, whose cosmological beliefs did not preclude celestial change, had recorded the appearance of many new stars in the heavens at a much earlier date. Also, without even the aid of a telescope, the Chinese had systematically recorded the appearance of sunspots centuries before these were seen by Galileo and his contemporaries. Nor were sunspots and a new star the only examples of celestial change to emerge in the heavens of Western astronomy immediately after Copernicus. Using traditional instruments, some as simple as a piece of thread, late sixteenth-century astronomers repeatedly discovered that comets wandered at will through the space previously reserved for the immutable planets and stars. The very ease and rapidity with which astronomers saw new things when looking at old objects with old instruments may make us wish to say that, after Copernicus, astronomers lived in a different world. In any case, their research responded as though that were the case . . .

Jean-François Lyotard: Postmodernism and the Collapse of the Metanarratives ('Big Fables')

This is a brief extract from what is a seminal cultural/social text of the last decade. According to Lyotard, the postmodern condition is one in which the majority no longer believe in any of the great metanarratives (theories), religious or secular, that seek to explain social existence. In the title of a popular book of the late 1960s, we are 'without Marx or Jesus'.

People no longer live within over-arching belief systems but operate in more fluid, negotiable and localised contexts. Social life has become more varied and is characterised by more centres of independent activity and thought. Lyotard describes these tendencies as 'many different language games'. It helps to regard his usage of 'language games' as a metaphor. Much of social life involves 'playing with words' or using language to express meanings and to get what we want. Lyotard is suggesting that people increasingly 'play with' other systems of organisation (e.g. work, education, leisure etc.) in the fluid, individual and confident way some play with language. Hierarchies of belief, control and function are changed, if not subverted, by these tendencies.

Despite my extensive attempts to 'decode' Lyotard, the reader is recommended to approach the following passage armed with a large dictionary.

Reading 82 From Jean-François Lyotard, *The Postmodern Condition* (University of Minnesota Press, 1984), as reprinted in J. C. Alexander and S. Seidman, *eds., Culture and Society: Contemporary Debates* (C.U.P., 1990), pp. 330–31

I define postmodern as incredulity toward metanarratives. This incredulity is undoubtedly a product of progress in the sciences: But that progress in turn presupposes it. To the obsolescence of the metanarrative apparatus of legitimation corresponds, most notably, the crisis of metaphysical philosophy and of the university institution which in the past relied on it. The narrative function is losing its functors, its great hero, its great dangers,

Arguably, this 'crisis' is also occurring within the social sciences.

In the absence of the metanarratives, people live by lesser, sometimes unclear, beliefs/goals.

its great voyages, its great goal. It is being dispersed in clouds of narrative language elements – narrative, but also denotative, prescriptive, descriptive, and so on. Conveyed within each cloud are pragmatic valencies specific to its kind. Each of us lives at the intersection of many of these. However, we do not necessarily establish stable language combinations, and the properties of the ones we do establish are not necessarily communicable.

Thus the society of the future falls less within the province of a Newtonian anthropology (such as structuralism or systems theory) than a pragmatics of language particles. There are many different language games – a heterogeneity of elements. They only give rise to institutions in patches – local determinism.

Even in the absence of legitimising beliefs or ideology – the powerful seek legitimation in every situation ('all our games') – citing the justification of efficiency itself.

The decision makers, however, attempt to manage these clouds of sociality according to input/output matrices, following a logic which implies that their elements are commensurable and that the whole is determinable. They allocate our lives for the growth of power. In matters of social justice and of scientific truth alike, the legitimation of that power is based on its optimizing the system's performance – efficiency. The application of this criterion to all of our games necessarily entails a certain level of terror, whether soft or hard: be operational (that is, commensurable) or disappear.

The logic of maximum performance is no doubt inconsistent in many ways, particularly with respect to contradiction in the socio-economic field: It demands both less work (to lower production costs) and more (to lessen the social burden of the idle population). But our incredulity is now such that we no longer expect salvation to rise from these inconsistencies, as did Marx.

Here Lyotard dismisses newer claimants to 'metanarrative' status, including technological rationality and Habermas' principle that a truthful consensus can be achieved through honest discussion.

Still, the postmodern condition is as much a stranger to disenchantment as it is to the blind positivity of delegitimation. Where, after the metanarratives, can legitimacy reside? The operativity criterion is technological; it has no relevance for judging what is true or just. Is legitimacy to be found in consensus obtaining through discussion, as Jurgen Habermas thinks? Such consensus does violence to the heterogeneity of language games. And invention is always born of dissension. Postmodern knowledge is not simply a tool of the authorities; it refines our sensitivity to differences and reinforces our ability to tolerate the incommensurable. Its principle is not the expert's homology, but the inventor's paralogy . . .

In contemporary society and culture – postindustrial society, postmodern culture – the question of the legitimation of knowledge is formulated in different terms. The grand narrative has lost its credibility, regardless of what mode of unification it uses, regardless of whether it is a speculative narrative or a narrative of emancipation . . .

Stephen Ball: Foucault – Discourse, Power-Knowledge and Fighting Fear

If Lyotard (Reading 82), is one of the better known postmodernists, Foucault is pre-eminent among poststructuralists. Like postmodernism, poststructuralism is about criticising the notion of given 'objective' external systems or structures.

Structures are dominant not because they are better or more 'real' than alternatives, but because those who control and most benefit from them have the power to enforce their will and their order. It is possible 'to take apart' or, in Foucault's terms, 'deconstruct' the nature of power and interest behind such structures as the education or health systems.

However, while intellectuals may be able to deconstruct dominant systems, those servicing them, particularly at lower levels, may not have the knowledge to do so. It is in this context, that a number of Foucault's concepts are relevant: discourse, power-knowledge, positioning and subjectivity. All except positioning are further explained in the text, but it will help to link them here. Most people's character, feelings, and understanding i.e. *subjectivity* are formed by the system they live and work within. The flow of *power-knowledge* (ideas put into practice) *positions* or places the least powerful in a situation in which they are constrained to conform, behaviourally and intellectually. The dominant ideology of a system is expressed in innumerable everyday discourses which seem to demonstrate the truth of the system but which, in fact, are self-fulfilling (see Reading 65). Thus, the ideology of educational competition is reinforced by the discourse of examination success and failure and the accompanying labelling of individuals.

Like Marx, Foucault exhorts us to look for alternatives to domination, but, unlike Marx, he offers no blueprints for escape.

Reading 83 From Stephen J. Ball, *Foucault and Education: Disciplines and Knowledge* (Routledge, 1992), pp. 1, 1–5, 6–7.

Michel Foucault is an enigma, a massively influential intellectual who steadfastly refused to align himself with any of the major traditions of western social thought. His primary concern with the history of scientific thought, the development of technologies of power and domination, and the arbitrariness of modern social institutions speak to but stand outside the main currents of Weberian and Marxist scholarship . . .

At the centre of his work, over a 25-year period, has been a series of attempts to analyse particular ideas or models of humanity which have developed as the result of very precise historical changes, and the ways in which these ideas have become normative or universal. Foucault has set himself staunchly against the notion of universal or self-evident humanity. Again in interview he explained:

> My role – and that is too emphatic a word – is to show people that they are much freer than they feel, that people accept as truth, as evidence, some themes which have been built up at a certain moment during history, and that this so-called evidence can be criticized and destroyed. To change something in the minds of people – that's the role of an intellectual.
>
> (Martin *et al.* 1988: 10)

Foucault has identified certain knowledges – human sciences – and certain attendant practices as central to the normalization of social principles and institutions of modern society. Among these are psychological, medical, penitential, and educational knowledges and practices. Our concern here is with the role of the latter, education, and its inter-relationship with politics, economics, and history in the formation and constitution of human beings as subjects. By normalization Foucault means the establishment of measurements, hierarchy, and regulations around the idea of a distributionary statistical norm within a given population – the idea of judgement based on what is normal and thus what is abnormal . . .

Discourse is a central concept in Foucault's analytical framework. Discourses are about what can be said and thought, but also about who can speak, when, and with what authority. Discourses embody meaning and social relationships, they constitute both subjectivity and power relations. Discourses are 'practices that systematically form the objects of which they speak . . . Discourses are not about objects; they do not identify objects, they constitute them and in the practice of doing so conceal their own invention' (Foucault 1974: 49). Thus the possibilities for meaning and for definition, are preempted through the social and institutional position held by those who use them. Meanings thus arise not from language but from institutional practices, from power relations. Words and concepts change their meaning and their effects as they are deployed within different discourses. Discourses constrain the possibilities of thought. They order and combine words in particular ways and exclude or displace other combinations. However, in so far as discourses are constituted by exclusions as well as inclusions, by what cannot as well as what can be said, they stand in antagonistic relationship to other discourses, other possibilities of meaning, other claims, rights, and positions. This is Foucault's 'principle of discontinuity': 'We must make allowance for the complex and unstable powers whereby discourse can be both an instrument and an effect of power, but also a hindrance, a stumbling block, a point of resistance and a starting point for an opposing strategy' (Foucault 1982: 101).

Implicit in the concept of discontinuity is that of change.

Discourse lies between the level of pure atemporal linguistic 'structure' (*langue*) and the level of surface speaking (*parole*): it expresses the historical specificity of what is said and what remains unsaid.

> [D]iscourses are composed of signs, but what they do is more than use these signs to designate things. It is this move that renders them irreducible to the language and to speech. It is this 'move' that we must reveal and describe.
>
> (Foucault 1974: 49)

The issue in discourse analysis is why, at a given time, out of all the possible things that could be said, only certain things were said: 'how is it that one particular statement appeared rather than another' (Foucault 1974:27). Further it is essential to reveal the 'density' and 'complexity' within discursive practices, to go beyond the boundaries of structure, or utterances, *langue*, and *parole*. The world is perceived differently within different discourses. Discourse is structured by assumptions within which any speaker must operate in order to be heard as meaningful. Thus the concept of discourse emphasizes the social processes that produce meaning.

In interactionist terms, the labelling of someone as deviant – educationally, medically or legally – illustrates the operation of discourse.

We are concerned here with educational sites as generators of an historically specific (modern) discourse, that is, as sites in which certain modern validations of, and exclusions from, the 'right to speak' are generated.

Educational sites are subject to discourse but are also centrally involved in the propagation and selective dissemination of discourses, the 'social appropriation' of discourses. Educational institutions control the access of individuals to various kinds of discourse.

> But we know very well that, in its distribution, in what it permits and what it prevents, it follows the lines laid down by social differences, conflicts and struggles. Every educational system is a political means of maintaining or modifying the appropriateness of discourses with the knowledge and power they bring with them.
>
> (Foucault 1971: 46)

This comment gives pause for thought about the current plethora of new tests in British education.

Above all, the distribution and appropriateness of discourses in education is mediated by the examination, that 'slender technique' in which is to be found 'a whole domain of knowledge, a whole type of power'. Indeed, Keith Hoskin argues that the examination is a key concept in understanding the nexus of power-knowledge relations. The act, the process of examining, embodies and relates power and knowledge in technological form.

Foucault's history is the history of the different modes by which, in our culture, human beings are made subjects. (Foucault in Dreyfus and Rabinow 1982: 208). That is the objectification of the subject by processes of classification and division. The latter, what Foucault called 'dividing practices' are clearly central to the organizational processes of education in our society. These divisions and objectifications are achieved either within the subject or between the subject and others. The use of testing, examining, profiling, and streaming in education, the use of entry criteria for different types of schooling, and the formation of different types of intelligence, ability, and scholastic identity in the processes of schooling are all examples of such 'dividing practices'. In these ways, using these techniques and forms of organization, and the creation of separate and different curricula, pedagogies, forms of teacher-student relationships, identities and subjectivities are formed, learned and carried. Through the creation of remedial and advanced groups, and the separation of the educationally subnormal or those with special educational needs, abilities are stigmatized and normalized.

To summarise, people (are forced to) become their category (or label).

These dividing practices are critically interconnected with the formation, and increasingly sophisticated elaboration, of the educational sciences: educational psychology, pedagogics, the sociology of education, cognitive and developmental psychology. These are the arenas in which 'truth games' about education are played out. For example, the development of the sociology of education in the 1960s and 1970s was organized around and informed and reinforced the 'problem of working-class underachievement'. The sociological findings of the period constructed a sophisticated and powerful social pathology of working-class family life as deficient and culturally deprived – abnormal. The problem of underachievement was defined as beyond the control and capabilities of the teacher, and as culturally determined and inevitable. Teachers were provided with a rich, pseudoscientific vocabulary of classifications and justifications for the inevitability of differences in intellectual performance between the social classes. Individuals drawn from the undifferentiated mass of school students could be objectified in terms of various fixed social class or other social indicators (Sharp and Green 1975) instituted in the school's spatial, temporal, and social compartmentalizations. Knowledge and practices drawn from the educational sciences provided (in Foucault's terms) modes of classification, control, and containment, often paradoxically linked to humanitarian rhetoric of reform and progress: streaming, remedial classes, off-site units and sanctuaries, informal or invisible pedagogies (Bernstein 1975).

In the processes of schooling the student is compiled and constructed both in the passive processes of objectification, and in an active, self-forming subjectification, the latter involving processes of self-understanding mediated by an external authority figure – for our purposes, most commonly the teacher. For example, this is apparent in the increasing use of profiling and records of achievement in schools (Hargreaves 1986).

The key term, power-knowledge relates social practice to ideology.

As indicated already, the key concepts in Foucault's exploration of the problem of the subject are those of power and knowledge, or more precisely that of power-knowledge, the single, inseparable configuration of ideas and practices that constitute a discourse. Power and knowledge are two sides of a single process. Knowledge does not reflect power relations but is immanent in them . . .

The bulk of Foucault's analytical effect is weighted towards the subjection of individuals to the accumulation of power in the state by the use of technologies of discipline and confession. He gives little attention to the ways in which such domination might be resisted or subverted by those subject to it. And yet, as indicated by the interview extract quoted earlier, he does see his work as providing a mechanism of critique, or a tool of subversion. He is reticent about specifying an ideal society beyond that which is, but he is adamant that there 'are more secrets, more possible freedoms, and more inventions in our future than we can imagine in humanism as it is dogmatically prescribed on every side of the political rainbow' (Martin *et al.* 1988: 13). Thus for Foucault

> the real political task in a society such as ours is to criticize the working of institutions which appear to be both neutral and independent; violence which has always exercised itself obscurely through them will be unmasked, so that we can fight fear.
>
> (Foucault 1974: 171)

This is very much the spirit in which this book was conceived and is offered. It is to be hoped that the application of Foucauldian analysis to education will unmask the politics that underlie some of the apparent neutrality of educational reform. We leave the last word to Foucault, who commented in an interview, 'I'm proud that some people think that I'm a danger for the intellectual health of students' (Martin *et al.* 1988: 13).

Immanuel Wallerstein: Some Thoughts Towards a Social Science Paradigm of the Capitalist World System

Immanuel Wallerstein has for some time been appreciated as a major theorist in the area of 'underdevelopment' – writing within a broad but uninhibited Marxist framework. However, it is clear from his more recent writings – many of which are reprinted in *Unthinking Social Science* (1991) – that he is claiming a still wider significance for his work.

He argues that a 'world-systems' perspective has replaced what he describes as 'the nineteenth century paradigms'. By these, Wallerstein means the fundamental, over-arching assumptions made by social scientists rather than the particular features of the thinking of, for instance, Adam Smith or Durkheim. Above all, Wallerstein wants to bury the notions of progress and benign capitalism he associates with modernisation theory which he sees as having been the dominant social scientific paradigm throughout the nineteenth and twentieth century.

In the opening section of this extract, Wallerstein briefly and amusingly indicates some of the problems associated with social scientific theorising. He then describes three 'defining characteristics of the world-systems perspective', these are:

1 that the most appropriate unit for the study of social or societal behaviour is a 'world system';
2 that the capitalist world system (and any previous or future world system) must be understood in terms of its historical development;
3 the world system we live in is the capitalist world system (Wallerstein then goes on to enumerate 12 characteristics of it).

In a more difficult section of the extract, Wallerstein goes on to sketch out what may be the main issues of a 'second phase' of analysis of the world capitalist system. These are:

1 the analysis of past world systems i.e. other than the capitalist one;
2 polarisation (roughly, inequality) within the capitalist world economy;
3 research into the choices that are available to us in moulding the future;
4 the development of a unidisciplinary perspective.

Wallerstein is writing here on the edge of theoretical speculation and this does not make for easy reading. Nevertheless for students who want a flavour of what may by a paradigm shift in sociology, it is worth persisting with this reading.

Reading 84 From Immanuel Wallerstein, *Unthinking Social Science: The Limits of Nineteenth Century Paradigms* (Polity Press, 1991), pp. 237–38, 266–272

"World-systems analysis" is not a theory about the social world, or about part of it. It is a protest against the ways in which social scientific inquiry was structured for all of us at its inception in the middle of the nineteenth century. This mode of inquiry has come to be a set of often-unquestioned a priori assumptions. World-systems analysis maintains that this mode of social scientific inquiry, practised worldwide, has had the effect of closing off rather than opening up many of the most important or the most interesting questions. In wearing the blinkers which the nineteenth century constructed, we are unable to perform the social task we wish to perform and that the rest of the world wishes us to perform, which is to present rationally the real historical alternatives that lie before us. World-systems analysis was born as moral, and in its broadest sense, political, protest. However, it is on the basis of scientific claims, that is, on the basis of claims related to the possibilities of systematic knowledge about social reality, that world-systems analyses challenges the prevailing mode of inquiry.

> Wallerstein is opposing world-systems theory to modernisation theory, which traces its traditian from Durkheim through Parsons.

This is a debate, then, about fundamentals, and such debates are always difficult. First of all, most participants have deep commitments about fundamentals. Second, it is seldom the case that any clear, or at least any simple, empirical test can resolve or even clarify the issues. The empirical debate has to be addressed at a very complex and holistic level. Does the sum of derived theorizing starting from one or another set of premises encompass known descriptions of reality in a more "satisfactory" manner? This involves us in all sorts of secondary dilemmas. Our known "descriptions" of reality are to some extent a function of our premises; future "descriptions" may of course transform our sense of reality. Does the "theorizing" said today to encompass reality really encompass it? And last but not least, what does it mean to encompass reality "in a satisfactory manner"? Is this latter criterion anything more than an aesthetic adjunct?

Not only are debates about fundamentals frustrating for all these reasons, but each side has a built-in handicap. The defenders of existing views must "explain away" the anomalies, hence our present challenge. But the challengers must offer convincing "data" in a situation where, compared to the 150 years or so of traditional social scientific inquiry, they have had far less time to accumulate appropriately relevant "data". In a subject matter inherently recalcitrant to experimental manipulation, "data" cannot be accumulated rapidly. So a dispute about fundamentals may be thought of as analogous to a heavyweight championship bout, but without a referee and between two somewhat dyspeptic boxers, each with his left hand tied behind his back. It may be fun to watch, but is it boxing? Is it science?

And who will decide? In some sense, the spectators will decide – and probably not by watching the boxers, but by fighting it out themselves. So why bother? Because the boxers are part of the spectators, who are of course all boxers . . .

World-systems analysis has existed under that name, more or less, for about 15 years. Some of its arguments, of course, have longer histories, even very long histories. Yet, as a perspective, it emerged only in the 1970s. It presented itself as a critique of existing dominant views in the various social sciences, and primarily of developmentalism and modernization theory which seemed to dominate social science worldwide during the 1960s.

The worldwide revolution of 1968 did not spare the world of social science, and world-systems analysis shared in, was part of, a wider reaction to the ideologized positivism and false apoliticism that had been the counterpart within world social science of the US hegemonic world view. Although world-systems analysis was only one variant of this critique, it stood out in retrospect by the fact that it broke more deeply with nineteenth-century social science than did other critiques, albeit probably not deeply enough.

It is hard to know how to assess "what we have learned." What I shall do is spell out what I think are the major premises or arguments that I believe have been reasonably explicated. I choose carefully the verb "explicited." It does not mean these premises or arguments have been widely adopted or that they have not been contested, in detail at least, even among those who think they share in the world-systems perspective. What it means is that there has been enough elaboration of the arguments such that they are familiar beyond the bounds of the initiates (and thus, for example, they might appear in textbooks as reflecting a "viewpoint"), and such that these premises and arguments might be seen as part of the defining characteristics of a world-systems perspective.

I see three such defining characteristics. The first and most obvious is that the appropriate "unit of analysis" for the study of social or societal behavior is a "world-system." No doubt this assertion has led to enormous discussion around the so-called macro-micro problem, which in this case translates into how much of local and/or national behavior is explained/determined by structural evolution at the level of the world-system. I believe this is a totally false problem, but I shall not argue that here. I merely point out that, formally, the macro-micro issue is no different if one decides that the boundaries of a "society" are those of a "world-system" or that these boundaries correlate more or less with those of "nation-states." There still can be said to be the macro-micro issue. The real novelty, therefore, is that the world-systems perspective denies that the "nation-state" represents in any sense a relatively autonomous "society" that "develops" over time.

The second defining characteristic has been that of the *longue durée*. This of course put us in the *Annales* tradition, as well as in that of the burgeoning field of "historical sociology." But I believe the world-systems perspective was more specific than either, and spelled out some elements that were blurry in the other two traditions. Long duration is the temporal correlate of the spatial quality of "world-system." It reflects the insistence that "world-systems" are "historical systems" that is, that they have beginnings, lives, and ends. This stance makes clear that structures are not "immobile." It insists, in addition, that there are "transitions" from one historical system to its successor or successors. It is this pair, the space of a "world" and the time of a "long duration," that combine to form any particular historical world-system.

The third element of world-systems analysis has been a certain view of one particular world-system, the one in which we live, the capitalist world-economy. Let me list the various elements that have been explicated.

Some of these were borrowed, directly or in modified form, from other earlier perspectives. Some others were relatively new. But it has been the combination of these arguments that has come to be associated with world-systems analysis. I merely list now the characteristics presumed to be the description of a capitalist world-economy:

1 the ceaseless accumulation of capital as its driving force;
2 an axial division of labor in which there is a core-periphery tension, such that there is some form of unequal exchange (not necessarily as defined originally by Arghiri Emmanuel) that is spatial;
3 the structural existence of a semiperipheral zone;
4 the large and continuing role of non-wage labor alongside of wage labor;
5 the correspondence of the boundaries of the capitalist world-economy to that of an interstate system comprised of sovereign states;
6 the location of the origins of this capitalist world-economy earlier than in the nineteenth century, probably in the sixteenth century;
7 the view that this capitalist world-economy began in one part of the globe (largely Europe) and later expanded to the entire globe via a process of successive "incorporations;"
8 the existence in this world-system of hegemonic states, each of whose periods of full or uncontested hegemony has, however, been relatively brief;
9 the non-primordial character of states, ethnic groups, and households, all of which are constantly created and re-created;
10 the fundamental importance of racism and sexism as organizing principles of the system;
11 the emergence of antisystemic movements that simultaneously undermine and reinforce the system;
12 a pattern of both cyclical rhythms and secular trends that incarnates the inherent contradictions of the system and which accounts for the systemic crisis in which we are presently living.

To be sure, this list is merely a set of premises and arguments that have been articulated, and that have become relatively familiar to many. It is not a list of truths, much less a list of creeds to which we all pay allegiance. No doubt much empirical work needs to be done on each of these items, and there may be in the future much theoretical reformulation of them. But, as a relatively coherent and articulated view of historical capitalism, they exist.

I should like now to talk about the "second phase" – the issues that have been raised, but are not yet well articulated, and that should, in my view, preoccupy us in the next decade or two.

The first is the elaboration of world-systems other than that of the capitalist world-economy. This work has been begun by Chris Chase-Dunn and Janet Abu-Lughod, as well as by a number of archaeologists whose writings are largely unread by world-systems analysts doing work on the modern world-system. As we pursue this kind of work, three things will probably happen. (a) We shall reevaluate what is in fact particular to our modern world-system. (b) We shall reevaluate what we mean by a world-system, both in terms of time and space. (c) We shall begin to compare different kinds of world-systems systematically. Whether this will then lead us astray and back into a new nomothetic world-view ("the science of comparative world-systems") or a new idiographic world-view ("the description of the unique world-system that has been evolving for at least 10,000 years") remains to be seen.

The second field is the elaboration of how we define and measure polarization within the capitalist world-economy. In the postwar period, polarization had become a relatively unpopular concept. World-systems analysis revived it, but has never really elaborated it. How do we prove its existence? Indeed, how do we measure its existence? There is first of all the technical difficulty that no measurements are useful or relevant that are not world-system-wide, and that the boundaries of the system have been constantly changing over time. Secondly, polarization is not theoretically between states but between economic zones, and between classes and peoples. Finally, statistics have not been collected by state-machineries in a manner pertinent to such analysis. The problems of measurement are thus daunting.

Quite aside from the necessary invention of new data bases, on which little real progress has been made in the past 15 years, there is the question of how we conceptualize polarization. If we measure it in some kind of monetary income terms, we face relatively well-known and long-considered, but not well-resolved, issues as to how to translate into monetary terms income that is not monetized but is nonetheless real. This is, however, the least of our problems. The bigger issue falls under the label of quality of life. For example, since there are more people in the world today, there is obviously less space per person. Less actual space? Surely. Less usable space? Possibly. How much space do people at polarized ends of the income distribution use, or have at their disposition, and how would we know? And what about trees? Do the world's upper strata have more trees to look at and the world's lower strata fewer than 500 years ago? Then there is the issue of health. If we all live on the average x years longer, but some of us live those x years at a level of health that permits good functioning and others are vegetating, this is a further polarization. The questions here are simultaneously technical (how to measure) and substantive (what to measure). They are knotty. They are also intellectually crucial in the debate with the still very much alive developmentalist perspective. Until we tackle convincingly the question of polarization, we cannot expect to become truly influential.

Thirdly, we must begin to do research on the historical choices that are before us in the future. If we believe that all historical systems come to an end, the one in which we are living will also do so. And if we believe that the secular trends of the existing system have brought it into the zone of systemic crisis or "transition," then it is more than time that we begin to engage in utopistics – not utopianism, but utopistics. Utopistics is the science of utopian utopias, that is, the attempt to clarify the real historical alternatives that are before us when a historical system enters into its crisis phase, and to assess at that moment of extreme fluctuations the pluses and minuses of alternative strategies.

In the rejection of nineteenth-century social science, world-systems analysis necessarily rejects its reigning faith, the belief in inevitable progress. I believe that a viable alternative model of change is that of nonlinear processes which eventually reach bifurcation points, whereupon slight fluctuations have large consequences (as opposed to determinate equilibria in which large fluctuations have small consequences). This is the model Prigogine has suggested for all complex systems ("order through chaos") – and the most complex of all known systems is a historical social system. Even for such simple systems as physical systems, the key variable becomes time, reconceptualizing reality as involving stochastic and irreversible processes, within which deterministic, reversible processes constitute a limited, special case. *A fortiori* for complex historical systems.

The fact that the solution of a bifurcation is indeterminate does not mean that it is something beyond the reach of rational research. We can clarify the network of forces at work, elaborate possible vectors (and therefore loci of possible conscious interference), and thereby illuminate the real historical choices that are before us. This is not a matter of speculation but of serious research. It is work that we should be doing.

I have left for the last what I believe to be the key issue, and the hardest nut to crack. We have said from the outset that our perspective is unidisciplinary. But we have merely paid lip service to this view. There is hard work to do, at three levels: theoretical, methodological, and organizational.

Theoretically, the issue is simple. Everyone in the social sciences uses regularly the distinction of three arenas: the economic, the political, and the socio-cultural. No one believes us when we say there is but a single arena with a single logic. Do we believe it ourselves? Some of us, no doubt, but not even all of us. And all of us fall back on using the language of the three arenas in almost everything we write. It is time we seriously tackled the question.

The theoretical question is whether this trinity of arenas of social action – the economy, or market; the polity, or state; the society, or culture – is at all useful, or whether it is in fact pernicious. Can any of the three be conceived to have, even hypothetically, autonomous activity? All economic activity assumes socio-cultural rules and preferences, and works within political constraints. Furthermore, markets are socio-political creations. Is there, for example, a true economic price that can somehow be stripped of its political and social base? All political activity serves the end of ensuring or pursuing economic advantage or need as well as the reinforcement of socio-cultural objectives. Can there be a pursuit of power that is stripped of these considerations? And socio-cultural activity is itself made possible and explained by economic and political location, and serves ends that are ultimately defined in these terms. How can one imagine social (and/or cultural) activity stripped of these factors?

Nor is it simply a question that the three arenas are closely interlinked. It is that human activity within a given world-system moves indiscriminately and imperceptibly in and among all three arenas. Do they really then constitute separate arenas? It is sometimes suggested that, although they were not separate arenas before the advent of a capitalist world-system, they became so in this system. But the descriptive work of world-systems analysis up to now on how historical capitalism has actually operated leads one to be very skeptical that the separation of spheres has had any functional reality even in that system. If so, then we are pursuing false models and undermining our own argumentation by continuing to use such language. It is urgent that we begin to elaborate alternative theoretical models.

This will then force us to face up to and spell out the methodological implications of world-systems analysis: that neither nomothetic nor idiographic modes of knowing in fact exist and that the only epistemology that is plausible lies in the swampy middle ground of the concept of a historical system. That is to say, our knowledge is about structures that reproduce themselves while they constantly change and consequently never reproduce themselves. We may discover the rules by which the cyclical rhythms seem to operate, except that they never truly describe any given empirical situation. The science of the complex is the science of the optimal description of the inherently imprecise.

We must not merely explicate this methodology. We have in addition the enormous task of creating world-systemic data that reflect this imprecise reality with maximum relevance. This is an intellectually difficult, materially and temporally exhausting, work of imagination and drudgery which will take a good 50 years by tens of thousands of scholars before it begins to pay off significantly. We have been dawdling too long.

Finally, we may be reluctantly forced to face the politically difficult organizational implications of our work: the wholesale reorganization of the social science sector of our universities and our libraries. It has taken 100 years for our present disciplinary divisions to institutionalize themselves, and they are now well entrenched. Social science is a mega-colossus, and even its feet of clay are large and not easy to chip at. Nonetheless, once we confront the theoretical and methodological issues, we may not be able to avoid the organizational implications of our radical views. But this is perhaps the third phase. The second phase is for the moment enormous enough.

Erving Goffman:
• The Effect of Performance Disruptions on Personality – Interaction – Society
• Staging and the Self

The inclusion of an extract from Erving Goffman in this section is to reassert the inextricable links between self and society which can easily get lost in discussions of macro-sociological theory. Goffman presents the self as both active and social (or interactive).

In the first section of this extract, Goffman indicates how a disrupted 'performance' of a given 'role' can effect the personality of the 'performer', the 'team' or group of associates, and the social institution of which the individual's performance is a 'part'. Thus, he links the levels of personality, immediate group interaction and society. The example he gives of a disrupted performance by a surgeon makes his point very clearly.

As the terminology cited from Goffman in the previous paragraph indicates, he adopts what he refers to as a 'dramaturgical' model of social interaction. He develops this model in his book, *The Presentation of Self in Everyday Life* (1959). As in the theatre, so in life, individuals *perform* a *character* for an *audience*. In an important passage, Goffman describes the *self* as the performed character which is the product partly of the perception of others (the audience) and of co-actors who provide supporting performances, as well as of the performer him or herself.

The self is social, existing in and through society and also contributing to it. Despite Goffman's effective use of the dramaturgical metaphor, it is worth noting his warning that the world is not a stage and that the socially constructed self tends to persist longer than a theatrical role. However, many of the same and similar techniques are involved in the construction of both.

Reading 85 From Erving Goffman, *The Presentation of Self in Everyday Life* (Penguin, 1969), pp. 234–35, 244–46.

Personality–interaction–society

In recent years there have been elaborate attempts to bring into one framework the concepts and findings derived from three different areas of inquiry: the individual personality, social interaction, and society. I would like to suggest here a simple addition to these inter-disciplinary attempts.

When an individual appears before others, he knowingly and unwittingly projects a definition of the situation, of which a conception of himself is an important part. When an event occurs which is expressively incompatible with this fostered impression, significant consequences are simultaneously felt in three levels of social reality, each of which involves a different point of reference and a different order of fact.

First, the social interaction, treated here as a dialogue between two teams, may come to an embarrassed and confused halt; the situation may cease to be defined, previous positions may become no longer tenable, and participants may find themselves without a charted course of action. The participants typically sense a false note in the situation and come to feel awkward, flustered, and, literally, out of countenance. In other words, the minute social system created and sustained by orderly social interaction becomes disorganized. These are the consequences that the disruption has from the point of view of social interaction.

Secondly, in addition to these disorganizing consequences for action at the moment, performance disruptions may have consequences of a more far-reaching kind. Audiences tend to accept the self projected by the individual performer during any current performance as a responsible representative of his colleague-grouping, of his team, and of his social establishment. Audiences also accept the individual's particular performance as evidence of his capacity to perform the routine and even as evidence of his capacity to perform any routine. In a sense these larger social units – teams, establishments, etc. – become committed every time the individual performs his routine; with each performance the legitimacy of these units will tend to be tested anew and their permanent reputation put at stake. This kind of commitment is especially strong during some performances. Thus, when a surgeon and his nurse both turn from the operating-table and the anaesthetized patient accidentally rolls off the table to his death, not only is the operation disrupted in an embarrassing way, but the reputation of the doctor, as a doctor and as a man, and also the reputation of the hospital may be weakened. These are the consequences that disruptions may have from the point of view of social structure.

Finally, we often find that the individual may deeply involve his ego in his identification with a particular part, establishment, and group, and in his self-conception as someone who does not disrupt social interaction or let down the social units which depend upon that interaction. When a disruption occurs, then, we may find that the self-conceptions around which his personality has been built may become discredited. These are consequences that disruptions may have from the point of view of individual personality.

Performance disruptions, then, have consequences at three levels of abstraction: personality, interaction, and social structure. While the likelihood of disruption will vary widely from interaction to interaction, and while the social importance of likely disruptions will vary widely from interaction to interaction, still it seems that there is no interaction in which the participants do not take an appreciable chance of being slightly embarrassed or a slight chance of being deeply humiliated. Life may not be much of a gamble, but interaction is. Further, in so far as individuals make efforts to avoid disruptions or to correct for ones not avoided, these efforts, too, will have simultaneous consequences at the three levels. Here, then, we have one simple way of articulating three levels of abstraction and three perspectives from which social life has been studied . . .

Staging and the self

The general notion that we make a presentation of ourselves to others is hardly novel; what ought to be stressed in conclusion is that the very structure of the self can be seen in terms of how we arrange for such performances in our Anglo-American society.

In this report, the individual was divided by implication into two basic parts: he was viewed as a *performer,* a harried fabricator of impressions involved in the all-too-human task of staging a performance; he was viewed as a *character,* a figure, typically a fine one, whose spirit, strength, and other sterling qualities the performance was designed to evoke. The attributes of a performer and the attributes of a character are of a different order, quite basically so, yet both sets have their meaning in terms of the show that must go on.

First, character. In our society the character one performs and one's self are somewhat equated, and this self-as-character is usually seen as something housed within the body of its possessor, especially the upper parts thereof, being a nodule, somehow, in the psychobiology of personality. I suggest that this view is an implied part of what we are all trying to present, but provides, just because of this, a bad analysis of the presentation. In this report the performed self was seen as some kind of image, usually creditable, which the individual on stage and in character effectively attempts to induce others to hold in regard to him. While this image is entertained *concerning* the individual, so that a self is imputed to him, this self itself does not derive from its possessor, but from the whole scene of his action, being generated by that attribute of local events which renders them interpretable by witnesses. A correctly staged and performed scene leads the audience to impute a self to a performed character, but this imputation – this self – is a *product* of a scene that comes off, and is not a *cause* of it. The self, then, as a performed character, is not an organic thing that has a specific location, whose fundamental fate is to be born, to mature, and to die; it is a dramatic effect arising diffusely from a scene that is presented, and the characteristic issue, the crucial concern, is whether it will be credited or discredited.

In analysing the self, then, we are drawn from its possessor, from the person who will profit or lose most by it, for he and his body merely provide the peg on which something of collaborative manufacture will be hung for a time. And the means for producing and maintaining selves do not reside inside the peg; in fact these means are often bolted down in social establishments. There will be a back region with its tools for shaping the body, and a front region with its fixed props. There will be a team of persons whose activity on stage and in conjunction with available props will constitute the scene from which the performed character's self will emerge, and another team, the audience, whose interpretative activity will be necessary for this emergence. The self is a product of all of these arrangements, and in all of its parts bears the marks of this genesis.

The whole machinery of self-production is cumbersome, of course, and sometimes breaks down, exposing its separate components: back region control; team collusion; audience tact; and so forth. But, well oiled, impressions will flow from it fast enough to put us in the grip of one of our types of reality – the performance will come off and the firm self accorded each performed character will appear to emanate intrinsically from its performer.

Let us turn now from the individual as character performed to the individual as performer. He has a capacity to learn, this being exercised in the task of training for a part. He is given to having fantasies and dreams, some that pleasurably unfold a triumphant performance, others full of anxiety and dread that nervously deal with vital discreditings in a public front region. He often manifests a gregarious desire for team-mates and audiences, a tactful considerateness for their concerns; and he has a capacity for deeply felt shame, leading him to minimize the chances he takes of exposure.

These attributes of the individual *qua* performer are not merely a depicted effect of particular performances; they are psychobiological in nature, and yet they seem to arise out of intimate interaction with the contingencies of staging performances . . .

Mike O'Donnell: Some Current Issues in Sociological Theory

Introduction: the collapse of dominant sociological paradigms

Like the great myths or metanarratives of modernity, the major sociological paradigms no longer command conviction. The two main structural theories are Marxism and Functionalism (with which can be included the related industrial society or modernisation theory).

It is now clear that Marxism failed not so much because it was put into practice 'incorrectly', but because it is a theory with major flaws. I will do no more than indicate three of these here. First, Marxism presents an over-deterministic view of history and of human consciousness. Second, notwithstanding the significance of social class, Marx ultimately exaggerated its importance – particularly, the importance many people subjectively attach to it. A corollary to this is that Marxism has tended to underestimate the significance and durability of other bases of identity, particularly ethnic and religious identity. Third, a serious charge against Marxism is that it is undemocratic if not anti-democratic. Most Marxist regimes have failed to apply the principle of equality to the equalisation of power. (They have been more successful in equalising or redistributing resources.) The failure to address the issue of power inequalities is perhaps the central failure of Marxism. Again, this failure can be attributed to the theory itself, not merely to distorted practice. Weber had a much more subtle grasp than Marx of power dynamics, including the ways in which power can be abused.

Like Marxism, Functionalism offers a variety of concepts and analysis of continuing usefulness. However, also like Marxism, its inadequacy as a *total* sociological paradigm is now clear. Modernisation theory, a development of Functionalism, suffers from being over-deterministic, over-optimistic, and substantially wrong. What various theories of modernisation have in common is their contention that 'non-modern' societies become modern by adopting either the values, behaviour, technology or some other aspect of modern societies. In reality, few 'non-modern' societies have been allowed to develop in this imitative way. They have developed or underdeveloped in the context of, and largely as a consequence of, their relations with 'modern' powers. More often than not, these relations have been based on the political, economic and cultural domination of the weak by the strong (i.e. the 'modern'). In other words, underdevelopment/dependency theory is far more convincing as a model for explaining the issues modernisation theory purports to address (this is particularly true of the more recent formulations and extensions of underdevelopment theory – see Reading 54). In respect to the international context, therefore, neo-Marxist theory has much more descriptive and explanatory power than modernisation theory (although it is weak in explaining how things might feasibly be made different and better).

Reading 86 Mike O'Donnell: Towards a Sociology of the Capitalist World System

It is no longer possible to regard 'society' or 'the social system' as a distinct and integral unit or level of sociological analysis, as Durkheim did (see Reading 2). This is because all societies and nearly all localities within them, are, or soon will be, part of a single capitalist world system. This system is dominated and driven by transnational corporations. Their investment can make or break local and even 'national' economies. Their economic power gives them considerable direct and indirect political power, particularly if they act in concert with a powerful Western governments. Their commodities, from advanced military equipment to MacDonald burgers, can have enormous impact on a country's social and cultural life.

It is now hardly adequate to approach the sociology of Britain other than in the context of a world capitalist system. The employment of the nation's workforce, the vitality or decline of many localities, many of the services and commodities people consume, are all more or less dependent on international investment and skill. Equally, Britain's capitalist class, or what Sklair would term Britain's members of the transnational capitalist class, are major 'players' on the world stage. The success of 'their' companies and, indeed, their own wealth often depends mainly on overseas profits (see Reading 52).

Trends in class and stratification analysis

Increasing economic globalisation has had a radical effect on class structure and the relations between classes. The British capitalist class has long been relatively international in its economic power-base and, to that extent, well placed to resist attempts by governments or trade unions to control it. However, a transnational class, only some of whose members are British, is substantially more powerful still, relative to national governments and unions. For the top management of transnational companies, Britain is just one spot on the game-board.

In shaping and reshaping national and local economies, the transnational capitalist class also contributes to the reshaping of the class system at every level. It does so specifically by investment/disinvestment policy, by its control and use of technology, and by organisational strategies in relation to labour. Of course, improvements in technological efficiency such as those which have affected manufacturing and office production do have certain near-inevitable social consequences, including a decrease in labour intensiveness and the laying-off of labour. Thus, the shift in employment from the manufacturing to the service sector was largely a result of technological change. Granted that, the transnational (and domestic) capitalist class is by far the most powerful group in creating jobs and in determining the quality of those jobs.

In the face of the power of capital and their own dependency on it, there has been a decline in militancy among both white-collar and manufacturing employees. Apparently, the majority would rather 'conform' than get involved in a struggle they feel they cannot win. Three developments have reinforced this attitude. First, economic instability, including two major recessions, since the oil crisis of 1973 and a generally upward trend in unemployment has meant that fewer people are prepared to risk their jobs. Second, the standard of living of most of those in work has increased, particularly in the case of the growing number of families with a dual income (even where one of those incomes is very low). Finally, the grim presence of a sizeable 'underclass' serves as an exemplary reminder to members of the comfortable majority of what would happen to them if . . .

Of course, class militancy would return if times change. However, matters are unlikely to revert back to the circumstances of a predominantly manufacturing society. The traditional working class is largely gone for good and with it the related analysis.

The new social movements

It may be a mistake for sociologists to look for an alternative 'story' to that of the 'triumph of the working class' as a way of locating and interpreting the direction of global change. Perhaps great metanarratives do tend to oversimplify and mislead. The problems of the contemporary world would not seem to lend themselves to a single unified interpretation or solution. It is difficult to see a compelling common link between nuclear proliferation, environmental pollution, world poverty and hunger, racial and ethnic conflict, and gender inequality. A variety of interest groups and social movements have developed around these issues although some of them do combine either to protest or to pursue a joint cause. However, these groups lack the shared interest and experience and, therefore, the shared institutions and ideology which characterised 'the working-class movement' (Reading 59).

Further, no clear-cut left-right ideological break-down can be made in any of these groups. An individual could be involved in any of the above movements and also support a political party of either the left or right (although a case could be made that to a greater or lesser extent, they are all characterised by a 'radical left' tinge). It is arguable that in cutting across traditional, largely class-based, left-right divisions, the new social movements are changing the established basis of politics. As the perceived importance of class has diminished so has that of class-based party politics.

While there is no doubt about the strength and persistance of the main social movements, there is considerable doubt about their focus and direction and therefore about their likely impact in the future. Both the women's and black liberation movements were able to unite their members around civil rights 'equality packages', but once this was achieved it became much less clear what 'all' women or 'all' black people would agree about or collectively want. In so far as this is so, it may be that these movements will have a diffuse rather than a programmatic influence on society. They may express themselves primarily as diverse movements of life-style, culture and opinion rather than as specifically political movements with clearly defined objectives.

The social movements also differ from class-based movements in the looseness of their organisation and objectives. Class-based movements reflect the material interests of their members (indeed, it is on the basis of occupation/income/property that class is defined). Historically, socialist movements were characterised by a range of policies designed to meet the needs of the working class and, in fact, were very successful in attracting working-class support. There is no parallel way in which a political party has become primarily the vehicle for women's policies or black minorities' policies. Some have argued that the most effective way forward for women's and black politics, is in some form of co-operation with socialism (see Reading 62). Others argue, however, that the interests of women and black ethnic minorities are so varied and diverse that it is unlikely they will find a single dominant channel of expression in the form of a particular political party. In any case, many radical or socialist women and black people seem more attracted to issue-oriented, quasi-pressure group politics rather than mainstream party politics. It is true that 'Green' parties have arisen in certain continental European countries and achieved parliamentary representation. However, this has only been made possible by proportional representation which allows smaller parties parliamentary representation.

It seems certain that the social movements of the latter half of the twentieth century will remain powerful and influential into the third millenium. However, it is less clear how these movements might best achieve maximum impact. It may be that to meet the challenges of a new epoch they will need to break the mould of traditional party politics rather than simply seek to influence the 'old' parties.

'Race' – ethnicity – nationalism

Sociology needs to address the concepts of 'race', ethnicity and nationalism with clarity and vigour. It has not always done so. Often obscure analysis has rendered remote questions and issues which daily affect life and death. Yet, ethnicity, in particular, is a rising and rampant force in the contemporary world.

Sociology often starts to become obscure on these matters when the difference between 'race' and ethnicity is discussed. What is at issue is the distinction between supposed biological ('race') and cultural (ethnic) differences between groups. I intend to sidestep this question here in favour of making an urgent practical point. When people are prejudiced or discriminate against 'The other' they frequently make no very clear distinction about whether their feelings and behaviour are based on perceptions of biological or cultural differences. They might use both arguments, sometimes in a contradictory fashion. What matters most is the reality of the prejudice and discrimination that occurs and the catalogue of suffering, humiliation and deprivation caused. If academic analysis confuses rather than heightens students awareness of the racist obscenity of Fascism, of the re-emerging menace of racism in, particularly, Germany, and of the routine racism that occurs in Britain, it is, to put it mildly, missing a vital opportunity.

The second point I want to make under this heading relates to ethnicity. To put it at its simplest, there are two sides to ethnicity, a good and bad. On the positive side, cultural differences between groups are a matter of interest and celebration and provide opportunities for new experience and education. On the negative side, identification with one ethnic group can lead to intolerance, and worse, against others. This returns us to the question of prejudice and discrimination, the conquest of which is the central issue of contemporary European culture and civilisation (not to mention the global context which is now the sociologist's frame of reference).

I put the above point in such stark terms because it is one which has sometimes become lost in the mist of ideology masquerading as sociology. In particular, there is a tendency among some Marxists to reduce ethnicity to a sub-set of class. Ethnic identity is considered less 'real' or fundamental than class identity and ethnic identity which cuts across or reduces class identity is seen as 'false'. This does not seem to be the way many people actually experience their identity. Whatever the dangers inherent in ethnic identity, it is time to recognise the importance many attach to it.

There are good reasons for distinguishing the ethnic revivalism analysed above from nationalism or national revivalism. Many nation states contain a variety of ethnic groups, some of whom may see the nation state as an imposition on them – perhaps by a dominant ethnic group. Many nation states are of recent creation whereas ethnic groups invariably seek to trace their roots far back in history. Thus, for many Serbs, at least, the nation state of Yugoslavia did not coincide with a deeper sense of perceived (ethnic) identity. Ethnic feeling does not therefore equate with national feeling and, where it does not, it tends to run deeper. It is more akin to tribalism and, whatever one may think of it, like all the more fundamental forces, it merits treating with respect.

It is worth adding that, as with ethnicity, there is an acceptable and unacceptable face of nationalism. The more rational and discriminating a sense of nation is, the more acceptable it would seem to be. On the other hand, the drunken-cavortings of union-jack clad football 'hoolies' take nationalism in the direction of a sort of popular Fascism.

Currently, the nations in the European Community are struggling with the issue of what they want to retain in terms of national independence and what they are prepared to pool in the cause of a larger unity. These decisions are not, of course, made in a vacuum but are subject to wider forces, some of which, including the power of transnational corporations, have already been discussed here. It is not yet clear whether centrifugal or centripetal forces will pervail.

The concepts discussed in this reading illuminate developments in the Soviet Union and Eastern Europe, in South Africa, and in the relationship of the Muslim world to the West. There are hardly more vital matters than these. Ultimately, the most crucial may be the relationship of the Islamic world to the West. For many, Islam has come to represent anti-imperial, anti-American, anti-British, and anti-Western sentiments, including distaste for what is seen as the lax, self-indulgent, immoral and irreligious way of life dominant in the West. The ideology or creed of Islam could become the reference point for many of the world's dispossessed. It may yet provide a more formidable challenge to liberal capitalism than did communism.

Production, consumption, culture and citizenship

A further cluster of issues must be considered in any review of the main trends in contemporary sociology. Production is necessarily the primary economic activity. Without production there can be no consumption – other than living off nature. Nevertheless, the importance of production relative to consumption in richer societies has been reduced in popular experience and perception. This is partly because, with the decline in the length of the average working week, people spend less time producing and more time consuming. More can afford to consume a wider range and quality of products. Moreover, the shift in employment from the manufacturing to the service sector has put millions of people at one remove from material production – which can increasingly be left to the automated machine. Crudely, people are now relatively more interested in spending than earning (see Reading 45). This apparent shift in popular focus from work and production to leisure and life-style is a further aspect of the decline in the salience of class consciousness referred to above.

The rise of the consumer and consumer culture is so pervasive that it is possible not to notice it, to assume it is 'normal reality'. Increasingly, the media is commercially driven, with programmes mimicing adverts and adverts mimicing programmes. With designer labels, we ourselves become walking bill-boards for the brand-name products we have individually 'chosen' to wear. This happens whether we like it or not – in the frequent absence of alternative, 'unbranded' choices. Sports sponsorship has created a whole new expense hazard for parents when buying their children sports equipment. For instance, if a popular football team changes the brandname 'sported' on its equipment – so, too, will thousands of youngsters. These comments tend to stress the extent to which apparent consumer choices are over-determined by commercial pressures. This is an old theme but it gets replayed in endless variety as such pressures take new shapes and forms.

Paul Willis and others have emphasised the creative (productive) and unpredictable side of consumption. People create their own clothes, music and videos; they transform their own homes and sometimes the commodities they buy; they get their own meanings out of media 'messages' and sometimes ignore intended messages altogether. Whatever the balance of conformity or creativity in contemporary consumption, the consumer issue is one that needs to be more fully addressed in introductory sociology.

Consumption is increasingly central to the public as well as the private sector. Of course, virtually from the inception of the welfare state, pressure groups and voluntary organisations have attempted to influence the quality of the service. The concept of consumers' rights has been systematically adopted by the Major government in order to place the welfare state within a quasi free-market context (see next section). Other views, however, strongly resist the equation of citizenship with consumption whilst generally recognising the growing importance of consumer power. A further illustration of the increasing significance of consumer issues, already discussed here, is the environmental movement (Readings 53 and 65). Ultimately, there will be little left to consume unless we develop a mutually healthy relationship with the environment.

As a burgeoning literature attests, sociologists and cultural critics (in this context the difference between the two is becoming increasingly difficult to distinguish) are enthusiastically addressing consumer and cultural issues (see, for instance, the journal, *Theory, Culture and Society)*. However, a word of caution on this matter is perhaps in order: issues of inequality do not magically disappear in a 'consumer world'. Indeed, for those with little consumer power, inequality can become more conspicuous and painful. A sociology which addresses culture and consumption merely as style and ignores or avoids questions of access is destined to be relevant only to an elite. Occasional forays into popular culture will not compensate for this. Socio-cultural criticism without a concern for the disadvantaged risks disappearing up its own elegant vocabulary.

Whatever its flaws, Marxist and socialist cultural criticism did address issues of access for the majority. It may be that citizenship theory, discussed below, can be extended to include cultural as well as a range of other rights.

Citizenship, consumption and rights

If the 'free market' was the 'big idea' of the 1980s, 'citizenship' promises to be one of the 'big ideas' of the 1990s and – if it proves to address the needs of the time – perhaps beyond. In this section I will present two differing approaches to the concept of citizenship: the first, the Conservative approach, put forward by John Major; the second, a more radical approach adopted by certain intellectuals of the left such as Bryan Turner (see Reading 58).

There are certain features of citizenship in a 'modern' society about which virtually all commentators agree. Citizenship involves both rights and responsibilities. It involves equal status in law (civil rights) and the right to vote – the key political right. Freedom of speech is both a civil and political right. On the question of social rights, there is general agreement that a citizen has, at a minimum, the right to basic food and shelter. The current debate about citizenship is largely about how the concept can be re-interpreted and built upon to map the needs and aspirations of people in the late twentieth century.

There is some overlap and also significant differences between left and right re-workings of the theory of citizenship. Probably because it is the party in power, Conservative analysis tends to be more familiar in Britain. However, the idea of a Citizen's Charter was practised in a number of Labour local authorities, including York, before it was taken up by the Conservative Party at national level. A charter – say in relation to education or health – states that the user has the right to a certain level of specified services and a degree of democratic involvement in how the relevant service operates. John Major and his government has firmly contextualised the concept of the charter within the context of consumption and the market. By means of the public service charters, the citizen *as consumer* puts pressure on the public services to become more efficient. Ideally, this should involve cost-saving as well as the more effective delivery of services. Thus, the discipline of the market place has been applied to the public sector.

Two points which distinguish radical social democratic approaches to citizenship may be mentioned. The first is a much greater emphasis on the right to economic citizenship (which can be regarded as an aspect of social citizenship). This involves greater economic equality and participation than is supported by British Conservatives. Thus, the European Social Charter (opposed by the Major government) embodies both a minimum wage and a maximum number of hours in the working week. Thus, a 'bottom line' is drawn below which people are not allowed to sink. Another economic feature of this approach is workers' participation in the running of industry which is also practised by most members of the European Community other than Britain. Workers' participation, of course, involves a sharing of power as well as resources.

A second point which increasingly characterises radical social democratic theories of citizenship is a commitment to the principle that the rights of citizenship apply worldwide – as a goal if not as a feasible immediate reality. This view is argued both by John Clark and Bryan Turner (Readings 54 and 58). Presented in this way, the 'citizenship agenda' is potentially huge and transformative. It stands comparison with the political/philosophical 'isms' of the nineteenth and twentieth century and is, as yet at least, untainted with their ideological partiality and self-interest.

Citizenship is about rights: people possess these inherently, they do not have rights given to them by others. Equal rights apply beyond differences of sex, creed and 'race'. This is a practical point as well as one of principle. It is only by self-enpowerment, by implementing and *practising* their own rights, that people will hold on to them securely. Current right and left citizenship theory is radically democratic. It is also a powerful counter to the forces of fragmentation and mutual inhumanity described elsewhere in this reading. Acceptance of citizens' rights means not just that 'I' or 'we' have access to 'the good life' but 'they' do, too.

Social and cultural theory: post-everything – what new beginnings?

The predominant message of social and political theory during the last quarter of a century is that we are at the end of an epoch. Post-industrial society theory, post-Fordism, postmodernism and poststructuralism all seem to attest that we have come to the end of 'something'. Where these theories tend to be less convincing is in indicating what the new age – the one presumably coming after all the 'posts' – may be like. I will now briefly review the 'end of the epoch' theories.

The accusation that the above theories fail to define the nature of the presumably emerging epoch finds its exception in Daniel Bell's analysis of post-industrial society. As the sub-title of his book, *The Coming of Post-Industrial Society: A Venture in Social Forecasting* (1973), suggests the theory was a bold attempt at futurology. He argued that the development from industrial to post-industrial society would be characterised by the predominance of the service sector over manufacturing, of information over mechanised energy, and of professional and technical employees over manual workers. These developments were already well under way in the technologically advanced societies when Bell published his book and are now empirical fact. To that extent Bell's theory is correct. What he leaves unresolved are the questions of power and control in 'information society' and also the issue of to what purposes the new knowledge might be put.

The controversial theory of post-Fordism has already been sufficiently discussed and criticised in this book (see Readings 41 and 42). Here it is enough to point out that in arguing that the mass production method of Fordism is on the decline, post-Fordism broadly complements post-industrial society theory. An information intensive age requires a core of elite employees who manipulate systems of communication and information (sometimes linked to systems of production) as well as less skilled workers. Again, however, issues of power, control and purpose are not resolved in post-Fordist theory – except in so far as post-Fordism appears to suggest more managerial and capitalist control. Despite the current weakness of organised labour, it is not necessary to regard this situation as either permanent or desirable.

In the early 1990s, the two theories that occupy the intellectual centre-stage are postmodernism and poststructuralism. Both present the world in terms of diversity and even fragmentation rather than in terms of 'grand theory'. In his book, *The Postmodern Condition* (1984), Jean-François Lyotard says: 'I define postmodern as incredulity toward metanarratives'. By this, he means that it is no longer credible to believe that there is any emerging pattern to human history. Marxism is his main target, but he also has lesser 'creeds' in his sights. Associated with postmodernism is the rejection of the modern belief that the application of science brings inevitable progress. We have seen too much industrial and technological destruction to buy that particular story any longer.

Dominic Strinati states that 'the breakdown of the distinction between culture and society' (1992) is a distinguishing feature of postmodernist analysis. It is true that there is currently a vogue in sociology which seems to merge social structural issues with cultural criticism. This may be partly due to a growing acceptance that the social structure of capitalism – chameleon-like though it is – is the only structure there is or is likely to be. It has become more interesting to examine capitalism's superstructure of culture and consumption than to plumb the functionings and contraditions of its infrastruction. Goodbye class! Hello carnival!

The merging of structural and cultural analysis has a more serious justification than mere disenchantment with the grand theories of structual sociology such as Marxism. Post-structuralist theory is perhaps the key intellectual influence here. First, though, a word about structuralism. Going back to Durkheim, the social psychology of structuralism comes close to equating the social and the cultural: normative rules or structures are embedded in the individual mind through processes of cultural socialisation. Through language and imitation, the individual learns (culture) to fit into society (structure): structure and culture are a seamless robe. A stark illustration of this is that it is impossible to 'touch' social structure despite its 'heavy' name. Structure is a term for part of culture. Foucault's poststructuralism accepts the logic of this argument whereas Durkheim did not. Durkheim wants to describe social structure as some*thing* 'out there', almost an imprisonment of 'facts'. In contrast, Foucault sees social structure or institutions (sets of rules) as a sort of lived culture which takes its form from the ideology and discourses of social action (see Reading 65). While Foucault considers that it is easy, perhaps even 'normal', to become caught and confused within dominant ideologies and discourses, he also believes that people 'are much freer than they feel' – potentially.

However, for both postmodernists and poststructuralists there is no beaten path to freedom along which people can confidently be directed. Most definitely, there are no short cuts to utopia. To quote Lyotard again:

> In any case, there is no question here of proposing a 'pure' alternative to the system: We all now know . . . that any attempt at an alternative of that kind would end up resembling the system it was meant to replace.

So, rather than try to break the system, we play with it, testing its weaknesses and capacity for change, exposing its injustices and inequalities. In the absence of anything else, we try to make the system work – but better.

For those who seek the intoxicating fix of total solutions, postmodernism must seem defeatist and even decadent. Postmodernism does little to ease the crisis of identity and meaning felt by many in the absence of Marx or Jesus. Playing radical games within the system – which is virtually what Lyotard suggests – hardly has the attraction of either revolution or eternity.

Perhaps the most serious criticism of postmodernism is that it fails to offer a fundamental critique of capitalism. It is more a clever commentary on capitalism than an analysis of the system. Inequalities of resources and power are becoming more, not less, characteristic of capitalism as it emerges as the dominant system virtually throughout the globe. On this crucial issue, for all its diverting and clever playfulness, postmodernism is irresponsibly inarticulate and unconvincing.

Global change: sociological response

Capitalist world-system theory is an influential counter to the fragmentation that postmodernist theoretical diversity might create. Wallerstein's argument that transnational capitalism forms and penetrates at regional, national and local/'communal' level is increasingly accepted as the framework within which sociology is best practised. Few, if any, significant areas of work, organisation or culture are outside the influence of the capitalist world system. Even micro-level activity in households or classrooms is likely to be in some ways shaped or affected by global forces. However, having declared, like Lyotard, that the nineteenth century paradigms or 'meta-narratives' are defunct, Wallerstein is unlikely to want to impose a rigid 'twenty-first century' paradigm. His point is rather that the capitalist world system is the established and pervasive context in which virtually all global citizens live, and that it is necessary to understand the system in order to engage effectively with it. Understanding how global capitalism works is now a central purpose of sociology. Most, if not all, the theoretical influences within sociology referred to above, such as feminist and environmentalist sociology, are already characterised by a developed global dimension. It is almost as if a global focus is acting as a compelling magnetic force holding the discipline together.

Finally, Wallerstein also suggests that many of the issues sociologists seek to analyse can better be understood by social science than by sociology alone. In this respect, he resembles at least one nineteenth century thinker, Karl Marx. A base of political economy was essential to Marx's sociological analysis, if, indeed, the two can be separated. The complexities of the contemporary world require that the disciplinary boundaries of sociology be further extended. Among others, Anthony Giddens is increasingly demonstrating that sociology requires a psychological and cultural dimension. This does not mean that for the practical purposes of textbooks, syllabuses and exams, sociology should cease to be parcelled into comprehensible topics. However, sociology has never been a securely defined discipline. It is forever leaking into other subject areas. That, perhaps, is a strength in a world in which barriers and boundaries seem to be rapidly melting.

References

The purpose of this reading is to overview key theoretical themes raised in readings throughout this book and particularly in this section. Citations are given under the relevant reading. Additional references in this reading are:

Bell, D. *The Coming of Post-Industrial Society: A Venture in Social Forecasting* (New York, Basic Books, 1973)

Strinati, D. 'Postmodernism and Popular Culture' in *Sociology Review,* April, 1992, pp. 2–7.

Willis, P. *Common Culture: Symbolic Work at Play in the Everyday Cultures of the Young* (Open University Press, 1990).

Questions and Issues

Theory – Current Developments: Section 18

The most relevant readings are indicated in brackets after each question.

1 Do you find any application of Thomas Kuhn's paradigm theory to the current state of sociological theory? Illustrate your answer with examples. (Section 18)

2 'I define postmodern as incredulity toward metanarratives' (Jean-François Lyotard). What explanations can you offer for this 'incredulity' and how far do you consider it to be justified? (Section 18, especially Readings 82–84, 86)

3 'To change something in the minds of people – that's the role of an intellectual' (Michel Foucault). How far would you say that Foucault's comment describes the role of the sociologist? (Section 18, especially Reading 83)

4 Describe and discuss what you consider to be the major contemporary developments in 'macro' sociological theory? (Section 18, especially Reading 86)

INDEX